Big School of Drawing
People

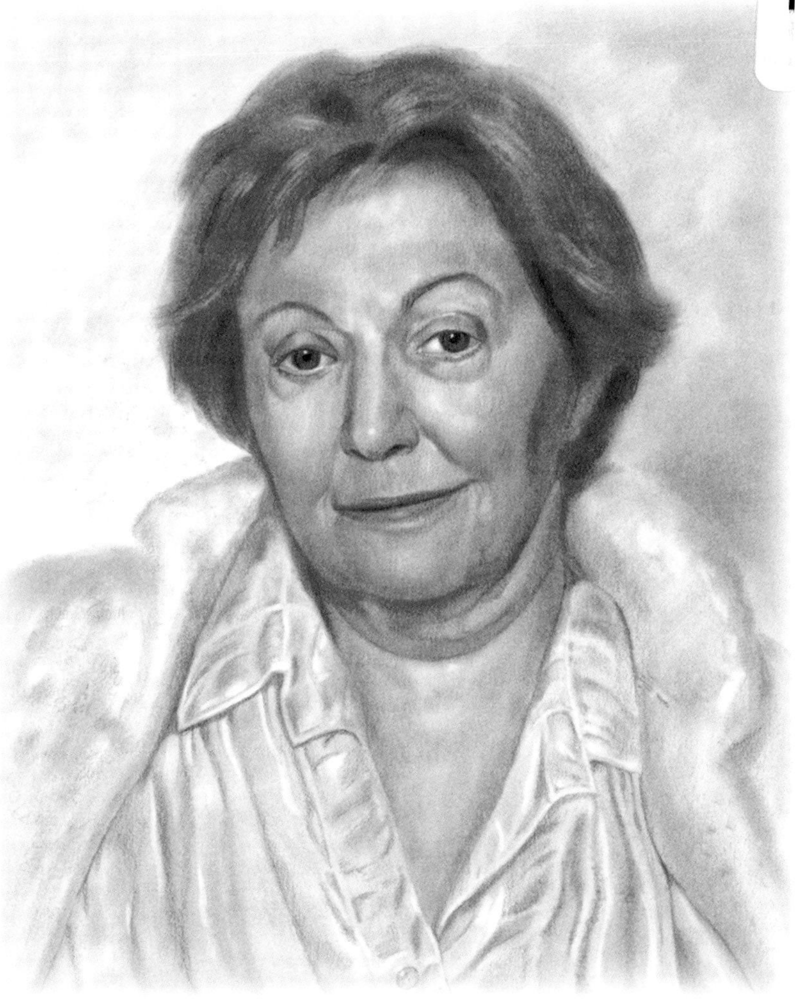

Well-explained, practice-oriented drawing
instruction for the beginning artist

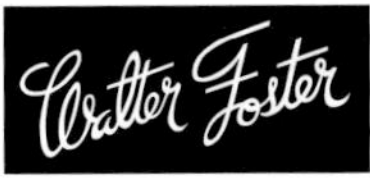

Contents

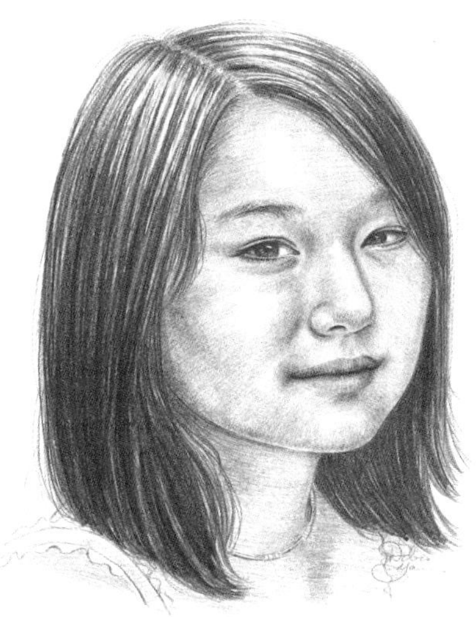

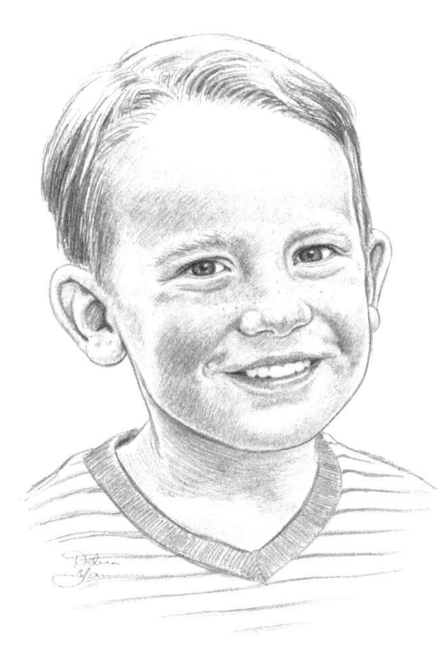

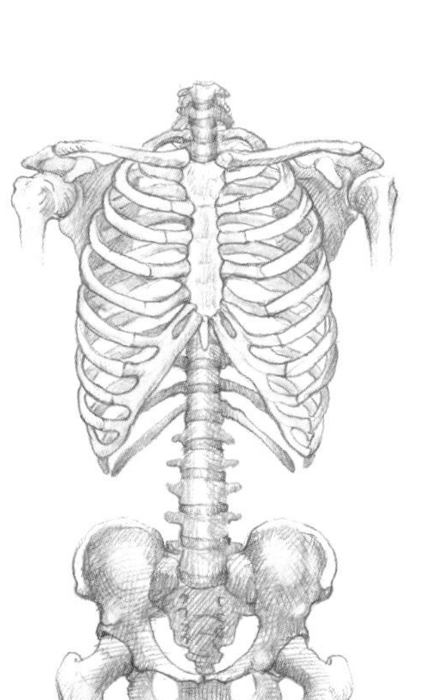

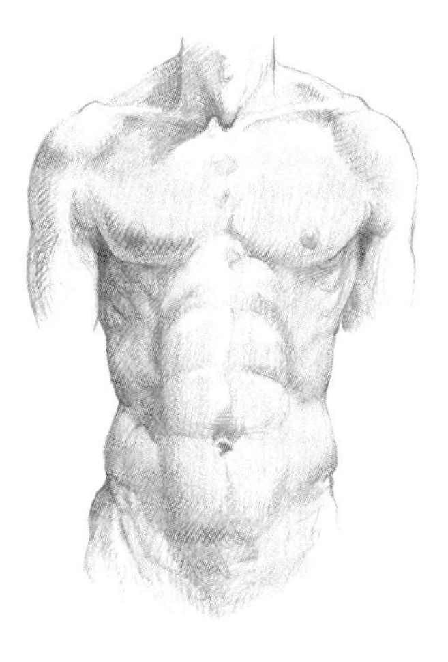

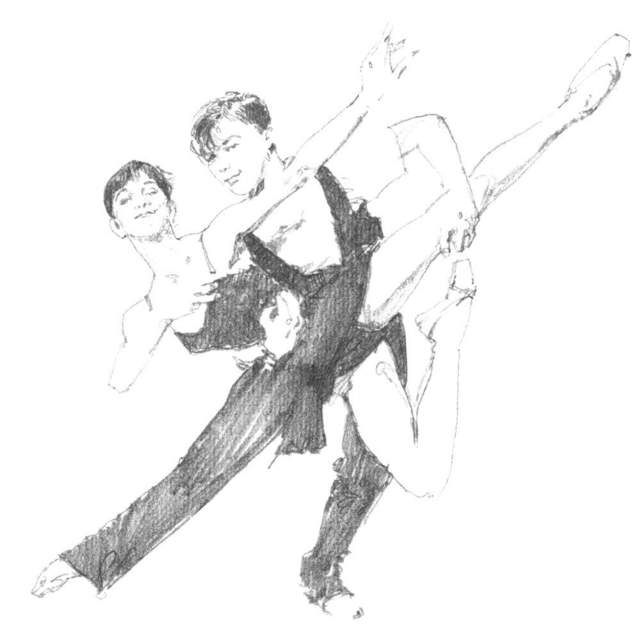

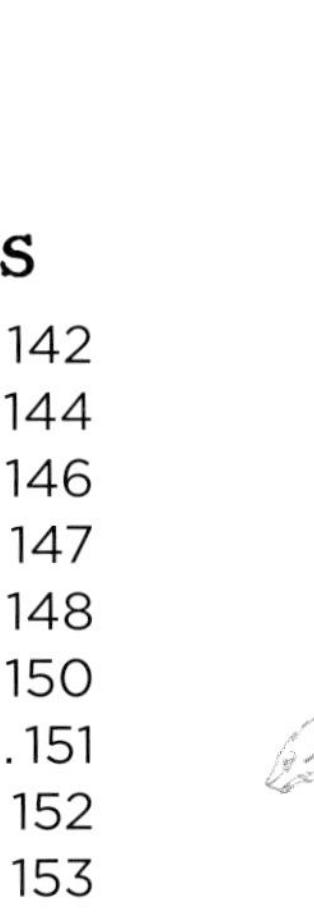

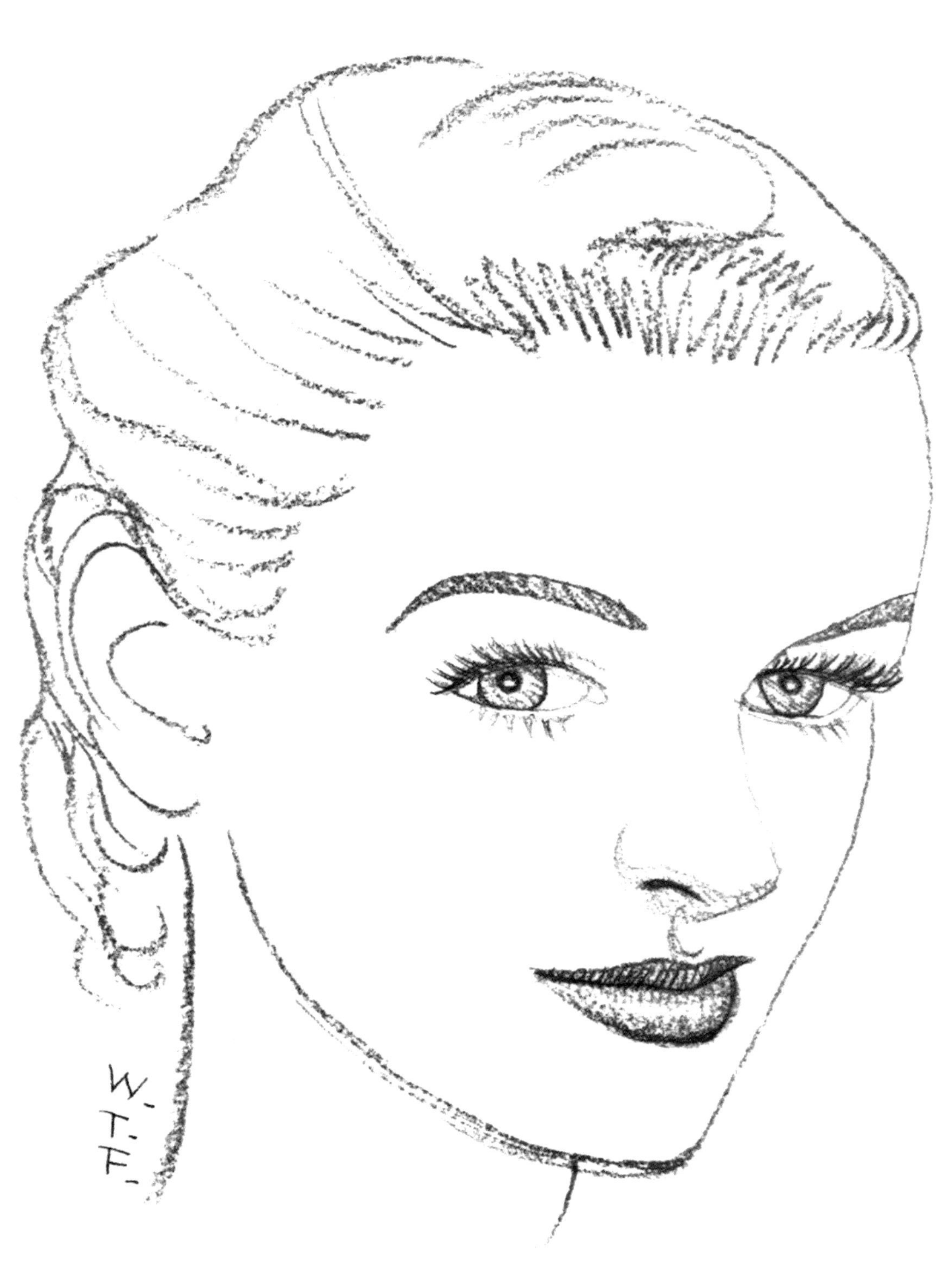

Getting Started

Learning to draw people in pencil is a rewarding endeavor that almost anyone can learn—and it requires just a few simple tools to get started. Whether you want to achieve lifelike results or create more stylized representations, pencil is a versatile medium that allows you to explore a variety of techniques. With practice and patience, beginners will be able to master the art of drawing people—even if they have never drawn before.

This chapter covers the basics, including tools and materials, the fundamentals of drawing, and a basic overview of facial views, proportions, and features in addition to a few step-by-step lessons. You will explore methods for creating depth, rendering texture, understanding perspective, placing figures in a composition, and more.

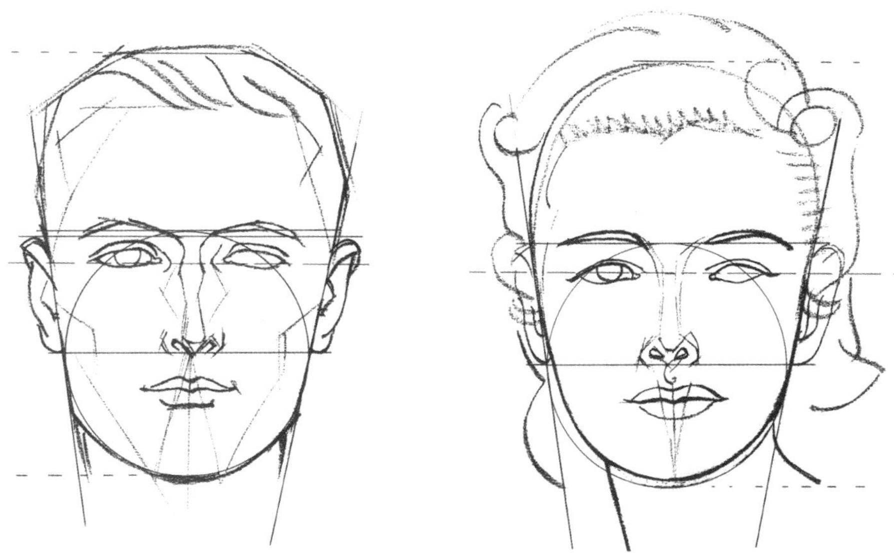

Tools & Materials

Drawing is not only fun, it also is an important art form. Even when you write or print your name, you are drawing! If you organize the lines, you can make shapes. When you carry that a bit further and add dark and light shading, your drawings begin to take on a three-dimensional form and look more realistic. One of the great things about drawing is that you can do it anywhere, and the materials are generally inexpensive. Whenever possible, purchase the best materials you can afford, and upgrade your supplies whenever you can. Although any tool that makes a mark can be used for drawing, you'll want to make sure your efforts will last over time. Here are some materials that will get you off to a good start.

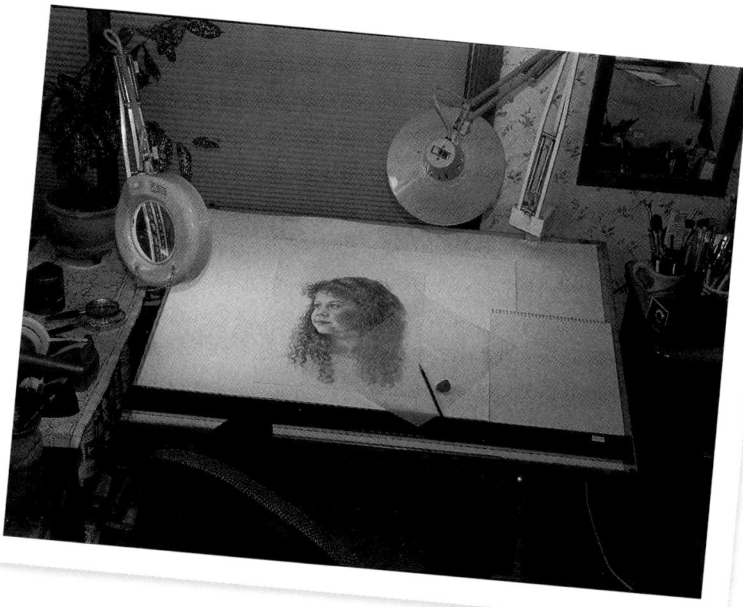

▲ **Work Station** Set up a work area that has good lighting and enough room for you to lay out your tools. A room with track lighting, an easel, and a drawing table is ideal. But all you really need is a place by a window for natural lighting. When drawing at night, you can use a soft-white light bulb and a cool-white fluorescent light so that you have both warm (yellowish) and cool (bluish) light.

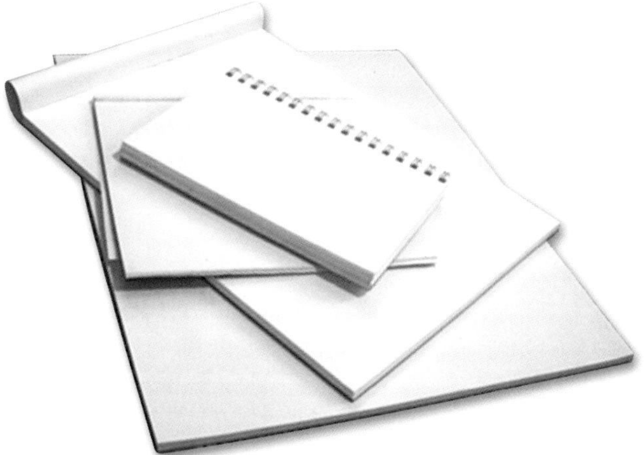

◀ **Sketch Pads** Drawing pads come in a wide variety of sizes, textures, weights, and bindings. They are particularly handy for making quick sketches and when drawing outdoors. You can use a large sketchbook in the studio for laying out a painting, or take a small one with you for recording quick impressions when you travel. Smooth- to medium-grain paper texture often is an ideal choice. (The texture of paper is also known as the "tooth.")

Charcoal Paper Charcoal paper and tablets also are available in a variety of textures. Some of the surface finishes are quite pronounced, and you can use them to enhance the texture in your drawings. These papers also come in a variety of colors, which can add depth and visual interest to your art.

Drawing Paper For finished works of art, using single sheets of drawing paper is best. They are available in a range of surface textures: smooth grain (plate and hot pressed), medium grain (cold pressed), and rough to very rough. The cold-pressed surface is the most versatile. It is of medium texture but it's not totally smooth, so it makes a good surface for a variety of different drawing techniques.

GATHERING THE BASICS

You don't need a lot of supplies to start; you can begin drawing with just a #2 or an HB pencil, a sharpener, a vinyl eraser, and any piece of paper. You always can add more pencils, charcoal, tortillons, and other tools later. Pencils are labeled with letters and numbers; these indicate the degree of lead softness. Pencils with B leads are softer than those with H leads, so they make darker strokes. An HB is in between, which makes it very versatile beginner's tool. The chart at right shows a variety of drawing tools and the kinds of strokes that are achieved with each one. As you expand your pencil supply, practice shaping different points and creating different effects with each by varying the pressure you put on the pencil. The more comfortable you are with your tools, the better your drawings will be!

ADDING ON

Unless you already have a drawing table, you may want to purchase a drawing board. It doesn't have to be expensive; just get one large enough to accommodate individual sheets of drawing paper. Consider getting one with a cut-out handle, especially if you want to draw outdoors, so you easily can carry it with you.

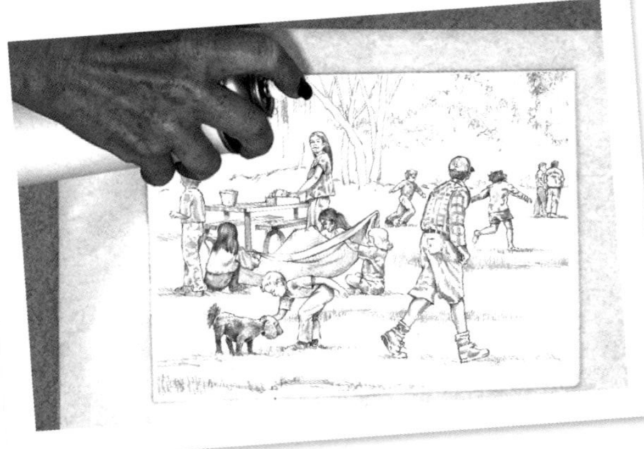

Spray Fixative A fixative "sets" a drawing and protects it from smearing. Some artists avoid using fixative on pencil drawings because it tends to deepen the light shadings and eliminate some delicate values. However, fixative works well for charcoal drawings. Fixative is available in spray cans or in bottles, but you need a mouth atomizer to use bottled fixative. Spray cans are more convenient, and they give a finer spray and more even coverage.

HB, sharp point

HB, round point

HB An HB with a sharp point produces crisp lines and offers good control. With a round point, you can make slightly thicker lines and shade small areas.

4B, flat point

Flat sketching

Flat For wider strokes, use the sharp point of a flat 4B. A large, flat sketch pencil is great for shading large areas, but the sharp, chiseled edge can be used to make thinner lines too.

4B charcoal

Vine charcoal

White charcoal

Charcoal 4B charcoal is soft, so it makes a dark mark. Natural charcoal vines are even softer, and they leave a more crumbly residue on the paper. Some artists use white charcoal pencils for blending and lightening.

Conté crayon

Conté pencil

Conté Crayon or Pencil Conté crayon is made from very fine Kaolin clay. Once it came only in black, white, red, and sanguine sticks, but now it's also available in a wider range of colors. Because it's water soluble, it can be blended with a wet brush or cloth.

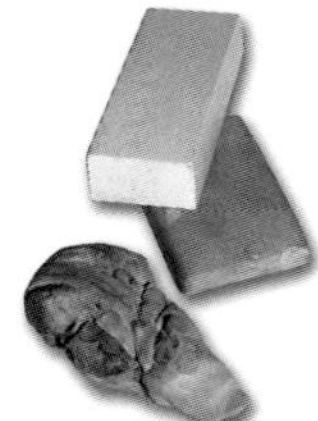

Artist's Erasers A kneaded eraser can be formed into small wedges and points to remove marks in very tiny areas. Vinyl erasers are good for larger areas; they remove pencil marks completely. Neither eraser will damage the paper surface unless scrubbed too hard.

◄ **Utility Knives** Utility knives (also called "craft" knives) are great for cleanly cutting drawing papers and mat board. You also can use them for sharpening pencils. (See page 11.) Blades come in a variety of shapes and sizes and are easily interchanged. But be careful; the blades are as sharp as scalpels!

▶ **Tortillons** These paper "stumps" can be used to blend and soften small areas where your finger or a cloth is too large. You also can use the sides to quickly blend large areas. To clean them, simply rub them on a cloth.

Basic Pencil Techniques

You can create an incredible variety of effects with a pencil. By using various hand positions and shading techniques, you can produce a world of different lines and strokes. If you vary the way you hold the pencil, the mark the pencil makes changes. It's just as important to notice your pencil point, which is every bit as essential as the type of lead in the pencil. Experiment with different hand positions and techniques to see what your pencil can do!

GRIPPING THE PENCIL

Many artists use two main hand positions for drawing. The writing position is good for very detailed work that requires fine hand control. The underhand position allows for a freer stroke with more arm movement—the motion is almost like painting. (See below for more information on using both hand positions.)

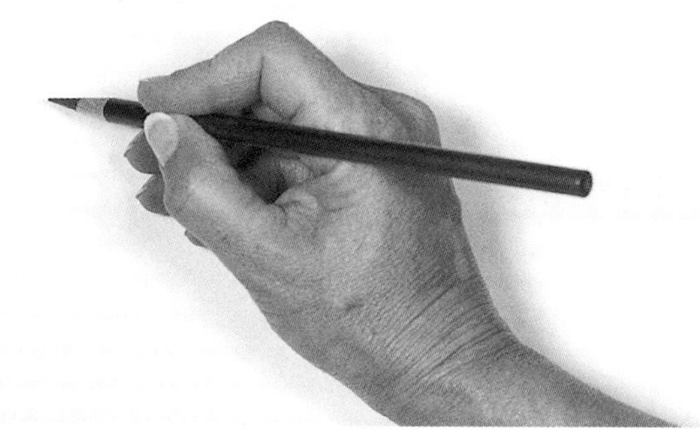

Using the Writing Position This familiar position provides the most control. The accurate, precise lines that result are perfect for rendering fine details and accents. When your hand is in this position, place a clean sheet of paper under your hand to prevent smudging.

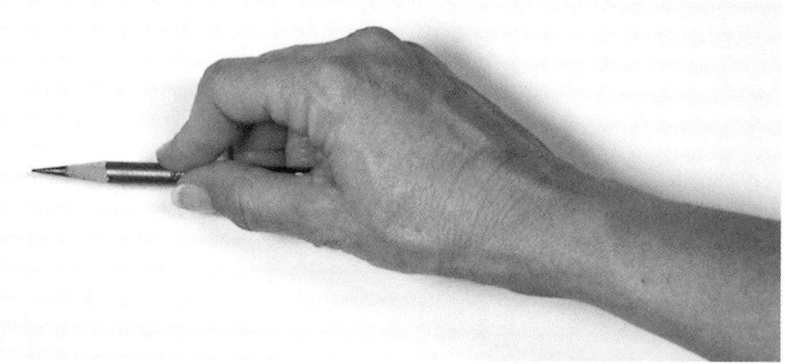

Using the Underhand Position Pick up the pencil with your hand over it, holding the pencil between the thumb and index finger; the remaining fingers can rest alongside the pencil. You can create beautiful shading effects from this position.

Hatching This basic method of shading involves filling an area with a series of parallel strokes. The closer the strokes, the darker the tone will be.

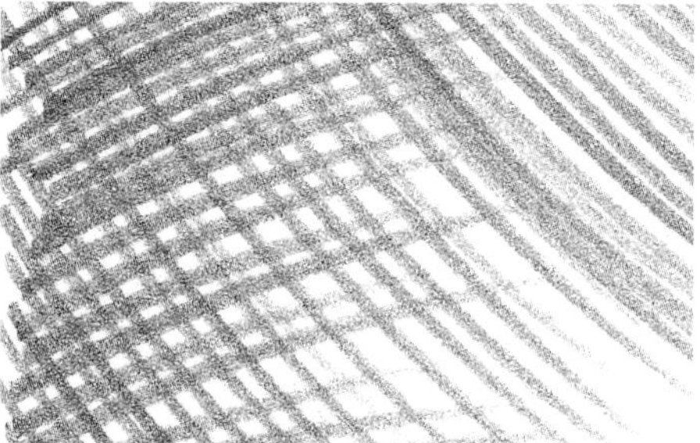

Crosshatching For darker shading, place layers of parallel strokes on top of one another at varying angles. Again, make darker values by placing the strokes closer together.

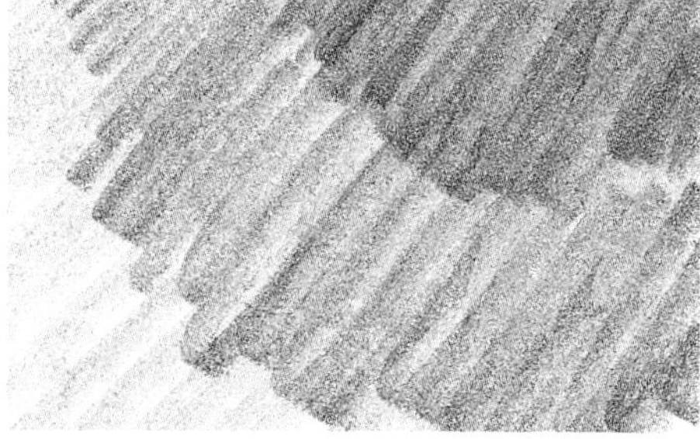

Gradating To create graduated values (from dark to light), apply heavy pressure with the side of your pencil, gradually lightening the pressure as you stroke.

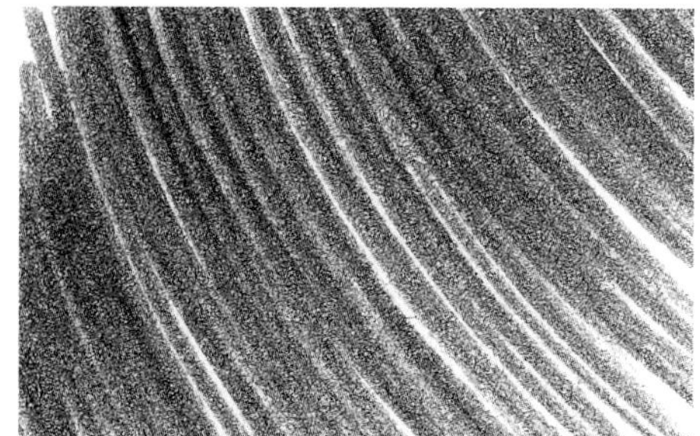

Shading Darkly By applying heavy pressure to the pencil, you can create dark, linear areas of shading.

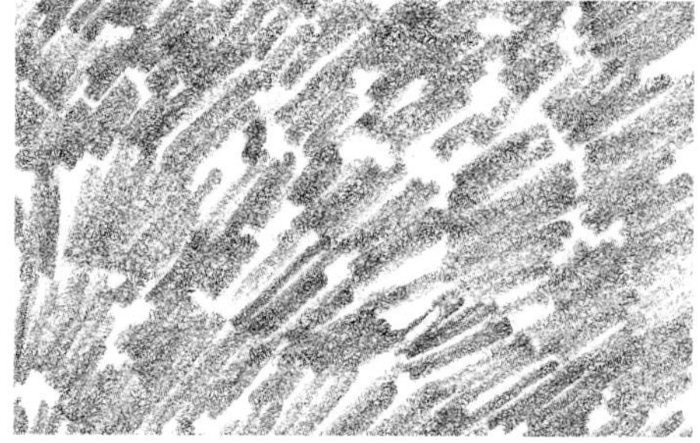

Shading with Texture For a mottled texture, use the side of the pencil tip to apply small, uneven strokes.

Blending To smooth out the transitions between strokes, gently rub the lines with a tortillon or tissue.

Other Ways to Shade

PRACTICING LINES

When drawing lines, it is not always necessary to use a sharp point. In fact, sometimes a blunt or rounded point may create a more desirable effect. When using larger lead diameters, the effect of a blunt point is even more evident. Play around with your pencils to familiarize yourself with the different types of lines they can create. Make every kind of stroke you can think of, using both a sharp point and a blunt point. Practice the strokes below to help loosen up your hand.

As you experiment, you will find that some of your doodles will bring to mind certain imagery or textures. For example, little Vs can be reminiscent of birds flying, whereas wavy lines can indicate water.

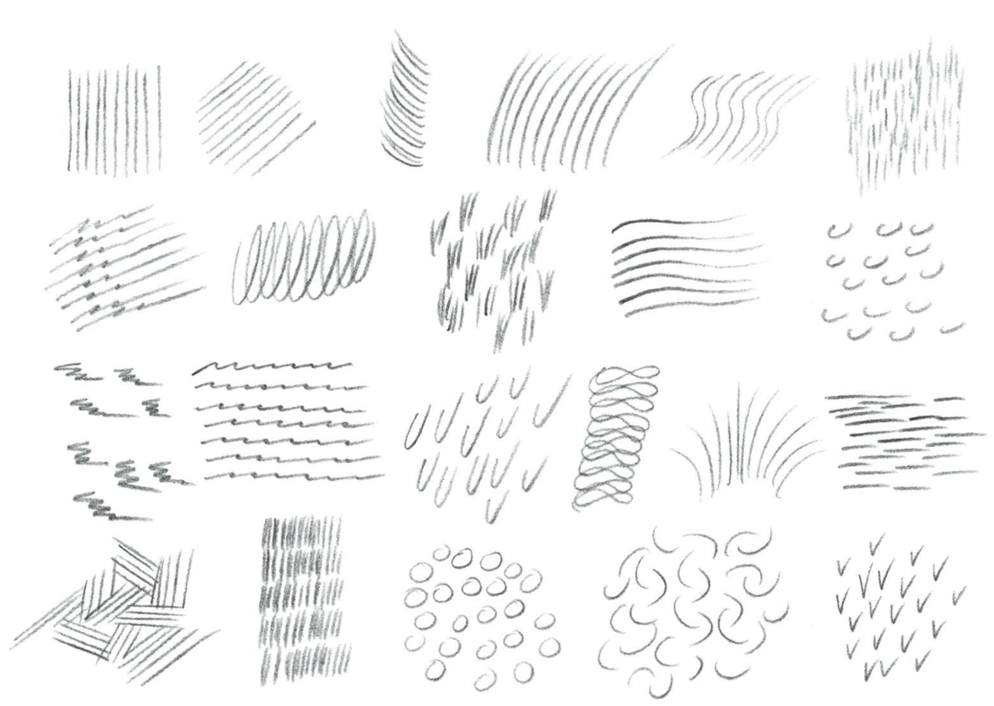

Drawing with a Sharp Point
First draw a series of parallel lines. Try them vertically; then angle them. Make some of them curved, trying both short and long strokes. Then try some wavy lines at an angle and some with short, vertical strokes. Try making a spiral and then grouping short, curved lines together. Then practice varying the weight of the line as you draw. Some of the most common letter shapes in drawing are O, U, and V.

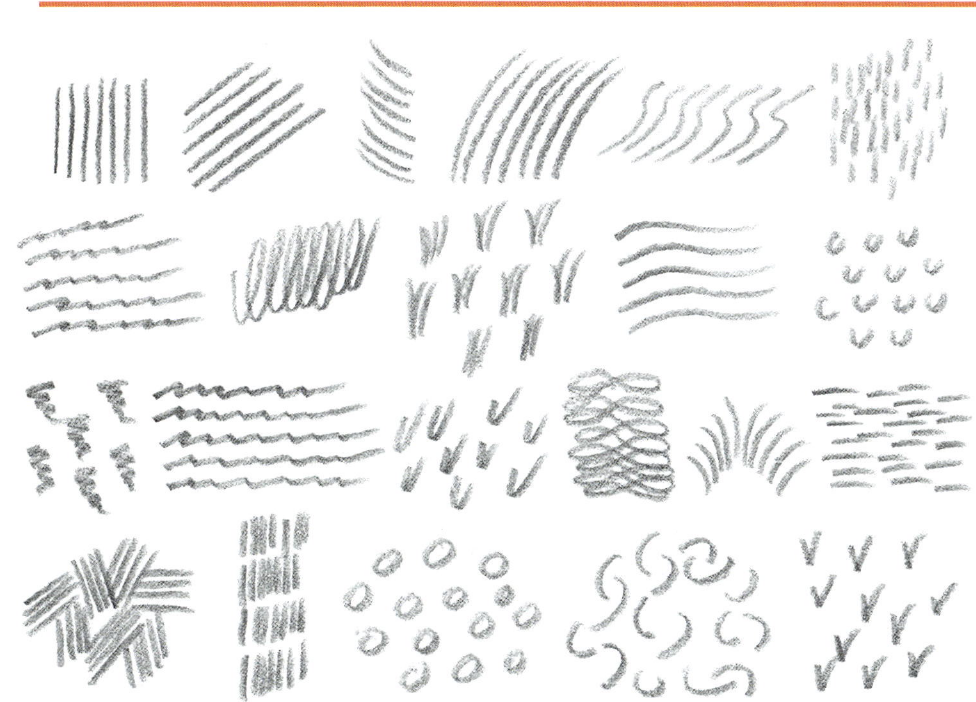

Drawing with a Blunt Point
Take the same exercises, and try them with a blunt point. Even if you use the same hand positions and strokes, the results will be different when you switch pencils. Take a look at these examples. The same shapes were drawn with both pencils, but the blunt pencil produced different images. You can create a blunt point by rubbing the tip of the pencil on a sandpaper block or on a rough piece of paper.

"PAINTING" WITH PENCIL

When you use painterly strokes, your drawing will take on a new dimension. Think of your pencil as a brush, and allow yourself to put more of your arm into the stroke. To create this effect, try using the underhand position, holding your pencil between your thumb and forefinger and using the side of the pencil. (See page 8.) If you rotate the pencil in your hand every few strokes, you will not have to sharpen it as frequently. The larger the lead, the wider the stroke will be. The softer the lead, the more painterly an effect you will have. These examples were all made on smooth paper with a 6B pencil, but you can experiment with rough papers for more broken effects.

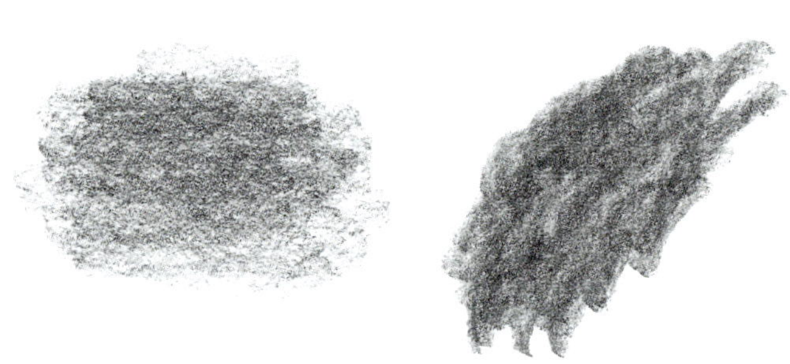

Starting Simply First experiment with vertical, horizontal, and curved strokes. Keep the strokes close together, and begin with heavy pressure. Then lighten the pressure with each stroke.

Varying the Pressure Randomly cover the area with tone, varying the pressure at different points. Continue to keep your strokes loose.

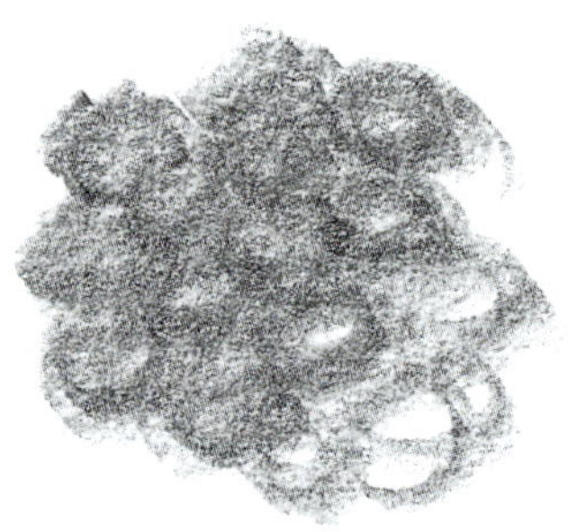

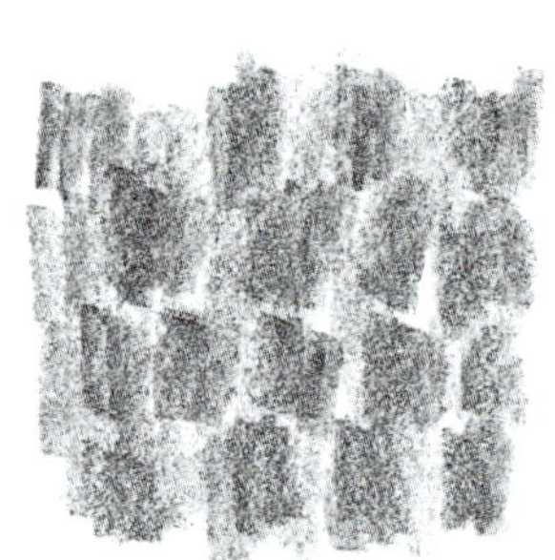

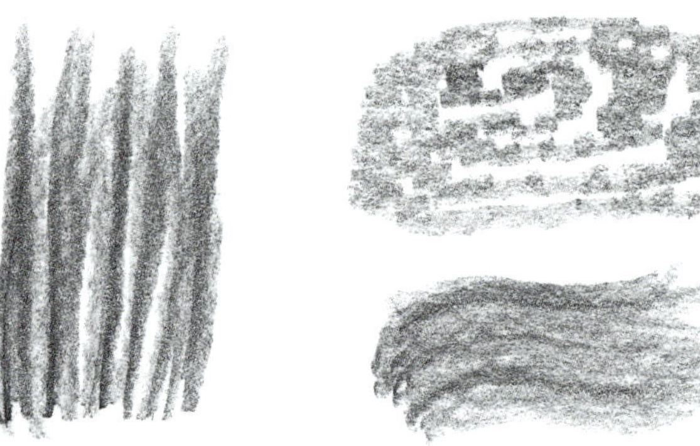

Using Smaller Strokes Make small circles for the first example. This is reminiscent of leathery animal skin. For the second example, use short, alternating strokes of heavy and light pressure to create a pattern that looks similar to stone or brick.

Loosening Up Use long vertical strokes, varying the pressure for each stroke until you start to see long grass (left). Then use somewhat looser movements that could be used for water (bottom). First create short spiral movements with your arm. Then use a wavy movement, varying the pressure (top).

EXERCISE: FEELING THE PENCIL ON THE PAPER

After some time, you will develop a sense of how the pencil will feel in your hand when you practice different types of shading. You will also have a better understanding of how much pressure you need to apply when creating graphic figures. First draw a conglomerate of various interlocking circles and ovals. Then fill the areas and shapes with different shadings and tonal values. The most important thing is that you develop a routine when working with the pencil.

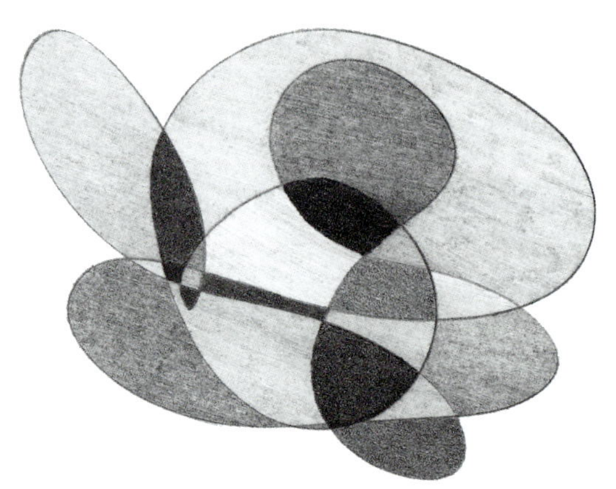

FINDING YOUR STYLE

Many great artists of the past can now be identified by their unique experiments with line. Van Gogh's drawings were a feast of calligraphic lines; Seurat became synonymous with pointillism; and Giacometti was famous for his scribble. Can you find your identity in a pencil stroke?

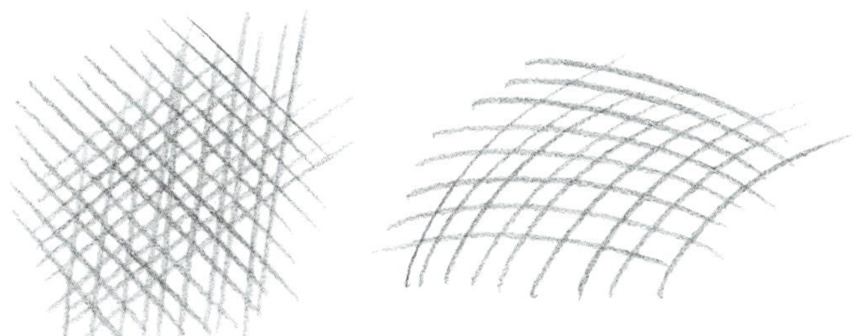

Using Criss-Crossed Strokes If you like a good deal of fine detail in your work, you'll find that crosshatching allows you a lot of control (see page 8). You can adjust the depth of your shading by changing the distance between your strokes.

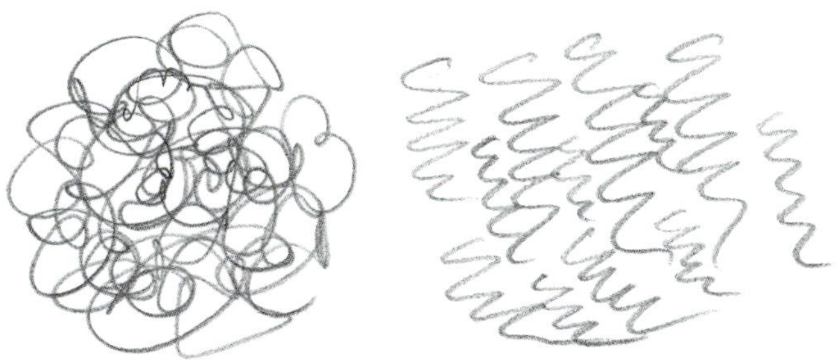

Sketching Circular Scribbles If you work with round, loose strokes like these, you are probably very experimental with your art. These looping lines suggest a free-form style that is more concerned with evoking a mood than with capturing precise details.

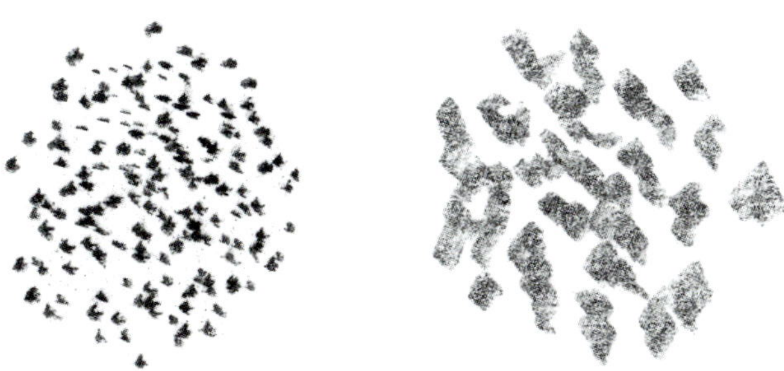

Drawing Small Dots This technique is called "stippling"—many small dots are used to create a larger picture. Make the points different sizes to create various depths and shading effects. Stippling takes a great deal of precision and practice.

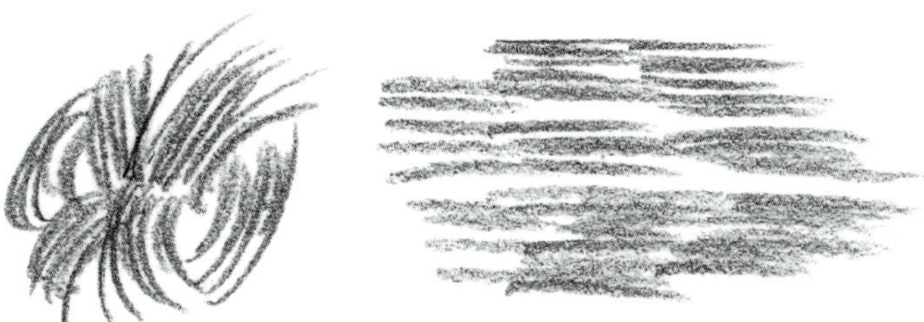

Simulating Brushstrokes You can create the illusion of brushstrokes by using short, sweeping lines. This captures the feeling of painting but allows you the same control you would get from crosshatching. These strokes are ideal for a more stylistic approach.

SHARPENING YOUR DRAWING IMPLEMENTS

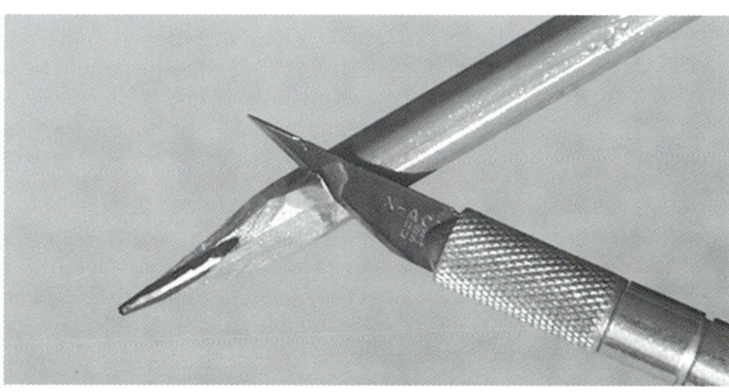

A Utility Knife can be used to form different points (chiseled, blunt, or flat) than are possible with an ordinary pencil sharpener. Hold the knife at a slight angle to the pencil shaft, and always sharpen away from you, taking off only a little wood and graphite at a time.

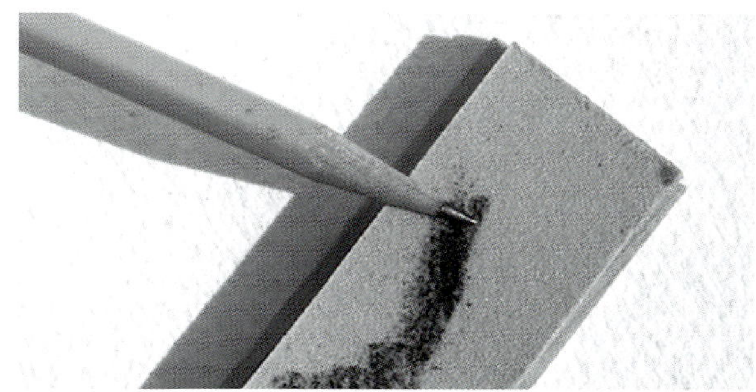

A Sandpaper Block will quickly hone the lead into any shape you wish. It also will sand down some of the wood. The finer the grit of the paper, the more controllable the resulting point. Roll the pencil in your fingers when sharpening to keep the shape even.

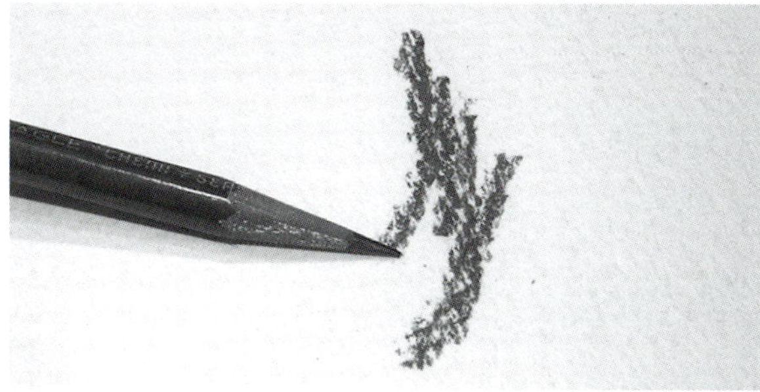

Rough Paper is wonderful for smoothing the pencil point after tapering it with sandpaper. This also is a great way to create a very fine point for small details. Again, it is important to gently roll the pencil while honing to sharpen the lead evenly.

The Elements of Drawing

Drawing consists of three elements: line, shape, and form. The shape of an object can be described with simple one-dimensional lines. The three-dimensional version of the shape is known as the object's "form." In pencil drawing, variations in value (the relative lightness or darkness of a color) describe form, giving an object the illusion of depth. In pencil drawing, values range from black (the darkest value) through different shades of gray to white (the lightest value). To make a two-dimensional object appear three-dimensional, you must pay attention to the values of the highlights and shadows. When shading a subject, you must always consider the light source, as this is what determines where your highlights and shadows will be added or placed.

MOVING FROM SHAPE TO FORM

The first step in creating an object is establishing a line drawing or outline to delineate the flat area that the object takes up. This is known as the "shape" of the object. The four basic shapes—the rectangle, circle, triangle, and square—can appear to be three-dimensional by adding a few carefully placed lines that suggest additional planes. By adding ellipses to the rectangle, circle, and triangle, you've given the shapes dimension and have begun to produce a form within space. Now the shapes are a cylinder, sphere, and cone. Add a second square above and to the side of the first square, connect them with parallel lines, and you have a cube.

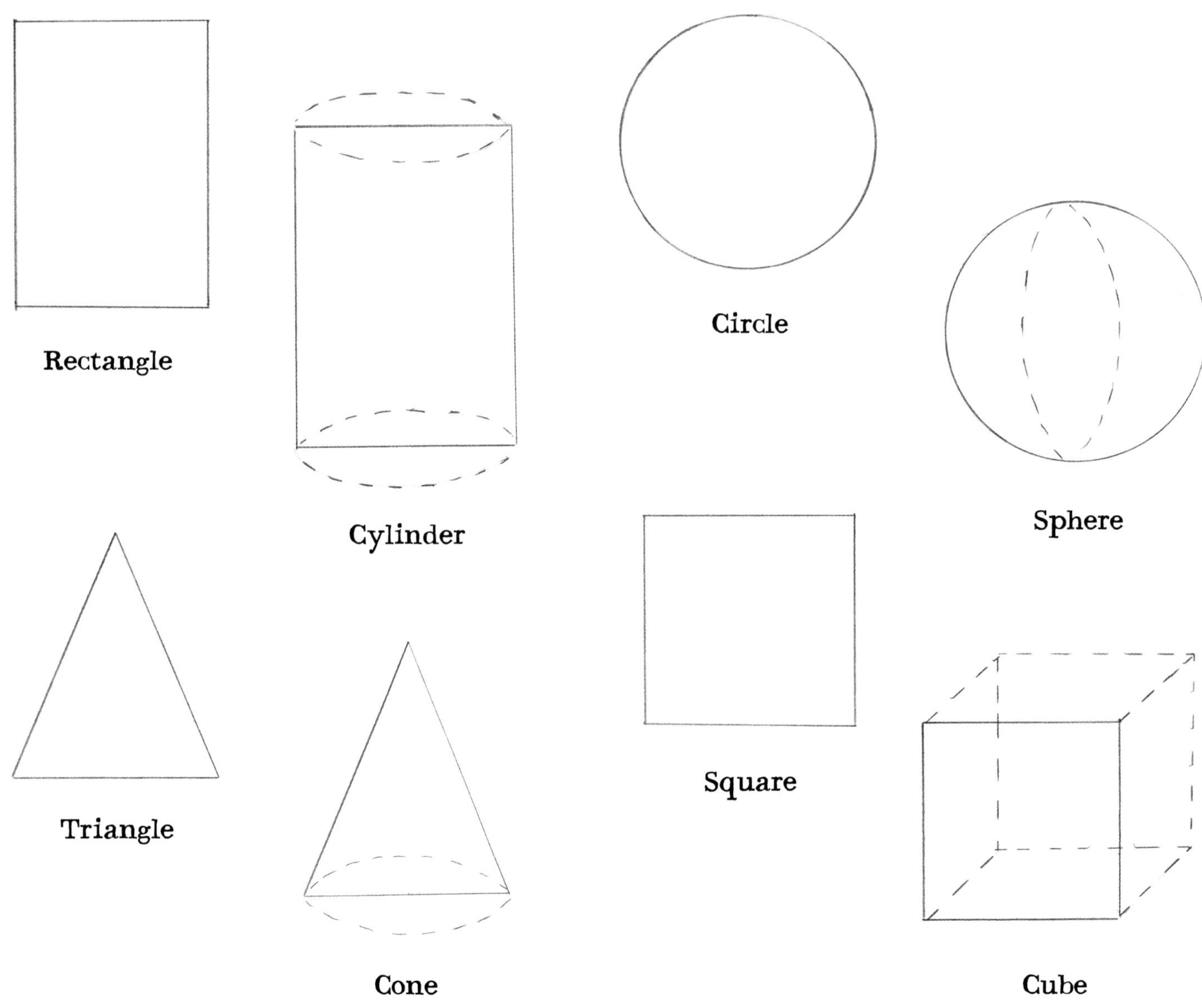

ADDING VALUE TO CREATE FORM

A shape can be further defined by showing how light hits the object to create highlights and shadows. First note from which direction the source of light is coming. (In these examples, the light source is beaming from the upper right.) Then add the shadows accordingly, as shown in the examples below. The core shadow is the darkest area on the object and is opposite the light source. The cast shadow is what is thrown onto a nearby surface by the object. The highlight is the lightest area on the object, where the reflection of light is strongest. Reflected light, often overlooked by beginners, is the surrounding light reflected into the shadowed area of an object.

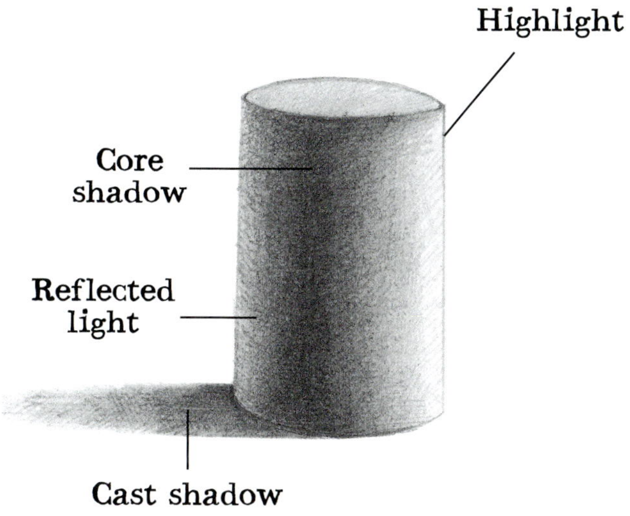

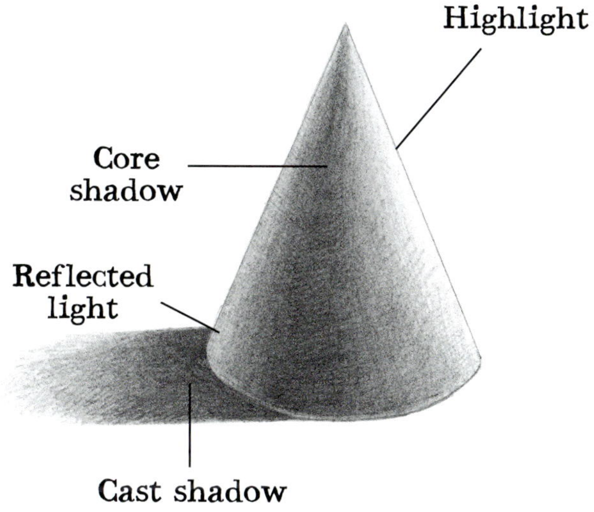

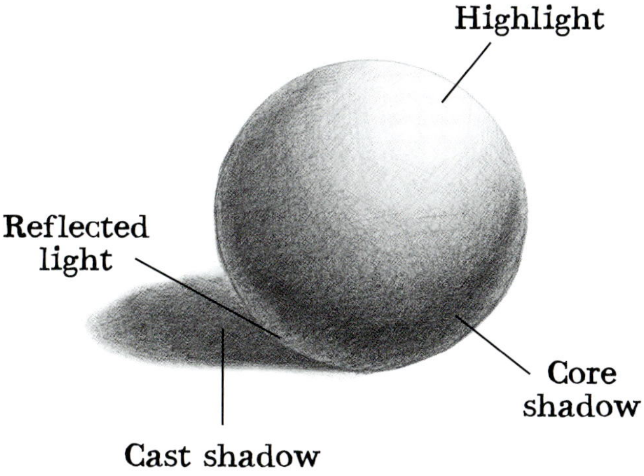

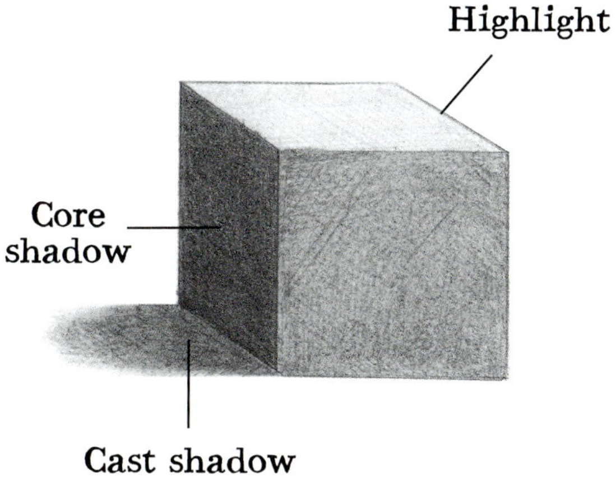

CREATING VALUE SCALES

Just as a musician uses a musical scale to measure a range of notes, an artist uses a value scale to measure changes in value. You can refer to the value scale so you'll always know how dark to make your dark values and how light to make your highlights. The scale also serves as a guide for transitioning from lighter to darker shades. Making your own value scale will help familiarize you with the different variations in value. Work from light to dark, adding more and more tone for successively darker values (top right). Then create a blended value scale (bottom right). Use a tortillon, or blending stump, to smudge and blend each value into its neighboring value from light to dark to create a gradation.

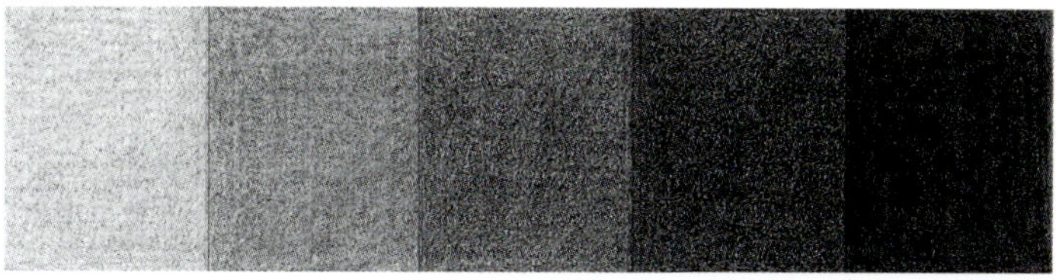

Learning to See

Many beginners draw without really looking carefully at their subject. Instead of drawing what they actually see, they draw what they think they see. Try drawing something you know well, such as your hand, without looking at it. Chances are your finished drawing won't look as realistic as you expected. That's because you drew what you think your hand looks like. Instead, you need to forget about all your preconceptions and learn to draw only what you really see in front of you (or in a photo). Two great exercises for training your eye to see are contour drawing and gesture drawing.

PENCILING THE CONTOURS

In contour drawing, you pick a starting point on your subject and then draw only the contours—or outlines—of the shapes you see. Because you're not looking at your paper, you're training your hand to draw the lines exactly as your eye sees them. Try doing some contour drawings of your own; you'll be surprised at how well you're able to capture the subjects.

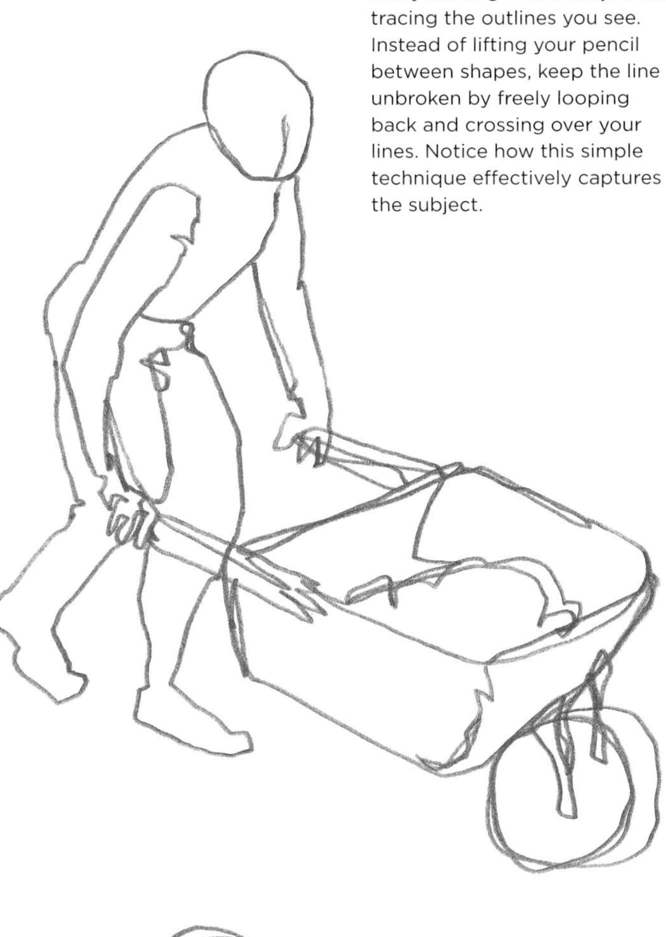

Drawing with a Continuous Line When drawing this man pushing a wheelbarrow, try glancing only occasionally at your paper to check that you are on track. Concentrate on really looking at the subject and tracing the outlines you see. Instead of lifting your pencil between shapes, keep the line unbroken by freely looping back and crossing over your lines. Notice how this simple technique effectively captures the subject.

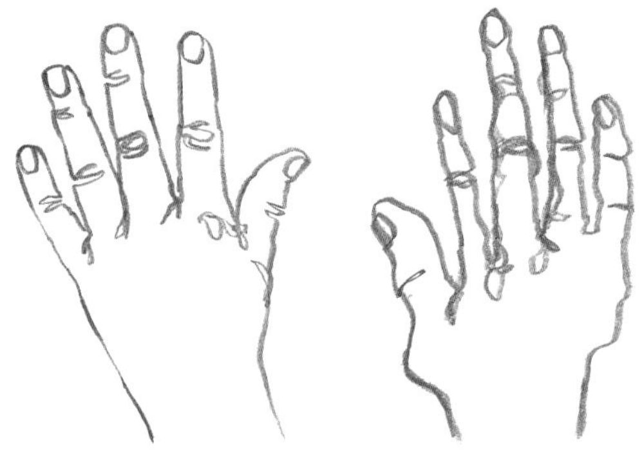

Drawing "Blind" For the contour drawing on the left, the artist occasionally looked down at the paper. The drawing on the right is an example of a blind contour drawing, where the artist drew without looking at the paper even once. It's a little distorted, but it's clearly a hand. Blind contour drawing is one of the best ways of making sure you're truly drawing only what you see.

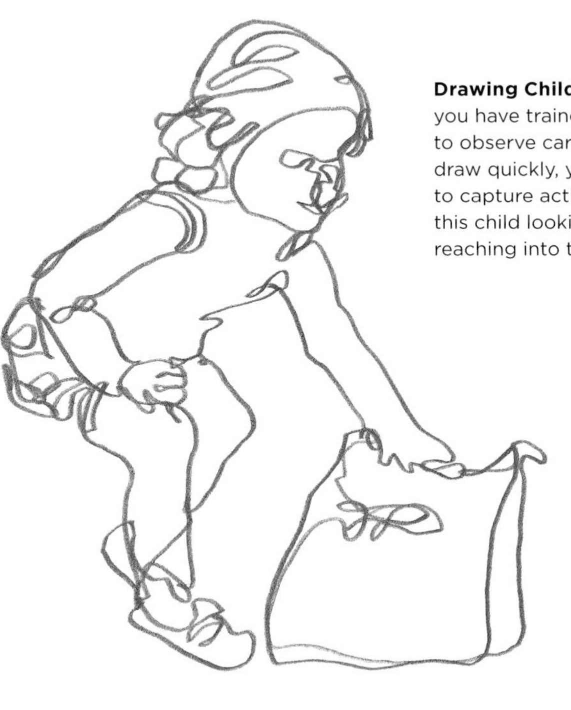

Drawing Children Once you have trained your eye to observe carefully and can draw quickly, you'll be able to capture actions such as this child looking and then reaching into the bag.

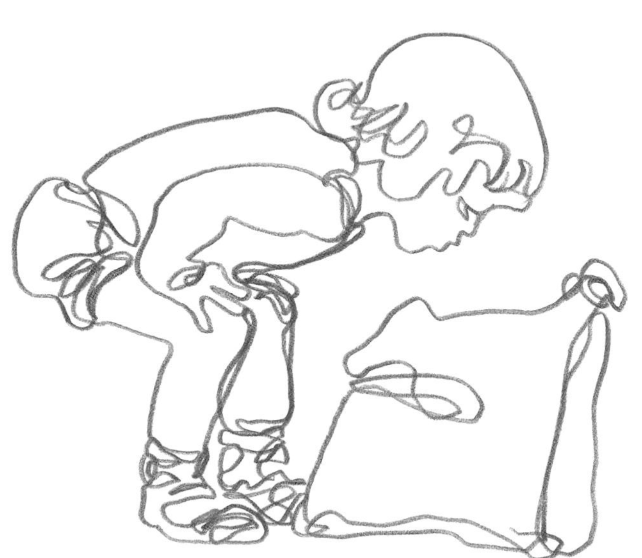

DRAWING GESTURE AND ACTION

Another way to train your eye to see the essential elements of a subject—and subsequently train your hand to record them rapidly—is through *gesture drawing.* Instead of rendering the contours, gesture drawings establish the *movement* of a figure. First determine the main thrust of the movement, from the head, down the spine, and through the legs; this is the *line of action,* or the *action line.* Then briefly sketch the general shapes of the figure around this line. These quick sketches are great for practicing drawing figures in action and sharpening your powers of observation.

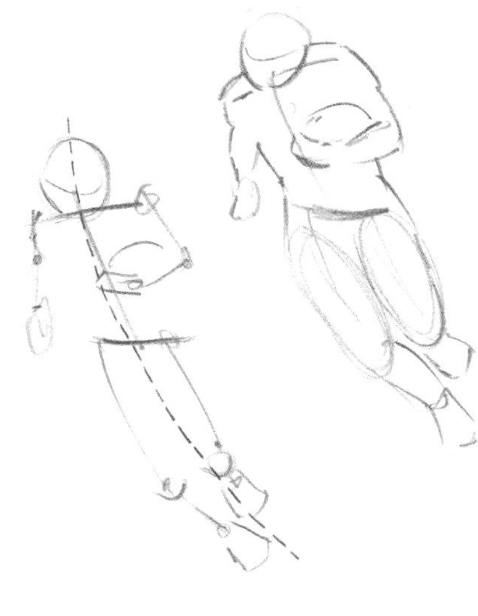

Starting with an Action Line Once you've established the line of action, try building a "skeleton" or stick drawing around it. Pay particular attention to the angles of the shoulders, spine, and pelvis. Then sketch in the placement of the arms, knees, and feet and roughly fill out the basic shapes of the figure.

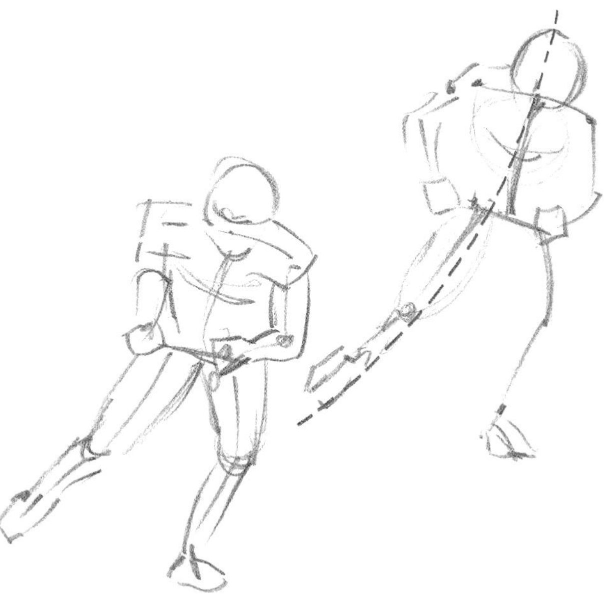

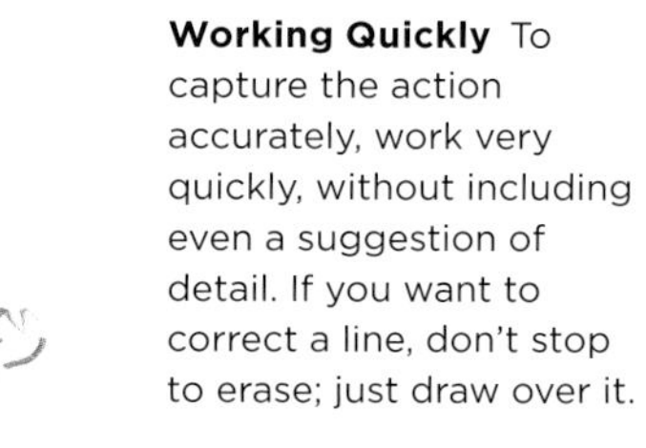

Working Quickly To capture the action accurately, work very quickly, without including even a suggestion of detail. If you want to correct a line, don't stop to erase; just draw over it.

Studying Repeated Action Group sports provide a great opportunity for practicing gesture drawings and learning to see the essentials. Because the players keep repeating the same action, you can observe each movement closely and keep it in your memory long enough to sketch it correctly.

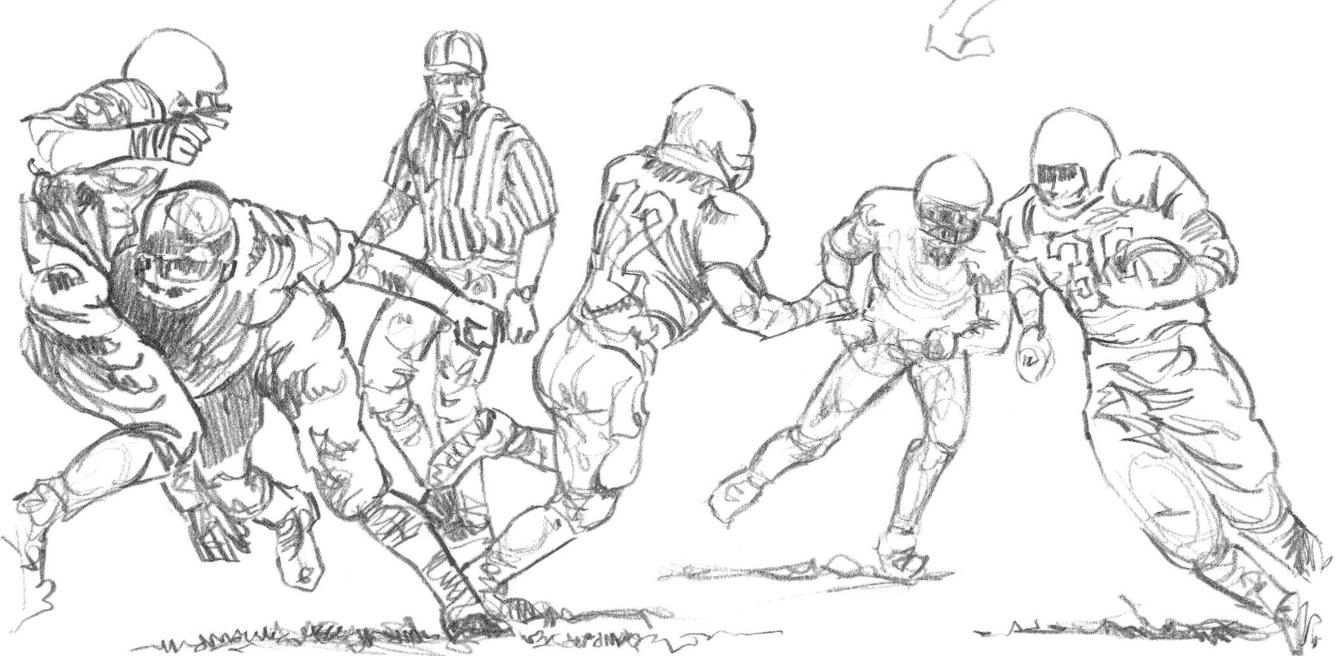

Drawing a Group in Motion Once you compile a series of gesture drawings, you can combine them into a scene of people in action.

Basic Facial Proportions

Drawing a person really is no different than drawing anything else. A human face has contours just like a landscape, an apple, or any other subject, and these contours catch the light and create shadow patterns just as they do on any other object. The difference is that the contours of the face change slightly from individual to individual. The "trick" to portraiture is observing these differences and duplicating them in your drawings.

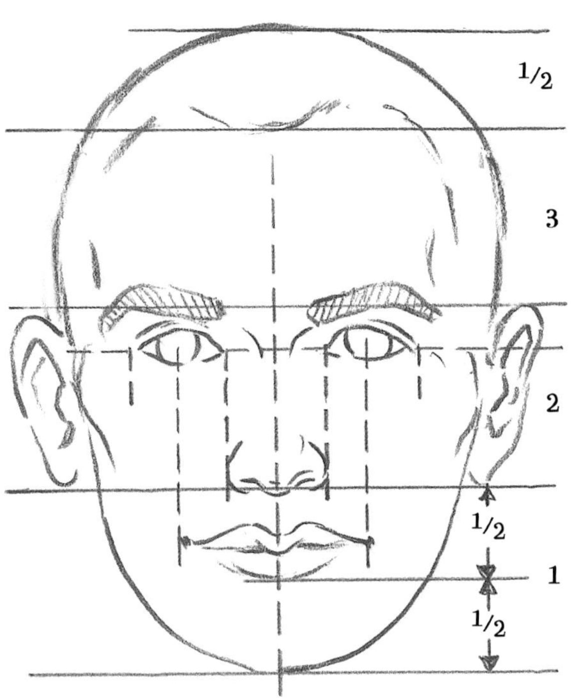

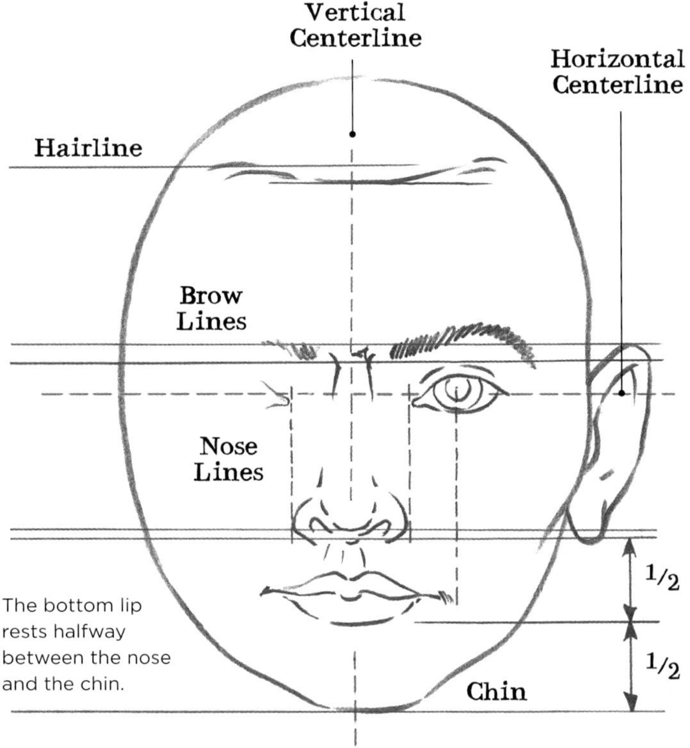

The bottom lip rests halfway between the nose and the chin.

Facial Proportions The charts on these pages show some general guidelines for facial proportions. The eyes sit in the middle of the head. The distance from the hairline to the brow line is usually the same distance as from the brow line to the bottom of the nose, and from the bottom of the nose to the chin. The lower lip rests halfway between the bottom of the nose and the chin. The eyes are one eye-width apart, and each eye is the same width as the nose. The width of the mouth is the distance from the center of one eye to the center of the other eye. The top of the ear aligns with the brow line; the bottom of the ear aligns with the nose.

To place the ear, divide the cranial mass into thirds.

CAPTURING A LIKENESS

You don't need to memorize all the bones, muscles, and tendons in the human head to draw a portrait; just follow the general rules of proportions, as shown in the chart on page 17. Simply divide the face into thirds, and note where the features fall in relation to the face and to one another. Then study your model to determine how his or her face differs from the chart (that is, how it is unique). Look for subtle changes, such as a wider nose or thinner lips, wide- or close-set eyes, and a higher or lower forehead. It also is important to practice drawing faces from different viewpoints—front, side, and three-quarter views—keeping the proportions the same but noting how the features change as the head turns. Remember: Draw what you really see and your portrait will look like your model!

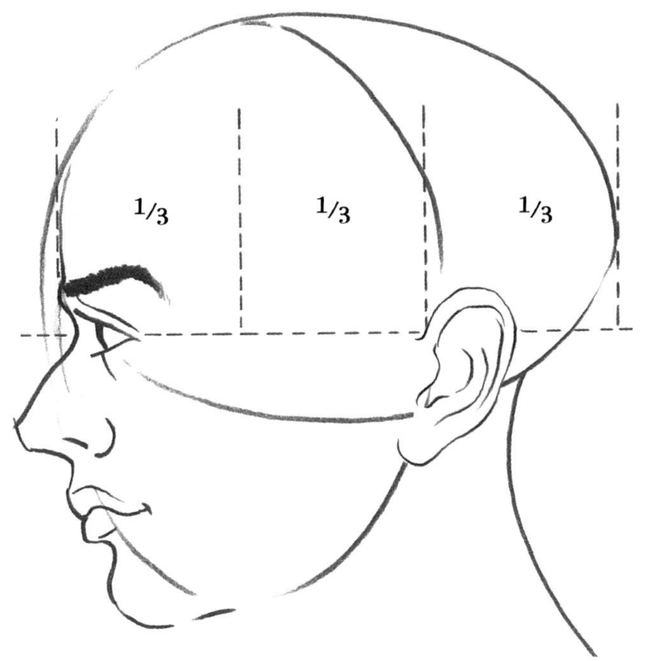

The length of the face is approximately equal to the depth of the head.

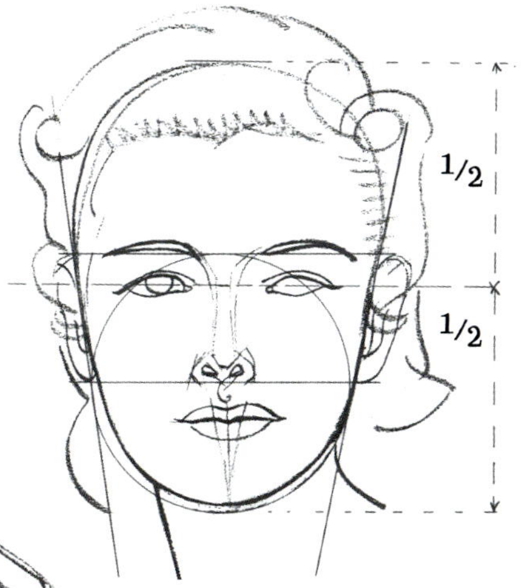

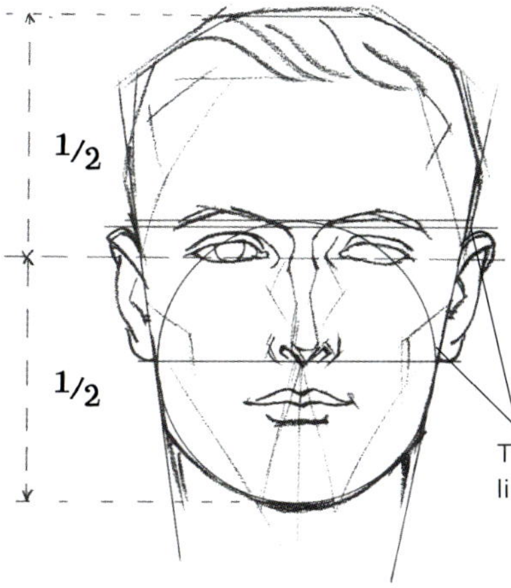

The ears extend from the brow line to the bottom of the nose.

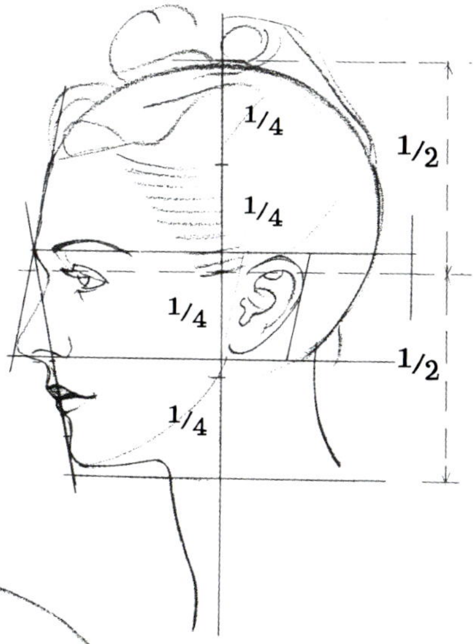

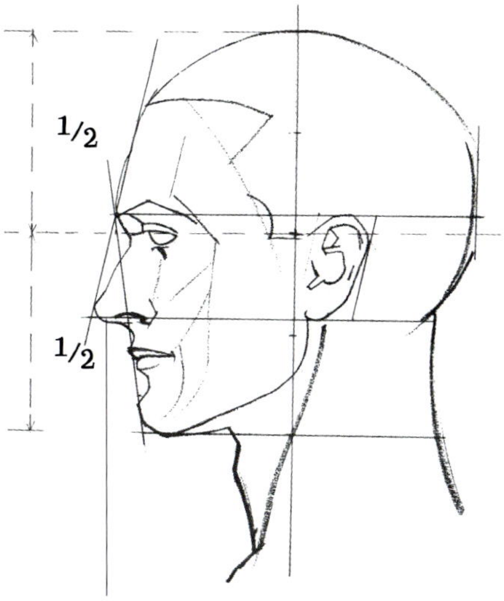

The bottom of the nose lies halfway between the brow line and the bottom of the chin.

ADULT HEAD PROPORTIONS

Learning proper head proportions will enable you to accurately draw the head of a person. Study the measurements on the illustration on the left. Draw a basic oval head shape, and divide it in half with a light, horizontal line. On an adult, the eyes fall on this line, usually about one "eye-width" apart. Draw another line dividing the head in half vertically to locate the position of the nose.

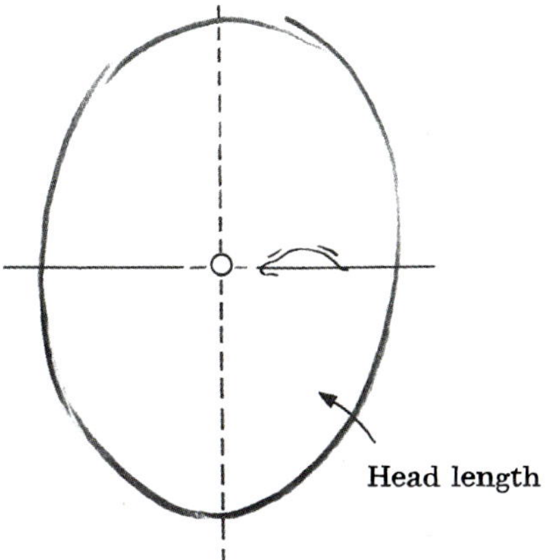

The diagram below illustrates how to determine correct placement for the rest of the facial features. Study it closely before beginning to draw, and make some practice sketches. The bottom of the nose lies halfway between the brow line and the bottom of the chin. The bottom lip rests halfway between the nose and the chin. The length of the ears extends from brow line to the bottom of the nose.

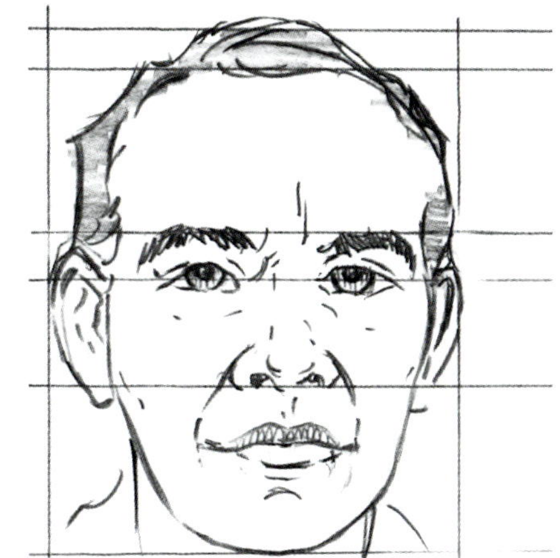

Art by William F. Powell

Focusing on Adult Proportions

Look for the proportions that make your adult subject unique; notice the distance from the top of the head to the eyes, from the eyes to the the nose, and from the nose to the chin. Look at where the mouth falls between the nose and the chin and where the ears align with the eyes and the nose.

Head Positions

The boxes shown here correlate with the head positions directly below them. Drawing boxes like these first will help you correctly position the head. The boxes also allow the major frontal and profile planes, or level surfaces, of the face to be discernable. Once you become comfortable with this process, practice drawing the heads shown on this page.

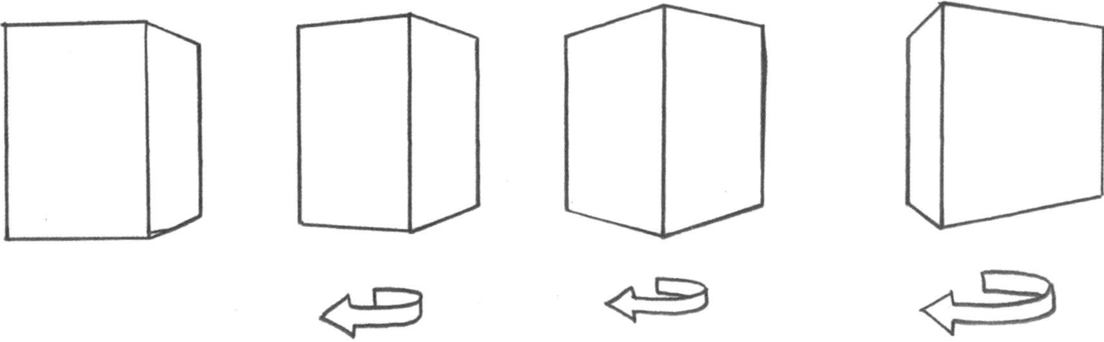

When drawing, pay attention to rules of perspective on the small space you are using. Once you start feeling more familiar with working with invisible vanishing points, you can venture into drafting the rough shape of a face (See page 29.)

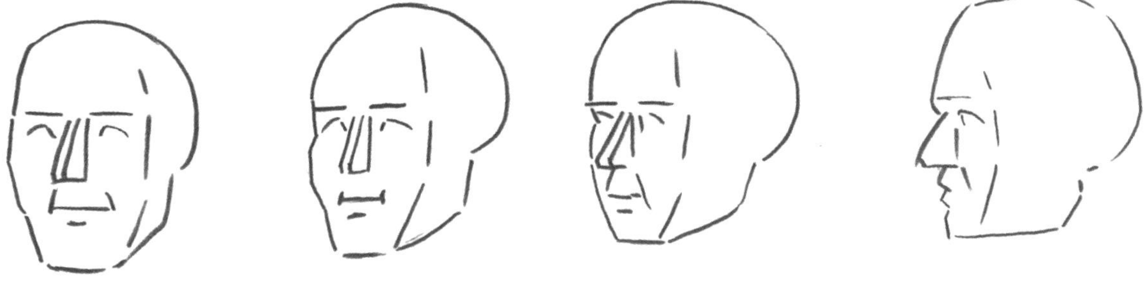

With just a few strokes, this rough shape of a smiling male face starts to take form. Place these few strokes with care following the rules of perspective.

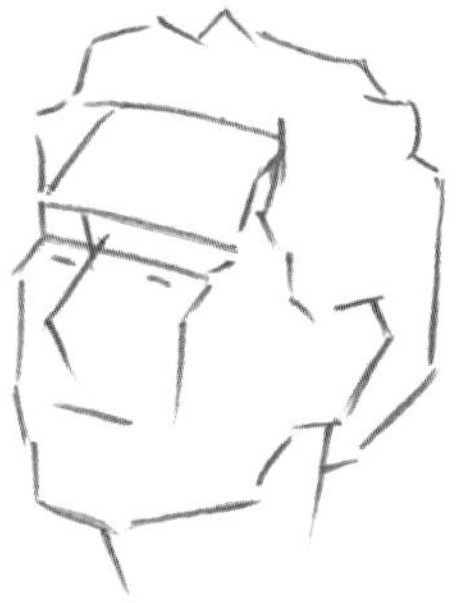

Keep all guidelines very light so they won't show in your actual drawing.

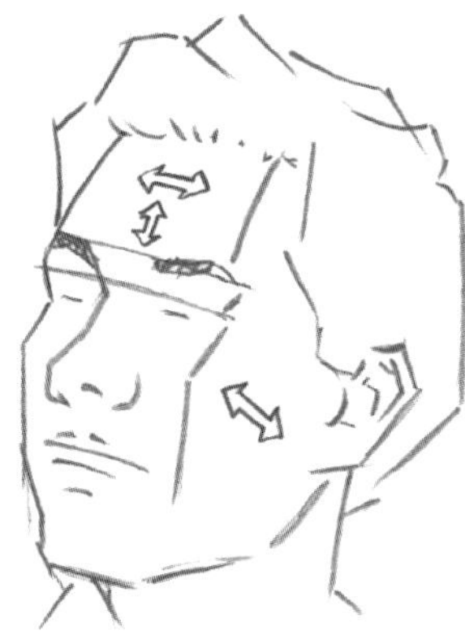

Your shading strokes should follow the arrow directions to bring out the contours of the face.

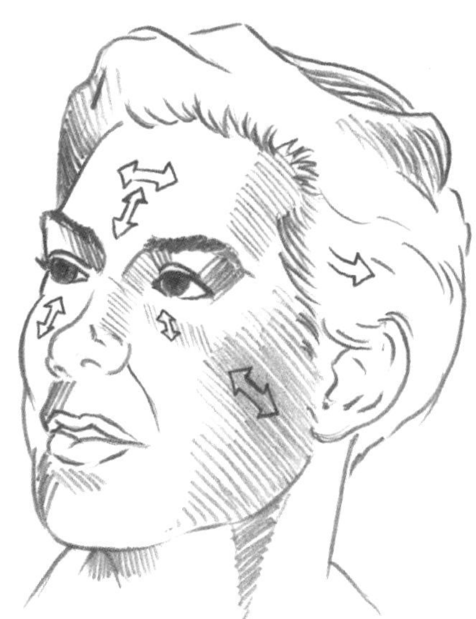

THE THREE-QUARTER VIEW

Although the three-quarter view may seem difficult, it can be drawn by following all of the techniques you've already learned. With an HB pencil, use the proper head proportions to lightly sketch the guidelines indicating where the main features will be located.

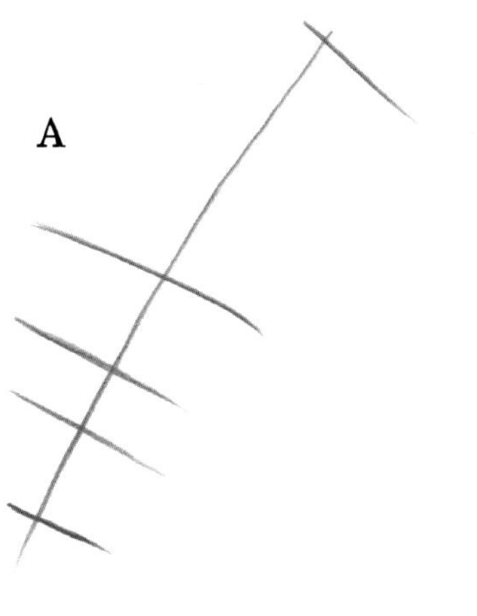

A

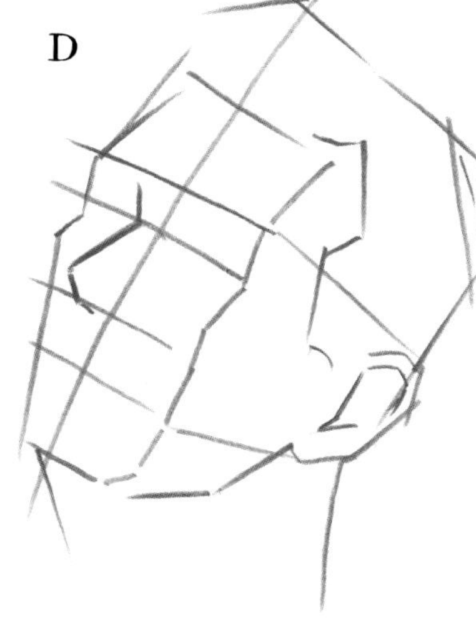

D

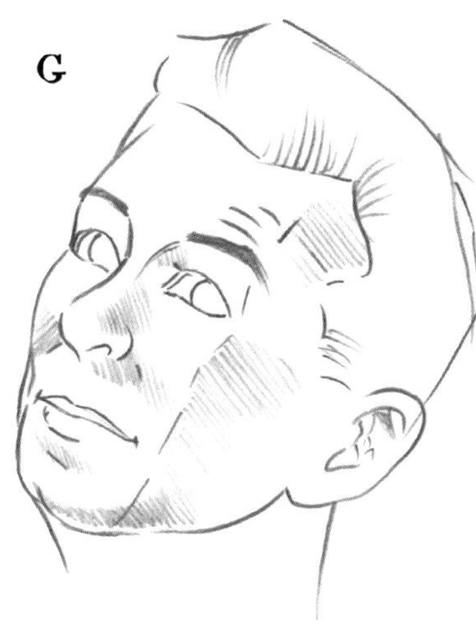

G

Begin to smooth out your block-in lines, shading lightly with an HB pencil to bring out the face's three-dimensional form. Fill in the creases and details with a sharp-pointed pencil; then use a kneaded eraser molded into an edge or point to pull out the highlights in the hair.

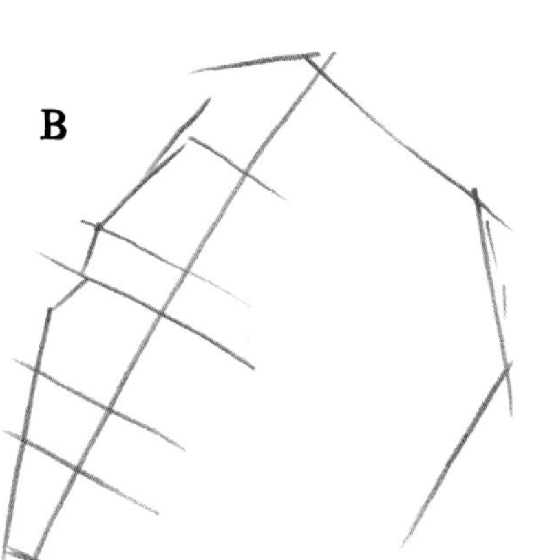

B

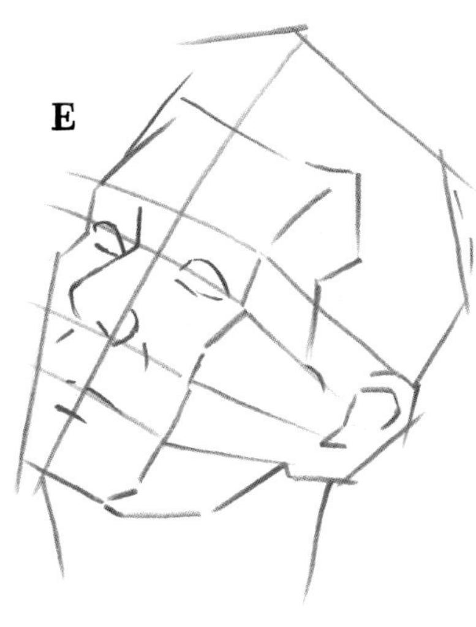

E

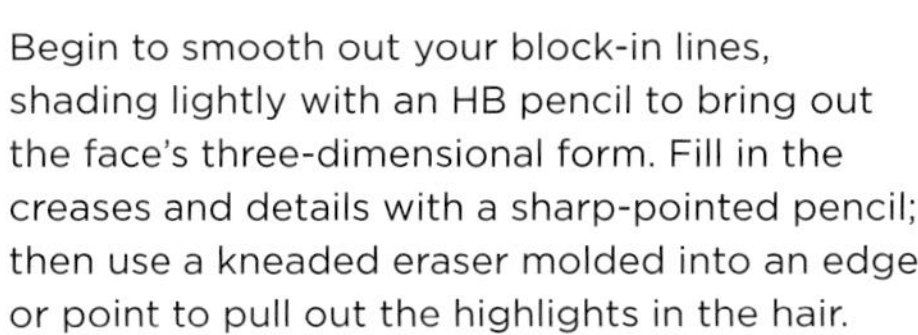

Begin blocking in the shape of the head; then add the hairline, and sketch the ear. Bring out the planes of the face (imagine a box), and position the nose correctly. Sketch the eyes and mouth on the guidelines you've drawn.

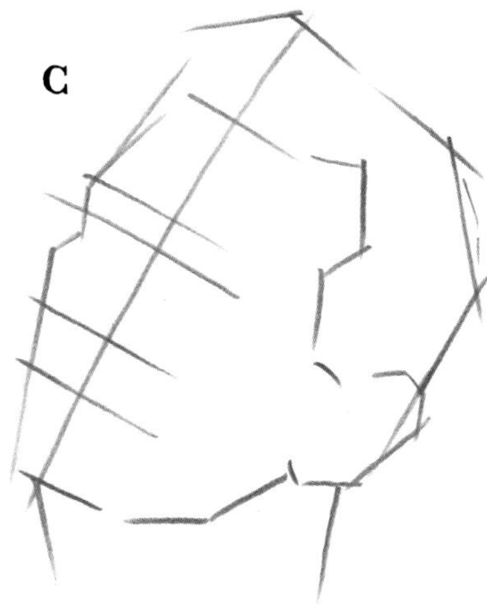

C

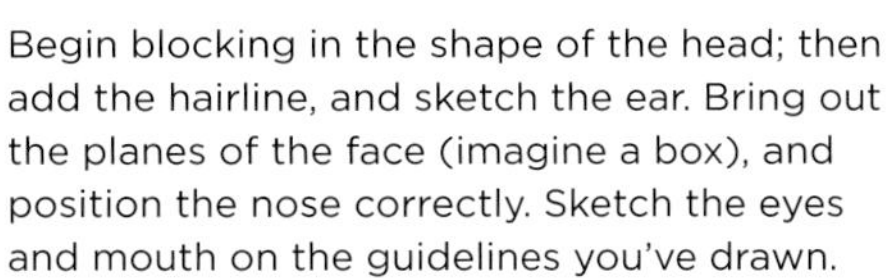

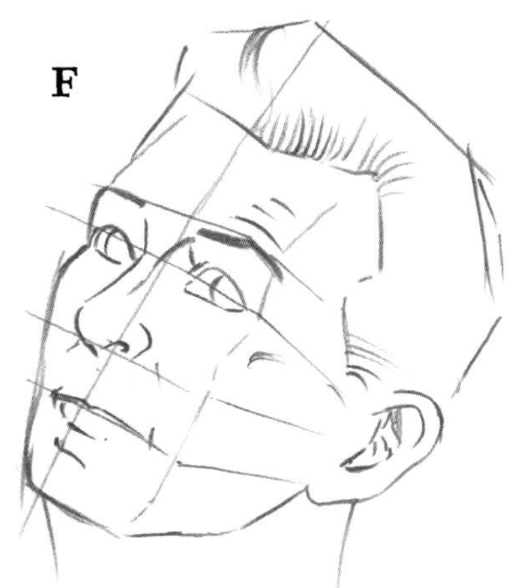

F

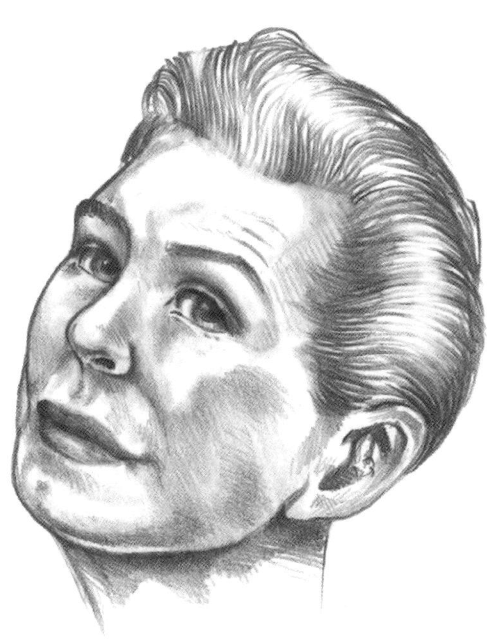

Basic Facial Shapes

Many people believe that drawing the human face is difficult, but it's really only a matter of proportion and properly placing the features. The lines and forms involved are just simple curves and basic shapes. The easiest way to learn to draw people is to start with individual features such as the eyes and mouth. It's best to draw from a photo or a live model. A reference makes rendering facial features easier.

Eye

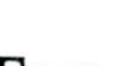

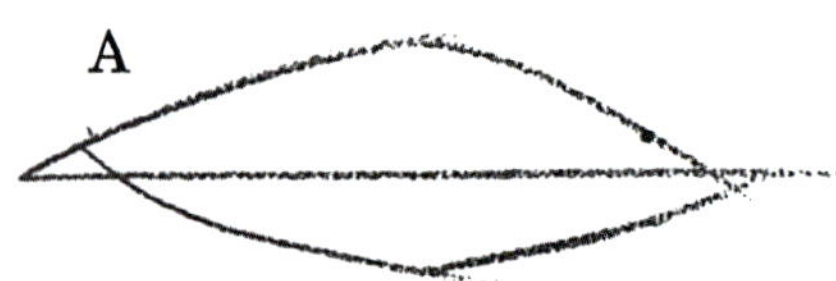

In this view, the iris is set somewhat off center, so place your guidelines just to the right of center.

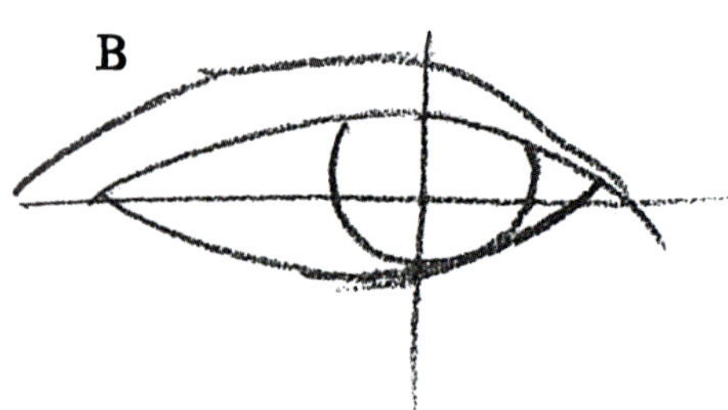

Highlight

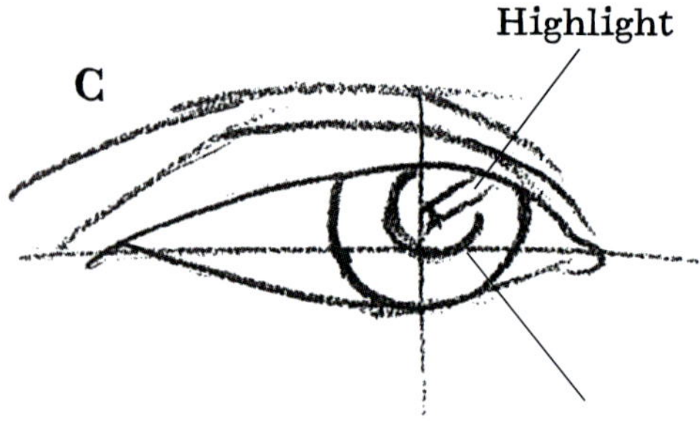

Whether from a frontal view or in profile, eyes and lips are drawn around horizontal and vertical guidelines. Both guidelines are perpendicular in the frontal view, and the vertical line is slanted slightly in the profile view. You can build on these guidelines with circles and simple curved lines. Study the outlines on this page, and practice drawing them several times.

Eye in Profile

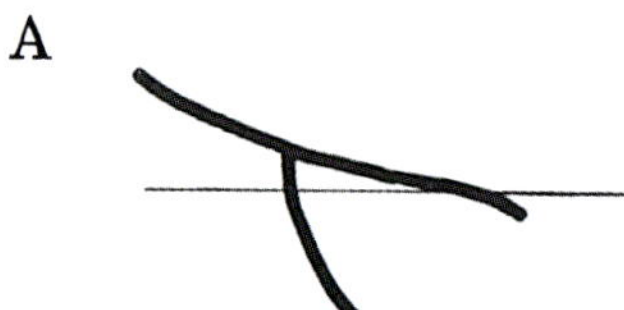

Notice that a good portion of the eyeball is covered by the eyelid, no matter what the viewpoint.

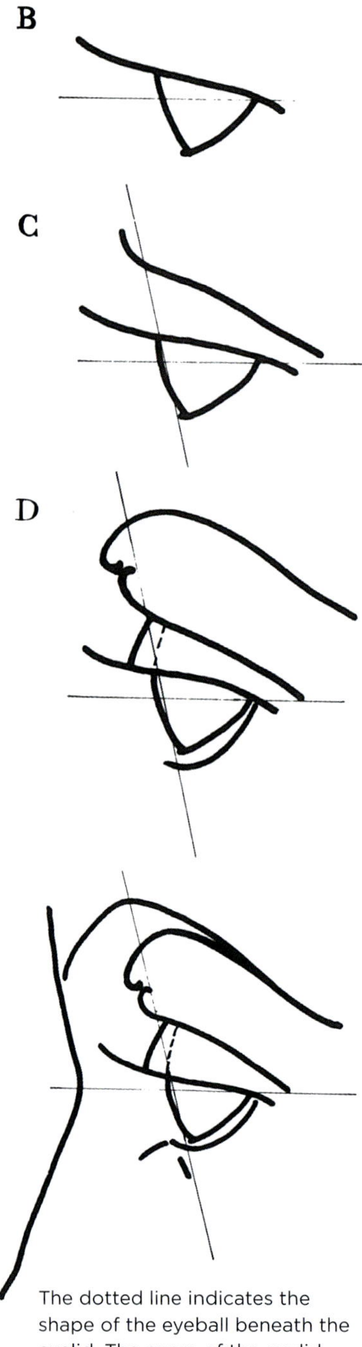

The dotted line indicates the shape of the eyeball beneath the eyelid. The curve of the eyelid follows the curve of the eyeball.

Mouth

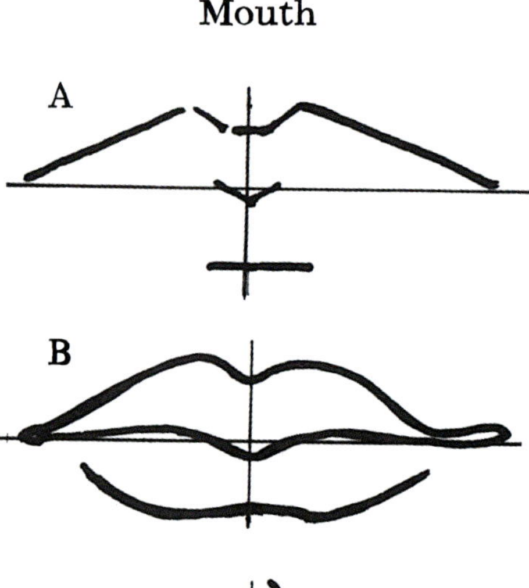

Mouth in Profile

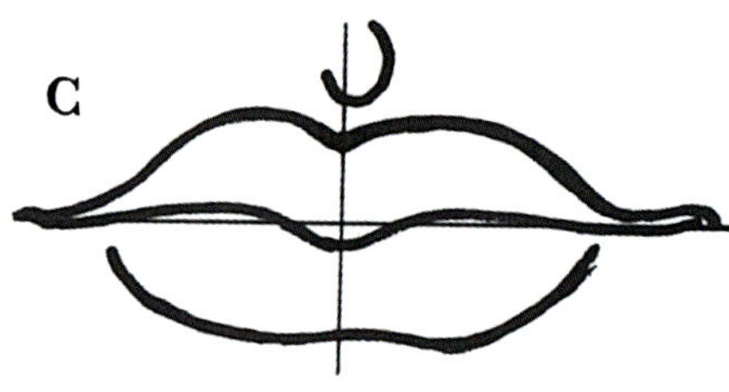

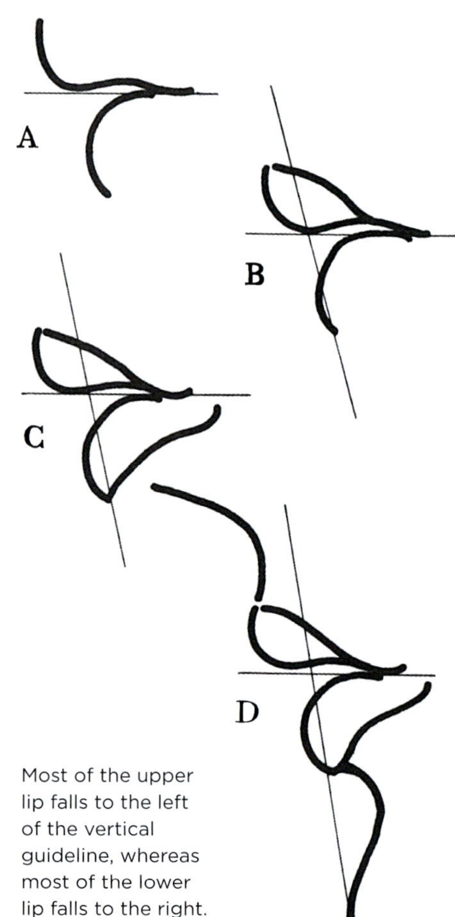

Most of the upper lip falls to the left of the vertical guideline, whereas most of the lower lip falls to the right.

These human profiles are built on two slanted
guidelines: one for the line of the plane of the face,
and one for the line of the nose. There are a variety
of sizes and shapes of noses, eyes, and mouths;
study your subject closely, and make several practice
sketches of his or her features. Then combine the
features into a simple profile.

For the full profile, start with
a slanted guideline from the
eyebrow to the chin. Then add
horizontal guidelines to place the
features. In adults, the bottom of
the nose is approximately halfway
between the eyebrow and the
bottom of the chin. The bottom
lip is about halfway between the
nose and the chin. Note that these
are just general rules of human
proportion. The precise placement
of features will vary slightly from
individual to individual and
between men and women.

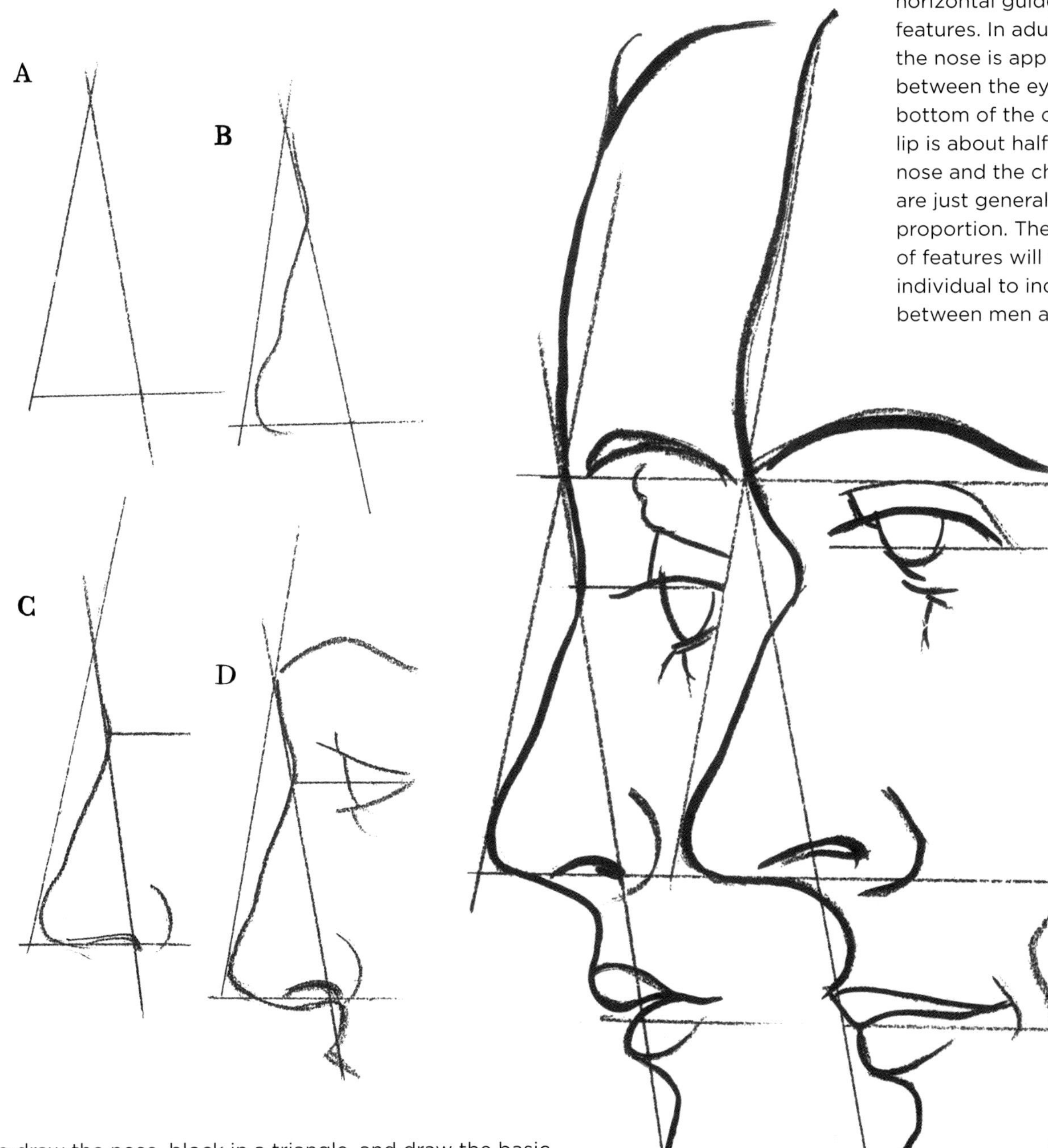

To draw the nose, block in a triangle, and draw the basic
outline of the nose within the triangle, as in steps A and B.
Refine the outline, and add a small curve to
suggest the nostril in step C.

Then add the centerline for the eye at the top of the bridge
of the nose. Next place the eye, eyebrow, and upper lip in
step D. Once you are satisfied with your sketches, try a
complete profile.

Basic Profile View

Like the previous drawings, this profile is a good exercise for becoming accustomed to placing the features correctly as well as practicing how to draw the individual features. Pay close attention to the shapes of the nose and chin; these features will greatly affect the overall appearance.

In step A, begin with a slightly curved vertical line, and add guidelines according to the proportions you've learned. Then lightly block in the features. In step B, begin to refine the shapes. Ask yourself what your subject's nose looks like. Is it long or short? Broad or narrow? Does the tip turn up or down? Is the bridge sloped, or does it have a bump? These are the factors that will determine whether you achieve a likeness or not.

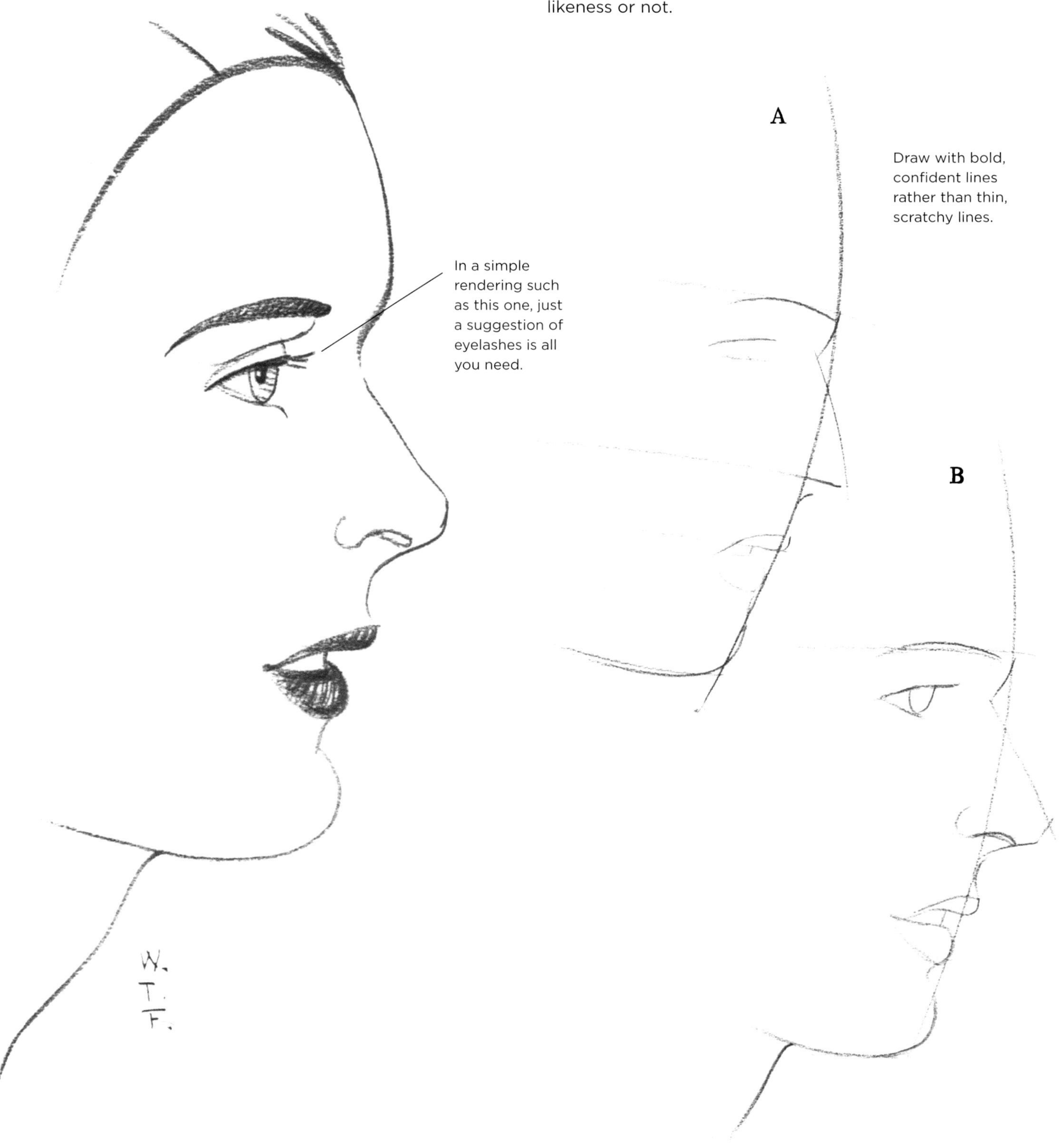

These heads were drawn from photos. Try profile views like the ones you see here, keeping them fairly simple. Don't worry about rendering the hair for now; spend time learning how to draw the face, and work on the hair later. Step A illustrates the proportions of the face. In this close-up profile, the bottom of the nose is about halfway between the eyebrows and chin. The mouth is about halfway between the bottom of the nose and the chin. Once the proportions are established, sketch the actual features. Study each one closely to achieve an accurate resemblance.

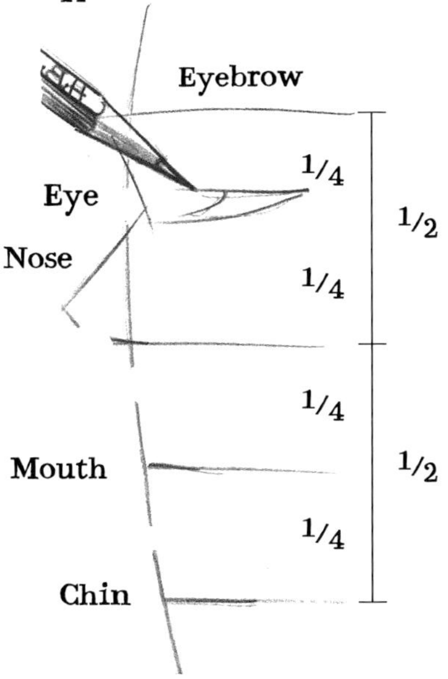

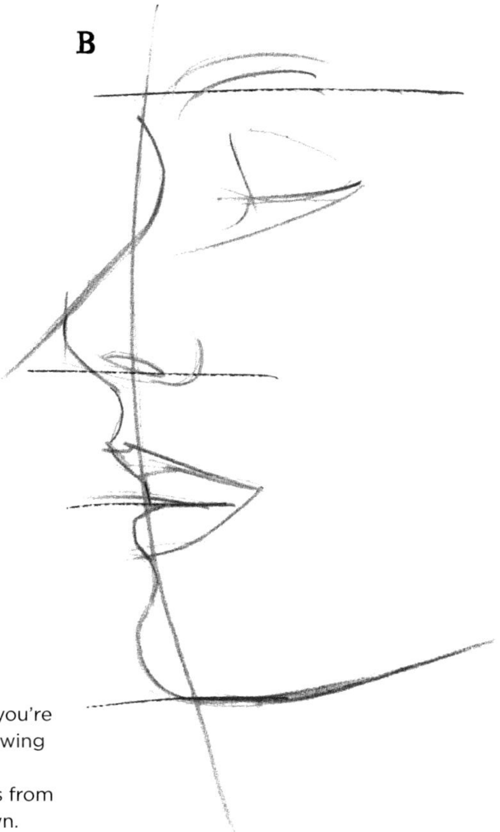

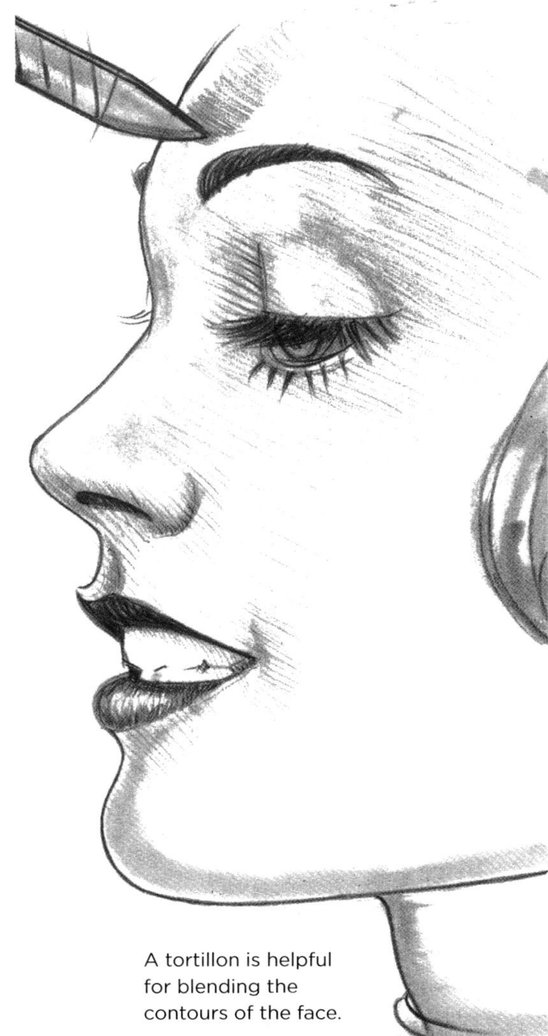

When drawing portraits, make sure you're comfortably seated and that the drawing board is at a good angle. Rotate the drawing often to prevent your hands from smudging areas you've already drawn.

Tortillon

A tortillon is helpful for blending the contours of the face.

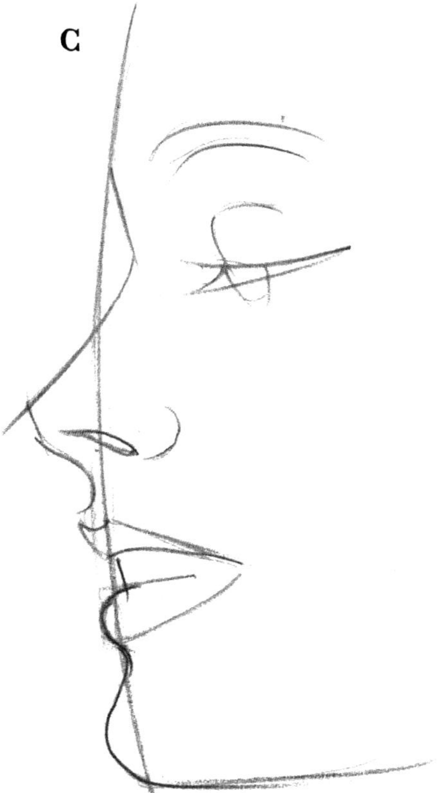

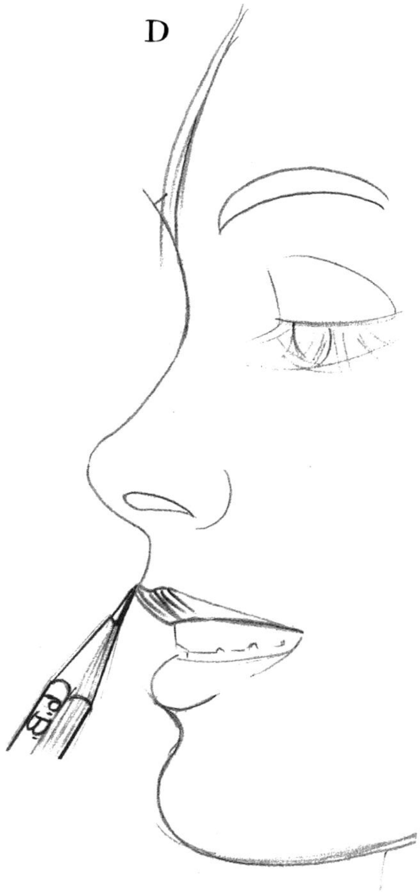

Basic Front View

For these front-view drawings, you will need to pay special attention to the position of the features. In a profile, for example, you don't have to worry about aligning the eyes with each other. Study your subject closely, because a small detail, such as the distance between the eyes, may determine whether your drawing achieves a strong likeness to your model.

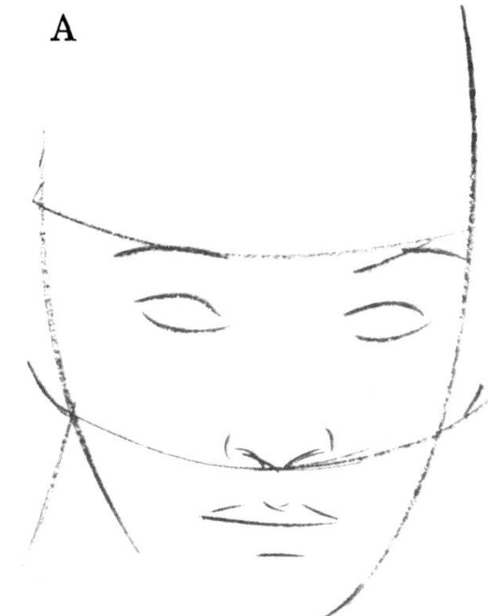

A

Step A shows minimal proportion guidelines. You will be able to start with fewer lines as you become more comfortable with your drawing and observation skills. Even the two lines shown are helpful for determining placement of the features.

A few loose, curving strokes with a chisel-tipped pencil can create the appearance of a full head of hair.

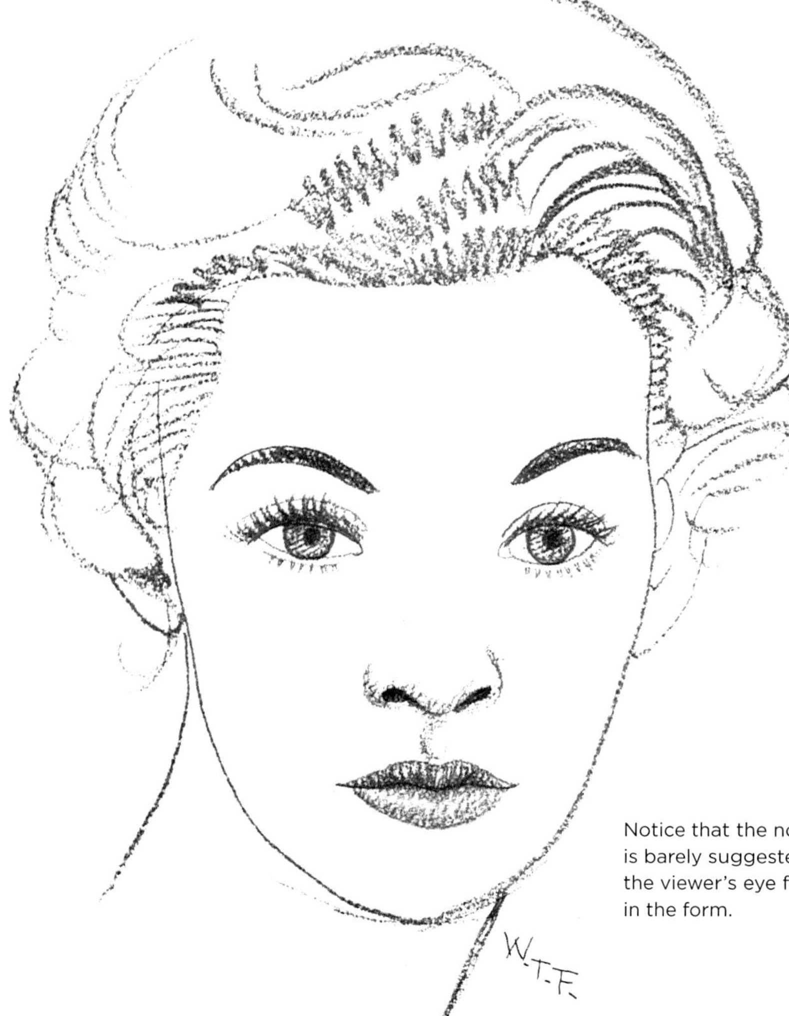

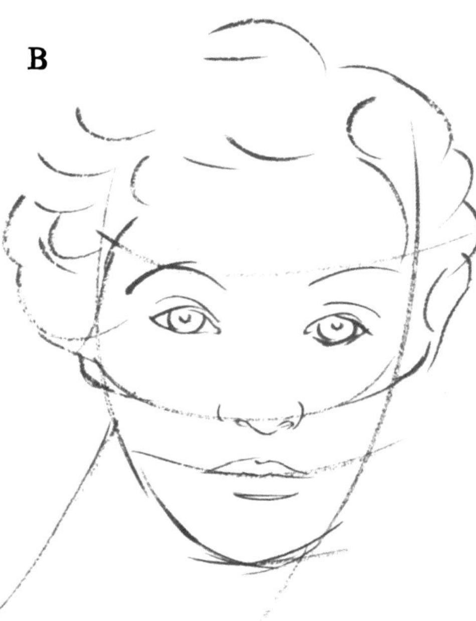

B

Notice that the nose is barely suggested; the viewer's eye fills in the form.

In step B, make the facial features more recognizable, and begin to suggest the hair. Notice that features rarely are symmetrical; for instance, one eye usually is slightly larger than the other. To finish the drawing, create depth by shading the eyes, nose, and lips. If you wish, practice developing form by shading along the planes of the face and around the eyes.

The features of this subject's face differ from those in the previous drawing. Here the nose is much thinner, and the eyes are closer together. You will need to make these adjustments during the block-in stage. In step A, use an HB pencil to block in the proportions. Use the guidelines to place and develop the features in step B. Notice the types of strokes used for the hair; they are loose and free. Quick renderings like this one are good for practice; do many of them!

A

B

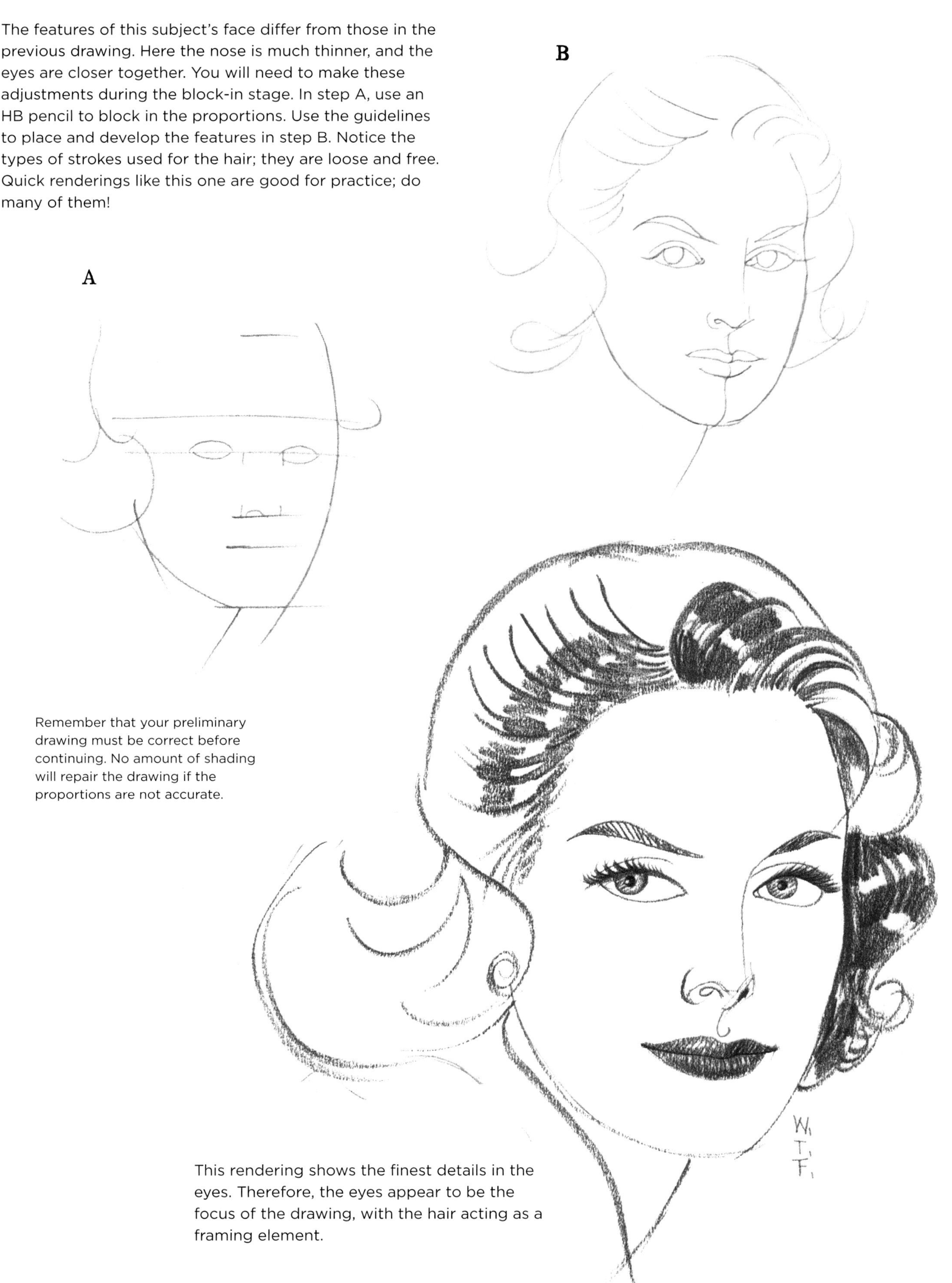

Remember that your preliminary drawing must be correct before continuing. No amount of shading will repair the drawing if the proportions are not accurate.

This rendering shows the finest details in the eyes. Therefore, the eyes appear to be the focus of the drawing, with the hair acting as a framing element.

Basic Three-Quarter View

Accurate proportions are important when drawing the three-quarter view. Start with curved guidelines to help you determine where to place the features. Light shading can help add dimension to your drawing.

A

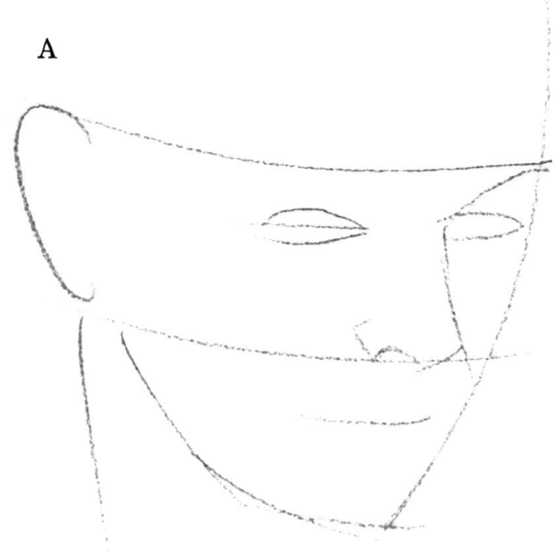

When you block in the hair, think of it as one mass that has a curved outline. You can suggest some of the individual hairs later.

B

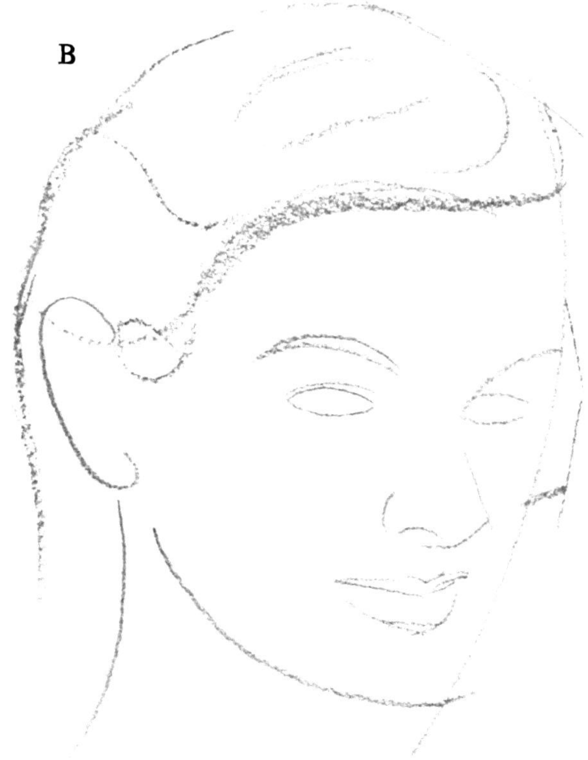

C

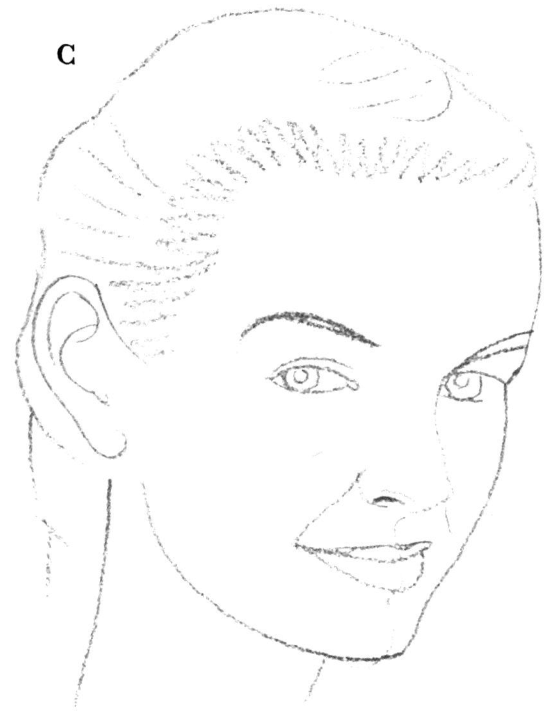

Check the proportions and the placement of the features. When you're happy with your sketch, refine the features, and add some light shading to finish off your drawing. Shade as much or as little as you like; sometimes simpler is better.

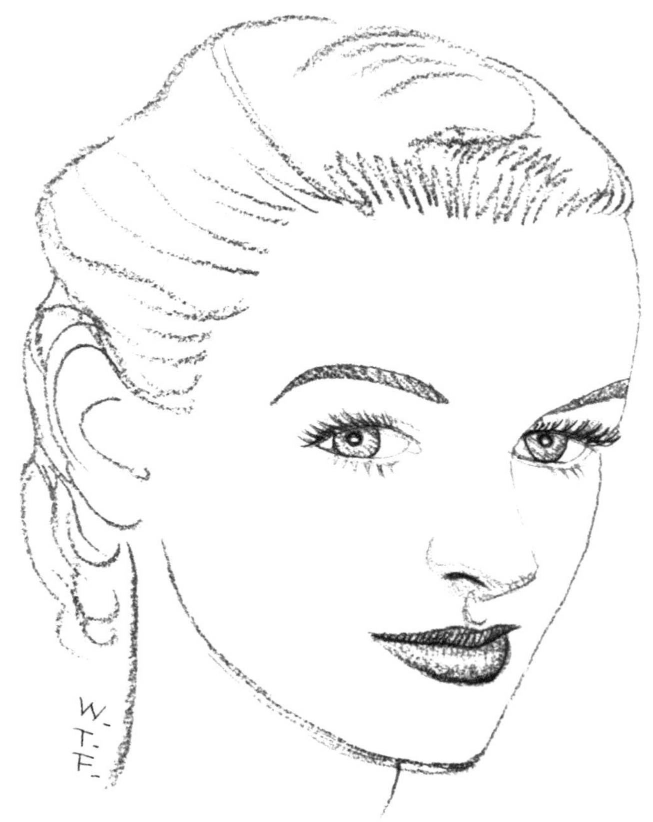

Browse through books and magazines for subjects to draw, or look in the mirror and draw yourself. The more you practice and the more diverse your subjects, the better your drawings will become. Young or old, male or female, all portraits start with the same basic steps.

A

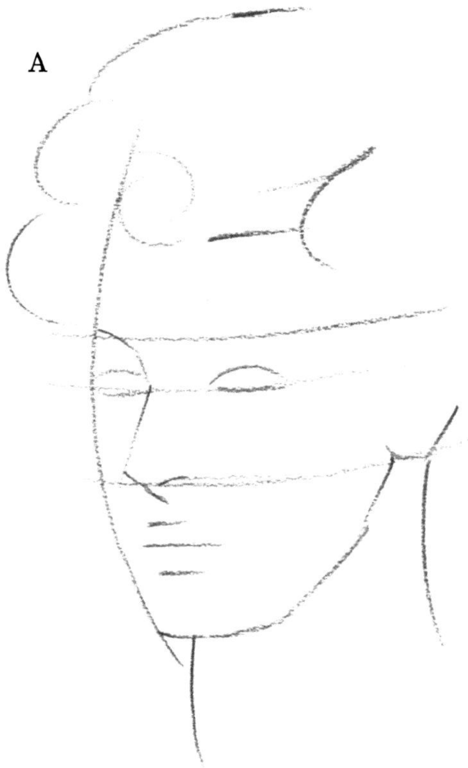

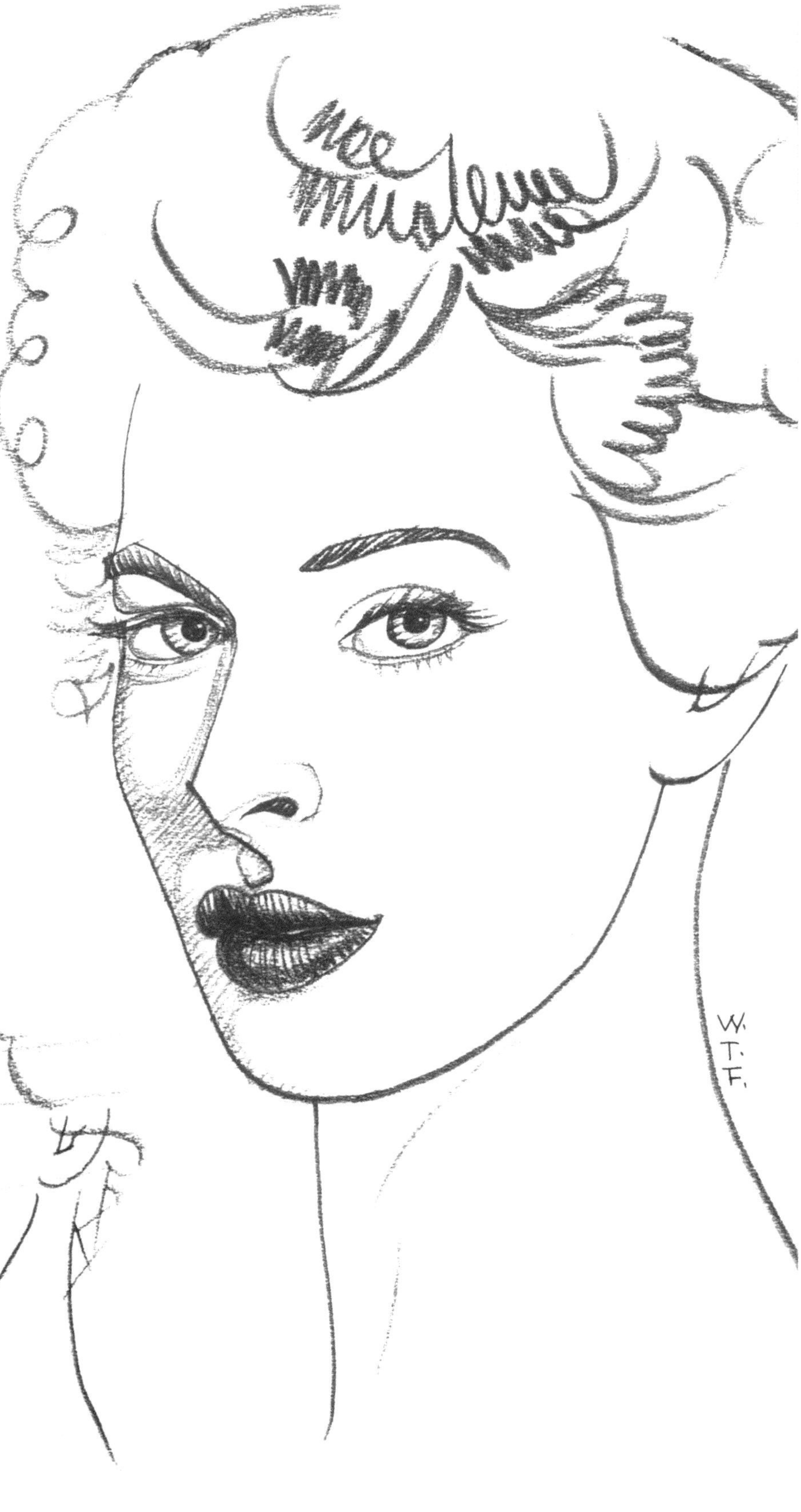

B

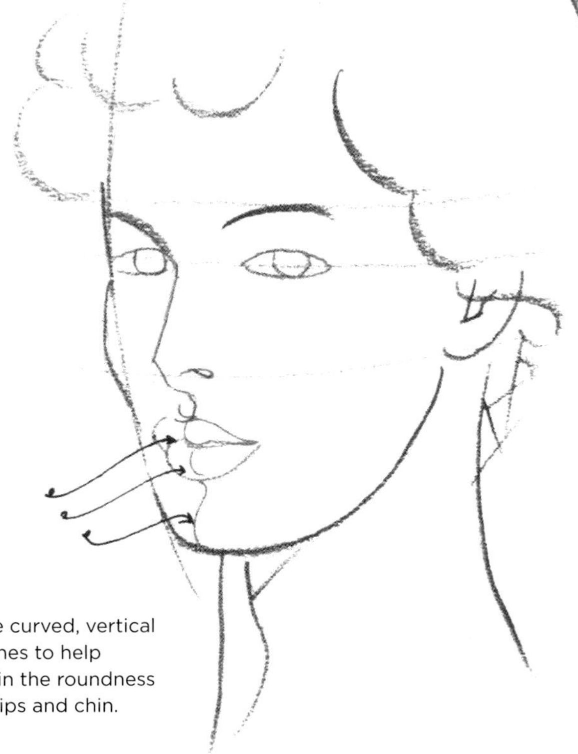

Use the curved, vertical guidelines to help maintain the roundness of the lips and chin.

Learning Perspective

Knowing the principles of perspective (the representation of objects on a two-dimensional surface that creates the illusion of three-dimensional depth and distance) allows you to draw more than one person in a scene realistically. Your eye level changes as your elevation of view changes. In perspective, eye level is indicated by the horizon line. Imaginary lines receding into space meet on the horizon line at what are known as "vanishing points." Any figures drawn along these lines will be in proper perspective. Study the diagrams below to help you.

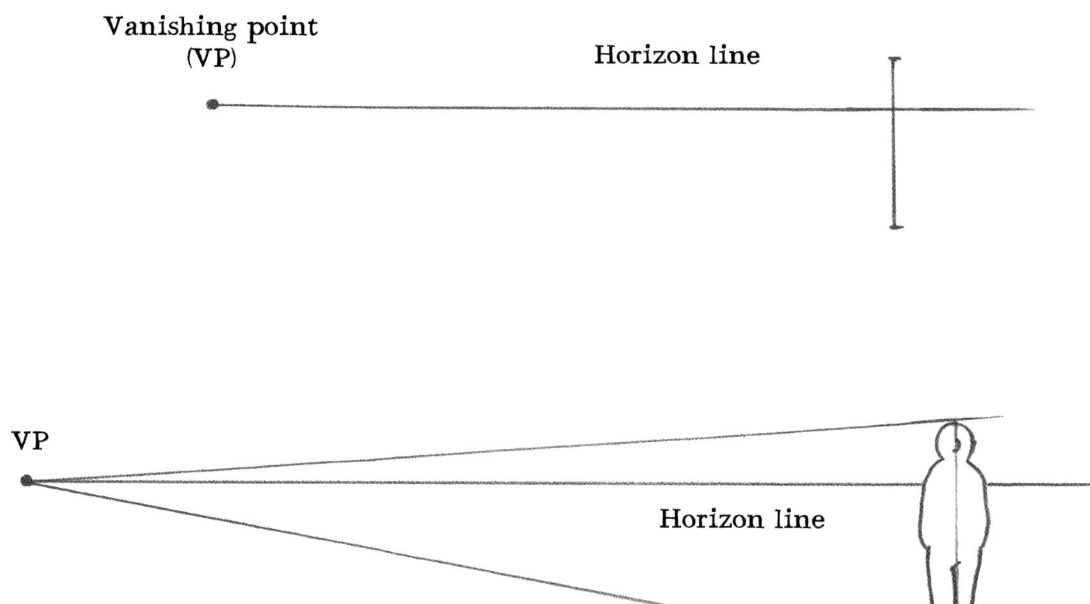

Note that objects appear
smaller and less detailed as
they recede into the distance.

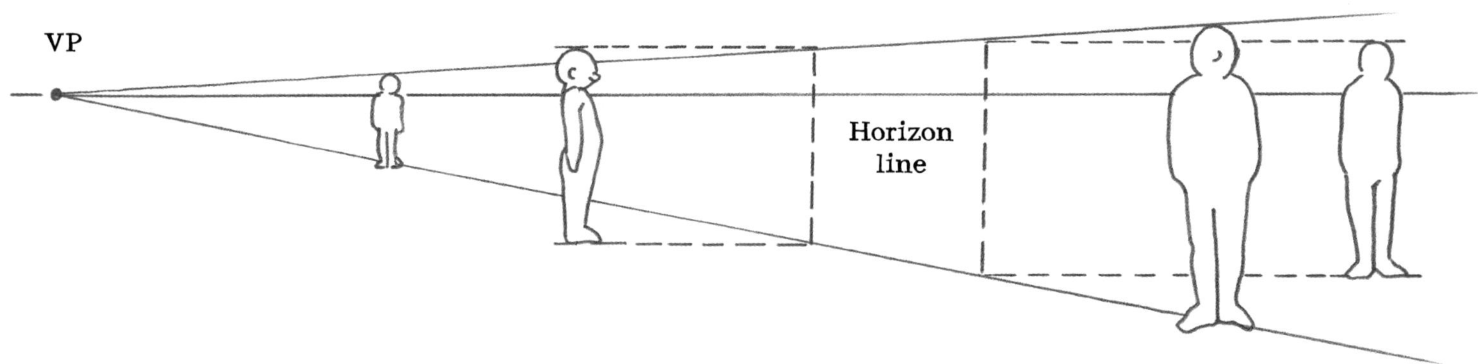

Try drawing a frontal view of many heads as if they were in a theater. Start by establishing your vanishing point at eye level. Draw one large head representing the person closest to you, and use it as a reference for determining the sizes of the other figures in the drawing. The technique illustrated below can be applied when drawing entire figures, shown in the diagram at the bottom. Although all of these examples include just one vanishing point, a composition can even have two or three vanishing points.

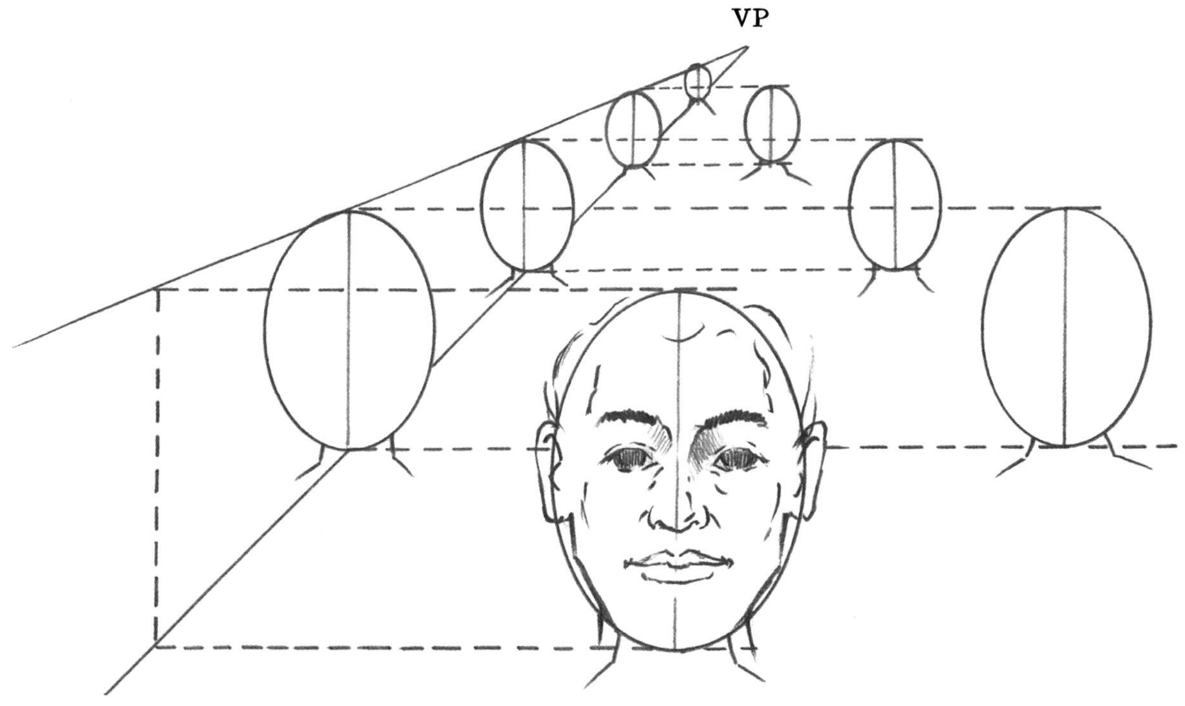

If you're a beginner, you may want to begin with basic one-point perspective, shown on this page. As you progress, attempt to incorporate two- or three-point perspective.

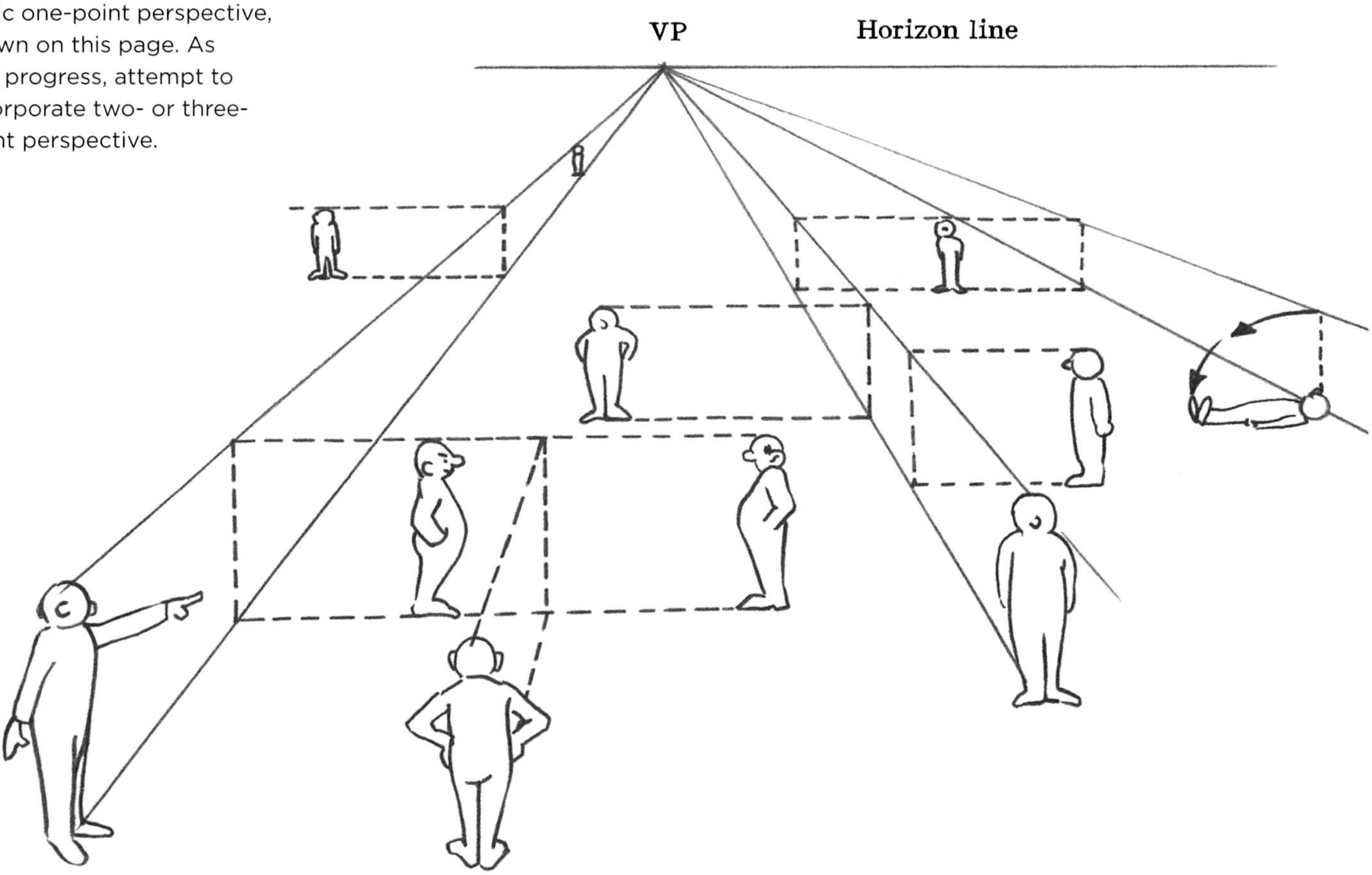

Figures in a Composition

Creating a composition that shows a complete person can be challenging. A standing figure is much taller than it is wide, so the figure should be positioned so that its action relates naturally to the eye level of the viewer and the horizon line. To place more than one figure on the picture plane, use perspective as we did with the portrait heads. Remember that people appear smaller and less distinct when they are more distant. For comfortable placement of people in a composition, they should be on the same eye level as the viewer with the horizon line about waist high.

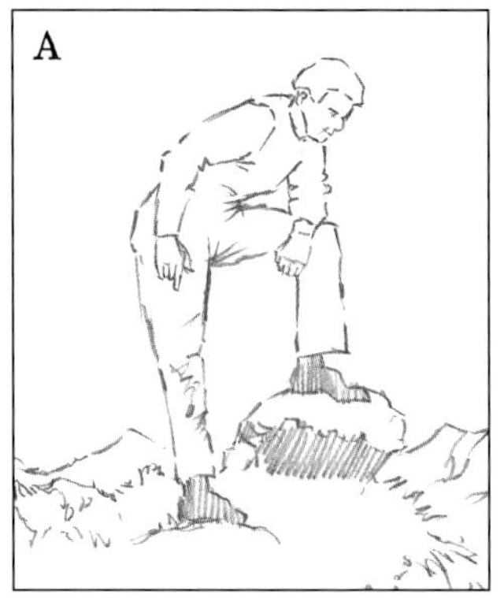

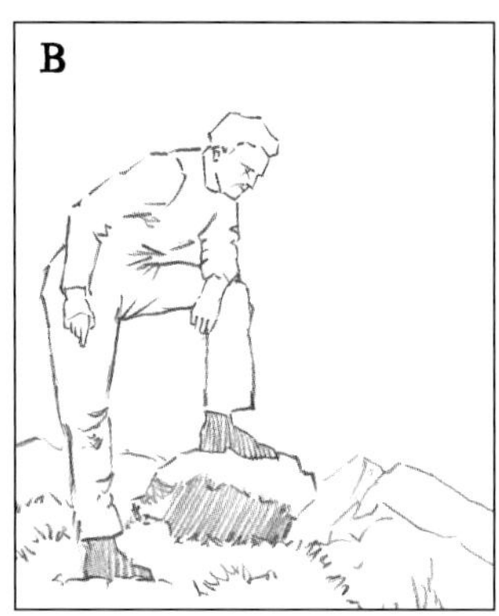

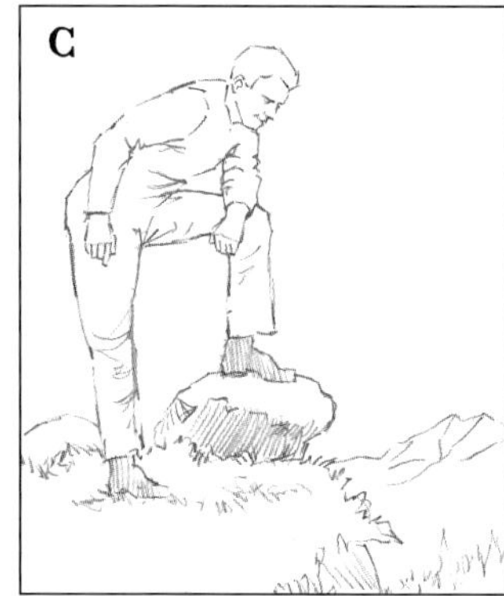

Full Figure Placement In thumbnail A, the subject is too perfectly centered in the picture plane. In thumbnail B, the figure is placed too far to the left. Thumbnail C is an example of effective placement of a human figure in a composition.

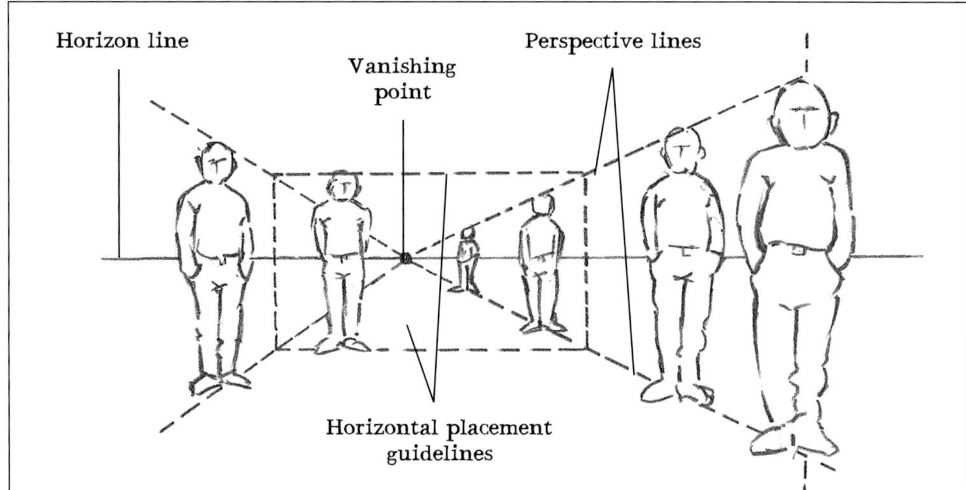

Sizing Multiple Figures For realistic compositions, we need to keep figures in proportion. All the figures here are in proportion; we use perspective to determine the height of each figure. Start by drawing a horizon line and placing a vanishing point on it. Then draw your main character (on the right here) to which all others will be proportional. Add light perspective lines from the top and bottom of the figure to the vanishing point to determine the height of other figures. If we want figures on the other side of the vanishing point, we draw horizontal placement guidelines from the perspective lines to determine his height, and then add perspective lines on that side.

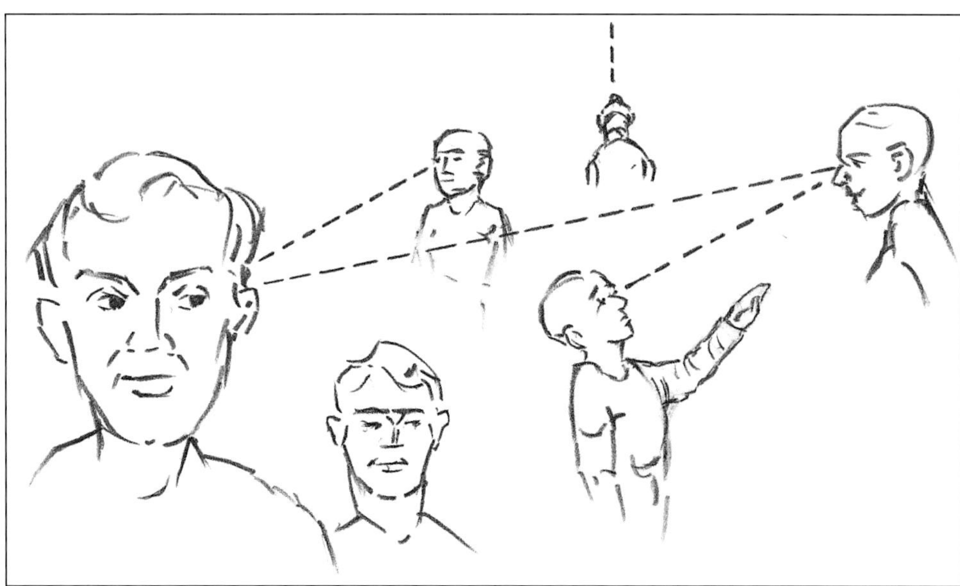

Line of Sight Figures in a composition like this one can relate to one another or to objects within the scene through line of sight (shown here as dotted lines). You can show line of sight with the eyes, but also by using head position and even a pointing hand. These indications can guide the viewer to a particular point of interest in the composition. Though the man on the left is facing forward, his eyes are looking to our right. The viewer's eye follows the line of sight of those within the drawing and is guided around the picture plane as the people interact. The man at the top is looking straight up.

PLACEMENT OF SINGLE AND GROUPED FIGURES

Artists often use the external shape and mass of figures to assist in placing elements within a composition—individual figures form various geometric shapes based on their pose, and several figures in close proximity form one mass. Establish a concept of what you want to show in your composition, and make thumbnail studies before attempting the final drawing. The following exercise is based on using the shape and mass of single and grouped figures to create the drawing at the bottom of the page.

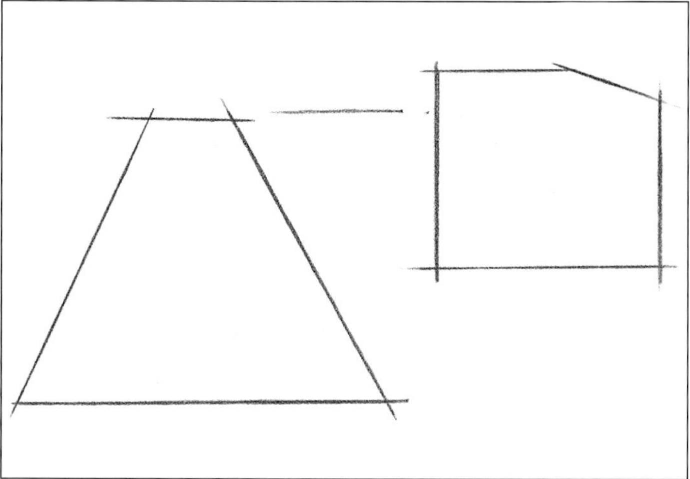

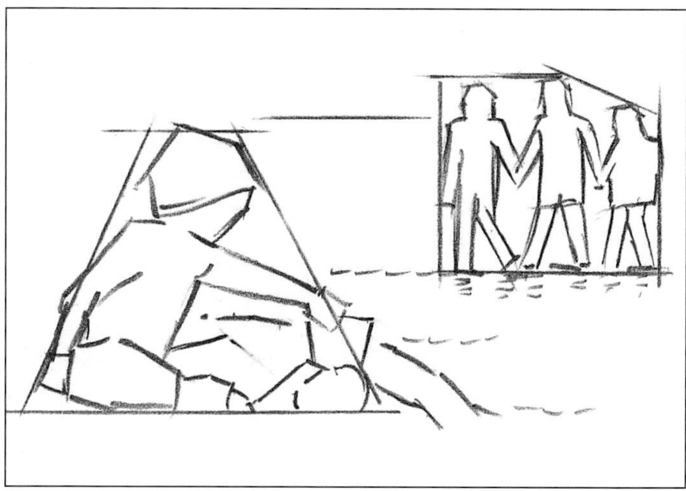

Step 1 Begin by considering the overall setting—foreground, middle ground, and background—for a subject like these children at the beach. You can use elements from different photos and place them in one setting. Block in the basic shapes of your subjects; the boy in the foreground is a clipped triangular shape, and the group of children forms a rough rectangle. Determine balanced placement of the two masses of people.

Step 2 Next, sketch in outlines of the figures. The little boy with the shovel and pail occupies an area close to the viewer. The three children occupy a slightly smaller mass in the middle ground at the water's edge. Even though there are three children in this area, they balance the little boy through size and placement at the opposite corner. The wave and water line unite the composition and lead the eye between the two masses.

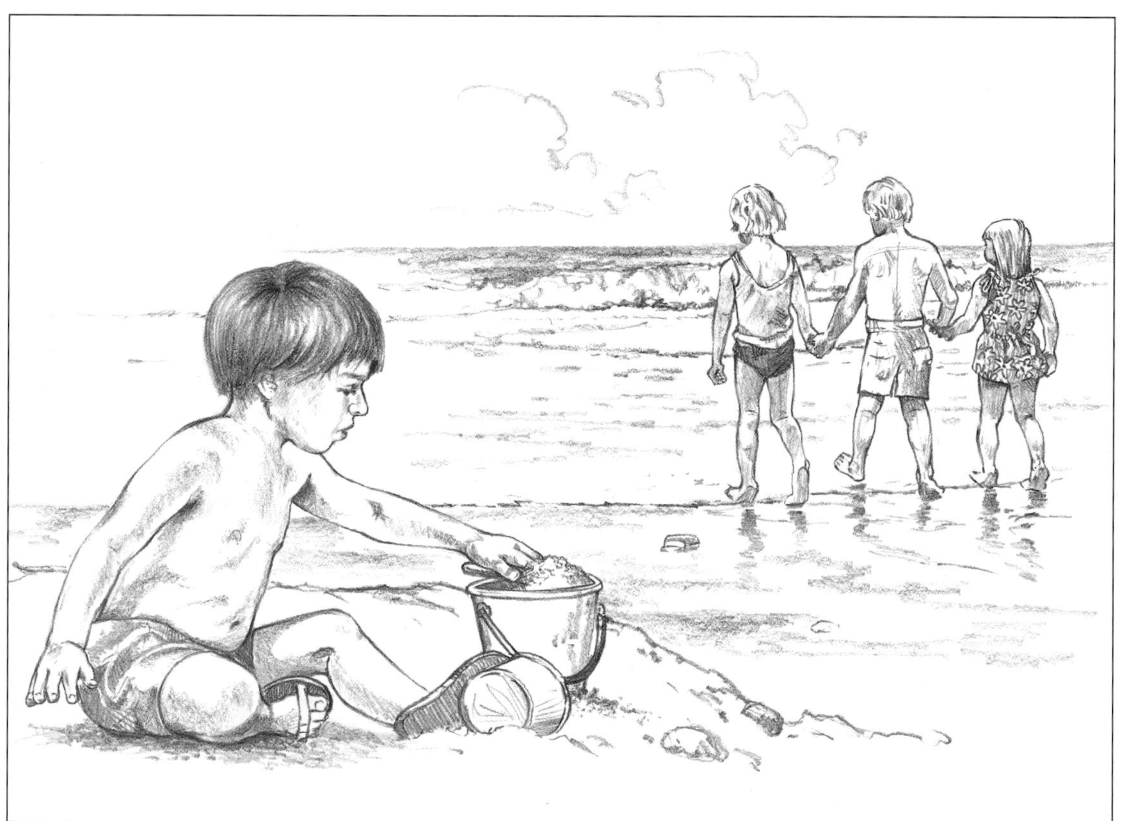

Step 3 Place your figures so that they fit comfortably on the picture plane. Add detail and shading to elements that are important in the composition. Use an element in the foreground to help direct the viewer's eye to other areas, such as the outstretched arm of the boy. Placing the small rock between the middle- and foreground creates a visual stepping stone to the three children at right.

Understanding Placement

The positioning and size of a person on the picture plane (the physical area covered by the drawing) is of utmost importance to the composition, or the arrangements of elements on your paper. The open or "negative" space around the subject generally should be larger than the area occupied by the subject, providing a sort of personal space surrounding them. Whether you are drawing only the face, a head-and-shoulders portrait, or a complete figure, thoughtful positioning will establish a pleasing composition with proper balance. Practice drawing thumbnail sketches of people to study the importance of size and positioning.

BASICS OF PORTRAITURE

Correct placement on the picture plane is key to a good portrait, and the eyes of the subject are the key to placement. The eyes catch the viewer's attention first, so they should not be placed on either the horizontal or vertical centerline of the picture plane; preferably, the eyes should be placed above the centerline. Avoid drawing too near the sides, top, or bottom of the picture plane, as this gives an uneasy feeling of imbalance.

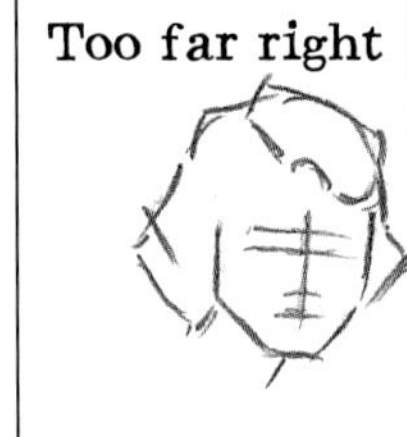

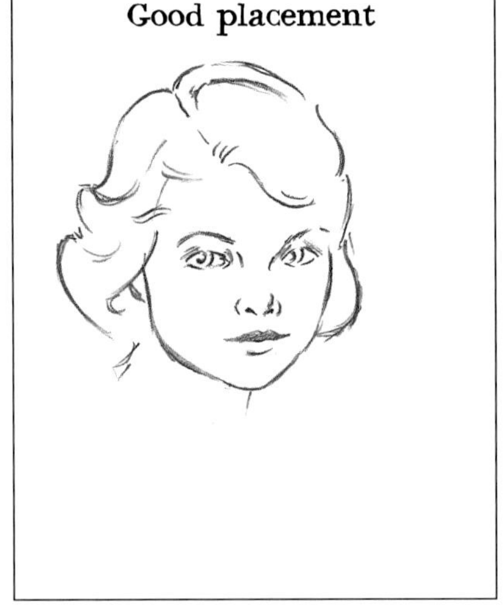

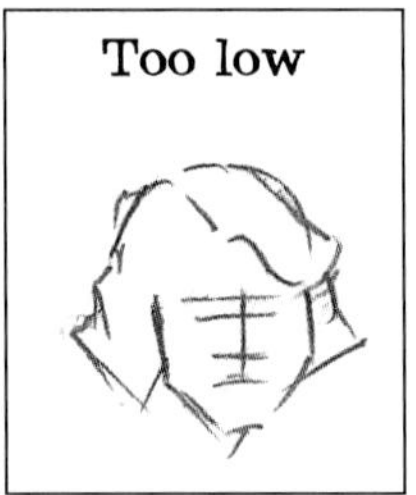

Placement of a Portrait The smaller thumbnails here show the girl's head placed too far to the side and too low in the picture plane, suggesting that she might "slide off" the page. The larger sketch shows the face at a comfortable and balanced horizontal and vertical position, which allows room to add an additional element of interest to enhance the composition.

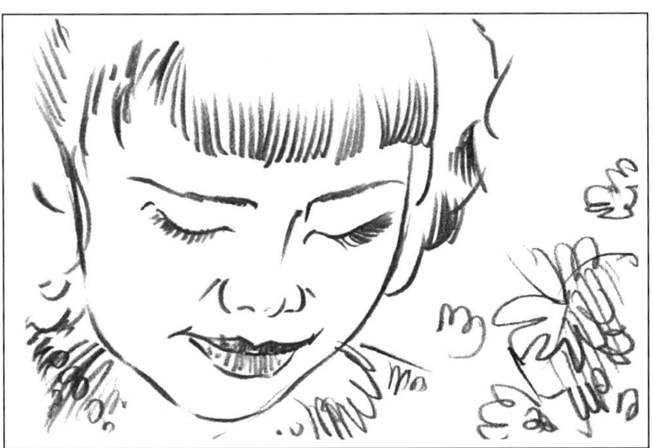

Intentionally drawing your subject larger than the image area, as in the example above, can create a unique composition. Even if part of the image is cut off, this kind of close-up creates a dramatic mood.

ADDING ELEMENTS TO PORTRAITS

Many portraits are drawn without backgrounds to avoid distracting the viewer from the subject. If you do add background elements be sure to control the size, shape, and arrangement of elements surrounding the figure. Additions should express the personality or interests of the subject.

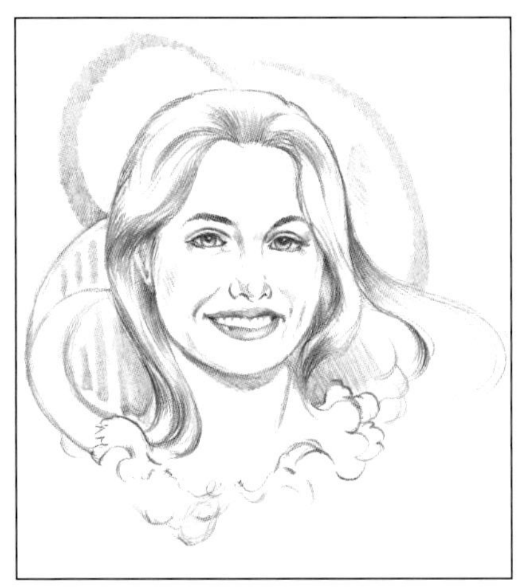

Repetition of Shapes within the Portrait The delicate features of this young woman are emphasized by the simple, abstract elements in the background. The flowing curves fill much of the negative space while accenting the elegance of the woman's hair and features. Simplicity of form is important in this composition; the portrait highlights only her head and neck. Notice that her eyes meet the eyes of the viewer—a dramatic and compelling feature.

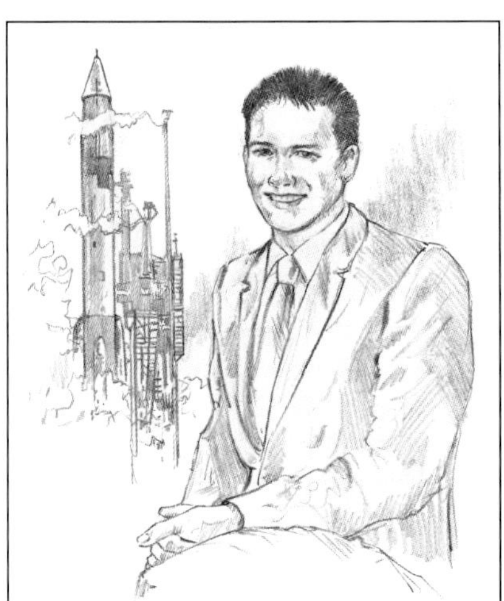

Depicting the Subject's Interest This portrait of a young man includes a background that shows his interest in rocketry. The straight lines in the background contrast the rounded shapes of the human form. Although the background detail is complex, it visually recedes and serves to balance the man's weight. The focus remains on the man, but we've generated visual interest by adding elements to the composition.

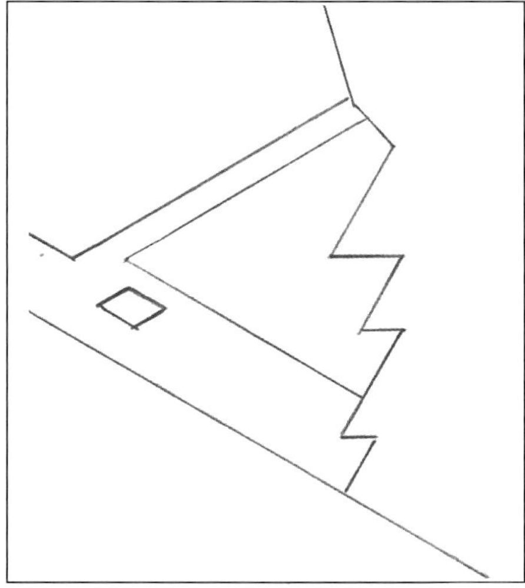

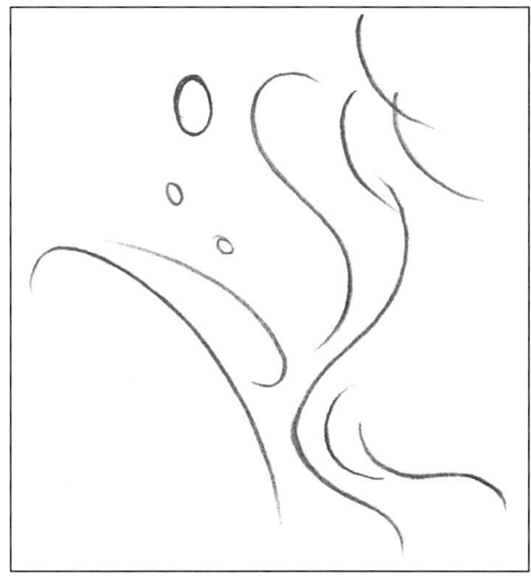

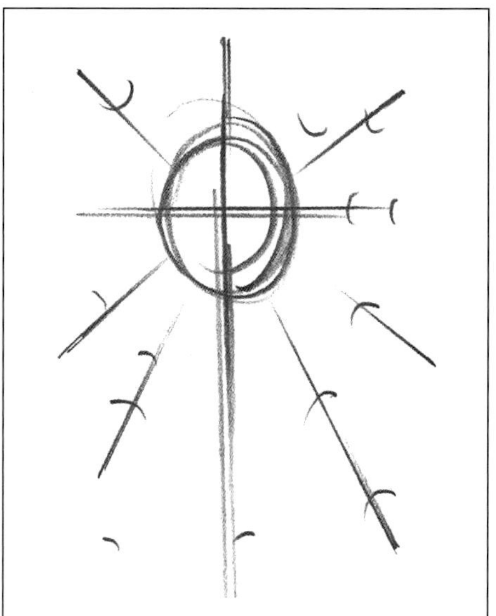

Sharp angles can produce dramatic compositions. Draw a few straight lines in various angles, and make them intersect at certain points. Zigzagging lines also form sharp corners that give the composition an energetic feeling.

Curved lines are good composition elements—they can evoke harmony and balance in your work. Try drawing some curved lines around the paper. The empty areas guide you in placing figures around your drawing.

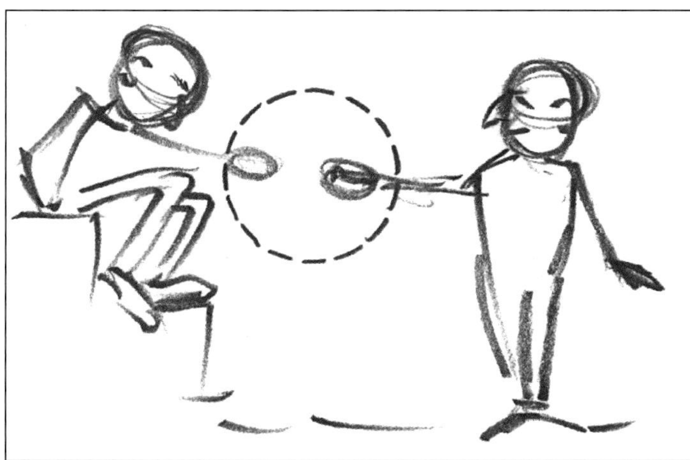

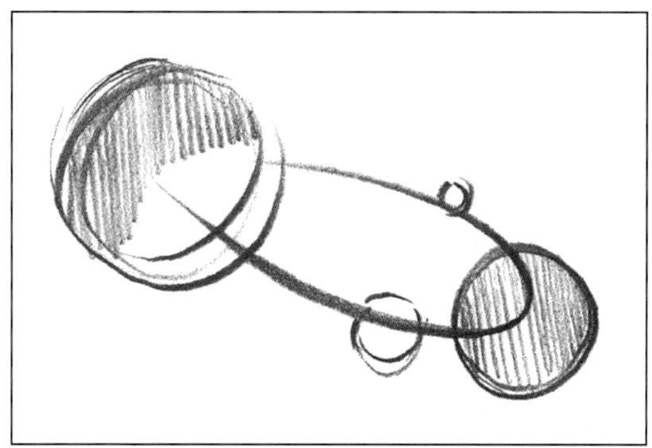

You can create a flow or connection between multiple subjects in a composition by creatively using circles and ellipses, as shown above.

Guiding the Eye The compositions above and to the right illustrate how arm position, eyesight direction, and line intersection can guide the eye to a particular point of interest. Using these examples, try to design some of your own original compositions.

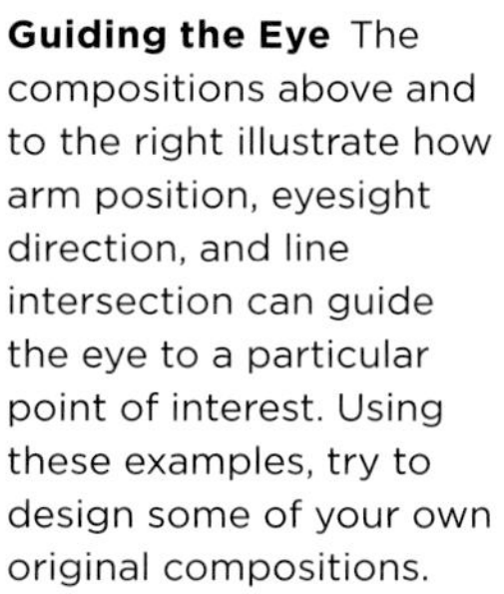

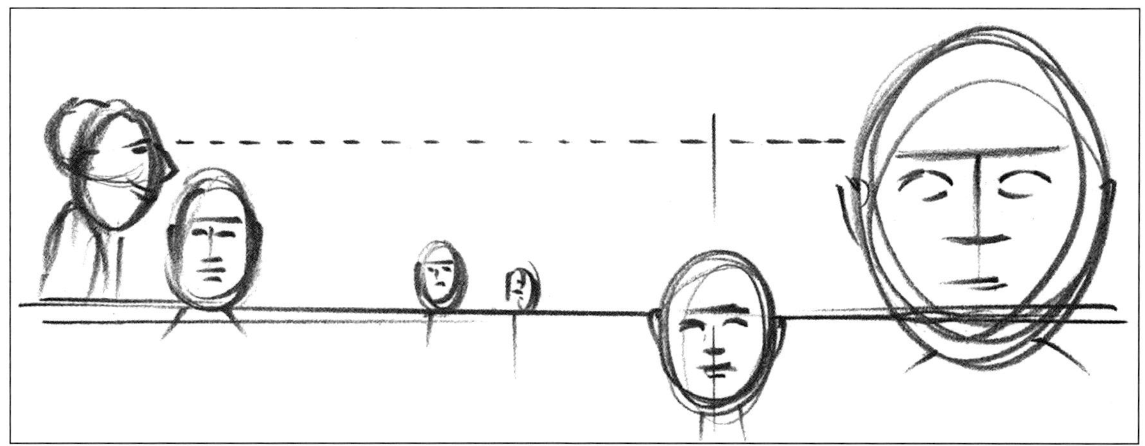

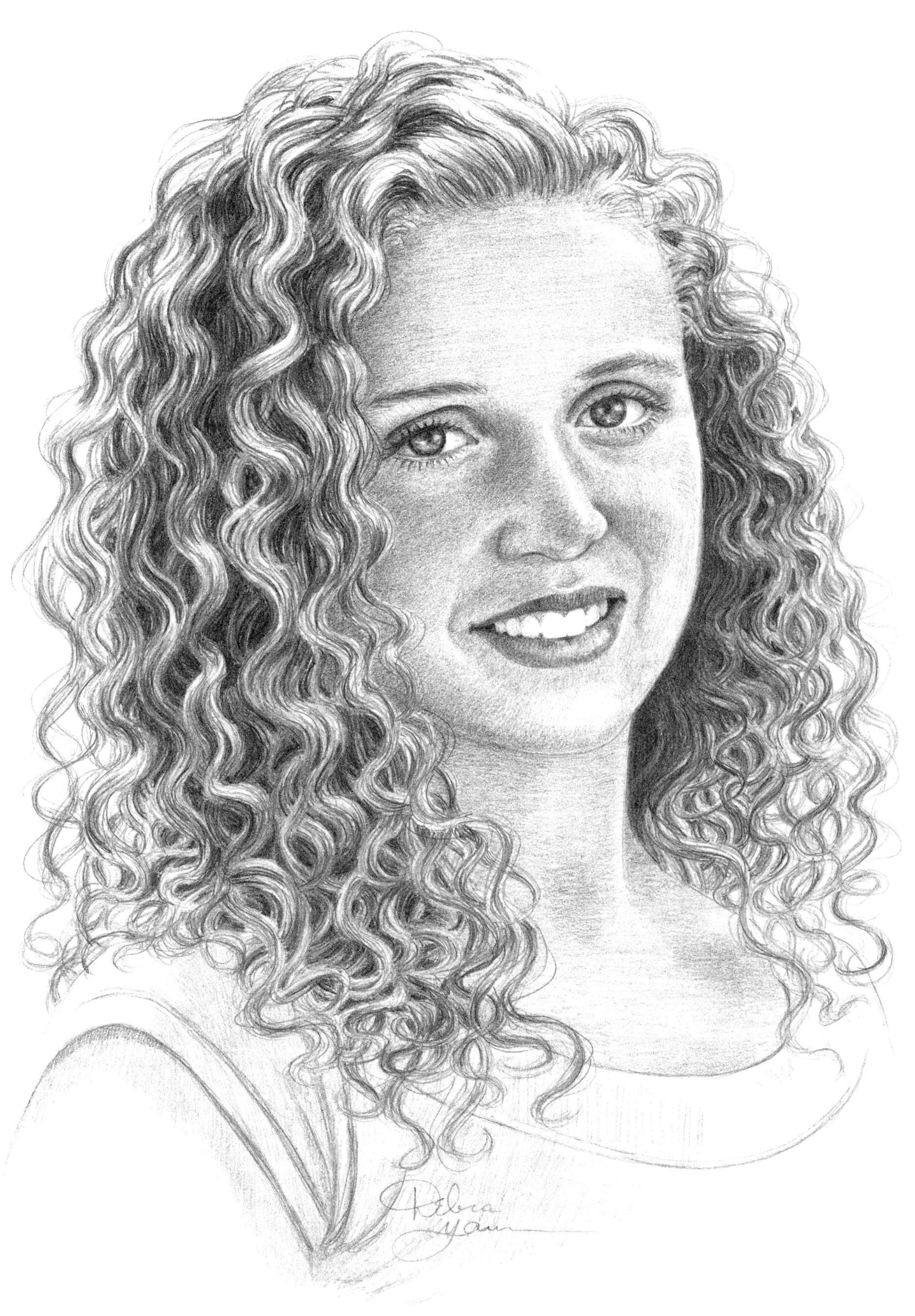

Drawing Portraits

Even if facial features are unique to every person, it isn't too difficult to learn how to draw a portrait. This is because the anatomy of our faces follows simple rules, which you can learn by reading through this chapter. The more people you draw, the quicker you will notice what makes every face distinctive. In addition, helpful tips on mastering light and shade, focusing on the details, and working from a photograph or with a live model will also help improve your skills.

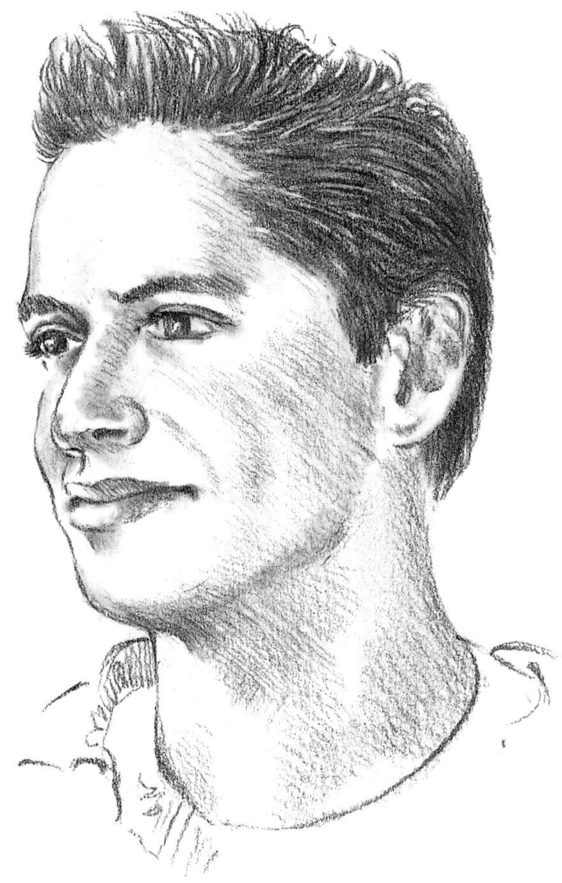

Beginning Portraiture

A good starting point for drawing people is the head and face. The shapes are fairly simple, and the proportions are easy to measure. Portraiture is also very rewarding. You can feel a great sense of satisfaction when you look at a portrait you've drawn and see a true likeness of your subject, especially when the model is someone near and dear to you, like a child.

DRAWING A CHILD'S PORTRAIT

Once you've practiced drawing features, you're ready for a full portrait. You'll probably want to draw from a photo, though, since children rarely sit still for very long! Study the features carefully, and try to draw what you truly see, and not what you think an eye or a nose should look like. But don't be discouraged if you don't get a perfect likeness right off the bat. Just keep practicing!

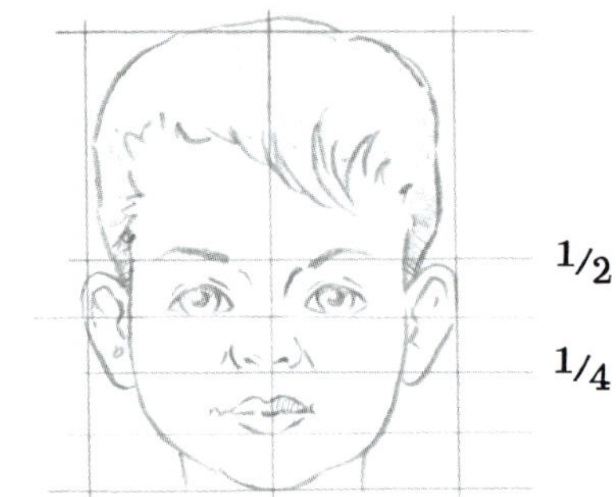

Understanding a Child's Proportions Draw guidelines to divide the head in half horizontally; then divide the lower half into fourths. Use the guidelines to place the eyes, nose, ears, and mouth, as shown.

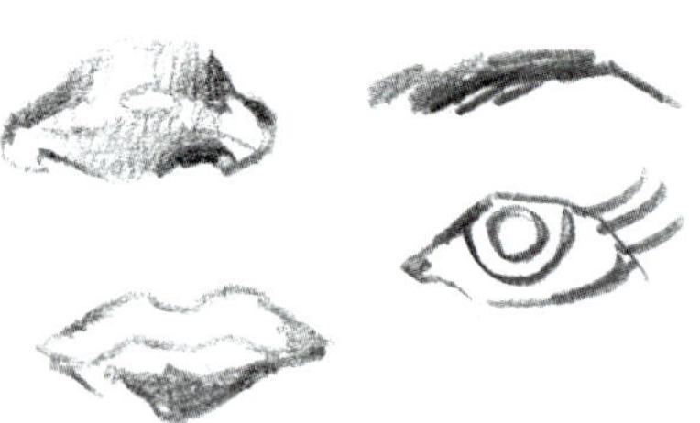

Separating the Features Before you attempt a full portrait, try drawing the features separately to get a feel for the shapes and forms. Look at faces in books and magazines, and draw as many different features as you can.

Starting with a Good Photo When working from photographs, some artists prefer candid, relaxed poses over formal, "shoulders square" portraits. You can also try to get a closeup shot of the face so you can really study the features.

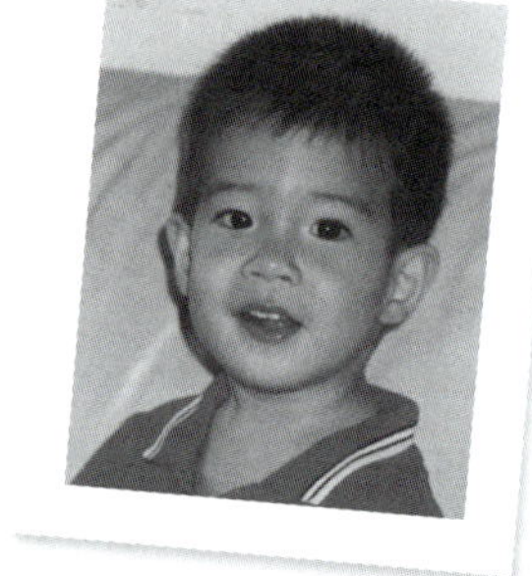

Sketching the Guidelines First pencil an oval for the shape of the head, and lightly draw a vertical center line. Then add horizontal guidelines according to the chart at the top of the page, and sketch in the general outlines of the features. When you are happy with the overall sketch, carefully erase the guidelines.

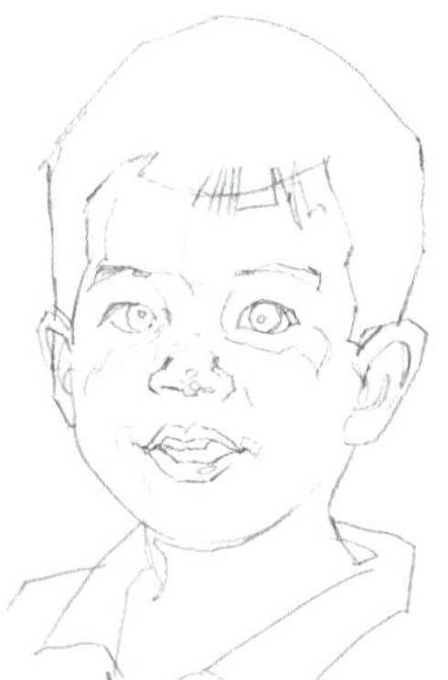

Finishing the Portrait With the side of a pencil, start laying in the middle values of the shadow areas, increasing the pressure slightly around the eye, nose, and collar. For the darkest shadows and the straight, black hair, use the side of a 2B and overlap your strokes, adding a few fine hairs along the forehead with the sharp-pointed tip of the pencil.

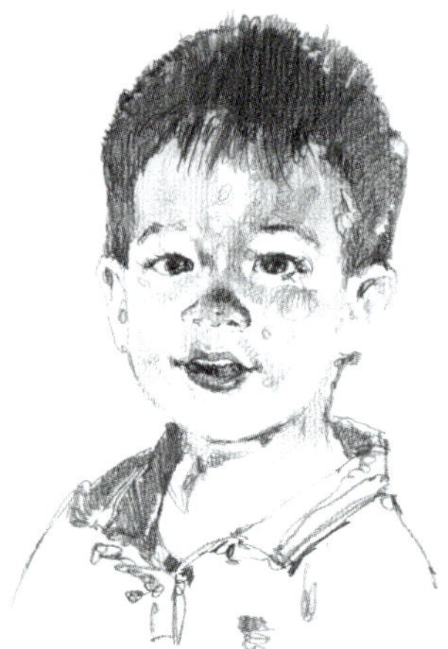

COMMON PROPORTION FLAWS

Quite a few things are wrong with these drawings of this child's head. Compare them to the photo at left, and see if you can spot the errors before reading the captions.

Thin Neck
The child in the photo at left has a slender neck, but not this slender! Refer to the photo to see where his neck appears to touch his face and ear.

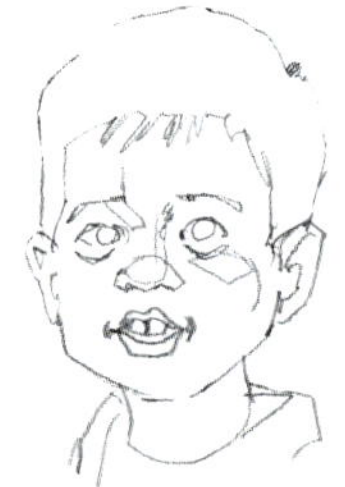

Not Enough Forehead
Children have proportionately larger foreheads than adults do. By making the forehead too small in this example, I've added years to the child's age.

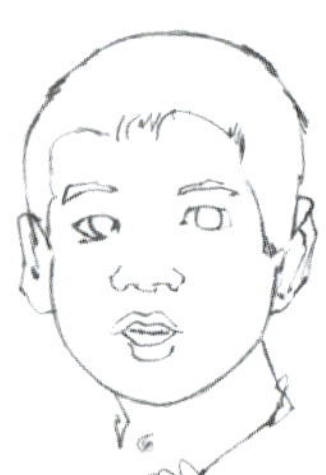

Cheeks Too Round
Children do have round faces, but don't make them look like chipmunks. And be sure to make the ears round, not pointed.

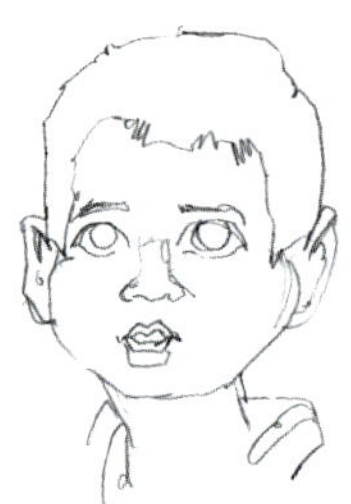

Sticks for Eyelashes
Eyelashes should not stick straight out like spokes on a wheel. And draw the teeth as one shape; don't try to draw each tooth separately.

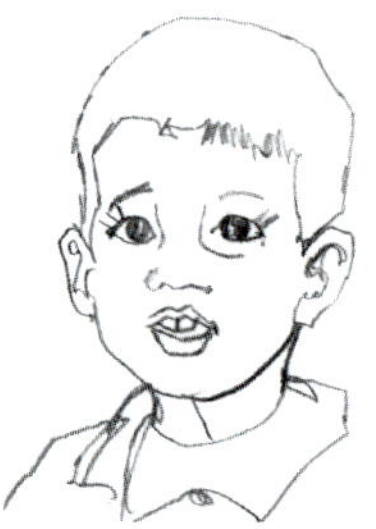

DRAWING THE ADULT HEAD

An adult's head has slightly different proportions than a child's head (see page 16 for more precise adult proportions), but the drawing process is the same: Sketch in guidelines to place the features, and start with a sketch of basic shapes. And don't forget the profile view. Adults with interesting features are a lot of fun to draw from the side, where you can really see the shape of the brow, the outline of the nose, and the form of the lips.

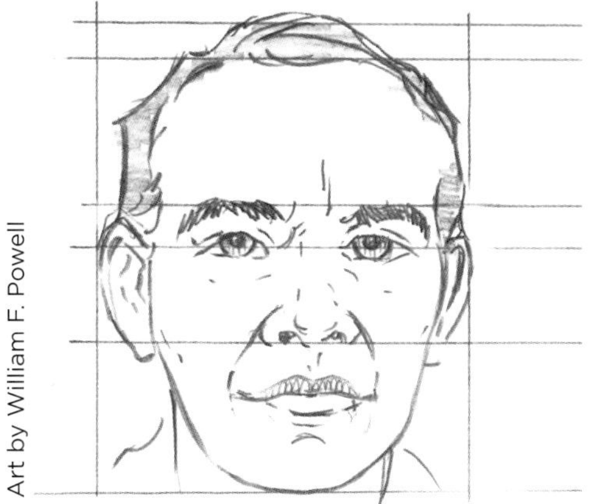

Art by William F. Powell

Focusing on Adult Proportions Look for the proportions that make your adult subject unique; notice the distance from the top of the head to the eyes, from the eyes to the nose, and from the nose to the chin. Look at where the mouth falls between the nose and the chin and where the ears align with the eyes and the nose.

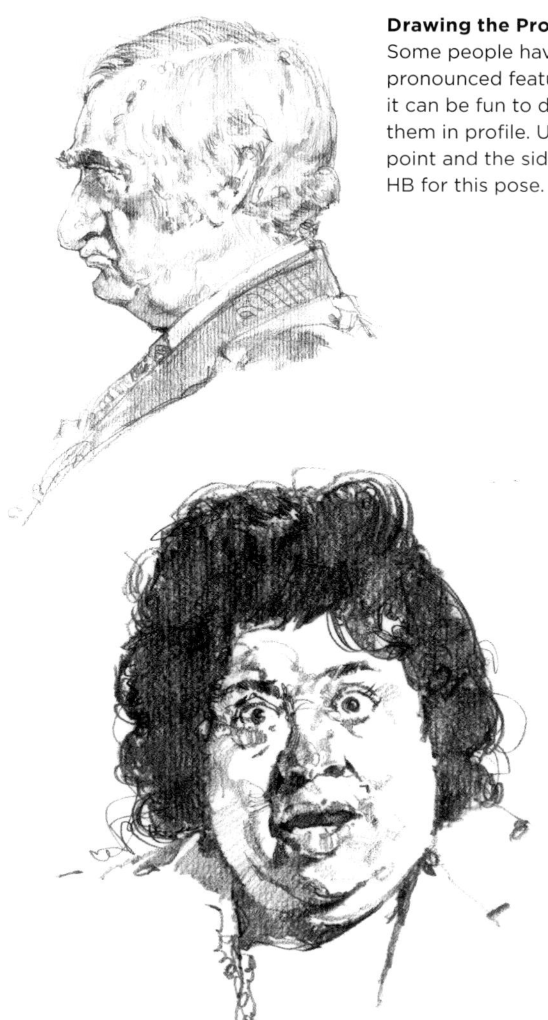

Drawing the Profile Some people have very pronounced features, so it can be fun to draw them in profile. Use the point and the side of an HB for this pose.

EXPRESSING EMOTION

Drawing a wide range of different facial expressions and emotions can be quite enjoyable, especially ones that are extreme. Because these are just studies and not formal portraits, draw loosely to add energy and a look of spontaneity, as if a camera had captured the face at just that moment. Some artists don't bother with a background, as they don't want anything to detract from the expression. But do draw the neck and shoulders so the head doesn't appear to be floating in space.

Depicting Shock When you want to show an extreme expression, focus on the lines around the eyes and mouth. Exposing the whole, round shape of the iris conveys a sense of shock, just as the exposed eyelid and open mouth do.

Portraying Happiness
Young children have smooth complexions, so make the smile lines fairly subtle. Use light shading with the side of your pencil to create creases around the mouth, and make the eyes slightly narrower to show how smiles pull the cheek muscles up.

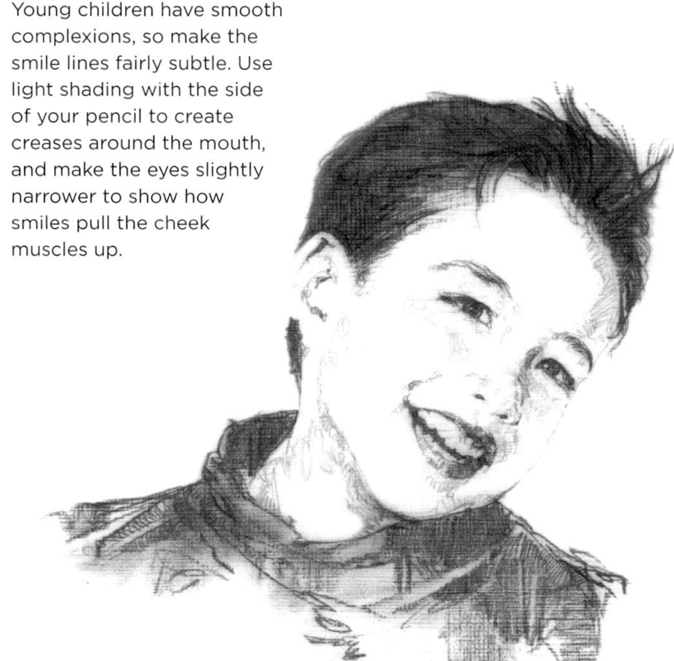

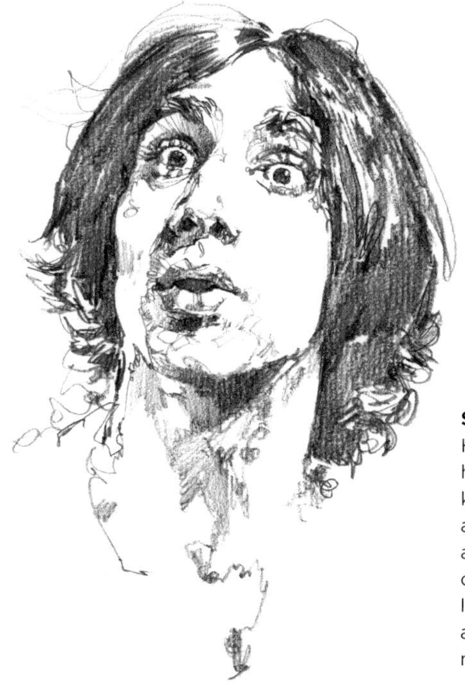

Showing Surprise
Here a lot of the face has been left white to keep most of the attention on the eyes and mouth. Use the tip of the pencil for the loose expression lines and the side for the mass of dark hair.

Understanding Anatomy

When drawing faces, it is important to be aware of the underlying structures of the head. Although the bones and muscles aren't visible in a final portrait, they provide the framework for the drawing, establishing the shape of the head and guiding the placement of the features. Having an understanding of this basic anatomy will lend realism and credibility to your drawings.

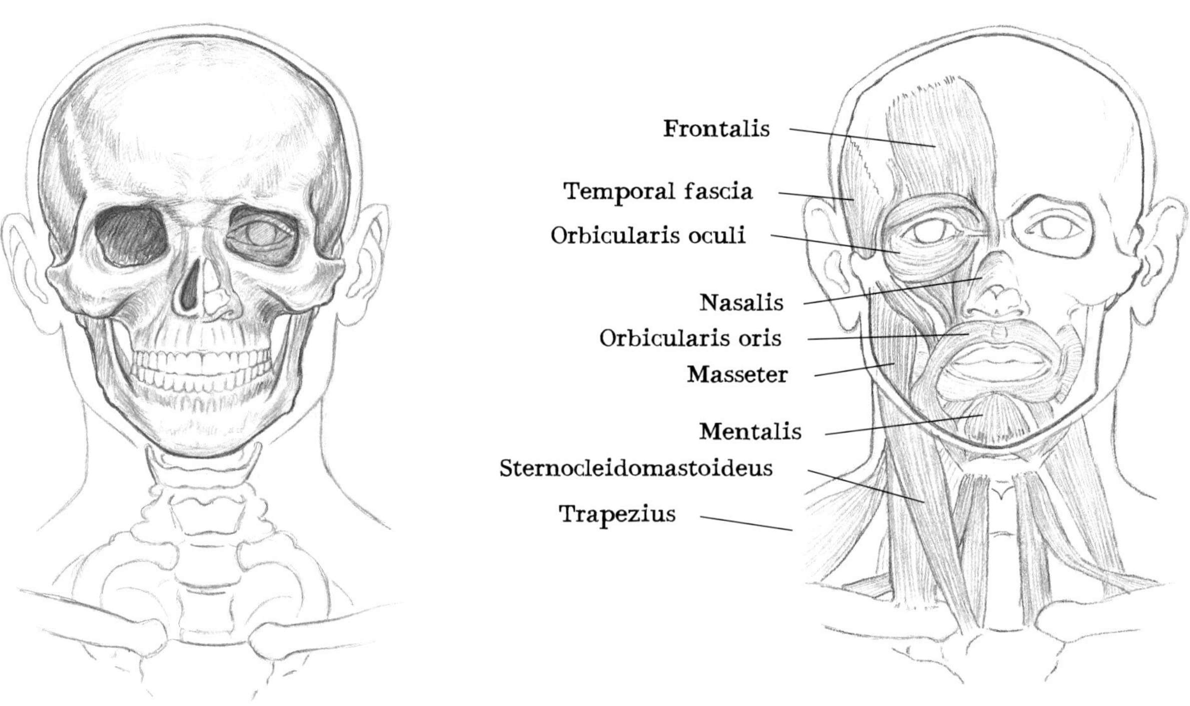

Understanding Bone Structure Becoming familiar with the bones of the skull and the way they affect the surface of the skin is essential for correctly placing the curvatures, ridges, and other prominent features of the head.

Understanding Muscle Structure When facial muscles contract, they affect the shape of the skin, cartilage, and underlying fatty tissues that cause the bulges, furrows, and other forms that create various facial expressions.

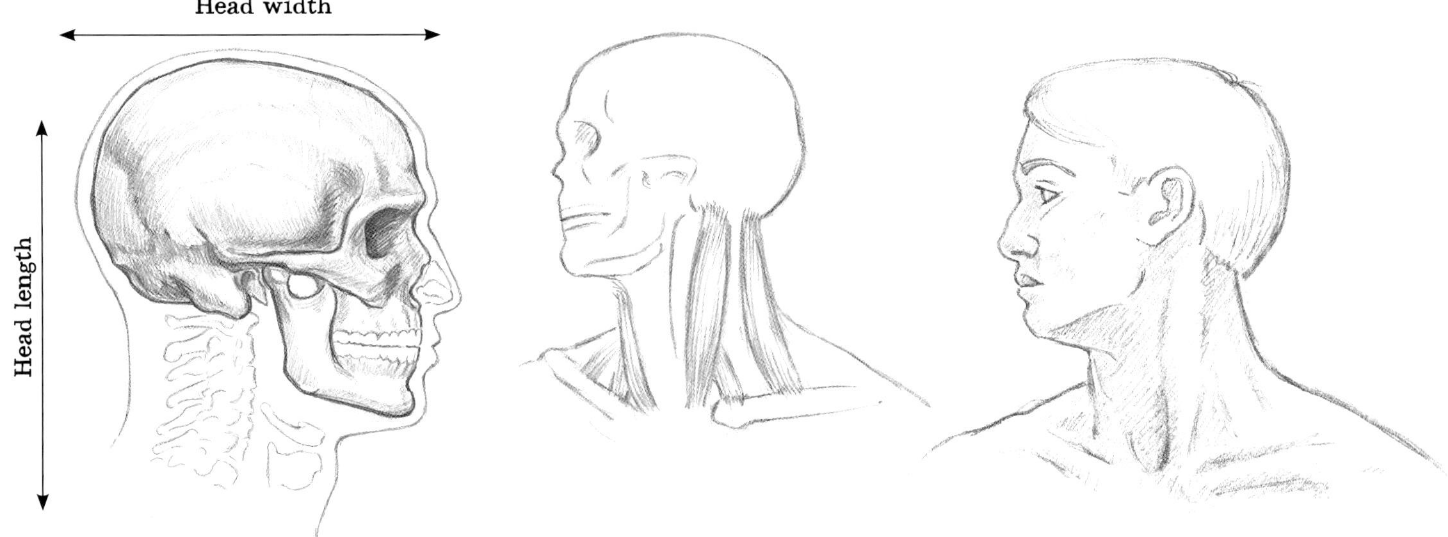

Visualizing the Underlying Muscles The large muscles of the neck and the clavicle bone twist when the head is turned. The muscles and clavicle are visible, even underneath the skin; they can create a bulge or tension that is evident on the surface.

Highlights & Shadows

Once you understand the basic structure of the head, you can simplify the complex shapes of the skull into geometric planes. These planes are the foundation for shading; they act as a guide to help you properly place highlights and shadows.

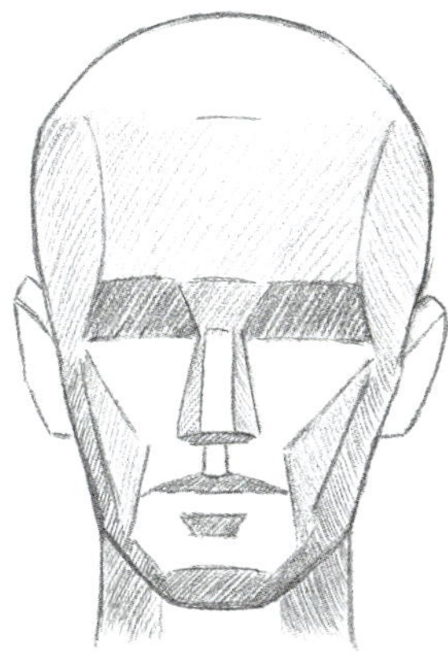

Lighting the Planes from Above
When light comes from above, the more prominent planes of the face—such as the bridge of the nose and the cheekbones— are highlighted. The eyes, which recede slightly, are shadowed by the brow; the sides of the nose, bottom of the chin, and underside of the neck are also in shadow.

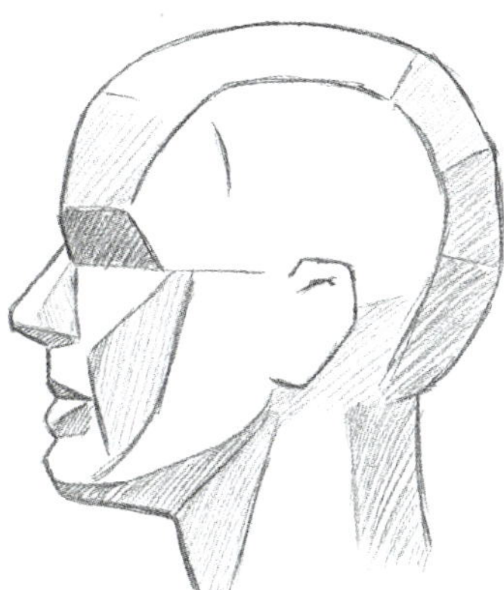

Lighting the Planes from the Side
Features are shaded differently when light hits the side of the face. The eyes are still in shadow, but the side of the face and neck are now highlighted. The shading on the head becomes darker as it recedes toward the neck; the sides of the cheeks appear "sunken"; and the ear casts a shadow on the back of the head.

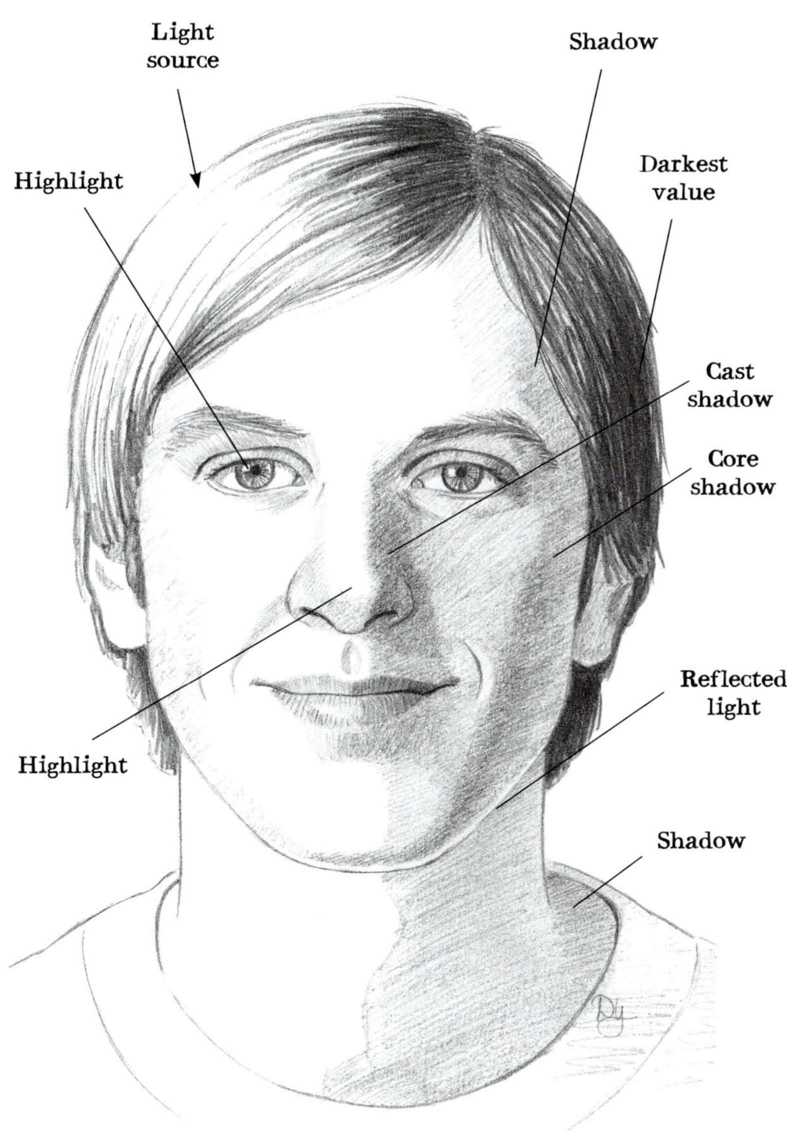

Shading the Planes of the Face Shadows contribute to the piecing together of the planes of the face. *Core shadows*—or the main value of the shadows—are a result of both the underlying structure and the light source. Protruding objects, such as the nose, produce *cast shadows,* like the dark area on the side of this subject's nose. Highlights are most visible when directly in the light's path. Here, the light source is coming from above left, so the lightest planes of the face are the top of the head and the forehead. The darkest areas are directly opposite the light source. In the drawing above, these are the left side of the subject's face and neck. Even in shadow, there are areas of the planes that receive spots of reflected light, such as those shown on the chin and under the eye.

Frontal View of the Face

Understanding the basic rules of human proportions (meaning the comparative sizes and placement of parts to one another) is imperative for accurately drawing the human face. Understanding proper proportions will help you determine the correct size and placement of each facial feature as well as how to modify them to fit the unique, individual characteristics of your subject.

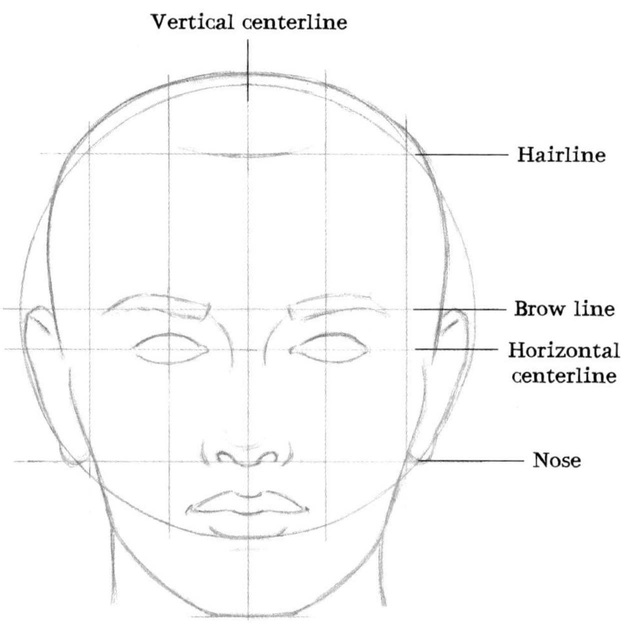

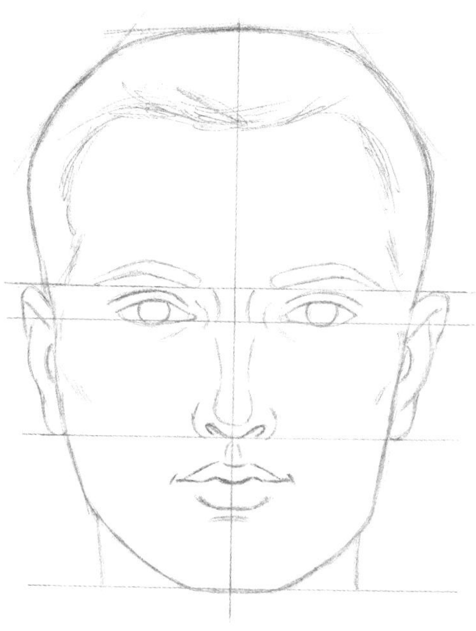

Establishing Guidelines Visualize the head as a ball that has been flattened on the sides. The ball is divided in half horizontally and vertically, and the face is divided horizontally into three equal parts: the hairline, the brow line, and the line for the nose. Use these guidelines to determine the correct placement and spacing of adult facial features.

Placing the Features The eyes lie between the horizontal centerline and the brow line. The bottom of the nose is halfway between the brow line and the bottom of the chin. The bottom lip is halfway between bottom of the nose and the chin, and the ears extend from the brow line to the bottom of the nose.

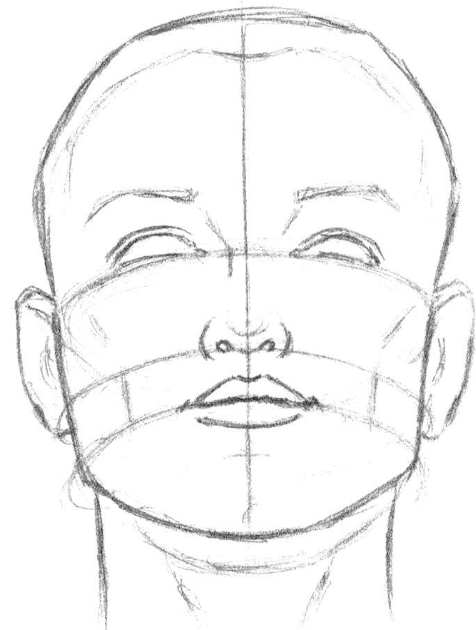

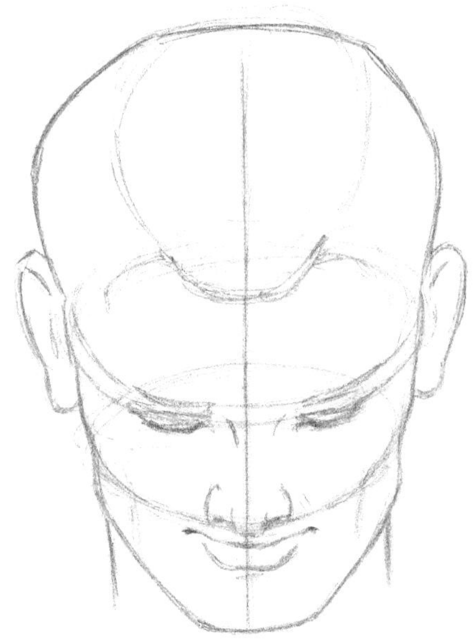

Looking Up When the head is tilted back, the horizontal guidelines curve with the shape of the face. Note the way the features change when the head tilts back: The ears appear a little lower on the head, and more of the whites of the eyes are visible.

Looking Down When the head is tilted forward, the eyes appear closed and much more of the top of the head is visible. The ears appear higher, almost lining up with the hairline, and they follow the curve of the horizontal guideline.

Exploring Other Views

Beginning artists often study profile views first, as this angle tends to simplify the drawing process. For example, in a profile view, you don't have to worry about aligning symmetrical features. But the rules of proportion still apply when drawing profile views as well as the more complex three-quarter views.

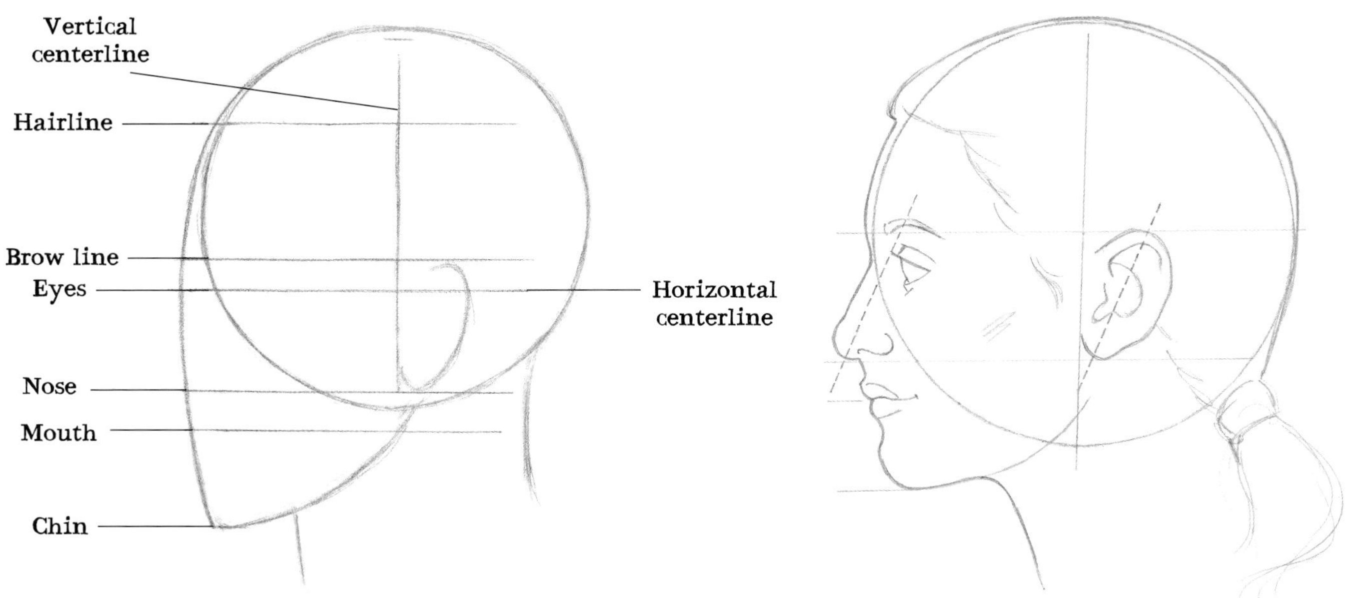

Simplifying the Profile To draw an adult head in profile, start by blocking in the cranial mass with a large circle. Add two curved lines that meet at a point to establish the face and chin. Place the ear just behind the vertical centerline.

Placing the Features Use the large cranial circle as a guideline for placing the features. The nose, lips, and chin fall outside the circle, whereas the eyes and ear remain inside. The slanted, broken lines indicate the parallel slant of the nose and ear.

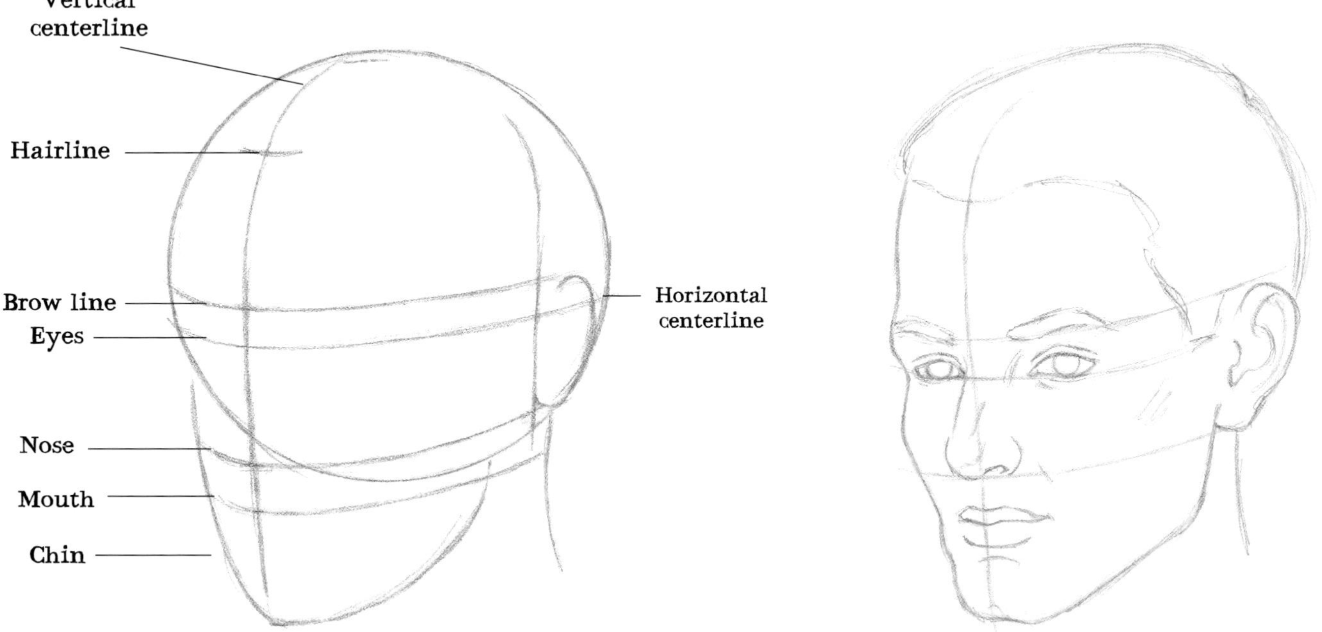

Drawing a Three-Quarter View In a three-quarter view, the vertical centerline shifts into view. More of the left side of the subject's head is visible, but you still see only the left ear. As the head turns, the guidelines also curve, following the shape of the head.

Distorting the Features When the head turns, the eye closest to the viewer (in this case the left eye) appears larger than the other eye. This is a technique called "foreshortening," in which elements of a drawing are distorted to create the illusion of three-dimensional space; objects closer to the viewer appear larger than objects that are farther away.

Focusing on the Details

If you're a beginner, it's a good idea to practice drawing all the facial features separately, working out any problems before attempting a complete portrait. Facial features work together to convey everything from mood and emotion to age. Pay attention to the areas around the features as well. Wrinkles, moles, and other characteristics help make your subject distinct.

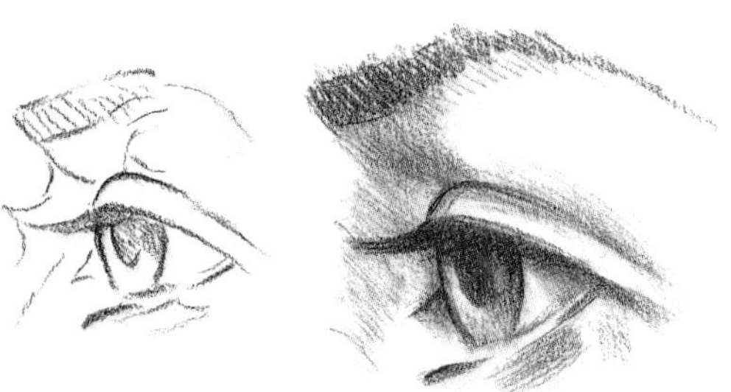

Eyes In a side view, the eye has a triangular shape. The iris has an oval shape, and the eyelids slightly cover it at the top and bottom. When shading, concentrate on developing the iris, lashes, and lids, leaving most of the brow white.

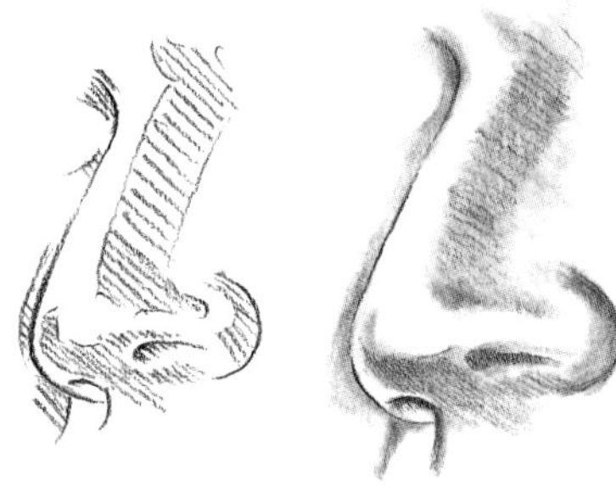

Nose In a three-quarter view, the far nostril is partially hidden from sight. The light strikes most strongly on the center ridge, so create the form by shading the side of the nose, under the tip, and outside the nostril.

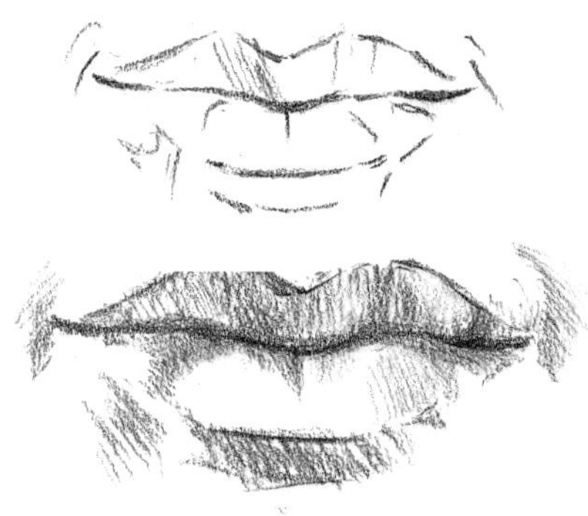

Lips In a frontal view, the upper lip has two "peaks" and a slight protrusion in the center. The lower lip is fleshier and has no sharp peaks. When shading, define the bottom edge of the lower lip by shading the area directly below it.

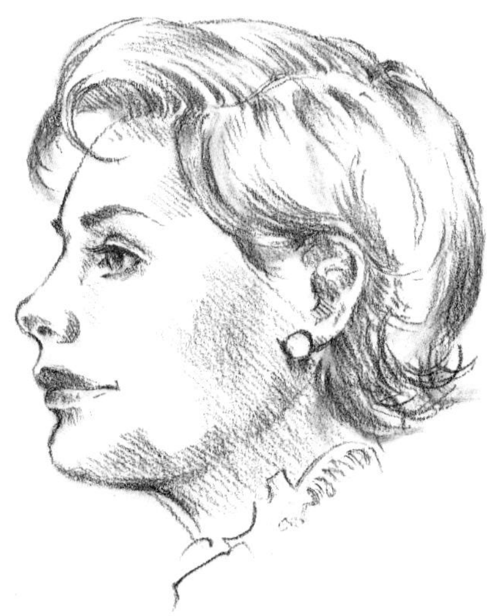

Profile The head shape changes in a side view, but the features remain in the same relative positions. Although the nose is a prominent feature in profile, take care not to let it dominate the face. Also pay attention to where the eye sits and how the lower lip curves into the chin.

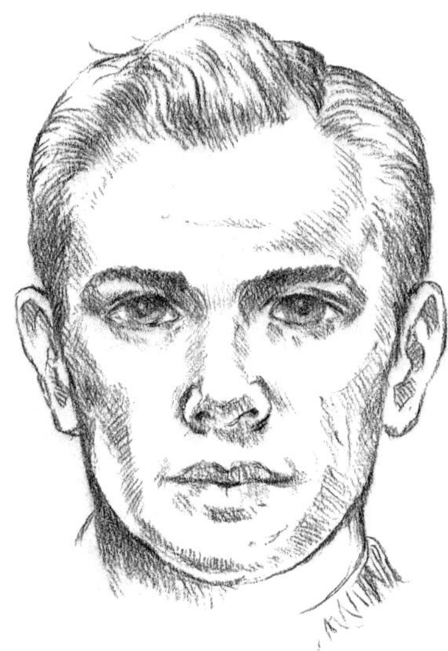

Front View In a frontal view, we can see that the face is not perfectly symmetrical. One eye is generally smaller than the other, or one might sit at a slightly different angle. The same is true of the ears, cheeks, and the sides of the nose and the mouth.

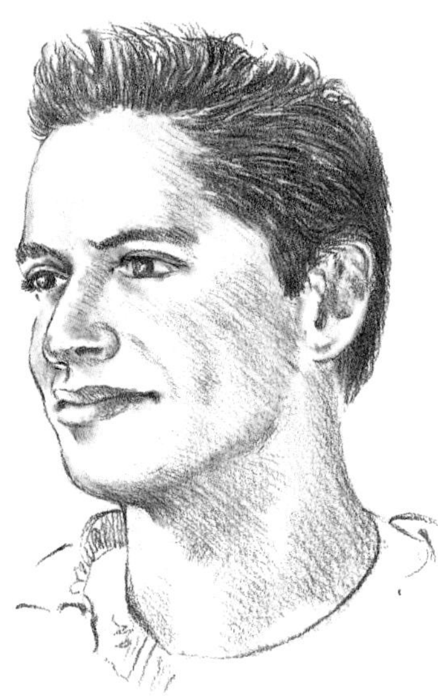

Three-Quarter View This view can be challenging because you have to distort the features to make them look realistic. Change the eye and lip shapes to curve with the face. You might want to start with a contour drawing to work out how the features really look.

Eyes

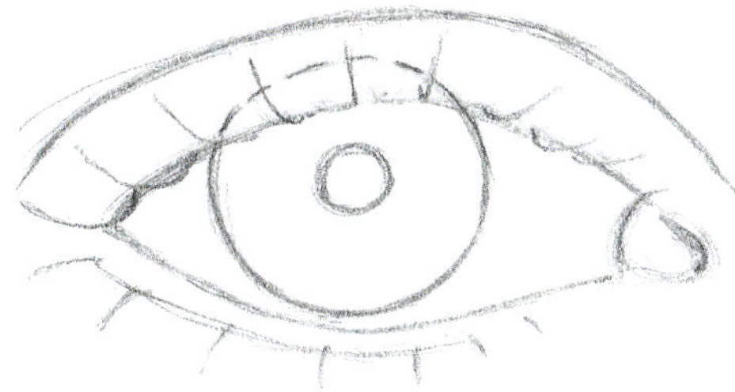

Step 1 Make a circle for the iris first; then, draw the eyelid over it. (Drawing an entire object before adding any overlapping elements is called "drawing through.") Note that part of the iris is always covered by the eyelid.

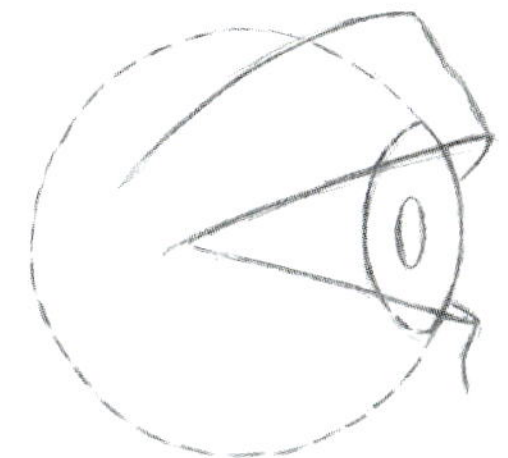

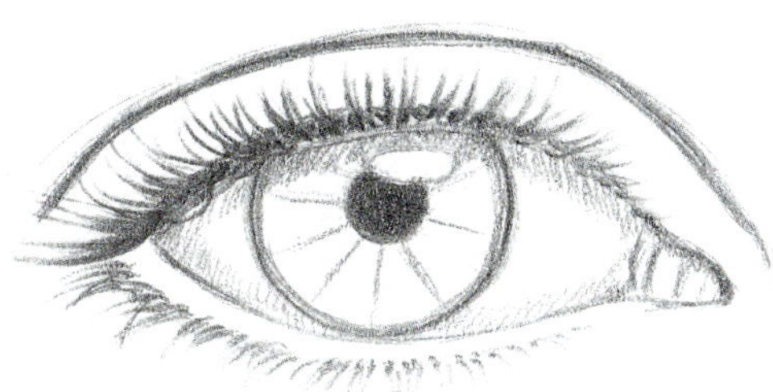

Step 2 Start shading the iris, drawing lines that radiate out from the pupil. Then add the eyelashes and the shadow being cast on the eyeball from the upper lid and eyelashes, working around the highlight on the iris.

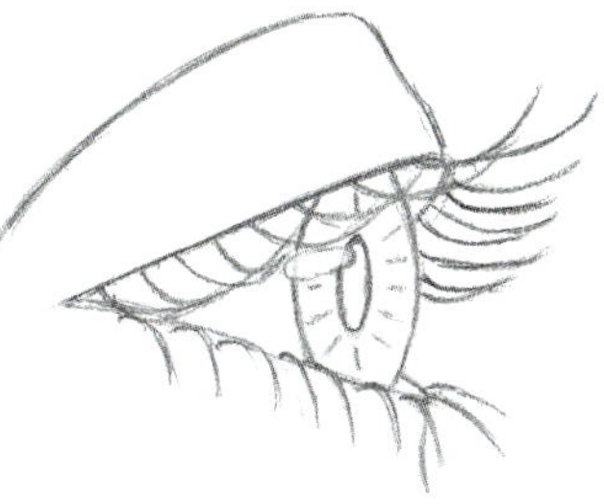

Step 2 To draw eyelashes in profile, start at the outside corner of the eye and make quick, curved lines, always stroking in the direction of growth. The longest lashes are at the center of the eye.

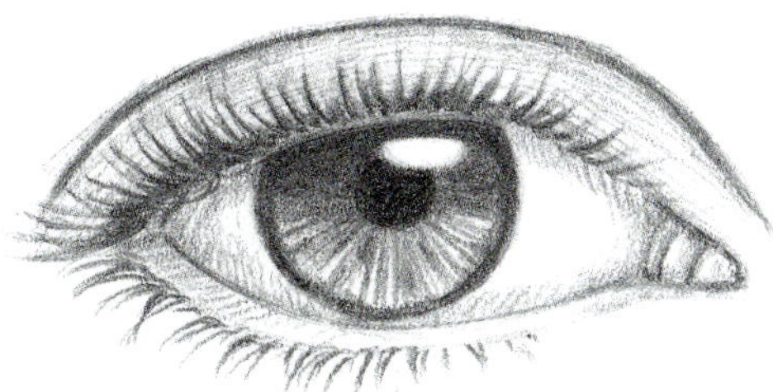

Step 3 Continue shading the iris, stroking outward from the pupil. Then shade the eyelid and the white of the eye to add three-dimensional form.

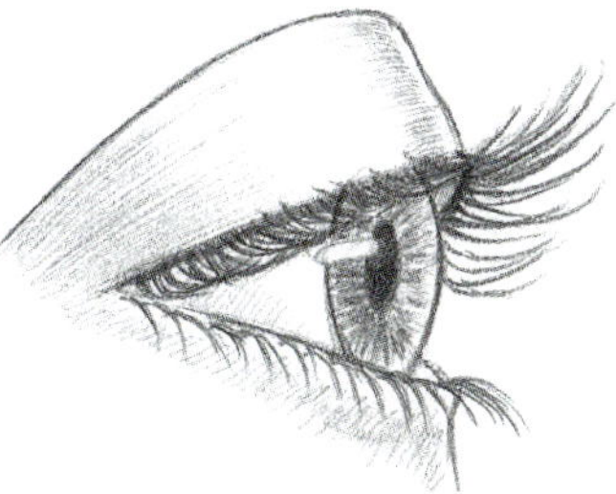

Step 3 When shading the eyelid, make light lines that follow the curve of the eyelid. As with the frontal view, the shading in the iris radiates out from the pupil.

DRAWING TIPS

The sclera (A) is the white of the eye. The iris (B) is a colored disc that controls the amount of light entering the round opening of the pupil (C). The domelike, transparent cornea (E) sits over the iris. The inner canthus (D) at the corner of the eye is an important feature of the shape of the eye.

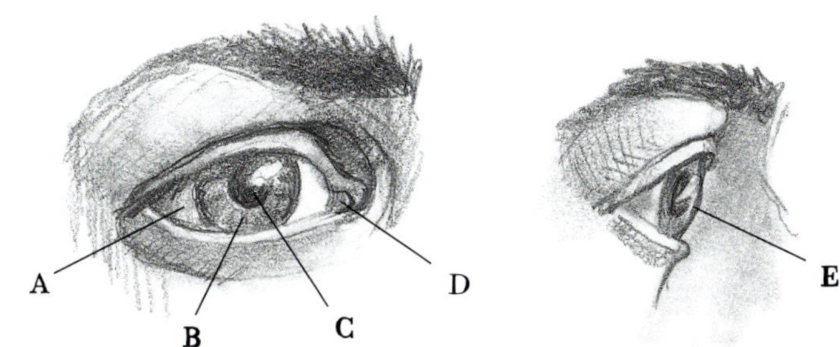

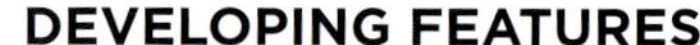

DEVELOPING FEATURES

After becoming comfortable with drawing the eye itself, start developing the features around the eye, including the eyebrows and the nose. Be sure to space adult eyes about one eye-width apart from each other. And keep in mind that eyes are always glossy—highlights help indicate this. It's best to shade around the highlights, but if you accidentally shade over the area, you can pull out the highlight with a kneaded eraser.

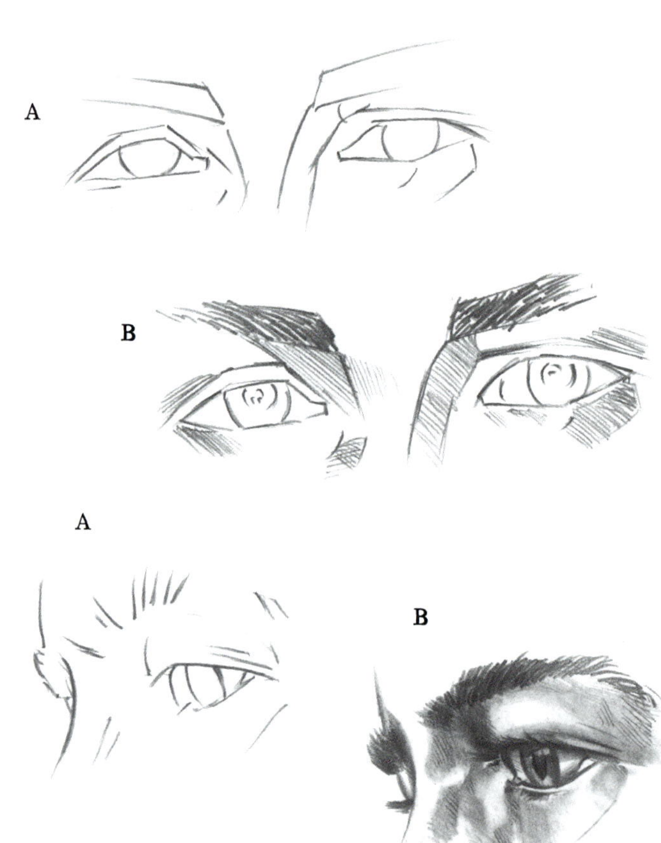

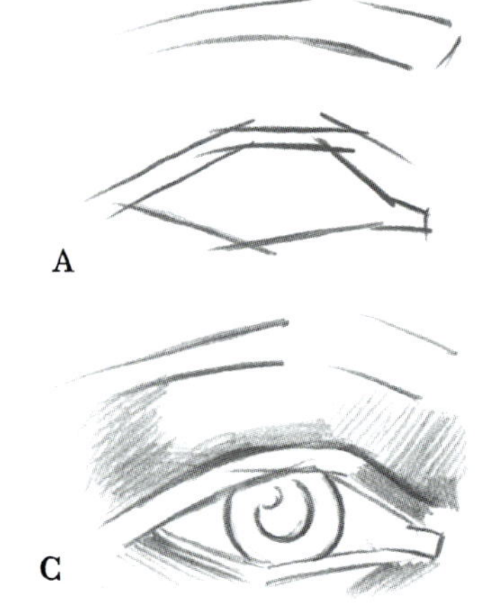

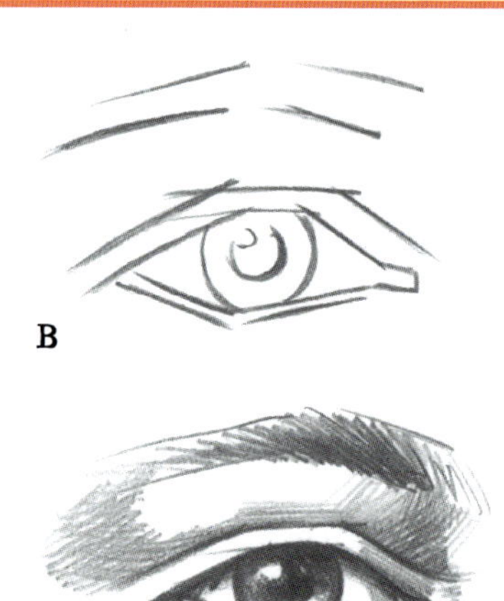

PRACTICE EXERCISE

Eyes are a crucial element for every portrait, and they are astonishingly easy to draw. Review the basic steps on page 43 and then complete this exercise. When you are comfortable with your results, move on to the other drawings on these pages.

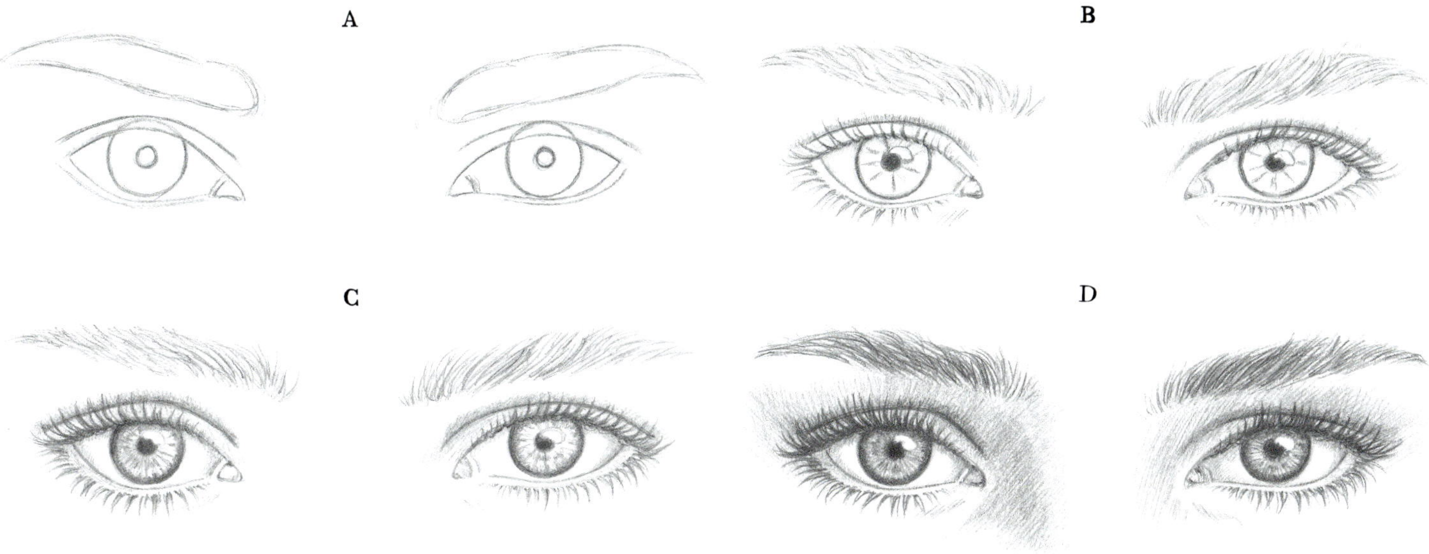

VARYING QUALITIES

There are several characteristics that influence how eyes are drawn and perceived by the viewer. These include the shape of the eyes, position of the eyebrows, length and thickness of the eyelashes, and the number of creases and wrinkles, which can denote everything from age to mood. Study the examples below to see how these different elements work together.

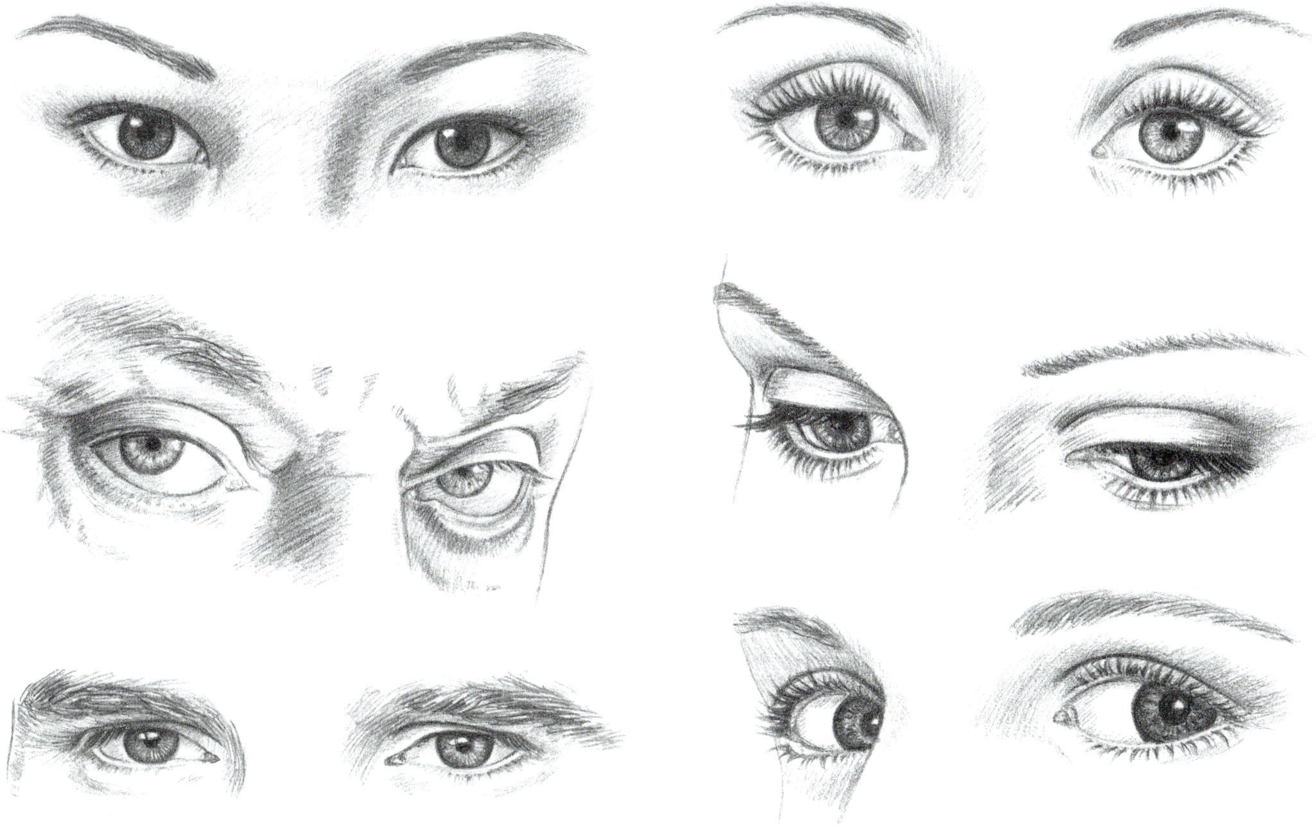

Ears

The ears aren't vertical to the head but are placed at a slight angle. The angle is individual to every person. Your portrait will benefit from rendering the angle exactly. In many cases, the shapes of both ears can vary significantly. Some people may have one protruding ear, while the other ear looks proportional. All of these unique characteristics add realism to your work.

A

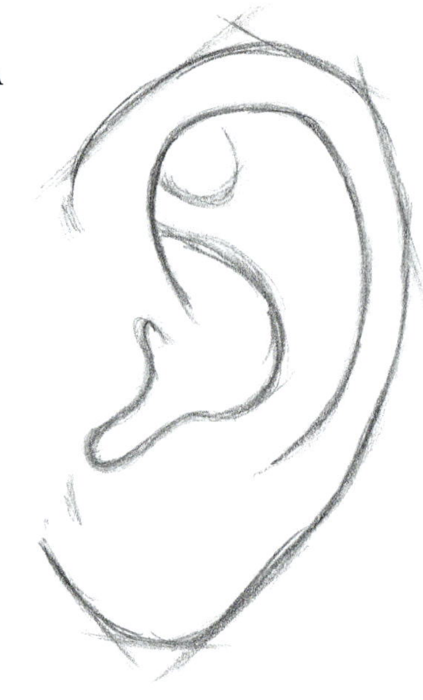

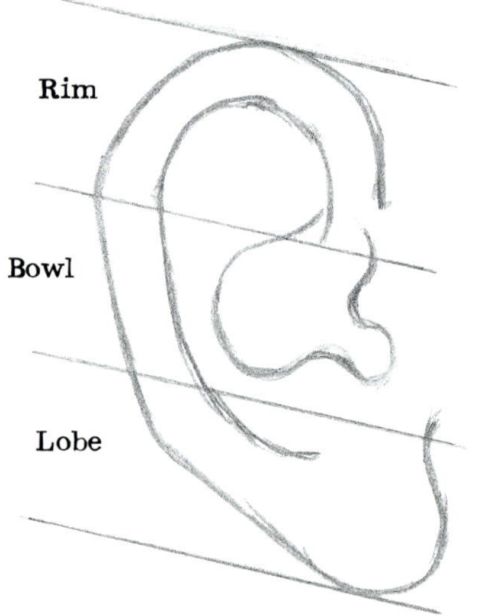

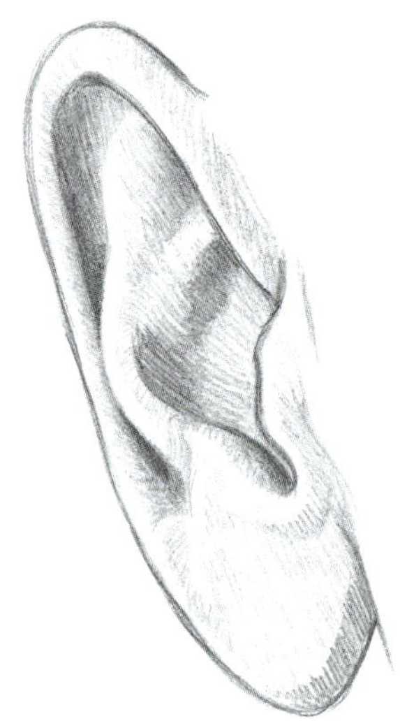

Dividing the Ear The ear is shaped like a disk that is divided into three parts: the rim, the bowl, and the lobe.

Sizing the Ear The ear usually connects to the head at a slight angle; the width is generally about one-half of the length.

B

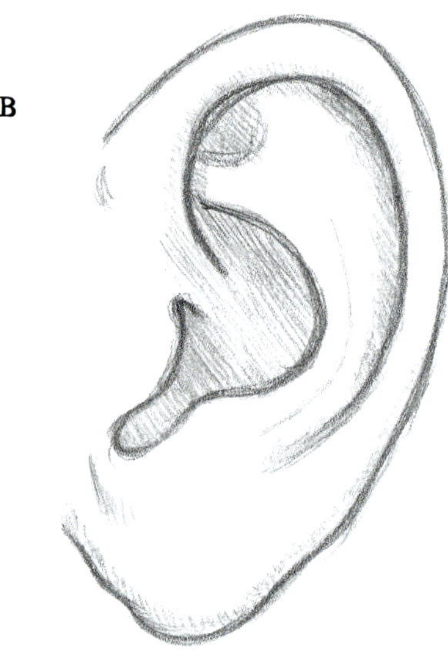

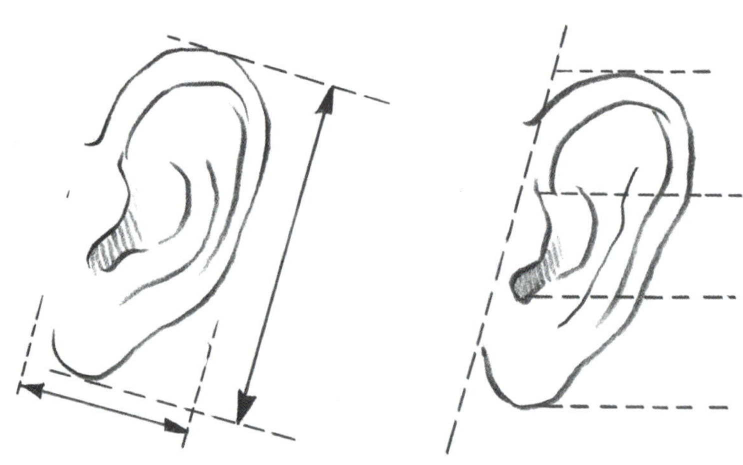

DEVELOPING THE EAR IN PROFILE

First block in the general shape, visually dividing it into its three parts. Next, start shading the darkest areas, defining the ridges and folds. Then shade the entire ear, leaving highlights in key areas to create the illusion of form.

C

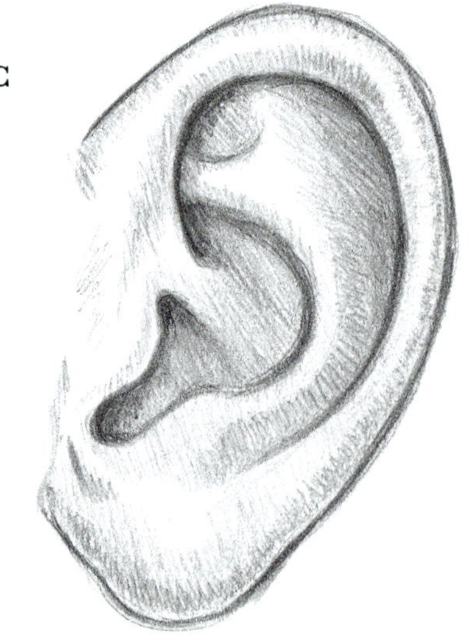

Noses

Noses easily can be developed from simple straight lines. The first step is to sketch the overall shape as illustrated by the sketches below. Then smooth out the corners into subtle curves in accordance with the shape of the nose. A three-quarter view also can be drawn with this method. Once you have a good preliminary drawing, begin shading to create form. The nostrils enhance the personality of the nose as well as the person. Make sure the shading inside the nostrils isn't too dark or it might not look natural. Observe your subject closely to ensure that each feature of your drawing is accurate.

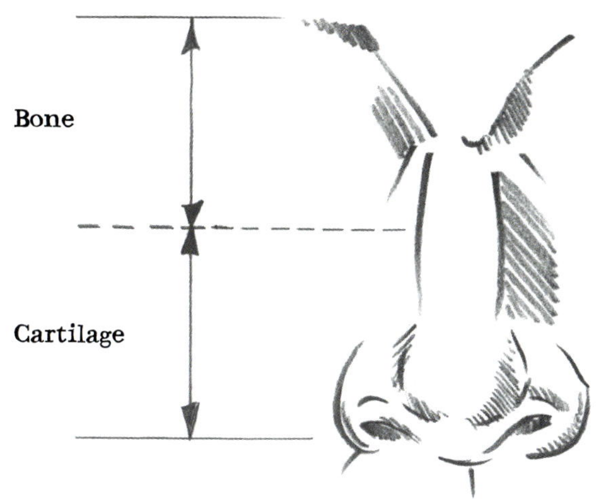

The lower portion of the nose is made of cartilage, whereas the upper portion is supported by bone. Also, the tip of the nose usually has a slight ball shape.

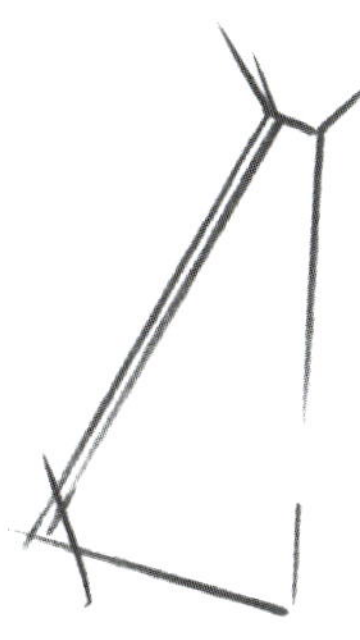

Profile view

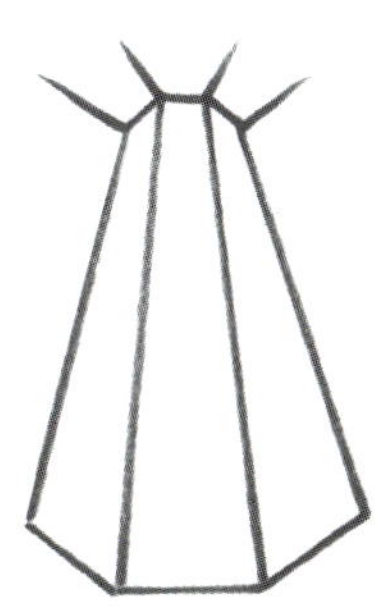

Frontal view

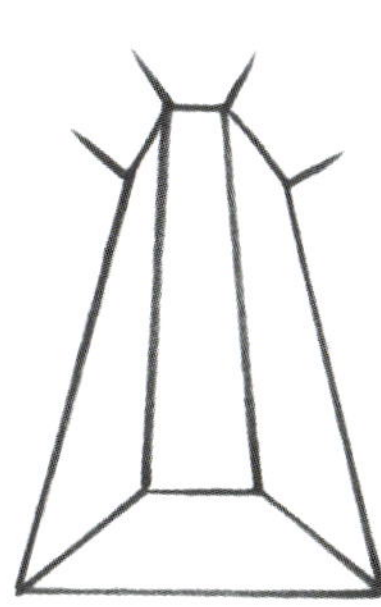

Upward view

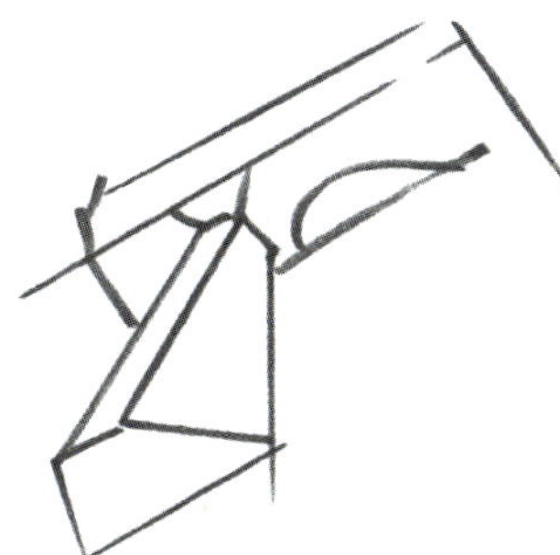

Upraised three-quarter view

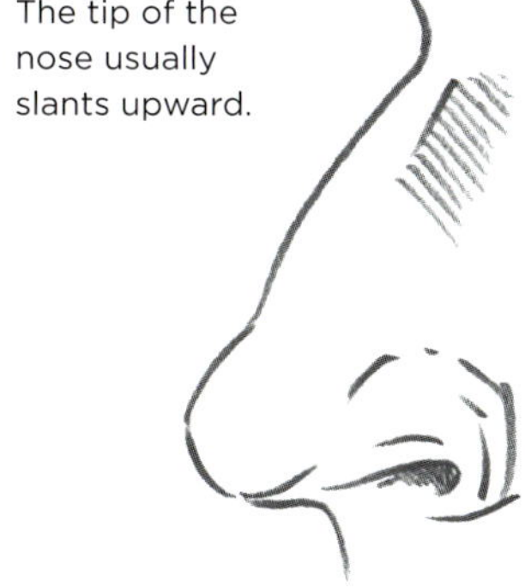

The tip of the nose usually slants upward.

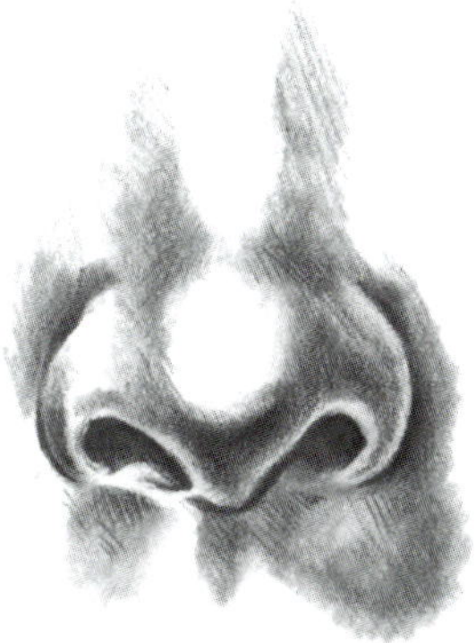

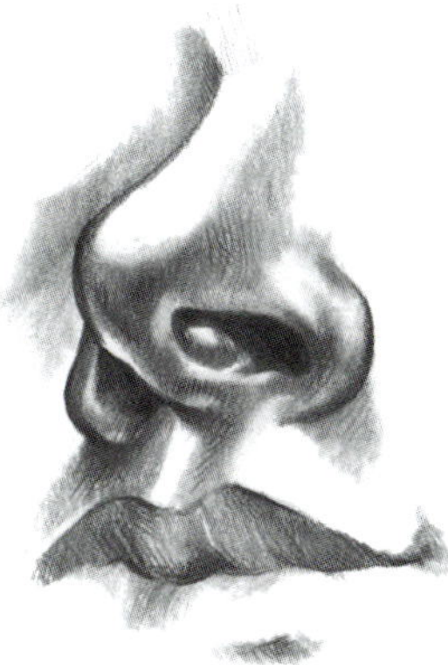

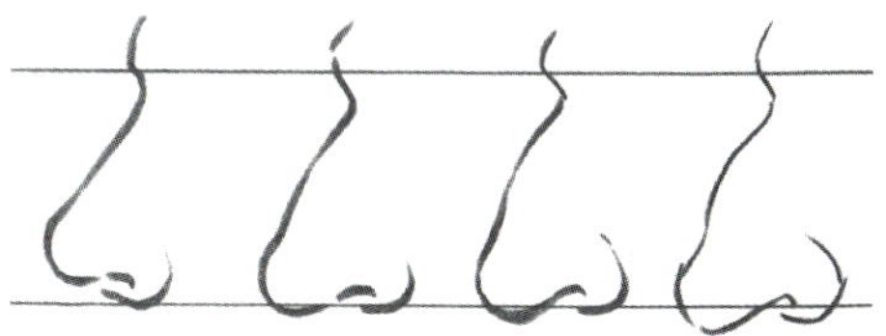

Process of an aging nose

The diagram above illustrates how the nose changes as a person ages. In many cases, the tip begins to sag and turn downward. All of these details are important for producing a realistic work.

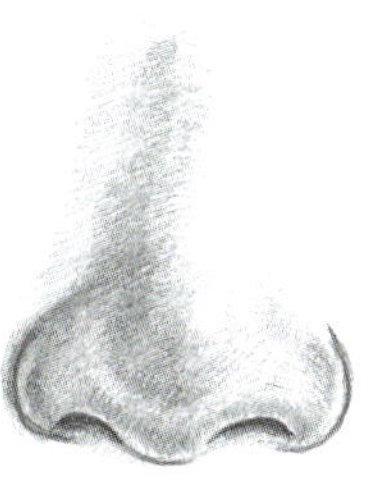

Round nose

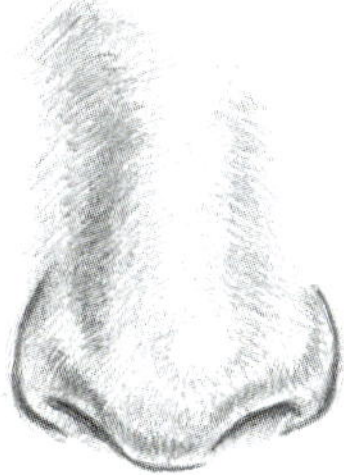

Flat nose

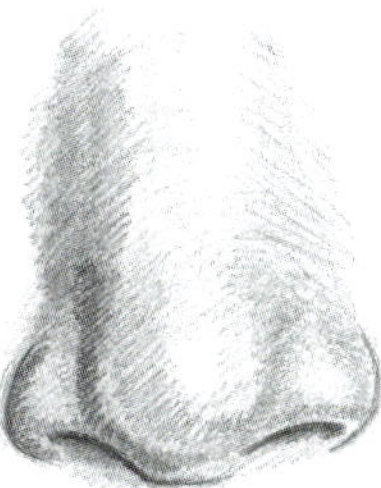

Bulbous nose

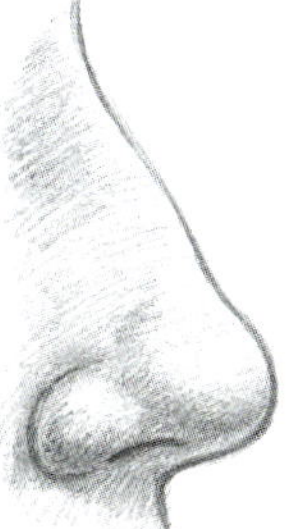

Ridged nose

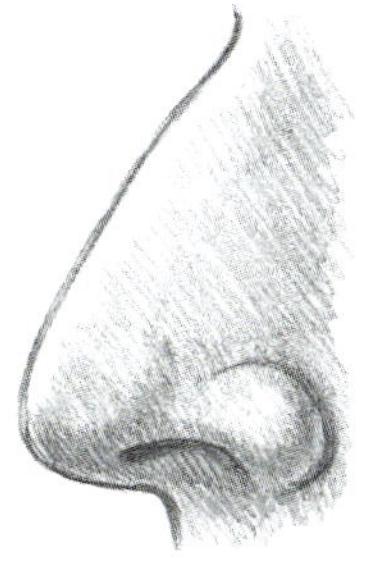

Hooked nose

Mouths & Lips

Lips are easy to draw once you have a little practice in rendering the basic shape. With time it will become easier to recognize the individual form of the mouth of the person you are drawing. Study the basic lip shapes shown on this page. These have been drawn freely and demonstrate the basic shape shown from a side angle.

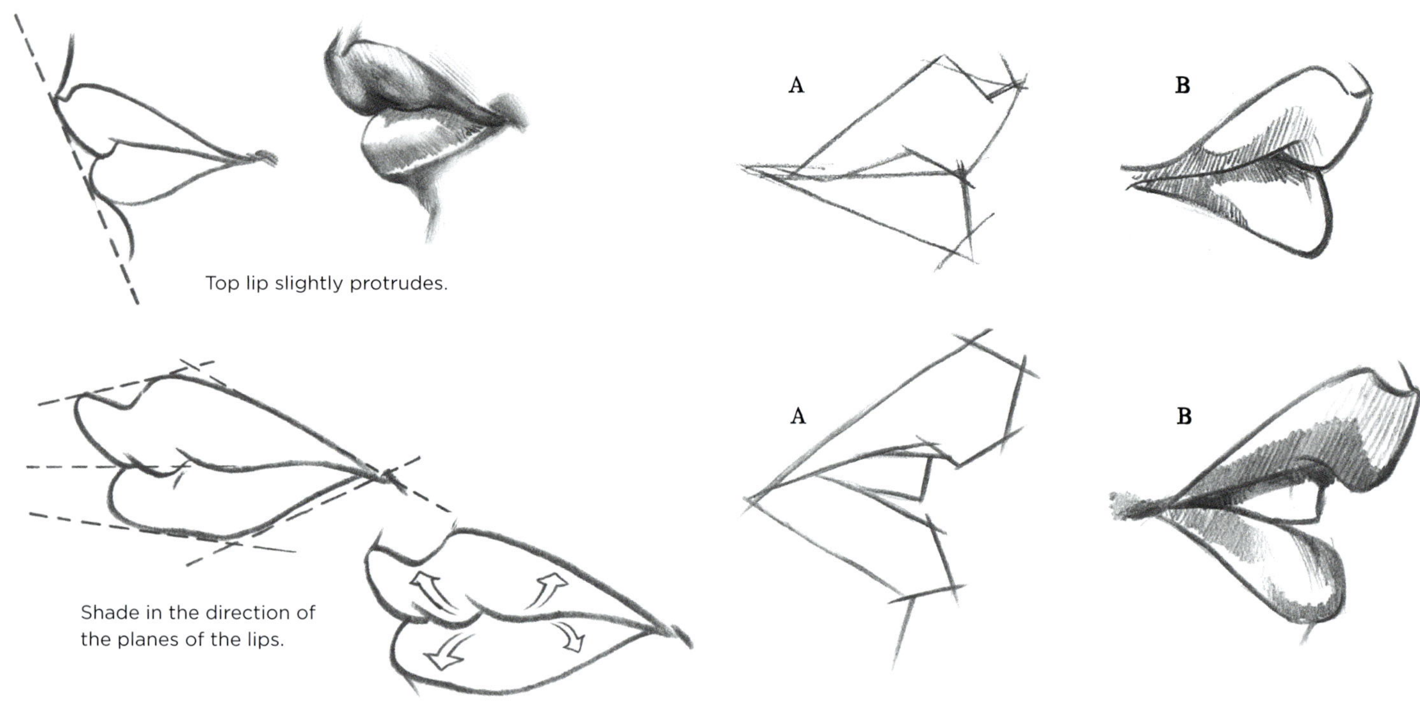

COMBINING FEATURES

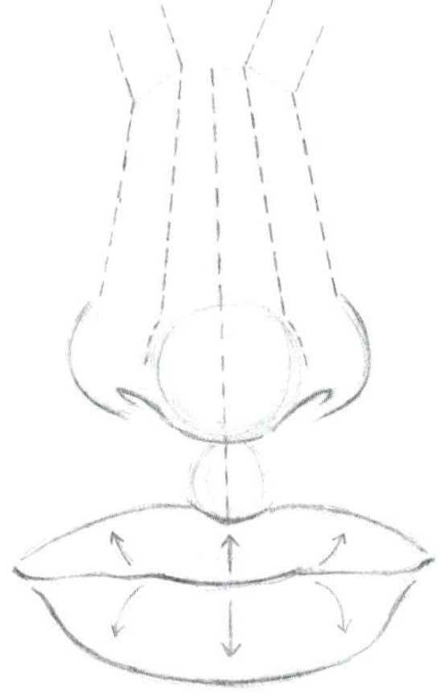

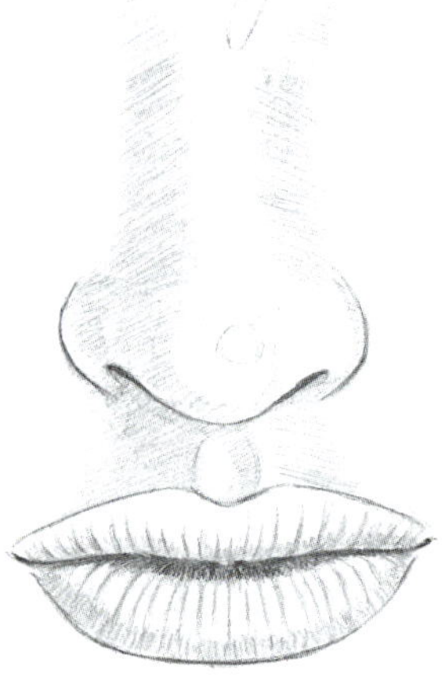

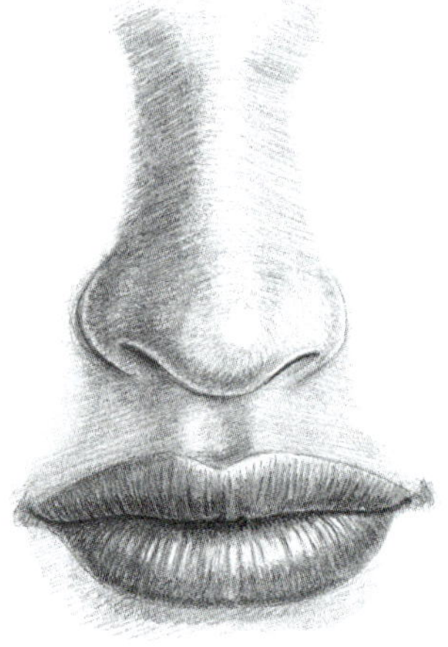

Step 1 First simplify the nose by dividing it into four planes—plus a circle on the tip to indicate its roundness. Then draw the outline of the lips. Add a small circle to connect the base of the nose with the top of the lip. The arrows on the lips indicate the direction in which to shade them.

Step 2 Now, lightly shade the sides of the nose as well as the nostrils and the area between the nose and lips. Begin shading the lips in the direction indicated by the arrows in step 1. Then, shade the dark area between the top and bottom lips. This helps separate the lips and gives them form.

Step 3 Continue shading to create the forms of the nose and mouth. Where appropriate, retain lighter areas for highlights and to show reflected light. For example, use a kneaded eraser to pull out highlights on the top lip, on the tip of the nose, and on the bridge of the nose.

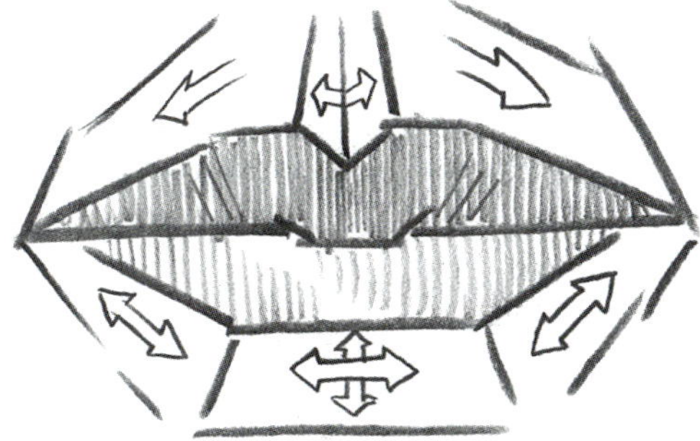

Facial planes around the mouth

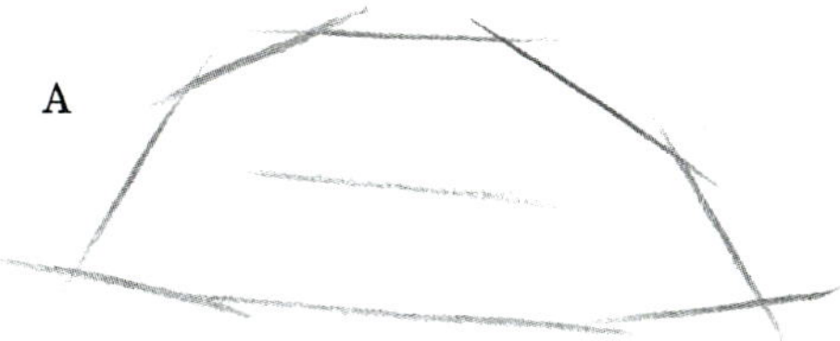

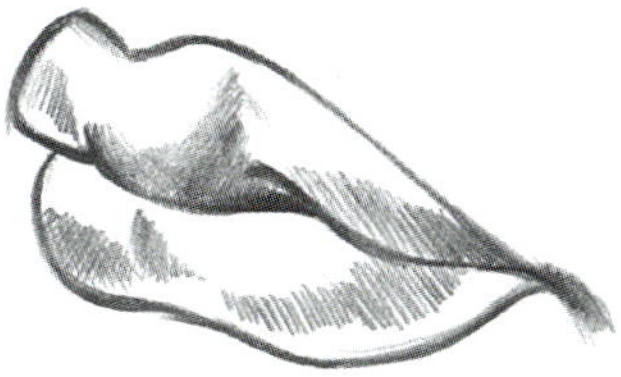

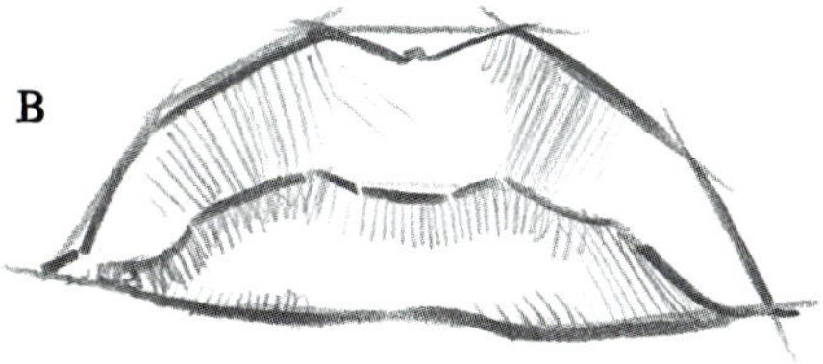

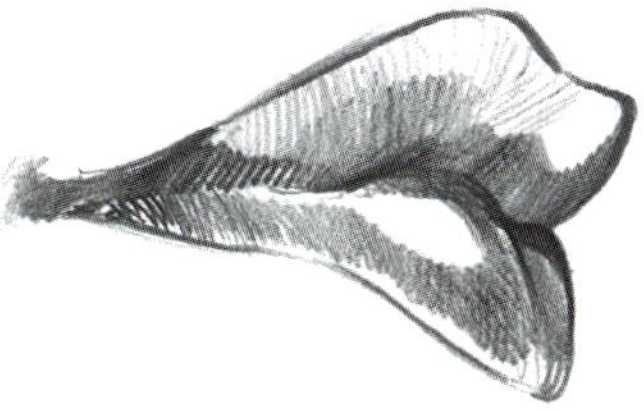

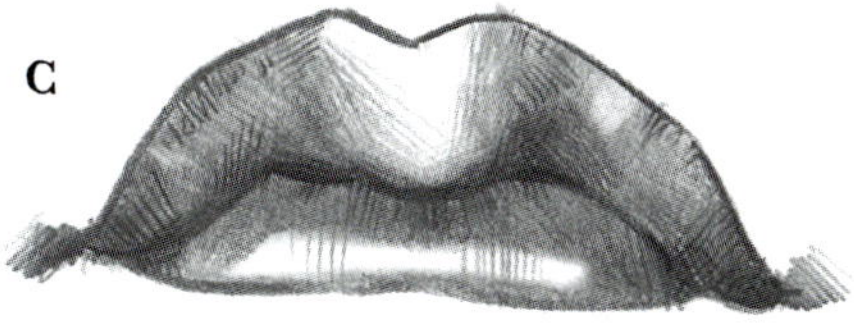

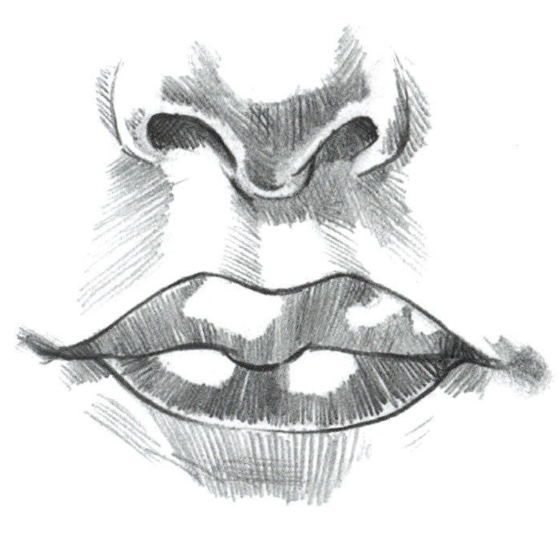

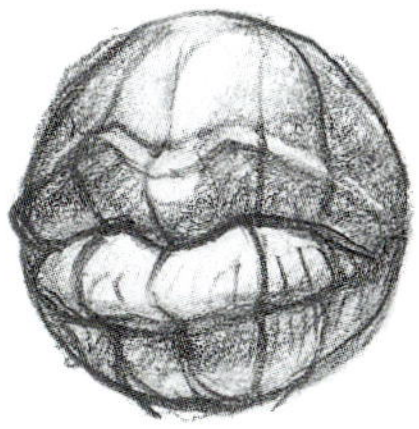

To draw the lips, block in the overall mouth shape with preliminary guidelines. Once you have a satisfactory line drawing, you can begin shading, paying particular attention to where the highlights are located. Highlights enhance the lips' fullness.

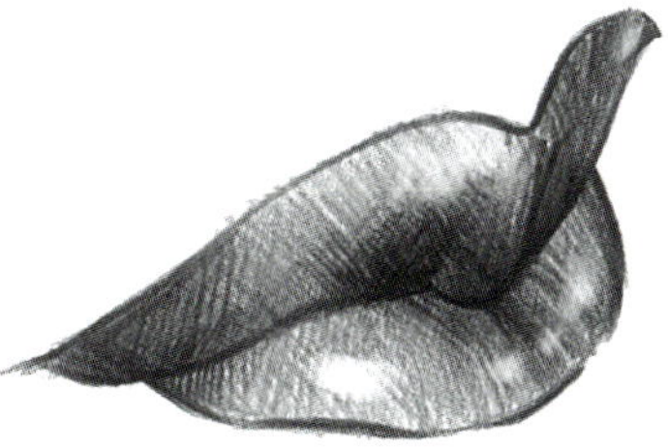

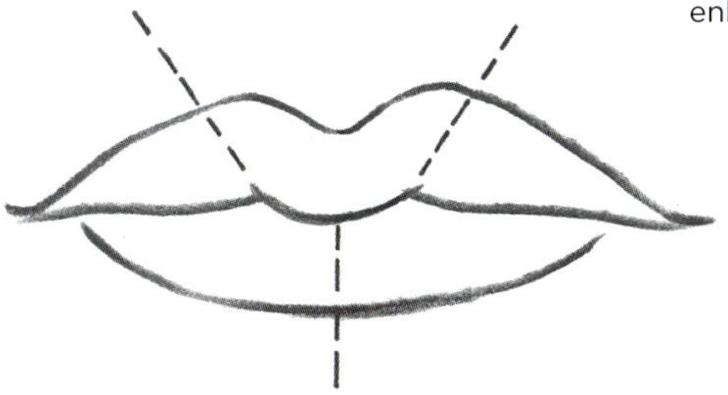

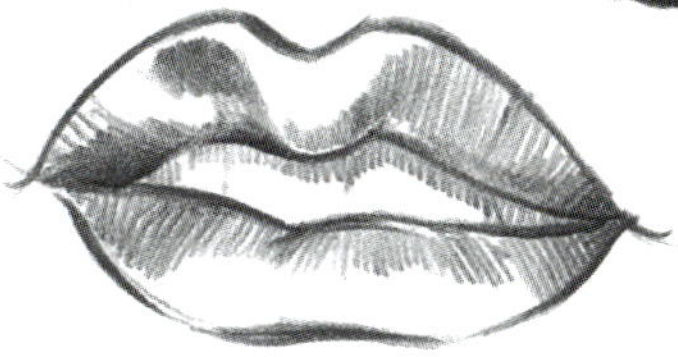

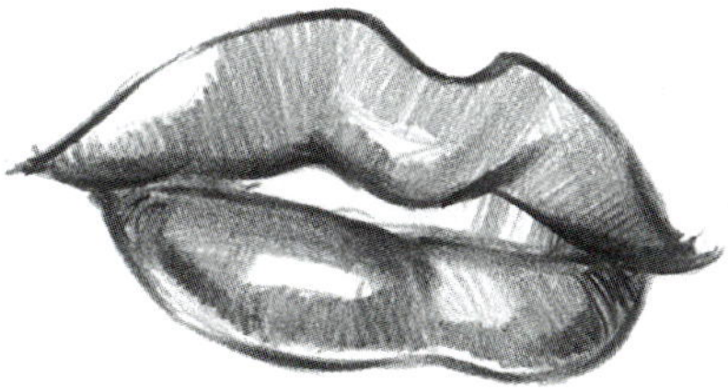

Divide the upper lip into three parts and the lower lip into two parts, as shown above. These light division lines will help you draw the top and bottom lips in proportion with each other.

DRAWING TIPS

The vertical furrow between the nose and upper lip is the philtrum (A). The tubercle (B) of the upper lip is a small rounded form surrounded by two elongated forms; it fits into the middle of the two elongated forms of the lower lip. The node (C) is an oval muscular form on the outer edge of the mouth.

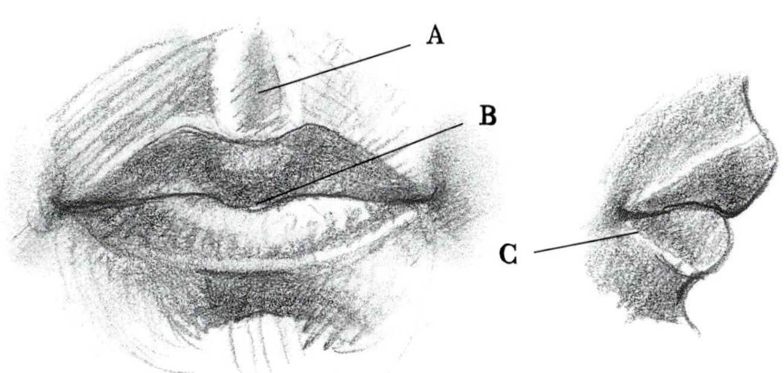

Because the lips curve around the cylinder of the teeth, it's helpful to draw and shade the mouth as if it were a sphere.

A

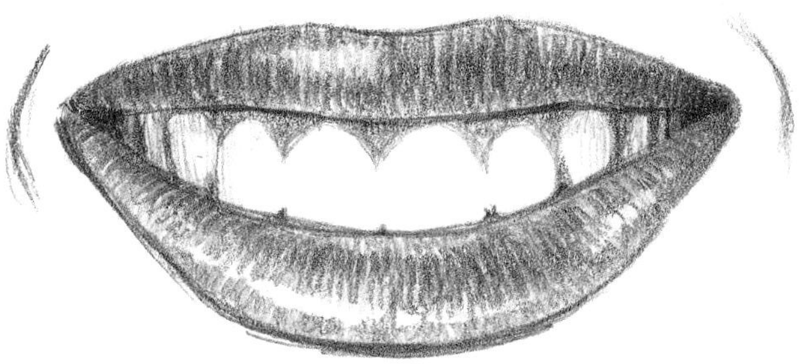

B

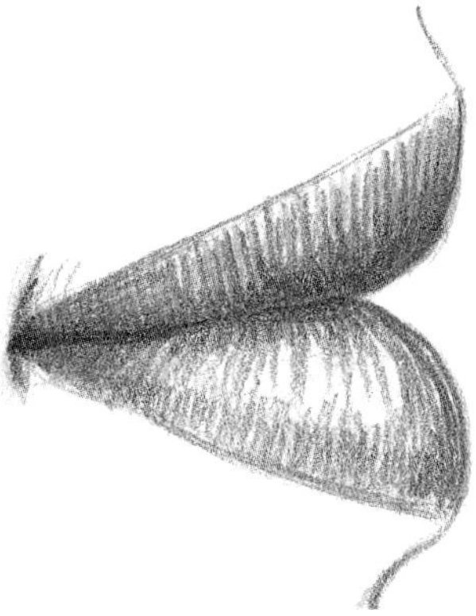

C

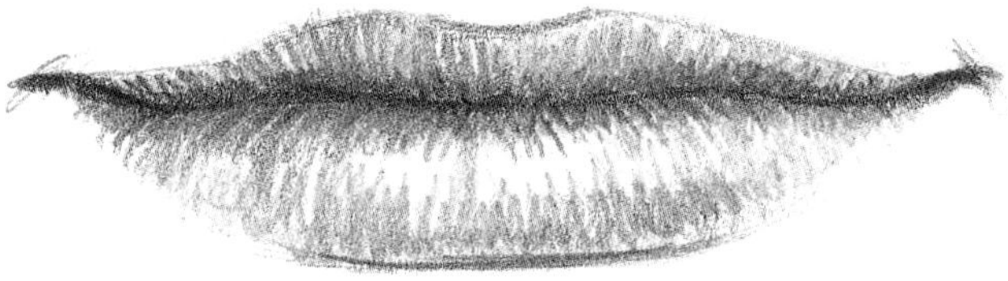

D

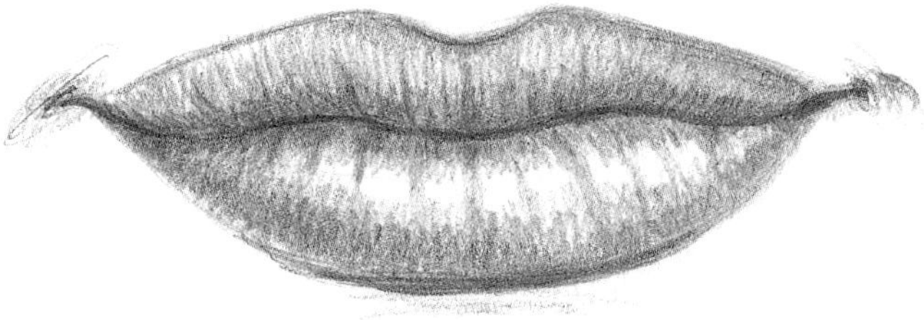

E

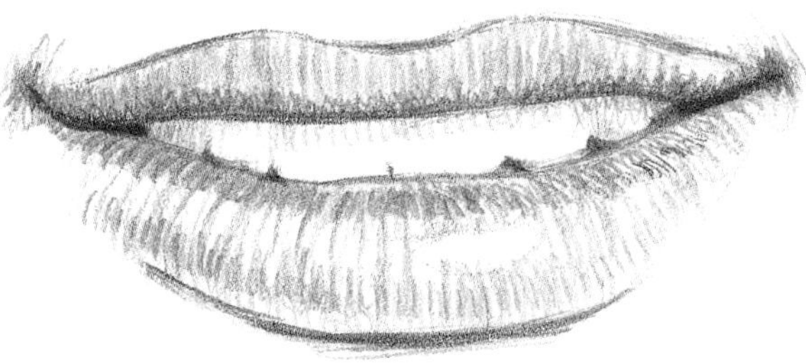

F

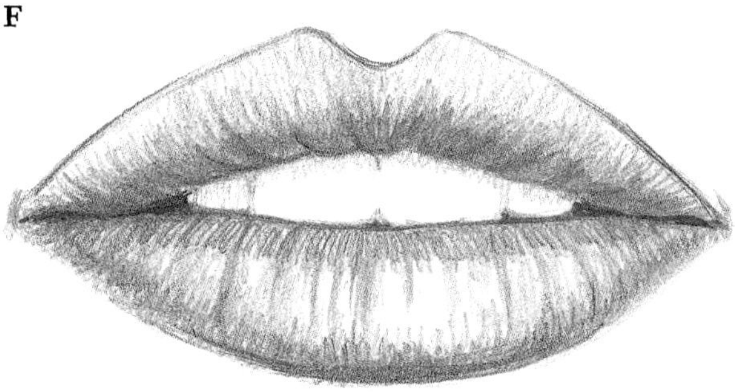

Detailing the Lips Determine how much detail you'd like to add to your renderings of lips. You can add smile lines and dimples (A, B, and D), you can draw clearly defined teeth (A) or parts of the teeth (E and F), or you can draw closed lips (B, C, and D).

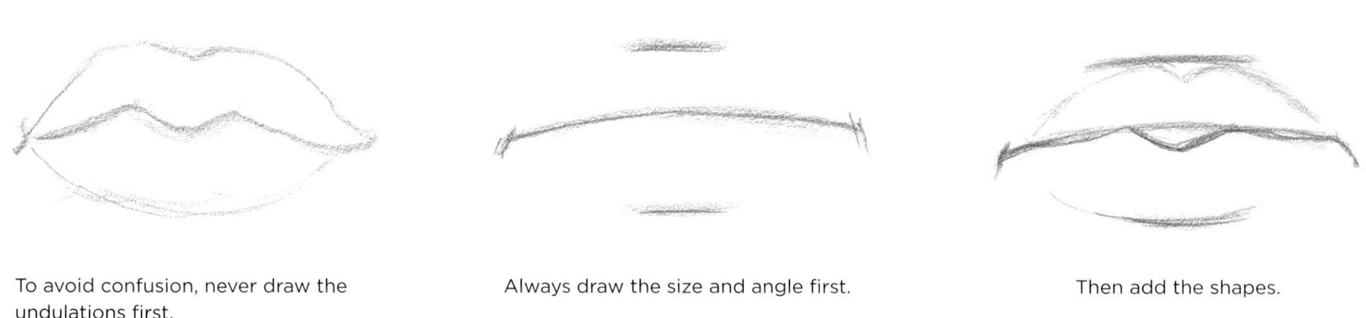

To avoid confusion, never draw the undulations first.

Always draw the size and angle first.

Then add the shapes.

Achieving a Likeness

For these frontal-view drawings, you will need to pay special attention to the position of the features. In a profile, for example, you don't have to worry about aligning the eyes with each other. Study your subject closely, because a small detail, such as the distance between the eyes, may determine if your drawing achieves a strong likeness to your model.

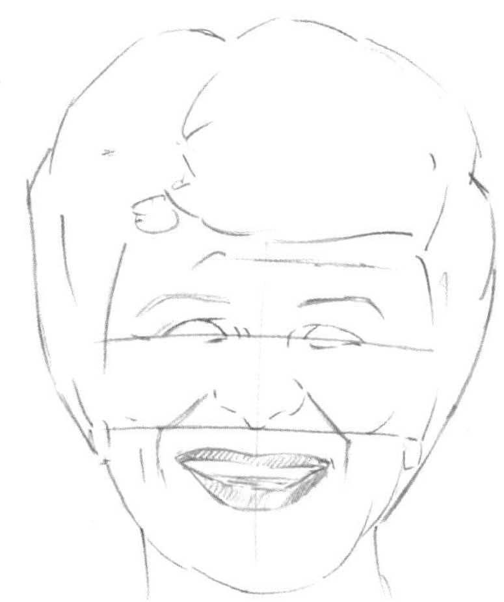

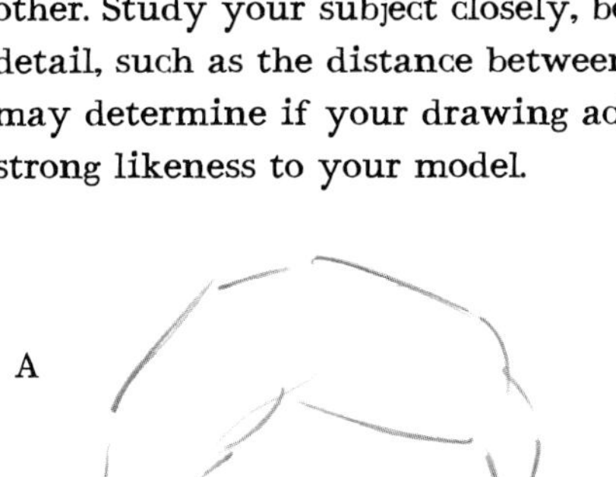

When a person smiles, the rest of the facial features are affected. For example, the bottom eyelids move slightly upward, making the eyes appear smaller.

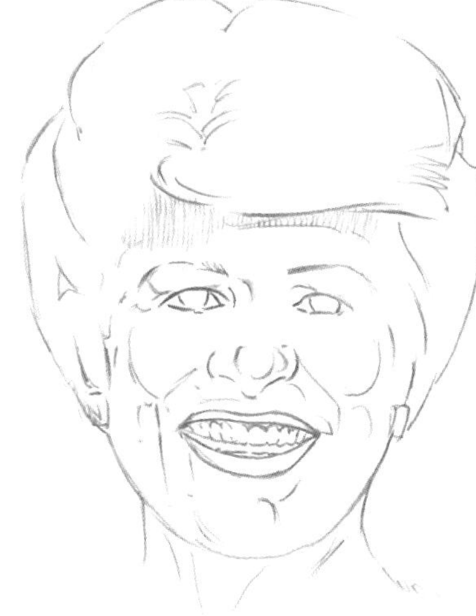

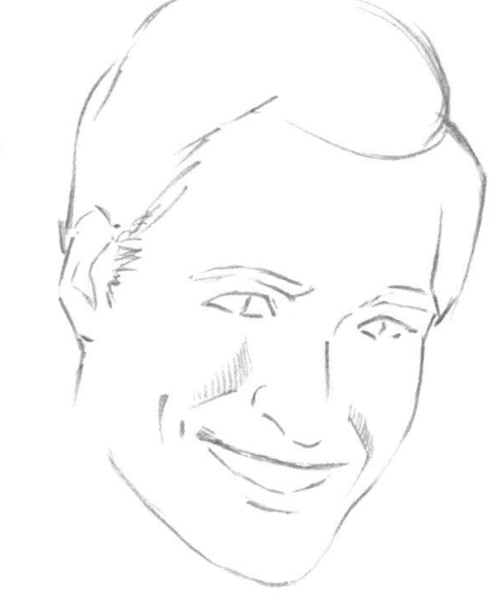

Once you've mastered drawing separate facial features, combine them to build the entire face. Use the head proportions you've already learned to correctly place the features.

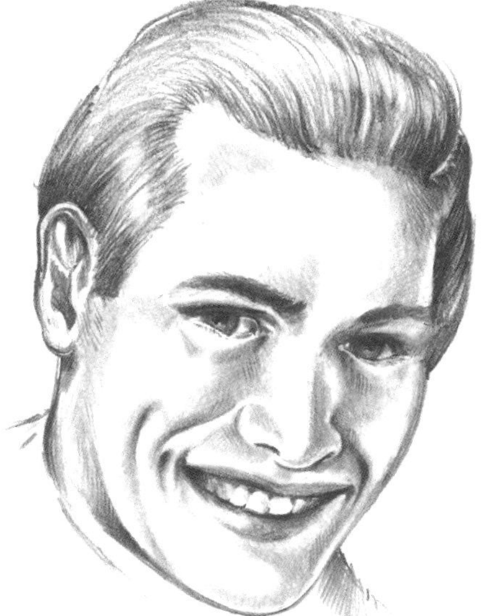

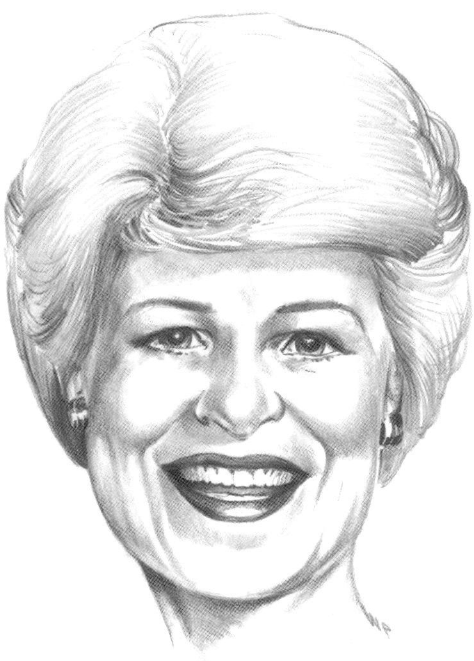

Smiling also causes creases around the mouth and produces more highlights on the cheek area because the cheeks are fuller and rounder. The lips, on the other hand, require fewer highlights because the smile causes them to slightly flatten out.

Capturing Unique Features

I n this photo, you can see the subject's delicate features, smooth skin, and sparkling eyes. But you should also to try to capture the features that are unique to her: the slightly crooked mouth, smile lines, and wide-set eyes. Note also that you can barely see her nostrils. It's details like these that will make the drawing look like the subject and no one else.

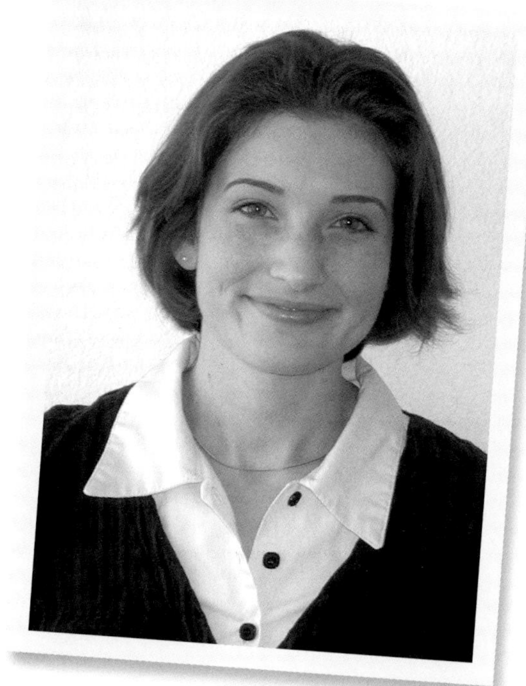

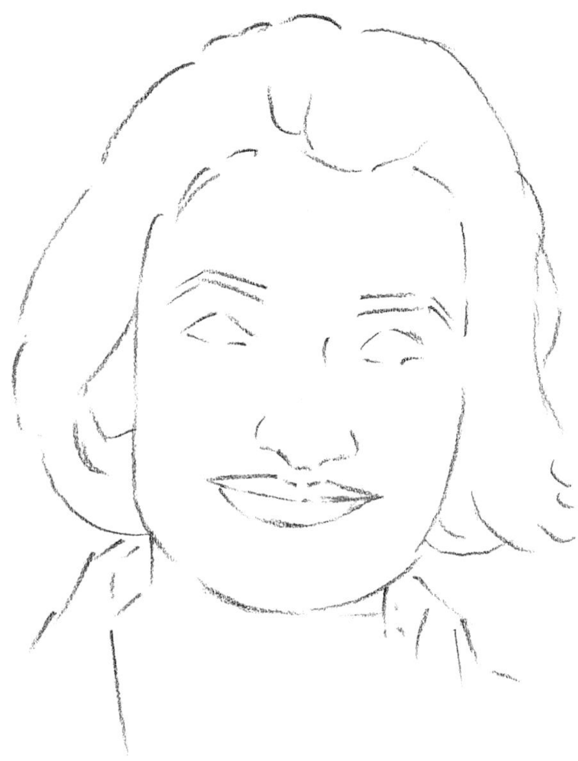

Step 1 Start with a sharp HB charcoal pencil and very lightly sketch the general shapes of the head, hair, and shirt collar. (Charcoal is used for this drawing because it allows for very subtle value changes.) Then lightly place the facial features.

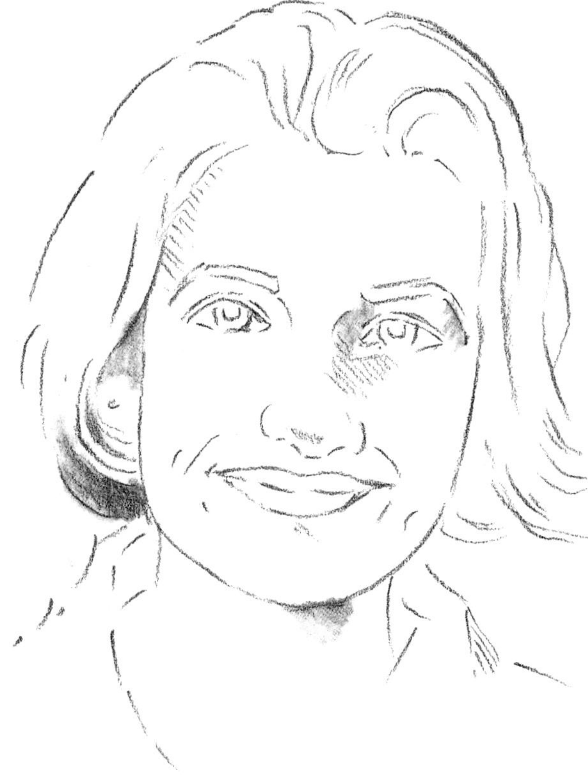

Step 2 Begin refining the features, adding the pupil and iris in each eye, plus dimples and smile lines. At this stage, study the photo carefully so you can duplicate the angles and lines that make the features unique to your subject. Then begin adding a few shadows.

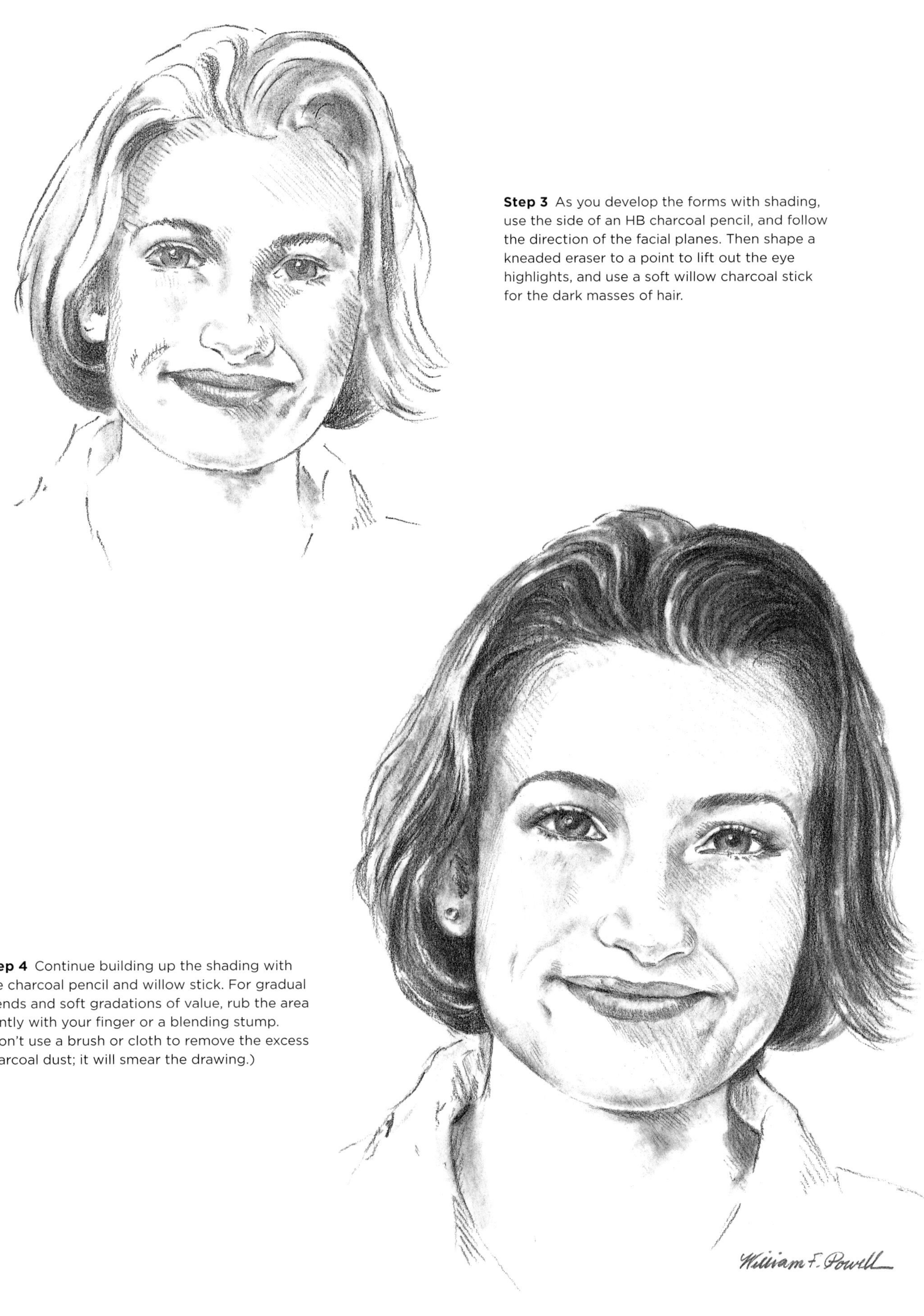

Step 3 As you develop the forms with shading, use the side of an HB charcoal pencil, and follow the direction of the facial planes. Then shape a kneaded eraser to a point to lift out the eye highlights, and use a soft willow charcoal stick for the dark masses of hair.

Step 4 Continue building up the shading with the charcoal pencil and willow stick. For gradual blends and soft gradations of value, rub the area gently with your finger or a blending stump. (Don't use a brush or cloth to remove the excess charcoal dust; it will smear the drawing.)

Drawing a Profile

A profile view can be very dramatic. Seeing only one side of the face can bring out a subject's distinctive features, such as a protruding brow, an upturned nose, or a strong chin. Because parts of the face appear more prominent in profile, be careful not to allow any one feature to dominate the entire drawing.

Managing Proportions When drawing a subject in profile, be careful with proportions, as your facial guidelines will differ slightly. In a profile view, you see more of the back of the head than you do of the face, so be sure to draw the shape of the skull accordingly.

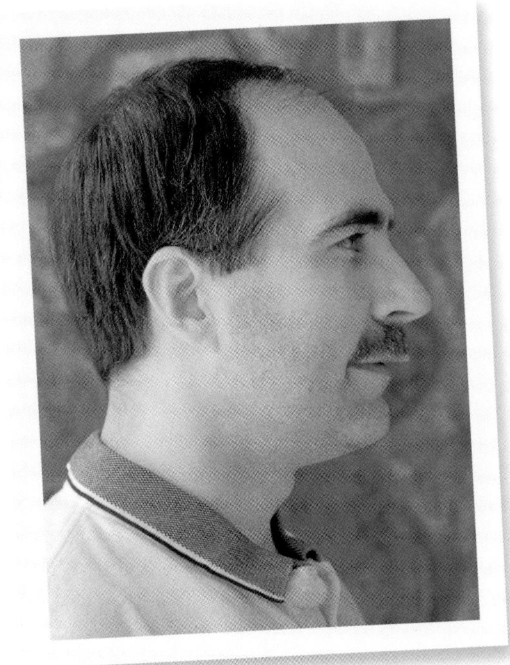

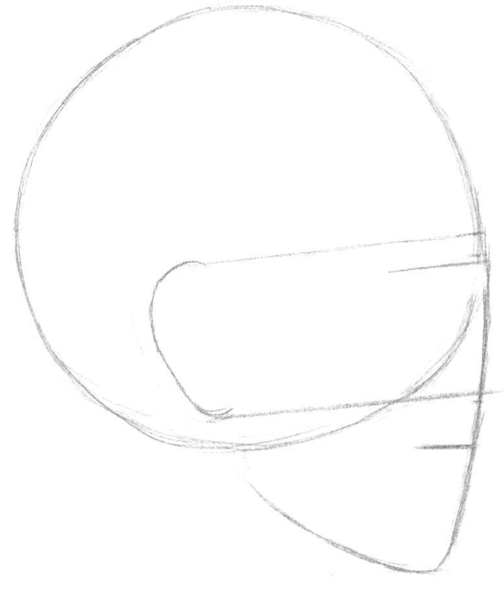

Step 1 After lightly drawing a circle for the cranial mass, use an HB pencil to block in the general shapes of the face, chin, and jawline. Add guidelines for the eyes, nose, mouth, and ear.

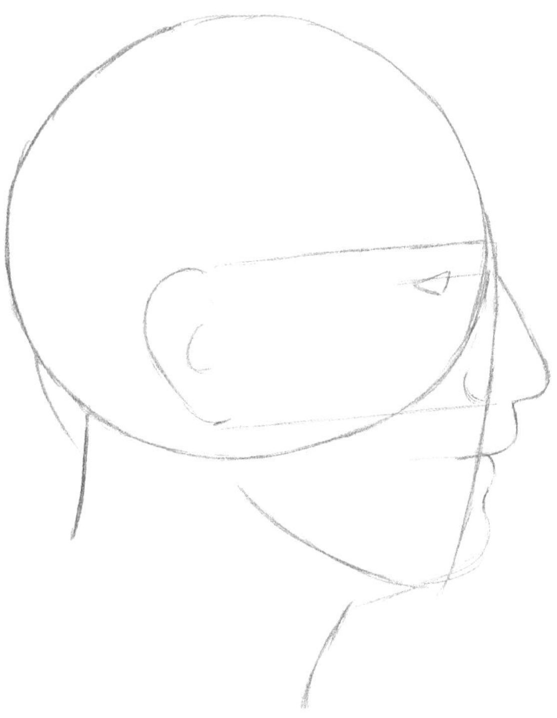

Step 2 Following the guidelines, rough in the shapes of the features, including your subject's slightly protruding upper lip. Sketch a small part of the eye, indicating how little of the iris you actually see in a profile view.

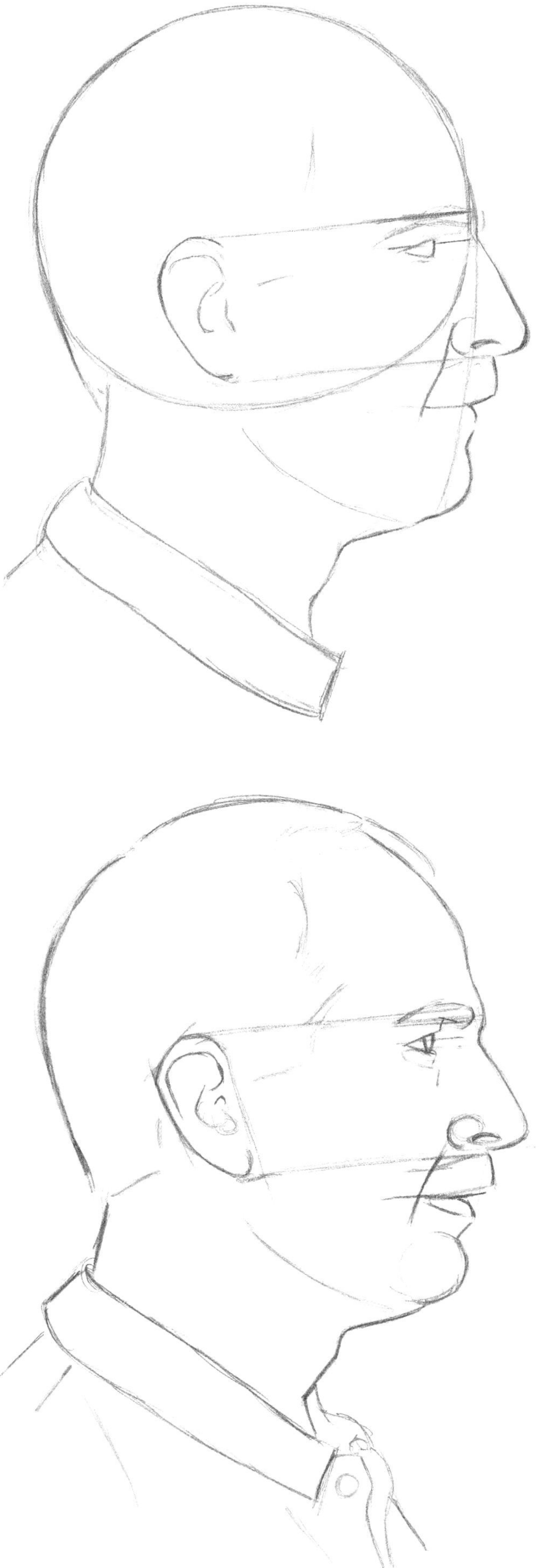

Step 3 Sketch the eyebrow, paying particular attention to the space between the eye and the eyebrow. In this case, the subject's eyebrow is fairly close to his eye. It also grows past the inside corner of his eye, very close to his nose, and tapers toward the outside corner of the eye. Continue refining the profile, carefully defining the shapes of the chin and the neck (including the Adam's apple).

Step 4 In a profile view, the hairline is important because it affects the size and shape of the forehead. This subject has a high forehead, so the hairline starts near the vertical centerline of the cranial mass. Once you're happy with the shapes of the face and hairline, start refining the features, giving them form.

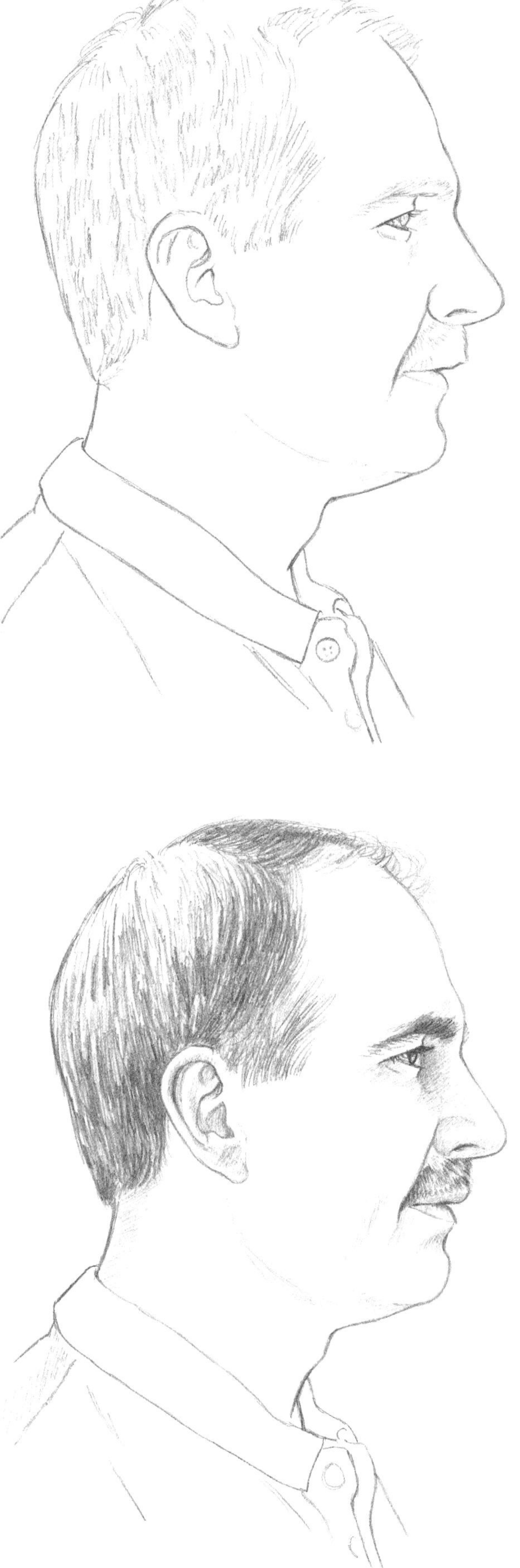

Step 5 Here you can see that the drawing is really starting to resemble the subject. Switch to a 2B pencil and continue building up the forms: round out the nose and chin; add light, soft strokes to the area above the lip for the mustache; and suggest the hair using short, quick strokes. Add more detail to the eye and develop the ear and the eyebrow.

Step 6 Still using the 2B, continue to develop the hair, eyebrows, and mustache, always stroking in the direction that the hair grows. Leave plenty of white areas in the hair to create the illusion of individual strands. Next, begin to suggest the curves and shadows of the face by shading the eye, ear, and nose.

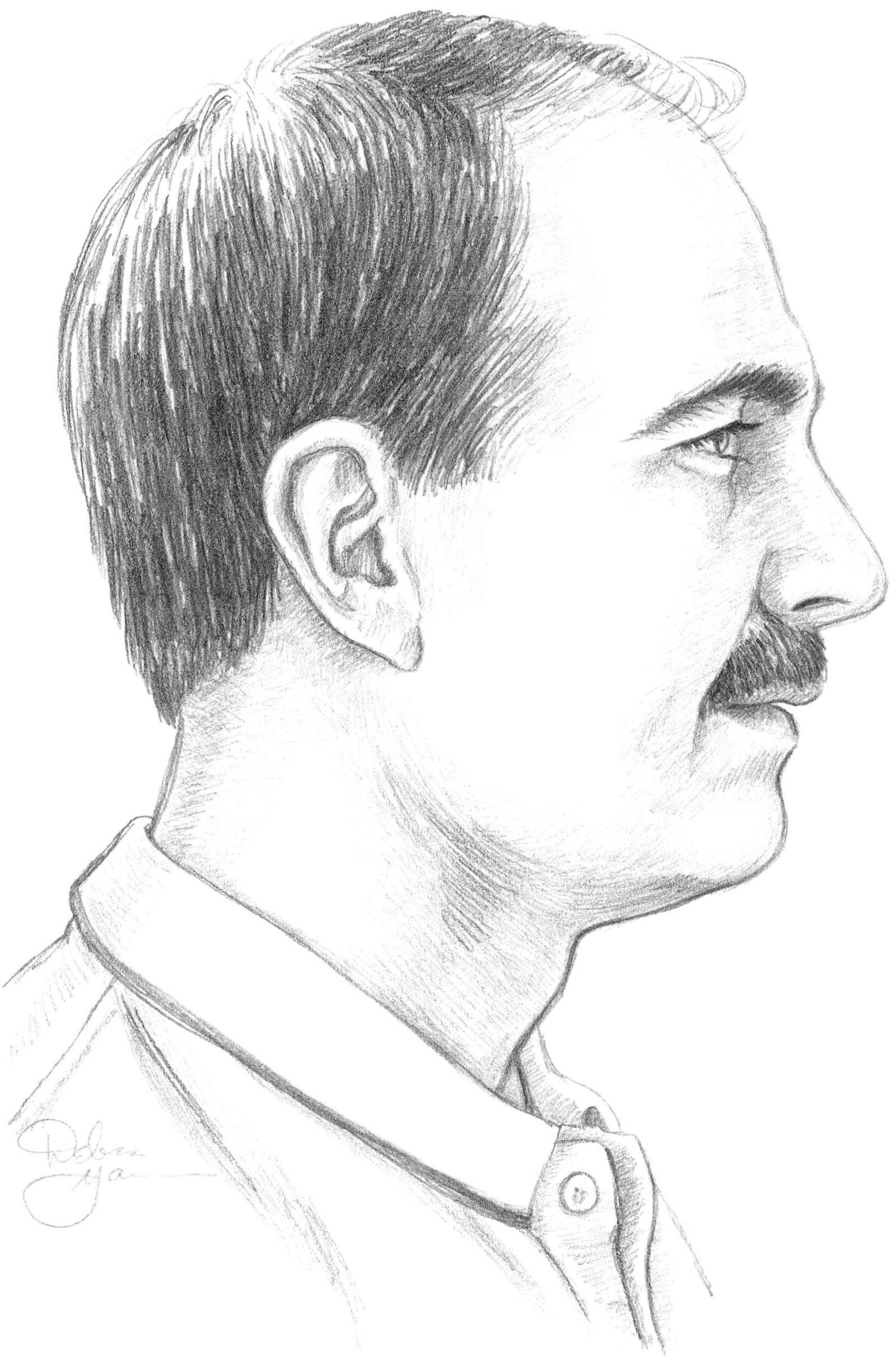

Step 7 Continue shading the lips, pulling out a white highlight on the bottom lip with a kneaded eraser. Then shade more of the ear and add even darker values to the hair, leaving highlights on the crown of the head, as it is in the direct path of the light source. Shade the forehead, the nose, and the chin. Leave the majority of the cheek and the middle part of the forehead white. This helps indicate that the light source is coming from above, angled toward the visible side of the face.

Drawing from Photographs

Once you've practiced drawing the individual features, you're ready to combine them in a full portrait. Use your understanding of the basics of proportion to block in the head and place the features. Study your subject carefully to see how the facial features are unique.

Drawing What You See Working from a photo helps you draw what you really see—as opposed to what you expect to see—because you can change your viewpoint. Try turning both the photo and your drawing upside-down as you work; you'll find that you can represent many shapes more accurately.

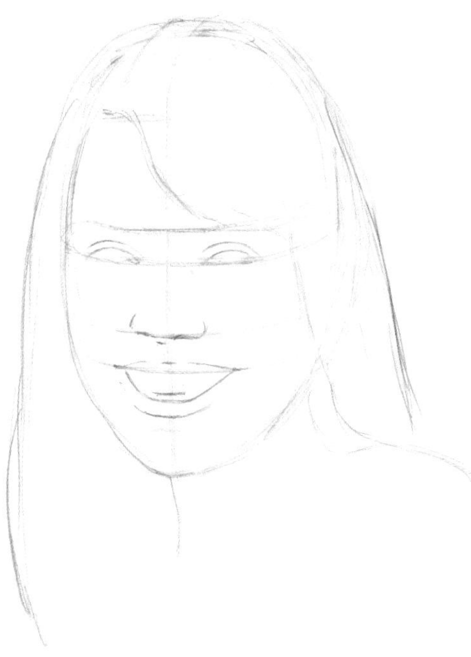

Step 1 Using an HB pencil, sketch the general outline of the subject's face. Then place the facial guidelines before blocking in the eyes, nose, and mouth. (Notice that the mouth takes up about one-fourth of the face.) Block in the shape of her hair, including the bangs.

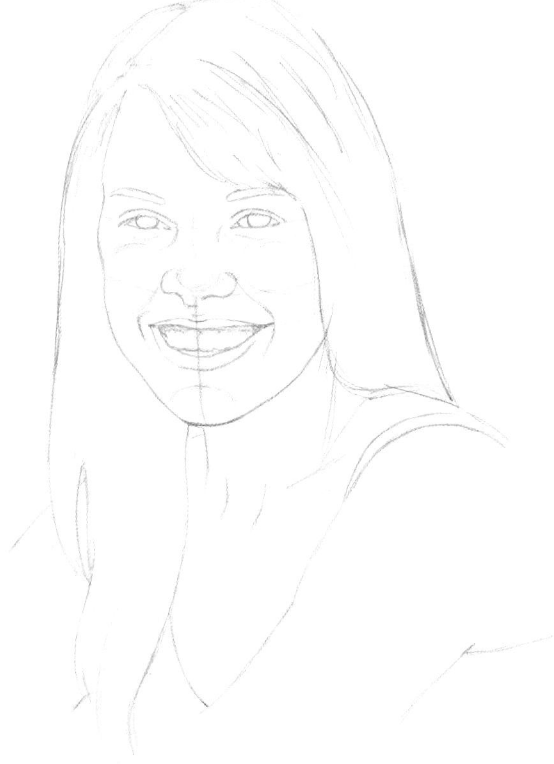

Step 2 Switch to a 2B pencil. Indicate the roundness of the facial features. Compare your sketch to the photograph often, making sure you've captured the things that make this individual unique, like the turned-up nose, slightly asymmetrical eyes, and wide smile.

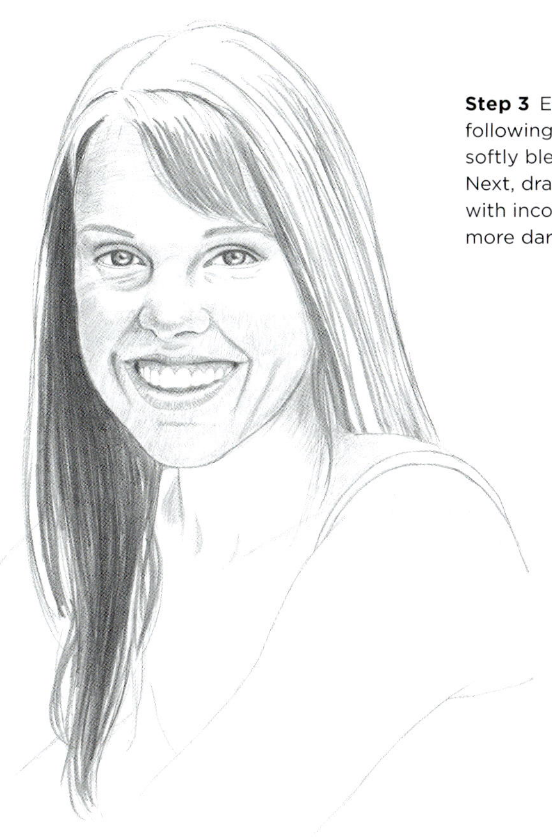

Step 3 Erase your guidelines and then begin shading, following the form of the face with the 2B pencil and softly blending to create the smoothness of the skin. Next, draw the teeth, lightly indicating the separations with incomplete lines. Switch to a 3B pencil to lay in more dark streaks of hair.

FOCUSING ON FEATURES

This drawing shows the same young lady with a different hair style, expression, and pose. Although she's in costume, she is still recognizable as the same subject because the artist was faithful to the facial characteristics that are specific to this individual.

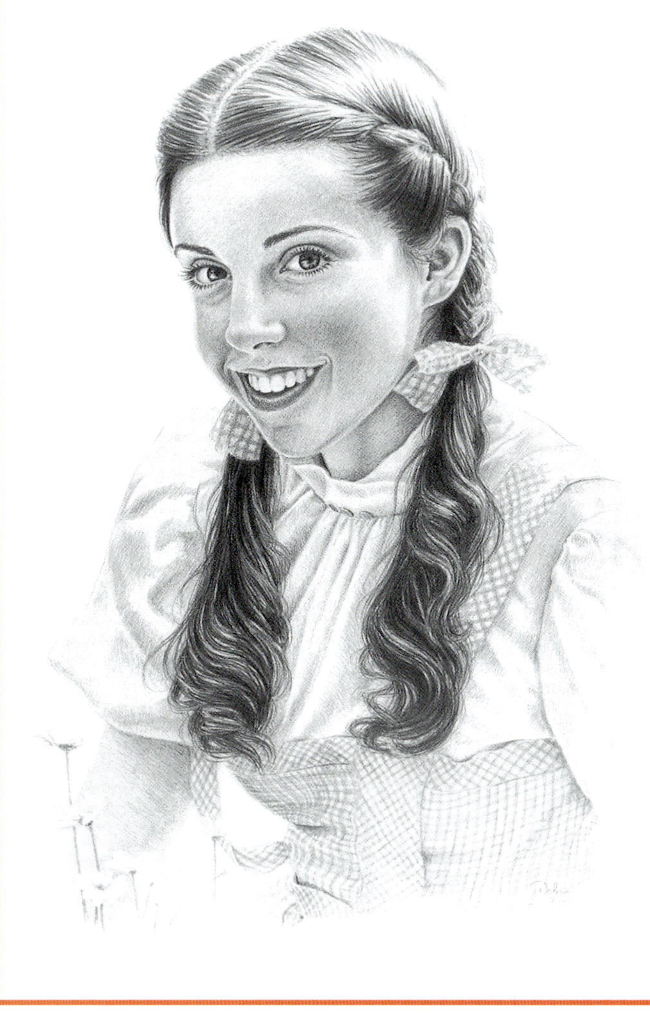

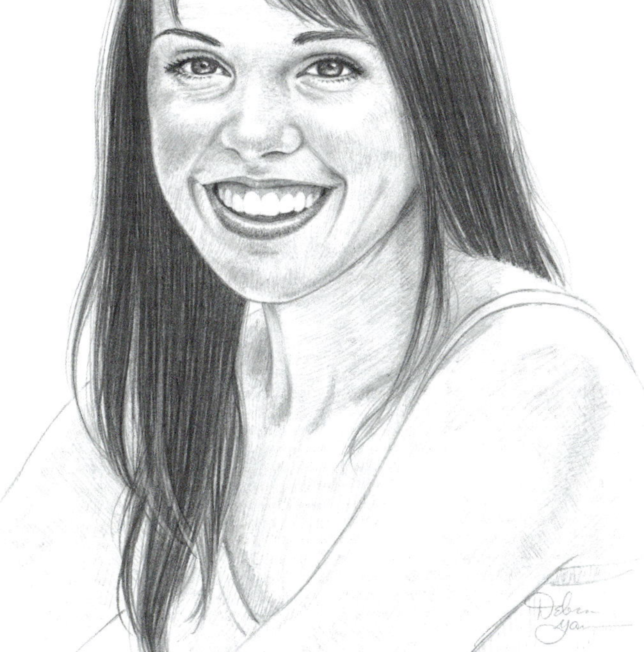

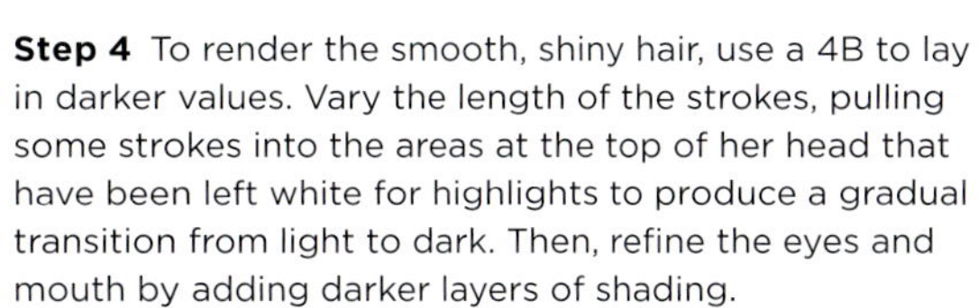

Step 4 To render the smooth, shiny hair, use a 4B to lay in darker values. Vary the length of the strokes, pulling some strokes into the areas at the top of her head that have been left white for highlights to produce a gradual transition from light to dark. Then, refine the eyes and mouth by adding darker layers of shading.

Including a Background

An effective background will draw the viewer's eye to the subject and play a role in setting a mood. The background should always complement a drawing, and it should never overwhelm the subject. Generally, a light, neutral setting will enhance a subject with dark hair or skin, and a dark background will set off a subject with light hair or skin.

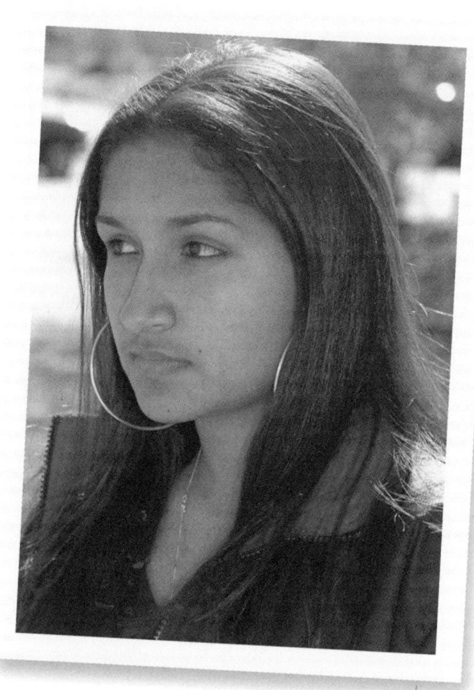

Simplifying a Background When working from a photo that features an unflattering background, simply alter the overall values to make it more interesting.

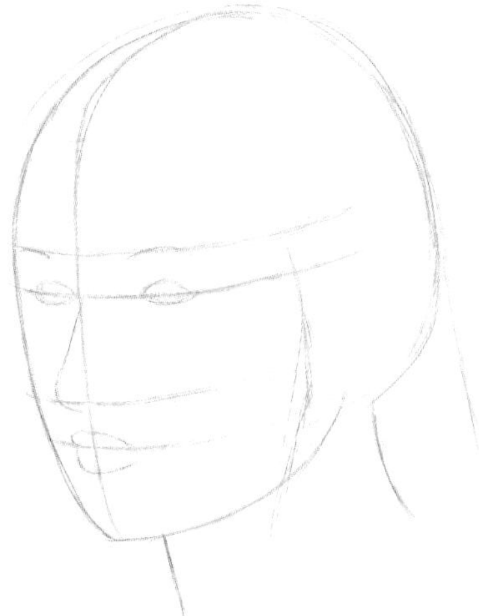

Step 1 With an HB pencil, sketch the basic head shape and the guidelines. Block in the position of the eyes, brows, nose, and mouth. (Notice that the center guideline is to the far left of the face because of the way the head is turned.) Next, indicate the neck and the hair.

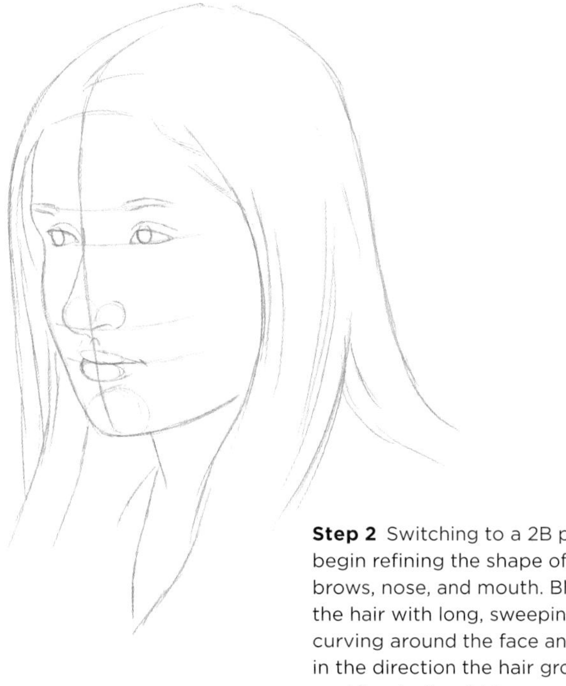

Step 2 Switching to a 2B pencil, begin refining the shape of the eyes, brows, nose, and mouth. Block in the hair with long, sweeping strokes, curving around the face and drawing in the direction the hair grows. Add a neckline to the shirt.

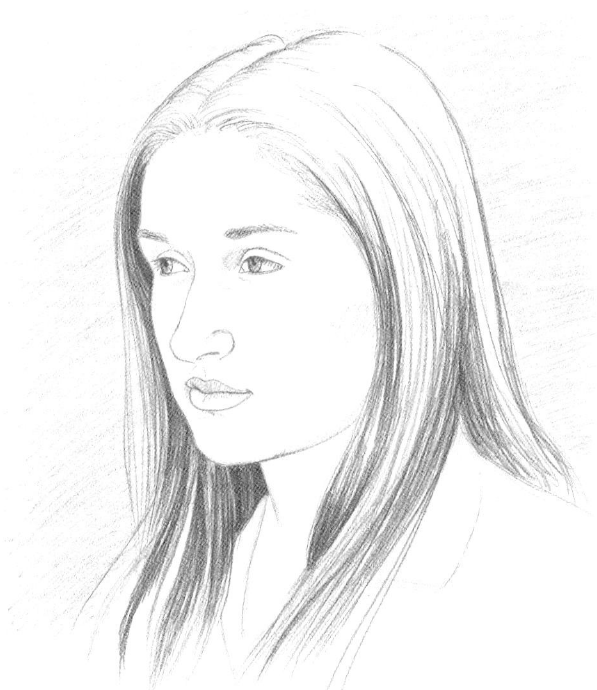

Step 3 First shade the irises with a 2B pencil. Then begin shading the background using diagonal hatching strokes. Once the background is laid in, use a 3B to build up the dark values of the hair. (Create the background before developing the hair so your hand doesn't smear the delicate strands of hair.)

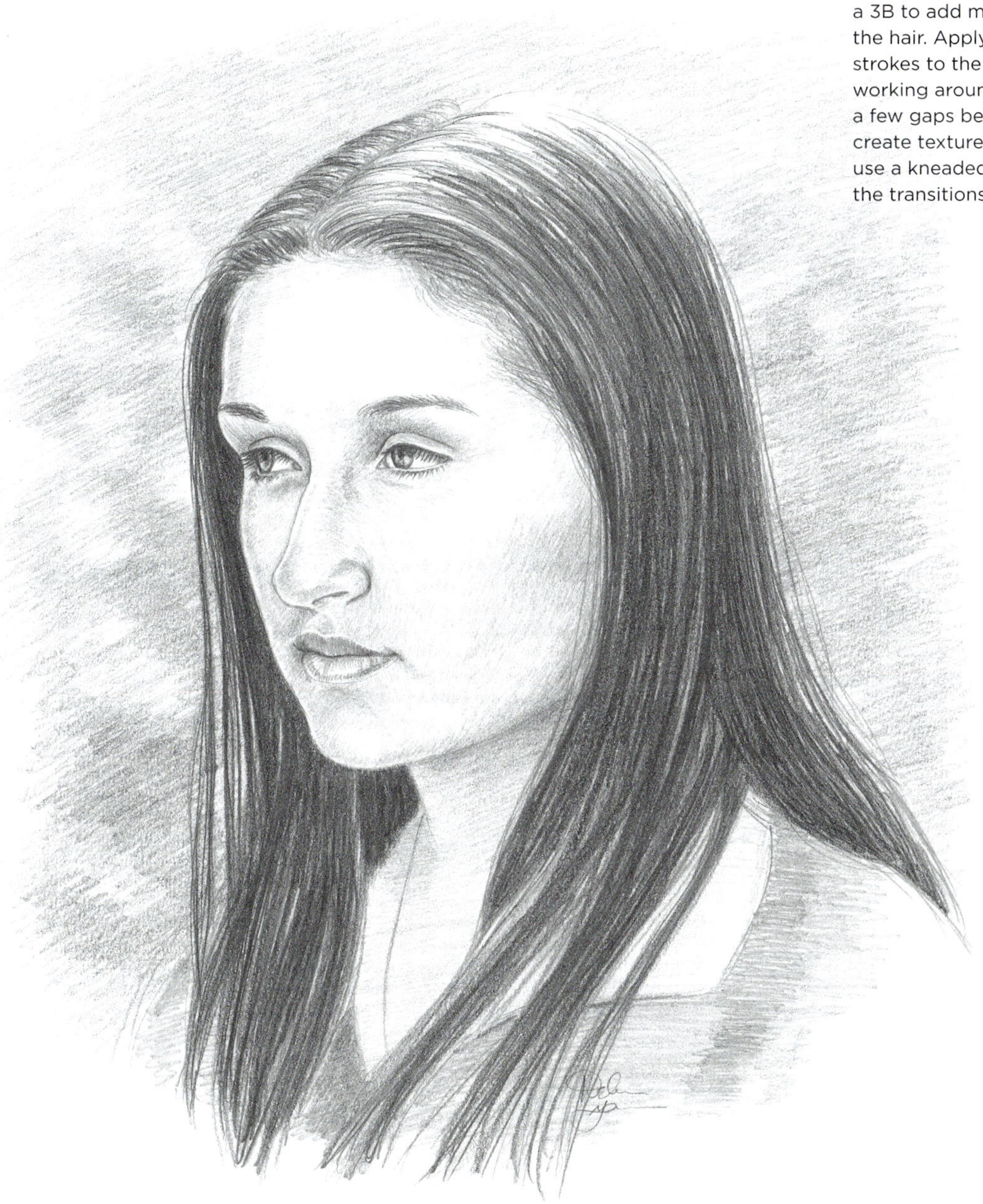

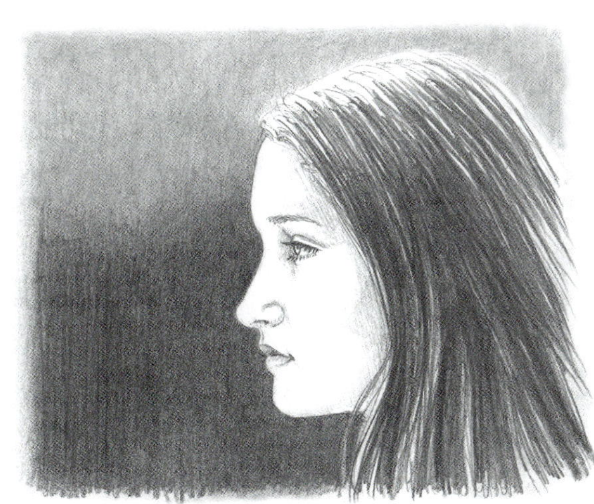

CREATING DRAMA

A darker background can add intensity or drama to your portrait. Here, the subject is in profile, so the lightest values of her face stand out against the dark values of the background. To ensure that her dark hair does not become "lost," create a gradation from dark to light, leaving the lightest areas of the background at the top and along the edge of the hair for separation.

Working with Lighting

Whether you're drawing from a photo or from life, lighting is extremely important to the overall feeling of your portrait. Lighting can influence the mood or atmosphere of your drawing—intense lighting creates drama, whereas soft lighting produces a more tranquil feeling. Lighting also can affect shadows, creating stronger contrasts between light and dark values. Remember that the lightest highlights will be in the direct path of your light source, and the darkest shadows will be opposite the light source.

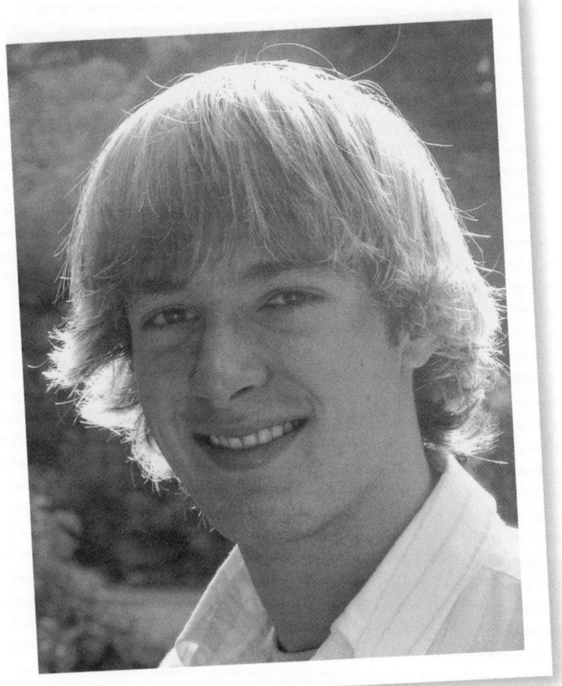

Using Backlighting Here, the light source is coming from behind the subject—the face is in shadow, but the hair is highlighted. When drawing a backlit subject, try leaving some areas of paper white around the edges of the head. This keeps the hair from looking stiff and unrealistic, and it also separates the hair from the background.

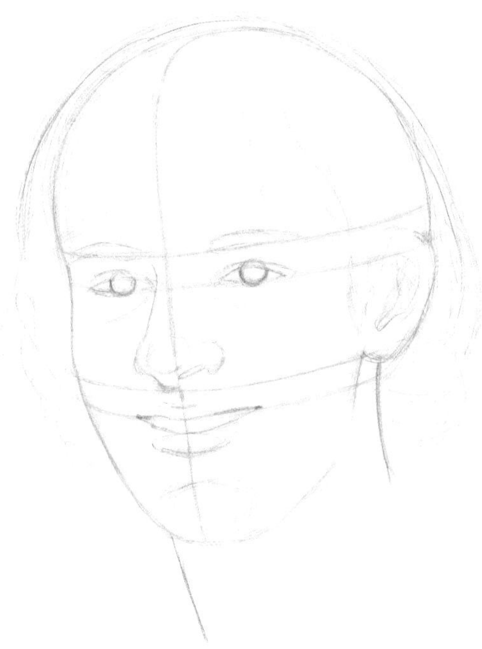

Step 1 Sketch the basic shape of the head, neck, and hair with an HB pencil. The subject's head is turned in a three-quarter view, so curve the guidelines around the face accordingly. (See page 41.) Sketch the facial features, indicating the roundness of the nose and the chin.

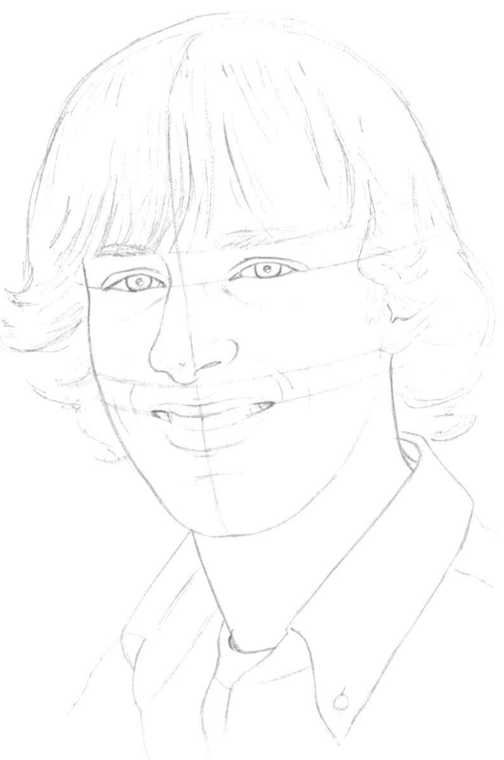

Step 2 Switching to a 2B pencil, define the features and fill in the eyebrows. Also sketch a few creases near the mouth and around the eyes. Then add the collar, button, and neckband to the shirt.

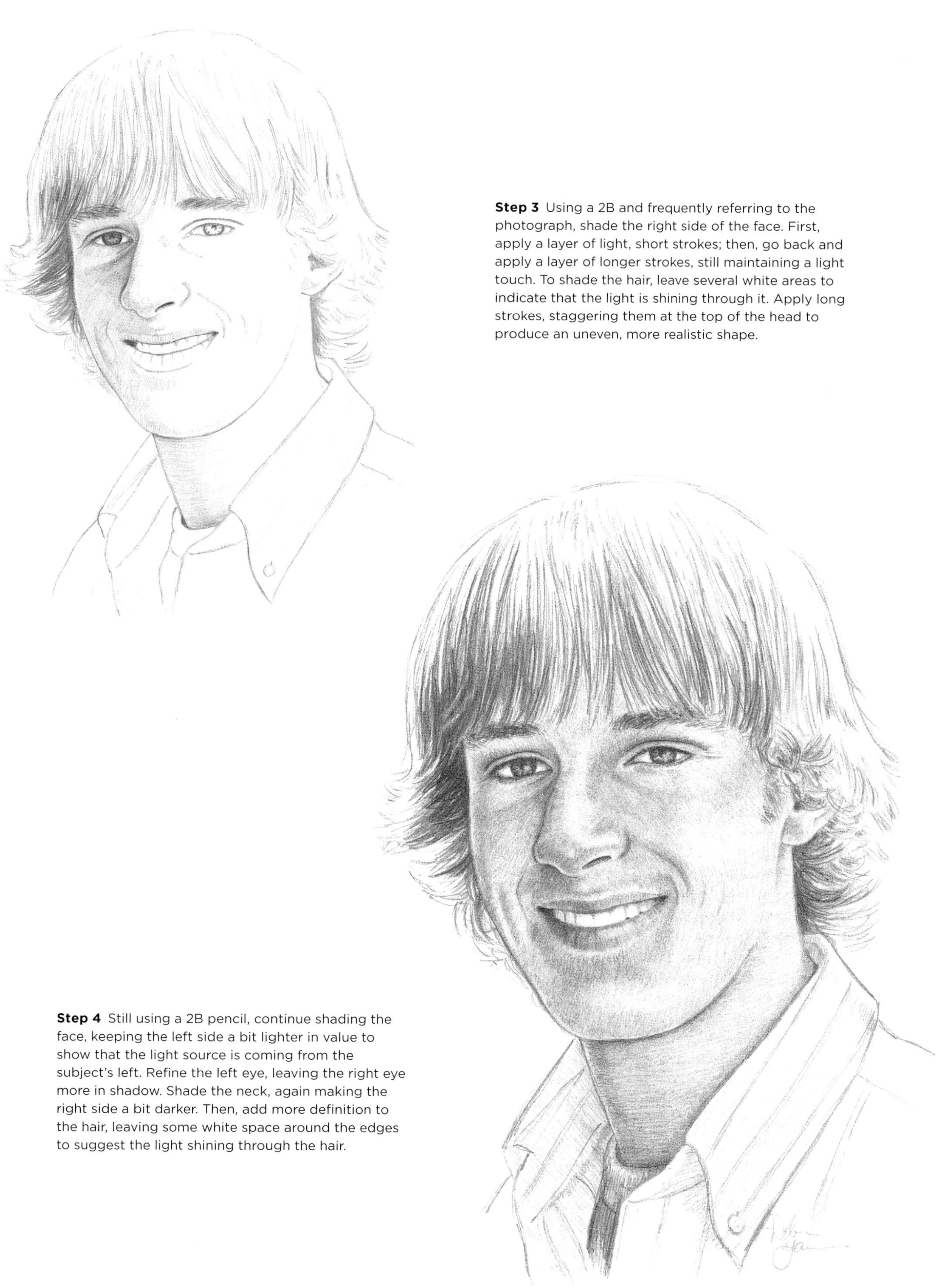

Step 3 Using a 2B and frequently referring to the photograph, shade the right side of the face. First, apply a layer of light, short strokes; then, go back and apply a layer of longer strokes, still maintaining a light touch. To shade the hair, leave several white areas to indicate that the light is shining through it. Apply long strokes, staggering them at the top of the head to produce an uneven, more realistic shape.

Step 4 Still using a 2B pencil, continue shading the face, keeping the left side a bit lighter in value to show that the light source is coming from the subject's left. Refine the left eye, leaving the right eye more in shadow. Shade the neck, again making the right side a bit darker. Then, add more definition to the hair, leaving some white space around the edges to suggest the light shining through the hair.

Drawing from Life

Having models pose for you as you draw (called "life drawing") is an excellent way to practice rendering faces. When drawing from life, you usually have control over the way your models are lit. If you're indoors, you can position the light source to your liking. If you're outdoors, you can reposition your model until you're satisfied.

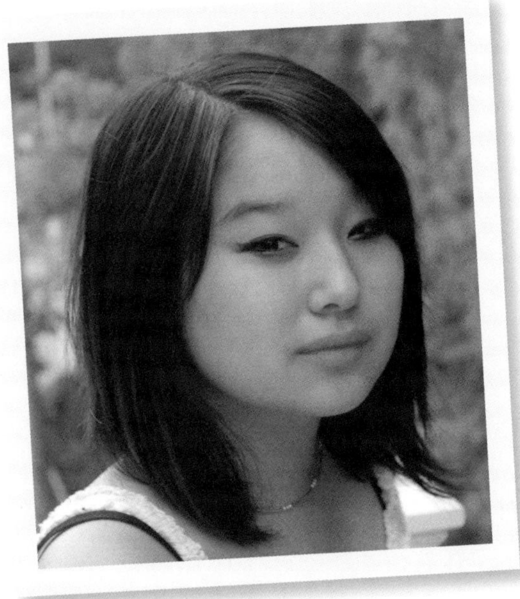

Creating a Comfortable Setup
When using live models, make sure they are comfortable and in a pose they can hold for a stretch of time. Don't forget to take regular breaks!

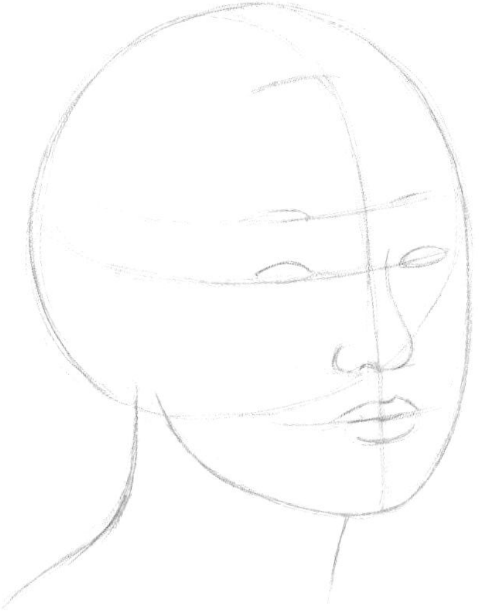

Step 1 Draw the basic shape of the head with an HB pencil. The subject's head is tilted at a three-quarter angle, so shift the vertical centerline to the right a bit (See page 41.) Use the guidelines to block in the eyes, nose, and mouth, and indicate the neck.

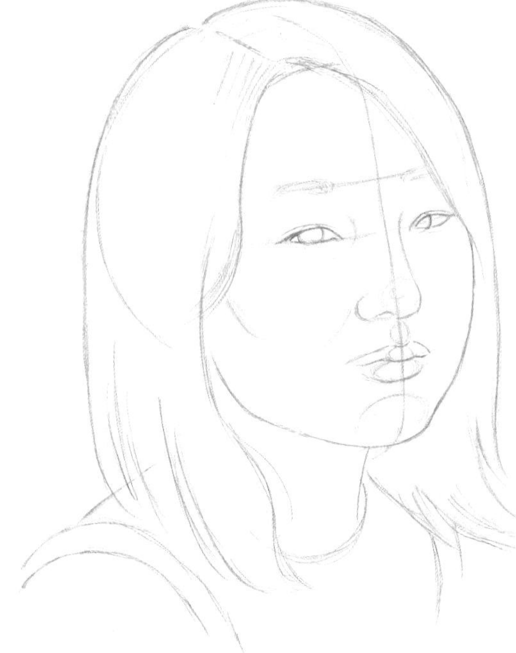

Step 2 Use the same HB pencil to foreshorten the subject's left eye, making it a little smaller than the right eye. Draw only one nostril, and make the mouth smaller on the left side. Making closer elements larger shows that the face is angled toward the viewer.

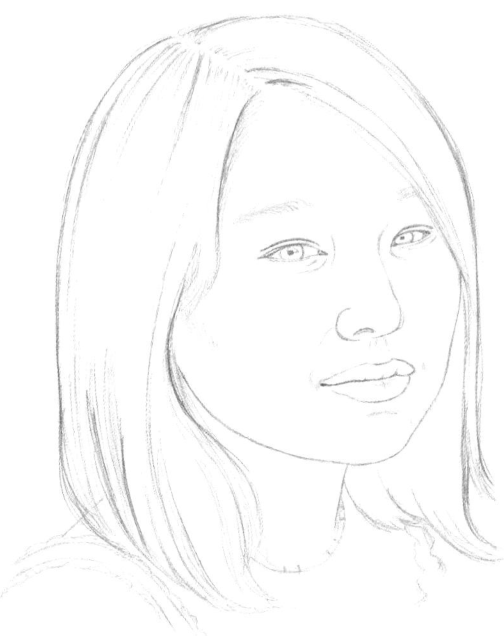

Step 3 Once you're satisfied with the placement of the features, begin to develop the eyes, nose, mouth, and eyebrows. Take note of what your model is wearing and begin to render the details accurately.

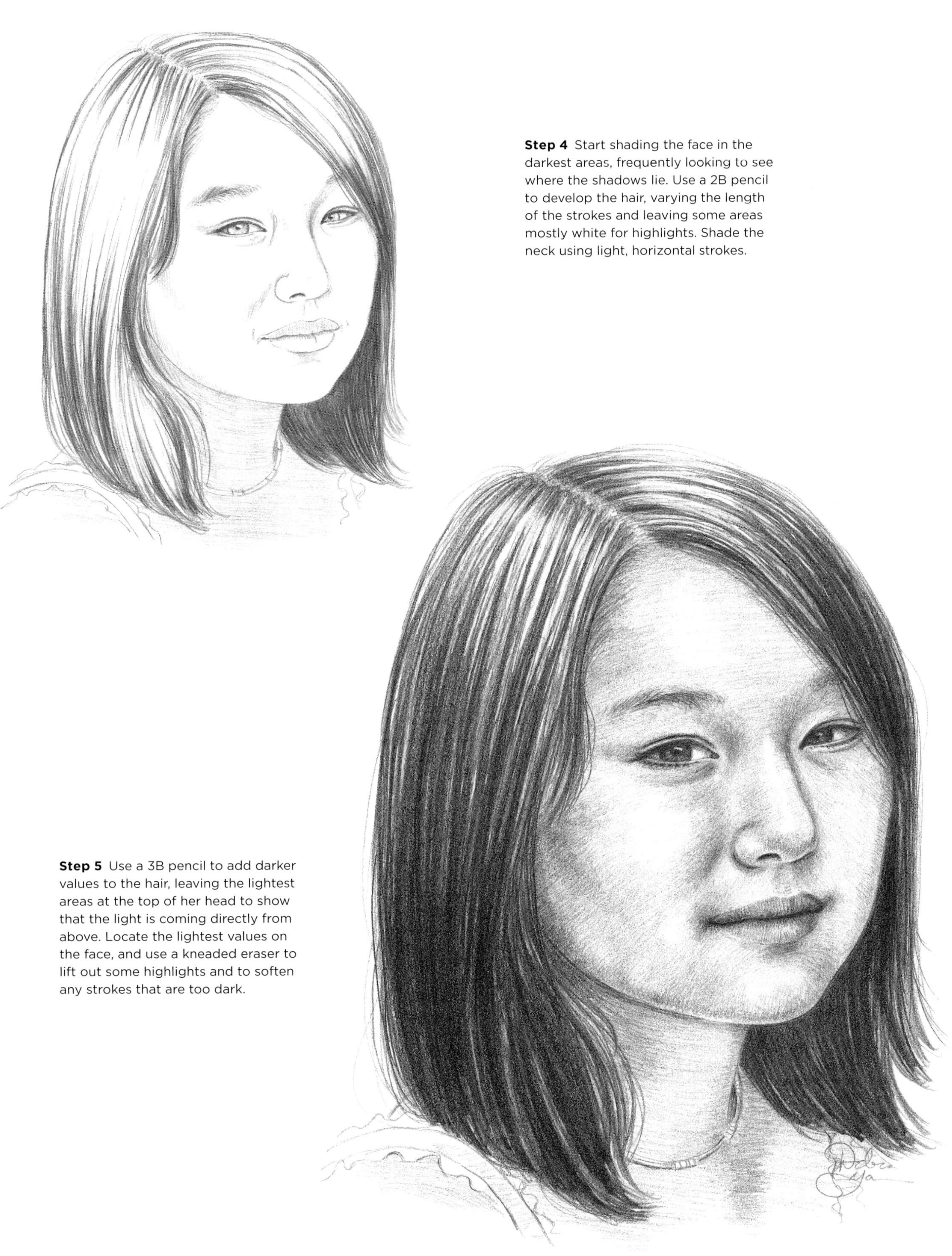

Step 4 Start shading the face in the darkest areas, frequently looking to see where the shadows lie. Use a 2B pencil to develop the hair, varying the length of the strokes and leaving some areas mostly white for highlights. Shade the neck using light, horizontal strokes.

Step 5 Use a 3B pencil to add darker values to the hair, leaving the lightest areas at the top of her head to show that the light is coming directly from above. Locate the lightest values on the face, and use a kneaded eraser to lift out some highlights and to soften any strokes that are too dark.

Developing Hair

There are many different types and styles of hair—thick and thin; long and short; curly, straight, and wavy; and even braided. And because hair is often one of an individual's most distinguishing features, knowing how to render different types and textures is essential. When drawing hair, don't try to draw every strand; just create the overall impression and allow the viewer's eye and imagination to fill in the rest.

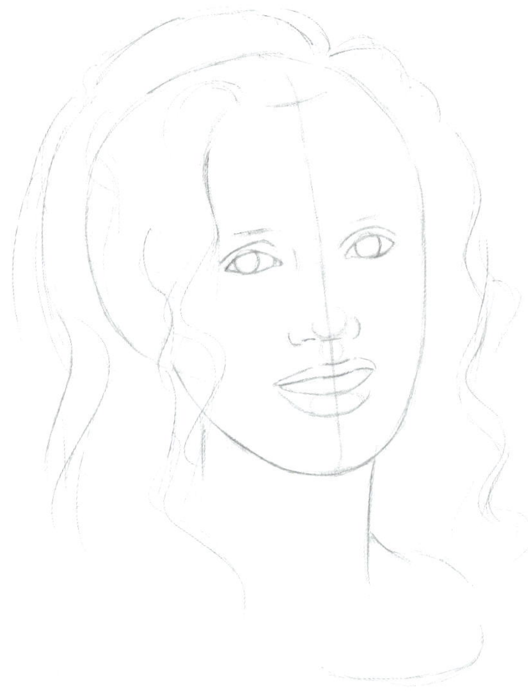

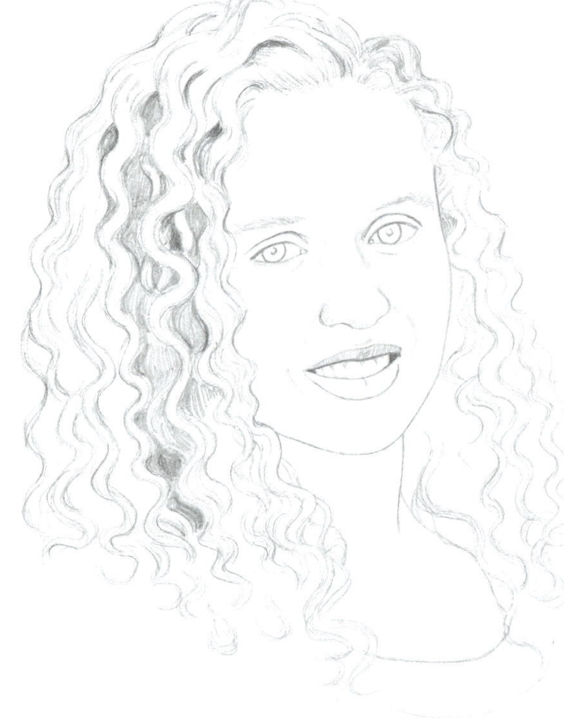

Step 1 Use an HB pencil to sketch the shape of the head and place the features. Then use loose strokes to block in the general outline of the hair. Starting at the part on the left side of the head, lightly draw the hair in the direction of growth on either side of the part. At this stage, merely indicate the shape of the hair; don't worry about the individual ringlets yet.

Step 2 Switching to a 2B pencil, start refining the eyes, eyebrows, nose, and mouth. Then define the neckline of her shirt with curved lines that follow the shape of her body. Returning to the hair, lightly sketch in sections of ringlets, working from top to bottom. Start adding dark values underneath and behind certain sections of hair, creating contrast and depth. (See "Creating Ringlets" below.)

CREATING RINGLETS

Step 1 First sketch the shapes of the ringlets using curved, S-shaped lines. Make sure that the ringlets are not too similar in shape; some are thick and some are thin.

Step 2 To give the ringlets form, squint to find the dark and light values. Leave the top of the ringlets (the hair closest to the head) lighter and add a bit more shading as you move down the strands, indicating that the light is coming from above.

Step 3 To create the darkest values underneath the hair, place the strokes closer together.

Step 4 Add even darker values, making sure that your transitions in value are smooth and that there are no abrupt changes in direction.

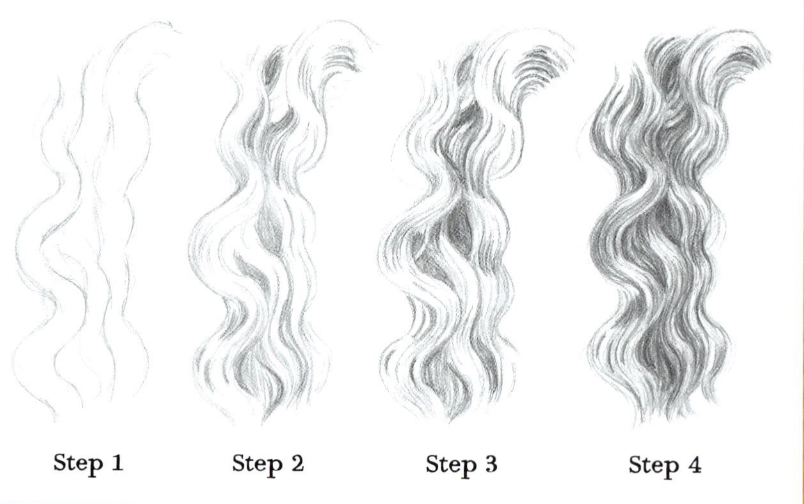

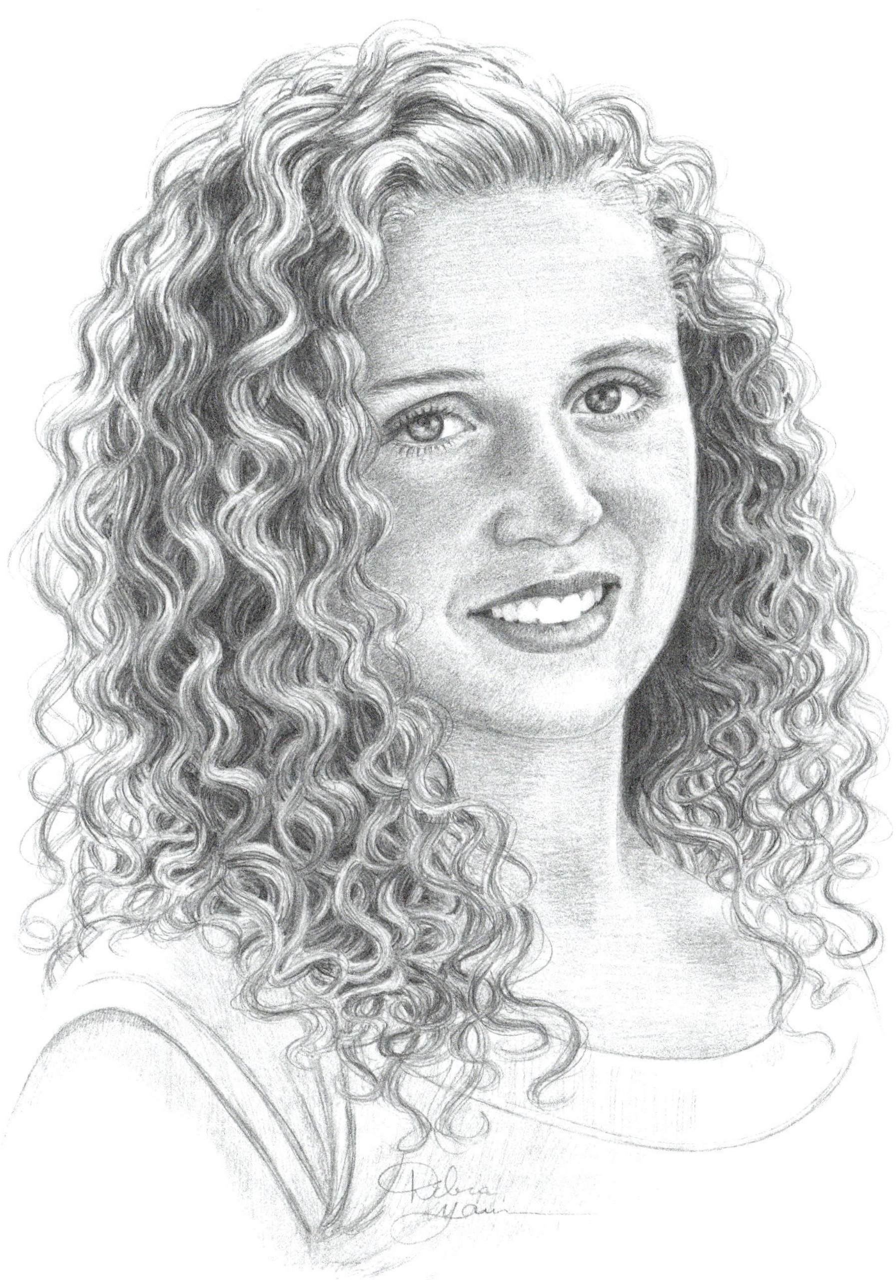

Step 3 Shade the face, neck, and chest using linear strokes that reach across the width of the body. Then define the eyes, lips, and teeth, and add her shoulder and the sleeve of her shirt. Next, continue working in darker values within the ringlets, leaving some areas of hair white to suggest blond highlights. Although the hair is much more detailed at this final stage, simply indicate the general mass, allowing the viewer's eye to complete the scene. Finally, draw some loose strands along the edges of the hair, leaving the lightest values at the top of the subject's head.

RENDERING BRAIDS

Step 1 First sketch the outline of each braid. Taper the ends a bit, adding a line across the bottom of each to indicate the ties that hold the braids together.

Step 2 Now start shading each section, indicating the overlapping hair in each braid. Add some wispy hair "escaping" from the braids to add realism.

Step 3 Continue shading the braids using heavier strokes. Add even more "escaped" strands of hair. Then use a kneaded eraser to pull out highlights at the bottom of each braid, emphasizing the ties. To finish, pull out some highlights in the braids themselves.

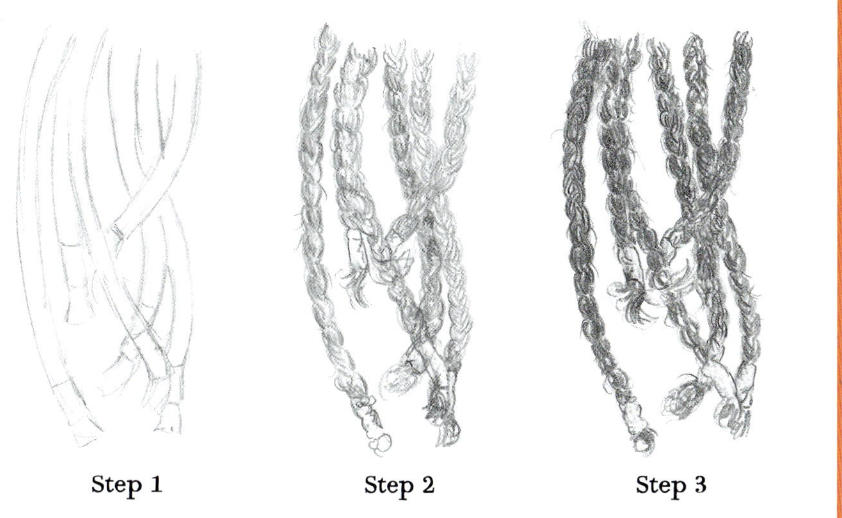

Step 1   Step 2   Step 3

Depicting Age

As people age, their bodies change. Skin loses elasticity and wrinkles appear, especially around the eyes; hair might turn gray; and certain other features, such as noses, ears, and lips, may not appear as smooth. Accurately rendering these characteristics is essential to creating successful portraits of mature subjects.

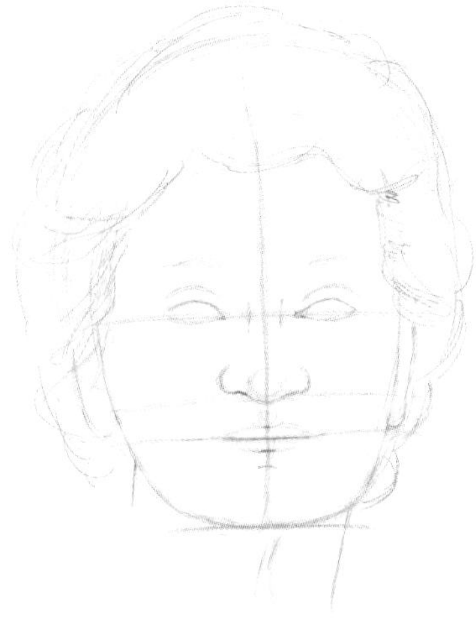

Step 1 Block in the face with an HB pencil. Then add guidelines to place the eyes, nose, ears, eyebrows, and mouth. Sketch the wavy outline of the hair.

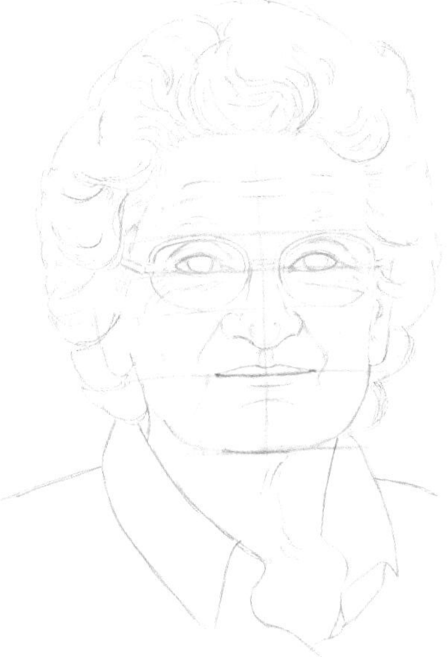

Step 2 Draw the basic shape of the eyeglasses. Begin to suggest the subject's age by adding delicate lines around the eyes and across the forehead. Round out the jaw and chin. Add a few lines on the neck and on either side of the nose.

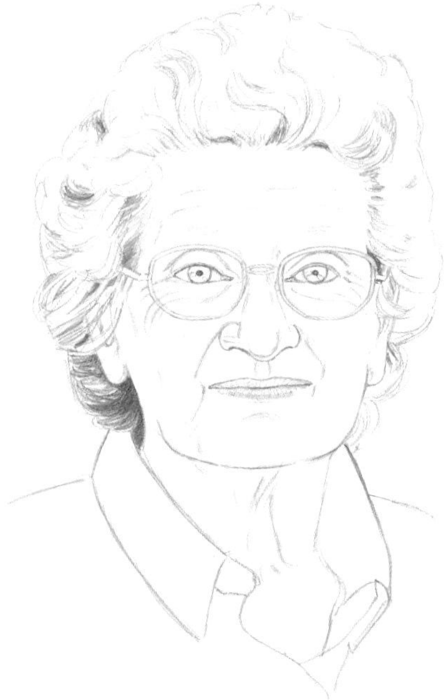

Step 3 Switching to a 2B pencil, begin shading the hair and developing the eyes, adding light, curved lines around and under them. Accentuate the wrinkles slightly where they can be seen through the glasses. (See "Rendering Wrinkles" on page 69.)

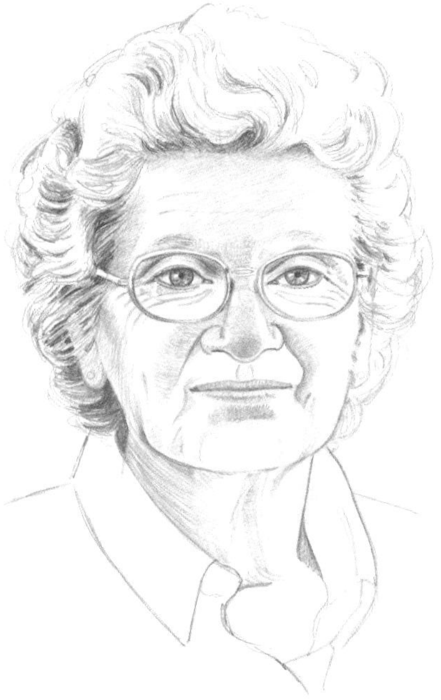

Step 4 Still using a 2B, shade the face and neck, adding strokes to the side of the neck for wrinkles. Finish shading the irises and the eyelids. Shade the area between the right side of the cheek and the jawbone. Add shading around the nose and mouth to make the skin appear full. Then add darker values to the hair and earrings.

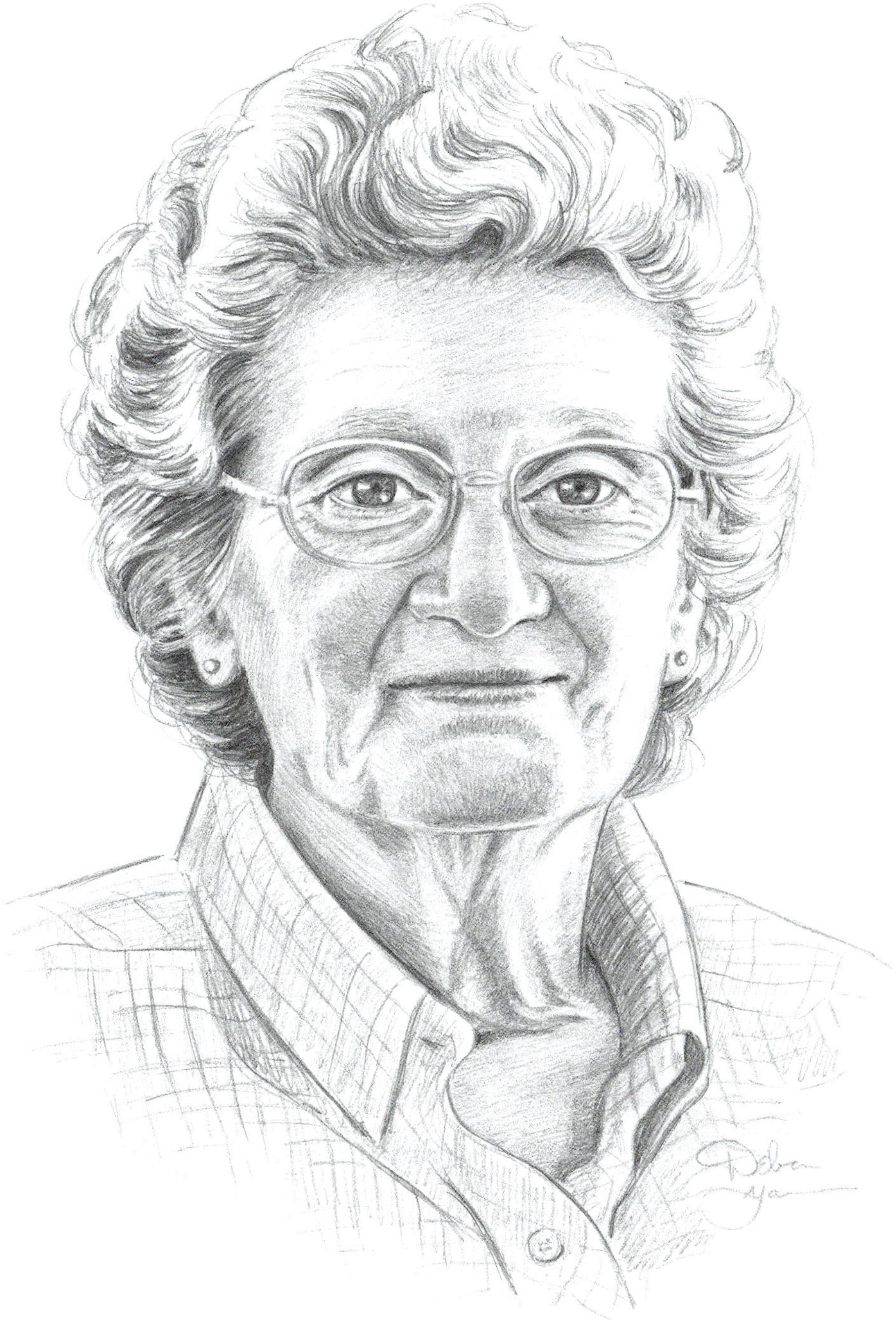

Step 5 As you continue shading the face, add more definition to the wrinkles around the eyes so they don't disappear into the shaded areas. Keep them subtle, smoothing out the transitions with a tortillon. Finally, add a buttonhole to the collar and create the plaid pattern of the shirt. Stand back from the drawing, and make any alterations as needed.

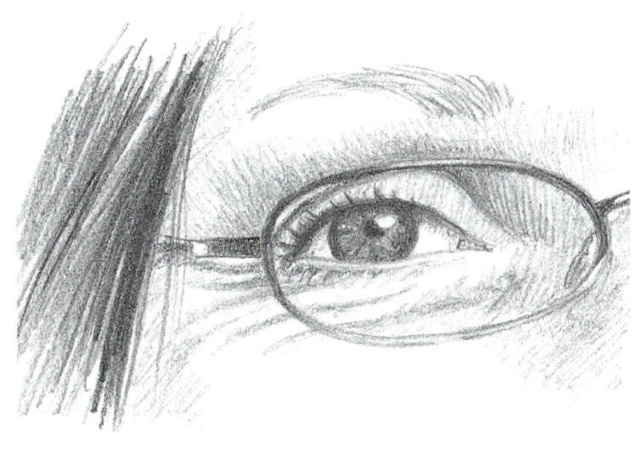

RENDERING WRINKLES

The key to drawing wrinkles is to keep them subtle. Indicate wrinkles with soft shading, not with hard or angular lines. You can best achieve this effect by using a dull pencil point. You also can use a cloth or a tortillon to softly blend the transitions between the light and dark values in the wrinkles. Or use a kneaded eraser to soften wrinkles that appear too deep.

When drawing a subject with glasses, as in the example at left, try to magnify the wrinkle lines that are seen through the lenses. You can do this by drawing the lines of shading a little larger and spacing them farther from one another.

Creating Facial Hair

Facial hair is another characteristic that distinguishes one individual from the next. Short, dark strokes are perfect for rendering a thick, coarse beard; whereas light, sweeping strokes are ideal for depicting a wispy mustache. Experiment with variations of light and dark lines when drawing a "salt-and-pepper" beard, and use a series of quick, short lines when indicating stubble.

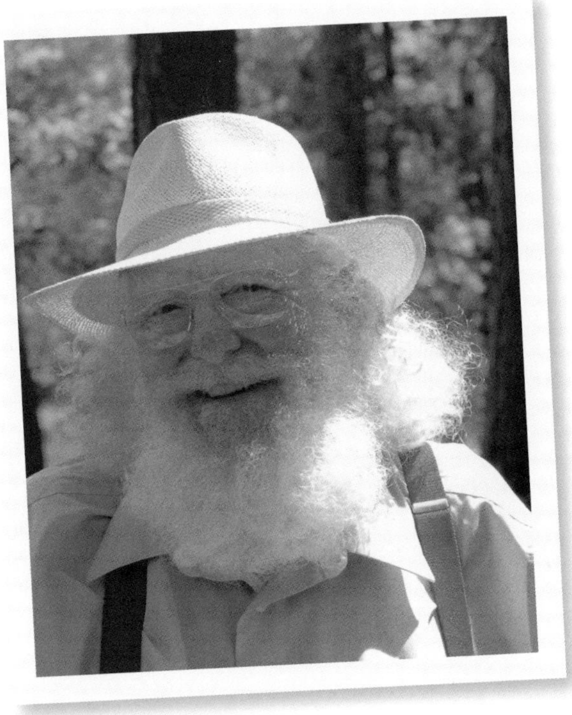

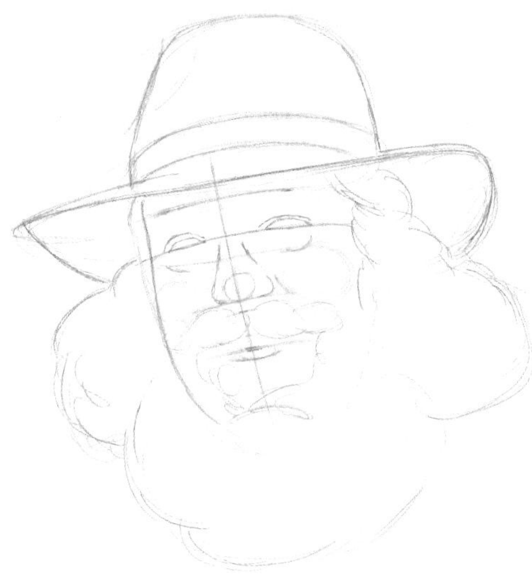

Step 1 Sketch the shape of the face with an HB pencil. Then, place the guidelines and the features. Next, draw the hat, including the band. Block in the masses of the hair, mustache, and beard with loose, curved lines. Just as when drawing any other type of hair, simply indicate the general shapes at this stage.

Drawing Through When drawing a face that is partly hidden by facial hair, it is important to draw the entire head and face. This is called "drawing through." After you've established the features, you can add the hair, beard, and accessories (such as the hat).

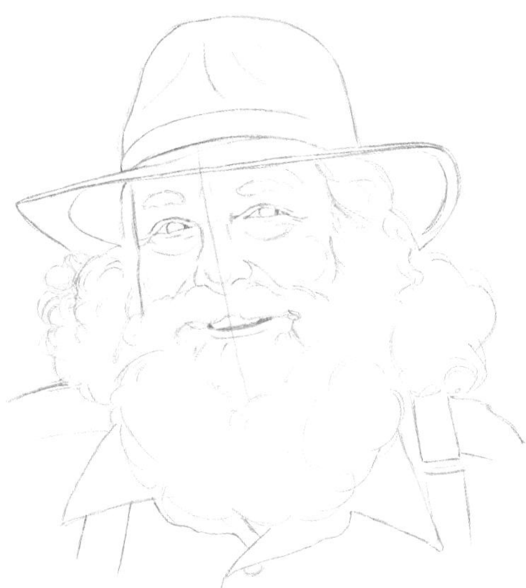

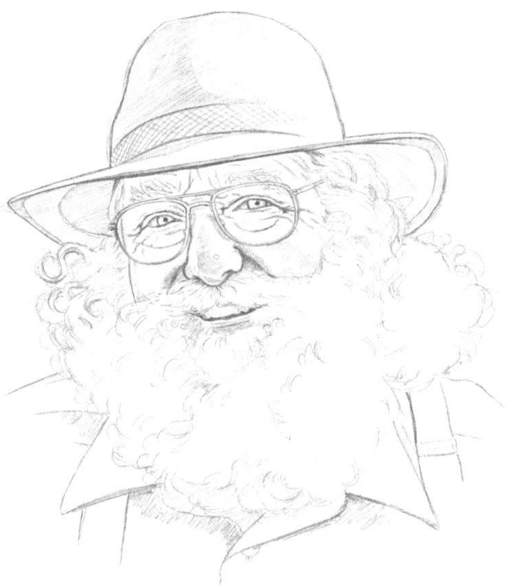

Step 2 Switching to a 2B pencil, refine the eyes, eyebrows, and teeth. Add wrinkles around the eyes and on the forehead; then, build up the hat, sketch the shirt collar, and draw the suspenders. Return to the hair, indicating the curls with circular strokes. Working from top to bottom, fill in the hair and develop the mustache, which partially covers the mouth.

Step 3 Erase your guidelines, and add the glasses. Next, define the eyes, shade the hat, and crosshatch a pattern on the band. Begin rendering the short, tight curls of the beard and the mustache. Then, add darker values to the curls on the left side of the face to separate them and to show the cast shadow of the hat.

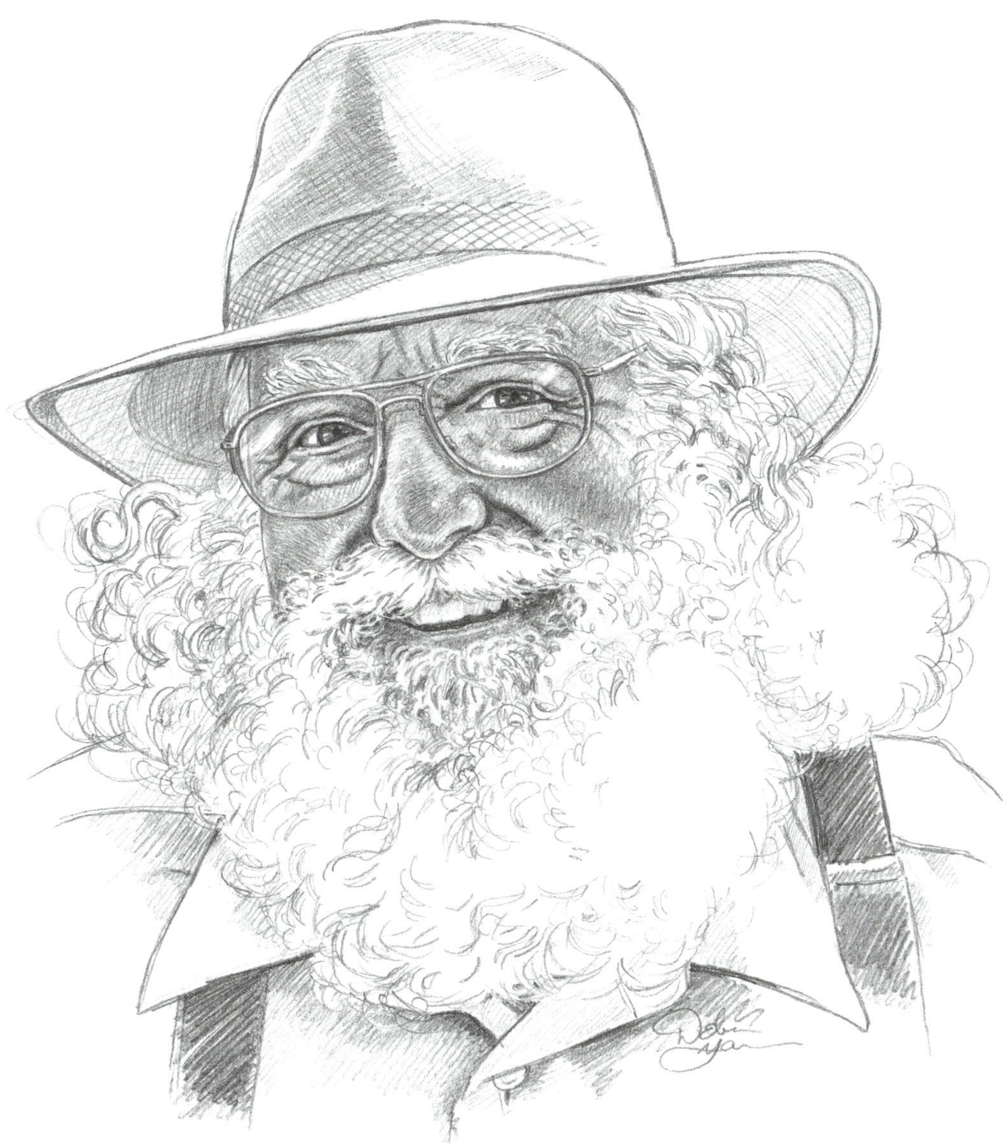

Step 4 Add a layer of shading to the irises, leaving white highlights in each eye. Using the edge of a kneaded eraser, lift out a highlight on each lens of the glasses to show the reflected light. Apply more shading to the hat to give it more of a three-dimensional look. Shade the suspenders and the shirt. Finally, finish the curls in the hair and beard, varying your strokes between tight, curved lines and quick, straight lines. Create the shortest, most defined lines in the mustache and around the mouth, leaving most of the beard to the viewer's imagination.

DRAWING BEARDS

When drawing a white beard, such as this one, group several lines together to create form, but leave some areas white. Also, try drawing the strokes in varying directions—this adds interest and movement. It's also a good idea to overlap your shading a bit where the skin meets the hair, indicating that the skin is showing through the beard.

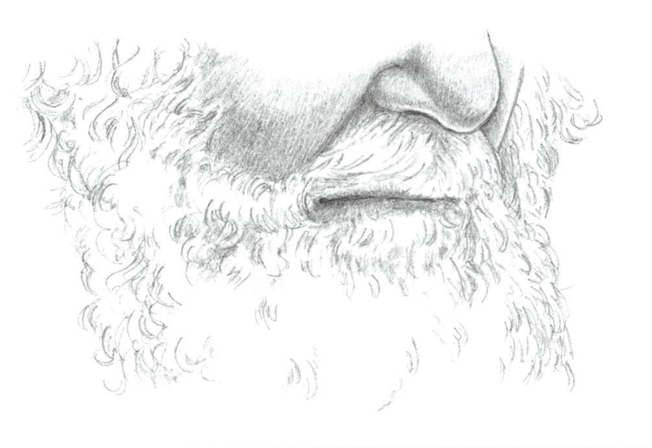

Elderly Man

Elderly men are good subjects for practicing a variety of techniques, such as wrinkles, thinning white hair, and aging features. Pay close attention to the details to create an accurate rendering.

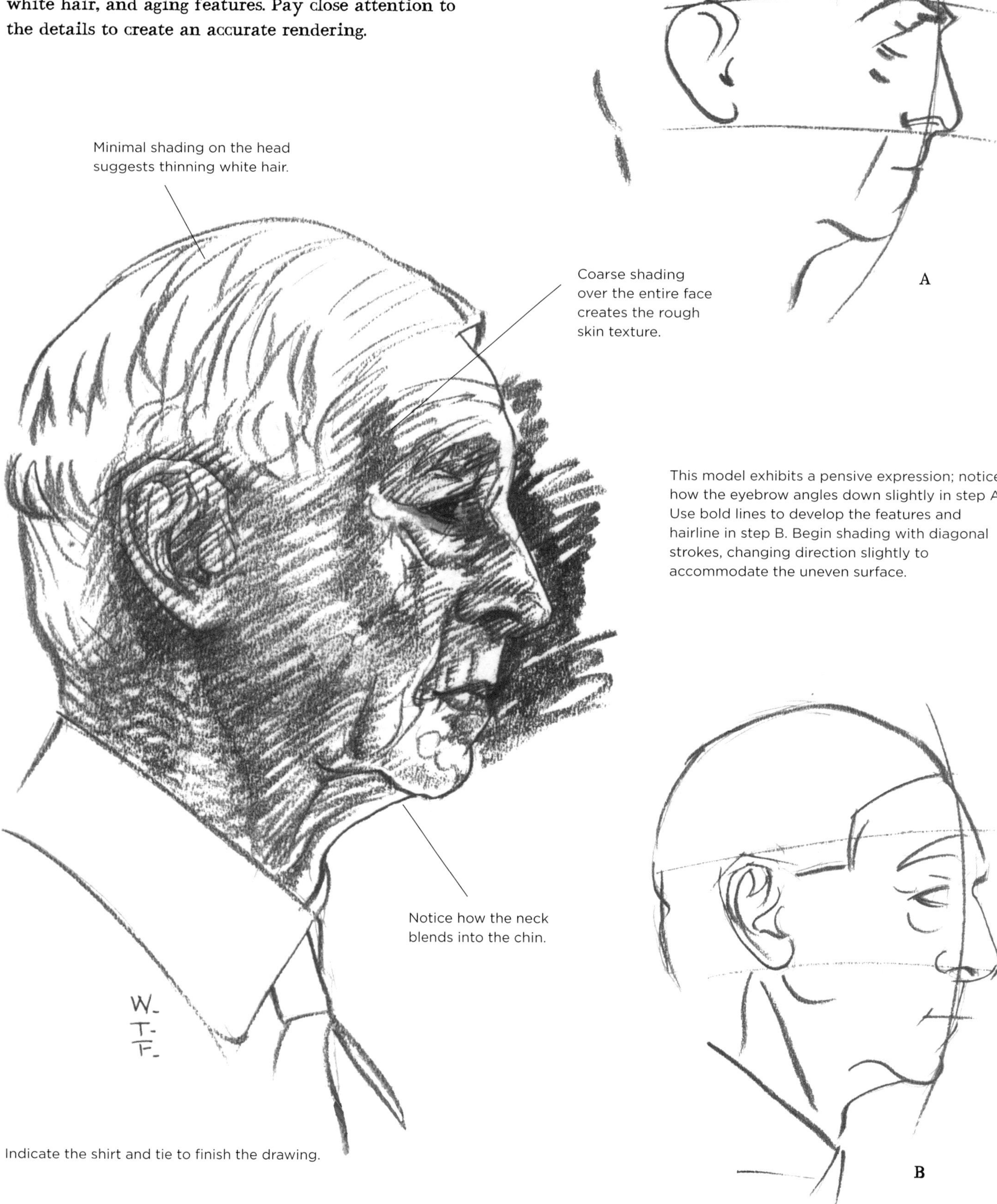

Minimal shading on the head suggests thinning white hair.

Coarse shading over the entire face creates the rough skin texture.

This model exhibits a pensive expression; notice how the eyebrow angles down slightly in step A. Use bold lines to develop the features and hairline in step B. Begin shading with diagonal strokes, changing direction slightly to accommodate the uneven surface.

Notice how the neck blends into the chin.

Indicate the shirt and tie to finish the drawing.

A

B

Portrait in Two Media

Two media were used for this drawing. A chisel-tipped 6B pencil was used for the shading on the face, and a brush and black India ink were used for the darkest details. Experiment with different drawing media to create new effects. Start at step A and move counterclockwise, following the steps.

A

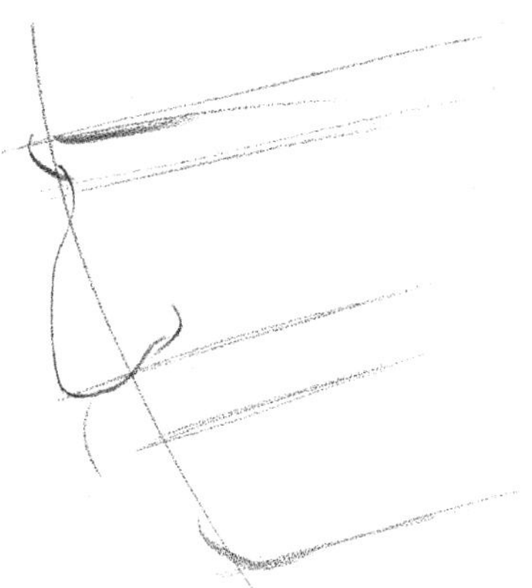

B

As always, begin with quick proportion guidelines (A). Then, sketch the basic shapes of the features, including the bushy mustache (B).

C

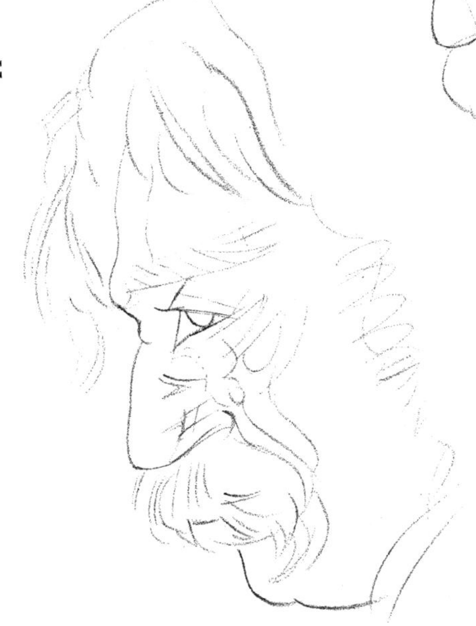

Keep referring to your subject, checking the proportions and shapes. Erase old guidelines (C). When the sketch is to your liking, begin shading.

D

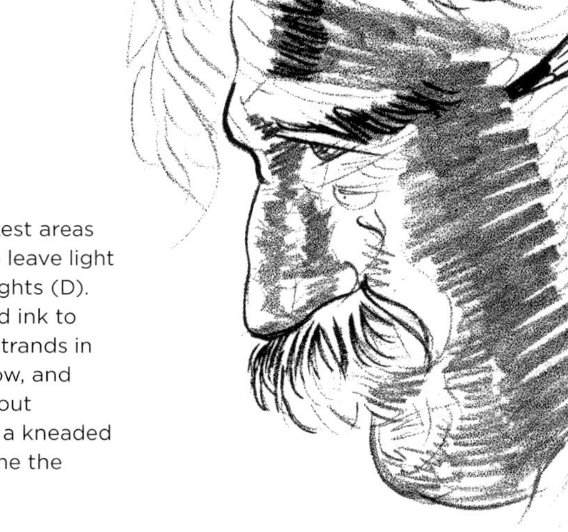

Shade the darkest areas first. Be sure to leave light areas for highlights (D). Use a brush and ink to bring out fine strands in the hair, eyebrow, and mustache. Lift out highlights with a kneaded eraser, and refine the details (E).

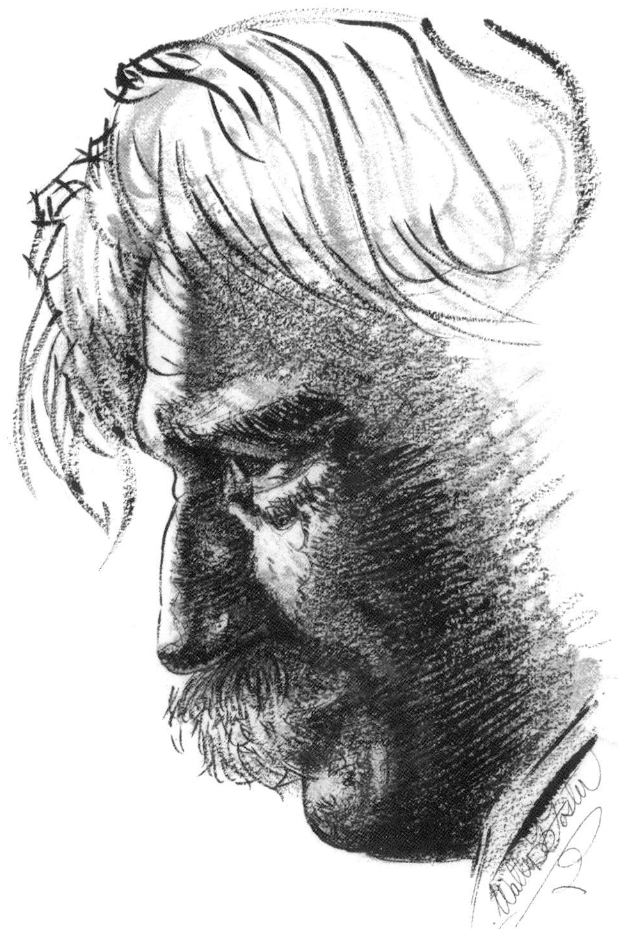

Young Faces

When drawing youthful faces, it is important to study their proportions closely. A clear understanding of children's proportions will help you create a close likeness of your subject. (See pages 36 and 80.)

A

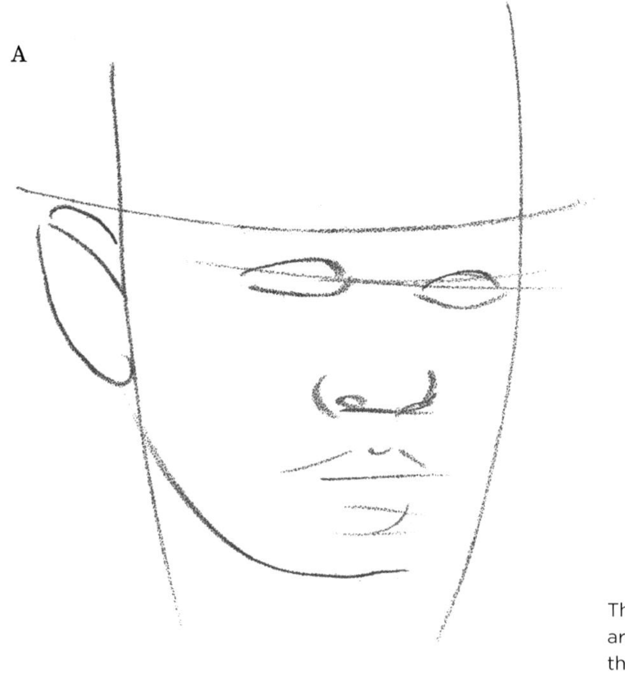

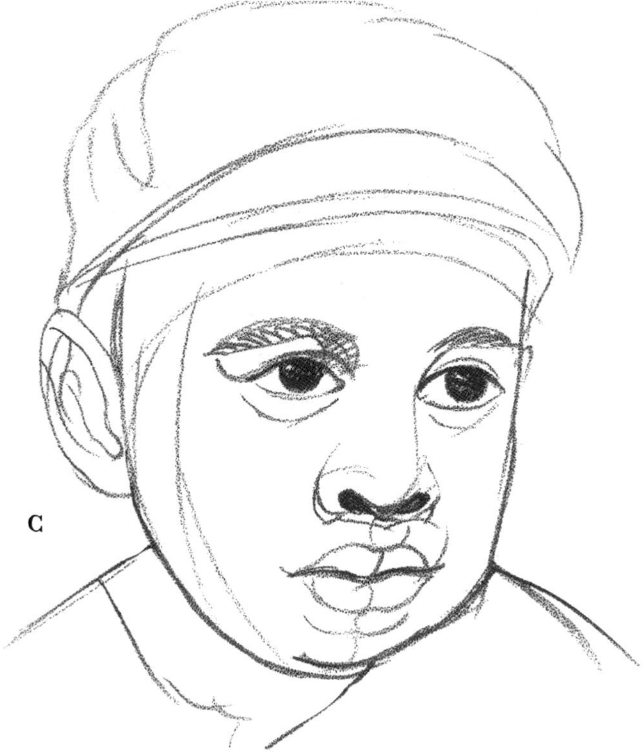

C

The slightly darker area here illustrates the cast shadow created by the bill of the cap.

Use charcoal or a soft-lead pencil to add shading with even, parallel strokes. Leave areas of white for highlights, especially on the tip of the nose and the center of the lower lip.

B

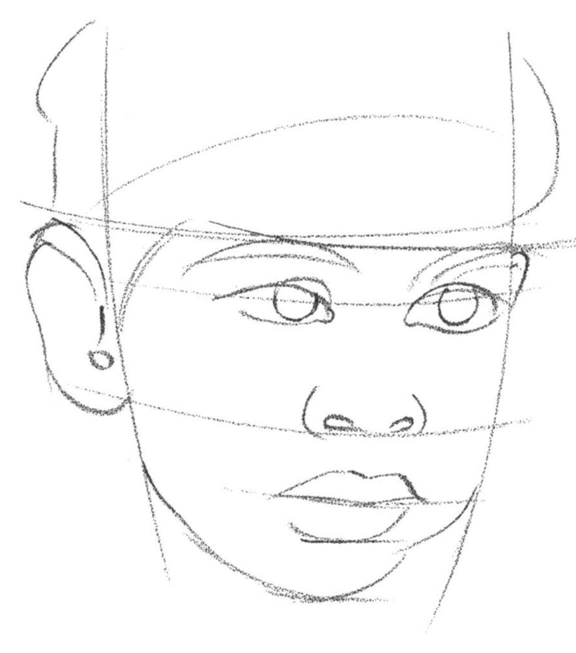

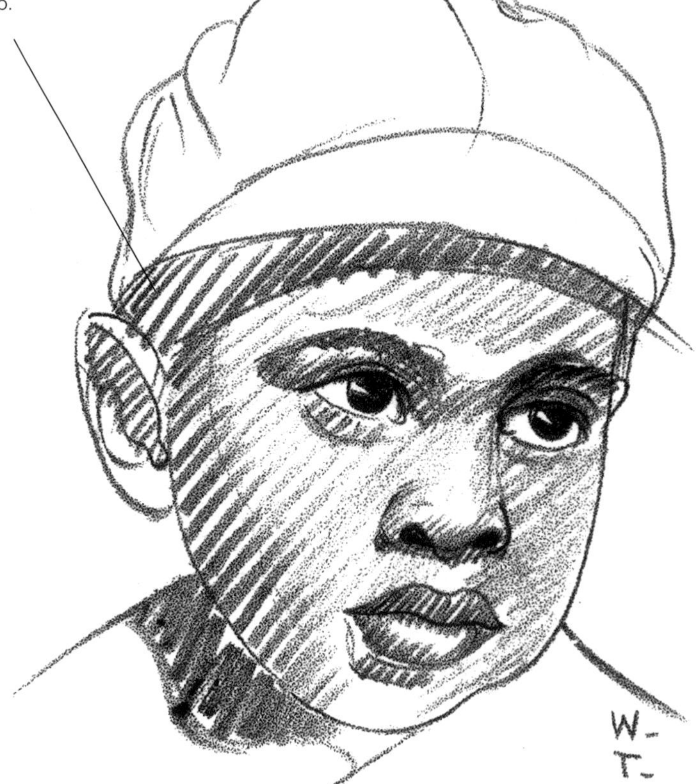

Ink Portrait

In this position, where the chin is close to the chest, the length of the face should be shortened, leaving a larger area for the top of the head. This adjustment is an example of foreshortening.

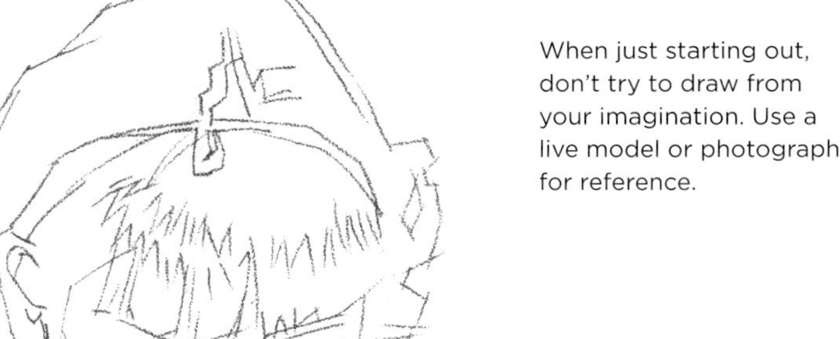

When just starting out, don't try to draw from your imagination. Use a live model or photograph for reference.

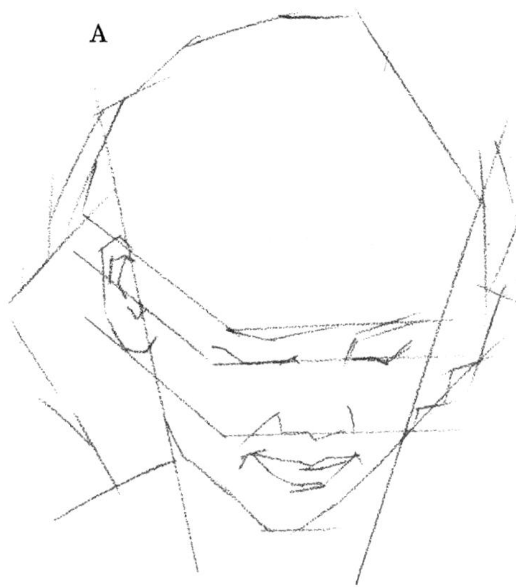

Observe your subject closely to determine the guidelines in step A. In steps B and C, develop the features, and suggest the hair and clothing. Leave small white areas for highlights, enhancing the sheen of the hair. In step E, add shading to the face to add dimension, and refine the details.

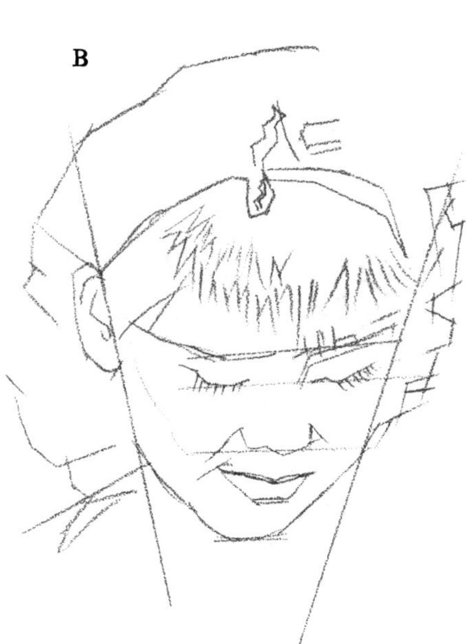

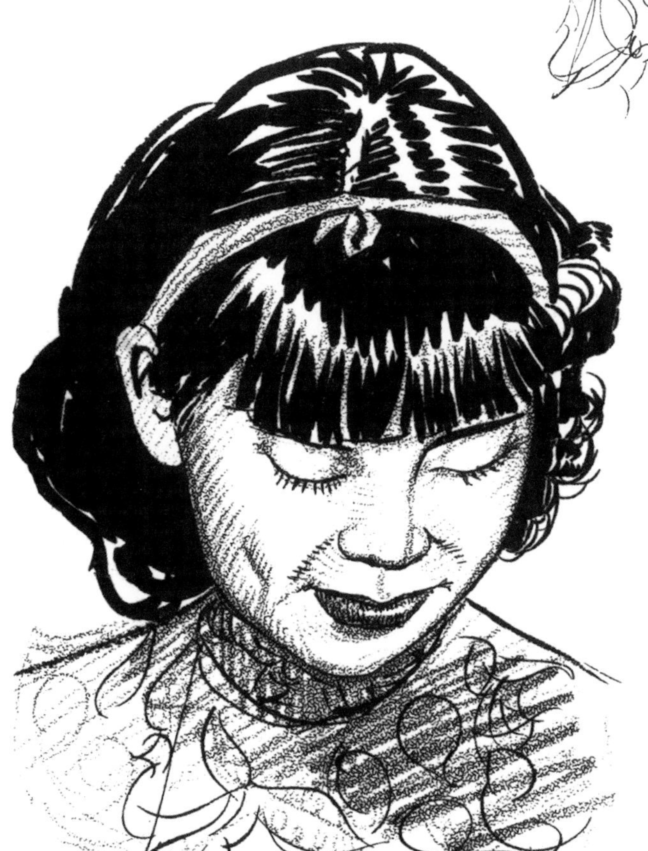

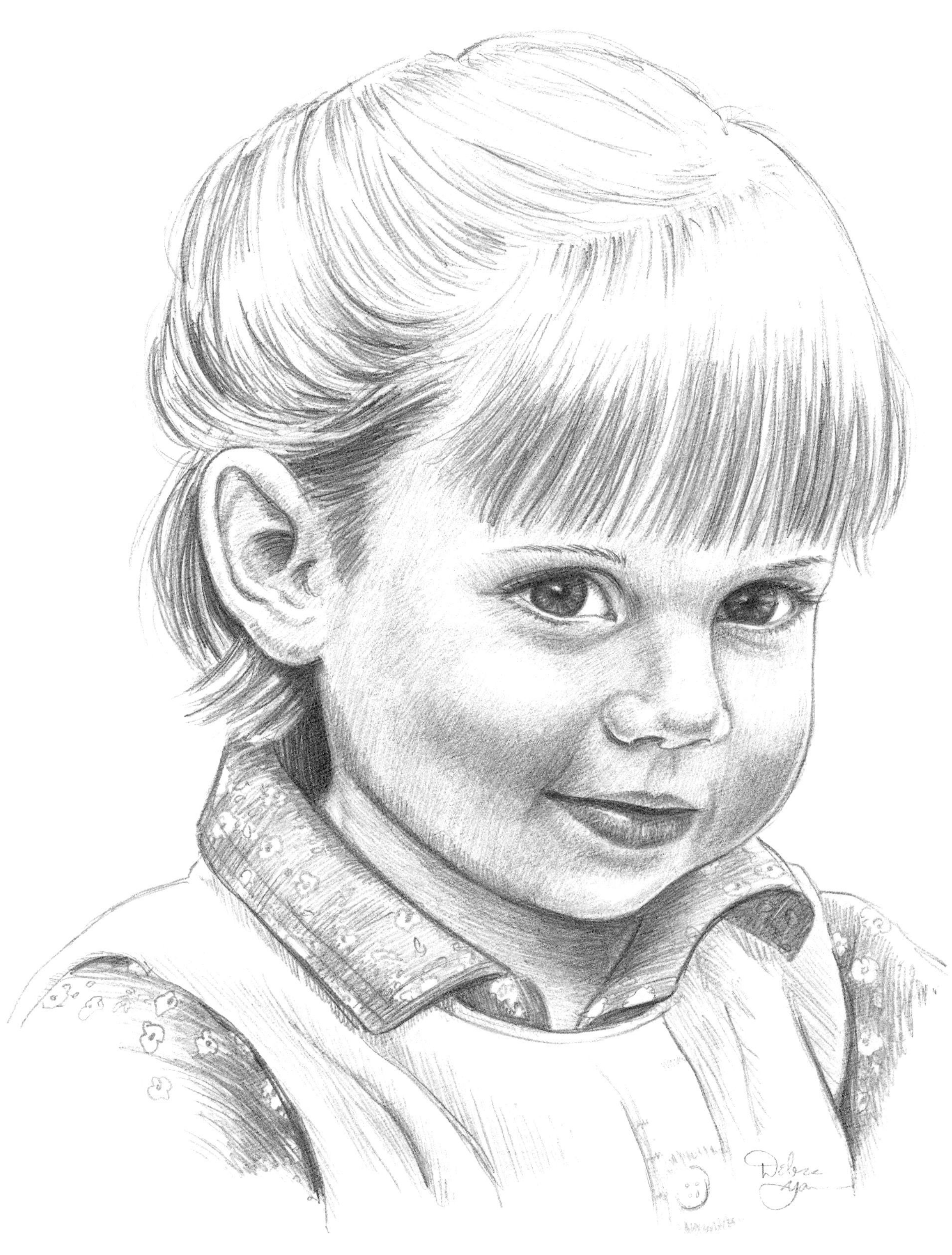

Drawing Children's Portraits

When they aren't asleep, children are constantly on the move. They discover new things all the time and marvel at the wonders of our world. They express their feelings much more directly than adults. They cry, scream, or laugh from the bottom of their hearts. Drawing children is rewarding for artists. Good observational skills, a feeling for the right moment, and an eye for children's proportions will help you create lifelike portraits that will capture the magic of childhood forever.

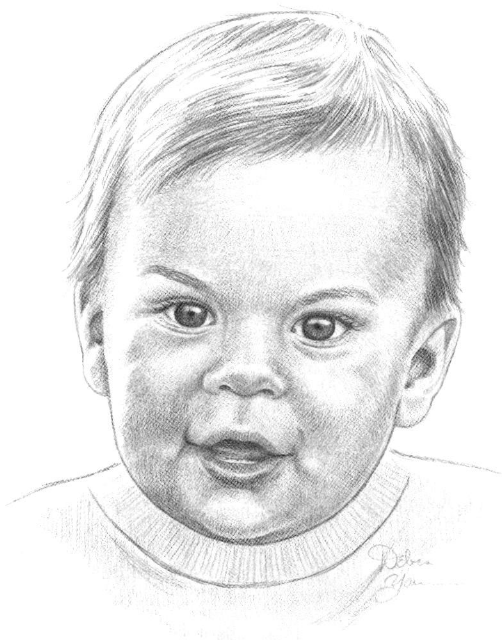

Portraying Children

Children are a joy to watch, and they make charming drawing subjects. If you don't have children of your own to observe, take a sketchpad to the beach or a neighborhood park, and make quick thumbnail sketches of kids at play. (Ask caregivers for permission first.) Sometimes it is better if you don't know your subject personally. It allows you to see the individual from a fresh and objective point of view.

MAKING QUICK SKETCHES

Children are generally free and flexible in their expressions, gestures, poses, and movements. To make sure you don't overwork your drawings of children, do speed sketches: Watch your subject closely for several minutes and then close your eyes, and form a picture of what you just saw. Next, open your eyes, and draw quickly from memory. This helps you keep your drawings uncomplicated—just as children are. Try it—it's a lot of fun!

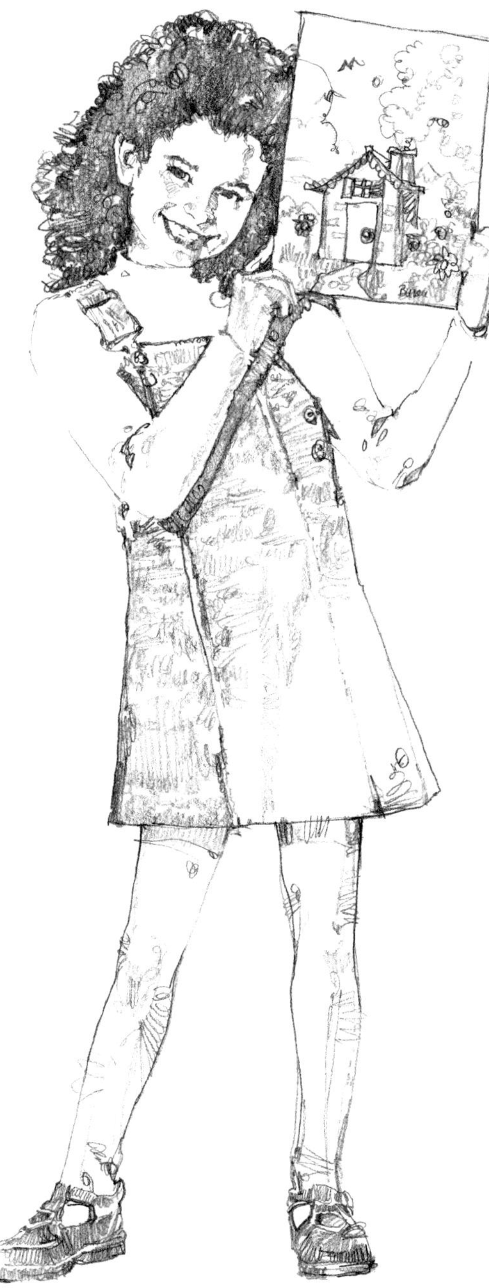

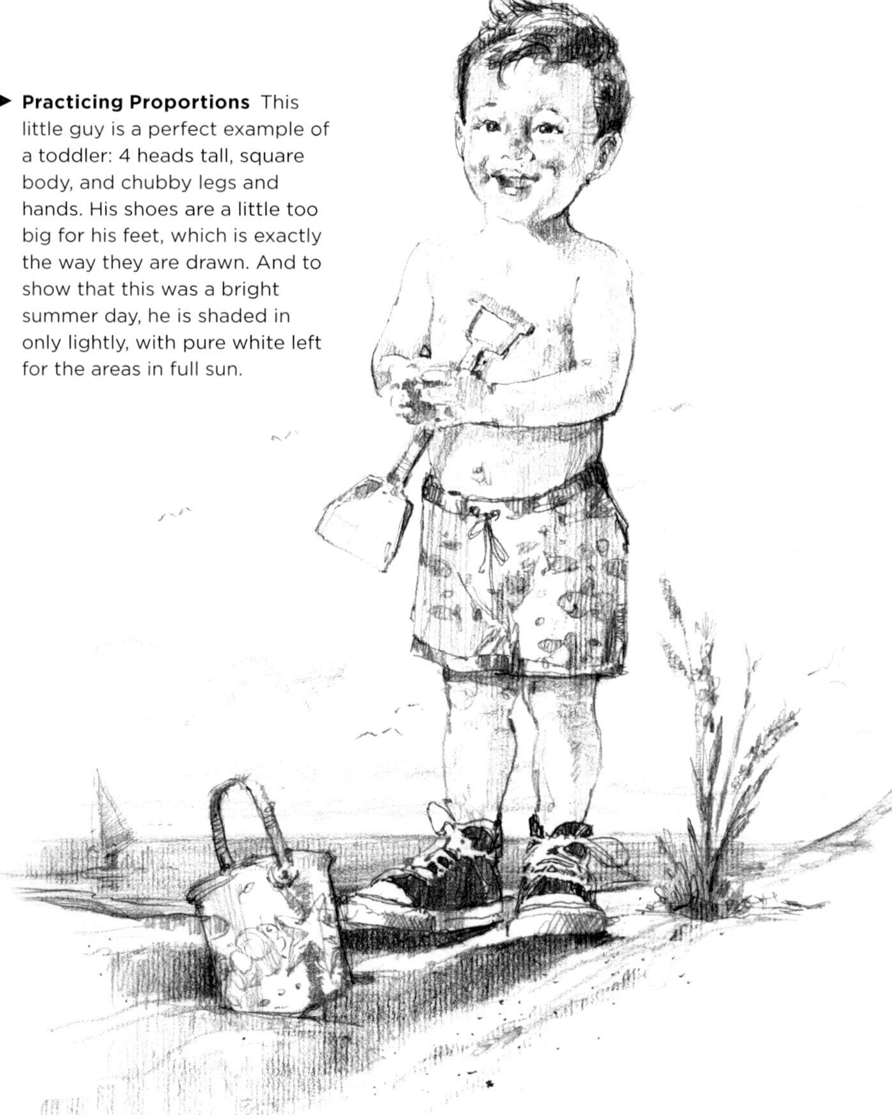

◀ **Showing Her Age** This girl has a charming expression as she shyly shows off her artwork. She is young but not a toddler, so her head and legs are more in proportion to her body than they are in a younger child.

▶ **Practicing Proportions** This little guy is a perfect example of a toddler: 4 heads tall, square body, and chubby legs and hands. His shoes are a little too big for his feet, which is exactly the way they are drawn. And to show that this was a bright summer day, he is shaded in only lightly, with pure white left for the areas in full sun.

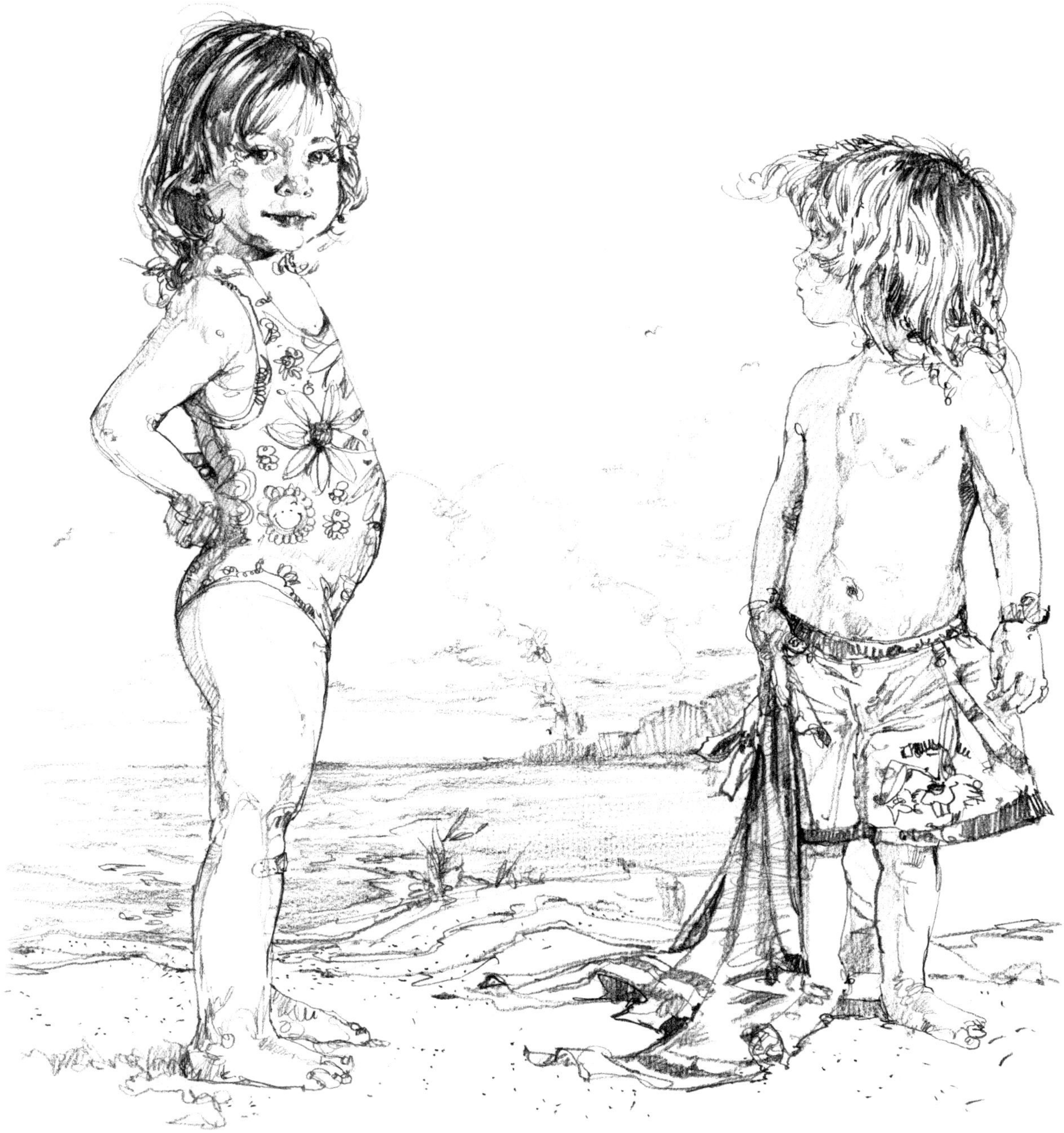

Drawing the Differences

Of course, there's more to drawing children than making sure they are the right number of heads tall. Their facial proportions are different from an adult's. (See pages 36 and 80.) They also have pudgier hands and feet with relatively short fingers and toes. They often have slightly protruding stomachs, and their forms in general are soft and round. Keep your pencil lines soft and light when drawing children.

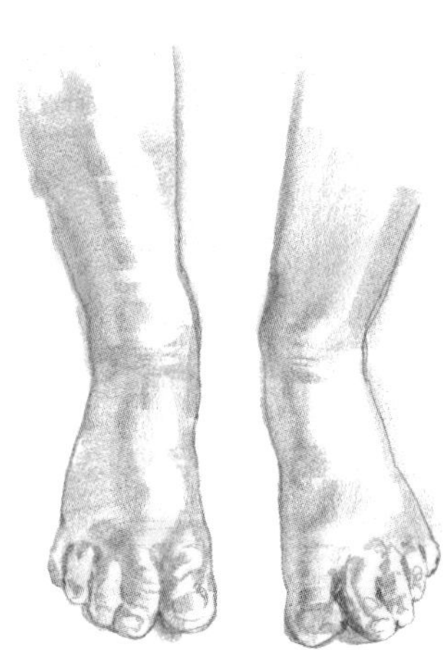

Studying Hands and Feet

Study these drawings of children's hands and feet and then compare them to your own. Children's fingers are short and plump, with an almost triangular shape. Their feet are soft and fleshy, with a predominantly square shape.

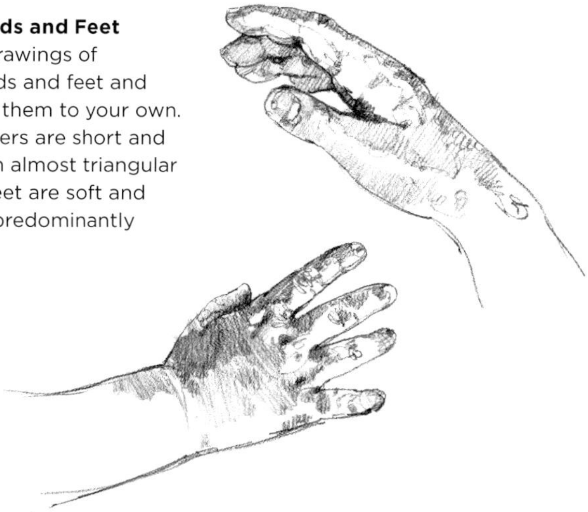

Children's Facial Proportions

Children's proportions are different than those of adults: Young children have rounder faces with larger eyes that are spaced farther apart. Their features also are positioned a little lower on the face; for example, the eyebrows begin on the centerline, where the eyes would be on a teenager or an adult. As a child ages, the shape of the face elongates, altering the proportions.

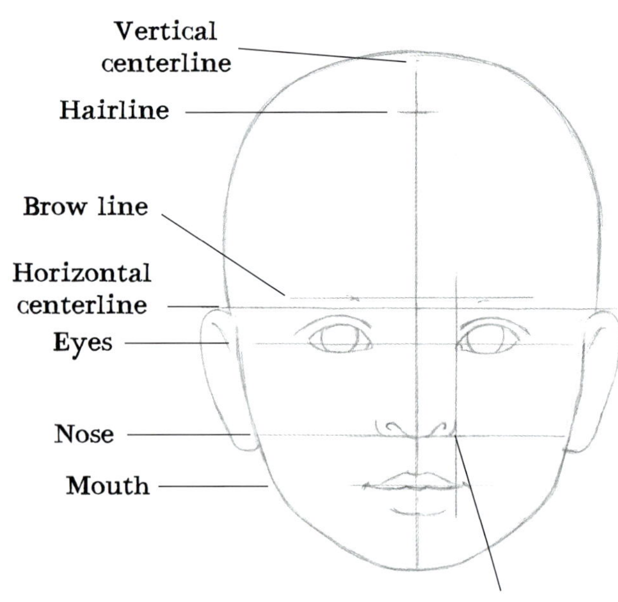

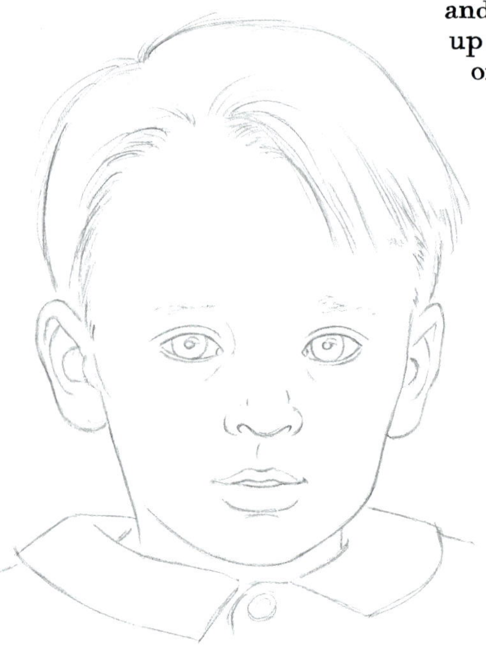

Placing the Features Based on the placement of this subject's features, you can estimate that he is around five or six years old. The face has elongated enough to shift the brow line so that it lines up with the tops of the ears, showing that the child is no longer a baby. But the eyes are spaced farther apart, indicating youth. The mouth is still relatively close to the chin, which also emphasizes his young age. (See the diagrams at right for more on the shifting of the features with age.)

CHANGING OVER TIME

The placement of the features changes as the face becomes longer and thinner with age. Use horizontal guidelines to divide the area from the horizontal centerline to the chin into equal sections; these lines can be used to determine where to the place the features.

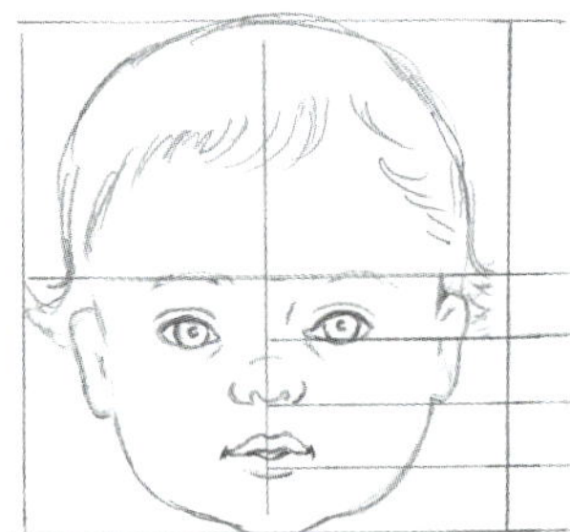

Drawing an Infant
A baby's head fits into a square shape. Babies have larger foreheads than adults do, so their eyebrows (not their eyes) fall on the horizontal centerline. Their eyes are large in relation to the rest of their features because the eyes are already fully developed at birth.

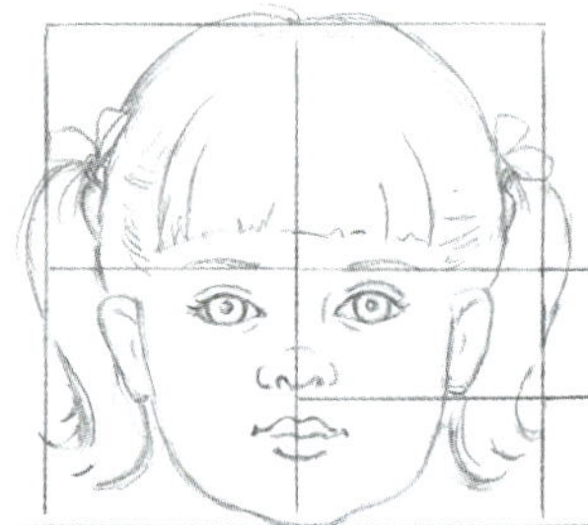

Drawing a Toddler
As a child grows, the forehead shortens a bit and the chin elongates, so the bottoms of the eyebrows now meet the horizontal centerline. The eyes are still more than one eye-width apart, but they are a bit closer together than an infant's eyes are.

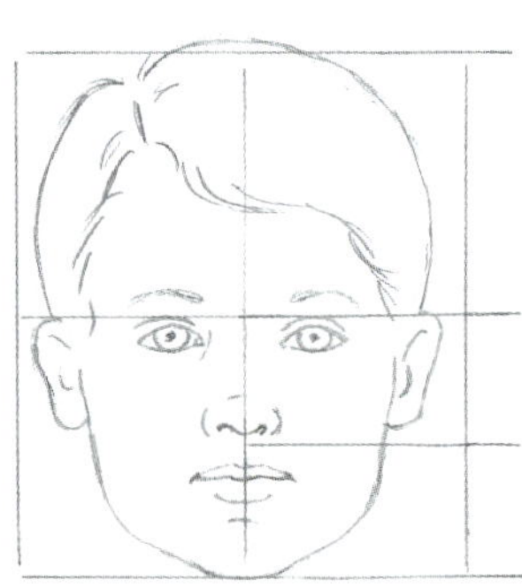

Drawing a Child
As a child nears seven or eight years of age, the face has lengthened and fits into more of a rectangular shape. The eyebrows are now well above the horizontal centerline and the eyes are a little closer to the centerline. The ears line up with the bottom of the nose.

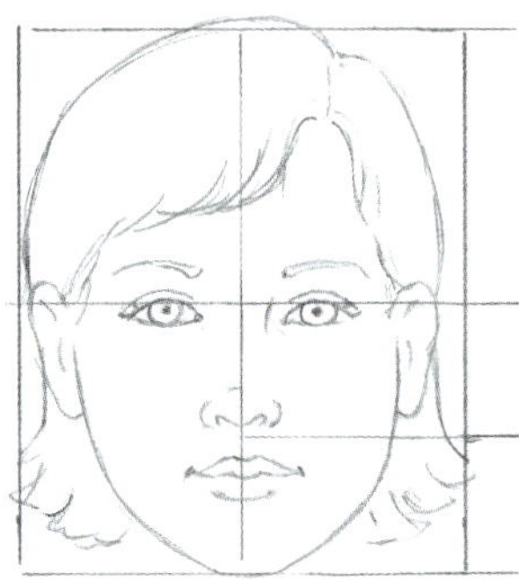

Drawing a Teenager
By age 13, the face is even longer and has lost most of its round shape; now it's more oval. The eyes are nearly at the centerline, as on an adult's face, but a teen's face and eyes are still slightly more rounded and full. The tops of the ears are about even with the eyebrows.

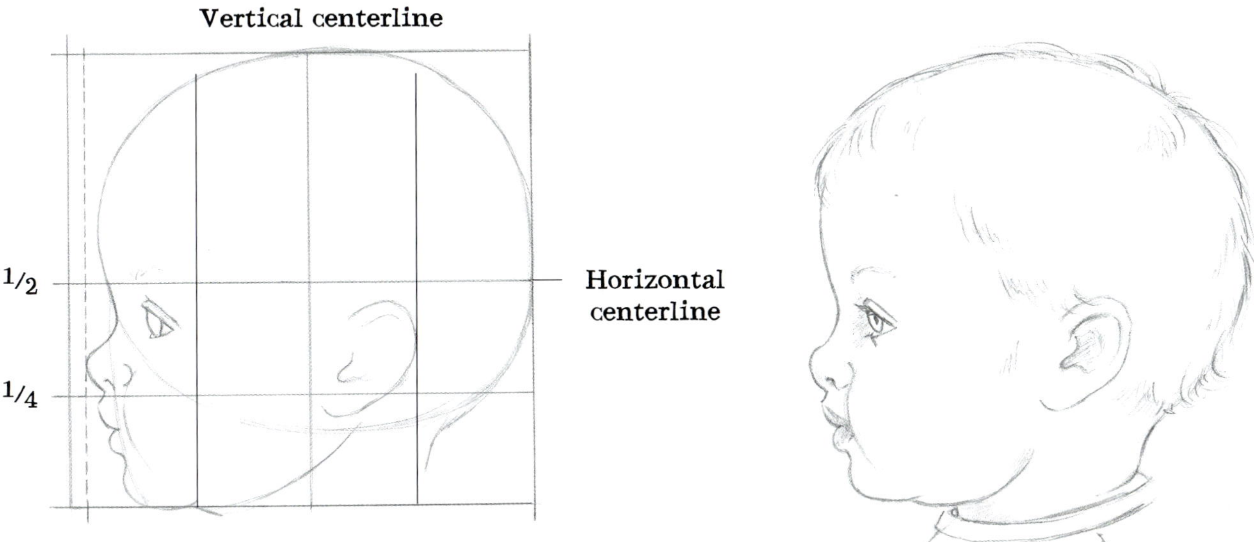

Drawing a Baby in Profile The profile of a child usually is very rounded. Youngsters generally have bigger, more protruding foreheads than adults do. Children's noses tend to be smaller and more rounded, as well. The shape of a baby's head in profile also fits into a square. Block in the large cranial mass with a circle; then sketch the features. The brow line is at the horizontal centerline, whereas the nose is about one-fourth of the way up the face. Study where each feature falls in relation to the dividing lines. In addition, light eyebrows and wispy hair help indicate a baby's age; as children get older, their hair grows in thicker.

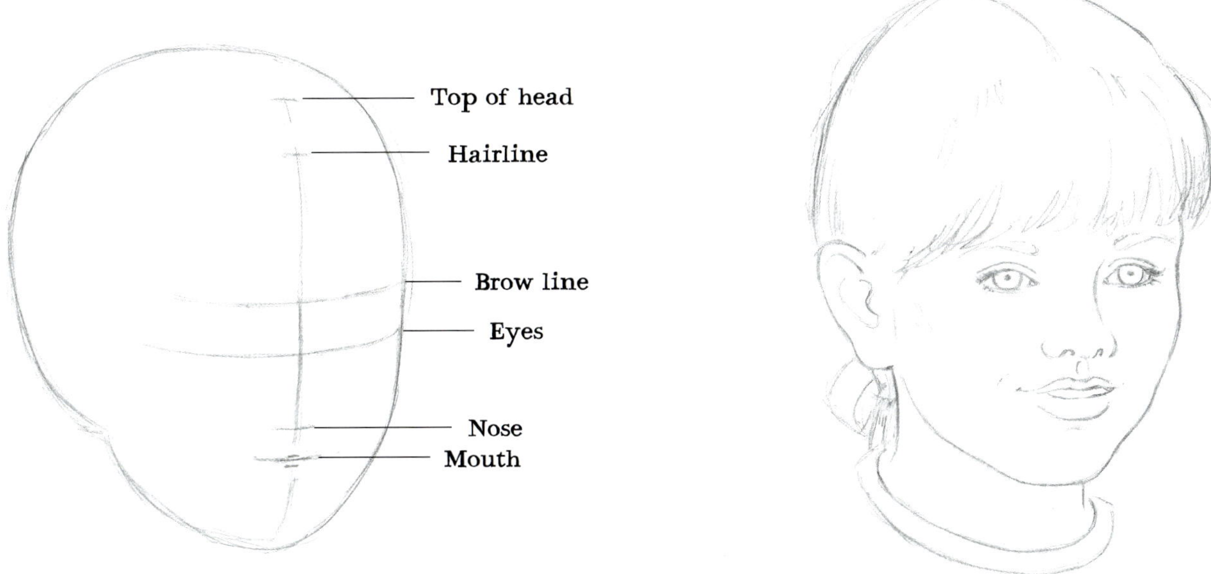

Adding Children's Details The features shift slightly in a three-quarter view, as shown here. Although a baby's features are placed differently on the head than an older child's are, their facial guidelines shift similarly, following the direction in which the head turns. Place the features according to the guidelines. Hair style and clothing—including accessories—also can influence the perceived age of your subject!

MODIFYING THE PROFILE

As children age, their profiles change quite a bit. The head elongates at each stage: The top of the baby's eyebrow lines up with the bottom of the toddler's eyebrow, the midway-point between the young boy's eyebrow and eyelid, and the top of the teenage girl's eyelid.

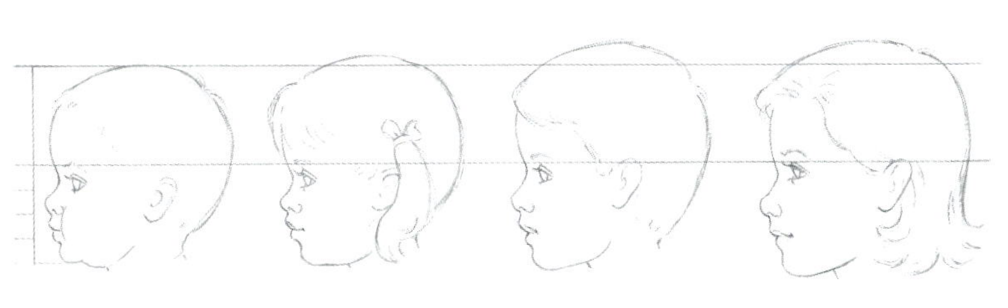

Drawing Children's Features

Children are fascinating drawing subjects, but they can be a challenge to draw accurately. It's important to get the right proportions for the particular age and to correctly render their features: Their eyes tend to be bigger and more rounded than those of adults, their nostrils are barely visible, and their hair is usually fine and wispy.

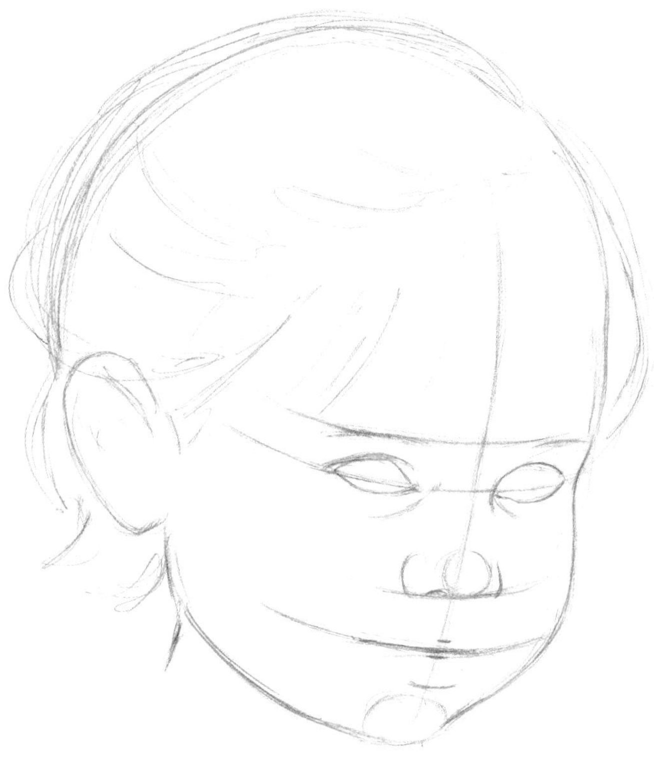

Step 1 With a sharpened 2B pencil, sketch the basic shape of the face. Lightly draw the guidelines, which curve slightly because of the viewpoint. Place the features below the horizontal centerline, where the eyebrows begin. Block in the round eyes, placing them a little more than one eye-width apart. Then sketch the round nose and small mouth and add some wispy hair to frame the face.

Step 2 Add details to the eyes and indicate highlights. (Prominent highlights give children's eyes that curious, youthful spark.) Then, develop the ear and fill out the lips. Draw a curved line from the tip of the girl's left nostril up to her left eye to build up the nose and draw another line connecting the nose to the mouth, giving her right cheek form. Sketch a few quick lines to indicate the slightly chubby area underneath her eyes, extending the cheek a bit to round it out. Add the bangs with light, soft strokes.

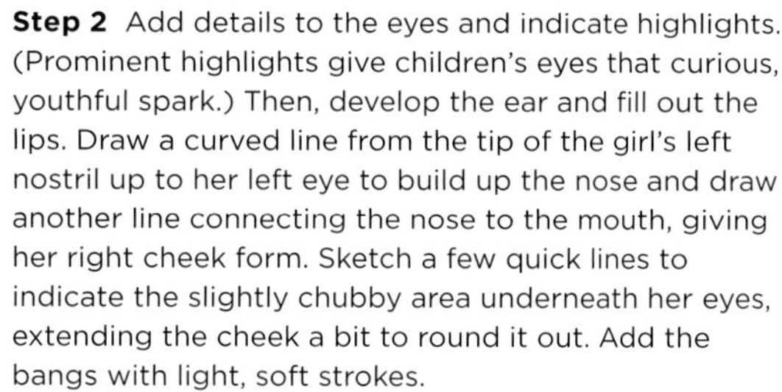

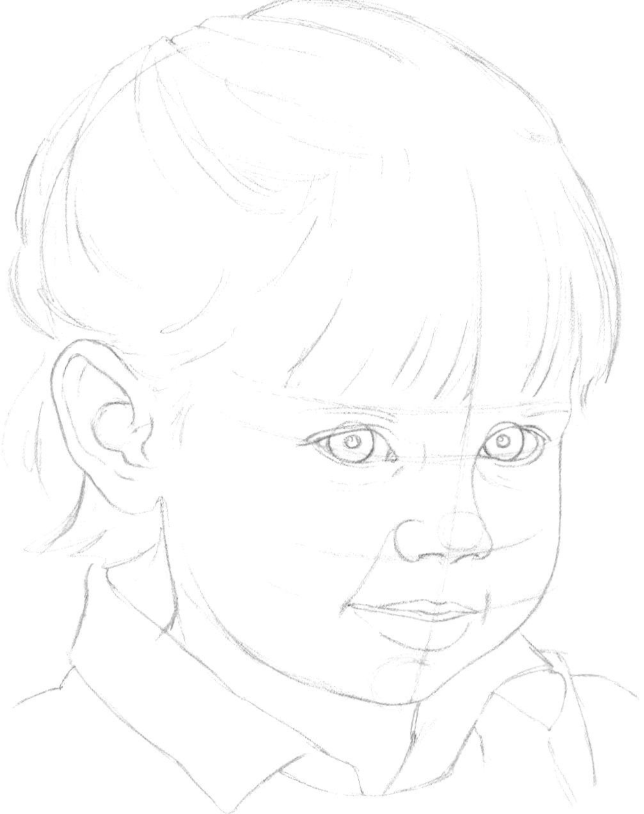

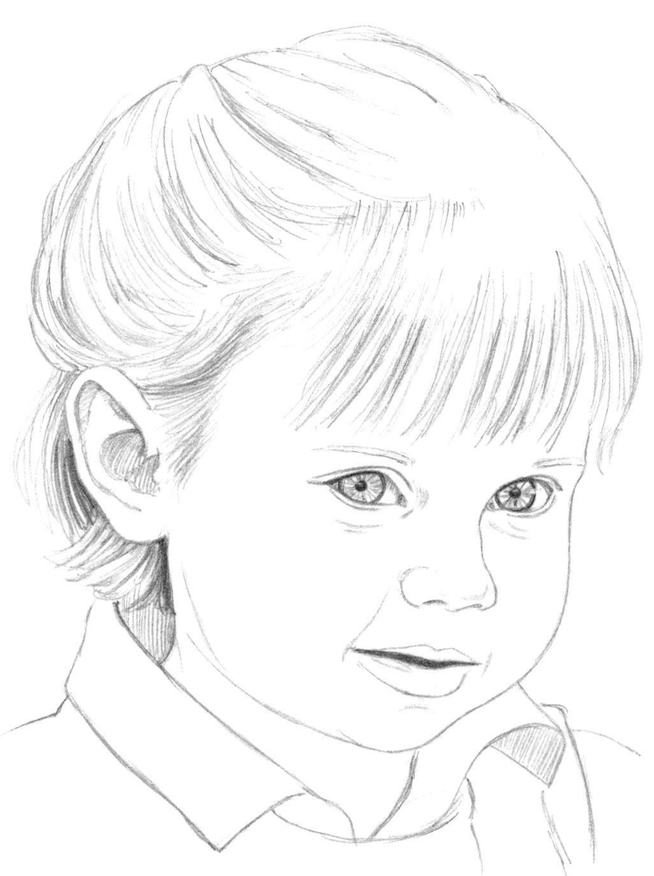

Step 3 With a 3B pencil, fill in the area between the lips and then shade the pupil and outline the iris. Add a few thin lines for hair between the scalp and the ear, darkening the hair where it is in shadow behind the ear. Keep the hair soft by sketching with light, short lines—this keeps the subject looking youthful. Switching back to the 2B pencil, shade the inside of the ear and the underside of the shirt collar, helping to show the direction of the light source. Define the lines around the eyes and the mouth.

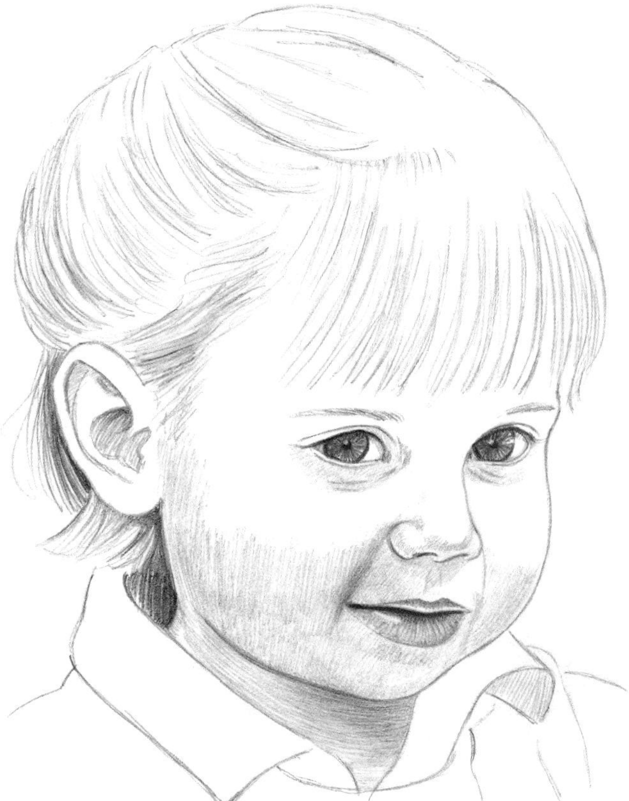

Step 4 Shade the lips with a 2B pencil, leaving a light area on the bottom lip to give it shine. Next, shade the neck using light strokes that follow the shape of the neck. With a few short lines, draw the eyebrows. Then, add light shading to the lower half of the face, filling out the cheeks and making them look rosy.

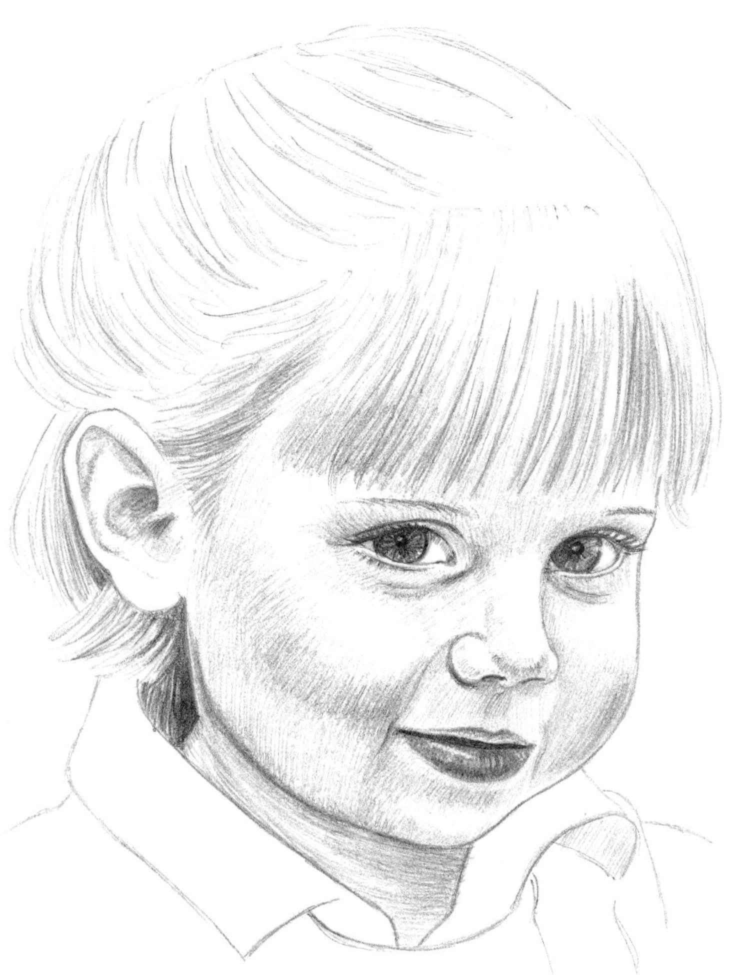

Step 5 Over each eyelid, sketch a series of small lines curving up to the eyebrows to show the youthful chubbiness. Add eyelashes using curved pencil strokes. To keep the subject looking young, draw very light eyebrows. Shade the forehead in an up-and-down motion, and then give her right cheek more form by darkening the areas around it. Use sweeping strokes to build up the bangs, leaving the paper white in areas for a shiny look.

Step 6 Still using the 2B pencil, further build up the ear. Shade a small area between the bottom of the nose and the top of the lips to suggest the indentation, and add shading to the creases around the mouth. Create more dark strokes in the back of the hair to show where the hair is layered. Draw a flower pattern on the shirt collar. Adding youthful patterns to your subject's clothing helps define their age; overalls, jumpers, ribbons, baseball caps, and bows also can imply youth.

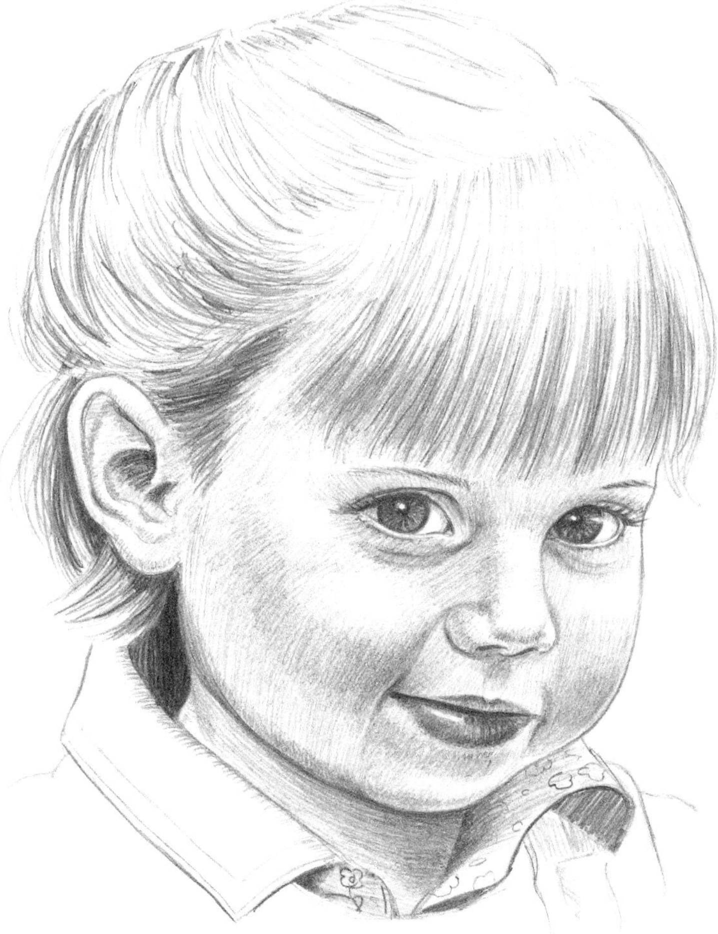

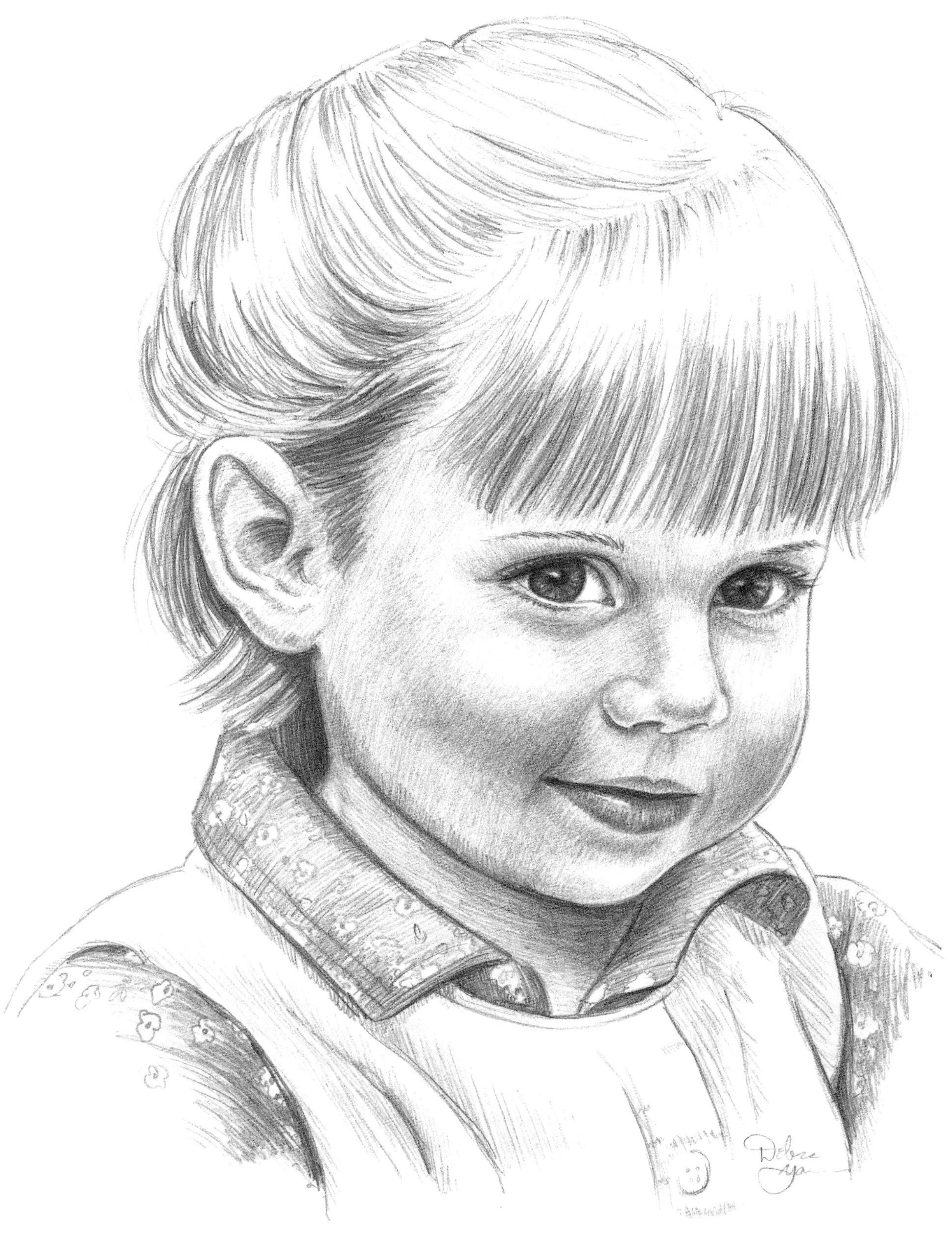

Step 7 Putting your pencil aside for a moment, carefully drag the edge of a kneaded eraser across the top of the bangs to create the appearance of blond hair. Using the 3B pencil, create texture on the jumper and shirt by spacing the lines of the corduroy slightly apart from one another. Then develop the floral pattern on the sleeves of her shirt and add a small button. Stand back from your portrait and make sure the transitions from light to dark values are smooth and that there are no harsh or angular lines that might make the subject appear older than she is.

Drawing a Baby

Drawing babies can be tricky because it's easy to unintentionally make them look older than they are. The face gets longer in proportion to the cranium with age, so the younger the child, the lower the eyes are on the face (and thus, the larger the forehead). In addition, babies' eyes are disproportionately large in comparison to the rest of their bodies, so draw them this way!

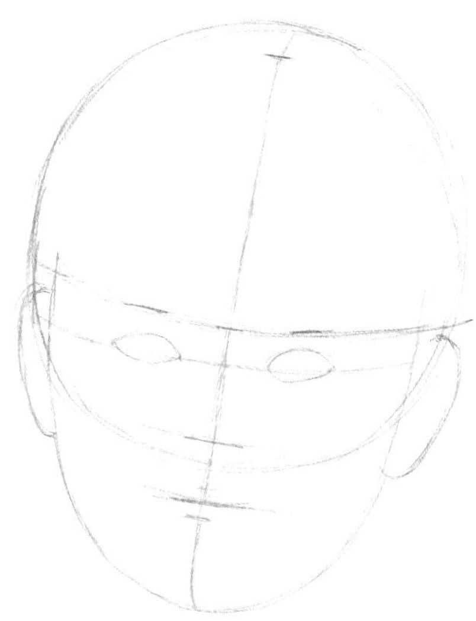

Step 1 Using an HB pencil, block in the cranial mass and the facial guidelines. The head is tilted downward and turned slightly to its left, so adjust the guidelines accordingly. Place the eyebrows at the horizontal centerline and the eyes in the lower half of the face.

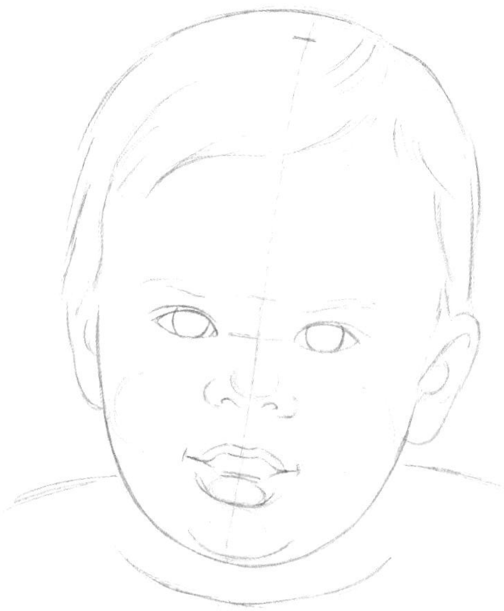

Step 2 Now create the fine hair using soft, short strokes and a B pencil. Draw the open mouth with the bottom lip resting against the chin. Add large irises that take up most of the eyes and suggest the small nose. Draw a curved line under the chin to suggest chubbiness; then indicate the shoulders, omitting the neck.

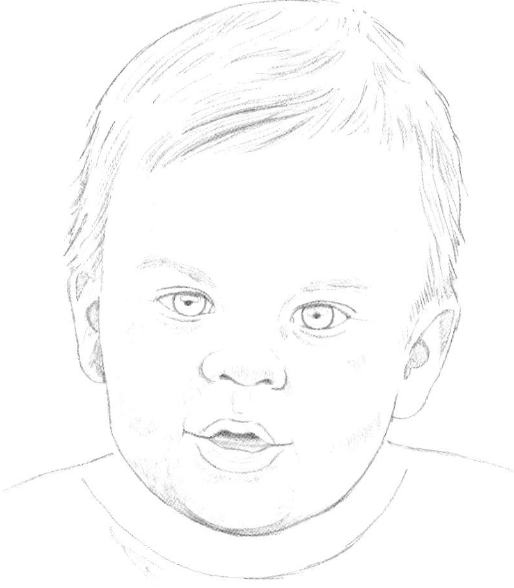

Step 3 Erasing guidelines as you draw, add pupils and highlights to the eyes with a B pencil. Lightly sketch more of the hair and eyebrows, and then shade under the chin to give it form. Shade inside the ears. Then connect and refine the lips, shading the upturned corners to suggest the pudgy mouth. Shade the inside of the mouth, showing that there aren't any teeth; then further define the neckline of the shirt.

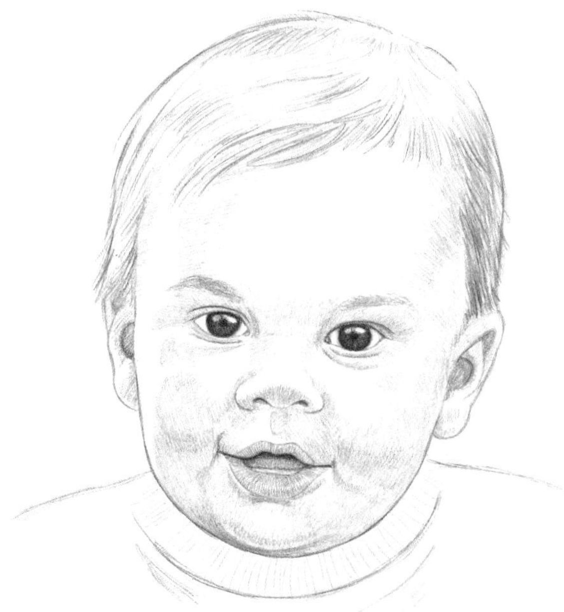

Step 4 With a 2B pencil, shade the irises, and then go back in and lighten the highlights with a kneaded eraser. Draw more soft strokes in the hair and eyebrows and shade the lips and face. Emphasize the pudgy mouth by softly shading the smile lines, then finally add curving lines to the neckline of the shirt.

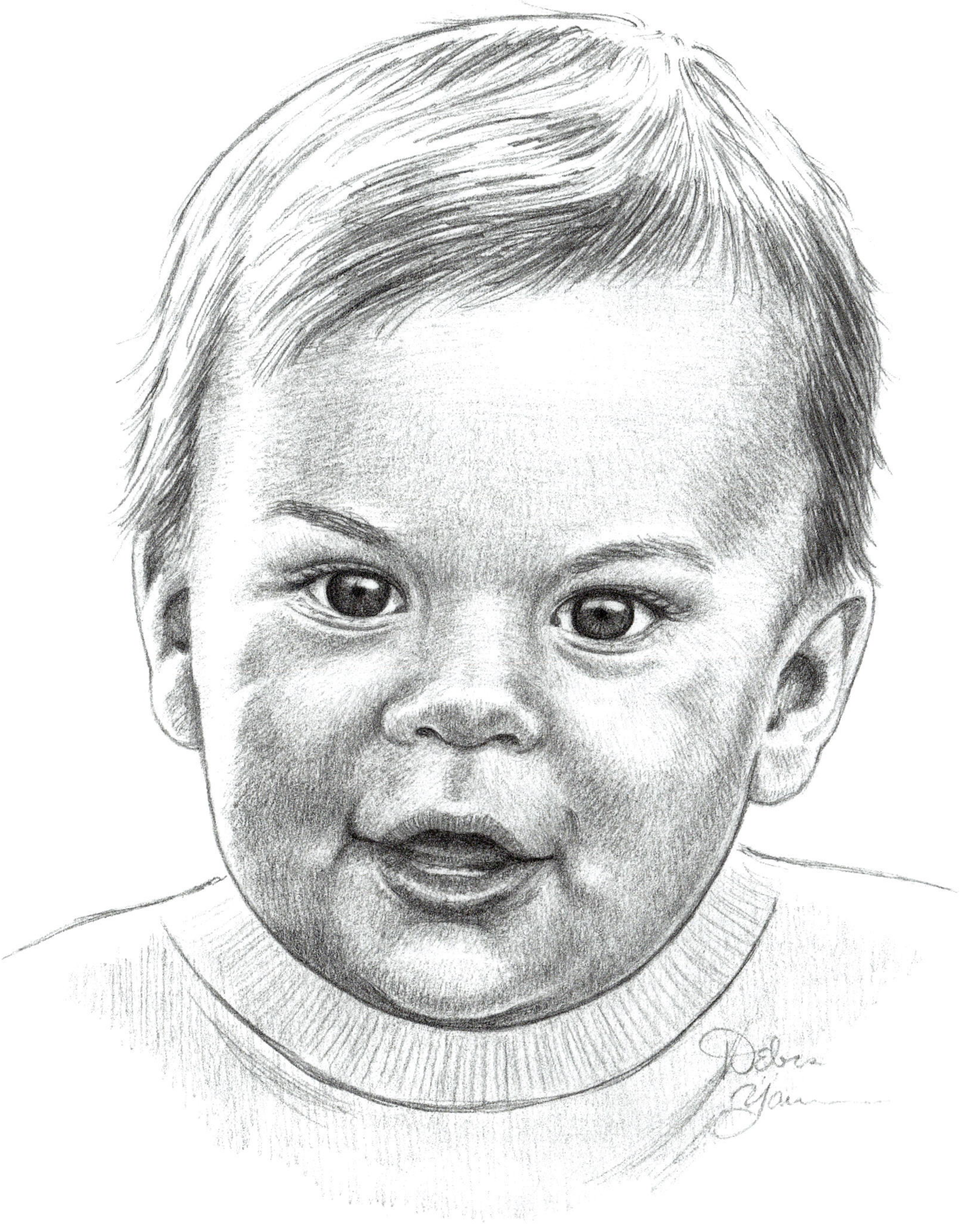

Step 5 Continue shading the face; then add another light layer of shading to the lips. Use the end of a kneaded eraser to pull out a highlight on the bottom lip. Then draw some very light eyelashes. Create darker values in the hair and eyebrows and round out the outline of the face. Lightly shade the shirt. Then take a step back from the portrait to assess whether you've properly built up the roundness in the cheeks, chin, eyes, nose, and mouth. Use a tortillon to softly blend transitions in your shading to make the complexion baby smooth.

DRAWING A BABY'S FEATURES

Babies often have wide-eyed, curious expressions. Try curving the eyebrows upward to create the appearance of childlike curiosity; pull out highlights in each eye to add life and interest to your drawing. A baby's lips have a soft, pudgy appearance, and the mouth usually is not as wide as an adult's mouth is. Adding highlights is important to convey a smooth texture, and creating creases at the corners of the mouth will help indicate youthful chubbiness.

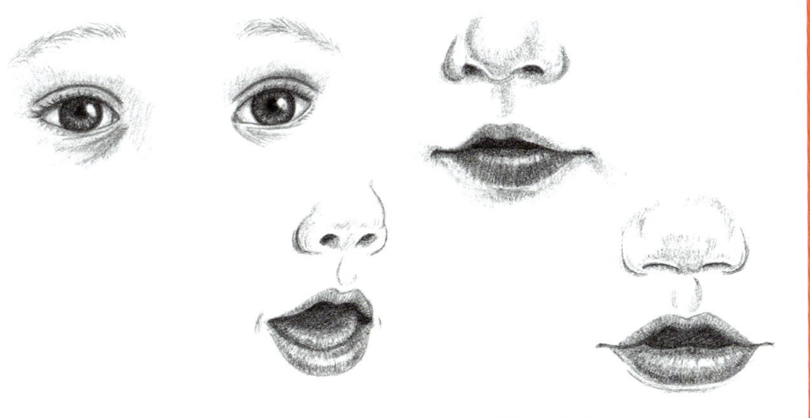

Choosing a Photo Reference

If you're using a photograph as a reference while you draw, it's usually best to have several different photographs from varying angles and with different light sources to choose from. Not only does this give you a wider selection of poses and lighting options, it also allows you to combine different elements from each photograph. For example, if you are satisfied with the lighting in one photograph but you're drawn to the facial expression in another, you can combine the best parts from each for your portrait.

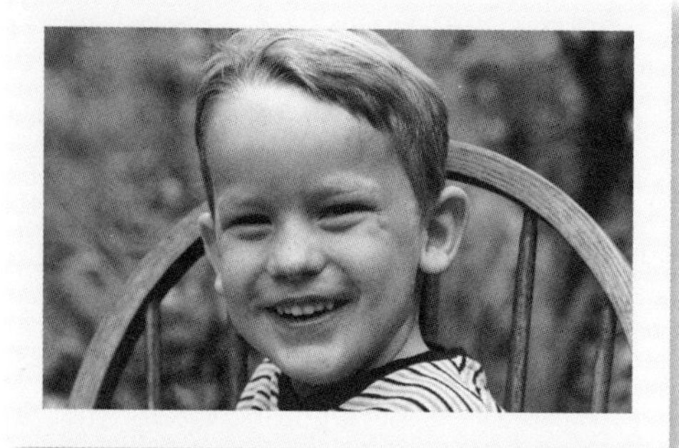

A

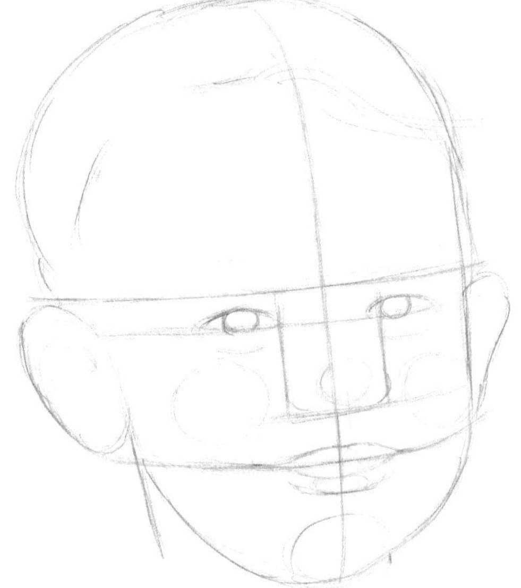

Step 1 After studying your selection of photographs, choose the best one and use it as a reference to block in the outline of the face, the guidelines, and the features.

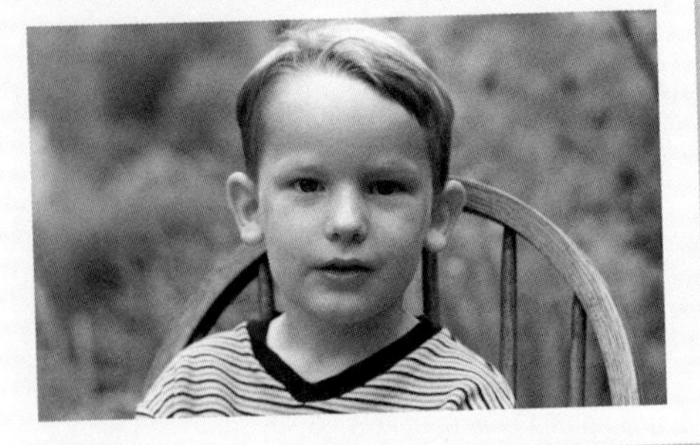

B

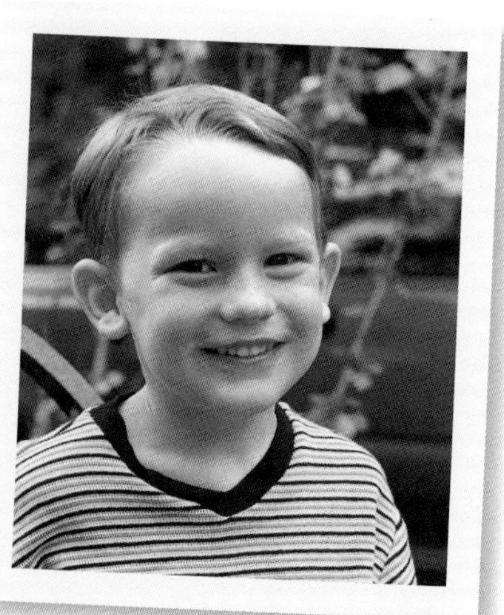

C

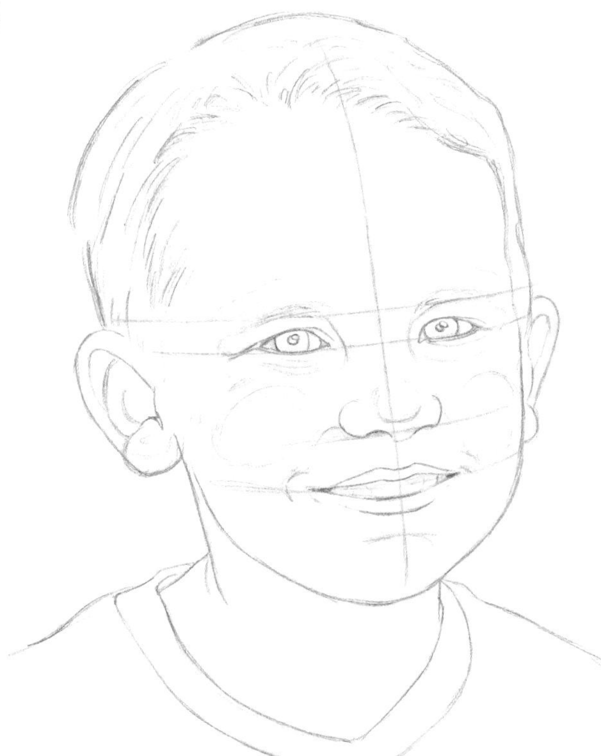

Step 2 Compare your initial sketch with the photograph and make necessary adjustments, indicating the roundness of the bottoms of the earlobes with light circles. Next, draw the slightly protruding teeth.

Finding the Best Pose In photo A, the subject's eyes are squinting just a tad too much. In photo B, the subject's pose seems stiff and stilted. But in photo C, his pose and expression are just right!

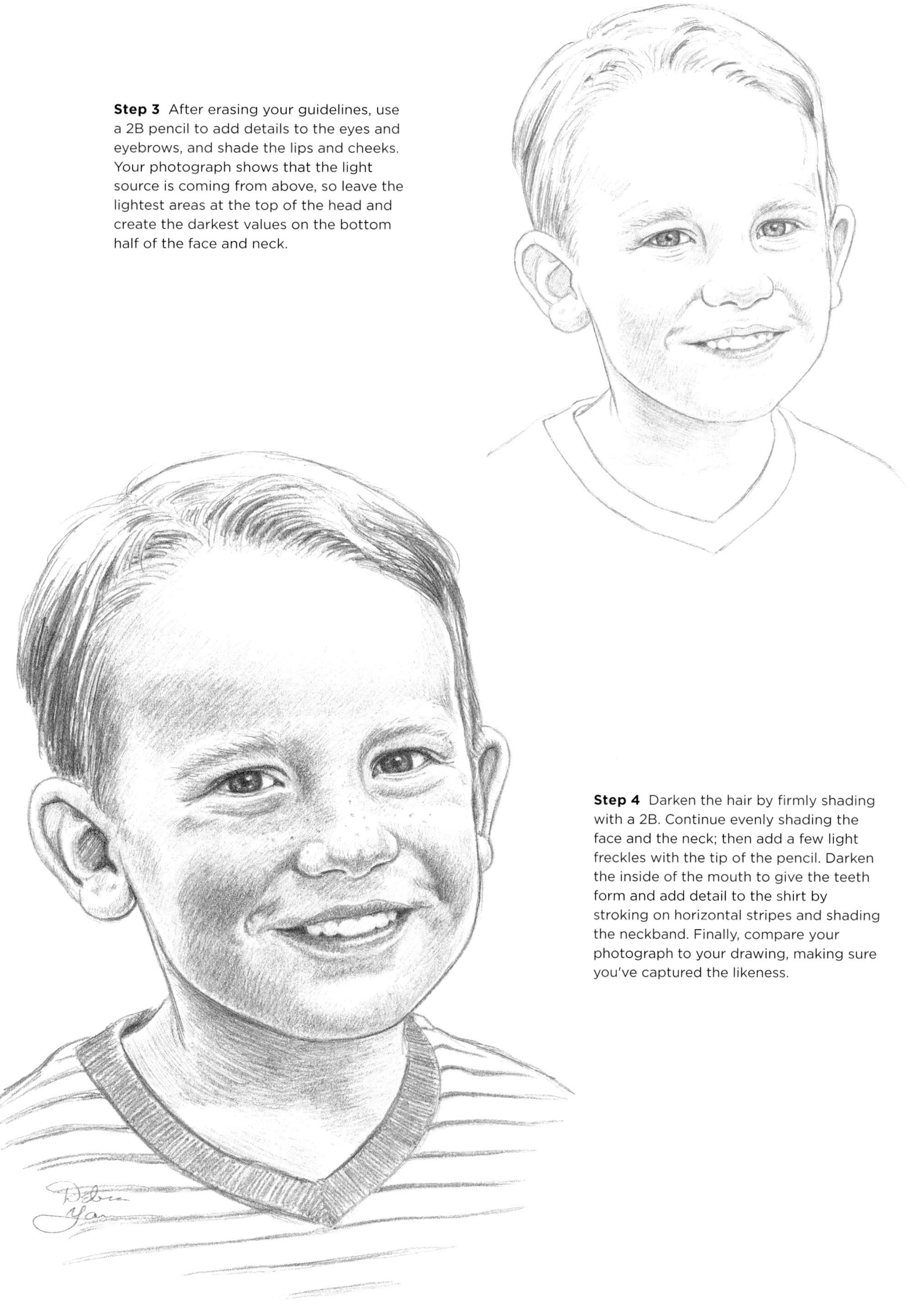

Step 3 After erasing your guidelines, use a 2B pencil to add details to the eyes and eyebrows, and shade the lips and cheeks. Your photograph shows that the light source is coming from above, so leave the lightest areas at the top of the head and create the darkest values on the bottom half of the face and neck.

Step 4 Darken the hair by firmly shading with a 2B. Continue evenly shading the face and the neck; then add a few light freckles with the tip of the pencil. Darken the inside of the mouth to give the teeth form and add detail to the shirt by stroking on horizontal stripes and shading the neckband. Finally, compare your photograph to your drawing, making sure you've captured the likeness.

Capturing Details

When drawing a subject with a fair complexion, keep your shading to a minimum. Apply just enough medium and dark values to create the illusion of form. Outline the general shape, adding a few carefully placed strokes to suggest the hairstyle and create some dimension.

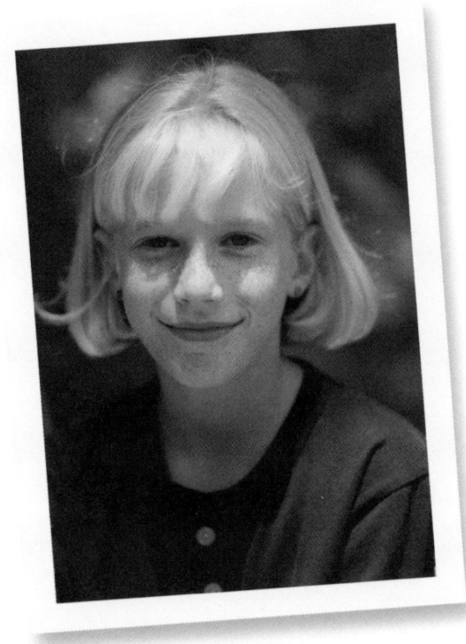

Shading Fair Skin and Hair In this photo, the overhead light makes the bangs, nose, and cheeks look nearly pure white.

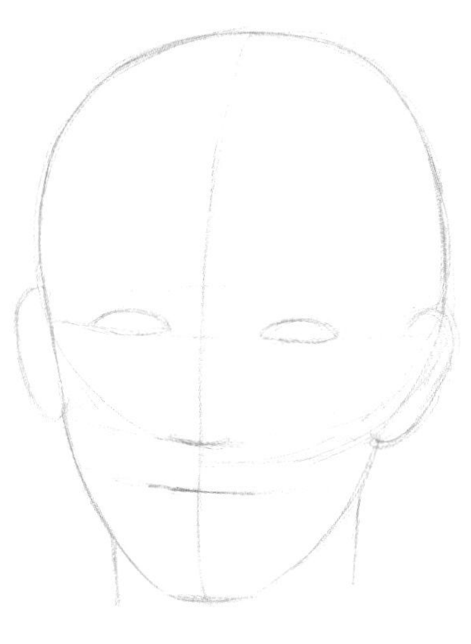

Step 1 First lay out the face with an HB pencil. The face is slightly tilted to the subject's left, so shift the vertical centerline to the left a bit. Lightly place the eyes, nose, mouth, and ears; then block in the neck.

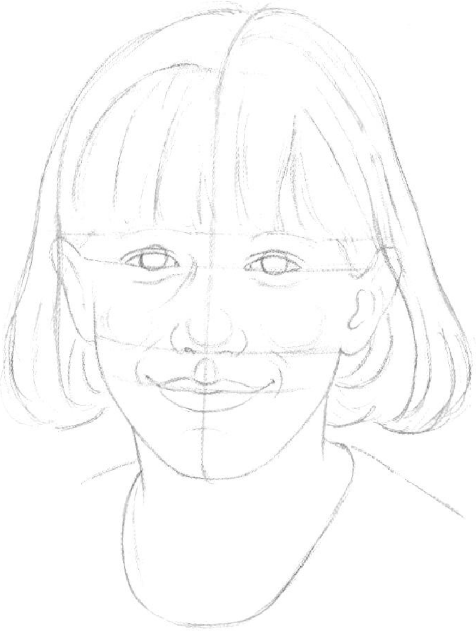

Step 2 Switching to a 2B pencil, develop the features. Follow the photo for reference, but use artistic license to adjust the rendering as you see fit. For example, you may want to straighten out some of the hairs.

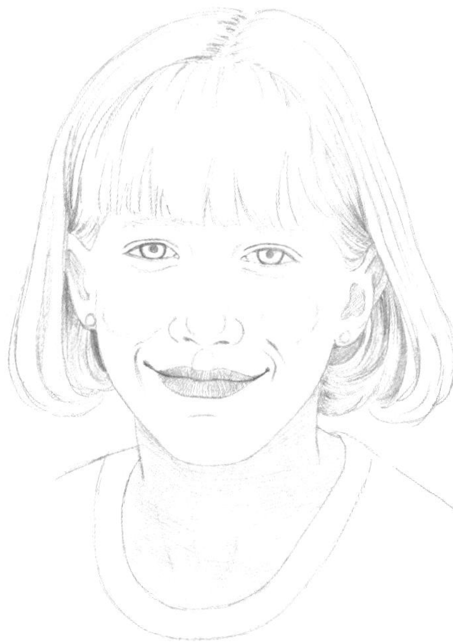

Step 3 Continue building up the hair, leaving the top and sides mostly white, adding only a few dark strands here and there. The darkest values are around the ears where the hair is in shadow. Next, add small circles for the earrings and shade the insides of the ears. Develop the lips, and then use horizontal strokes to shade the neck.

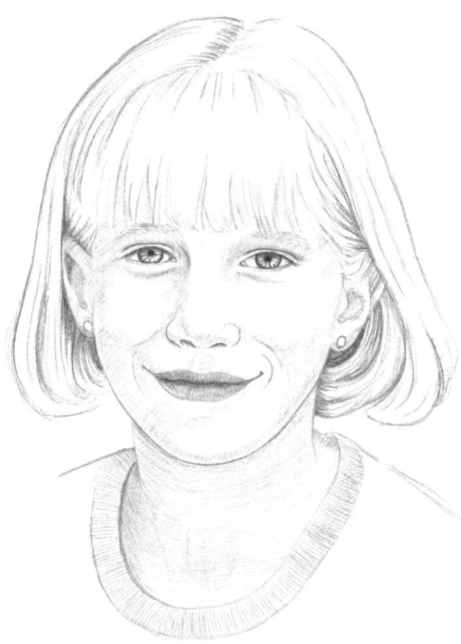

Step 4 Shade the face with light, soft strokes to depict the subject's skin. Make short, quick strokes for the eyebrows, keeping them light and soft to indicate blond hair. Next, shade the irises using strokes that radiate out from the pupil. Add some hatching strokes along the neckband of the shirt.

Step 5 Using a kneaded eraser, pull out a highlight on the bottom lip. Then create more dark strands of hair and further develop the eyes and eyebrows. Add freckles, making sure that they vary in size and shape. Finally, shade the shirt, using relatively dark strokes.

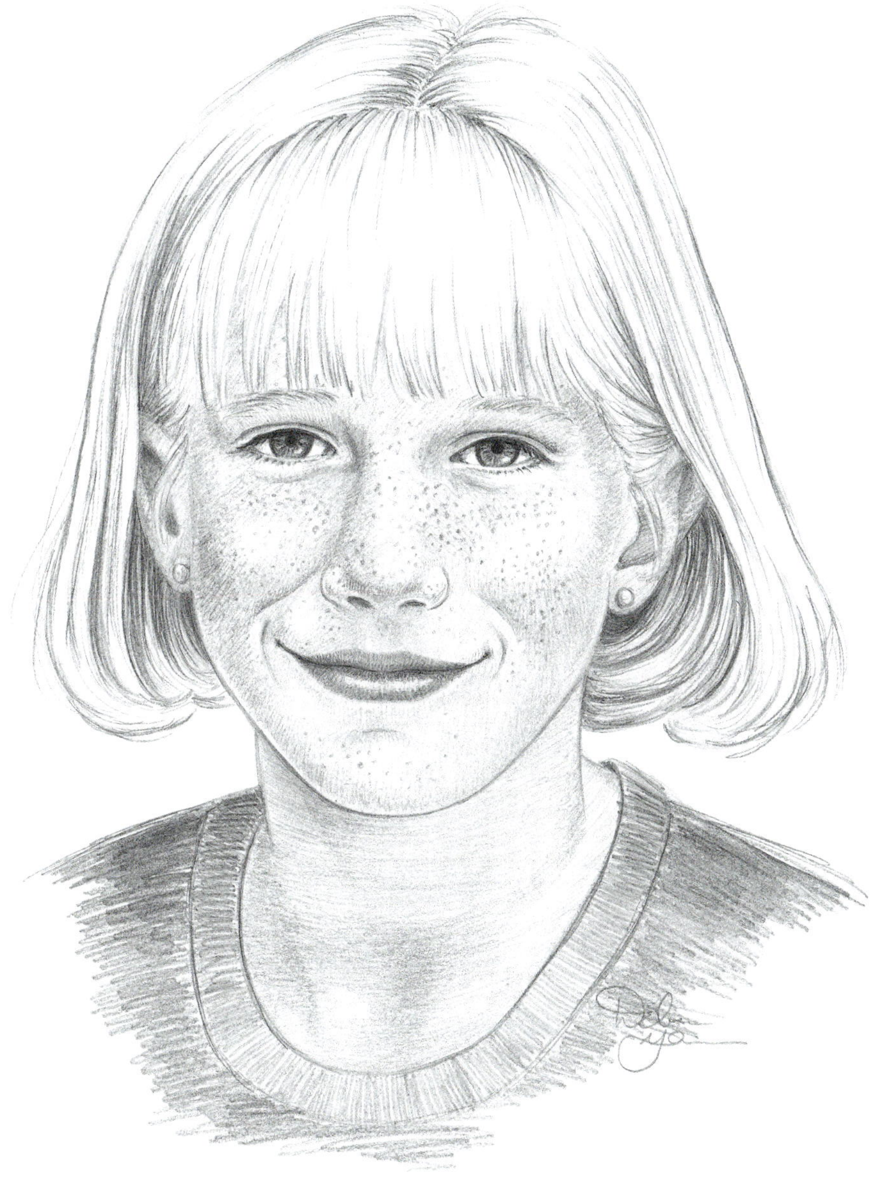

DEPICTING FINE HAIR

Draw fine hair in narrow sections, leaving plenty of white areas showing through the dark values. Add some short, wispy strands of hair at the forehead to frame the face.

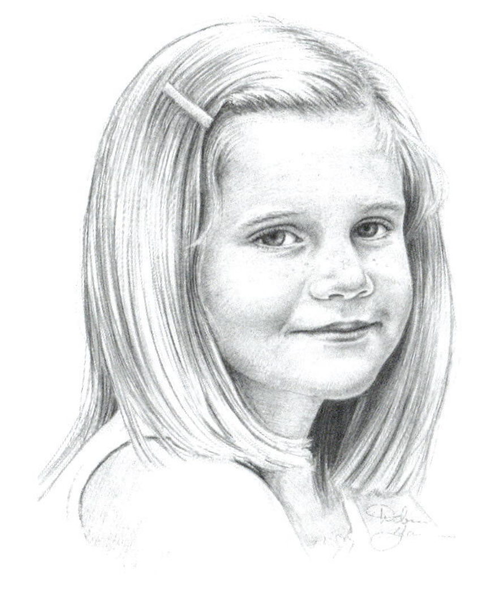

DRAWING FRECKLES

To draw freckles, space them sporadically, in varying sizes and distances from one other. You don't have to replicate every freckle on your subject's face—just draw the general shapes and let the viewer's eye fill in the rest.

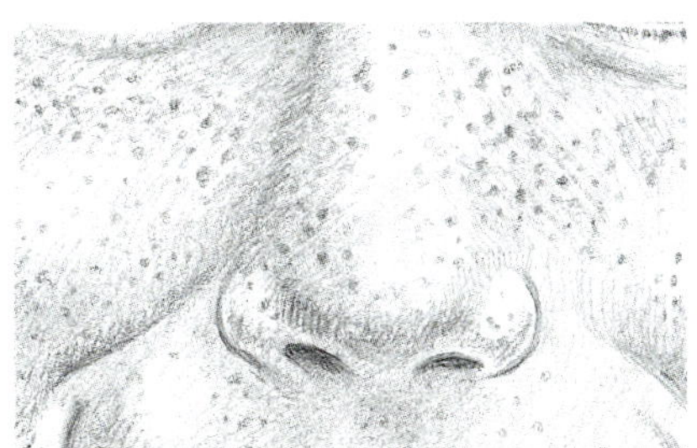

What to Do Make sure some of the freckles overlap, and make some light and some dark by varying the pressure you place on the pencil.

What Not to Do When drawing freckles, do not space them too evenly or make them equal in size, as shown here. These freckles look more like polka dots!

Establishing Values

When shading a portrait, vary the direction of your pencil strokes to follow the different planes of the face. Darken shadowed areas and leave highlights light to make the face appear three-dimensional. Pay attention to the value of the skin tone and how it compares with the values of other facial features.

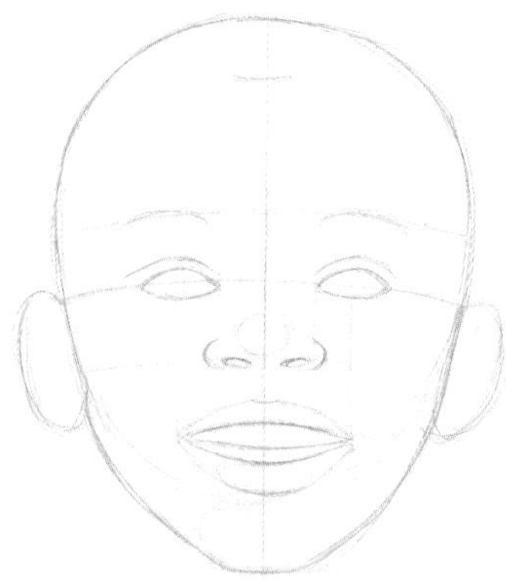

Step 1 With a 2B pencil, block in the basic head shape and place the features, following the guidelines. Draw the eyes, nose, and lips. Then block in the teeth and indicate the hairline, eyebrows, and ears.

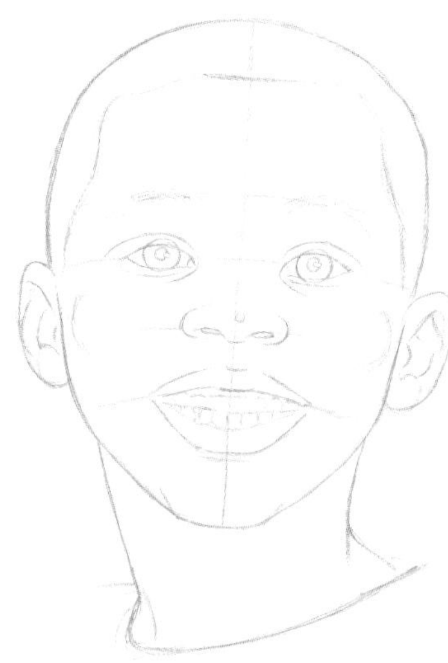

Step 2 Still using the 2B pencil, sketch in the neck and define the chin. Develop the eyes and use short, quick lines to draw the eyebrows.

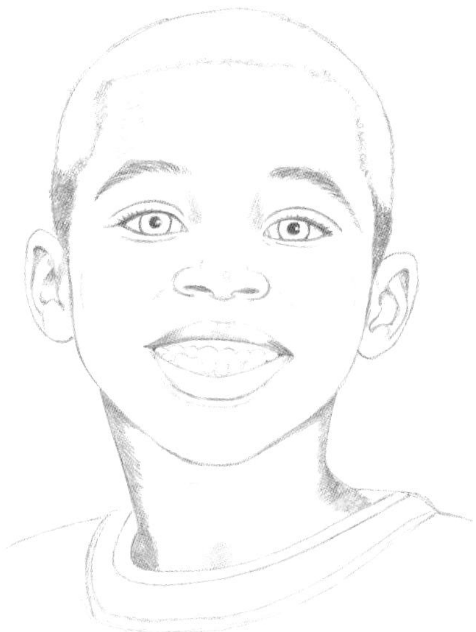

Step 3 Next, shade the nose, neck, and top lip. Using quick, circular strokes, render the short, curly hair. Then detail the eyebrows and eyes.

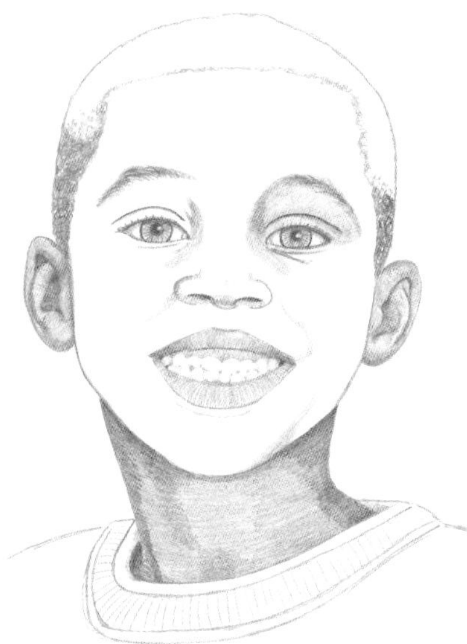

Step 4 Using strokes that follow the shape of the mouth, continue shading the lips; then shade the gums, carefully working around the teeth. Build up the hair with more circular strokes. Then move to the neck, using horizontal lines that curve with the shape of the neck. Notice how these lines overlap and blend into the shading that was applied in step 3.

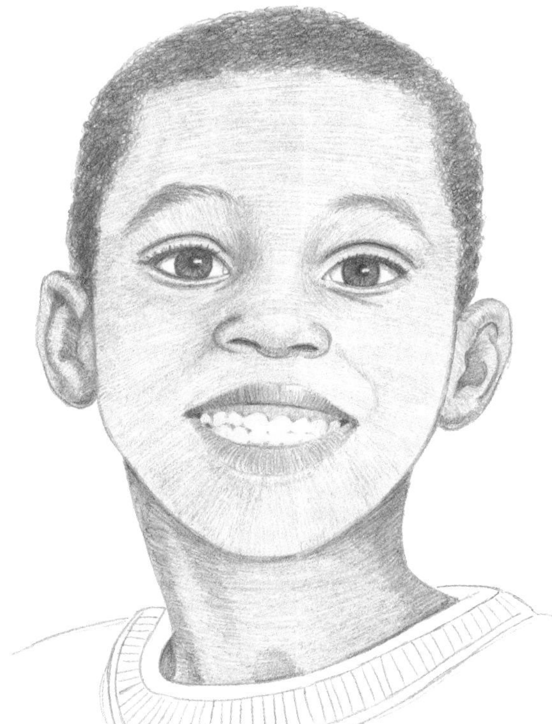

Step 5 Now apply a light layer of shading over the entire face, always varying the direction of strokes as necessary to follow the shapes of the different planes.

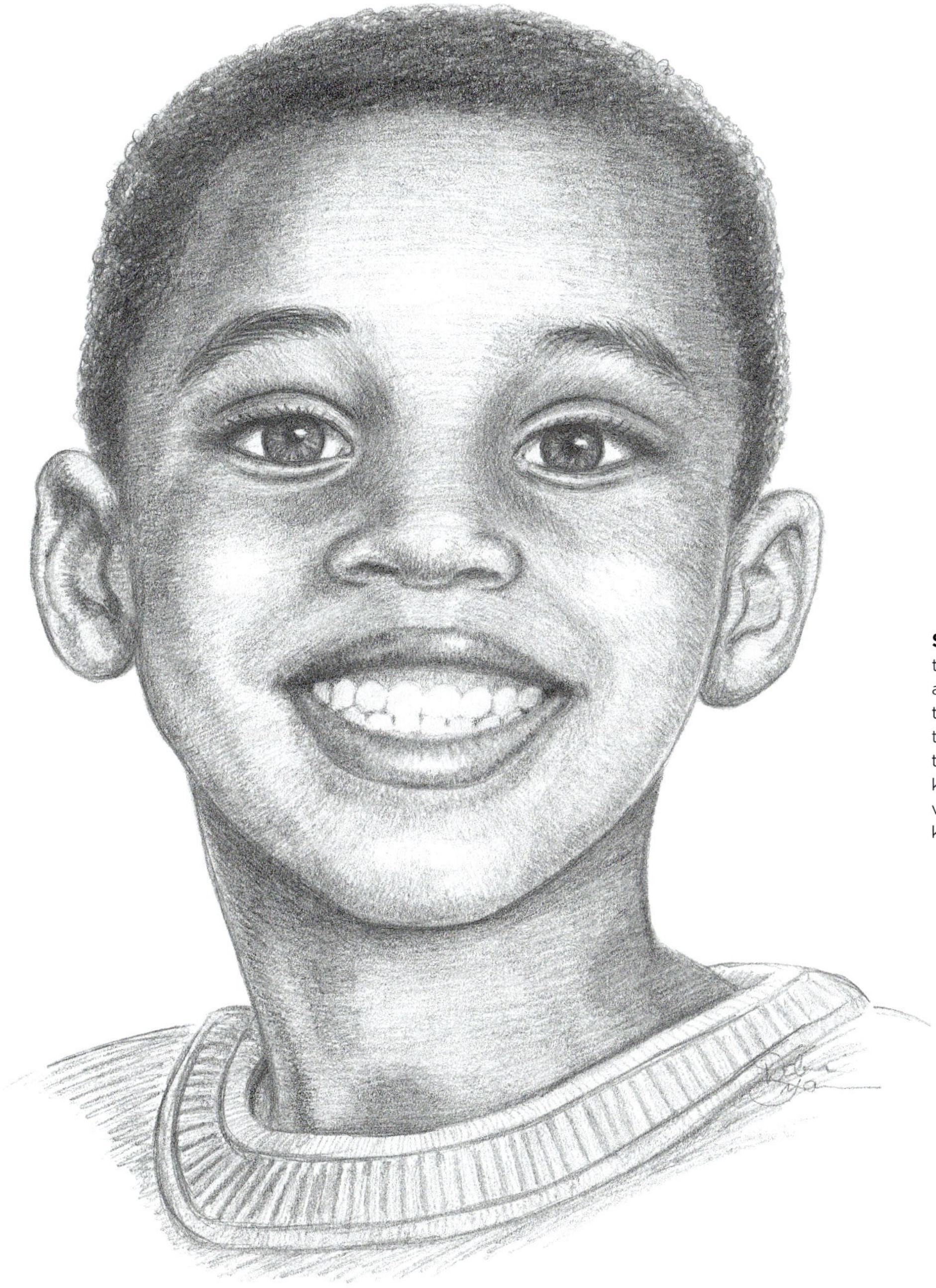

WORKING WITH VALUE

Every skin tone is made up of a variety of values—when drawing in graphite pencil, you can accurately capture these differing tones using varying degrees of light and shadow. Before you start drawing, be sure to study your subject to establish the richest darks and brightest lights.

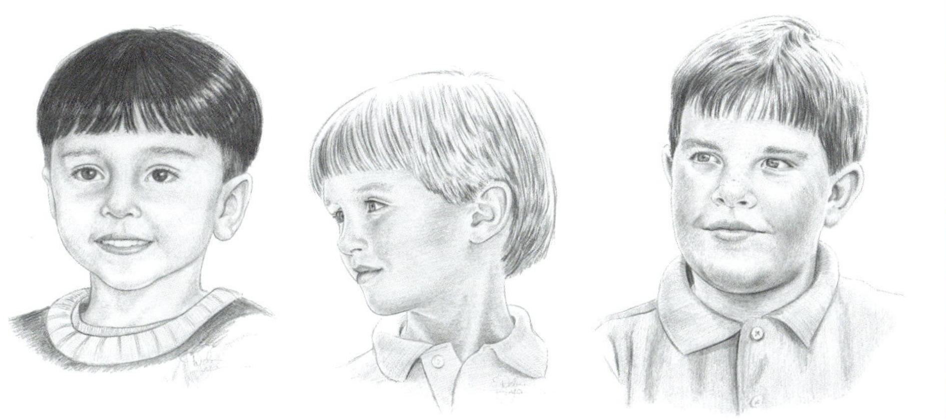

Working with Light

This seven-step portrait lesson shows an artistic way of dealing with light and shade. There are no auxiliary lines, not even in the beginning. Follow the subtle work of rendering the face using pencils in varying degrees of hardness and different tortillions.

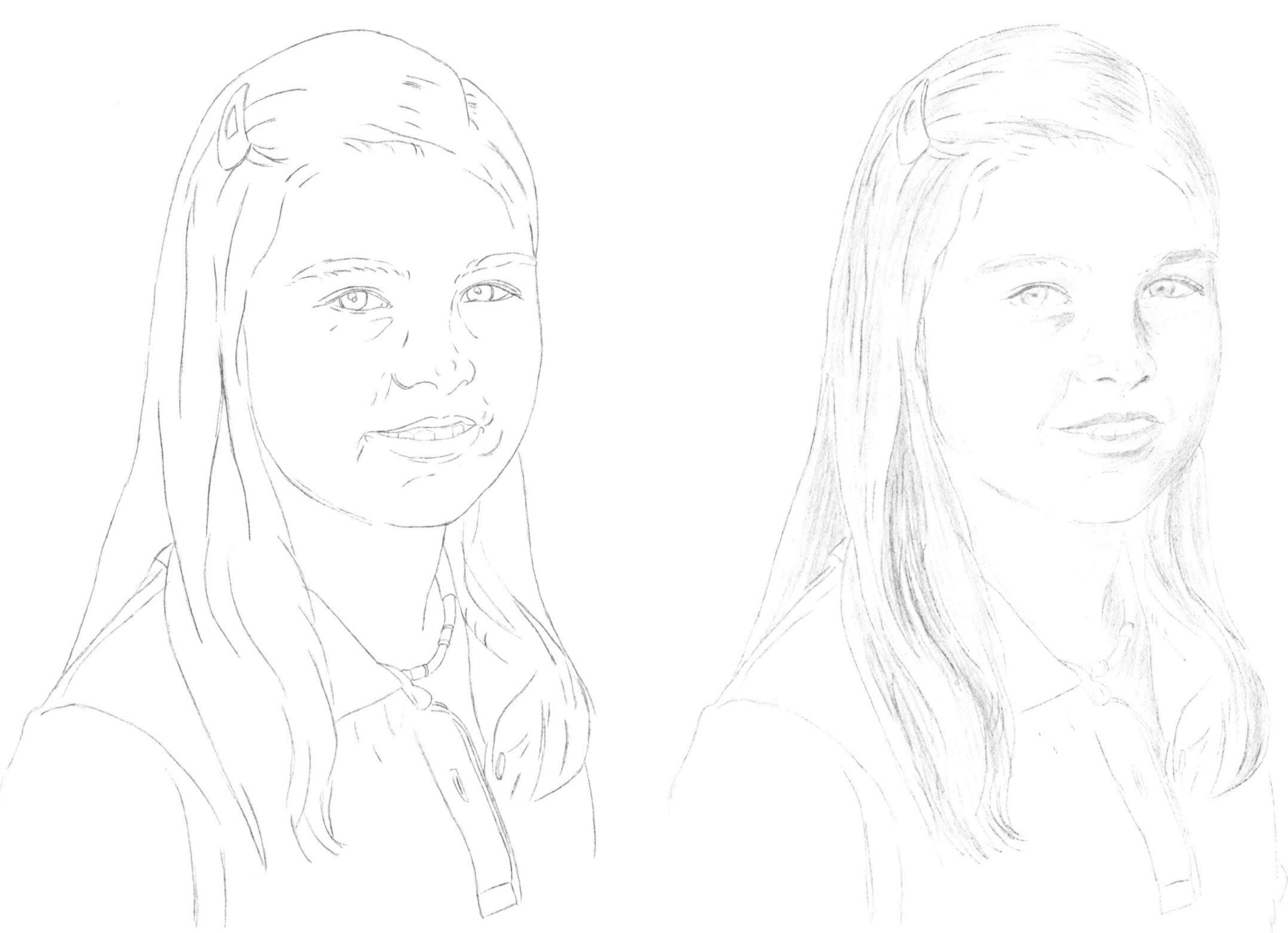

Step 1 When choosing the pose for a portrait, it is important to think about the qualities that are particularly special about your subject. Jewelry, such as necklaces and bracelets, can offer additional textural interest. For portraits, smooth Bristol paper is a great choice because it allows you to capture subtle details. Use a sharp HB pencil to outline the basic features of the head. Check and recheck the accuracy of your drawing, because the slightest errors in observation will take away from the likeness of the subject.

Step 2 Using the side of a 2B pencil, draw long, flowing strokes that follow the direction of the hair. Add light tone in the iris of each eye, using small, circular strokes. Under the eyebrow of her left eye, develop the shadow of the down plane by the nose. For the side of the nose, use longer strokes with a slight curve, but for the tip, think of a small sphere and use shorter, curved strokes. On the side of the face, use very light strokes that curve with the shape of the face. Indicate the shadow directly under the lower lip. Draw lines that indicate the cylindrical shape of the neck, and add some darker tone for the cast shadow under the collar.

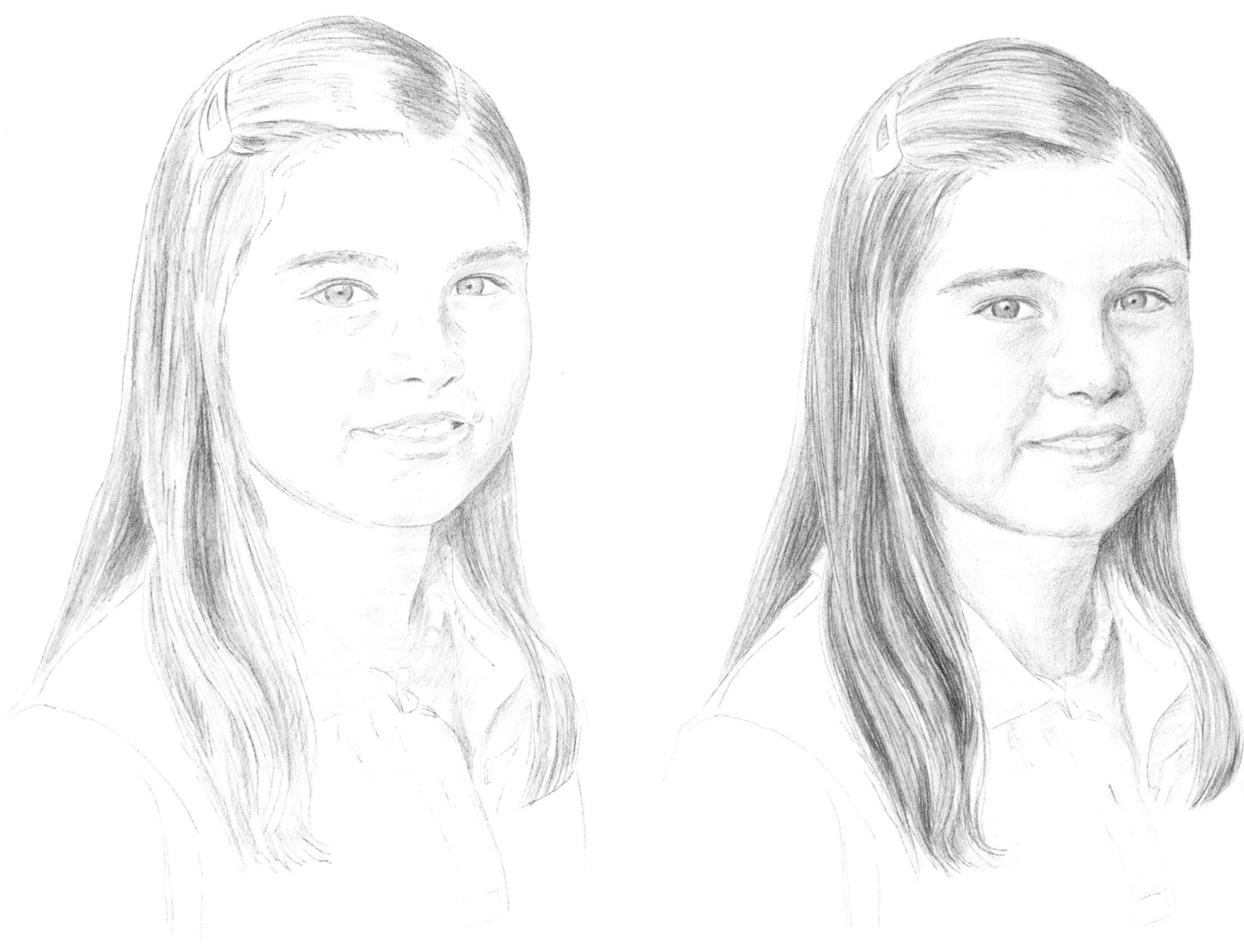

Step 3 Begin to blend the hair with a large stump. Then, lay in more tone with a 4B for definition around the area where the hair parts and around the side of the face. With the lightest touch, slightly blend the pencil strokes around the side of the face, following the rounded contour of the cheeks. With a smaller stump, lightly blend the areas around the eyes, mouth, nose, and eyebrows. Uisng your 2B pencil, lay in some deeper tone in the nostrils, the corner of the mouth, and the pupil of the eye. Darken the lines around the eye, making the line above the eye thicker to indicate the lashes. Work in light layers to slowly develop the form.

Step 4 Using the point of a 2B pencil, build up the tone and flow of the hair. Alternate between a pencil and a stump, being careful to retain the highlights. Work on the face, using a delicate buildup of crosshatching. Draw light, long strokes with an HB across the forehead. Shade around the eye area, always following the contour of the form. Do the same for the nose, lips, cheeks, and chin, building up tone slowly. Add subtle shading on the teeth—but don't make them too white. Deepen the tone of the irises with a 2B, and lift out to adjust the placement of the highlights. Move to the neck area, using heavy pressure in the cast shadow areas. Shade the collar of the shirt, keeping your strokes farther apart to start developing a feel of the knit fabric. Then use curved lines to indicate the necklace.

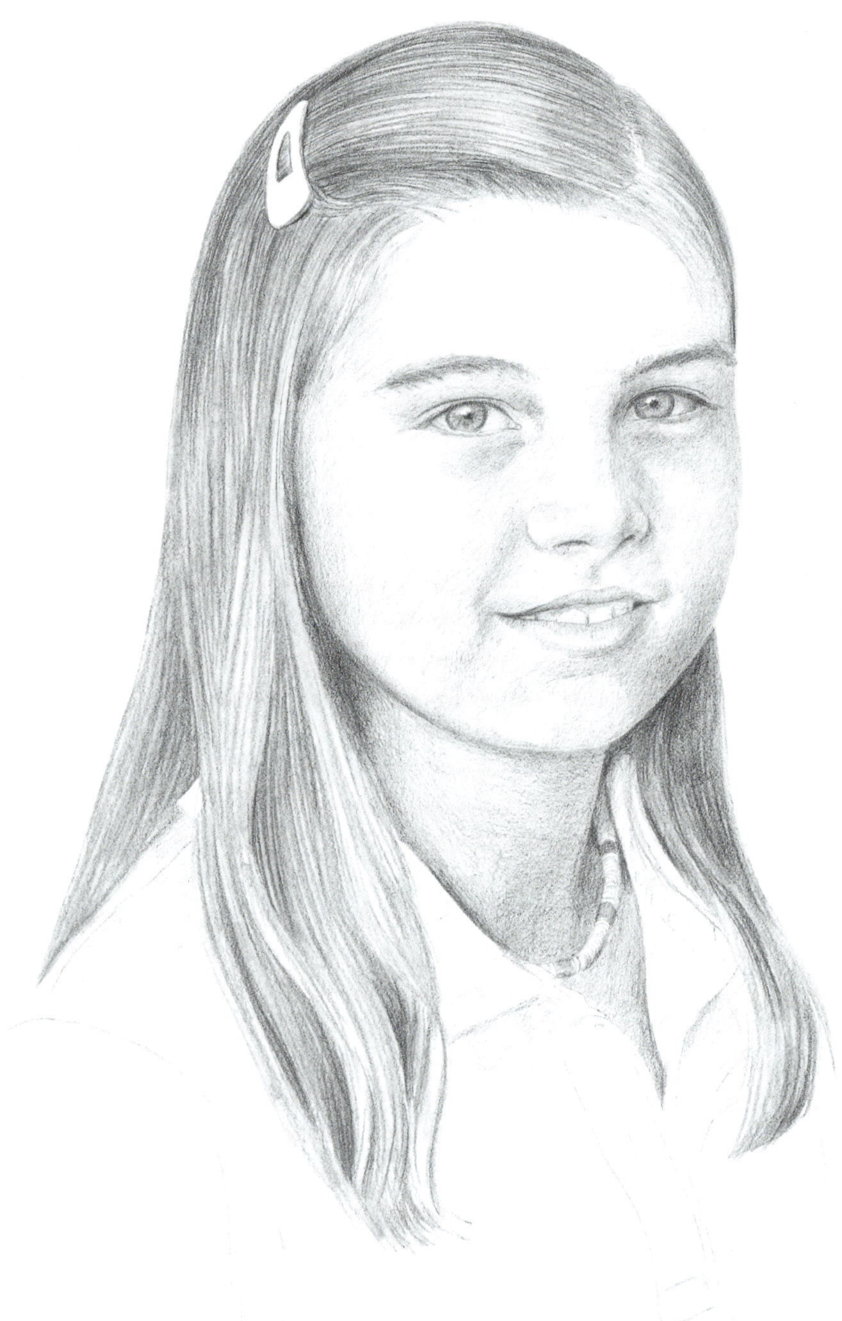

Step 5 At this point, the forms of the face are solidly established, so begin refining. Continue building up the tone of the silky hair, using a 4B for the darks and a 2B for the lights. Deepen the shadow areas between the face and the hair that will help give depth to the face. Use a kneaded eraser to delicately lift out where tones are built up too much—at times you may do as much work with your eraser as with a pencil! Deepen the eyebrows with short lines to show the variations in tone. Using radial strokes with a 2B, darken the irises. In the detailed areas where you need a sharper point, like the folds of the eyelids or the edges of the lips, use an HB. Continue to build up the neck, keeping it darker than the face to show the cast shadow. Shade the necklace, using separate, curved strokes to indicate the heavy fibers, and fill the smooth, dark beads with heavy, circular strokes.

DRAWING FROM A DIFFERENT ANGLE

Because of the way this young girl's head is tilted back, you see more of her chin and neck than you do the top of her head. The ears appear a bit lower on the head, and you see more of the bottom parts of her eyes. You can even see the underside of the upper eyelid beneath the eyelashes. Even when drawing children from a different angle, the features remain rounded and childlike. For example, you can still get a sense of this girl's wide-eyed, curious expression, although you see less of the eyes than you would in a forward-facing view. And although the nostrils are a little more prominent in this view, they still retain their soft, smooth shape.

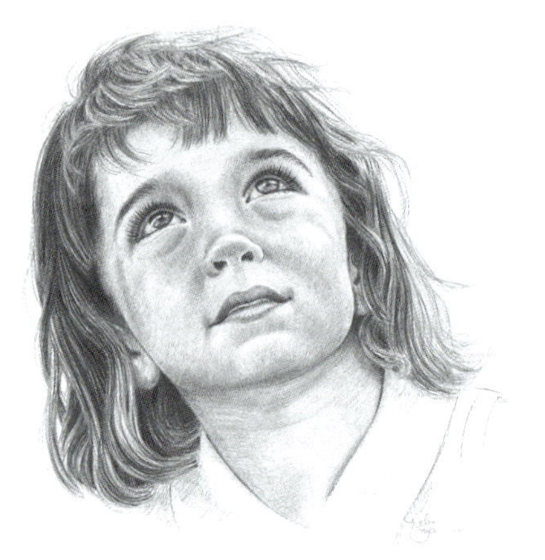

Step 6 Build up the tone of the hair and lightly shade the plastic barrette, putting in small cast shadows with a sharp point. Continue to crosshatch the face to refine the transition between the tones, while keeping the smoothness of her skin. Still use the HB, but also use a 2H in the lightest areas of the cheek. Deepen the upper and lower eyelashes with short lines. Refine the nose and mouth, using curved lines that are more prominent in the lower lip to give some texture. Deepen the tone of the gums, the lines between the teeth, and the shadow inside the mouth. For the fiber texture of the necklace, use a soft 6B to pick up a bit of the paper's grain. Lift out the sharp highlights of the metal beads. Finally work on the shirt, simulating the knit fabric with crosshatching. Add a line for the buttonhole and the round button.

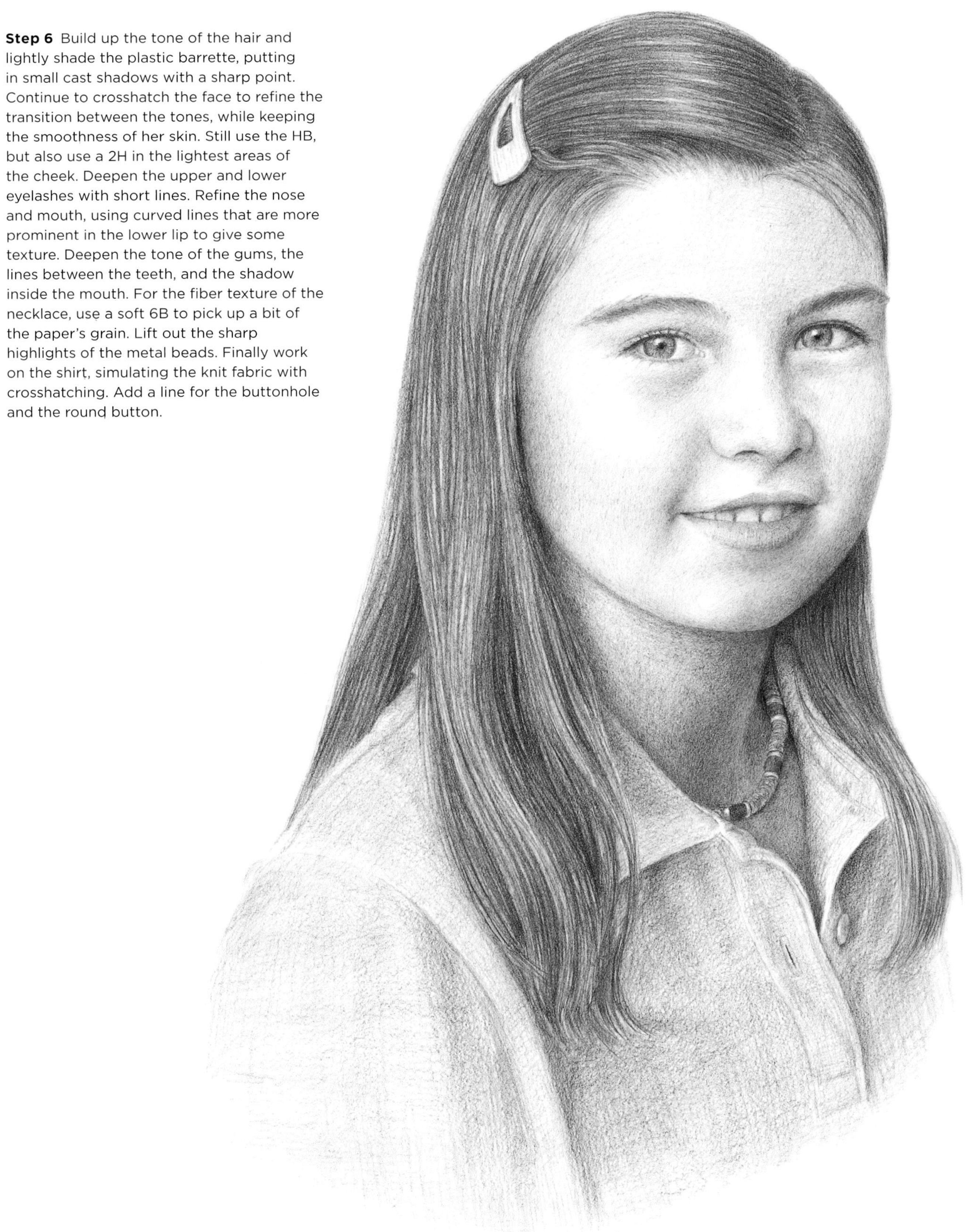

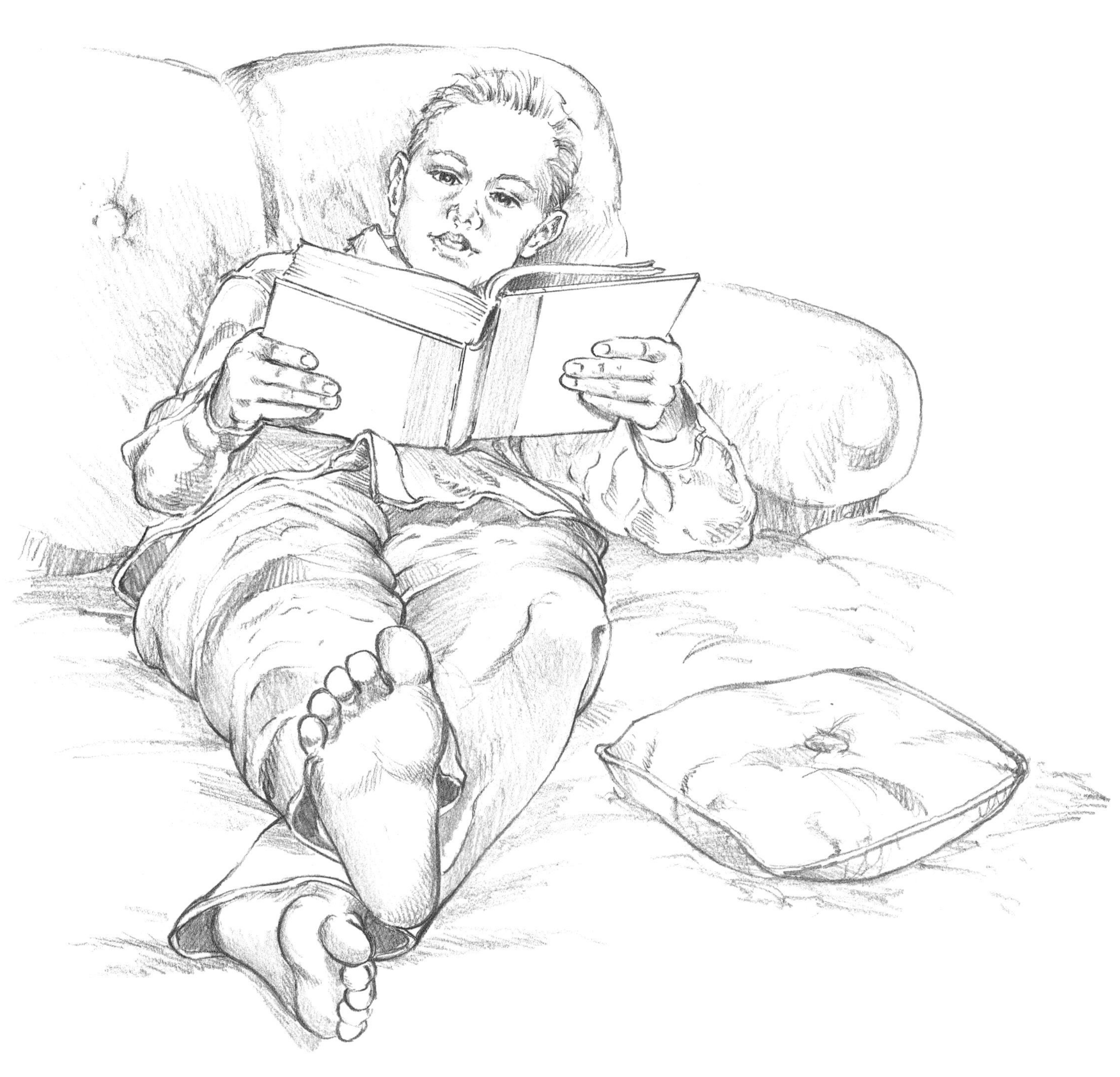

Drawing the Body

Even though it is very interesting to draw a face, it's only the rendering of the entire human body that completes a portrait. And although we all look very different, certain rules facilitate the artist's work. Our proportions follow certain norms, which an attentive observer will quickly understand. In this chapter, you will learn more about human anatomy and test your skills by following quick exercises. You will also discover how simple sketches allow you to grasp and render even the most complex movements. You will also discover optical foreshortening and learn many other tricks used by experienced artists.

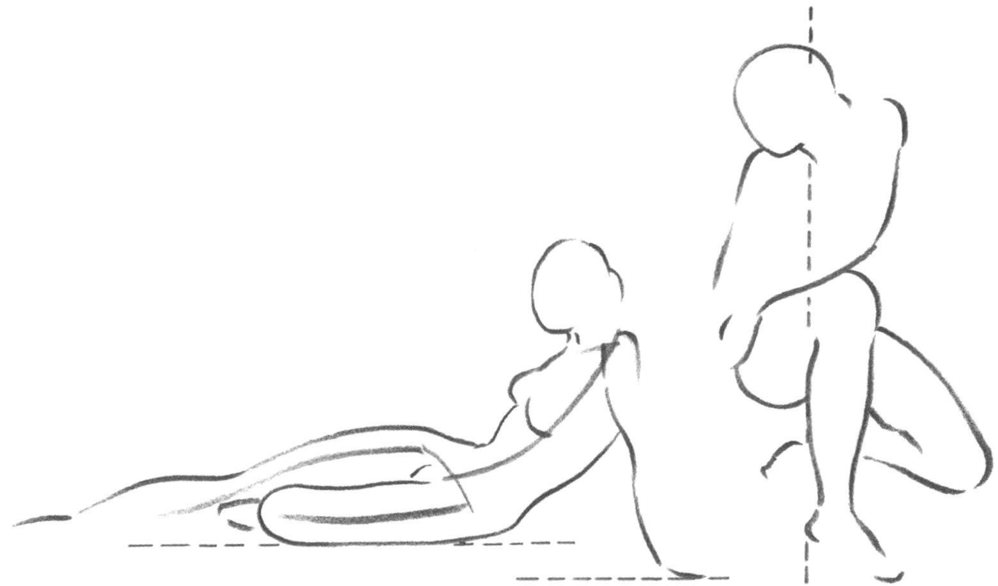

Figures in Action

To draw the human figure from head to toe, it helps to know something about the skeletal and muscular framework. Many art classes have students draw skeletons, which is good practice in visualizing how all the parts fit together. You don't have to try that exercise; simple drawings will suffice. But do start with simple stick figure sketches. Then once you have the proportions right, you can flesh out the forms.

CAPTURING ACTION

A gesture drawing is a quick, rough sketch that illustrates a moment of an action. The idea is just to capture the gesture—it isn't about trying to get a likeness. Give yourself 10 minutes to draw the entire figure engaged in a sport or full-body activity, working either from life or from a photo. Set a timer, and stop when the alarm goes off. Working against the clock teaches you to focus on the essentials and get them down on paper quickly.

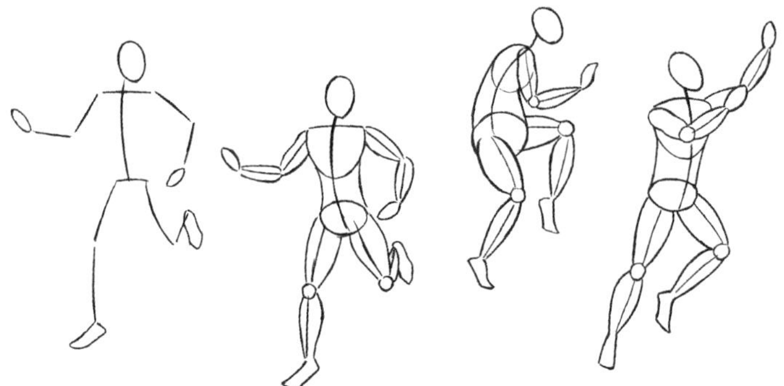

Using Basic Shapes and Forms The human figure can be broken down into several basic shapes. To help you see the human body in three-dimensional form, practice building a figure with cylinders, boxes and spheres.

Developing Gesture Drawings Start with a simple stick figure to catch the motion; then add circles and ovals and flesh out the forms.

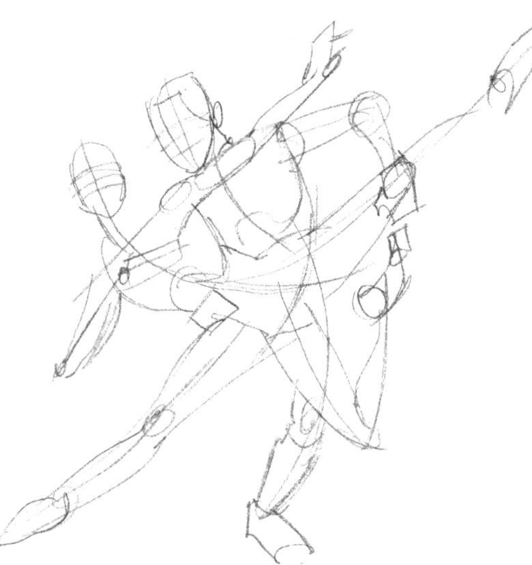

Suggesting Movement First sketch in diagonal center lines for the arms and legs, adding ovals and circles for the heads and joints. Then rough in the general outlines.

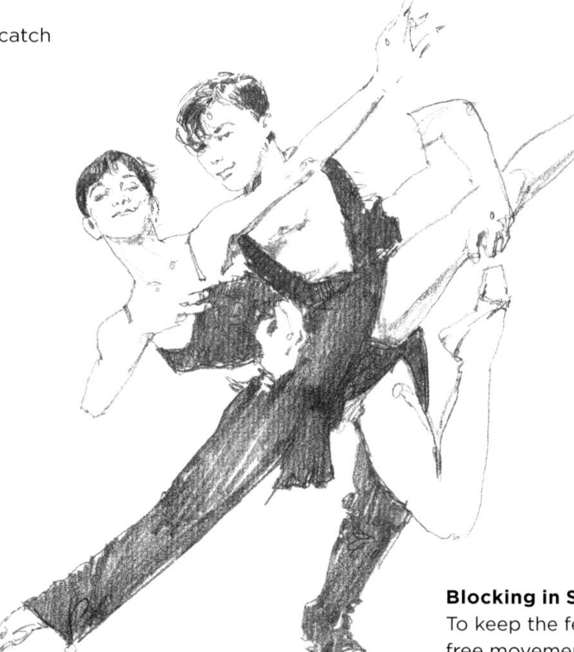

Blocking in Shadows To keep the feeling of free movement, don't draw perfectly refined lines and shadows. Instead, focus on making delicate outlines for the dancers, and quickly lay in broad, dark strokes for their clothing.

DRAWING SPORTS FIGURES

Sports figures are one of the best subjects for action drawings. Begin by drawing the action line. Then, build the rest of the figure around that line, paying careful attention to the way the body maintains its balance. It wouldn't do to have an athlete appear to fall over!

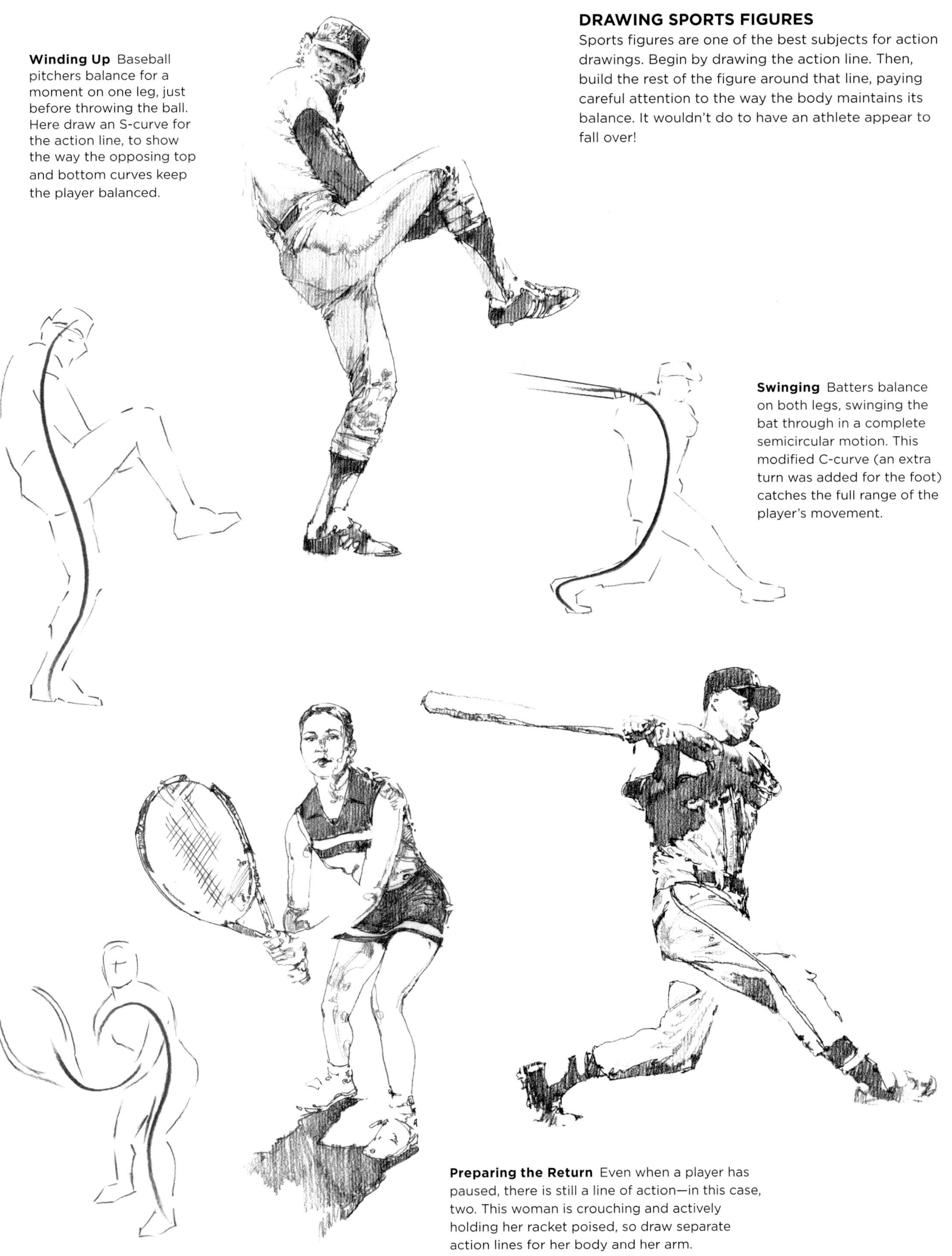

Winding Up Baseball pitchers balance for a moment on one leg, just before throwing the ball. Here draw an S-curve for the action line, to show the way the opposing top and bottom curves keep the player balanced.

Swinging Batters balance on both legs, swinging the bat through in a complete semicircular motion. This modified C-curve (an extra turn was added for the foot) catches the full range of the player's movement.

Preparing the Return Even when a player has paused, there is still a line of action—in this case, two. This woman is crouching and actively holding her racket poised, so draw separate action lines for her body and her arm.

Adult Body Proportions

The proportional measurements of the parts of the human body vary slightly for every person, making them unique. Paying attention to these variations will help you render accurate likenesses. But first, it's important to understand how we're all the same by studying the average proportions of the human body, which are apparent when we look at the skeletal and muscular views of the body. When drawing a figure, we measure in "heads": the vertical distance from the top of the head to the chin. Use rough measurements to help place the parts of your figure. If a head or other body part appears too large or too small, you can check the body's proportions to correct the problem.

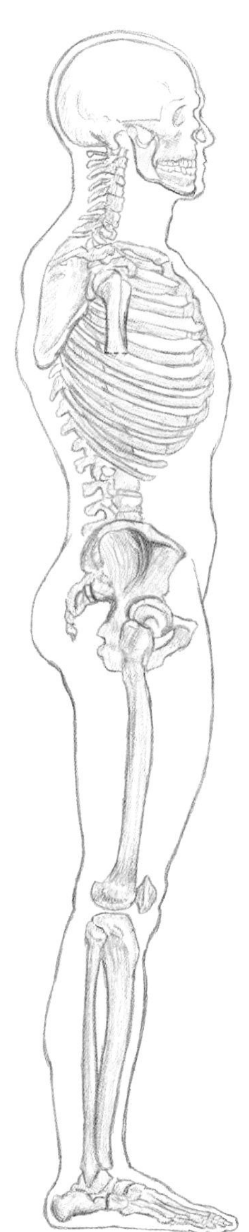

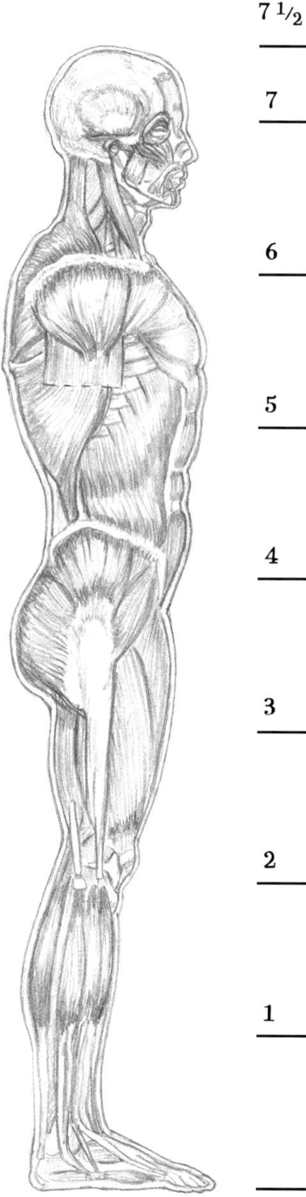

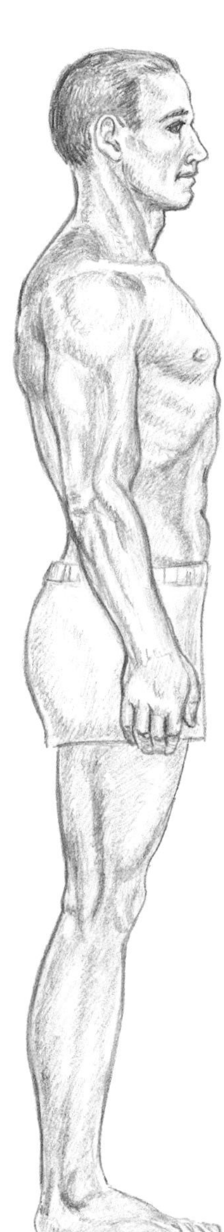

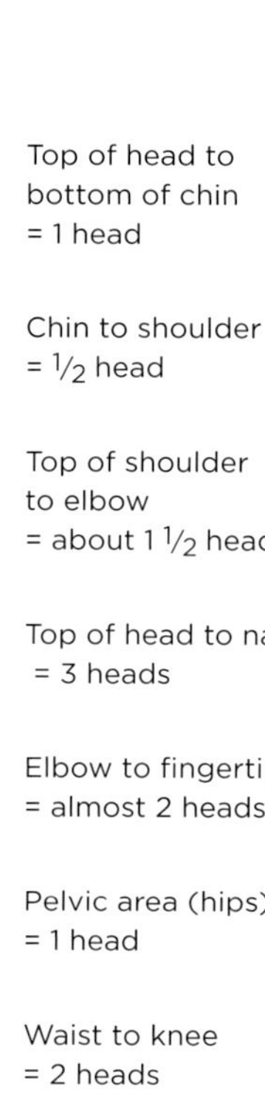

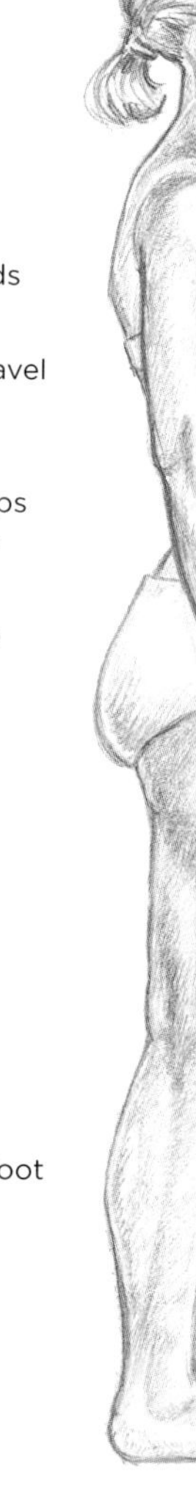

Skeletal Structure By studying bone structure, we can clearly see the relationship of the length of each part of the body to the whole.

Body Musculature Proportion doesn't apply to length alone—the thickness of the body also must be proportionate. This aspect of proportion varies depending on the fitness of the individual, but the drawing above will help you assess these proportions based on ideal human musculature.

Male Proportions The average male is approximately 7 1/2 heads high; of course, these proportions vary with different body types. Often artists use an 8-head-high figure for the male as an ideal proportion.

Female Proportions The average female is about half a head shorter than the male, or 7 heads high. Artists often elongate the female figure, especially in fashion drawings. Generally, the female has narrower shoulders and a smaller waist than a male, but proportionally wider hips.

Child Body Proportions

The illustrations at the bottom of the page explain how to use the size of the head as a measuring unit for drawing children of various ages. If you're observing your own model, measure exactly how many heads make up the height of the subject's actual body.

Begin the drawing below by lightly sketching a stick figure in the general pose. Use simple shapes such as circles, ovals, and rectangles to block in the body. Smooth out the shapes into the actual body parts, and add the outline of the clothing.

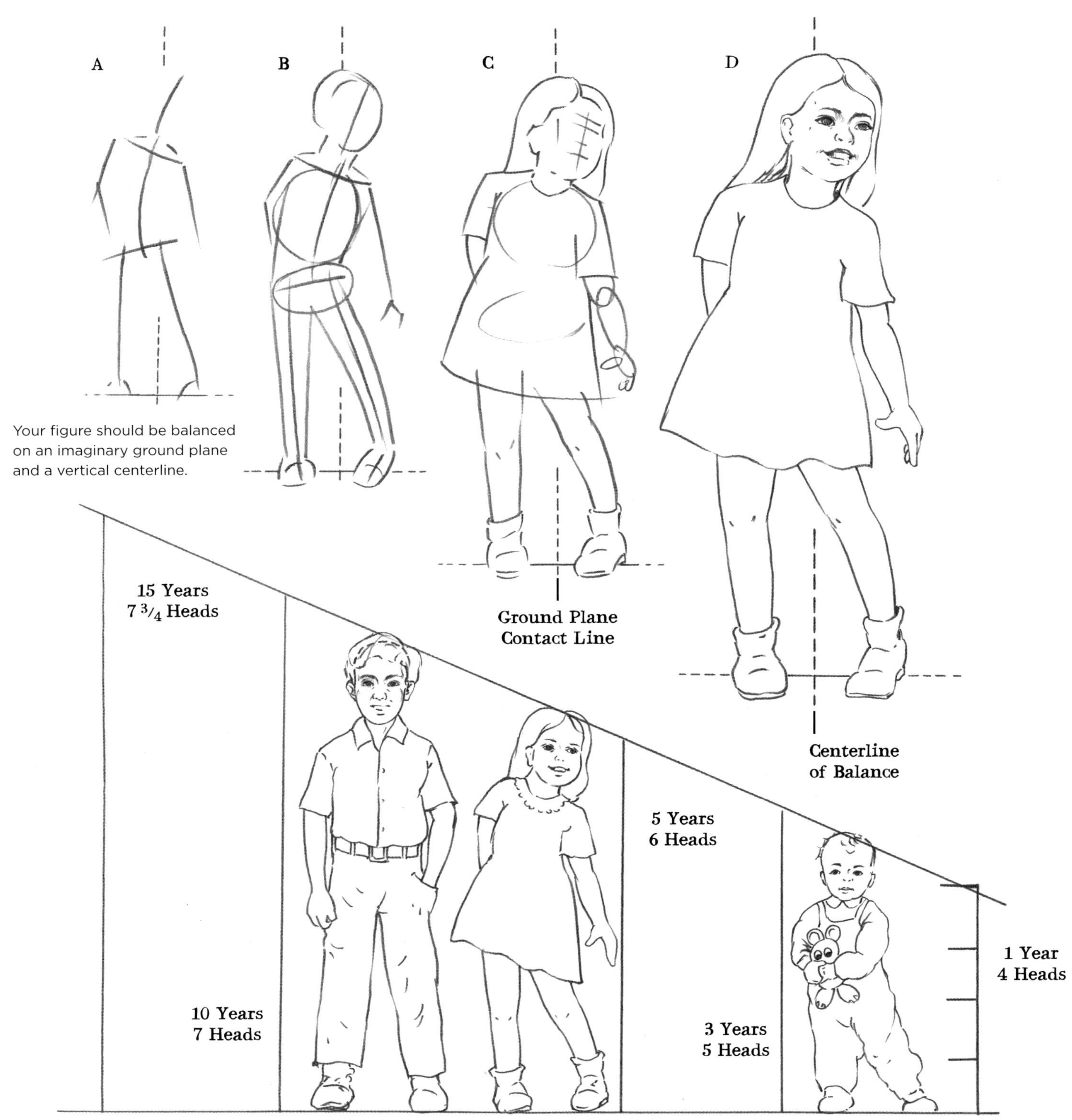

Exploring the Torso

FRONT VIEW

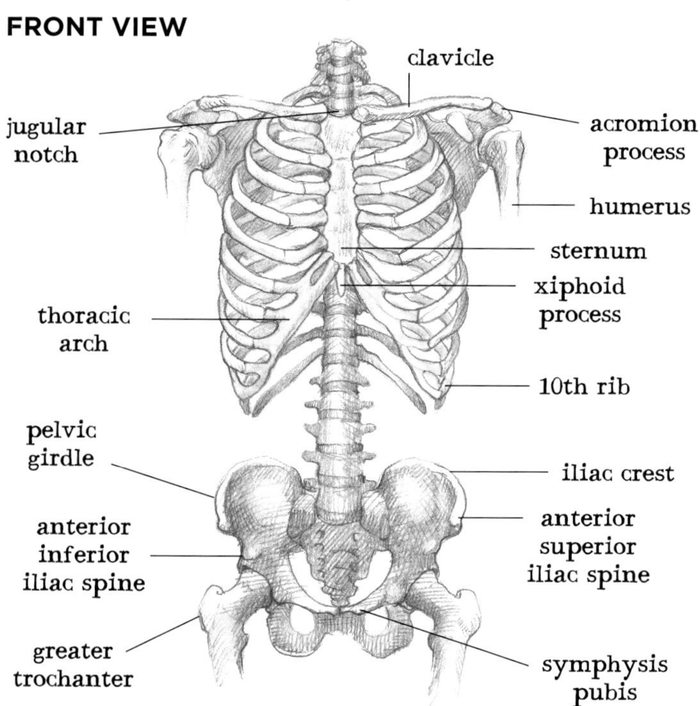

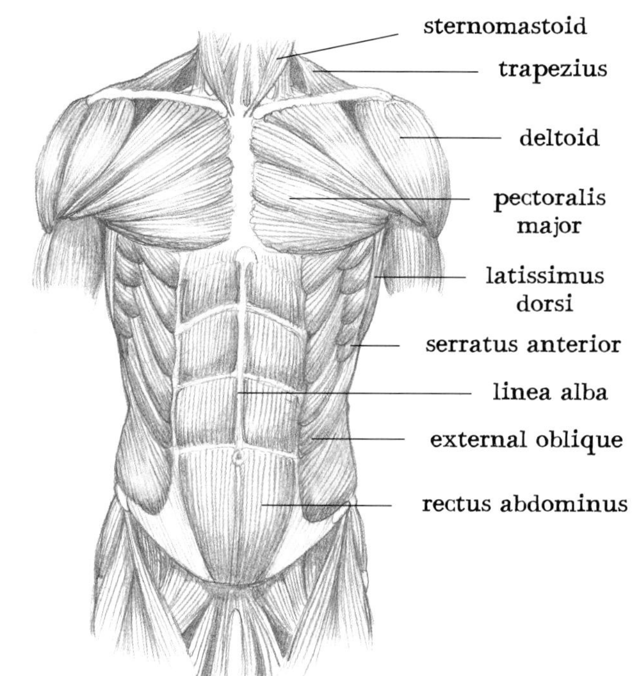

Skeleton Some parts of the skeletal system are important to the artist because they are prominent and serve as visual landmarks. Several bones of the torso's frontal skeleton are obvious even beneath the skin, including the clavicles, acromion processes, sternum, thoracic arch, 10th rib, anterior superior iliac spines, and greater trochanters. The spinal column comprises 24 vertebrae, divided into 3 sections: The cervical (or neck) region has 7 vertebrae, the thoracic (or chest) region has 12, and the lumbar (or lower back) region has 5.

Trunk Muscles The torso's movement is dependent on and restricted by the spine—both the chest and the pelvis twist and turn on this fixed, yet flexible, column. And the relationship between the rib cage, the shoulders, and the pelvis creates the shape of the trunk muscles. The pectoral (breast) muscles are divided by the sternum, the rectus abdominus is divided by the linea alba, and the external obliques—which are interwoven with the serratus anterior—bind the eight lowest ribs to the pelvic girdle.

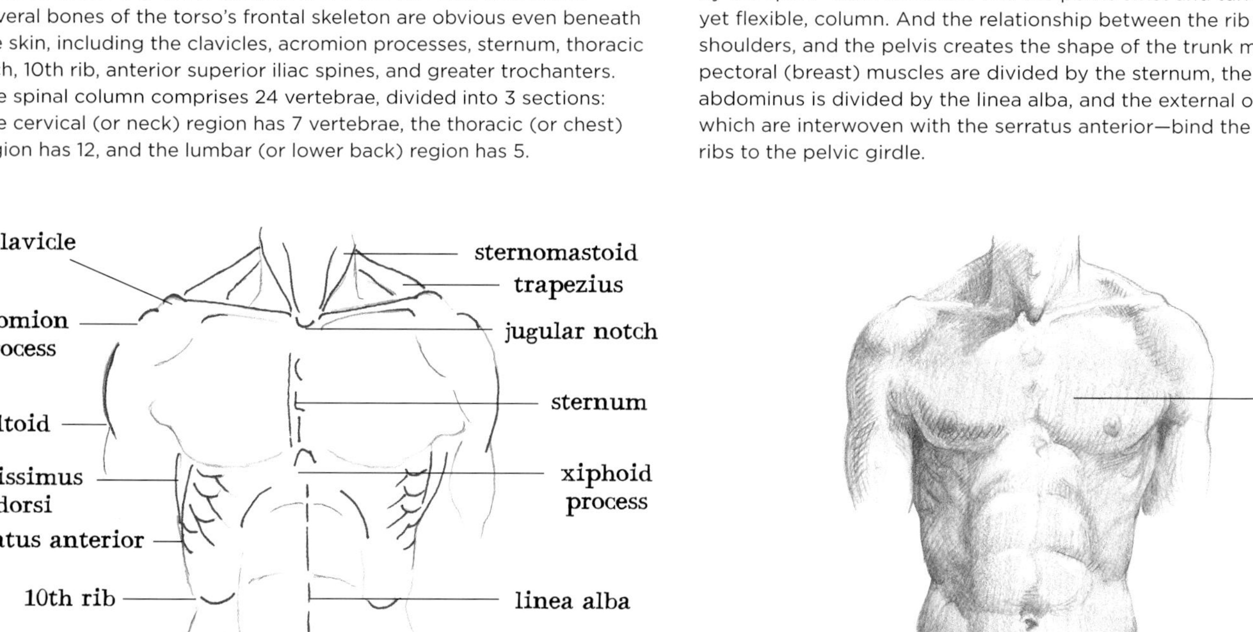

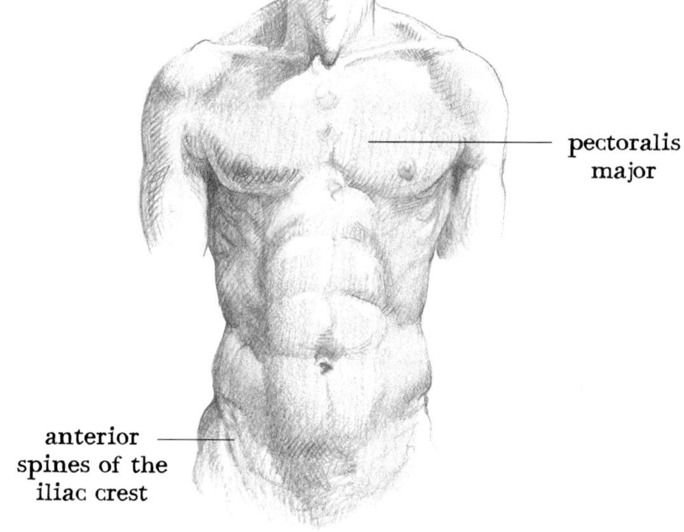

Diagram of Landmarks The observable muscles and bony landmarks labeled on the illustration above are the most important for artists who want to draw the torso's surface anatomy from the front view. Focus on accurately portraying these anatomical features to achieve a lifelike drawing, such as the example at right.

Drawing Tips Use the bony skeletal landmarks, which are apparent despite the layers of muscles, to guide the placement of the features. For example, the nipples align vertically with the anterior spines of the iliac crest. Note also that the pectoralis major sweeps across the chest and over to the arm, ending nearly horizontal to the nipples.

BACK VIEW

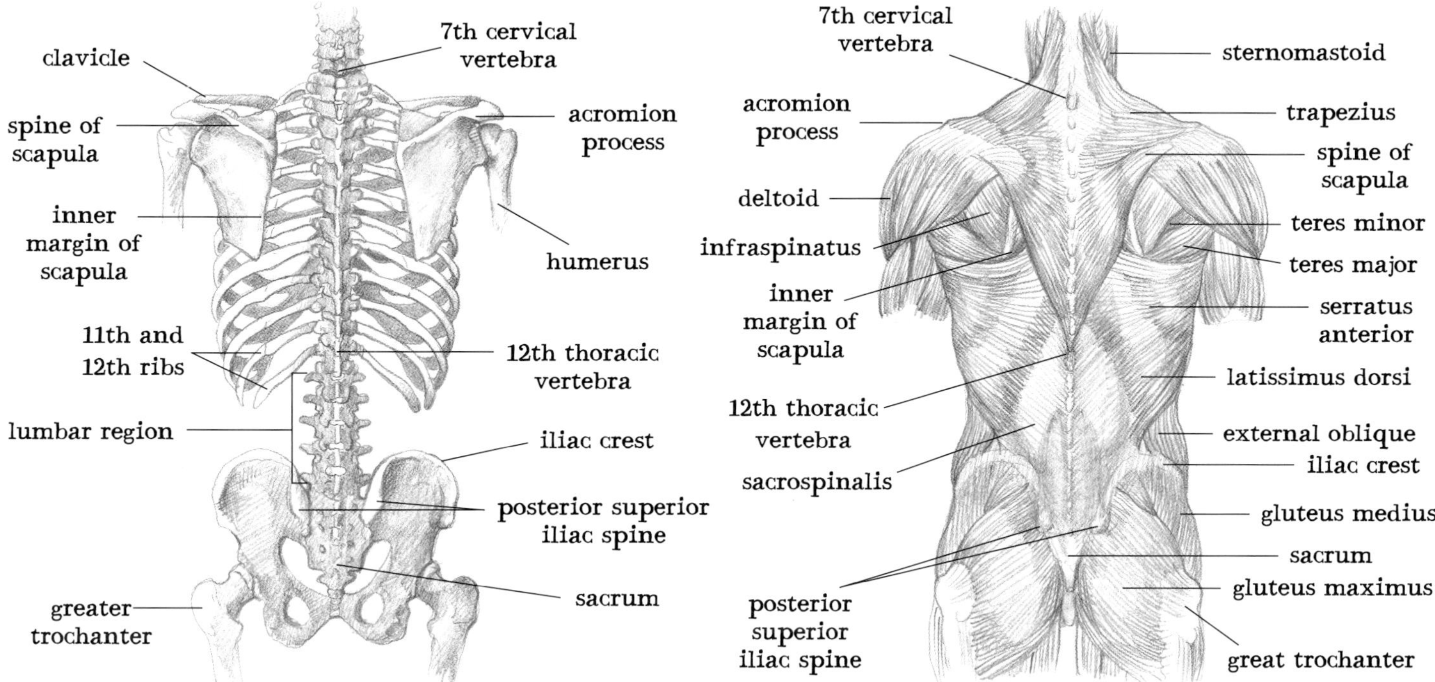

Skeleton The back is one of the most challenging parts of the body to draw because of its skeletal and muscular complexity. From the artist's point of view, the most important bones visible from the rear skeletal view are the 7th cervical vertebra, the posterior superior iliac spines (dimples on the pelvic girdle), and the sacrum, which together form the sacral triangle—a major anatomical landmark at the base of the spine.

Trunk Muscles The back has many overlapping muscles; our focus will be on the upper layer, which is more immediately apparent to the eye. The trapezius connects the skull to the scapula (shoulder blade) muscles—deltoid, infraspinatus, teres minor, and teres major—which connect to the arm. The latissimus dorsi attaches under the arm, extending to the pelvis. And the gluteus medius bulges at the hip before meeting with the gluteus maximus.

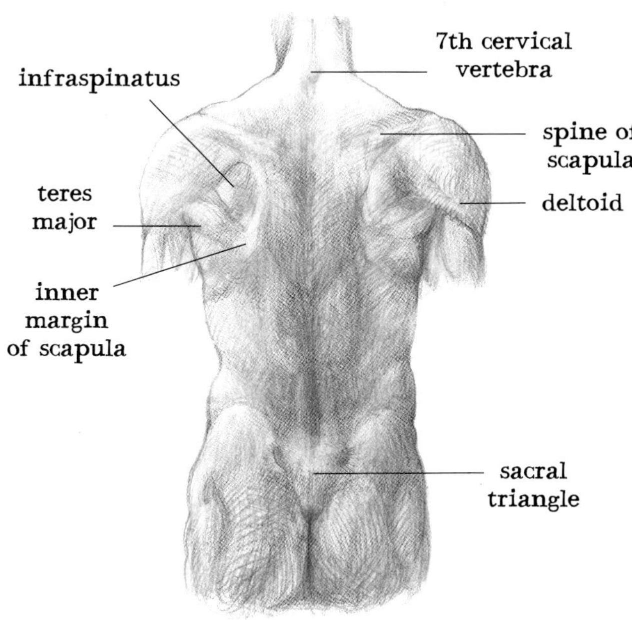

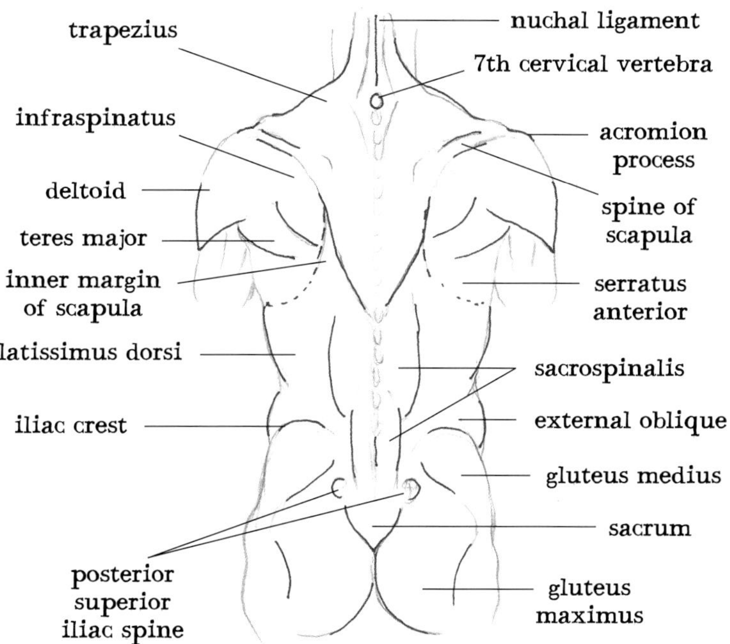

Drawing Tips Under the skin, back muscles are not easy to discern. However, the trapezius, 7th cervical vertebra, spine of scapula, inner margin of scapula, deltoid, infraspinatus, and teres major are all fairly evident. To depict the nuchal ligament, 7th cervical vertebra, spinal column, and sacral triangle, draw a long line and an inverted triangle.

Diagram of Landmarks The observable muscles and bony landmarks labeled on the illustration above are the most important for artists who want to draw the torso's surface anatomy from the rear view. Focus on accurately rendering these anatomical markers to achieve a lifelike drawing, such as the example at left.

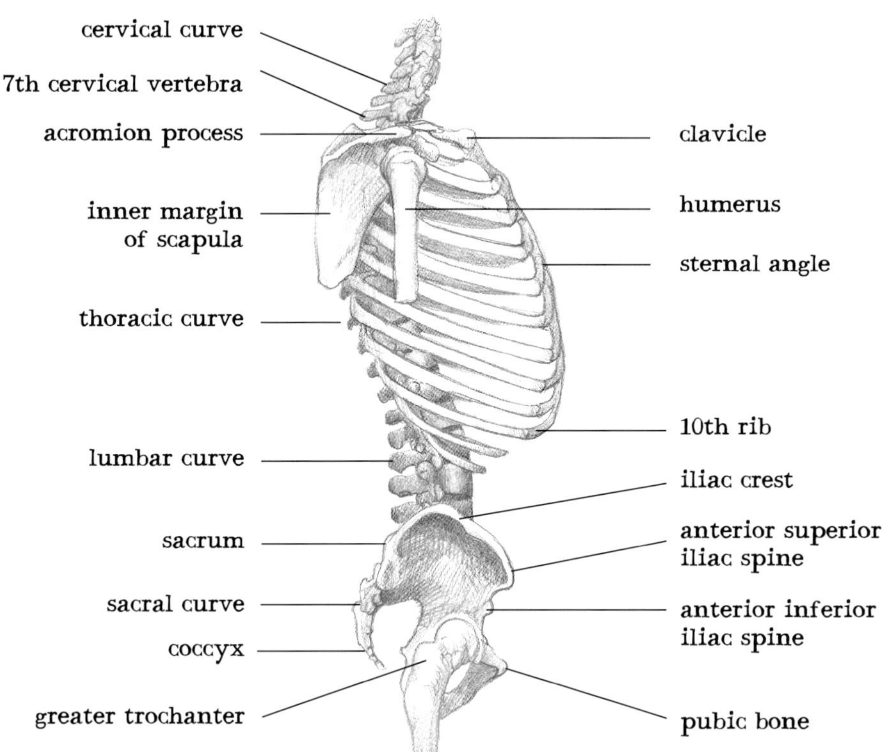

Skeleton The visual landmarks of the skeleton in profile are the 7th cervical vertebrae, acromion process, inner margin of scapula, and backbone. The backbone's four curves—cervical (forward), thoracic (backward), lumbar (forward), and sacral (backward)—arrange the head, chest, and pelvic girdle over the legs for balance.

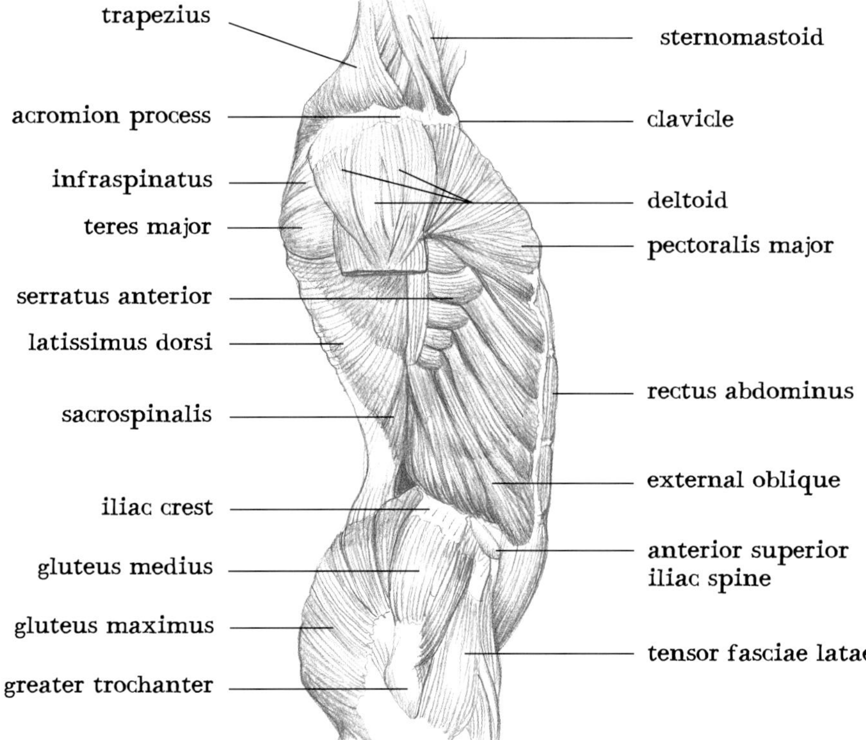

Trunk Muscles The upper torso muscles—as well as the scapula, which is anchored by muscle to the spine, ribs, and arms—follow and influence all arm movement. Mid-torso muscles, such as external oblique, rectus abdominus, and latissimus dorsi, bend, twist, and stabilize the rib cage and pelvis. Muscles below the pelvic girdle activate the legs.

Studying the Body

The human body is challenging to render; therefore, it's important to start with a quick drawing of the basic skeletal structure. The human skeleton can be compared to the wood frame of a house: It supports and affects the figure's entire form.

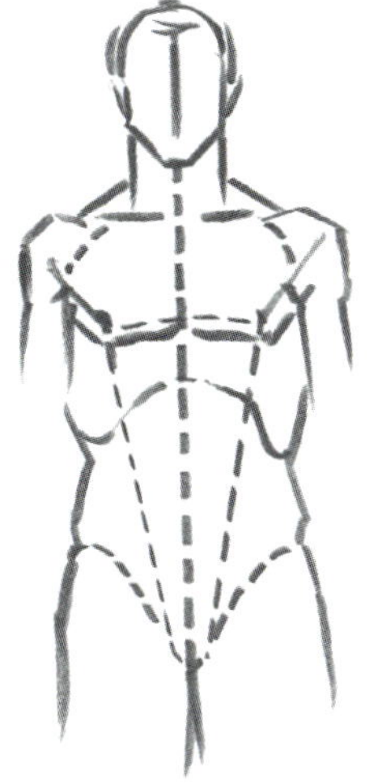

Frontal View

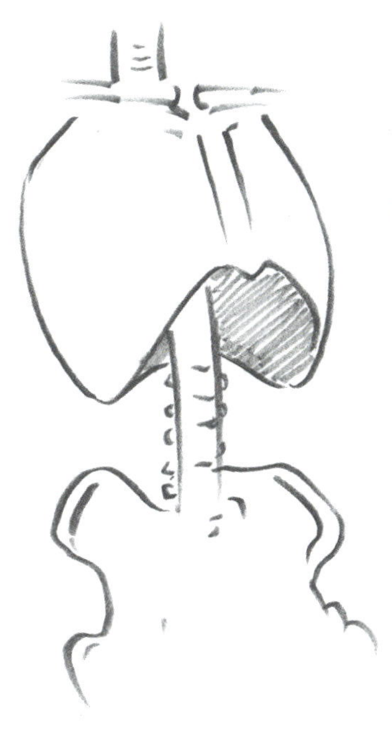

Torso forms into triangle shape.

Basic Skeletal Structure

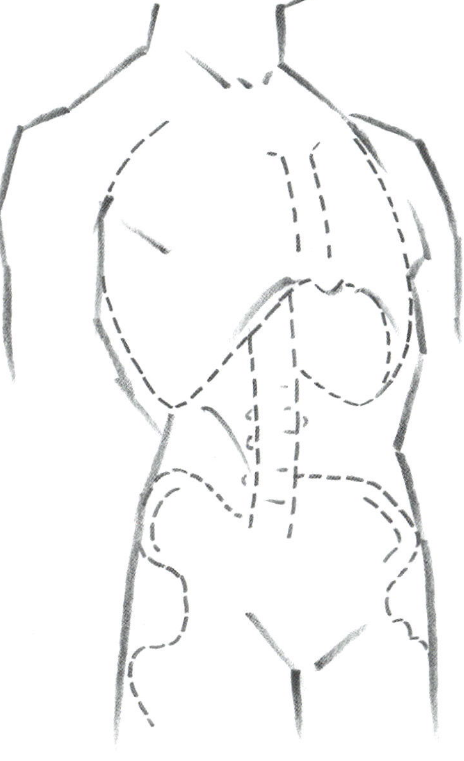

Skeletal Structure Inside Body

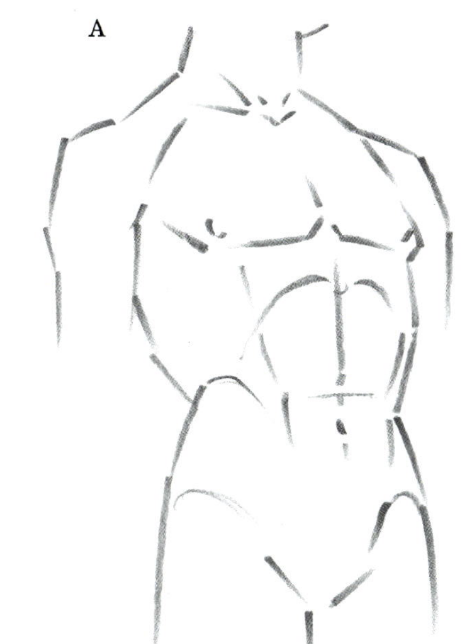

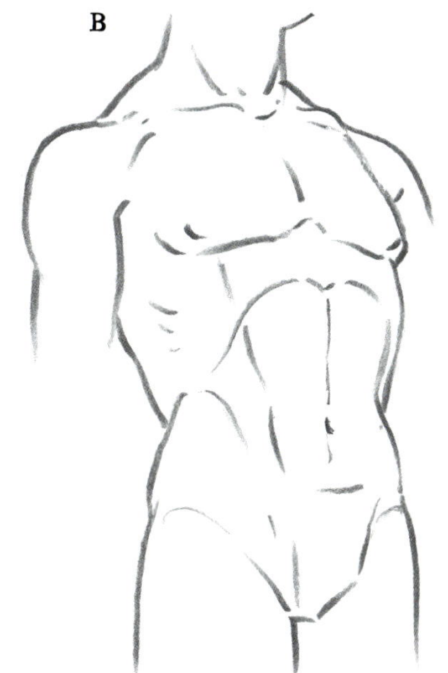

EXERCISE: DRAWING THE BODY

The frontal view illustrates the planes of the body that are created from the skeleton's form. In men's bodies especially, the torso forms a triangle shape between the shoulder blades and the waist. In women's torsos, the triangle shape is generally less pronounced, and their bodies can even resemble an inverted triangle. In other words, the widest part of the body may be at the hips.

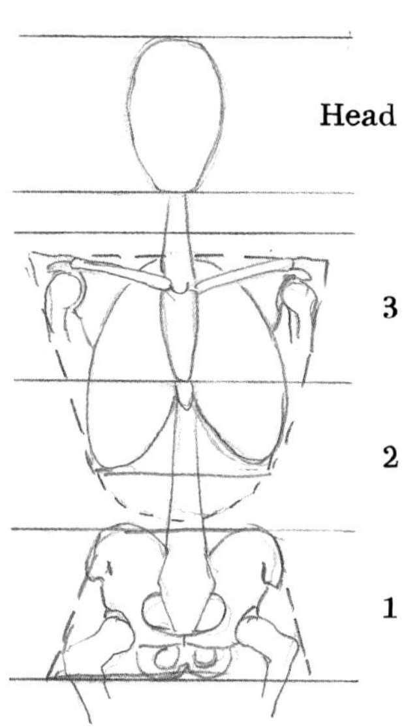

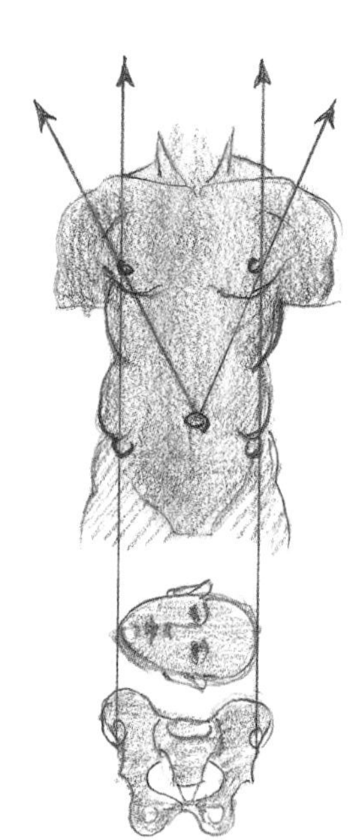

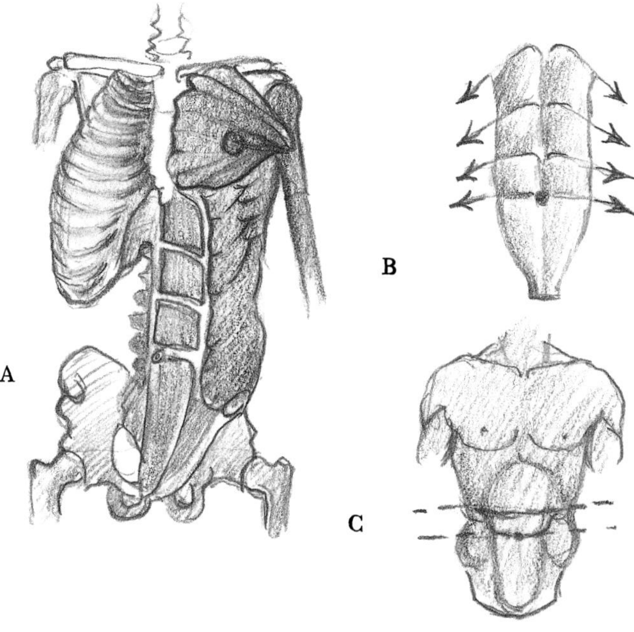

Proportion The pelvic girdle is about 1 head high, and the torso—from trochanters to 7th cervicle vertebra—is about 3 heads high.

Tips The nipples, 1 head-width apart, are vertically aligned with pelvic landmarks and diagonally aligned with the *acromion processes.*

Detail Note the relationship between the skeletal and muscular structures (A). The *linea alba* (interrupting tendons) of the *rectus abdominis* create a "six pack" appearance as they arch progressively higher toward the *sternum* (B). Two of the interrupting tendons line up with the 10th rib and the navel (C).

BACK VIEW

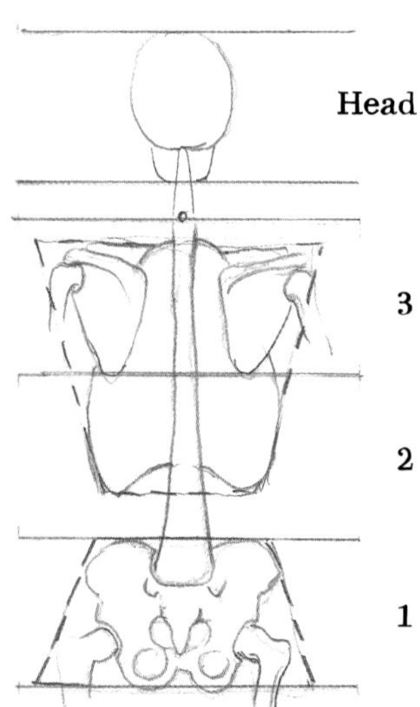

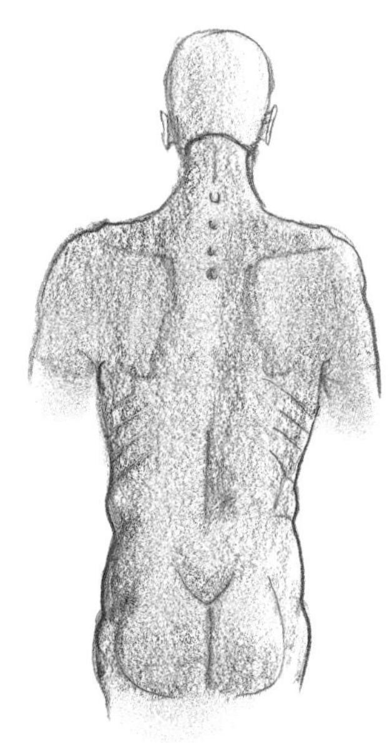

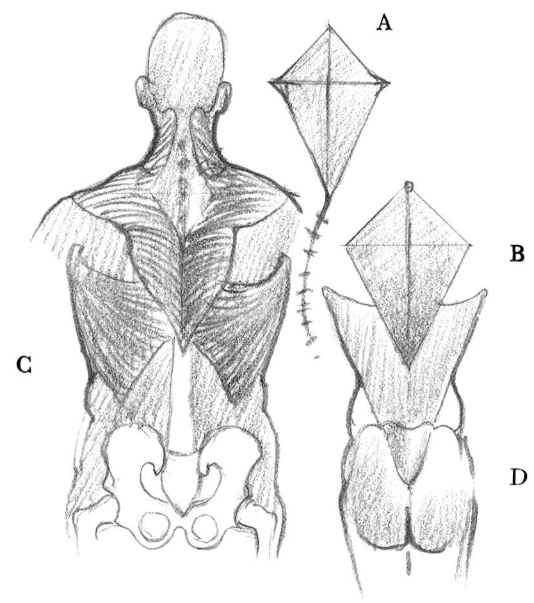

Trapezoids represent the overall bone structure of the torso from both front and rear views. Here you can see the same three-part division.

On an erect figure, the bones of both the lower ribs and the upper spine are apparent, while the *lumbar* region looks like a furrow.

The shape of the *trapezius* is similar to that of a kite (A) or a four-pointed star (C). The simplified shape of the *latissimus dorsi* suggests the appearance of an upside-down triangle (B), with a diamond-shaped sheath removed from its upside-down apex (D).

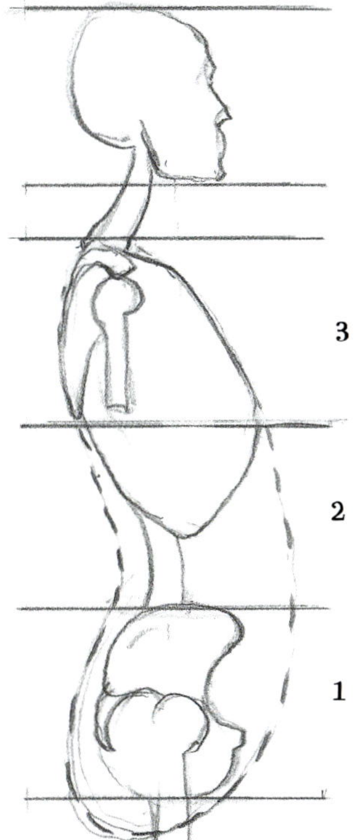

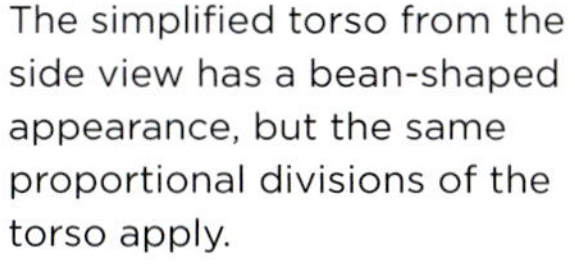

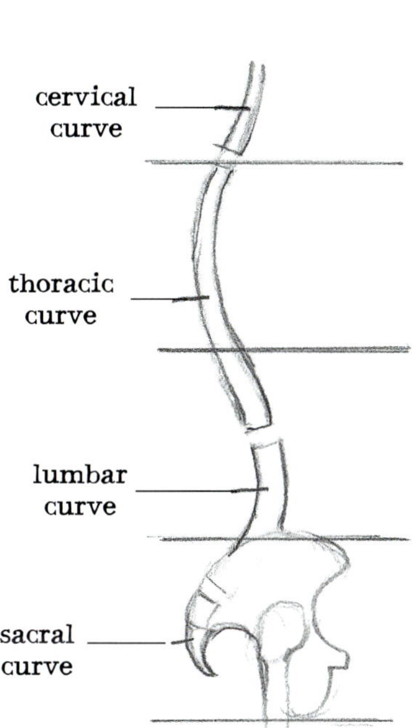

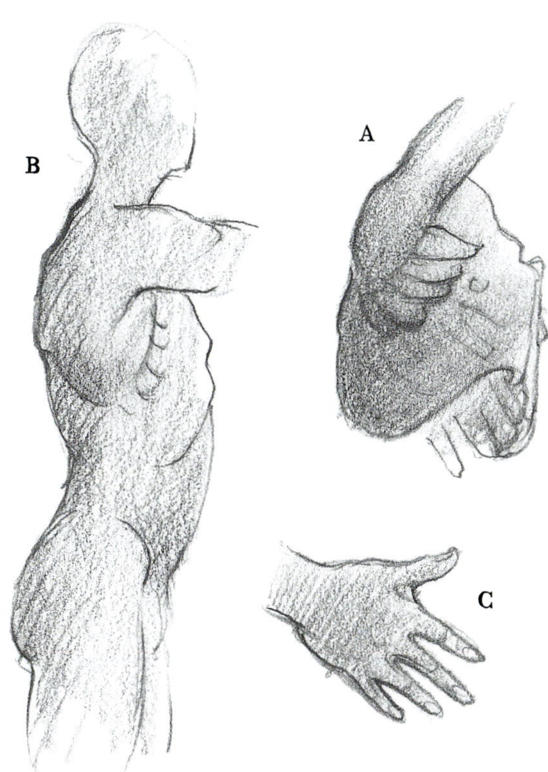

The simplified torso from the side view has a bean-shaped appearance, but the same proportional divisions of the torso apply.

Each spinal segment curves more as the column descends toward the *sacrum.* The *thoracic* region has the longest curve.

The serratus anterior muscle starts alongside the first eight ribs, then ends at the inner margin of the *scapula* (A). Its main mass appears as a bulge underneath the *latissimus dorsi* (B). At the muscle's origin (on the ribs), it looks a little like the fingers of a hand (C).

EXERCISE: UNDERSTANDING THE BODY'S SHAPE

Try to repeatedly draw these three views of the body until you are familiar with the basic body shape in all three views: front, back, and side. Being able to conceive a figure with a few strokes and simple shapes is the best base for any figure drawing. When drawing the back view, pay attention to an important detail of the body's balance—the line between the neck and the middle of the pelvis' sacrum. The standing side view reveals a bean shape and several ovals.

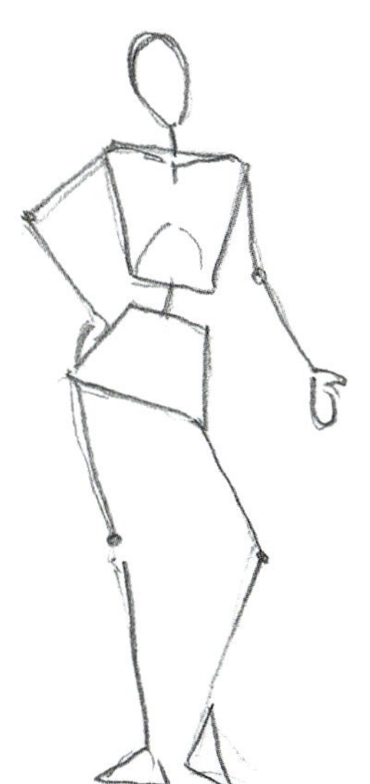

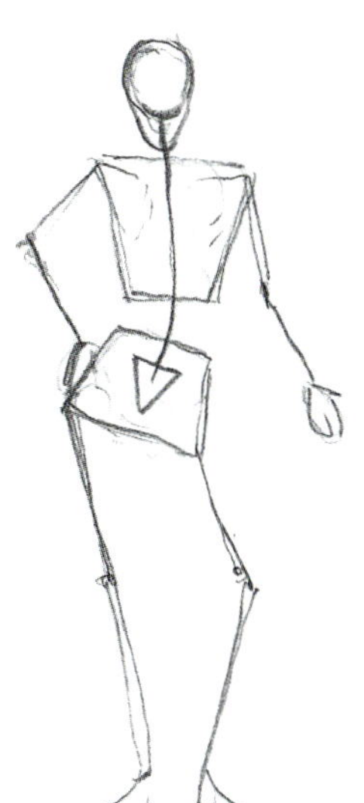

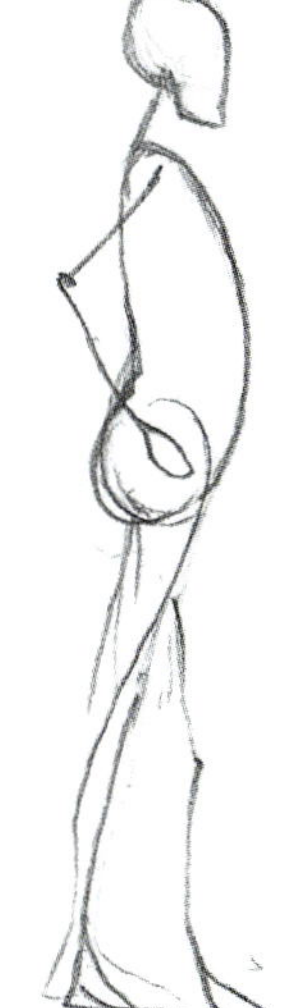

Front View   **Back View**   **Side View**

Drawing the Arm

FRONT VIEW

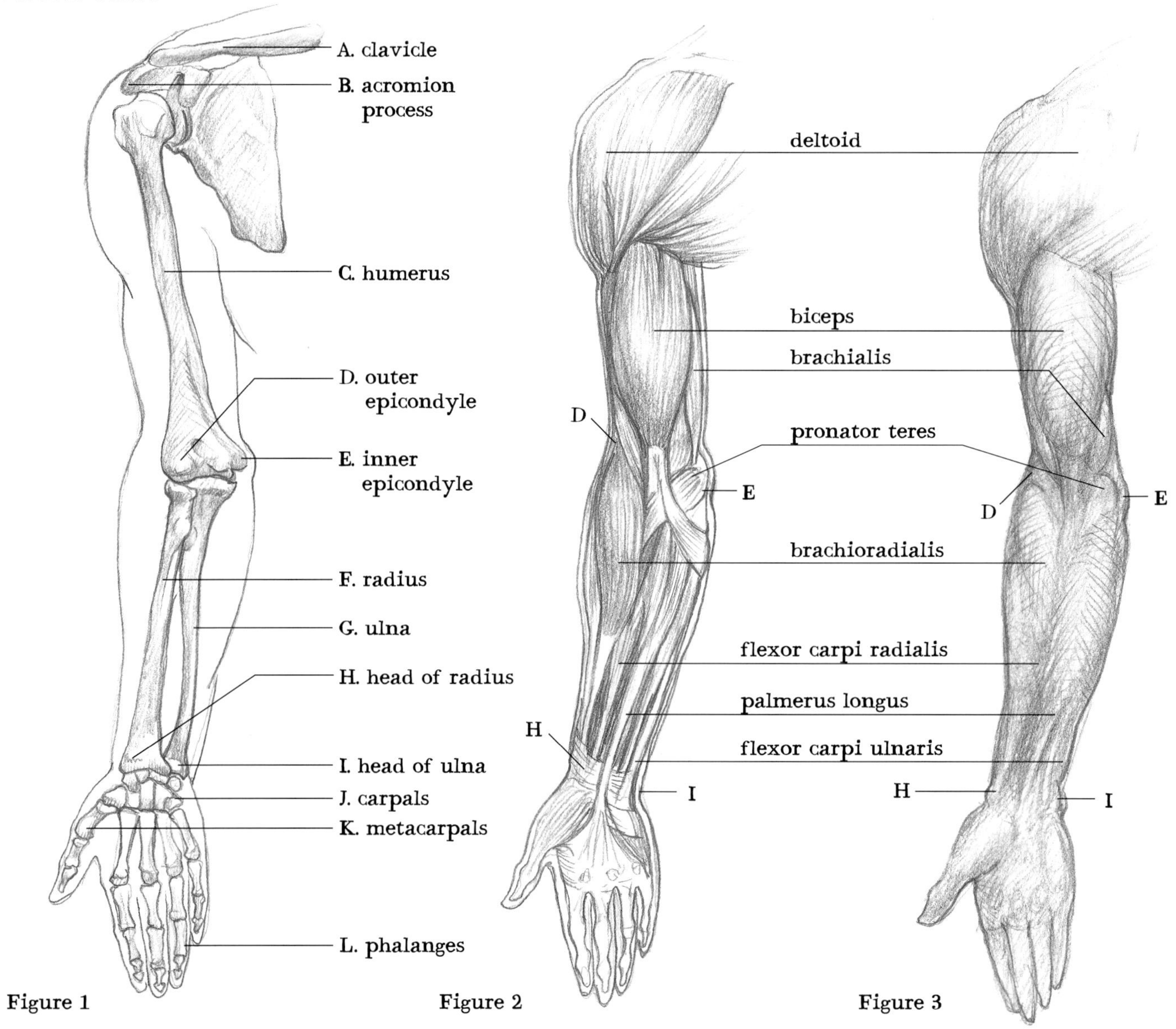

A. clavicle
B. acromion process
C. humerus
D. outer epicondyle
E. inner epicondyle
F. radius
G. ulna
H. head of radius
I. head of ulna
J. carpals
K. metacarpals
L. phalanges

Figure 1

deltoid
biceps
brachialis
pronator teres
brachioradialis
flexor carpi radialis
palmerus longus
flexor carpi ulnaris
D
E
H
I

Figure 2

deltoid
biceps
brachialis
pronator teres
D
E
H
I

Figure 3

Bones The underlying skeletal structure determines much of the overall shape of the arm (figure 1). Several elements of this substructure, such as the inner epicondyle (E), act as visual landmarks that are identifiable even under layers of muscle (figure 2) and skin (figure 3).

Muscles The upper and lower portions of the arm each consist of three major muscle masses. The bicep and brachialis of the upper arm bend the lower arm, the tricep straightens it, and the deltoid raises the entire arm. In the lower arm, the flexors (flexor carpi radialis, palmerus longus, and flexor carpi ulnaris) bend the palm and clench the fingers; the extensors on the back of the arm straighten the palm and open the fingers; and the supinators, attached to the outer epicondyle (D, figure 1) on the outside arm, rotate the hand outward. A fourth, smaller muscle, the pronator teres, rotates the palm inward.

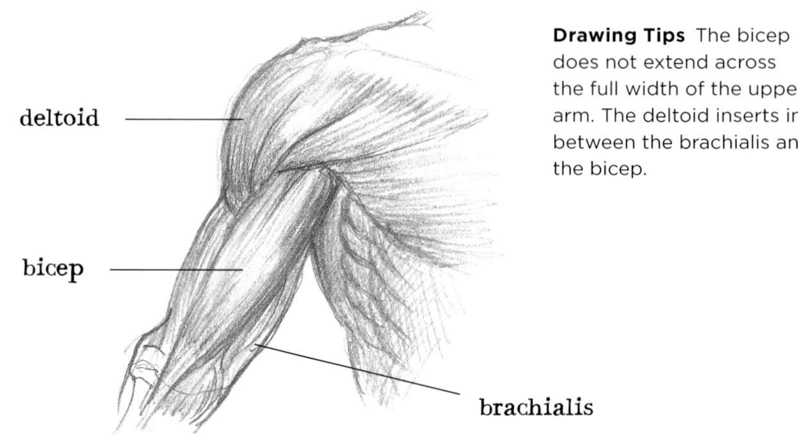

Drawing Tips The bicep does not extend across the full width of the upper arm. The deltoid inserts in between the brachialis and the bicep.

BACK VIEW

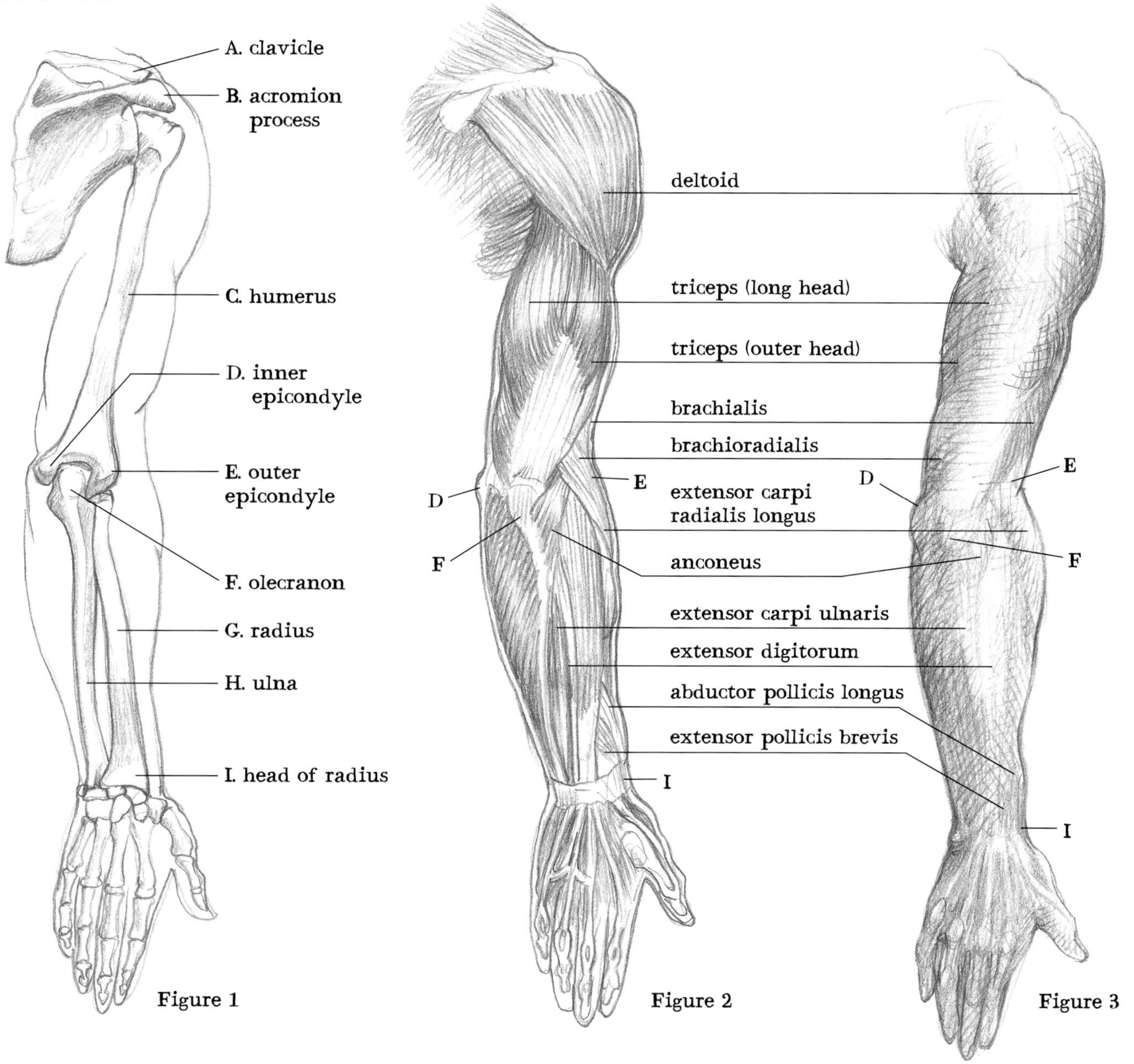

Figure 1

A. clavicle
B. acromion process
C. humerus
D. inner epicondyle
E. outer epicondyle
F. olecranon
G. radius
H. ulna
I. head of radius

Figure 2

deltoid
triceps (long head)
triceps (outer head)
brachialis
brachioradialis
D
E
extensor carpi radialis longus
F
anconeus
extensor carpi ulnaris
extensor digitorum
abductor pollicis longus
extensor pollicis brevis
I

Figure 3

E
D
F
I

Bones Much of the overall shape of the arm in the back view is determined by the underlying skeletal structure, just as with the front view. The inner and outer epicondyle (D and E), are again identifiable, even under layers of muscle. And from this view, the olecranon, or elbow (F), is also evident.

Muscles Muscles work in opposing pairs: Flexors pull and extensors extend, moving in the opposite direction. When a flexor or extensor muscle becomes active, its opposite becomes passive. From the back view, when the hand is pronate (illustrated in figures 2 and 3), extensor groups are the most prominent muscles. On the upper arm, the tricep is the most visible extensor. On the lower arm, extensor carpi radialis longus, extensor carpi ulnaris, and extensor digitorum, which all originate on the outer epicondyle, are evident.

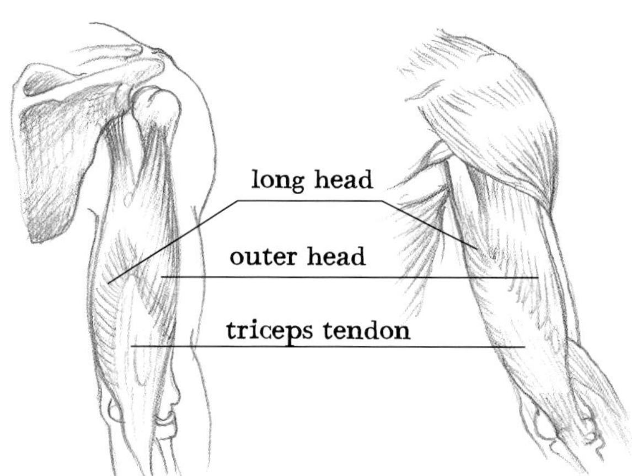

Drawing Tips The tricep has three heads (the long and outer heads are shown here; the medial head lies beneath). All share a common tendon: a flattened form on the back of the upper arm.

SIDE VIEW: CLENCHED FIST

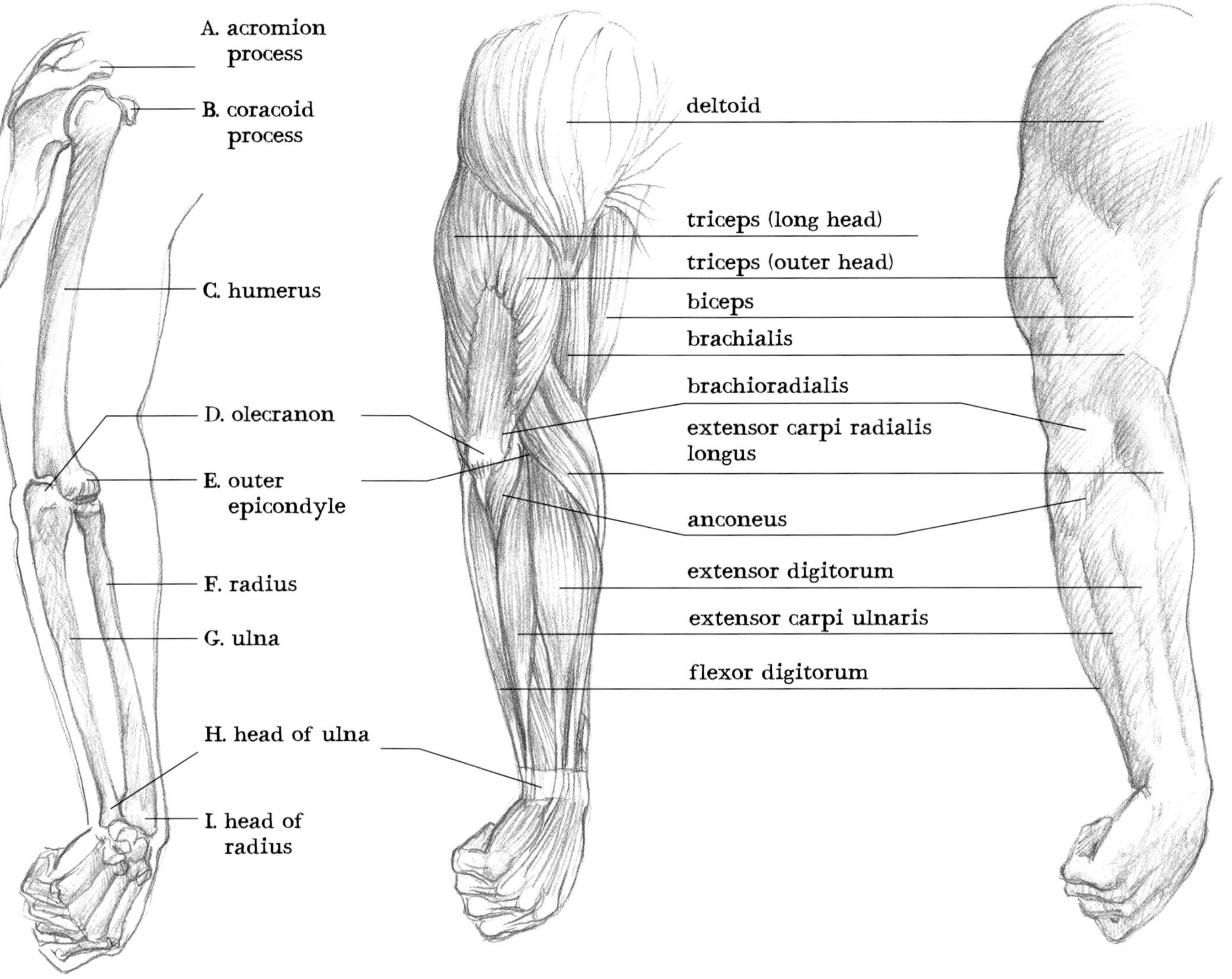

A. acromion process

B. coracoid process

C. humerus

D. olecranon

E. outer epicondyle

F. radius

G. ulna

H. head of ulna

I. head of radius

deltoid

triceps (long head)

triceps (outer head)

biceps

brachialis

brachioradialis

extensor carpi radialis longus

anconeus

extensor digitorum

extensor carpi ulnaris

flexor digitorum

Bones Here the arm is not viewed in full profile; rather, it is seen from an angle that is a combination of a side view and a back view. Because of the angle, the bony landmarks most apparent under the muscle are the olecranon, outer epicondyle, and head of ulna.

Muscles The side view provides a good angle for observing the extensors and flexors of the upper and lower arm. The brachioradialis, located where the upper and lower arms meet, is particularly important. It originates on the lateral side of the humerus (C), above the outer epicondyle (E), and then attaches to the lateral side of the wrist above the head of the radius (I).

Rotated Arm

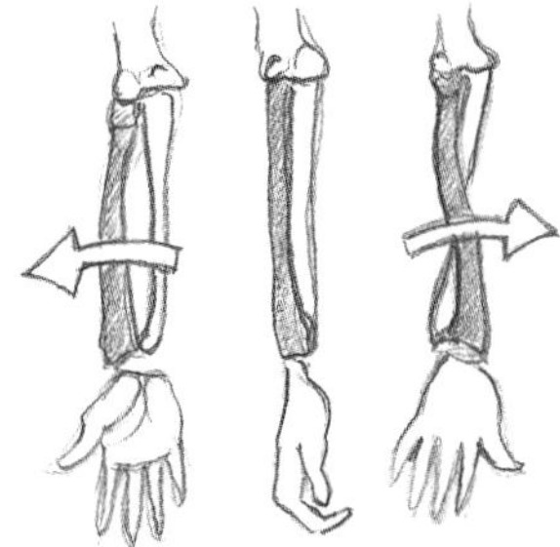

The brachioradialis is responsible for turning the palm up (supinate), and the pronator teres for turning the palm down (pronate). The radius (shaded) rotates around the fixed ulna, permitting pronation and supination of the palm.

Bent Arm

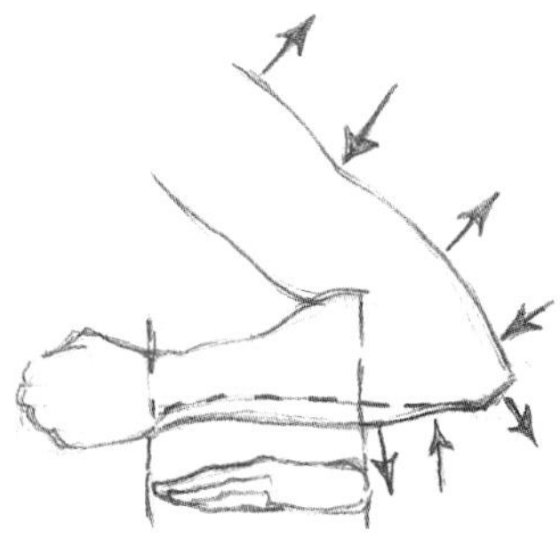

The span between the inside bend of the elbow and the wrist is usually about one hand length. The arrows show the inward and outward curvature of the muscles, and the dashed line shows the line of the ulna, called the "ulnar furrow."

Drawing the Leg

FRONT VIEW

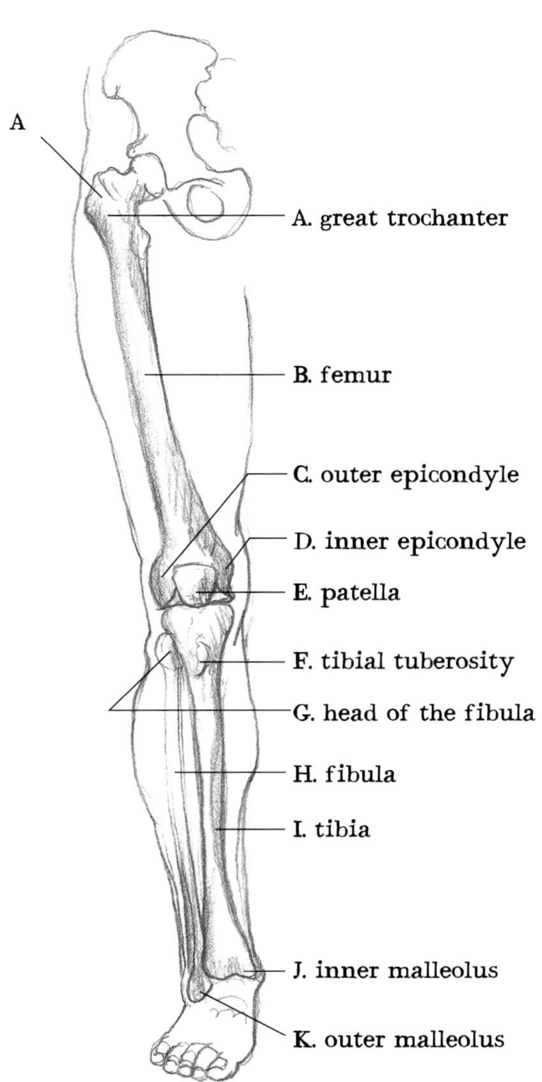

Figure 1

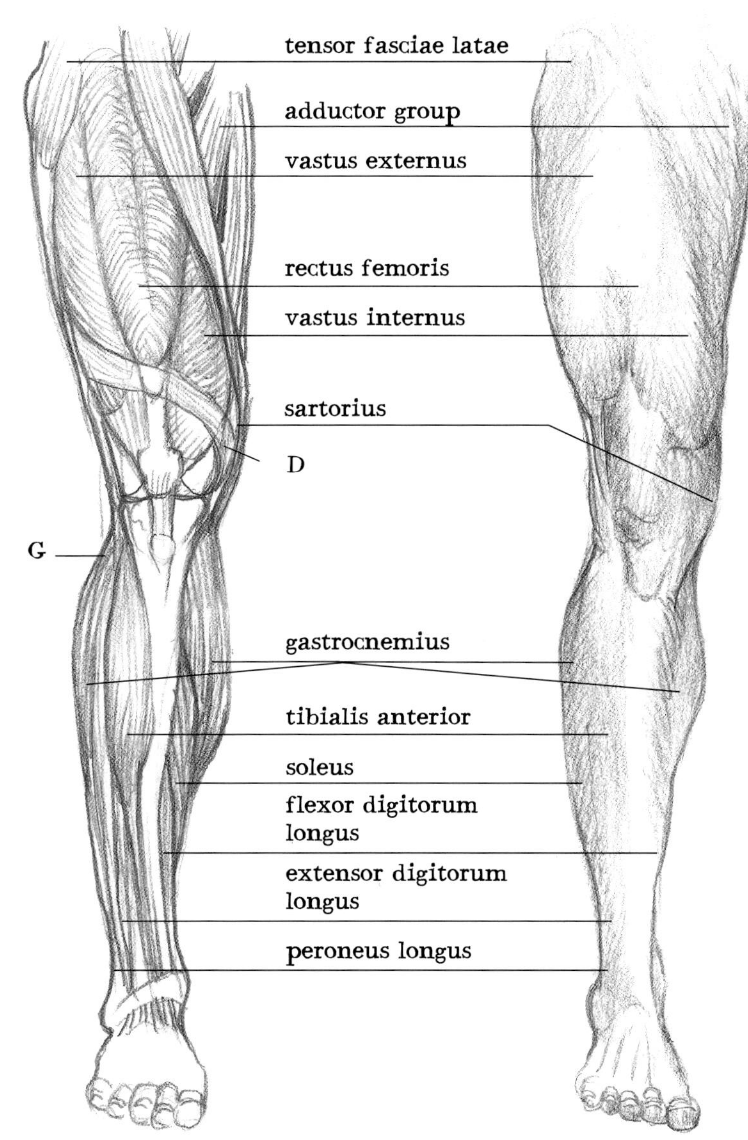

Figure 2   Figure 3

Bones The femur (B), with its great trochanter at the top (A) and outer epicondyles (C) and inner epicondyles (D) at the base, is the heaviest and longest bone of the skeletal system. The knee cap (patella) sits in between the outer epicondyles and inner epicondyles on the patellar surface. The lower leg consists of the thick tibia (I) and the slender fibula (H). The tibial tuberosity (F) and head of the fibula (G) are important landmarks at the top, as are the ankle bones (the inner malleolus and outer malleolus).

Muscles The upper leg has four major muscle masses: vastus externus, which attaches to the knee cap (E); rectus femoris, which engulfs the patella (E) and continues toward the tibial tuberosity (F); vastus internus, a medial bulge; and the adductor group on the inside of the leg. There are also two other masses: the tensor fasciae latae and the sartorius. The sartorius is the longest muscle in the body. The lower leg has six long muscles visible: gastrocnemius, protruding on both sides; tibialis anterior, running along the shin toward the big toe; soleus; flexor digitorum longus; extensor digitorum longus; and peroneus longus.

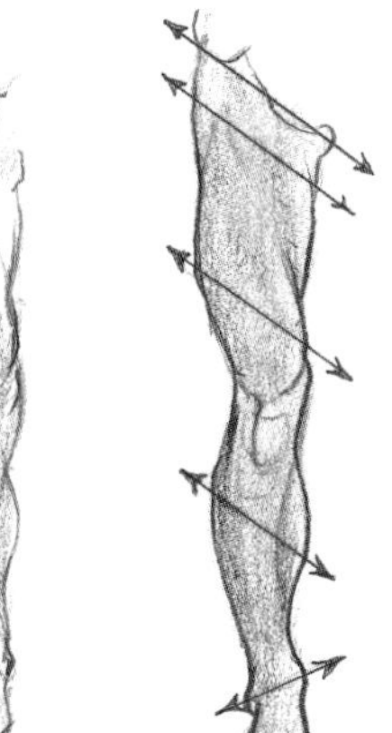
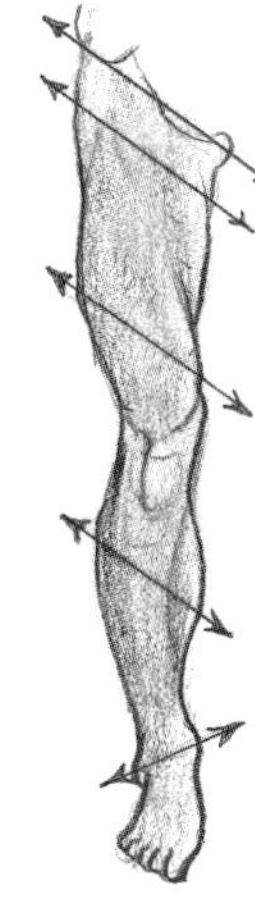

Figure 1   Figure 2   Figure 3

Drawing Tips The legs angle in toward the middle, positioning the body's weight over the gravitational center. (See figures 1 and 2.) The muscle masses on the outside of the leg are higher than those on the inside. (See figure 3.) The ankles are just the reverse—high inside, low outside.

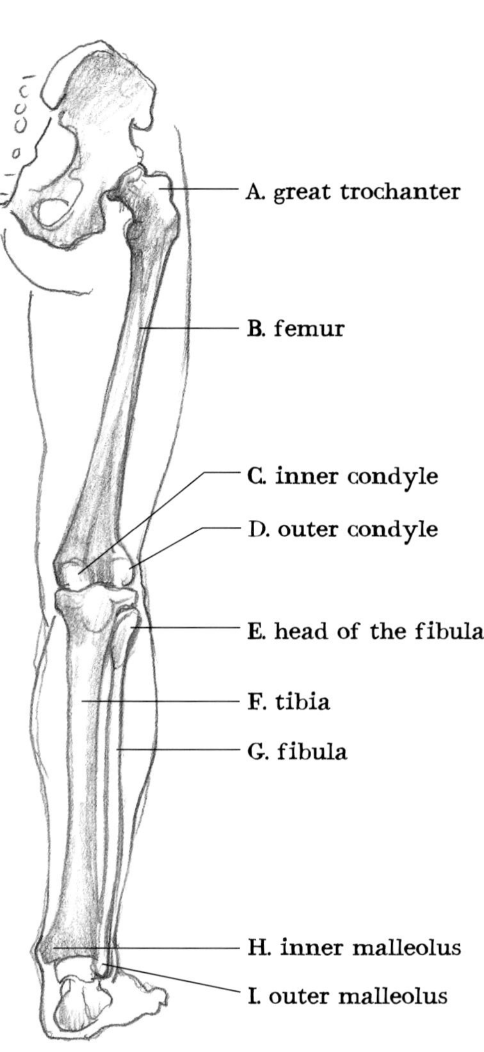

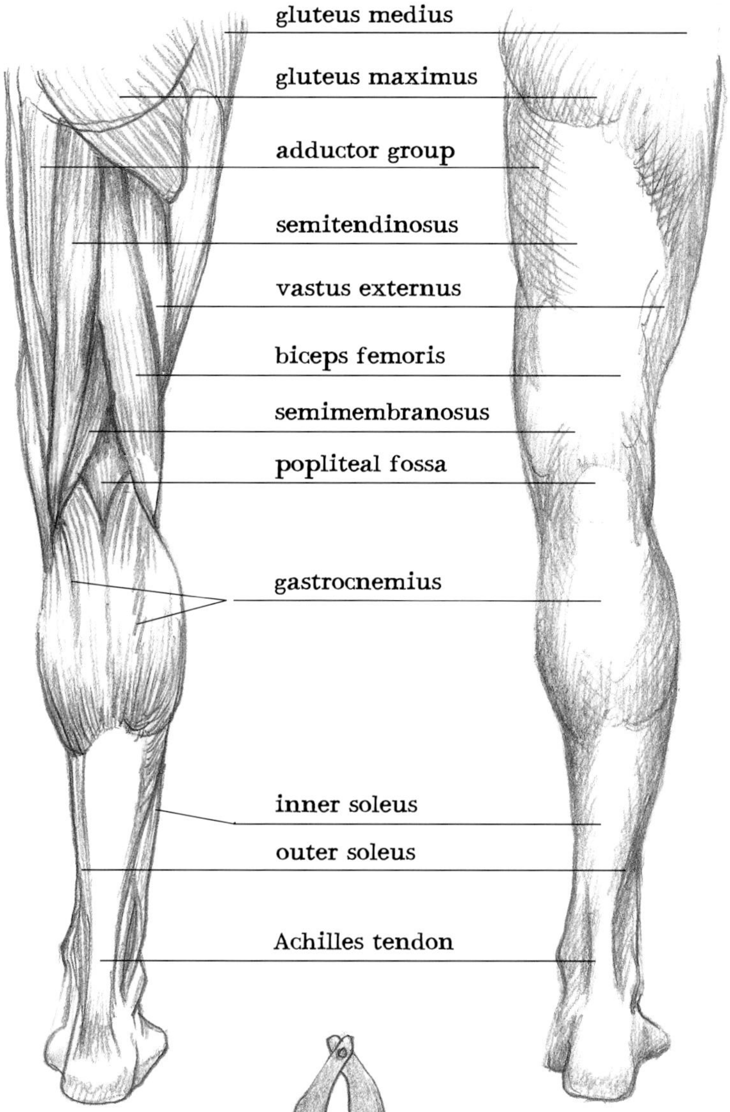

Bones From the back view, the same leg bones that appear in the front view are visible. Their appearance is slightly altered, however, because the bone attachments in the front are designed to allow muscles to extend, and the back attachment is designed for muscles to flex.

Muscles The upper leg consists of five large muscle masses: gluteus maximus; gluteus medius; the hamstring group (biceps femoris, semitendinosus, and semimembranosus); the adductor group; and the vastus externus, which can be seen peeking out from behind the biceps femoris. The lower leg also features five masses: three larger ones and two smaller. The larger masses are the two heads of the calf: the gastrocnemius and the Achilles tendon, which connects to the heel bone. The two smaller masses are the inner soleus and the outer soleus. Also notice the hollow area behind the knee where the calf tendons attach, called the "popliteal fossa;" this fatty hollow makes deep knee bends possible.

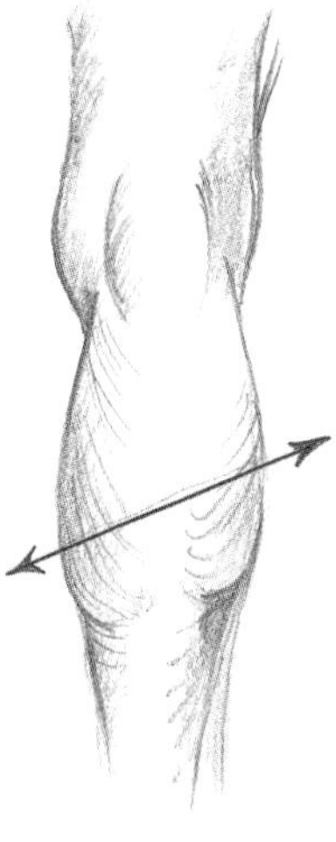

Figure 1 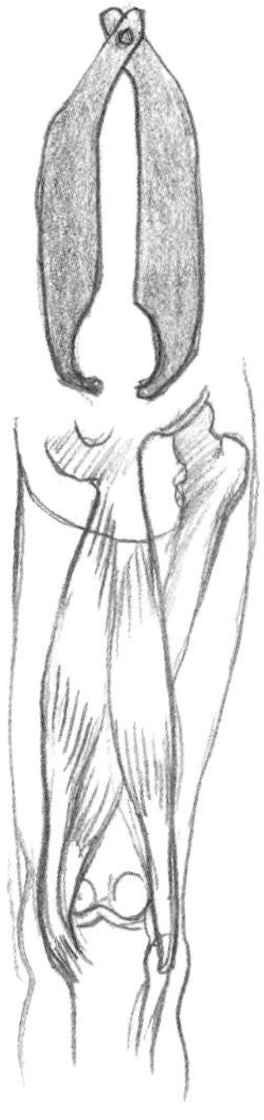   Figure 2

Drawing Tips The calf is lower and rounder on the inside than it is on the outside. (See figure 1.) The hamstring tendons grip below the knee on both sides, almost like a pair of tongs. (See figure 2.)

A. great trochanter
B. femur
C. patella
D. outer condyle
E. tibial tuberosity
F. head of fibula
G. fibula
H. tibia
I. outer malleolus

tensor fasciae latae
rectus femoris
vastus externus
illiotibial band
biceps femoris
popliteal fossa
patellar ligament
gastrocnemius
tibialis anterior
soleus
extensor digitorum longus
peroneus longus
Achilles tendon

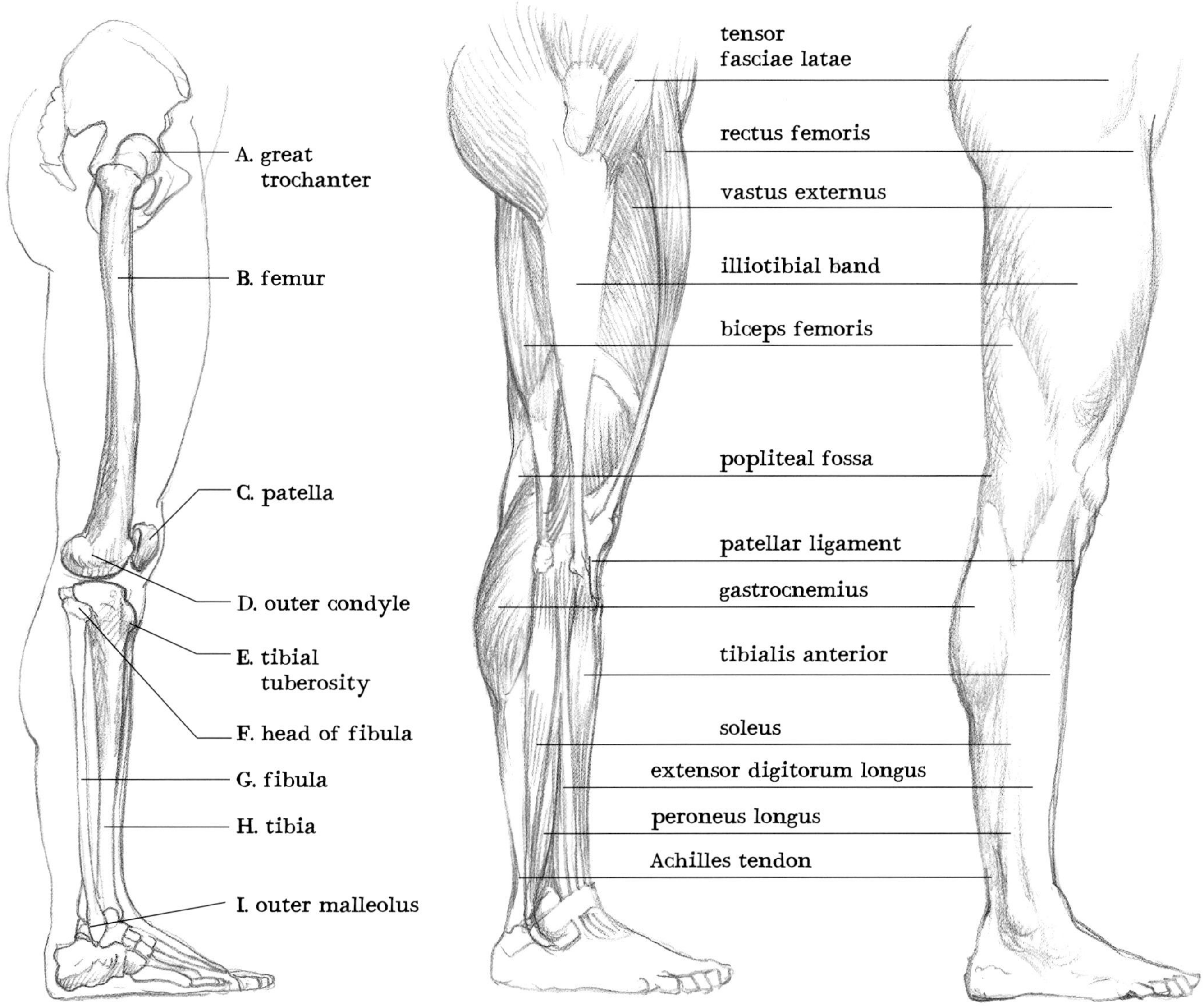

Bones and Muscles Because the long femur (B) and large tibia (H) carry the weight of the body, they sit directly on top of one another. But in a side-view drawing, the upper and lower leg appear staggered; the front of the shin lines up directly below the illiotibial band muscles and behind the upper-leg masses of the rectus femoris and vastus externus.

In the lower leg, the forms to look for are the gastrocnemius; the long, straight form of the Achilles tendon; the peroneus longus tendon, which passes behind the outer malleolus (I) and the bulk of the extensor digitorum longus; and the tibialis anterior, toward the front of the leg.

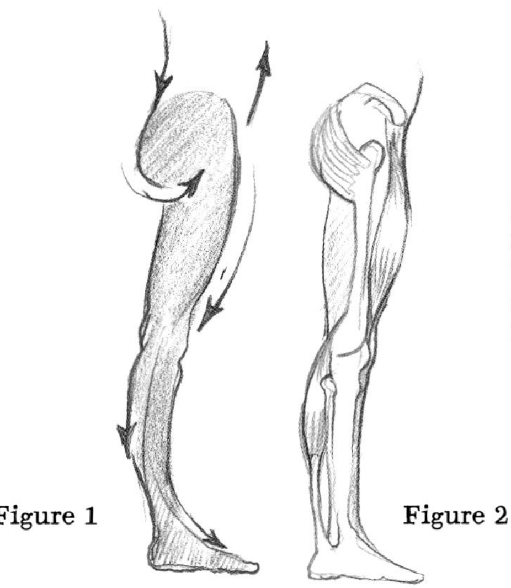

Figure 1

Figure 2

Drawing Tips The six arrows in figure 1 show the overall gesture of the leg. The upper thigh and lower calf create the gesture. (See figure 2.) Figure 3 shows the pattern of tendons in the foot. (See below.)

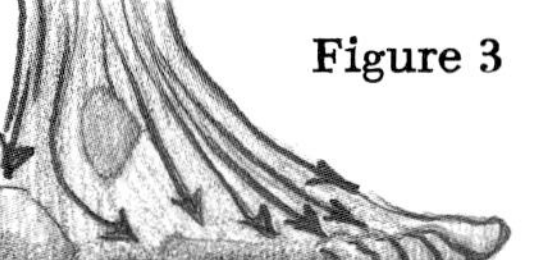

Figure 3

Drawing the Hand

Hands are complex and involve many moveable elements, which can be a challenge to draw. Some positions of the hand are more difficult to draw than others. You may want to try posing a hand—yours or a model's—in many different positions and drawing them for practice. Start by reviewing the anatomy of the hand before drawing.

OPEN PALM

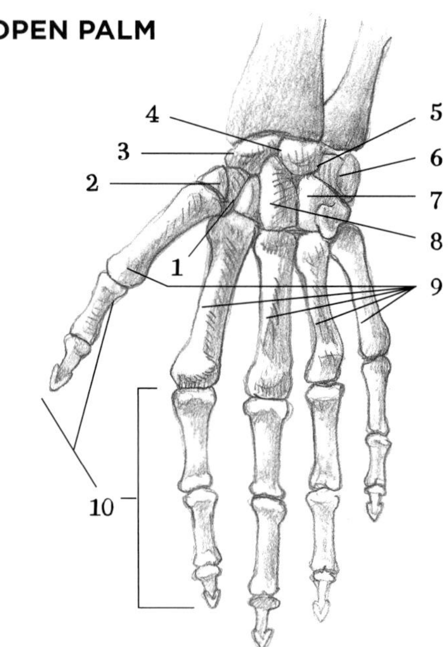

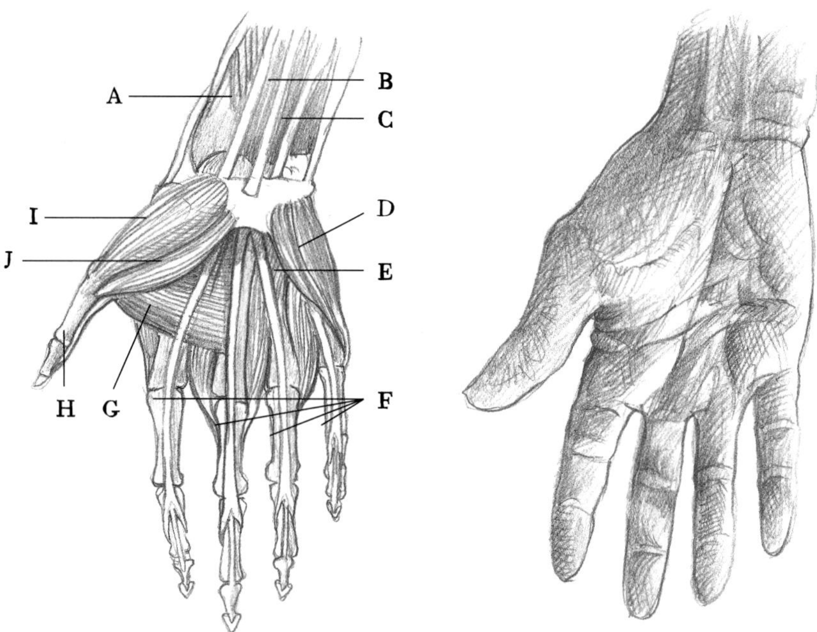

Bones The hand contains eight wrist (carpal) bones: minor multangular (1), major multangular (2), navicular (3), lunate (4), triquetrum (5), pisiform (6), hamate (7), and capitate (8). The hand also features five metacarpals (9) and fourteen phalanges (10).

Muscles The flexor tendons (A, B, C) from the forearm muscles extend into the hand. The teardrop-shaped muscle masses, the thenar eminence abductors of the thumb (I, J) and the hypothenar eminence abductor (D) and flexor (E) of the little finger, are known as the "palmer hand muscles." The adductor of the thumb (G) lies under the flexor tendons (F). The visible creases of the palm show the way the skin folds over the fat and muscles of the hand.

BACK

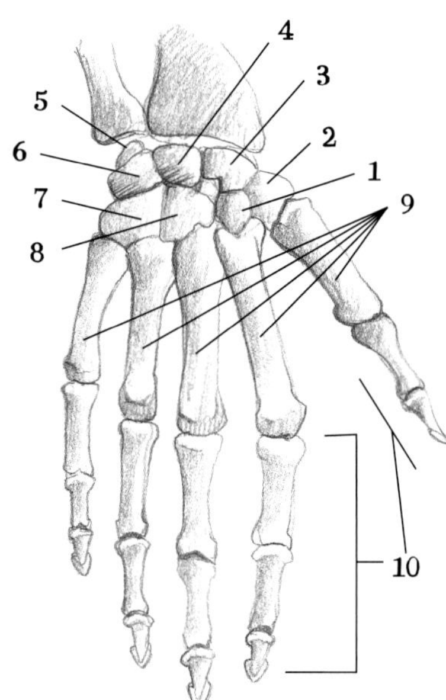

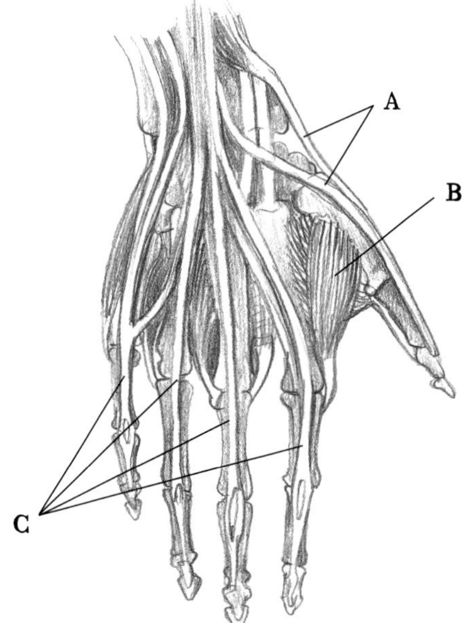

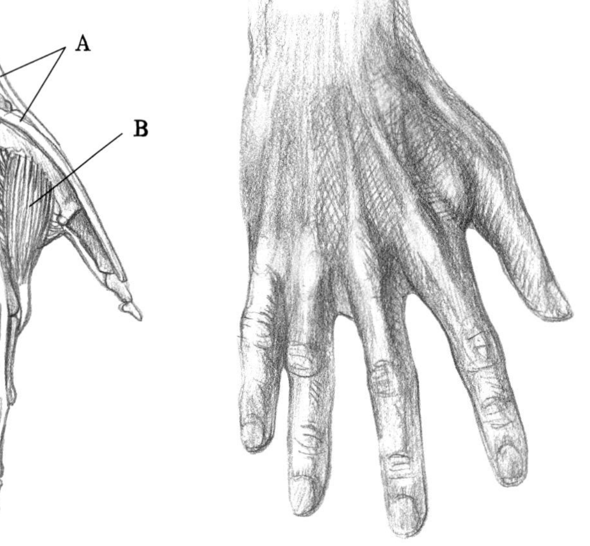

Bones From this view of the hand, all the same bones are visible, but the carpal bones appear convex rather than concave. From this angle, the bones have more influence on the shape of the fleshed-out hand.

Muscles Whereas the palm side of the hand is muscular and fatty, the back of the hand is bony and full of tendons. The extensor tendons of the thumb (A) are visible when contracted, as are the other four extensor tendons (C). The first dorsal interosseous (B) is the largest of the four dorsal interosseous muscles, and it is the only one that shows its form through the skin's surface; when the thumb is flexed, this muscle appears as a bulging teardrop shape.

HAND SIZE

In general, draw men's hands more angularly, with a heavier line quality; draw women's hands lightly with smooth, graceful lines. When sizing a hand to a figure, remember that a hand is about the same length as the face, from chin to hairline. If a hand is posed in a way that does not allow you to see all the fingers, don't be tempted to draw what you can't see or it will look unnatural. Try not to be discouraged if your first few drawings aren't lifelike; hands definitely take a lot of practice!

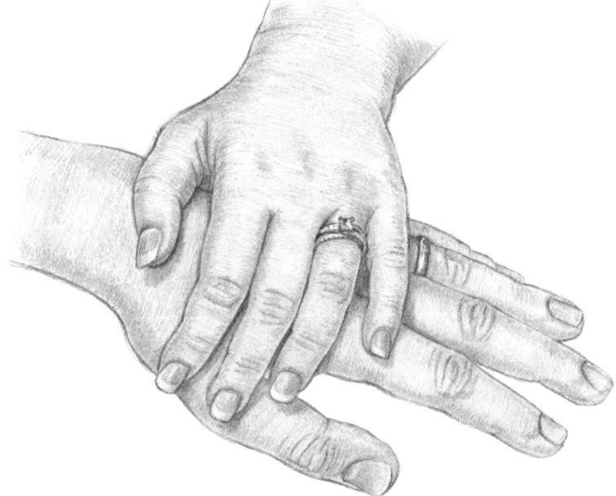

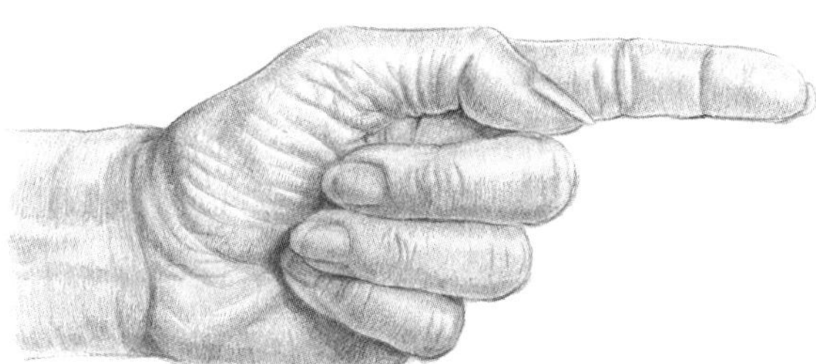

Extended Versus Folded Fingers The skin at the base of the thumb shows more modeling or folds than the other fingers. This view is lit from above, so the highlights are on the tops of the fingers, and the shadows are beneath.

Differences in Male and Female Hands Here the hands of a young married couple clearly show how male and female hands are drawn differently. The strong lighting is from above, creating bright highlights on the back of the woman's hand.

Showing an Open Palm An open-palm rendering of an adult female's hand could be at rest, showing us something in her hand, or reaching for something. With lighting from above, the highlights are on the tops of the fingers and palm, with the back of the hand in shadow.

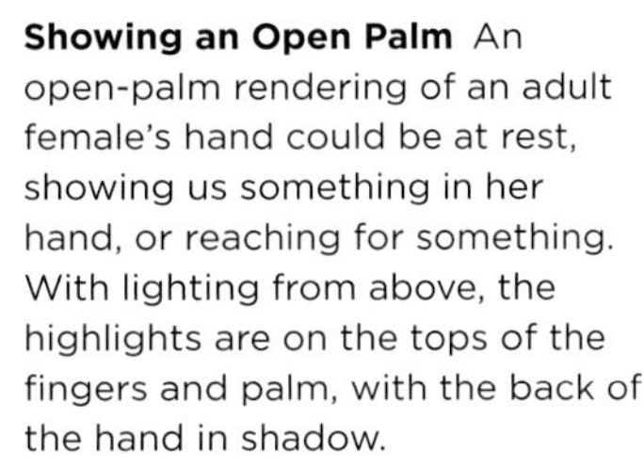

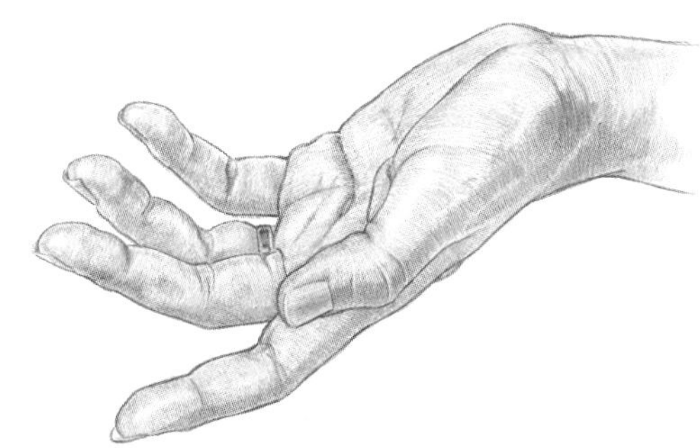

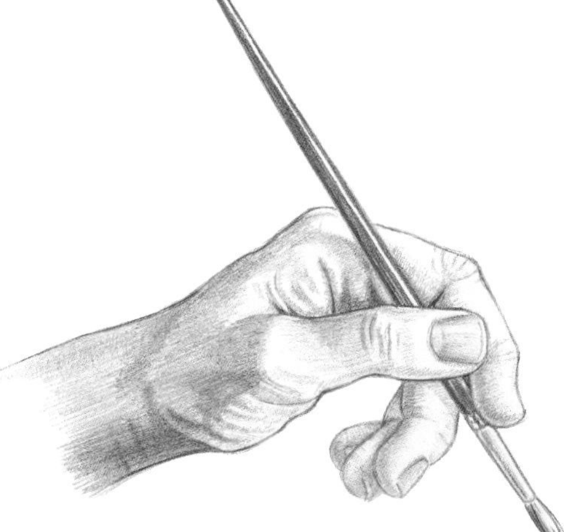

Playing an Instrument In this view of a young male's hands on a keyboard, several of the fingers are not visible. These hands also could depict reaching for something. The light here is from above, highlighting the backs of the hands.

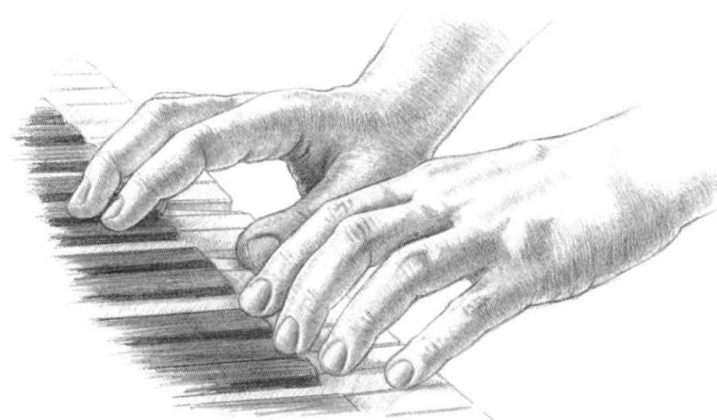

Holding a Pen or Brush This adult male hand holds a paintbrush, but the same pose could hold a pen or pencil. The strong light source from the right highlights the fingers and leaves the back of the hand and wrist shadowed.

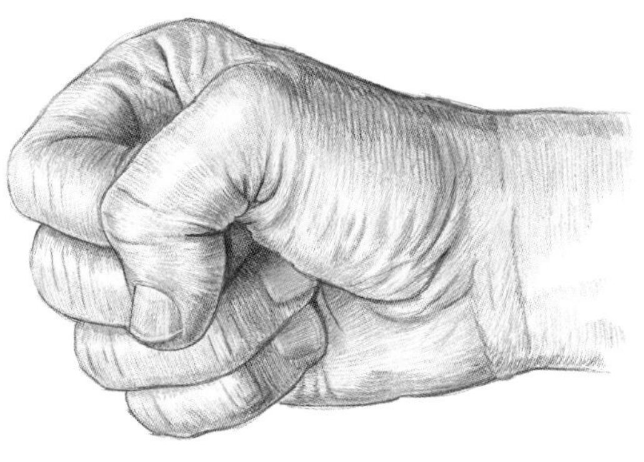

Making a Fist The middle-aged male fist here could be holding something tightly or using a tool. The lighting is soft and evenly distributed from a source that is to the viewer's left.

Drawing the Foot

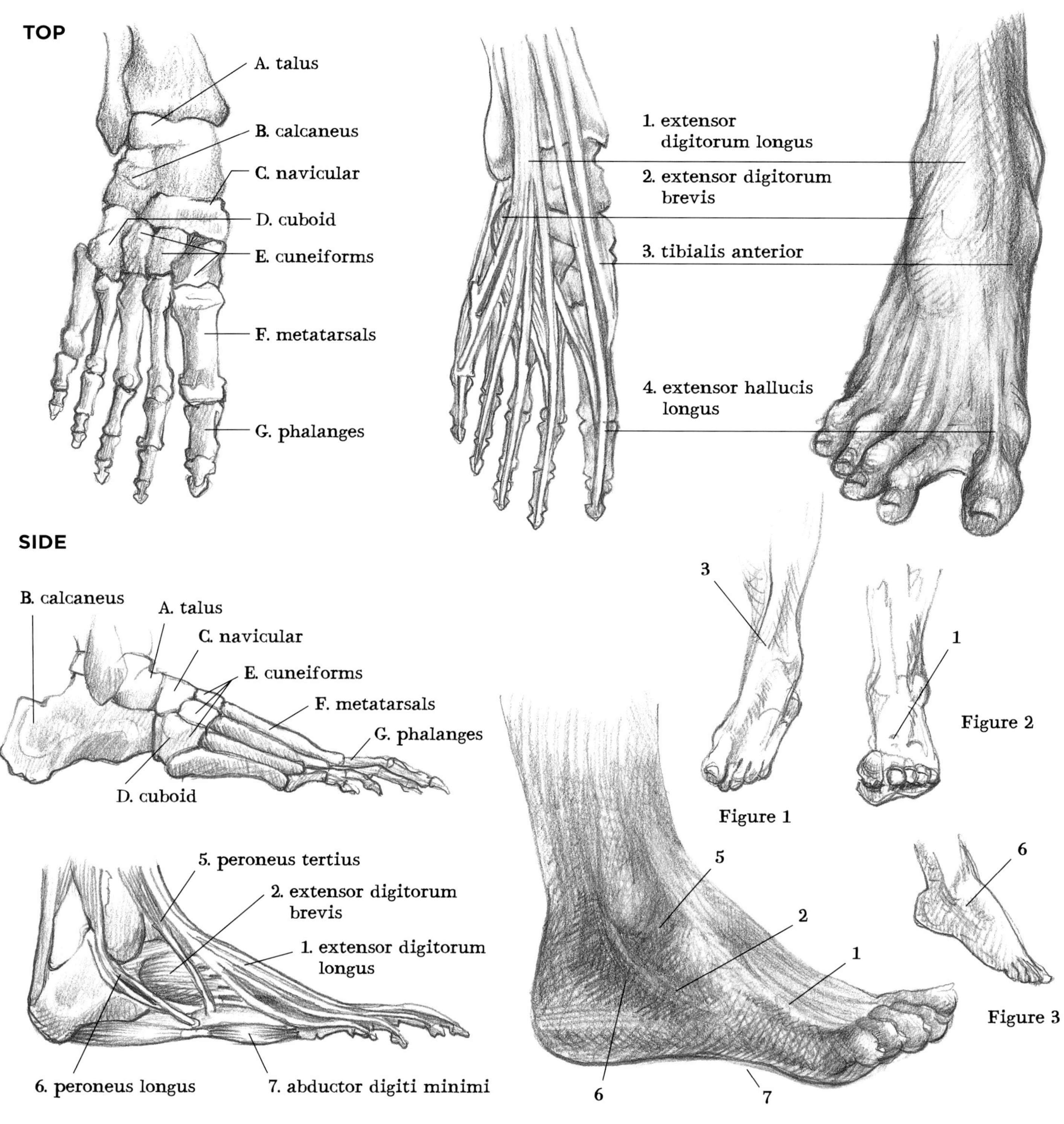

Bones Like the hand, the foot also comprises three parts: seven tarsal bones (A–E), five metatarsals (F), and fourteen phalanges (G). The tarsal bones include the ankle, heel, and instep. The metatarsals are longer and stronger than the five metacarpals of the hand, and they end at the ball of the foot. The phalanges of the toes are shorter than those of the fingers and thumb; the four small toes press and grip the ground surface, and the big toe tends to have a slight upward thrust.

Muscles When the foot is flexed upward, these tendons are evident: extensor digitorum longus (1), extensor digitorum brevis (2), tibialis anterior (3), and extensor hallucis longus (4). (From the side view, extensor digitorum brevis appears as a round shape inside a triangular pocket.) Peroneus longus (6) curves around the ankle, while abductor digiti minimi (7) appears as a bulge on the outer side of the foot.

Drawing Tips The tibialis anterior (3) is an obvious landmark on the inverted foot. (See figure 1, above.) In figure 2, dorsi-flexion makes visible the extensor digitorum (1). In figure 3, plantar-flexion lets you see the tendons of peroneus (6).

FEET

Toes are less flexible than fingers, so feet are not as complicated to draw as hands. Because feet have a unique structure, however, it is still helpful to study the bones, muscles, and tendons to assist you in rendering accurate drawings. Practice drawing feet in various views, as shown here, to build your skills.

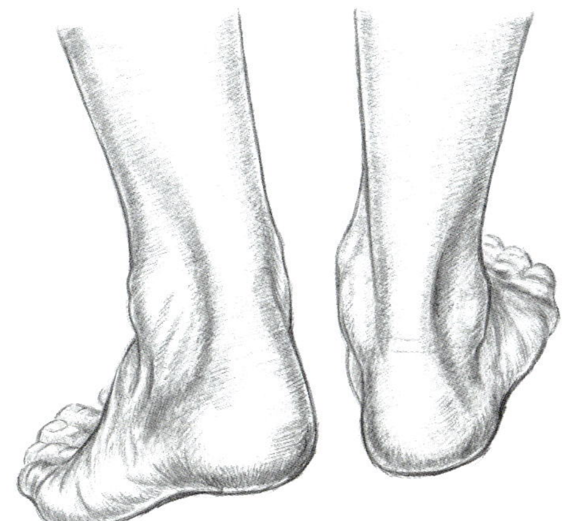

Back View of Feet When viewed from behind, the heel and leg bone catch the light and become one large area. Very little of the front of the feet are visible from this angle.

Crossed Feet From our viewpoint in front of this man's crossed feet, we see the entire bottom of his right foot. The left leg is crossed over the right and the foot is pointed at us, so there is severe foreshortening (See page 131). The toes are just ovals when they are seen straight on like this.

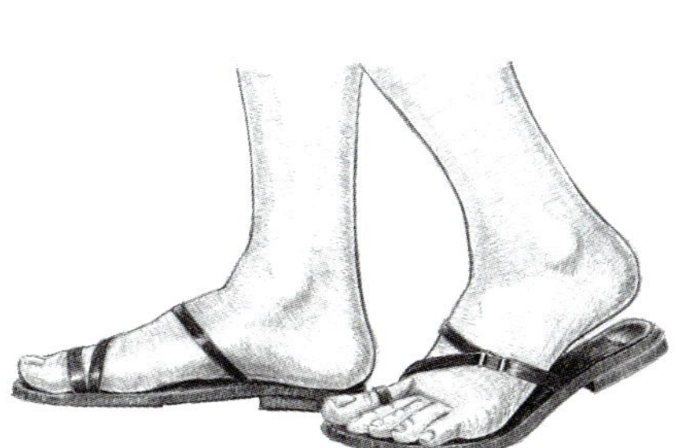

Young Female Feet The feet of this young girl are smooth on top because she is sitting with her feet extended in front of her. The strong lighting from above gives the tops of the feet bright highlights and casts dark shadows.

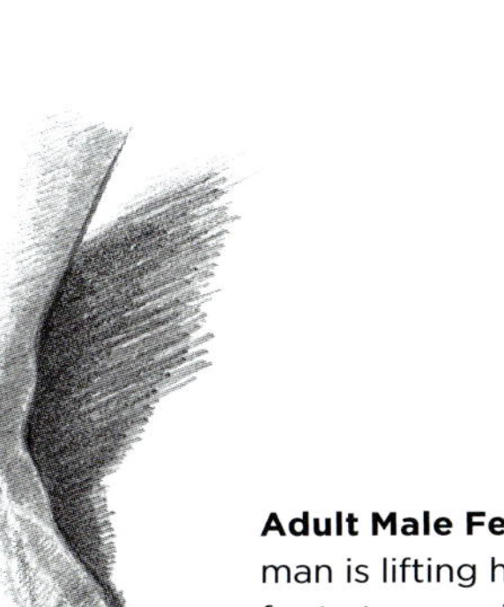

Adult Male Feet This man is lifting his right foot at an angle to take a step; it looks smaller than the other foot because it is farther away from the viewer. Notice how the raised foot catches the light, but the foot on the floor shows more intricate shading of light and dark areas.

Feet in Profile In this view of a woman walking, her right foot is a complete side view with only the big toe showing. Her left foot is bending at the toes and pointed slightly toward us, so we can see all the toes on that foot. Notice the difference between the shape of the foot when flat as opposed to when it is bent.

TODDLERS' LIMBS

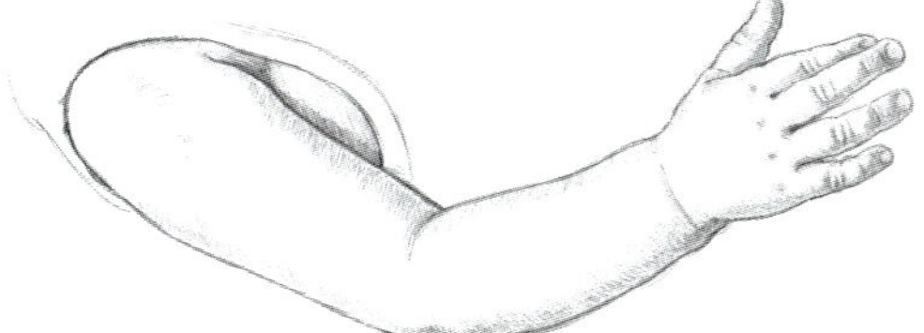

Arm and Hand The arm of a two-year-old usually is a bit pudgy and has wrinkles at the joints. Deep folds of skin at the inner elbow and wrist are fairly common, as are dimples on the elbow and knuckles.

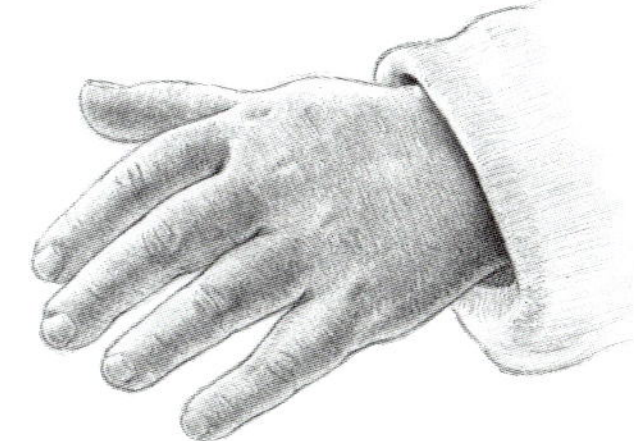

Hand and Fingers The back of a toddler's hand is chubby and rounded. The fingers are plump and fleshy, even at the tips.

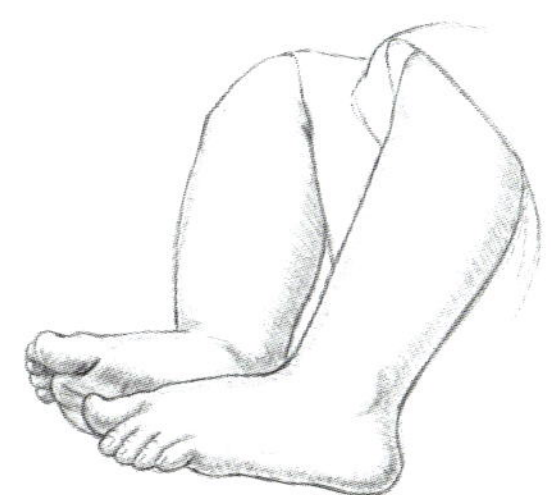

Legs and Feet The legs are short, which makes them look fairly thick. Plump, two-year-old toes are short, round, and nearly shapeless. The foot is just starting to form an arch at this stage.

Movement & Balance

Another way to make drawings more realistic is to draw the figures in action. Since people hardly ever sit or stand still, your figure drawings of them shouldn't either. You can begin by using simple sketch lines to lay out the dominant action of the figure.

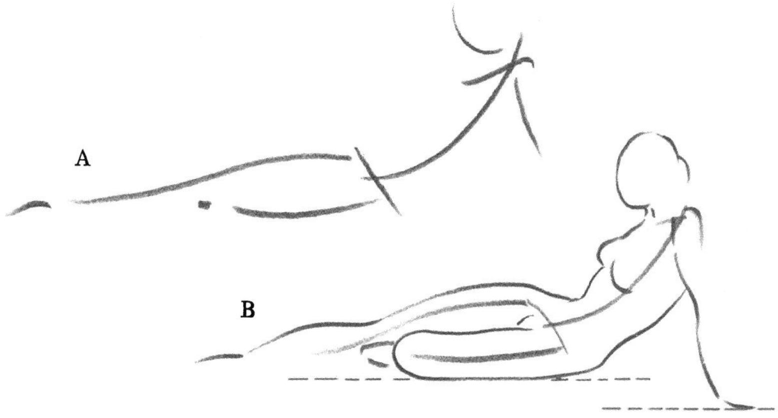

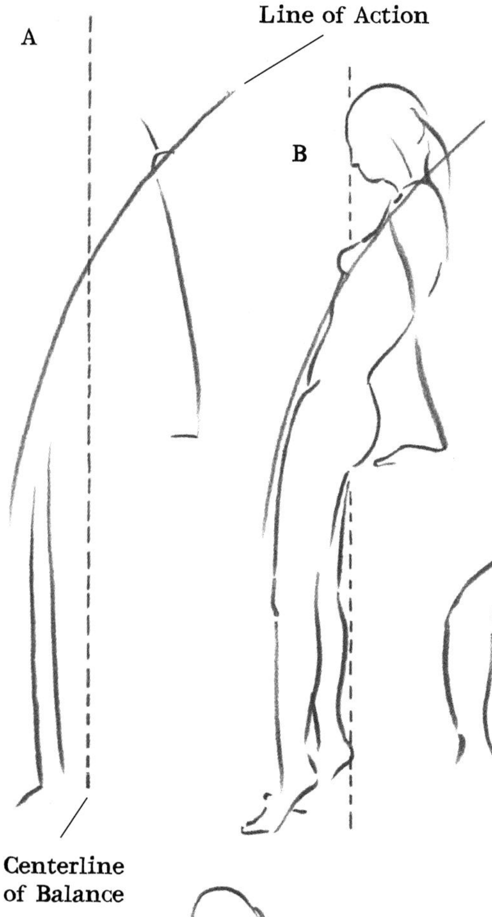

Line of Action

A

B

Centerline
of Balance

Try employing an imaginary centerline of balance that seems to hold or balance the figure in its position. Otherwise, the figure may look as though it's going to fall over. The best way to achieve balance is to place approximately the same amount of weight on either side of this centerline.

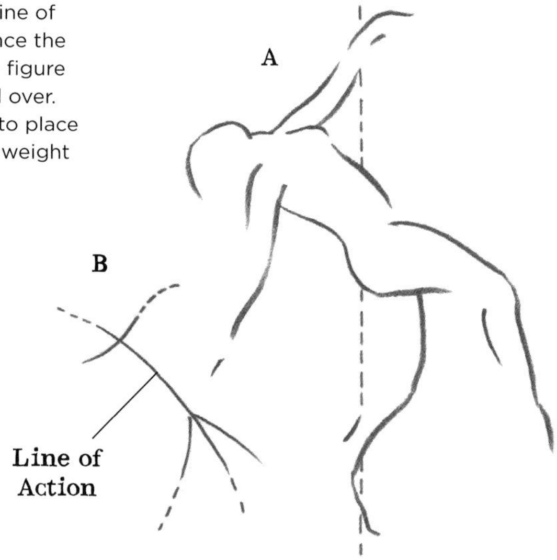

A

B

Line of
Action

Draw a line that represents the spine of the figure in its action pose; you can develop the pose from this line of action. Using both the centerline of balance and the line of action help establish effective action figure drawings.

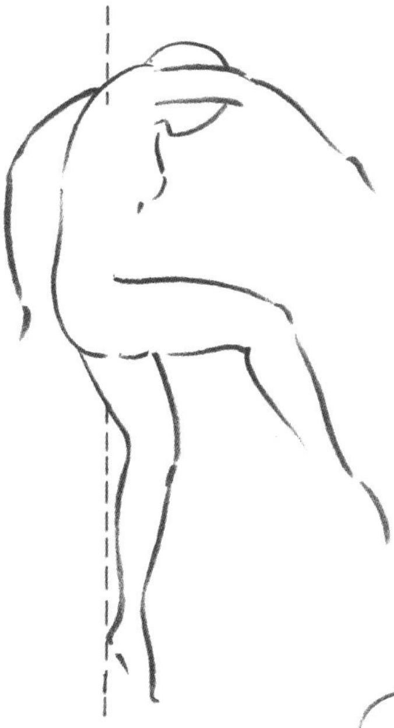

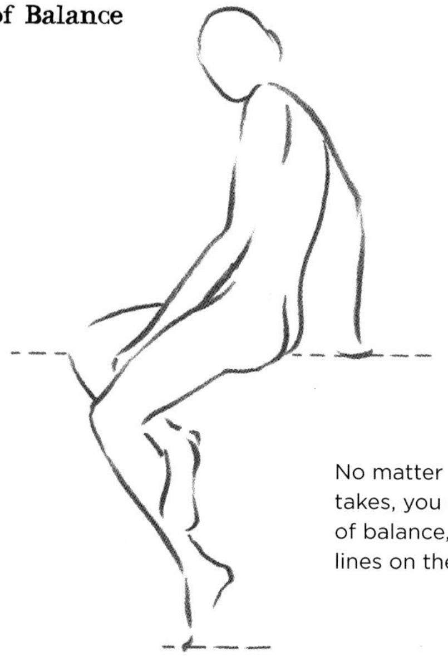

No matter what position a figure takes, you can always find a center of balance, illustrated by the dotted lines on these examples.

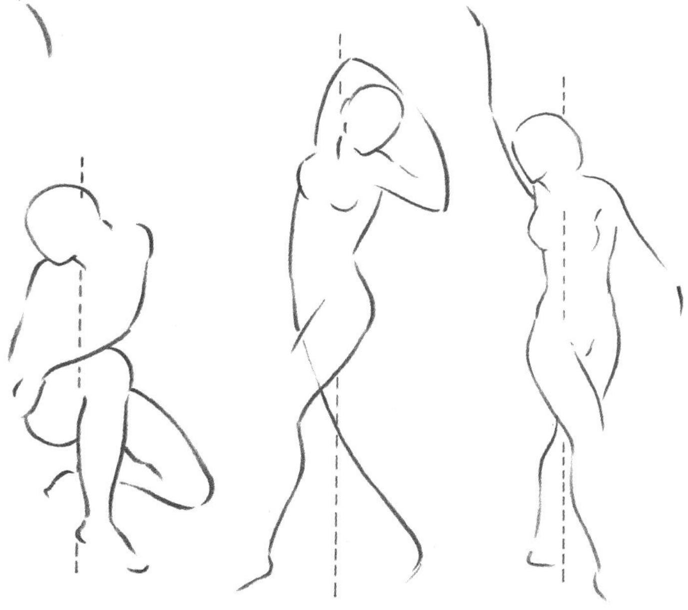

Proportion & Detail

For this figure drawing, emphasize the light and airy feel of a ballerina's pose. Just as the ballerina appears delicate, so should the shading you apply on her skin and costume. Use deep values sparingly.

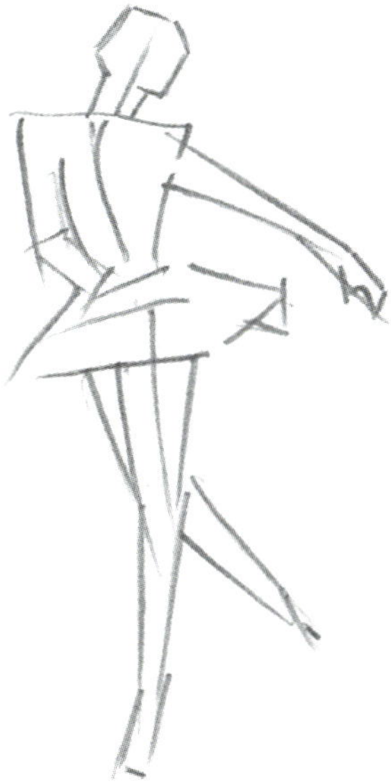

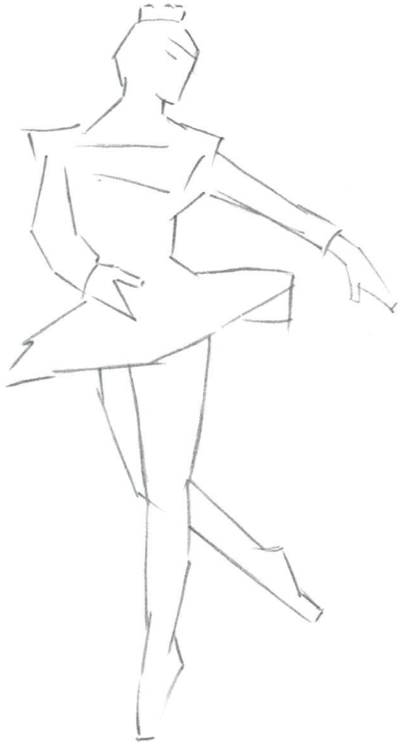

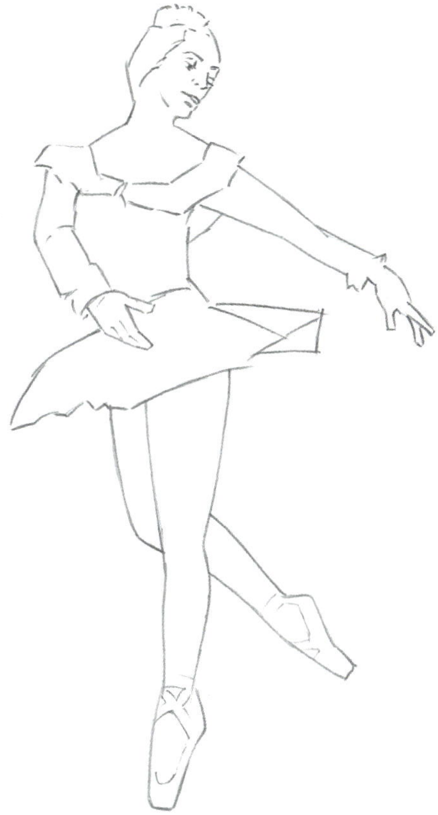

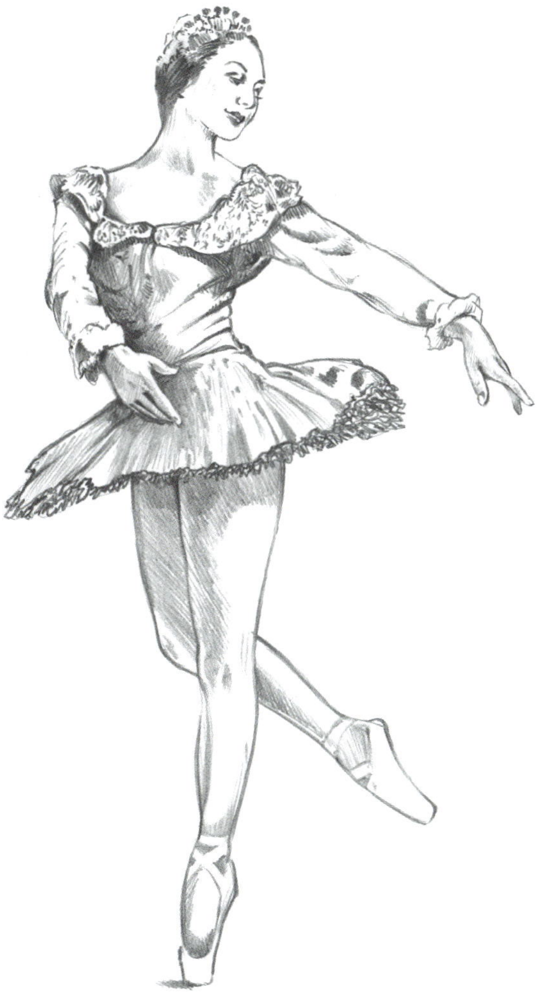

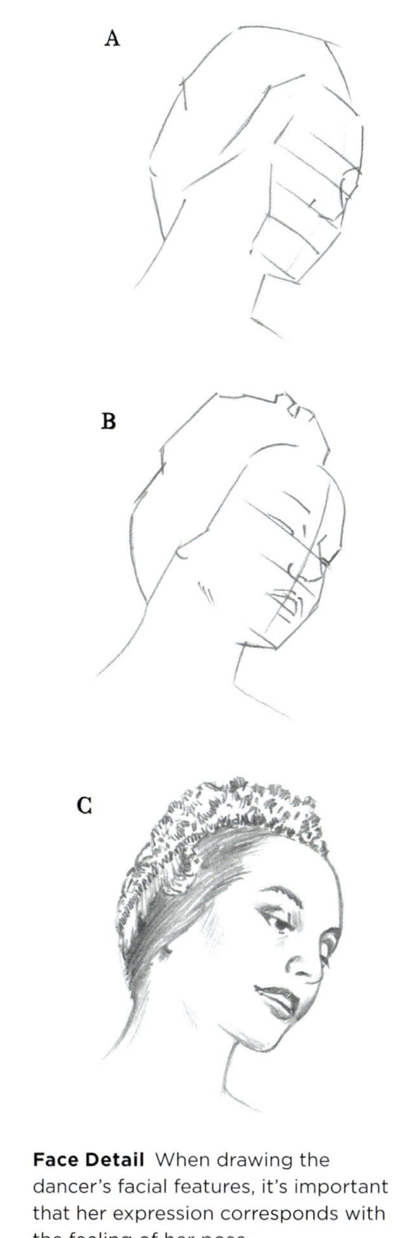

A

B

C

Face Detail When drawing the dancer's facial features, it's important that her expression corresponds with the feeling of her pose.

Drawing the Hands The graceful position of this subject's hands complements her serene pose.

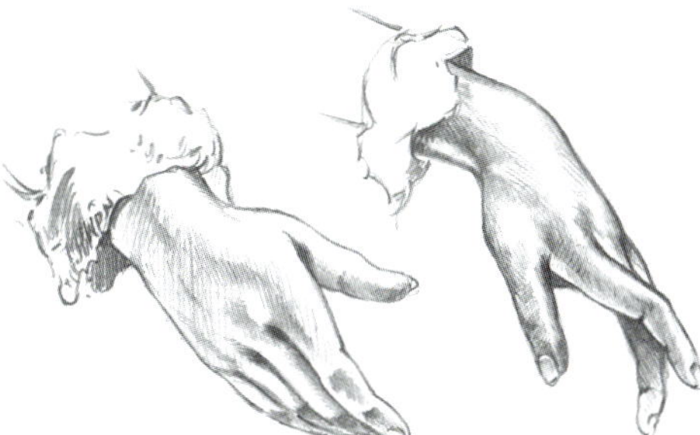

Showing Movement

All the parts of the body combine to show movement of the figure. Our jointed skeleton and muscles allow us to bend and stretch into many different positions. To create drawings with realistic poses, it helps to study how a body looks and changes when stretched or flexed as well as when sitting or standing. Begin by drawing the line of action (a line to indicate the curve and movement of the body) or "gesture" first; then build the forms of the figure around it.

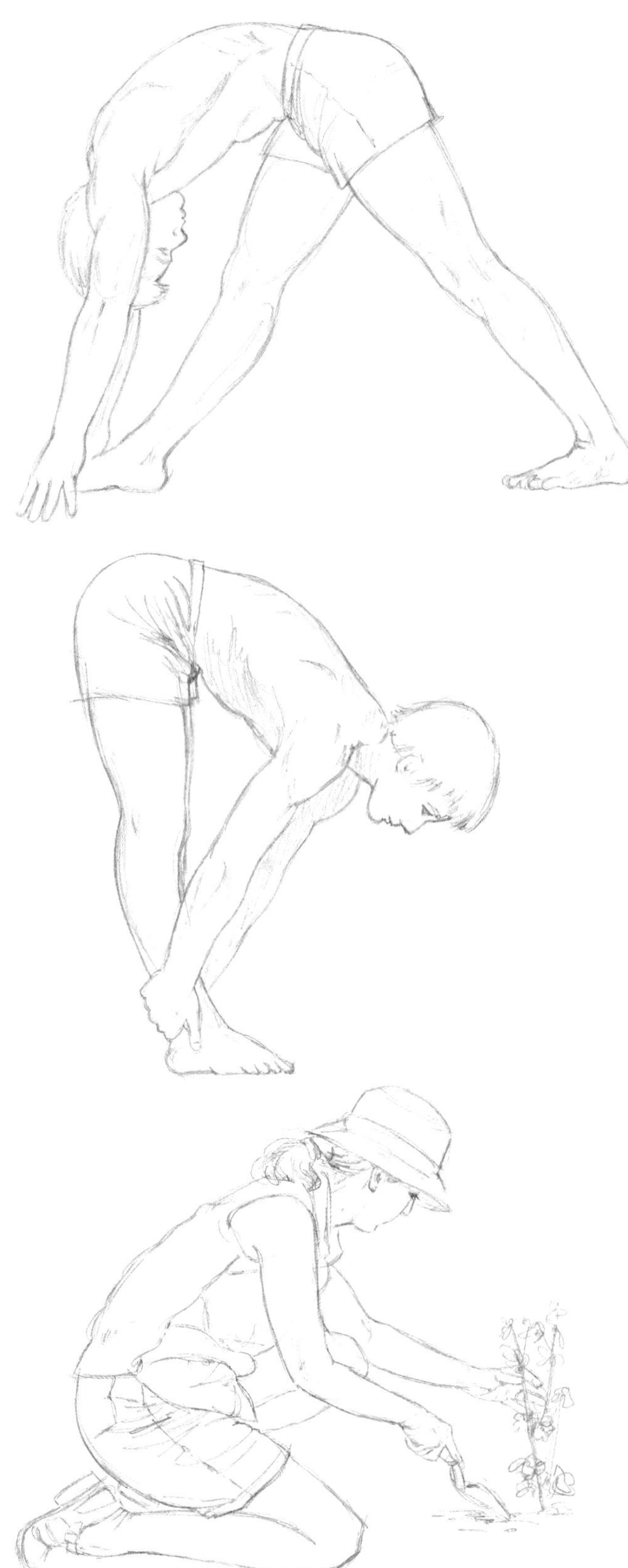

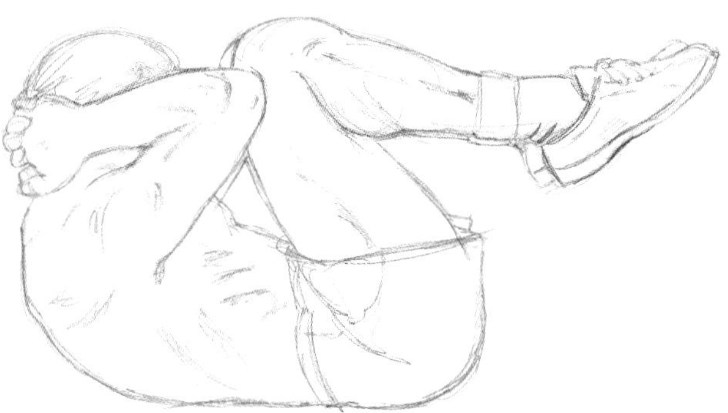

Extending and Contracting The spine is flexible and allows us to bend many ways while stretching and contracting our limbs. These three poses show how the shape of the body can change drastically while the proportions stay the same.

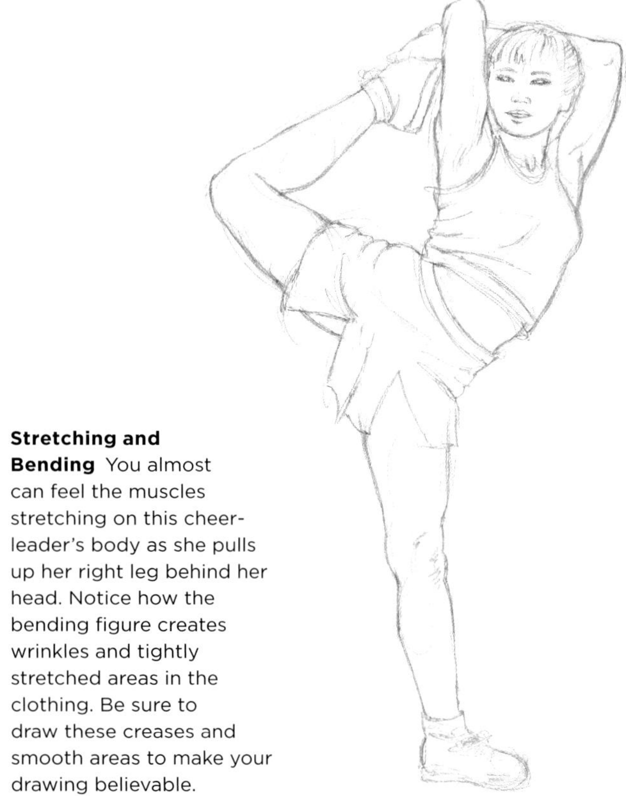

Stretching and Bending You almost can feel the muscles stretching on this cheerleader's body as she pulls up her right leg behind her head. Notice how the bending figure creates wrinkles and tightly stretched areas in the clothing. Be sure to draw these creases and smooth areas to make your drawing believable.

Everyday Action This woman kneeling in her garden is bending into an S shape. All wrinkles or folds in the fabric are on the inward side of the body's bend; the back side is fairly smooth. The curve of her turned head has only a slight influence on the line of action.

Bending & Twisting

When people are involved in something active, they bend and twist their bodies. You should be able to render these movements in your drawings. Clothing helps convey the appearance of a twisting body because the folds form into a twisting design.

When drawing figures in a twisting motion, use what you've already learned about shading folds, but keep in mind that folds on a twisting body will be tighter than folds on a person in a still pose.

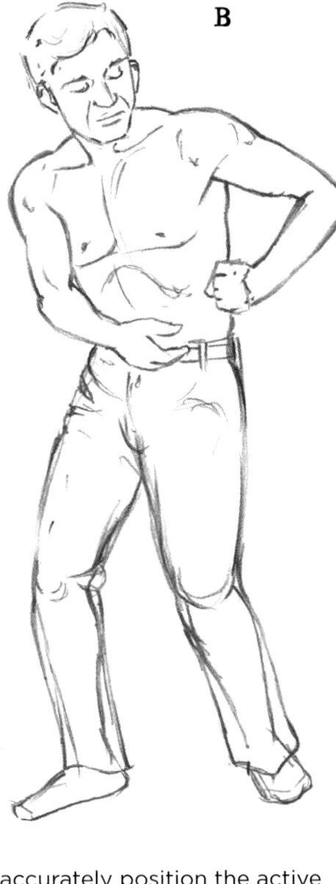

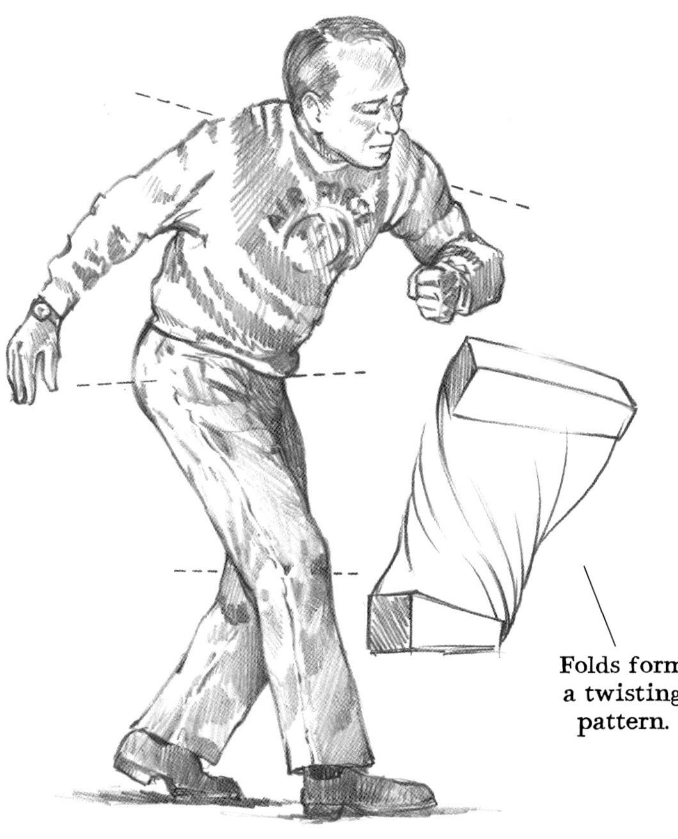

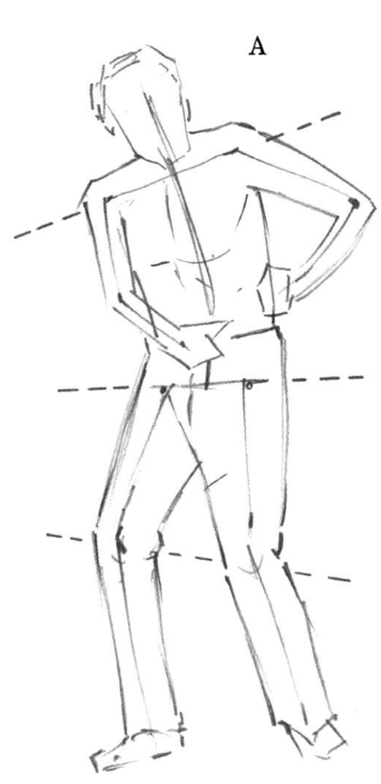

Folds form a twisting pattern.

To accurately position the active body, sketch some guidelines to indicate the angles of the shoulders, hips, and knees, as shown in the examples.

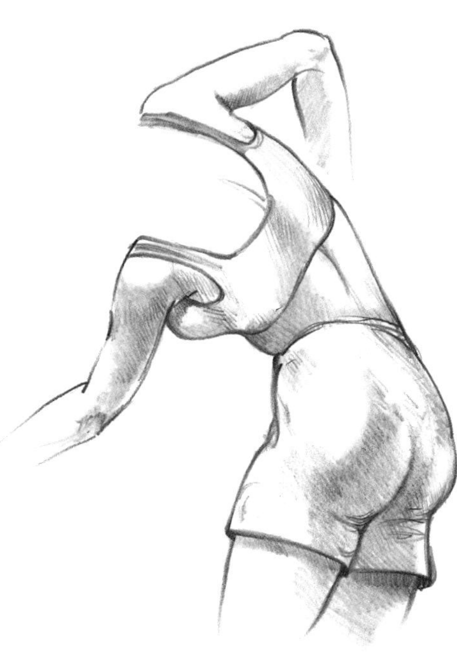

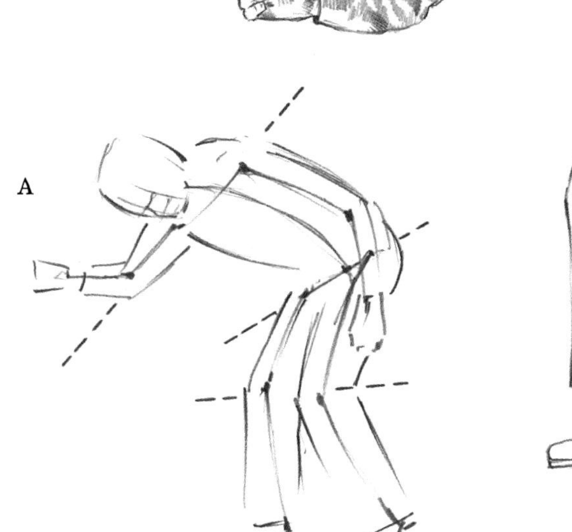

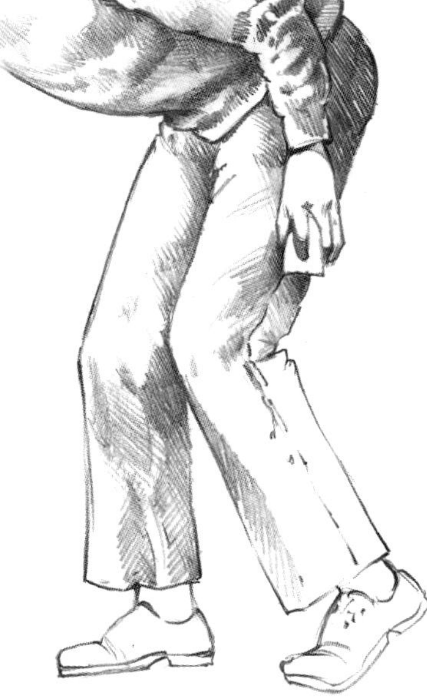

Children in Action

Drawing children in action presents a unique challenge. To capture their actions, train your eye to assess the essential elements of the movement, and then quickly draw what you see. One way to rapidly record details is through a gesture drawing, a quick sketch establishing a figure's pose. First determine the main thrust of the movement—or the line of action—from the head, down the spine, and through the legs. Then sketch general shapes around this line. As you can see here, a quick sketch is all you need to capture the main gesture—and you can always add details later.

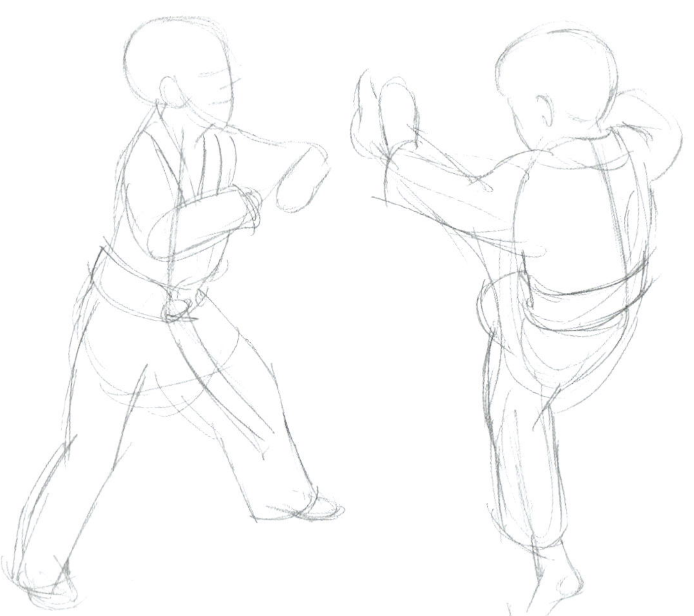

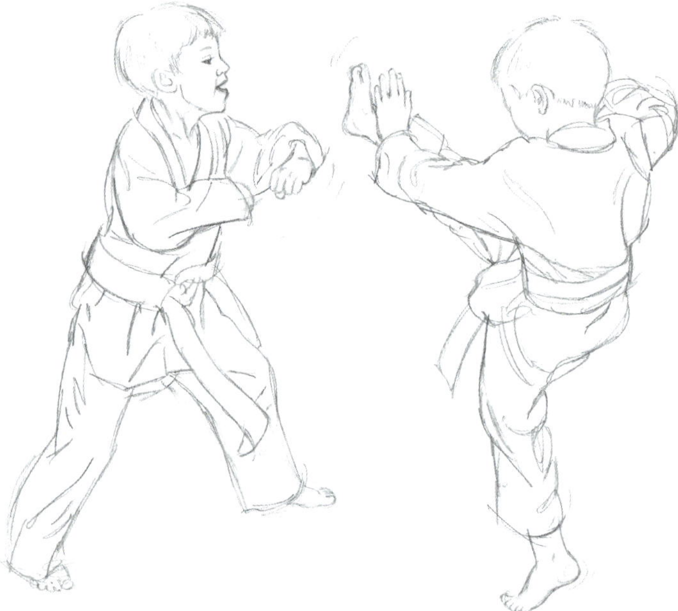

Step 1 To capture the gestures of these boys, first establish the lines of action; then block in the general shapes surrounding them. For the boy on the left, the line of action moves down his spine and through his left leg, where his weight is balanced. The boy on the right is kicking with his right leg—note the way the kick causes his body to bend forward in order to balance, curving the line of action at the base of his spine.

Step 2 After placing the lines of action correctly and blocking in the basic shapes, add a few details on their heads, hands, feet, and clothing, keeping the lines loose. Karate uniforms are loose fitting, but you can see how the boys' movements have pulled the fabric taut in some places.

GESTURE DRAWING

Gesture drawing generally refers to sketching figures in action. But it also can be a quick drawing of an object. Whatever the subject, the key is to capture its essence in a few seconds. Detail is unimportant—look more at your subject than at your drawing. Feel the structure and movement of line as you use the pencil. When gesture drawing, use your whole arm—your elbow needs to move without much shifting of your wrist.

Establishing a Gesture Gesture drawing is perhaps the most important of the warm-up exercises to employ before drawing figures, as it helps capture the movement of the body. As you create this type of sketch, refrain from shading or adding details.

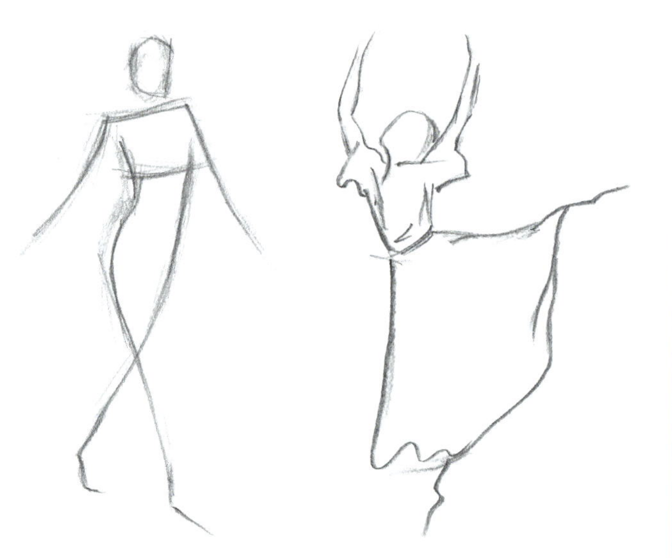

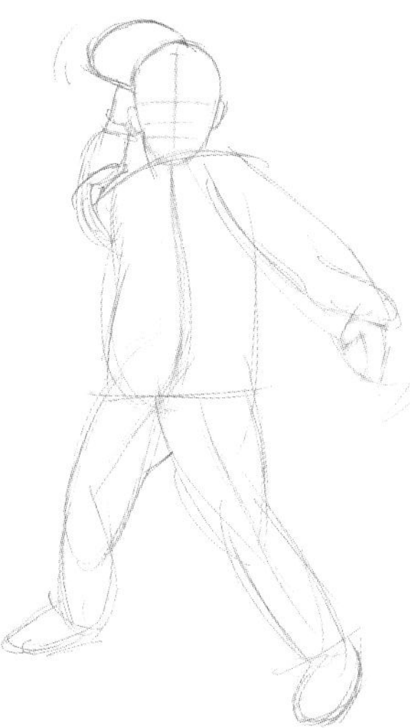

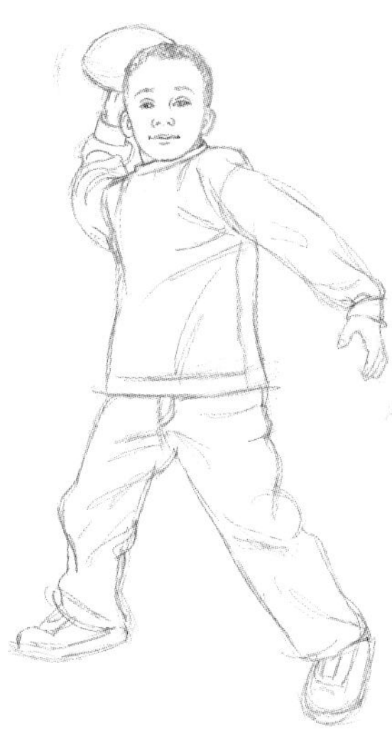

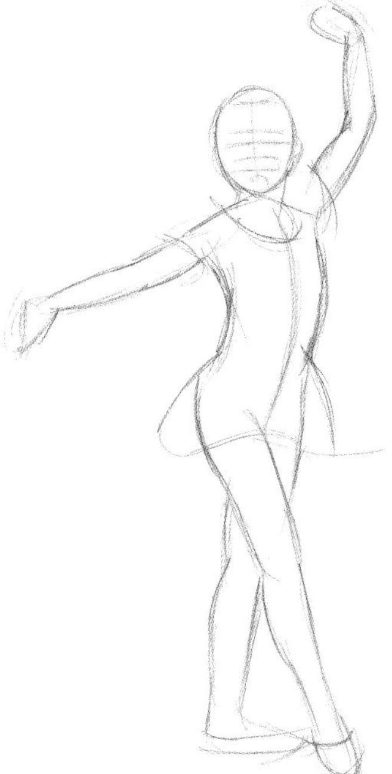

Step 1 This boy is leaning back on his right leg as he prepares to throw. His left arm and leg are used for counterbalance. The line of action flows down his spine and through his left leg, but a secondary line of action runs down his right leg.

Step 2 After establishing the basic shapes, add simple details that accompany the action. The folds of his clothes and direction of his gaze correspond with the pose.

Step 1 This ballet pose has two lines of action: The main line curves with the torso and runs down the left leg; the secondary line starts at the left hand and flows across the chest, down the right arm, and through the right hand. Most of the weight is on the left leg; the right leg is extended for balance. If the basic gesture isn't correct, the figure will look like she's falling over.

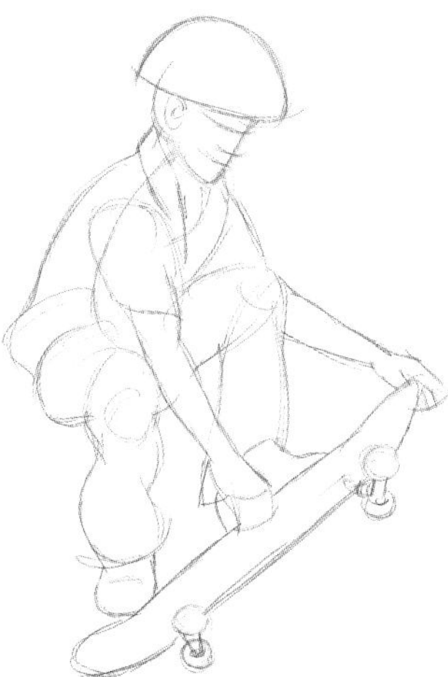

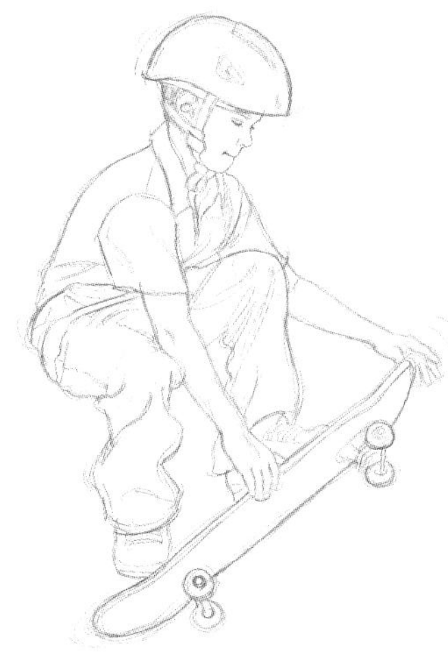

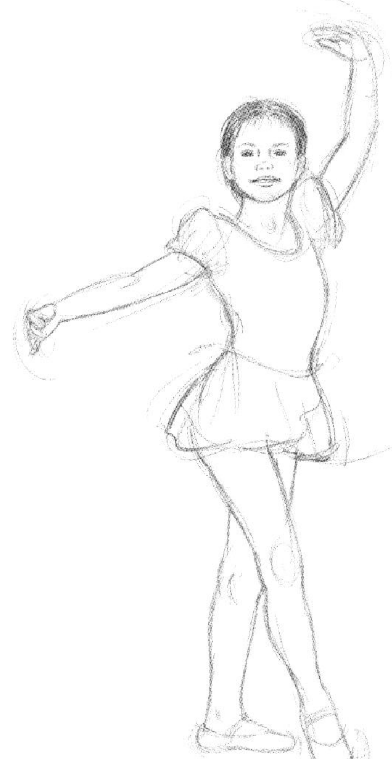

Step 1 This pose is challenging because skateboarders often appear to defy gravity, but the process is the same. Draw the line of action down the spine, sharply curving through the left thigh. Then add the arms and the right leg for balance. Keep the head in line with the spine.

Step 2 Here again, minimal shading and detail are the best ways to keep the movement from looking stiff. Loose speed lines around the boy's helmet, hand, and skateboard also indicate motion.

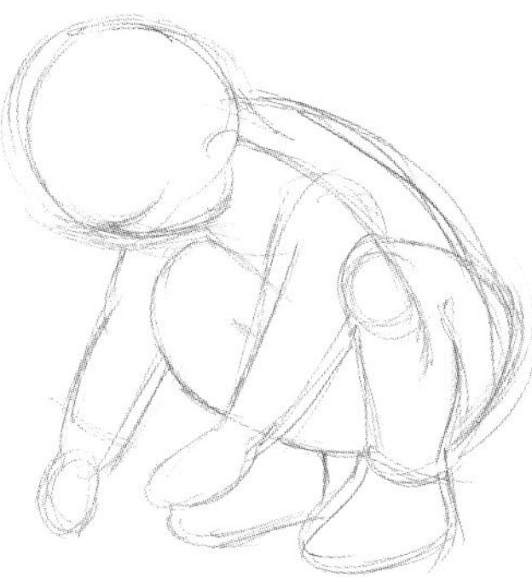

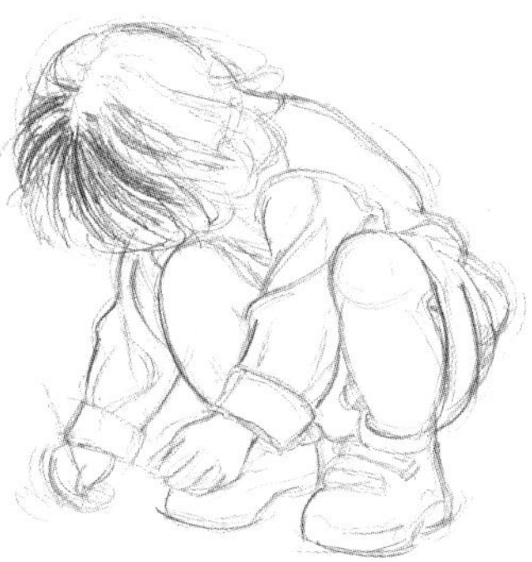

Step 1 As this child crouches to pick a flower, her weight is evenly balanced on both feet. The line of action starts at the top of her head and curves down her spine.

Step 2 Keep the action of the pose alive with loose details. Folds in the clothing and a natural tousle of the hair also enhance the sense of movement.

Step 2 When blocking in and refining the shapes of a complicated pose such as this one, it's important to keep in mind many of the concepts you've learned in this book, including the head and body proportions and how foreshortening affects them.

Clothing Folds

Drawing realistic clothing, including rendering folds, tucks, textures, and other details, is one of those techniques that will help improve the overall quality of your work.

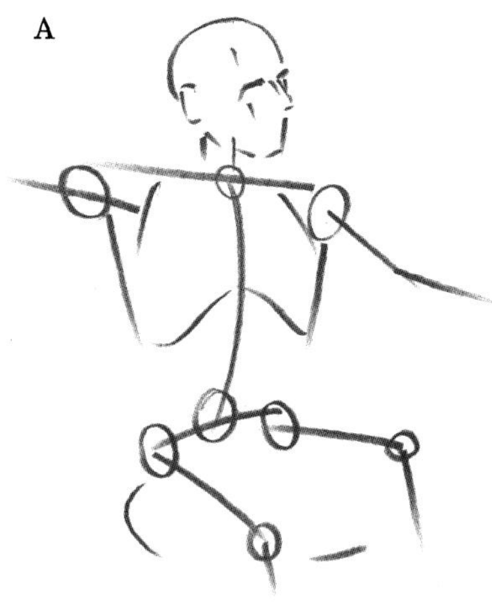

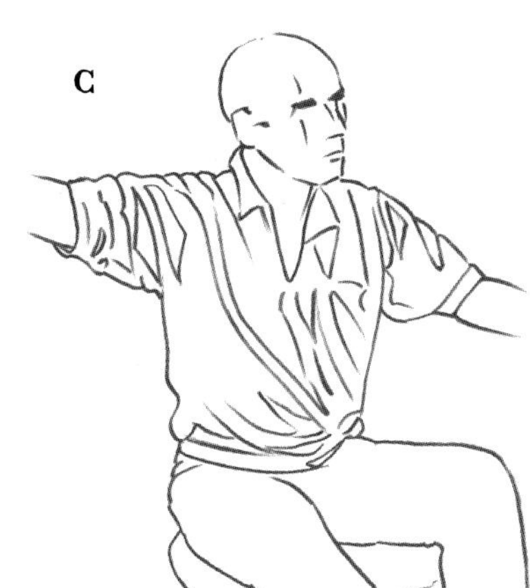

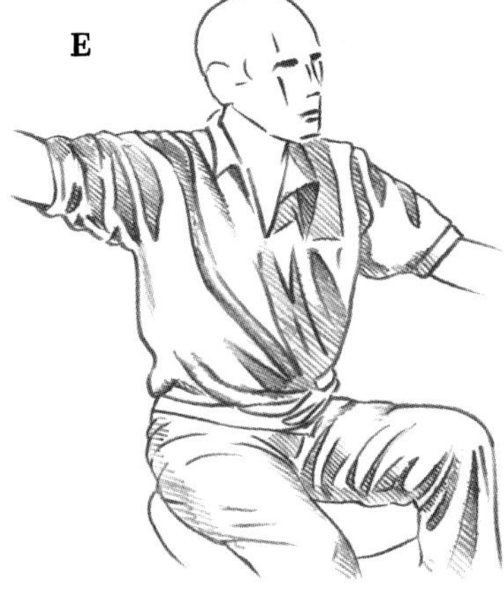

Begin by drawing a stick figure, indicating the location of each joint with some light circles (A). Then sketch the outline of the clothing, along with preliminary guidelines for the folds (B); these guidelines will later provide a map for your shading. Indicate only the major folds at this point, while continuing to add light guidelines. Continue to fill in the details of the form a little bit at a time (C, D).

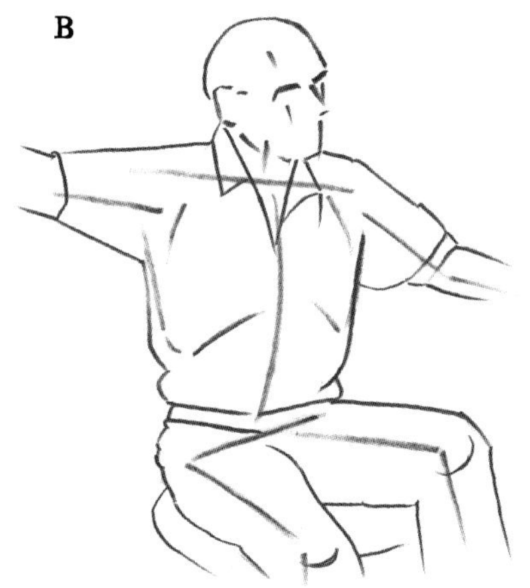

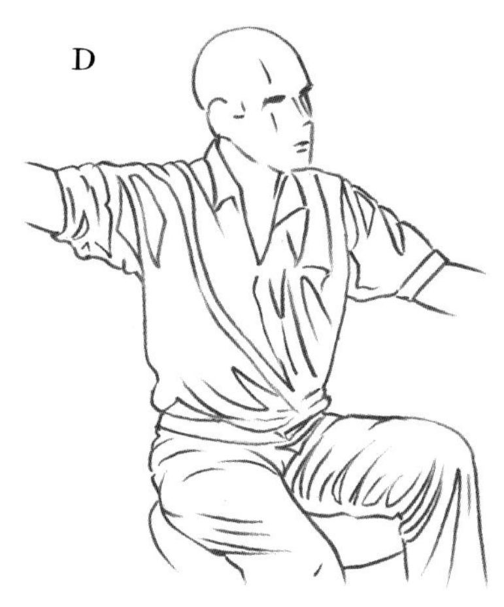

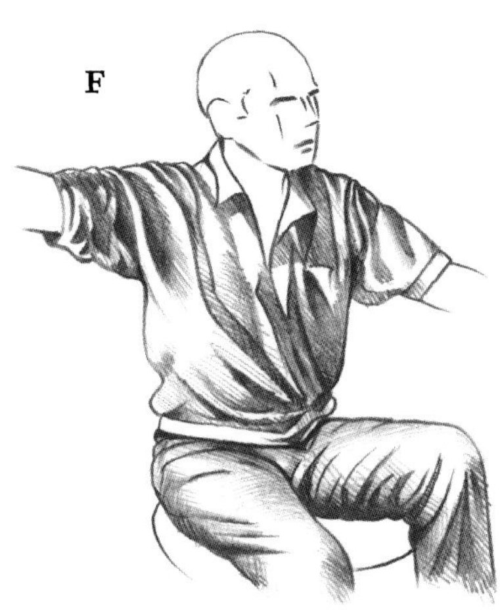

Begin to darken the areas inside the folds with short, diagonal strokes using the point of a 2B pencil (E). Overlap your strokes at different angles, making them darker toward the center of the folds. Use a paper stump for the finishing touches, blending the edges of the folded areas (F). You might also want to leave some shading lines to give the drawing an artistic feel.

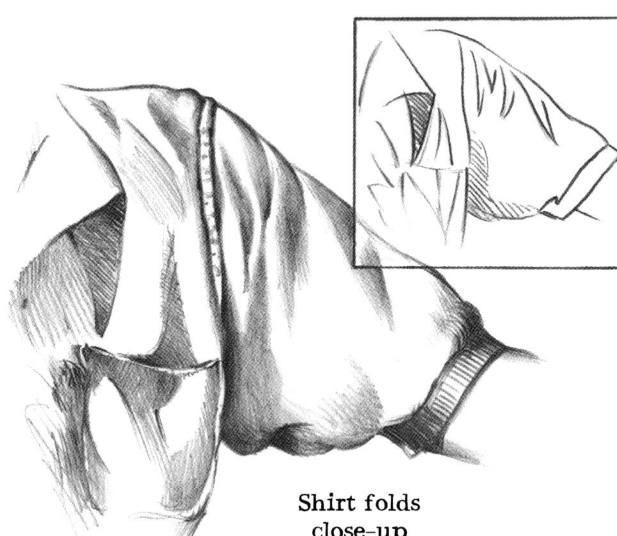

Shirt folds close-up

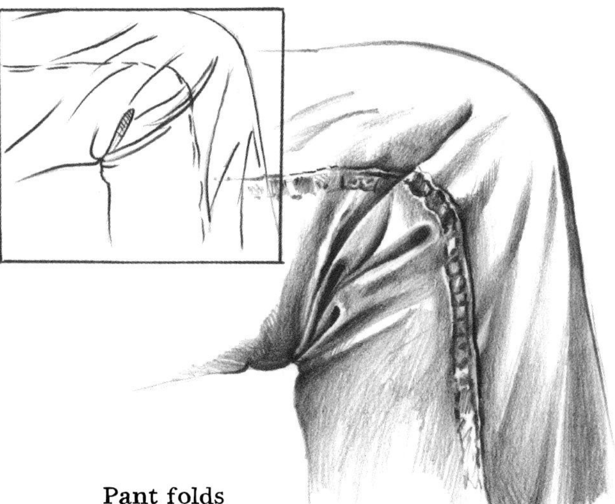

Pant folds close-up

Foreshortening

Foreshortening refers to the visual effect (or optical illusion) that an object is shorter than it actually is because it is angled toward the viewer—and that objects closer to the viewer appear proportionately larger than objects farther away. For example, an arm held out toward the viewer will look shorter (and the hand will look larger) than an arm held straight down by the subject's side.

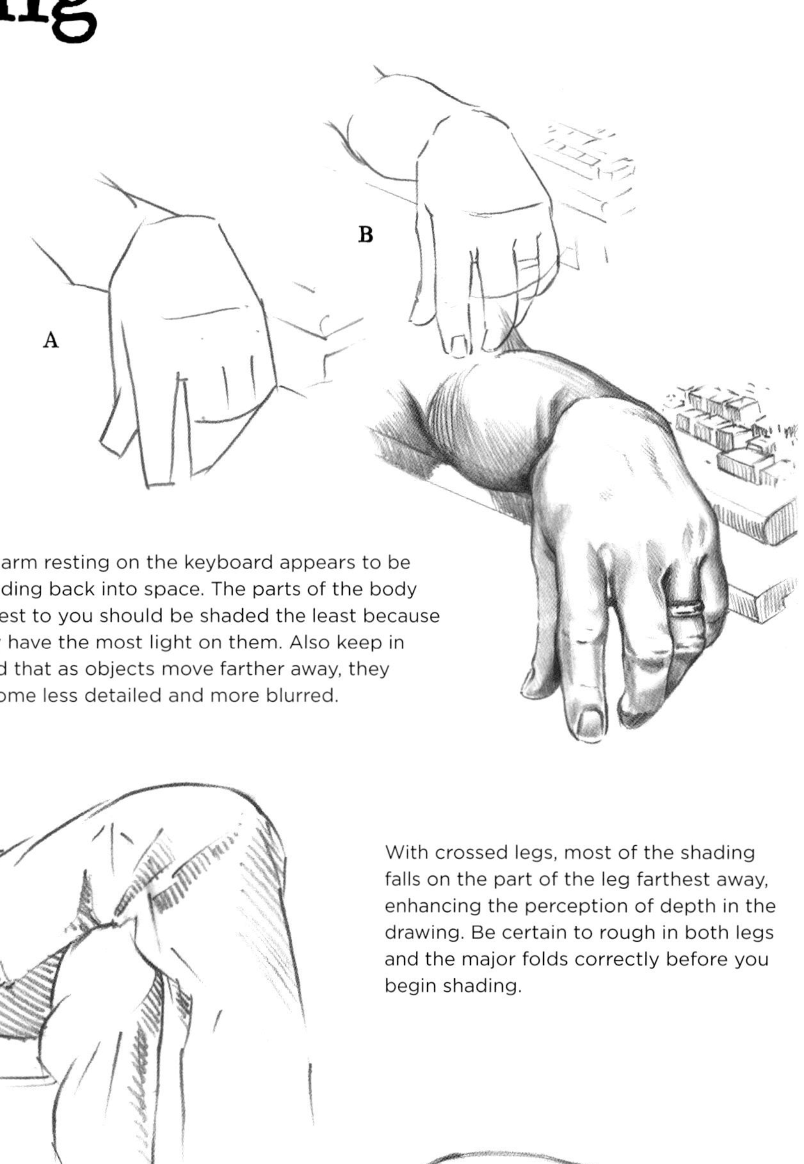

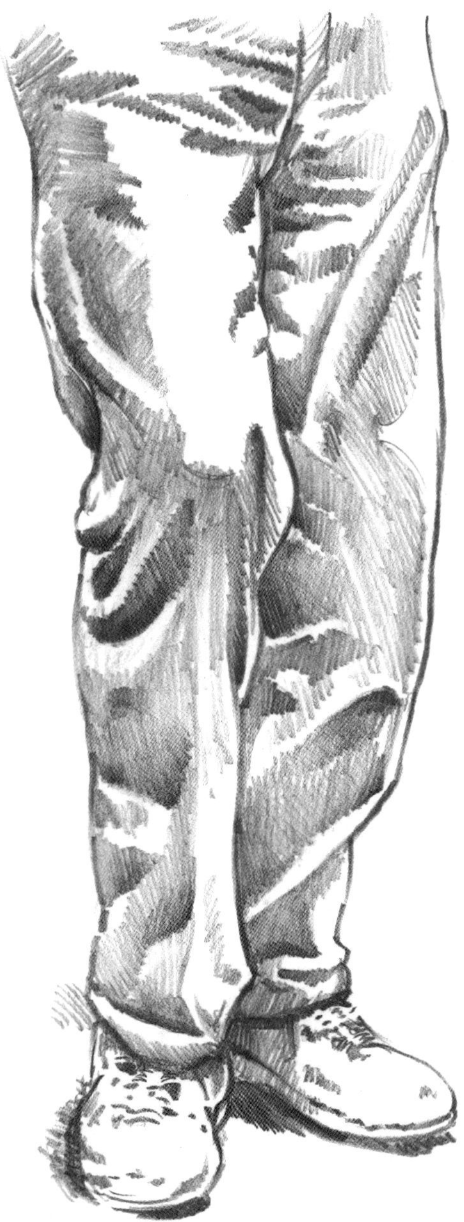

The arm resting on the keyboard appears to be receding back into space. The parts of the body closest to you should be shaded the least because they have the most light on them. Also keep in mind that as objects move farther away, they become less detailed and more blurred.

With crossed legs, most of the shading falls on the part of the leg farthest away, enhancing the perception of depth in the drawing. Be certain to rough in both legs and the major folds correctly before you begin shading.

More Foreshortening

To achieve realistic depth in your drawings, it's important to understand foreshortening. Foreshortening allows you to create the illusion of an object coming toward you in space. While the principles of perspective still exist, body parts are more difficult to draw in this manner because they don't have straight edges. In addition, the body proportions are somewhat skewed, or shortened, in a drawing that includes foreshortened subjects. When foreshortening something in a drawing, be sure to draw the object the way you really see it—not the way you think it should look. Foreshortening helps create a three-dimensional effect and often provides dramatic emphasis. Study the examples here to see how foreshortening influences their sense of depth.

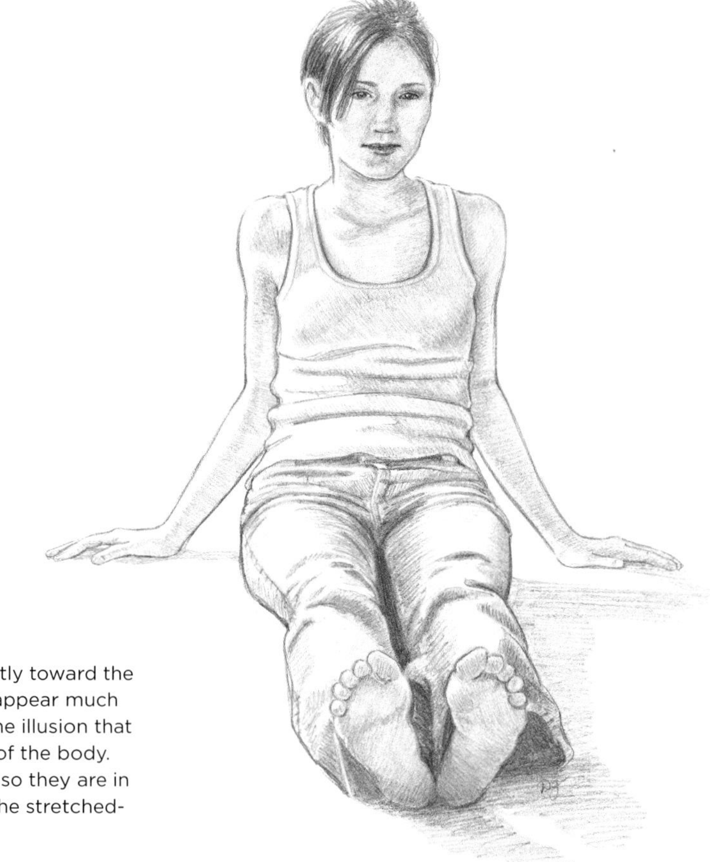

▶ **Straight-On View** Here, the legs are extended directly toward the viewer, so the legs are foreshortened, making them appear much shorter than they really are. This distortion creates the illusion that the feet are much closer to the viewer than the rest of the body. The torso, head, and arms are all on the same plane, so they are in proper proportion to one another. Notice here that the stretched-out legs appear to be only about 2 heads long.

▶ **Side View** In this view, the young woman's limbs are not distorted because the view is directly from the side, not at an angle. Her torso, head, and legs are all at roughly the same distance from the viewer. The fingers of her left hand are somewhat foreshortened because they are turned toward the viewer.

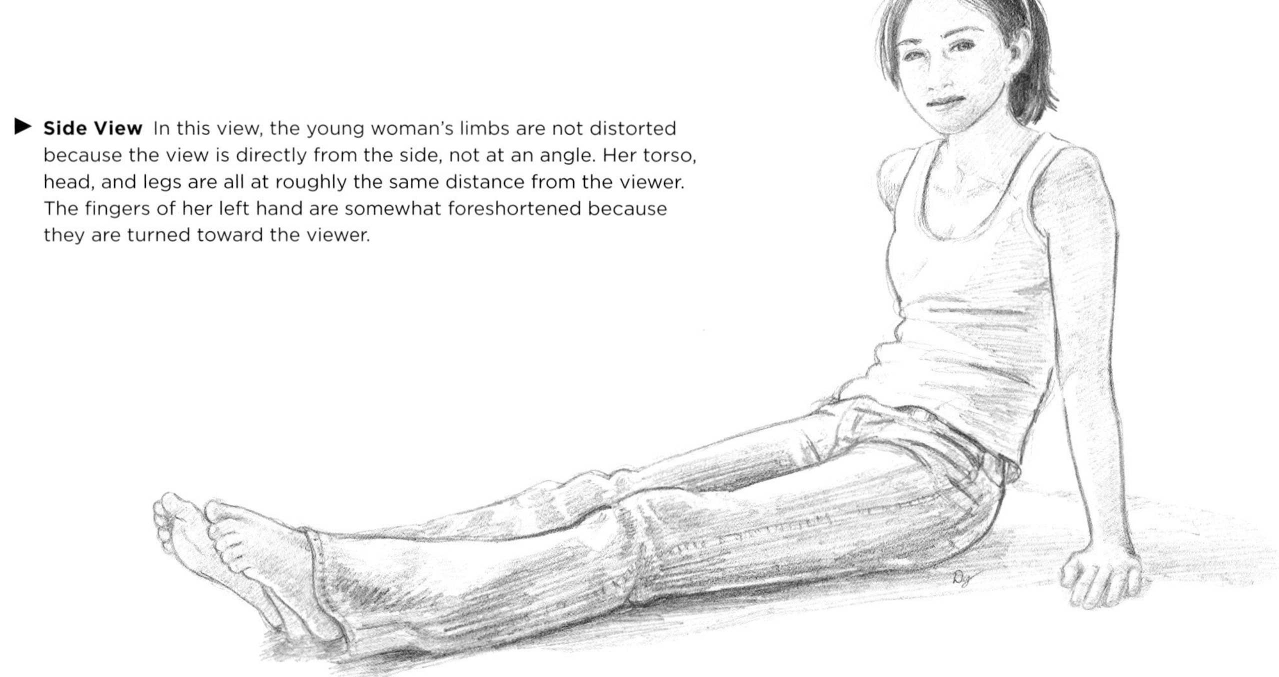

▶ **Angled View** In this view, the head is closer to the viewer than the feet. The thighs seem to disappear behind the hips. Only part of one foot is visible, and it is relatively small due to foreshortening. The right arm supporting the head is not distorted by perspective because the full length is parallel with the side of the picture plane (not angled toward or away from the viewer). The torso is slightly distorted by foreshortening; the shoulders are closer to us and appear a little larger in comparison with the hips.

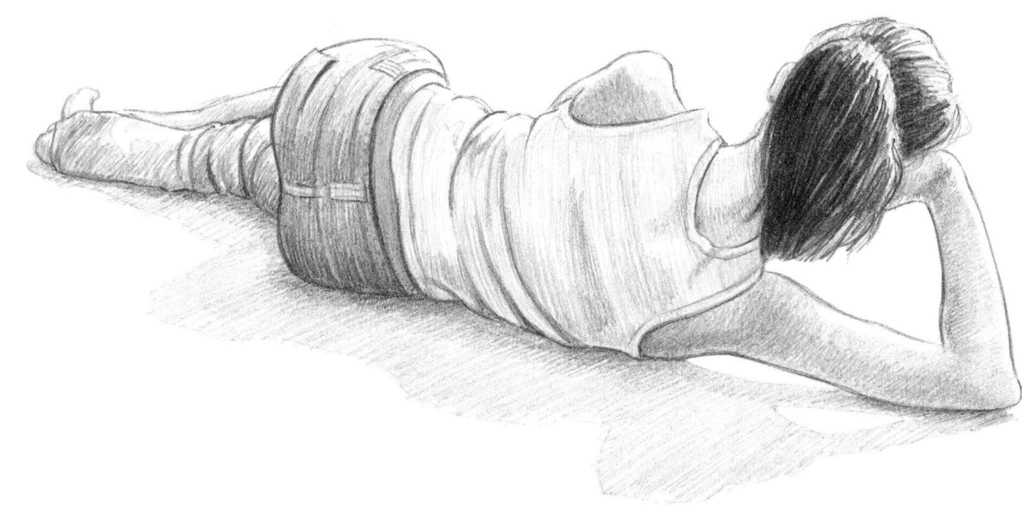

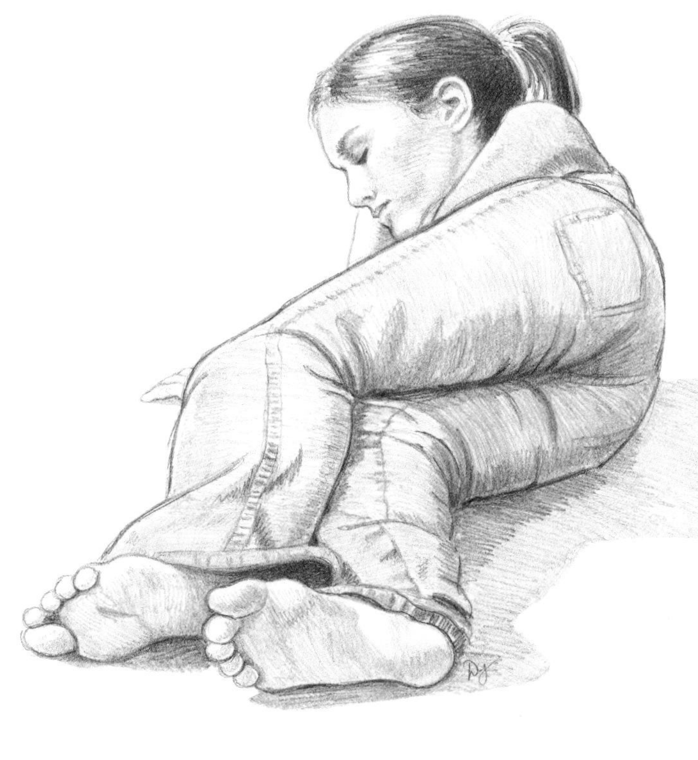

◀ **Foot to Head View** Here the feet are closest to the viewer, and the head is farthest away, so the feet appear relatively larger than they would normally. The lower legs are foreshortened because they are angled directly toward the viewer. Most of the torso and the arms are hidden behind the legs—remember that you shouldn't draw what you can't see!

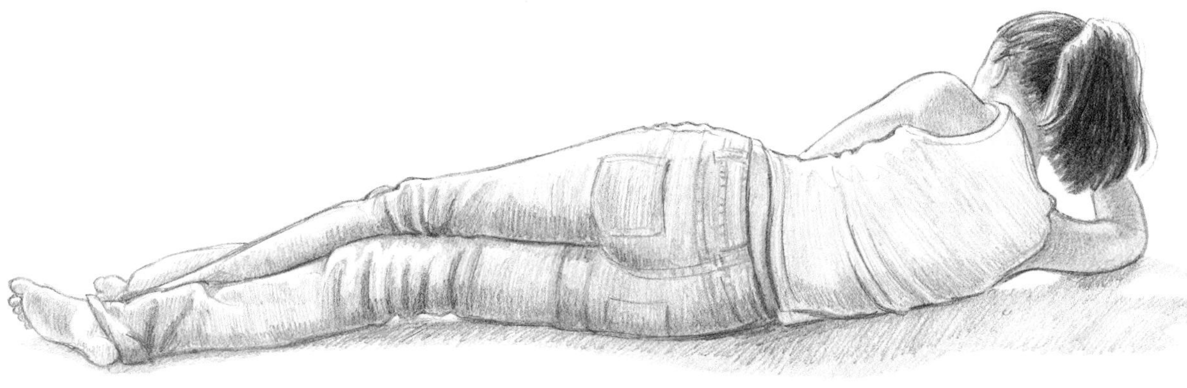

Back View with Angled Head and Arm In this view, most of the body is on the same plane (and parallel to the picture plane), but the head and arms are angled slightly away from the viewer, so they appear relatively small when compared with the rest of the body.

Mastering Depth

Drawing is all about illusion, but not the sleight-of-hand variety magicians perform. In a drawing, artists attempt to create the illusion of three dimensions in a variety of ways, but in every case they are just drawing what they see in front of them. Foreshortening is an important method of creating the illusion of depth, and it works hand in hand with perspective; that is, the part of the subject that is closest to us appears to be larger than the parts that are farther away.

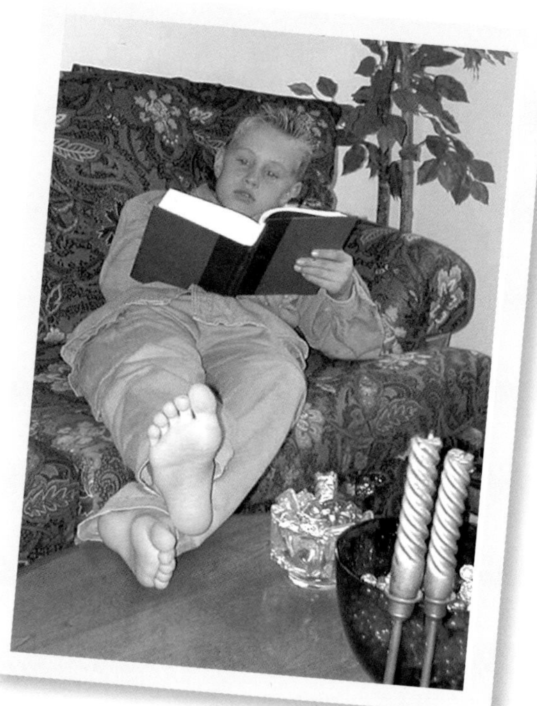

Recognizing Foreshortening This photo is an excellent example of foreshortening. Notice the difference in the size of his tiny head compared to his huge feet. This is because his feet are closer to us, so they appear much larger. Additionally, viewers know his legs must be longer than they appear from this viewpoint, and they know that his foot can't be the same length as his shin. But these are the size relationships seen from this point of view, so these are the size relationships that need to be drawn.

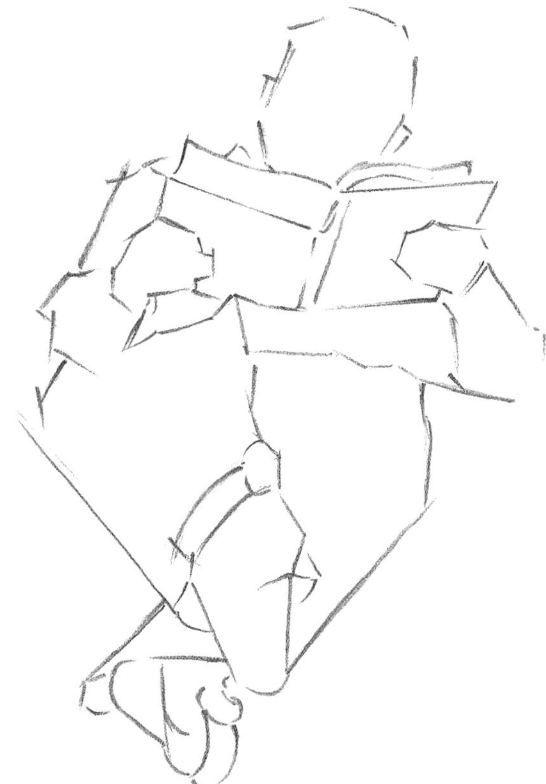

Step 1 Begin by lightly blocking in the outlines of only the major shapes—no details yet. The most important thing is to study the photo carefully and make sure all the size relationships are correct. In this photo, the book appeared to be unnaturally supported, so the artist added the right arm and hand. Even though "draw what you see" is a good path to follow, sometimes you need to take what is called artistic license and make a few changes to improve the composition.

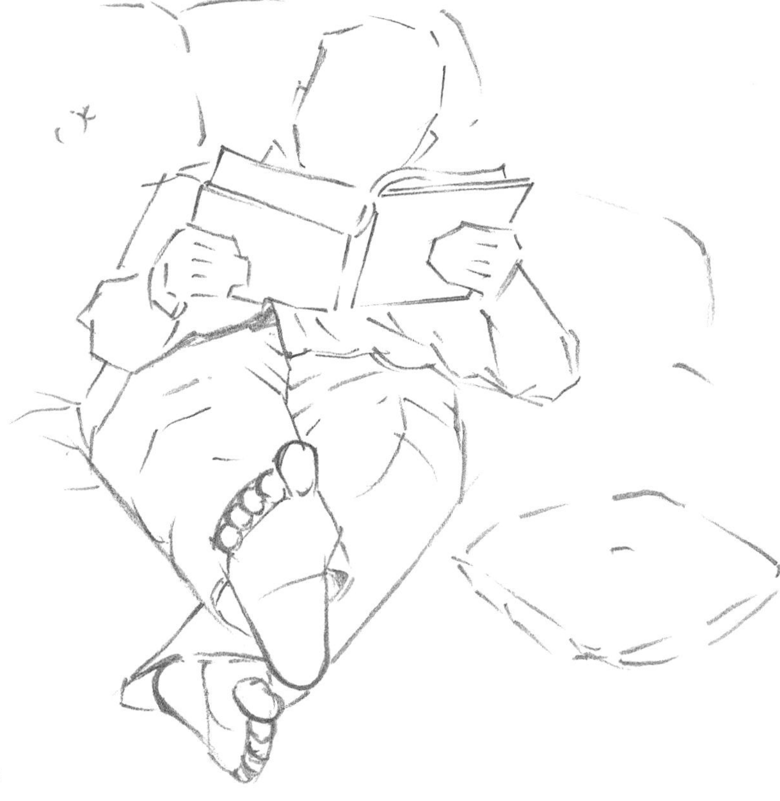

Step 2 Next, lightly add secondary curves to represent the roundness of the figure and the folds in the clothes. You are still blocking in basic information at this point, so keep these lines light so they wouldn't interfere when you refine the outlines.

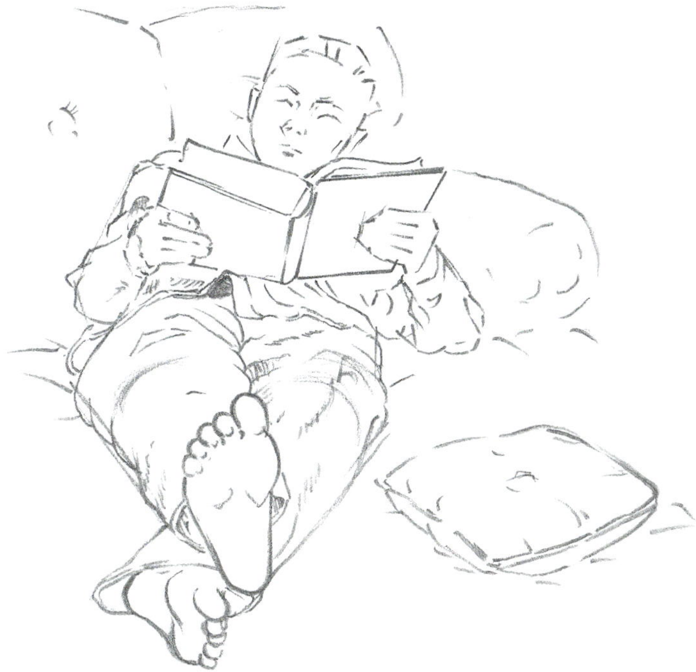

Step 3 As you refine the shapes, check your reference frequently. Notice how the darker, thicker lines on the feet already make them appear to come forward, whereas the thinner, fainter lines of the upper body recede. This technique enhances the sense of depth.

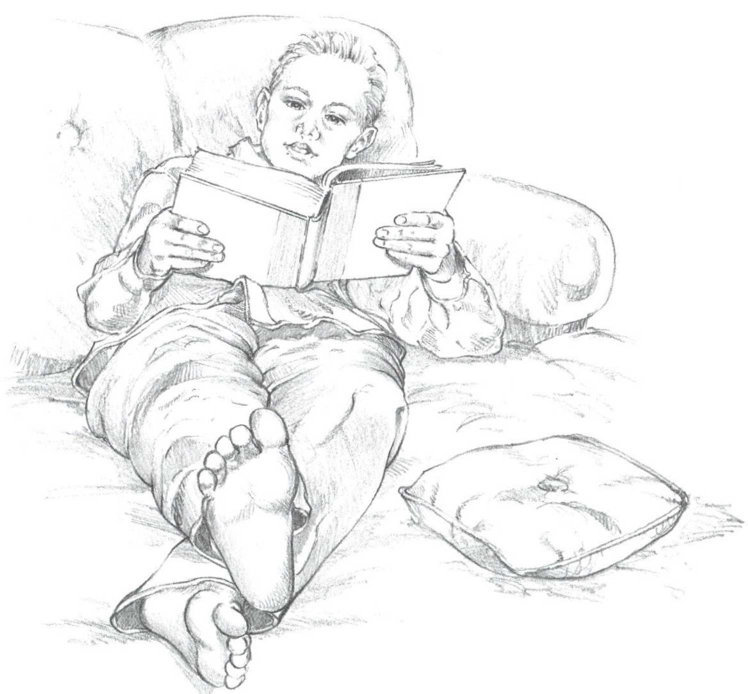

Step 4 Add light shading, and detail the fabric folds and facial features. Within the overall foreshortened pose, there are secondary areas of foreshortening. For instance, notice how the left foot is foreshortened (because it points toward the viewer) and his right one is not (because it points straight up). The backs of the hands, wrists, and forearms also are foreshortened (because they point toward us), whereas the fingers are not.

FORESHORTENING SIMPLIFIED

Fingers Straight Up Hold your hand in front of a mirror, palm forward. Notice that your fingers are the correct length in relation to your palm. Nothing is foreshortened here.

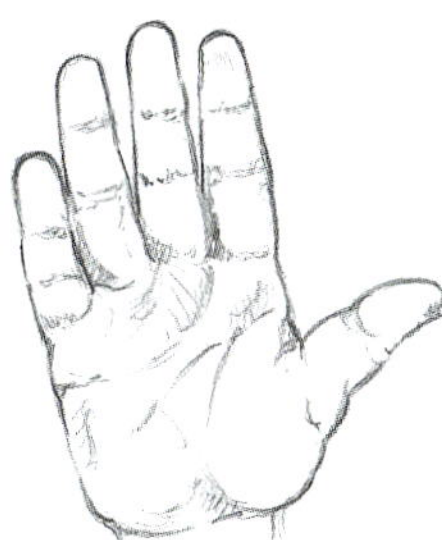

Fingers Angled Toward You Now tip your hand a little, and see how the length of the fingers and the palm appear shortened. This is subtle foreshortening. Of course, your fingers didn't really get shorter; it just looks that way!

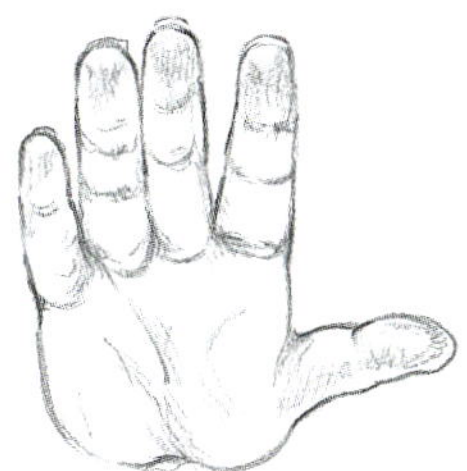

Fingers Pointing Front Now point them straight at you. This is the most extreme foreshortened view; the fingers appear to be mere stubs. Notice the shape of the fingernails as they curve over the cylindrical fingers.

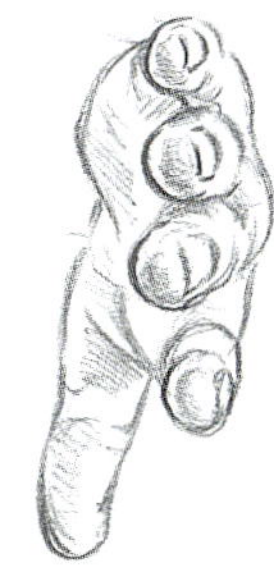

Fingers Angled Down The fingers appear longer now but still not full length, yet the fingertips are still visible. This pose shows some foreshortening; the fingers seem too long and thick in relation to the back of the hand.

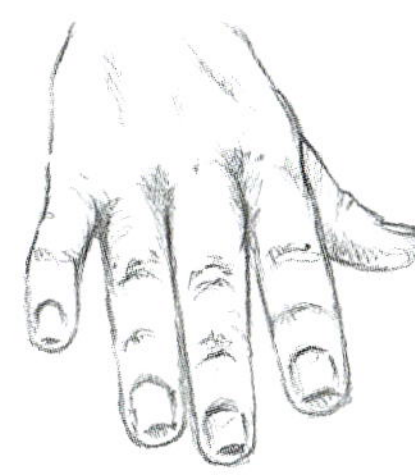

Fingers Pointing Straight Down No foreshortening is at work in this position—another frontal view. The tips of the fingers cannot be seen, and the length of the fingers and hand are not distorted.

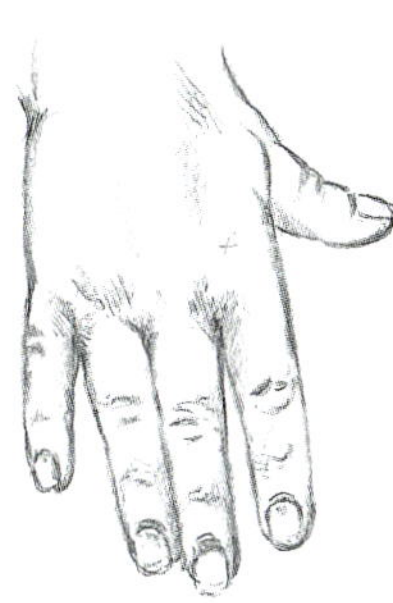

Drawing from Life

Drawing from a live model (also called "drawing from life" or "life drawing") is a wonderful exercise in drawing the human body in its various shapes and positions. Drawing from life helps you avoid overworking your drawing because you're instead focused on quickly recording the gesture and specific details of your model, resulting in a spontaneous, uncomplicated finished drawing. Take advantage of available models whenever possible. When drawing from life, be sure the pose is comfortable for the model. Allow short breaks for your models (also providing you time to rest), and don't require them to smile, as this can tire out their facial muscles. Because you're working at a faster pace, drawing from life will help you learn freedom and flexibility—both of which will benefit your drawings regardless of the type of reference. It will also help you appreciate the subtleties the eye perceives that the camera can't—such as a twinkle in the eye!

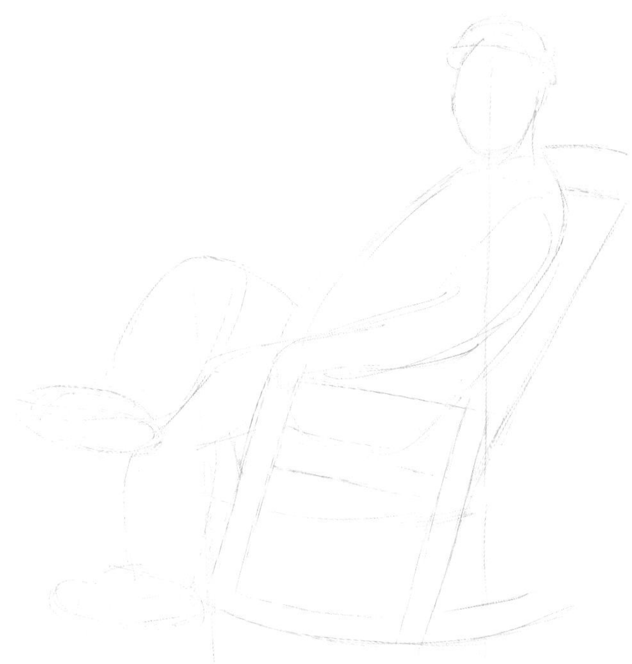

Step 1 Using an HB pencil, lightly block in the basic shapes of the figure and the rocking chair, paying particular attention to the vertical lines and balance to make sure the figure doesn't look as if he's going to tip over in the chair. Notice that the model's back curves forward while the back of the chair angles backward, and his head aligns vertically with the back of the chair leg. Foreshorten the right leg, and make the right foot larger than the left because the right leg is angled toward the viewer.

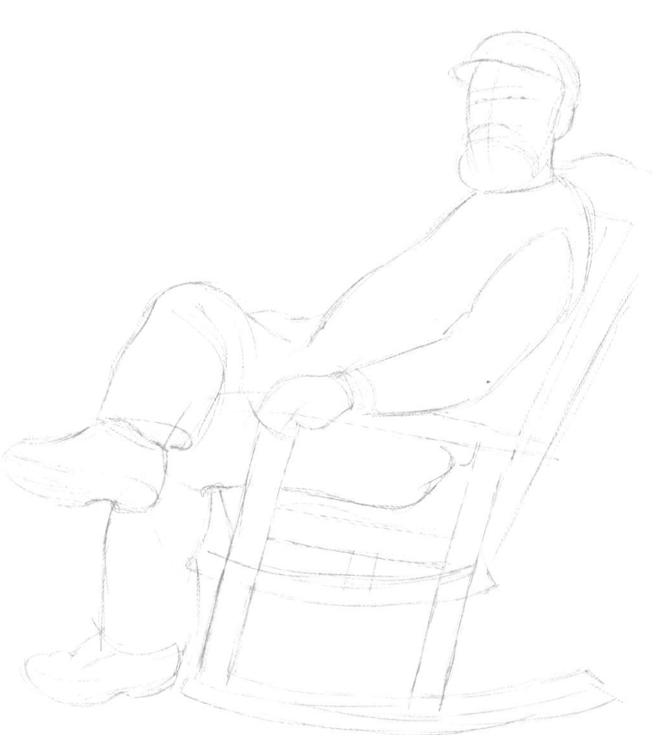

Step 2 Begin to refine the shapes, indicating the clothing and shoes. Then block in the mustache and beard, and place guidelines for the facial features.

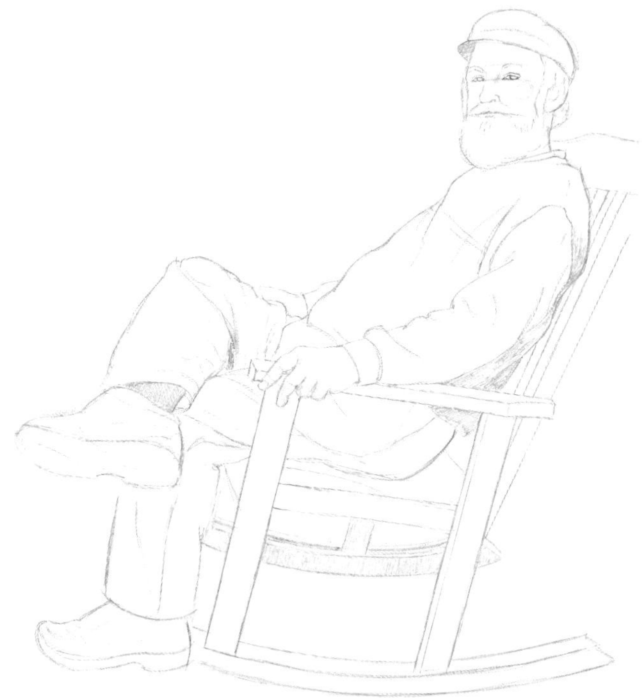

Step 3 With a B pencil, draw in the facial features and refine the shapes of the head, including the ear, hair, and hat. Then hone the rest of the body, drawing the folds and details of the fabric and adding the fingers on the left hand. Next, further develop the chair, using a ruler to create straight lines. Continue by shading the hat, the sock, the far rocker, and the model's back.

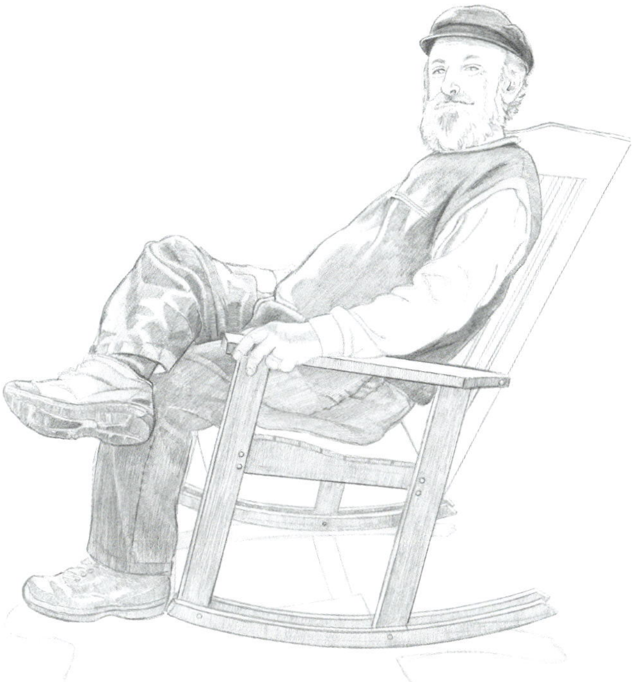

Step 5 Lightly shade the face, varying your strokes to follow the different planes. Add further details and shading to the eyes, nose, mouth, ear, hair, and facial hair. Study your model to see what details will help create a likeness. Then shade the clothing and chair, always keeping in mind where the light is coming from, and adjusting the lights and shadows as needed to enhance the illusion of depth. Use a 4B pencil for the darkest areas, and leave the lightest areas pure white. Soften any hard edges with an eraser, a blending stump, or a tissue. Finally, step back from your drawing, squint your eyes, and see if there are any areas that need to be corrected. If any areas are too light or too dark, adjust them as necessary.

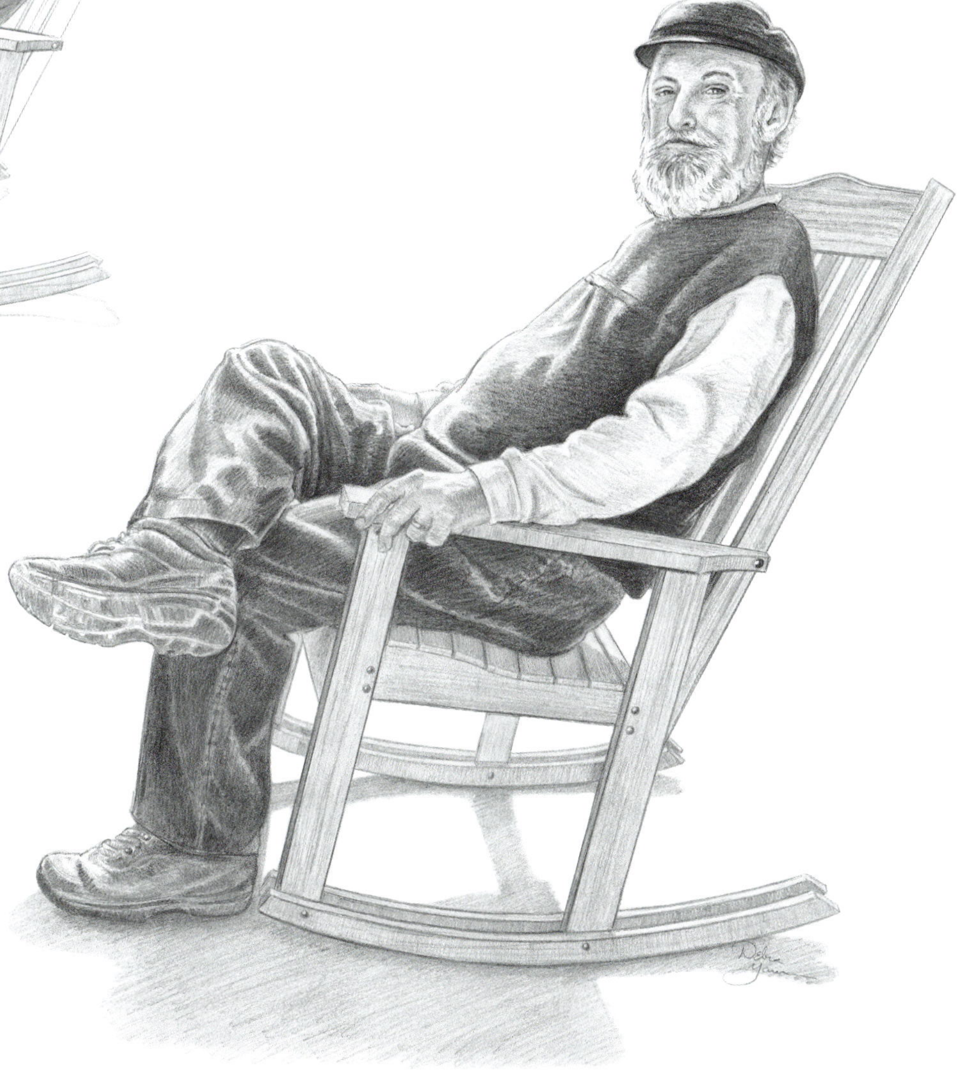

Step 4 Using a 2B pencil, begin shading the hat, leaving the top edge and a line on the brim white. Add some detailing to the hair and beard with short strokes, following the direction of growth. Shade the clothing, leaving the areas white along the side where the light hits. Watch the shapes of the wrinkles and how they affect the lights and shadows. Also shade some of the rocker, and lightly sketch in the shapes of the cast shadows.

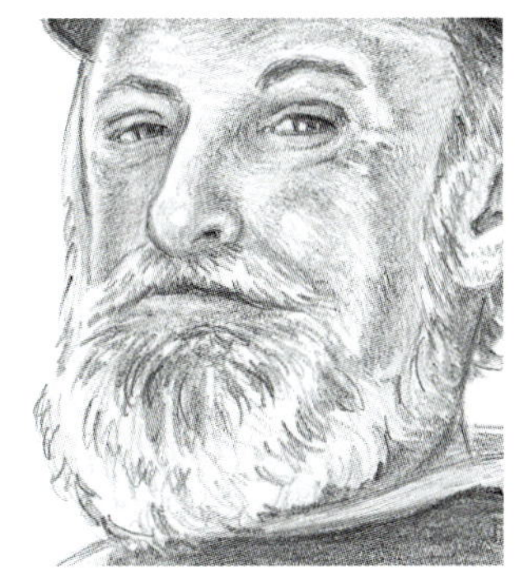

FACE DETAIL

To create the beard, apply very dark tone to areas of the beard, showing the gaps between groups of hair. Also leave some areas of the paper completely white to reflect the areas of the beard that are in the direct path of sunlight. When detailing the face, shade very lightly to indicate wrinkles and creases. The wrinkles should appear soft, so avoid using hard lines. To create the twinkle in the eyes, pull out a highlight in each pupil with a kneaded eraser.

Understanding Lighting

An important aspect of drawing—especially when drawing people—is lighting the subject. Lighting can have a dramatic effect on the figure's appearance, eliciting an emotional response from the viewer and setting the mood of the drawing. Subtle lighting often is associated with tranquility and can make a subject appear soft and smooth. This type of lighting tends to lighten the mood, generally lending a more cheerful feel to the composition. On the other hand, strong lighting makes it easier to see the contrasts between light and dark, which can add drama and make the subject appear more precisely formed. Longer shadows can mute the mood of a portrait, producing an air of pensiveness. Here strong shadows on the subject's face make her subtle smile seem reflective rather than content.

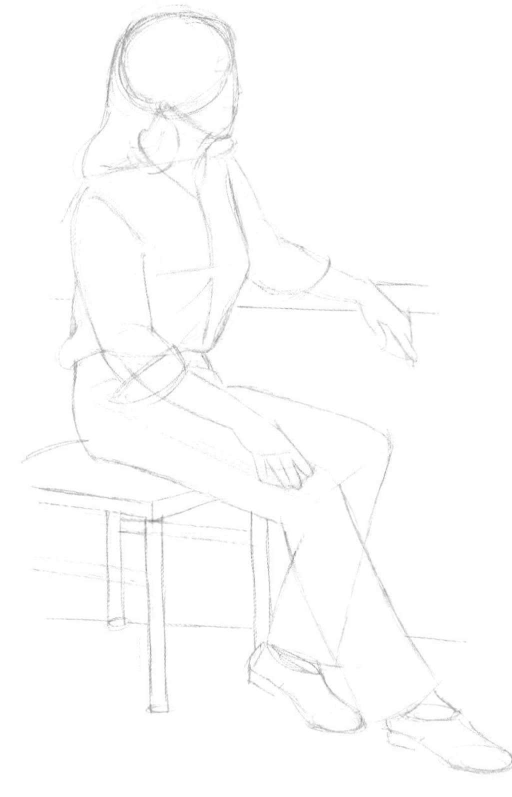

Step 1 First, sketch the outlines of the figure on white drawing paper, using an HB pencil. Start with the torso, and then add the shape of the head. This is a three-quarter view of the body, but the face is in complete profile as the subject looks out the window. Block in the lines of the shoulders and chest; then add the window frame and sketch both arms. Draw the seat of the chair, and indicate the chair legs. Then, add the subject's legs, with the subject's right leg stretched out in front of her and the left leg pulled back toward the chair. Lightly sketch the entire back leg, "drawing through" the front leg to help position the leg correctly, and then erase any unnecessary lines.

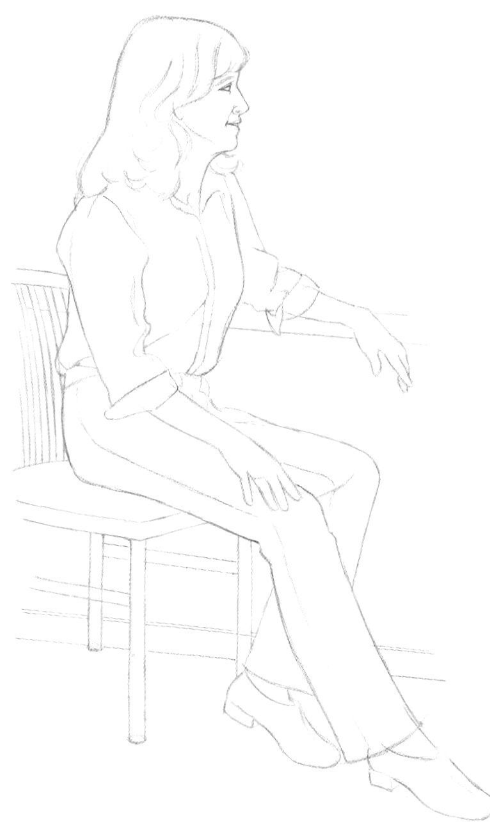

Step 2 Switch to a B pencil and begin refining the head by adding the features and the hair, erasing unneeded lines as the drawing progresses. Refine the shirt and jeans, adding details like the seam along the leg. Add the back of the chair, and refine the shape of the rest of the chair. Draw the lower window frame, and refine her fingers and the shapes of the shoes. The main concern at this stage is establishing the overall shape of the figure—shading to indicate lighting and mood will come next.

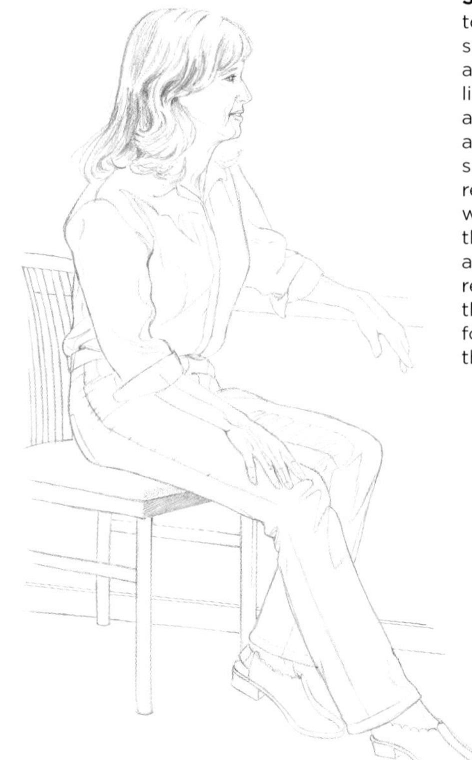

Step 3 Using a very light touch, draw the edges of the shadows along the face, neck, arms, hands, and ankles. These lines will serve as a guide for adding the shading later. Also add this shading line to the shirt and pants, following your reference photo. The shading will outline the areas where the lightest highlights will be, as this part of the paper will remain white. Begin to shade the hair, curving the strokes to follow its shape. Then shade the front of the chair.

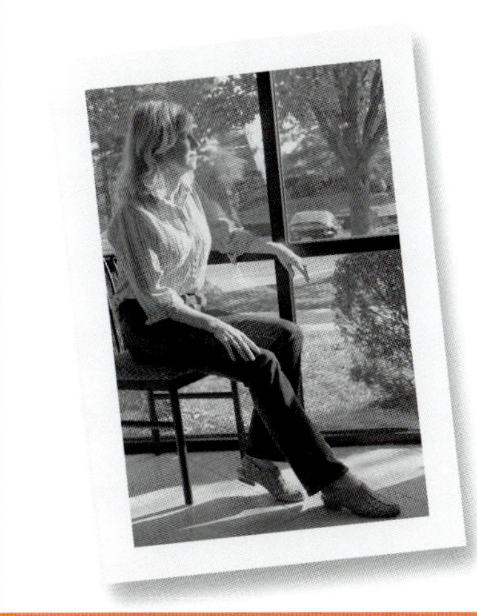

USING STRONG NATURAL LIGHT

The model for this drawing is sitting beside a floor-to-ceiling window. The sun is streaming through the glass from above and in front of her. The strong light creates visual interest by casting deep shadows and creating bright highlights.

Step 5 Switch back to a very sharp B pencil to add some details to the face. Using a 2B pencil, create more dark values in the hair, and shade the stripes on the shirt. Darken the rest of the jeans using strokes that follow the form of her legs. With a sharp pencil point, carefully add a layer of shading to the darker areas of the skin. Reflected light from the shirt lightens her jaw line. Reflected light also appears on her arms and fingers; stroke across the arms to give them form. Shade the rest of the chair, leaving white on the chair legs where the light hits them. Because this portrait utilizes strong contrasts in light, larger portions of the drawing will remain nearly white—including the highlights on her legs, her throat, and her chest. A portrait that comprises varying degrees of shadows without these large areas of highlight would lose drama and intensity. Next shade the shoes, making them darker where the woven pattern is more detailed. On the floor, use diagonal hatching strokes, angling away from the light to create the shadows cast by the legs of both the subject and the chair.

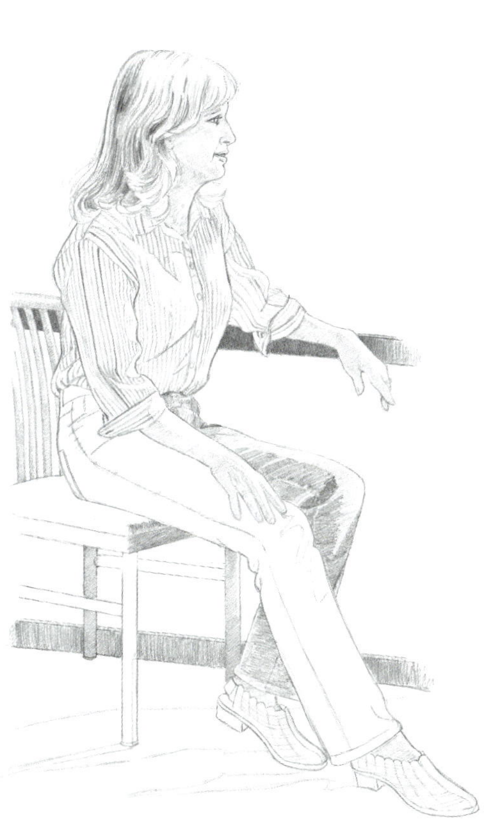

Step 4 Shade the skin using light, diagonal strokes, except where the highlight is strongest. Erase any remaining shading guidelines. Then draw the stripes of the subject's shirt, following the folds and curves of the fabric over her form and leaving the lightest areas white. After adding details to the shoes, use a 2B pencil to create dramatic contrasts in value—shading the inside of the left leg, adding a few more dark values to the hair, and drawing the outlines of the shadows on the floor. Look at your reference photo frequently to check the placement and strength of your highlights and dark values. Then apply additional shading to the back and legs of the chair, and shade the window frame.

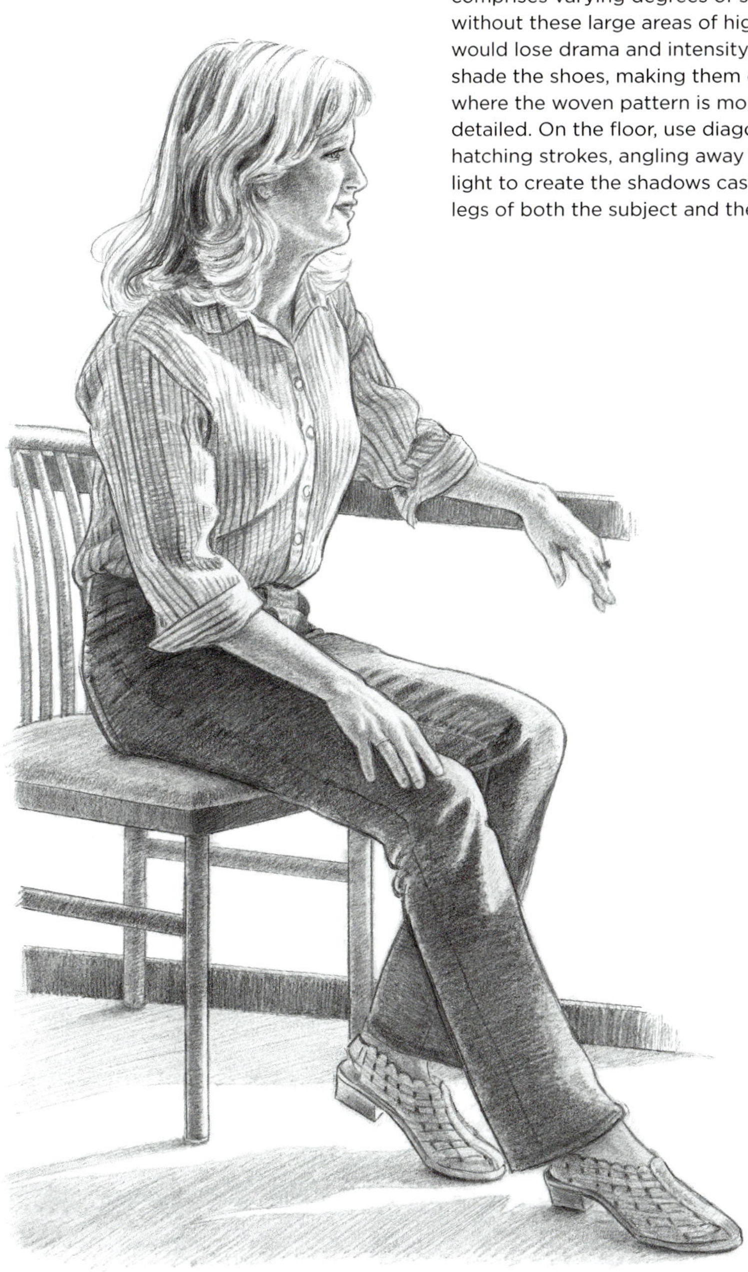

Choosing a Pose

Not every photo you take is going to be good, and not every pose your model strikes is going to be perfect. Look for poses that are natural and balanced, not stiff or boring. Some movement or tension can make the pose more interesting, but your subject should look stable and comfortable in the position. Unless in motion, the model should not have his or her arms and legs stretched out in all directions; instead, he or she should be more compact and relaxed. The pose should reflect the personality or interests of the subject. Take many photos to use as references, and evaluate them for suitability.

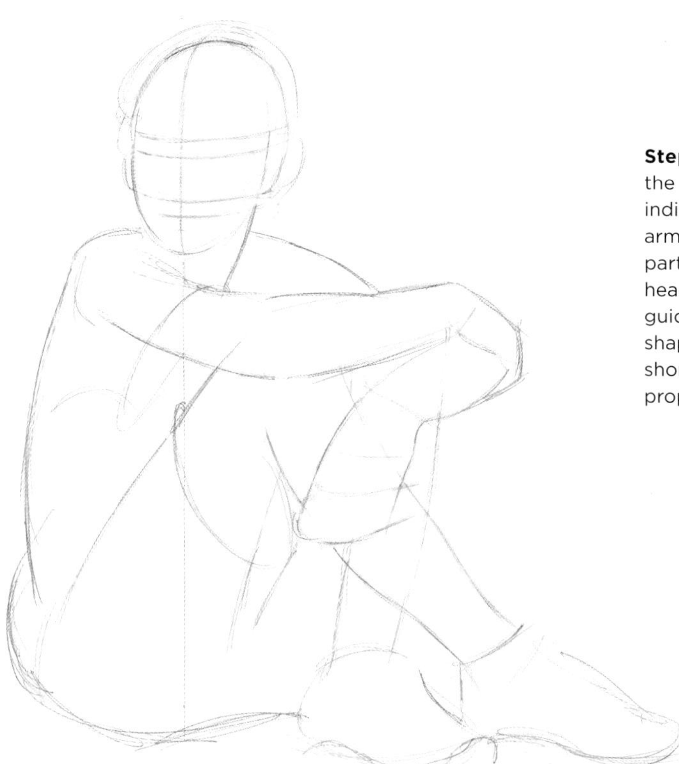

Step 1 Using an HB pencil, block in the figure. Place the head above the center of the main body mass, as indicated by the vertical line. Sketch the shapes of the arms and legs, drawing through the overlapping body parts for correct placement. The vertical centerline on the head shows the three-quarter view. Add the horizontal guidelines for the facial features. Sketch the general shapes of the shoes and the lines for the ends of the shorts and the shirt sleeve. Be sure the pose and proportions are accurate before adding any details.

Step 2 Now it's time for some definition. Place the facial features on the guidelines. Remember: The guides you learned about earlier are based on averages; to achieve a good likeness, be sure to follow your photo reference and adjust accordingly—for example, accounting for this boy's high forehead and wide-set eyes. Indicate the hair, and sketch in the clothing, showing some of the folds and wrinkles. Sketch in the shapes of the fingers of his left hand and the elbow of his right arm. Refine the shapes of the shoes, and indicate laces.

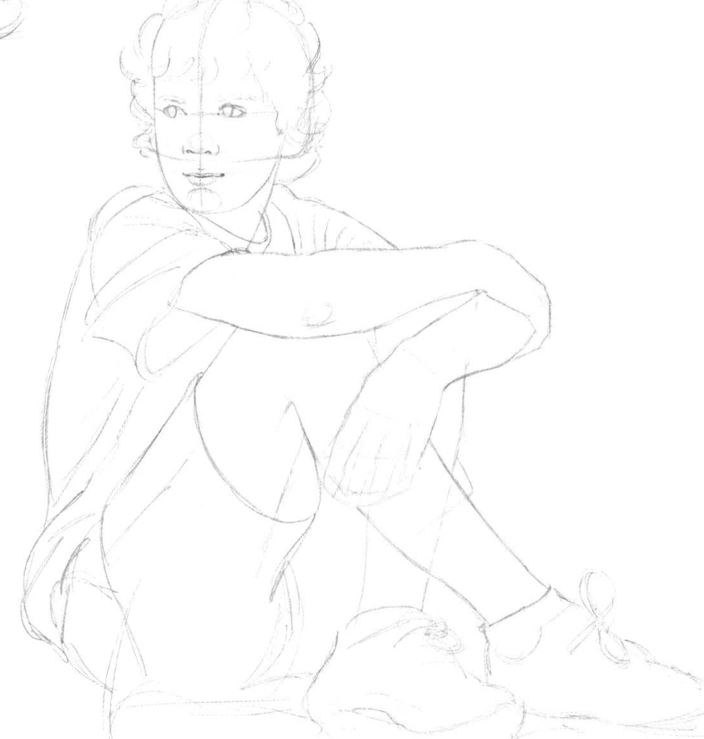

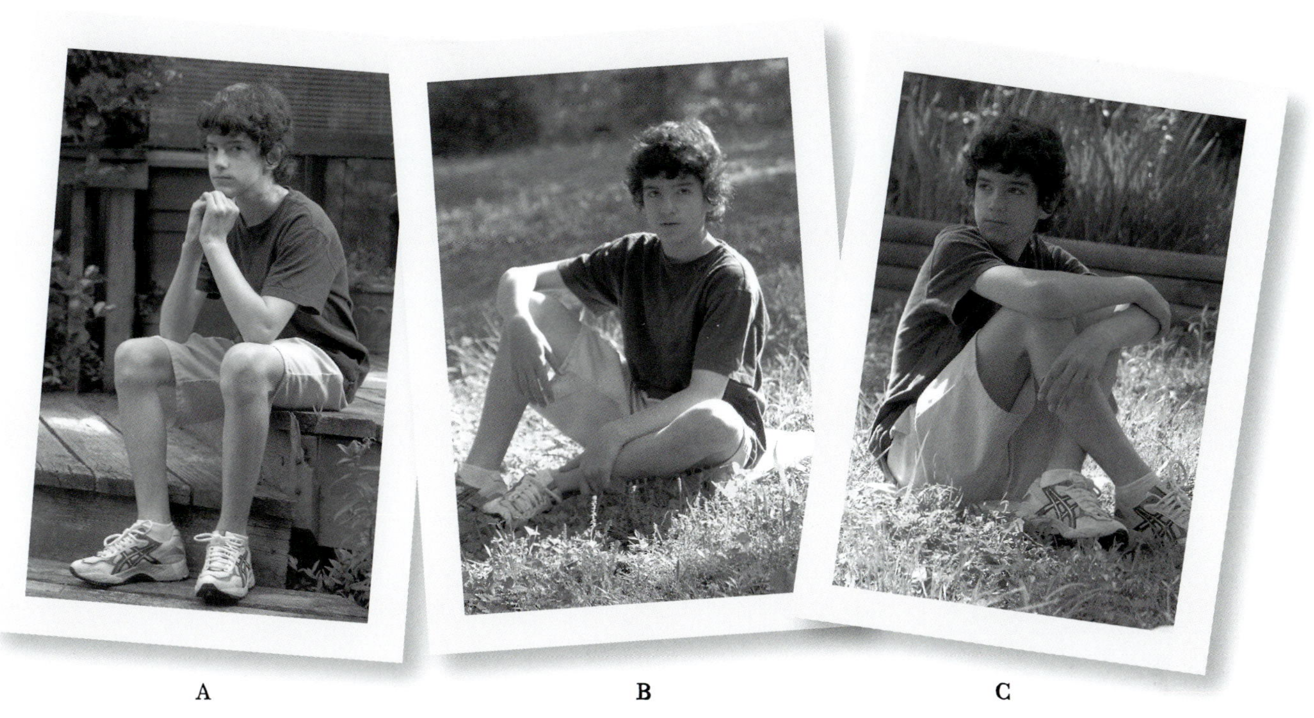

A   B   C

EVALUATING PHOTO REFERENCES

In photo A, the subject has a stable, compact pose, but he looks a bit stiff and bored; his personality doesn't show through. The pose in photo B is more relaxed, but the boy looks a little out of balance, and his arms and legs are in awkward positions; in addition, the light behind him is a bit harsh. Photo C is a great pose to represent this young man. He looks quite comfortable, and his hands and feet are in good, natural positions; his head is turned at a 90° angle to his body, which helps give some movement and interest to the pose. The lighting is more even as well. This is the best pose to use for a drawing.

Step 3 Erase the guidelines. Then use a B pencil to refine the facial features and the hair. Give the fingers a more precise shape, and add the fingernails. Refine the shapes of the arms, legs, and clothing, removing unneeded lines with a kneaded eraser. Using "artistic license" (the artist's prerogative to ignore what actually exists and to make changes, deletions, or additions), the author decides to change the shoelace so it is not awkwardly sticking up at an odd angle.

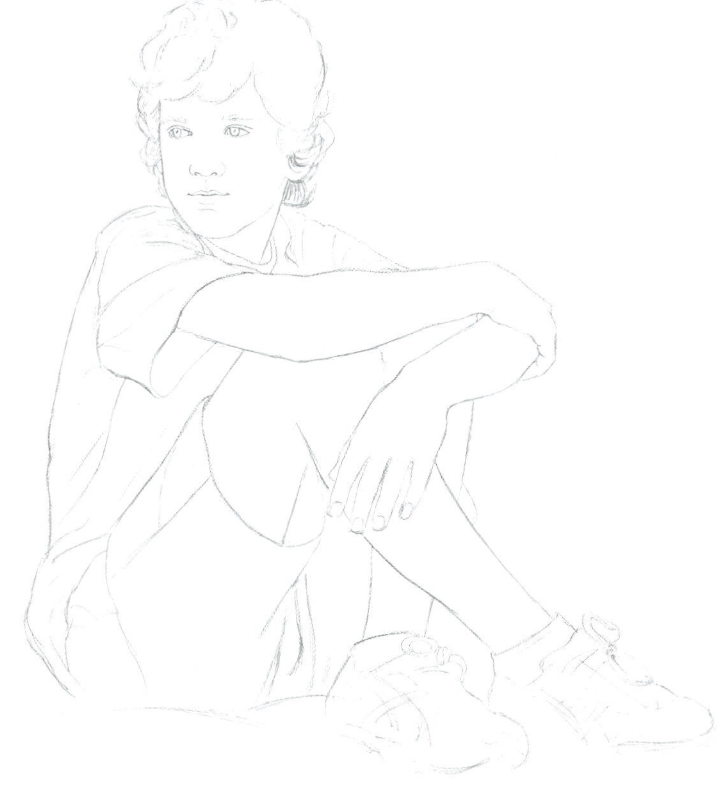

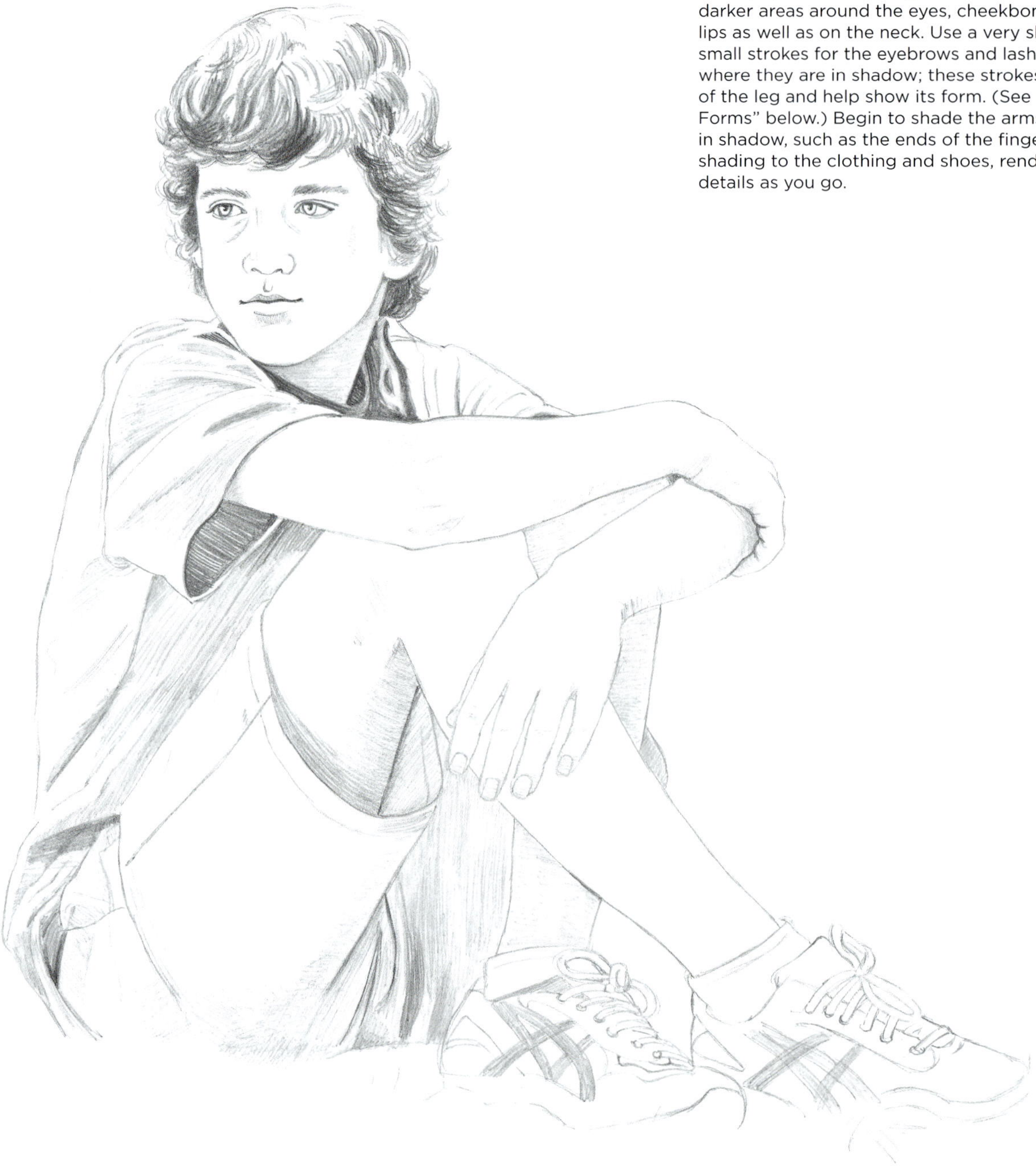

Step 4 Using a 2B pencil, begin shading the hair with strokes that follow the direction of growth. Leave areas of white paper where the light hits the hair. Shade some darker areas around the eyes, cheekbones, and under the lips as well as on the neck. Use a very sharp pencil and small strokes for the eyebrows and lashes. Darken the legs where they are in shadow; these strokes follow the curve of the leg and help show its form. (See "Shading the Forms" below.) Begin to shade the arms and other areas in shadow, such as the ends of the fingers. Add more shading to the clothing and shoes, rendering additional details as you go.

SHADING THE FORMS

Shading with varying values—from black through all shades of gray to white—enhances the illusion of depth in a drawing. Effective shading also adds life and realism to a drawing. When shading cylindrical elements, such as the arms and legs, make sure your pencil strokes follow the curved forms, as shown in the picture at right. This illustration has been exaggerated to demonstrate the different directions the shading lines should follow; your strokes, of course, will be smoother with subtle gradations and highlighting.

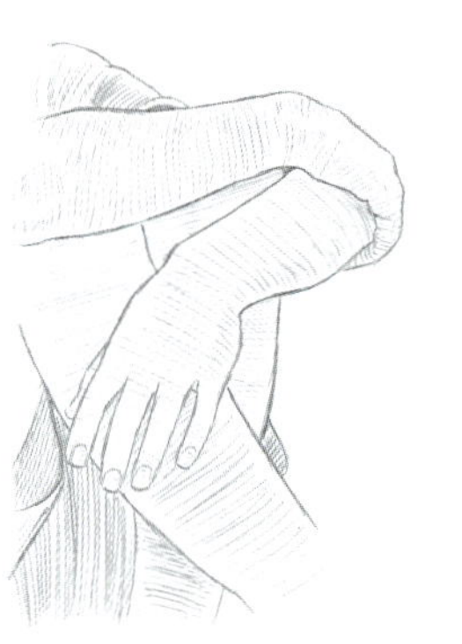

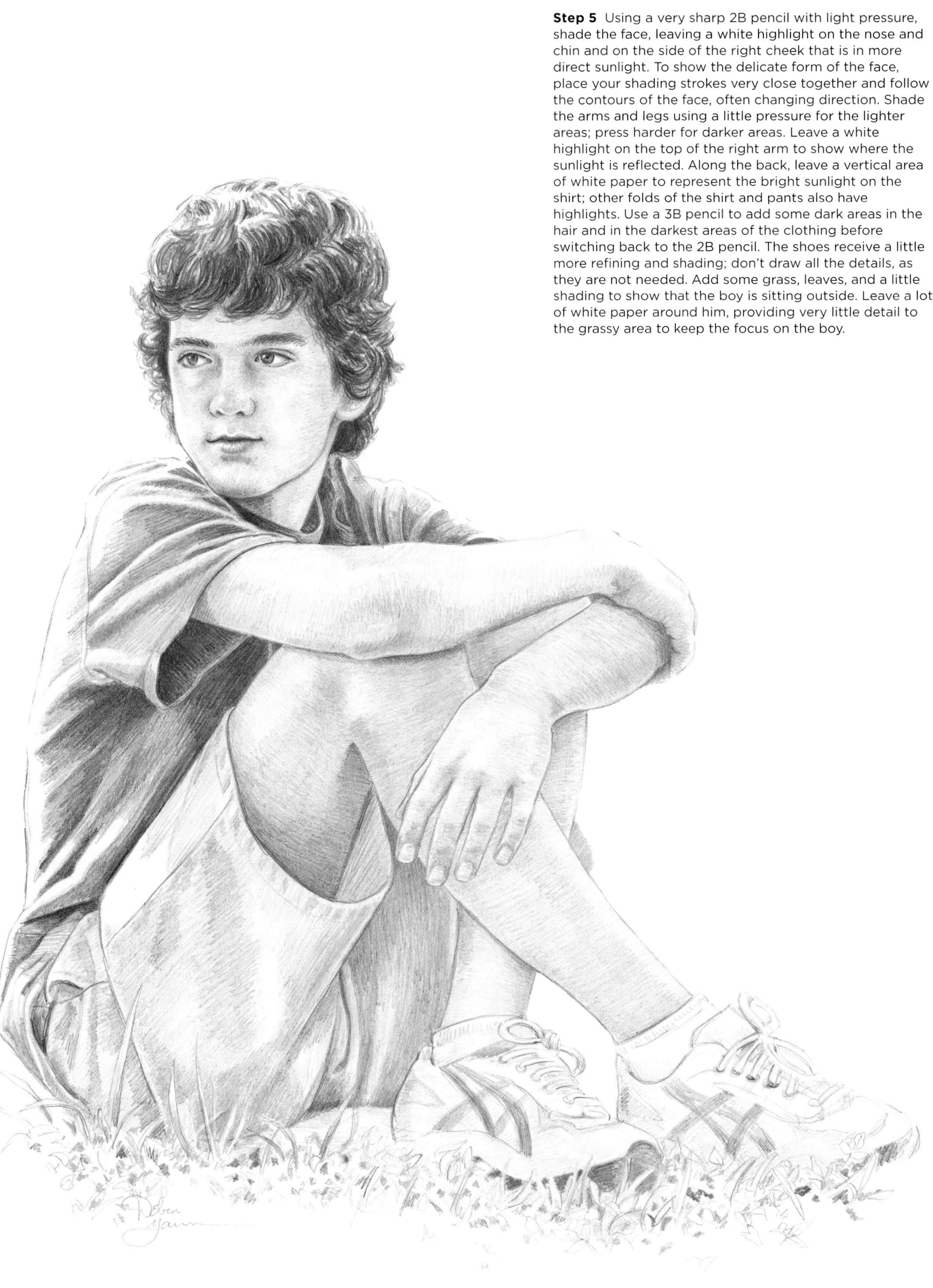

Step 5 Using a very sharp 2B pencil with light pressure, shade the face, leaving a white highlight on the nose and chin and on the side of the right cheek that is in more direct sunlight. To show the delicate form of the face, place your shading strokes very close together and follow the contours of the face, often changing direction. Shade the arms and legs using a little pressure for the lighter areas; press harder for darker areas. Leave a white highlight on the top of the right arm to show where the sunlight is reflected. Along the back, leave a vertical area of white paper to represent the bright sunlight on the shirt; other folds of the shirt and pants also have highlights. Use a 3B pencil to add some dark areas in the hair and in the darkest areas of the clothing before switching back to the 2B pencil. The shoes receive a little more refining and shading; don't draw all the details, as they are not needed. Add some grass, leaves, and a little shading to show that the boy is sitting outside. Leave a lot of white paper around him, providing very little detail to the grassy area to keep the focus on the boy.

Applying Your Skills

Now that you've mastered all of the techniques in this chapter, you can incorporate them into one finished work. As you can see, this drawing demonstrates principles of perspective, line of action, and center of balance. It also illustrates successful renderings of figures bending and twisting, sitting, and moving in a variety of action poses. It's important that you attempt to draw a challenging work like this to improve your artistic skills. On location, record your subjects with quick simple lines, creating a reference for a tighter, more polished work back at home. Success requires patience and a lot of practice!

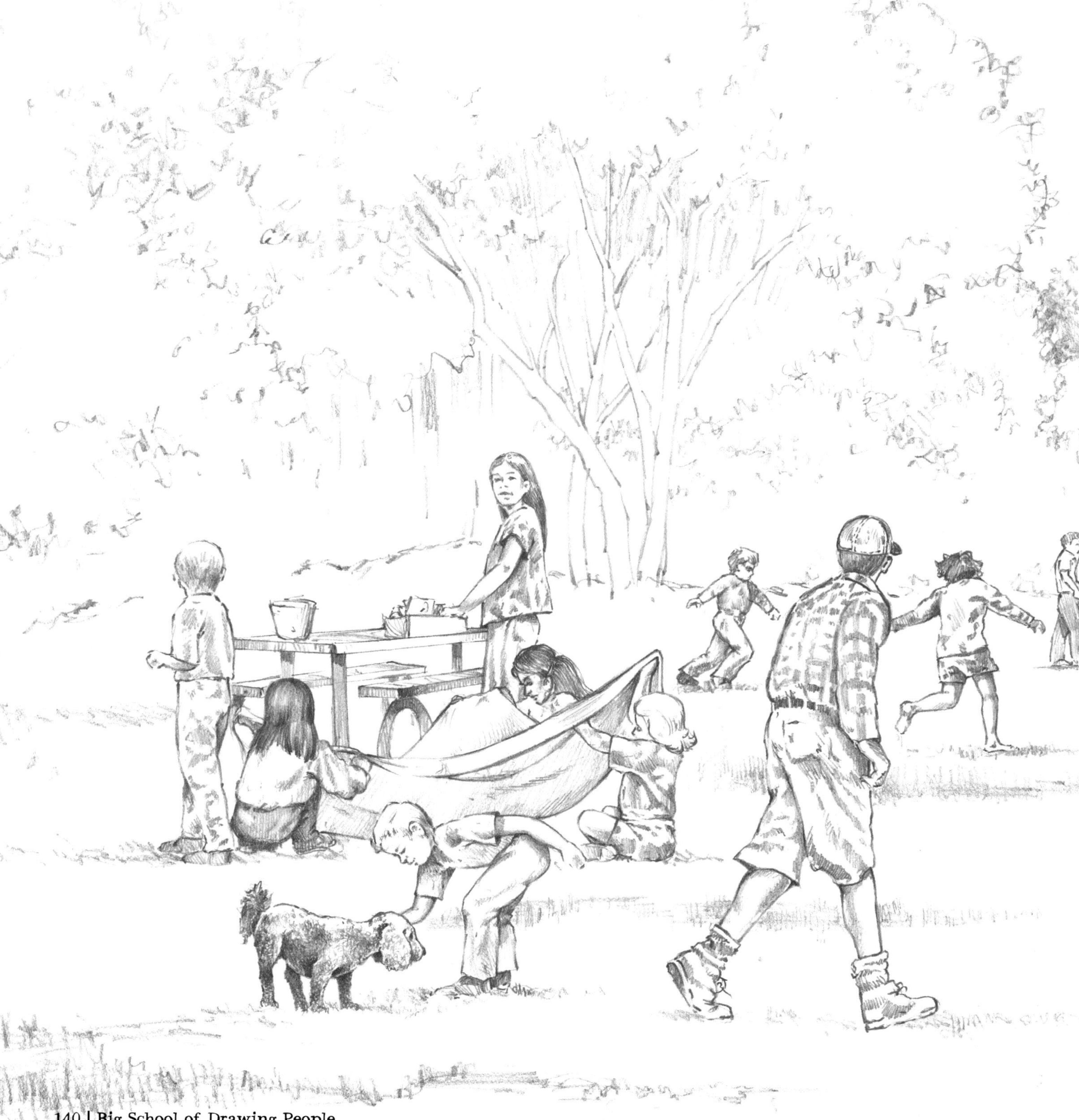

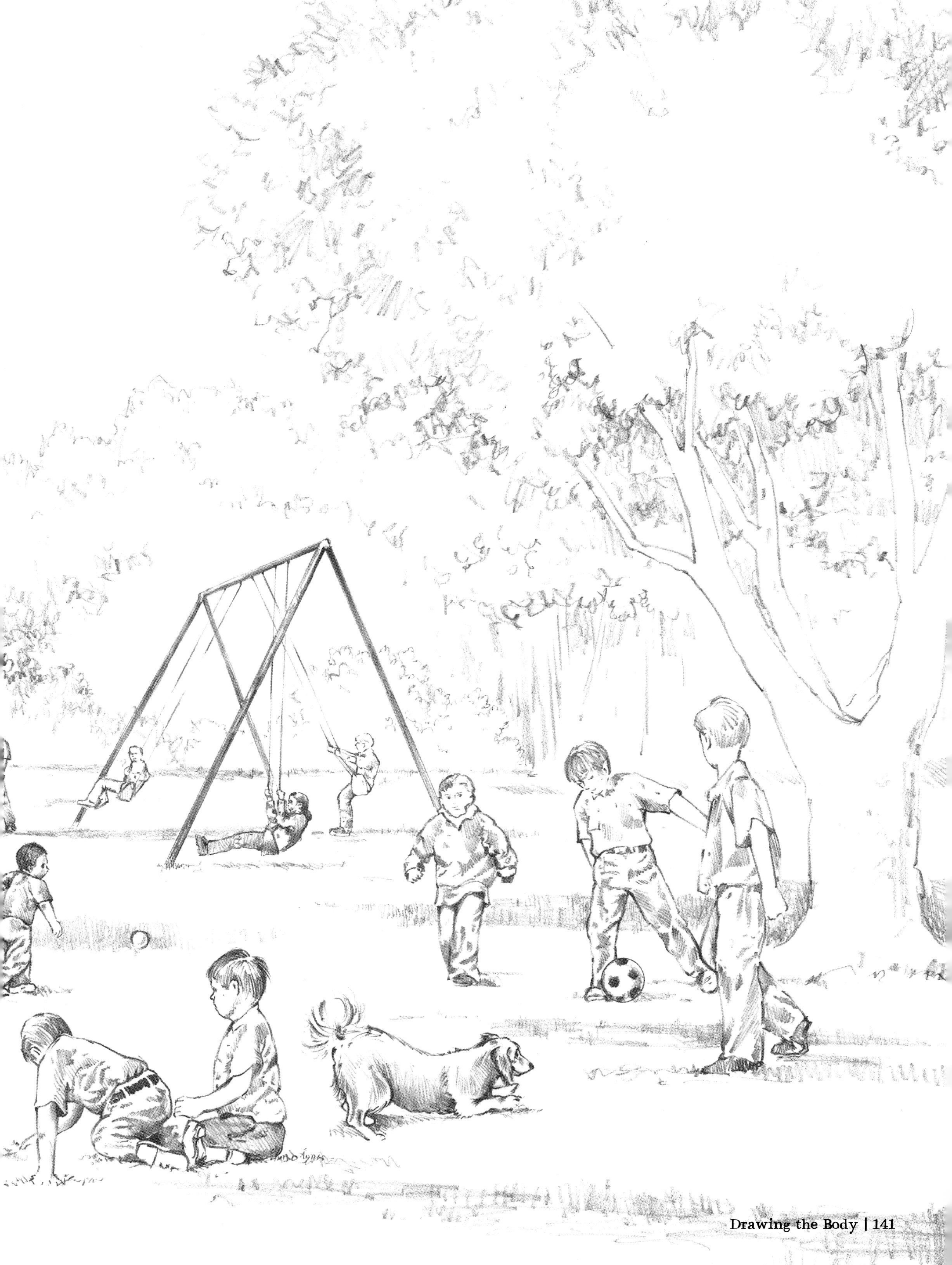

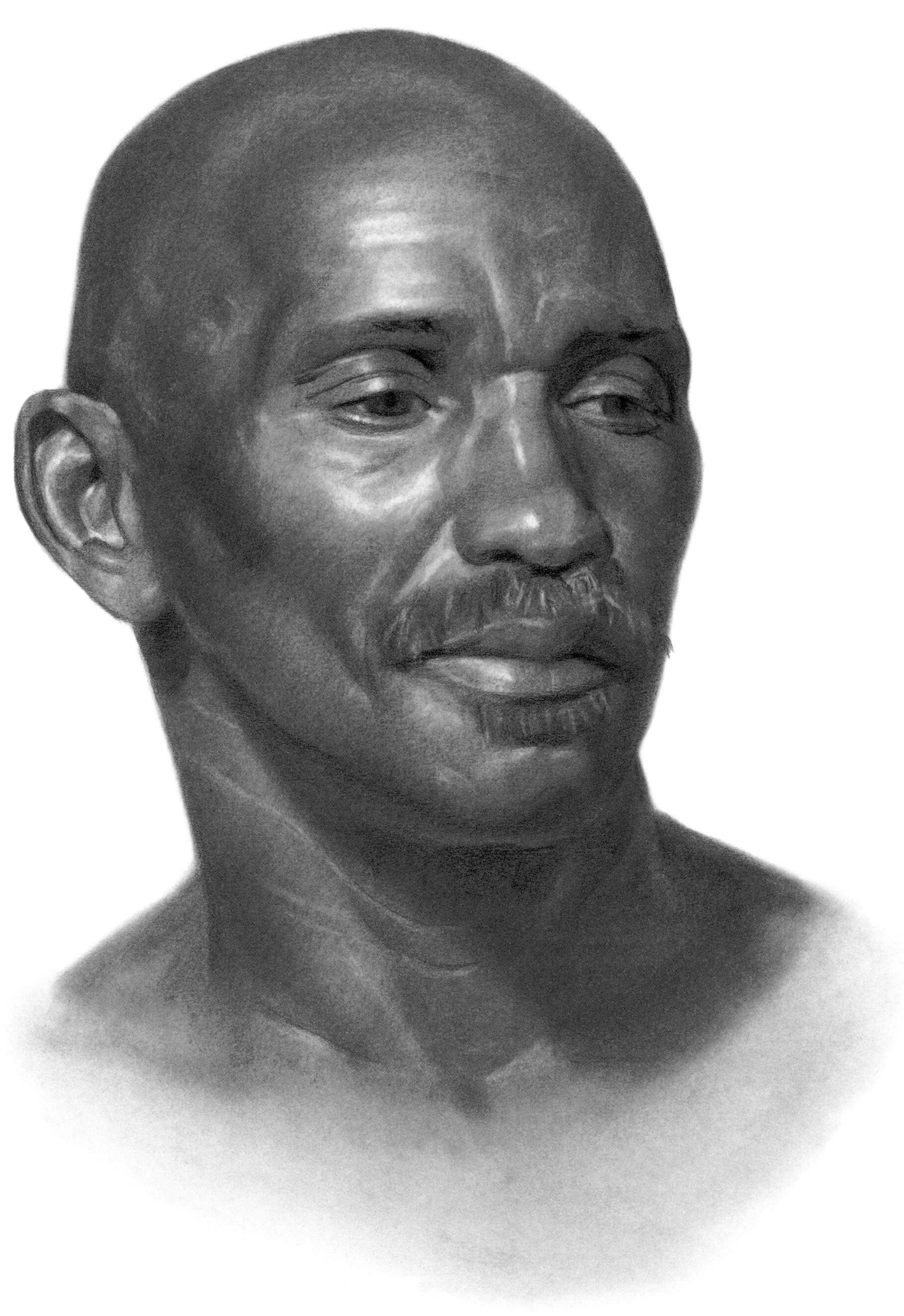

Master Class: Drawing Portraits in Graphite

In this chapter, you will learn a specific drawing method: drawing with graphite. You will also learn how to draw in graphite using a live model. Unlike working from a photograph, you can "measure" a live model in the studio using simple tools that allow you to draw facial features on paper. Once the first sketch is finished, you will follow a simple but efficient method that allows you to create striking, vivid drawings in six steps. An experienced artist can help you to better understand the anatomy and composition of a face. You will also learn how to spot and avoid mistakes.

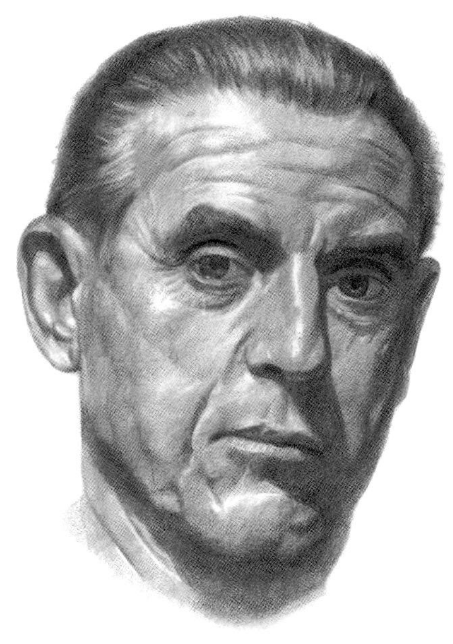

Materials & Techniques

Generally, graphite drawing requires a few simple tools, such as a pencil, eraser, and paper. However, a painterly approach to this medium (such as the realistic style shown in this chapter) requires the small list of materials below. You don't need anything else to complete the projects in this chapter.

1. Woodless graphite pencils: 9B, 2B, and 5B
2. Staedtler® 8B pencil (to achieve matte blacks)
3. Stumps (smooth, not ridged)
4. Graphite powder made using Design® Ebony Sketching Pencils (Matte Jet Black). Sand the tips into a jar to create a velvety black powder.
5. Powder puffs and eye make-up applicators for blending and applying graphite powder. (You'll find they can be used for things stumps can't.)
6. Kneaded, vinyl, and battery-operated erasers
7. A retractable, pen-shaped stick eraser
8. A knitting needle or ruler
9. Marker paper (at least 18 lb; thinner than this is too flimsy)
10. Bristol paper with a rough finish
11. A drawing board with clips to hold the paper or pad

PAPER

The two types of paper listed above must be handled differently. The 18-lb marker paper is the best paper for heads smaller than a fist and can be used for life-size heads. The rough Bristol paper should never be used for small heads; the tooth (or raised areas of textured paper) will obliterate the detail. Marker paper is essential whenever speed is an issue because it automatically looks smooth and requires very little blending. The Bristol paper is excellent for large, time-consuming drawings. It is much more resilient, and the tooth absorbs graphite, which results in marvelous darks and blends. Unfortunately, the tooth also makes it necessary to continually blend the graphite to achieve smooth gradations. You will want to try both papers.

SHADING

Draw with the woodless 9B graphite pencil, switching to the 5B and 2B only for finer details. Some artists use hatch lines for shading (see page 145), but this particular style strives to look like black-and-white paintings—highly realistic. Therefore, it calls for drawing with the side of the graphite (A) and uses the tip for fine detail and thin outlines (B).

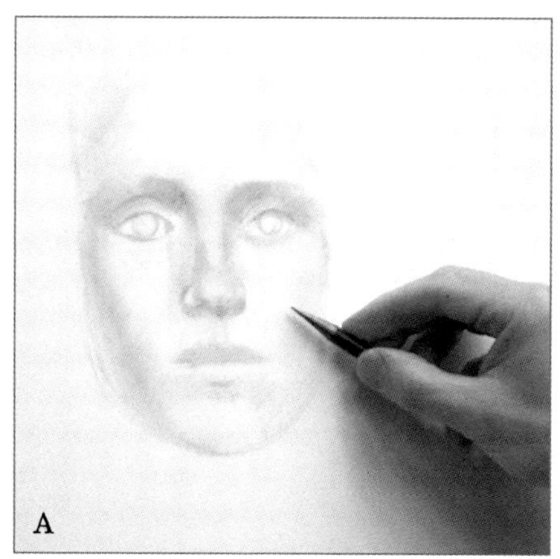

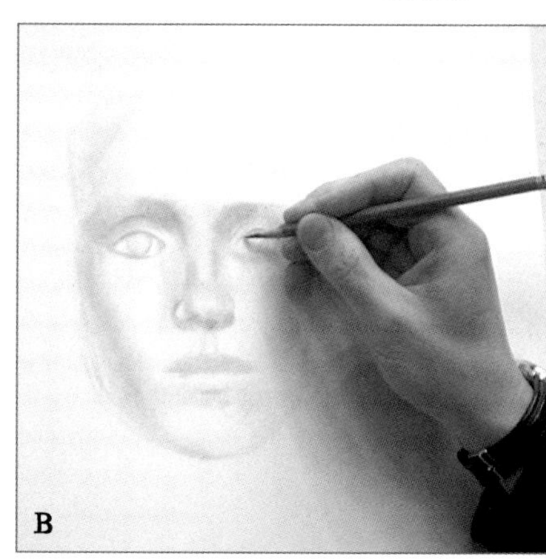

Below are a few methods for applying tone to your drawing as well as examples of what to avoid when shading. Practice the recommended methods before you begin the projects so you can achieve clean, controlled tone in your drawings. Use whichever method adequately describes the form.

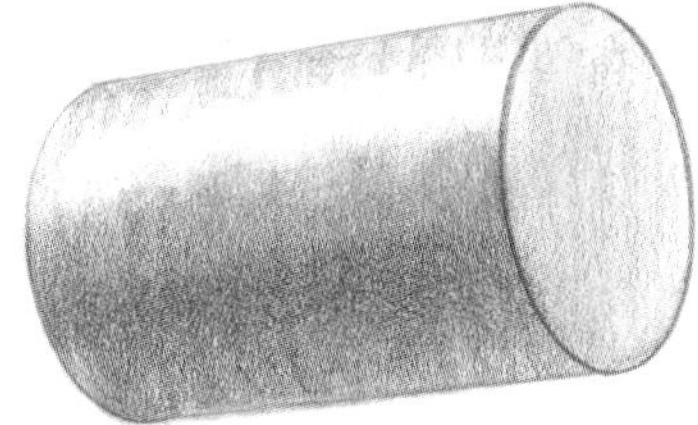

Shade Across the Form Create convincing form with pencil strokes that follow the width of the form.

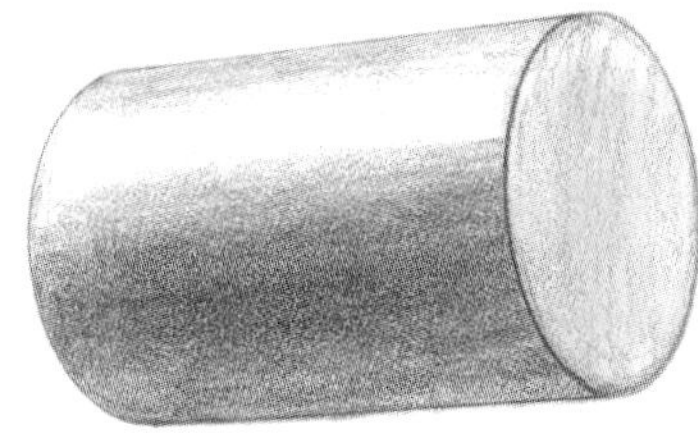

Shade Along the Form You can achieve similar results by shading evenly along the length of the form.

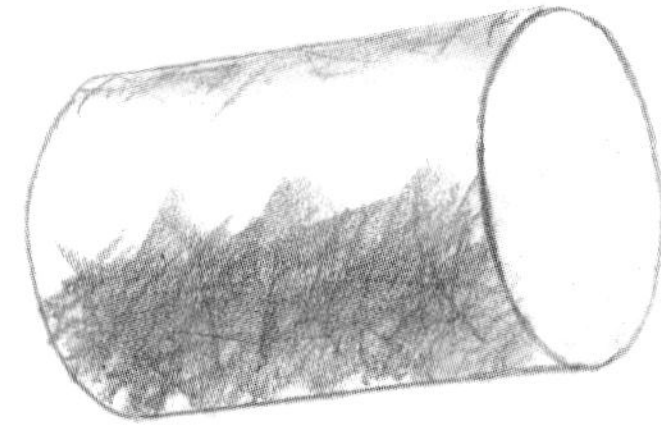

Don't Shade Chaotically Don't use several directions of shading over the form—this is messy and uneven.

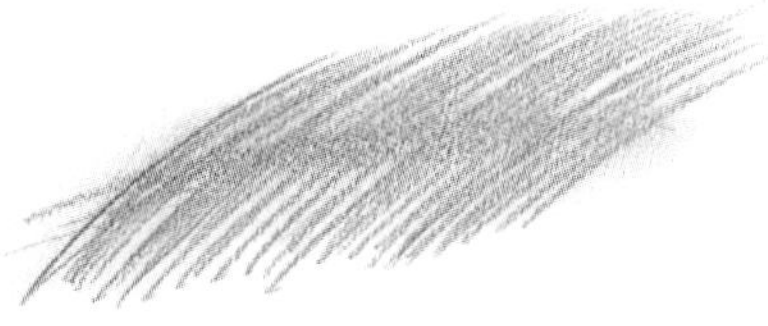

Hatching This involves applying parallel pencil strokes close together. This method is common but not used in this chapter.

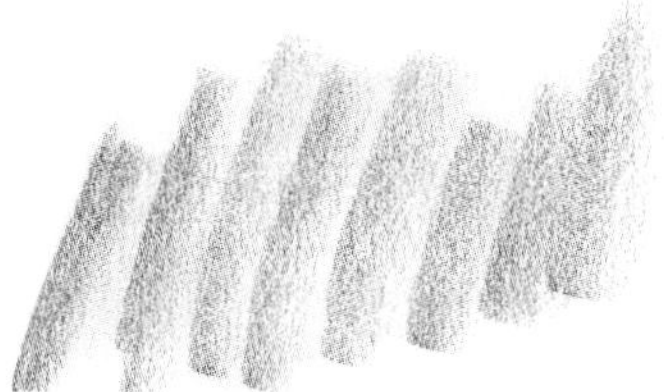

Don't Leave Gaps When shading with the side of the pencil, overlap each stroke to avoid separate bands of tone.

Avoid Using Uneven Pressure Shade with the same amount of pressure through an area—caress, don't slash.

STUMPING

After laying in a form's proportions, outlining it, and shading it, switch to a stump or a make-up applicator to blend and deepen the tones of the shadows. When the stump becomes coated with graphite, you can occasionally use it as a pencil.

RUBBING AND ADDING HIGHLIGHTS

After outlining, shading, and stumping the shadows, rub the entire drawing with a powder puff, and pull out highlights with a kneaded eraser. (For pure white highlights, gently use a battery-operated eraser.) Rubbing can be dangerous because artists tend to rub too early in the development of the drawing, which causes the drawing to look messy and lack precision. On the other hand, rubbing is almost indispensable for finishing a drawing on white paper. I've tried shading up to the highlights and stopping, but rubbing is more efficient. Here are the rules for rubbing: (1) Wait until the drawing is three-quarters of the way finished; (2) rub enough graphite over the light areas so you can see the difference when you pull out the highlights. (Don't be perturbed if you have to re-darken areas that become bland after they're smeared.)

A

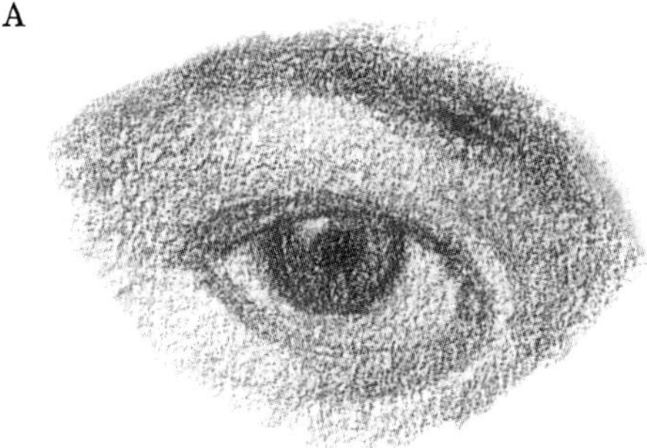

B

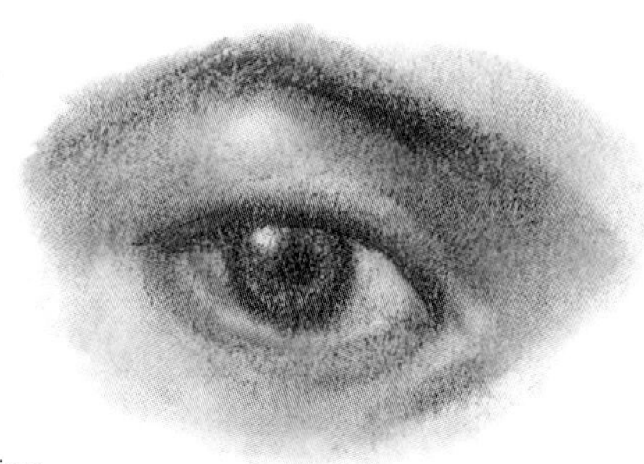

Creating a Polished Look Stumping and pulling out highlights creates a smooth and realistic finish. Compare the eye before (A) and after (B).

Shadows & Highlights

Below is a diagram that demonstrates the breakdown of light and shadow across a form. All forms—from faces and clothing to hills in a landscape—feature the same elements. In graphite drawing, these elements are represented by tone or value (the lightness or darkness of a color or of black). The more accurately your tones reflect the shadows and highlights of a form, the more you will convince the viewer of its three-dimensionality.

Basic Shadows and Highlights Shadows shouldn't be messy dark things. They come in predictable patterns that always break down into the same elements. Study the diagrams on this page, and then look for the shadows on the your model as you draw.

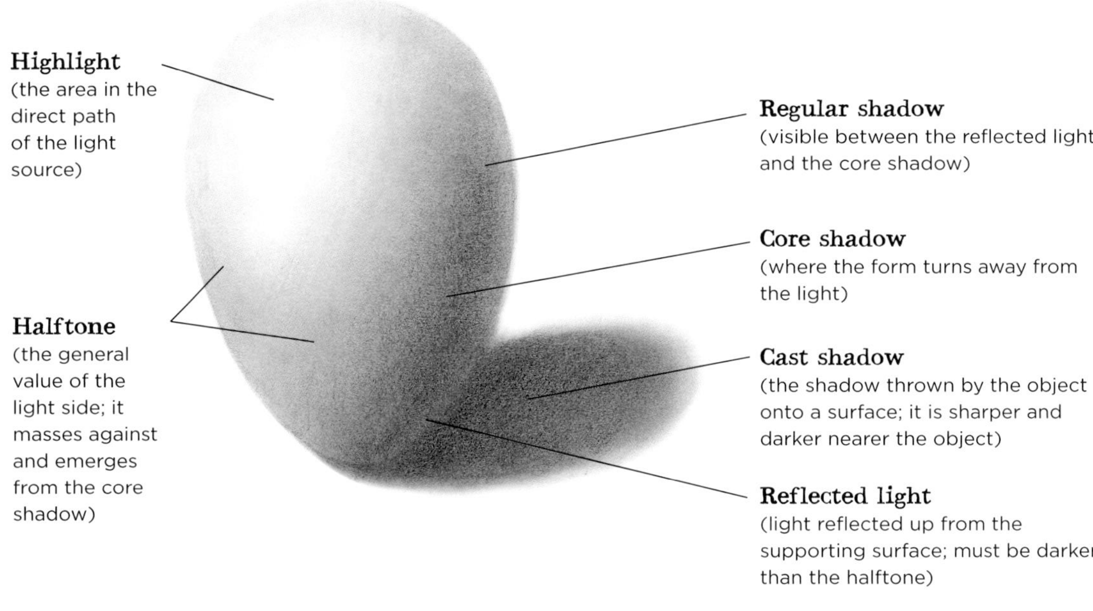

Shadows and Highlights of the Head This drawing was created deliberately in halftone (a middle value of graphite) so you can see the elements of shading more easily.

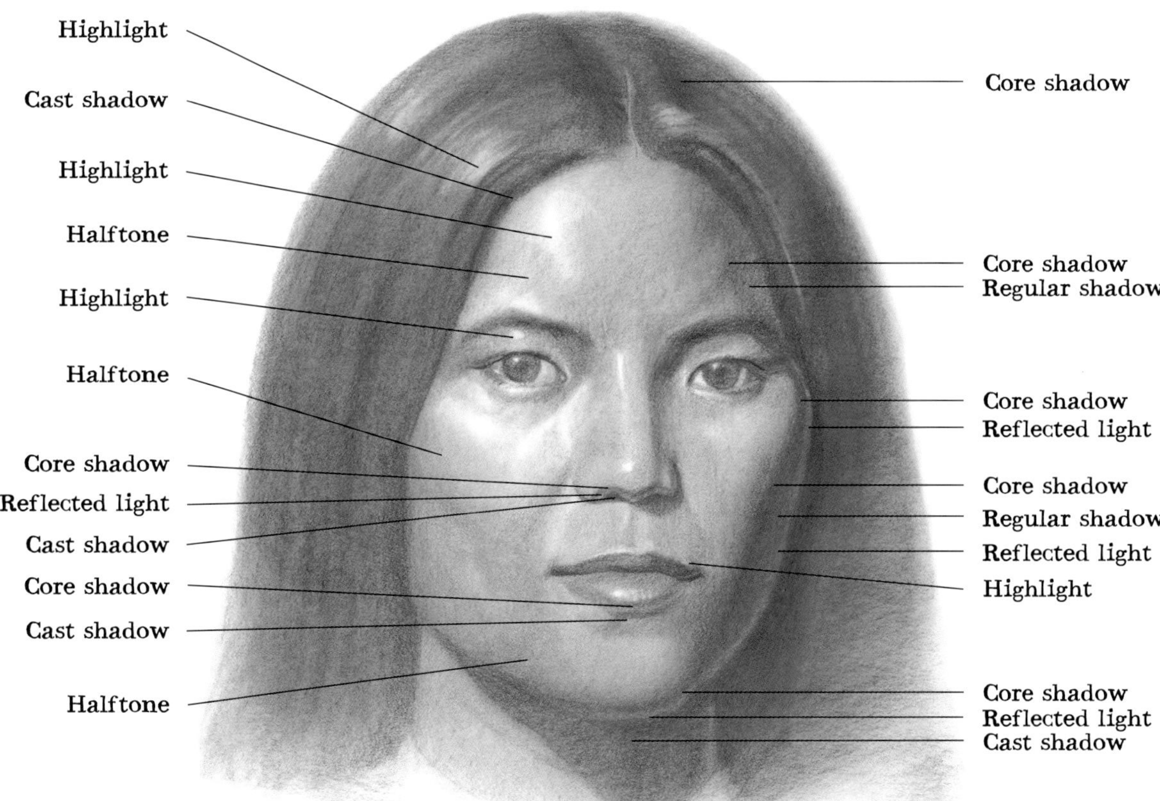

How to Light the Model

Always use only one dominant light on your model. It's OK to have some general light in the room, but several competing lights directed at the model will create forms that are flat or hard to read. Below are two drawings of the same woman done with two different lighting styles that were practiced by two master artists: Rembrandt and Van Dyke. One creates a harsh look with distinct shadows and more contrast (Rembrandt's high-contrast side lighting), whereas the other produces a more feminine, delicate image (Van Dyke's low-contrast front lighting).

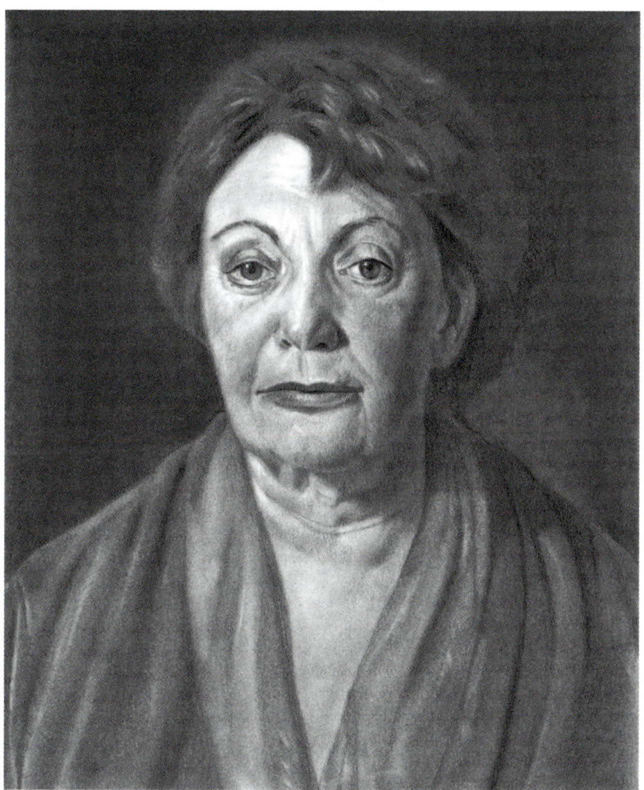

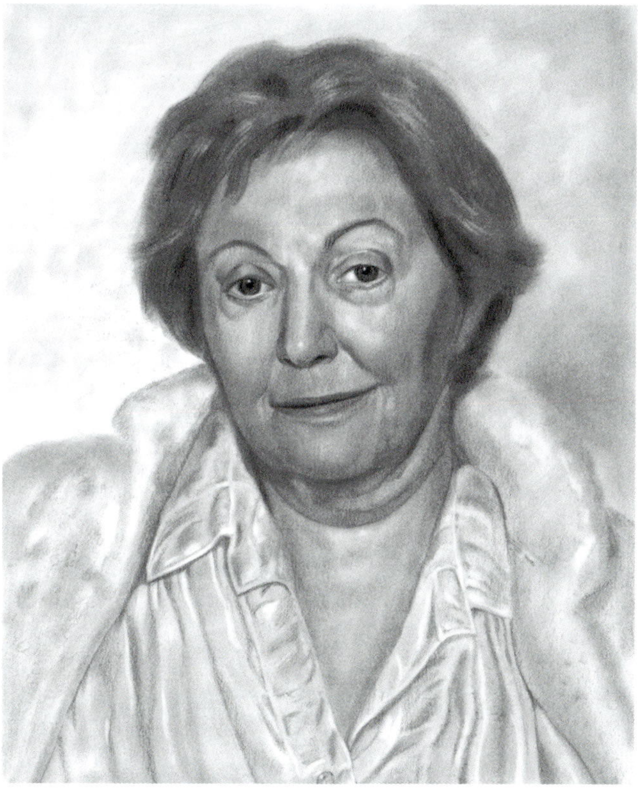

Side Lighting When drawing this portrait, the artist worked in a dark room with one light positioned to the model's right. Rembrandt often used this type of lighting for his portraits. This style makes the model look older and more serious, as the contrasts create harsh shadows, deepening and creating lines on the face and neck. This type of lighting is best for giving a model an air of power and gravitas.

Front Lighting Van Dyke used a different method of lighting his models, which involved using a well-lit room with one light positioned in front of the model. Ingres, another great portraitist, learned to use this lighting style in order to reduce shadows across the model, resulting in more flattering portraits of their clients. (When using this method, position the light as far away as possible to avoid hurting the model's eyes.)

TRICKS FOR LIGHTING TO ENHANCE EXPRESSION

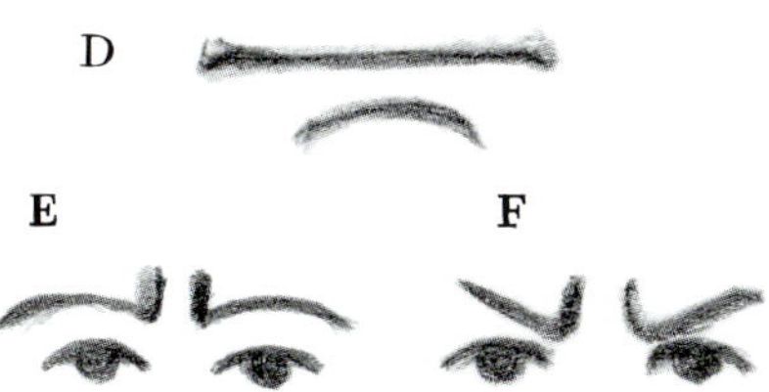

Be careful with slight smiles—they tend to look odd. Try to be a little bolder and make your smiles unambiguous. In the front-lit drawing, create a clear, gradual arc for the lips (A).

Raise the lower eyelids so the bottom of the iris is a bit flattened (B), which suggests a smile. In contrast, showing the bottom of the iris creates a serious eye (C).

The model's intelligence is emphasized in the side-lit drawing by the pushing up of the lower lip in judgement (D) and by the furrow between the eyes (E). Be careful not to lower the eyebrows—this would make her look mean (F).

General Proportions

Proportion (the comparative sizes and placement of parts to one another) is key to creating a likeness in your drawing. Although proportions vary among individuals, there are some general guidelines to keep in mind that will help you stay on track. Before you study the diagrams and tips below, memorize these two most important guidelines:

1. The face is usually divided into thirds: one-third from the chin to the base of the nose, one-third from the nose to the browridge, and one-third from the browridge to the hairline.
2. The midpoint of the head from the crown to the chin aligns with the tear ducts.

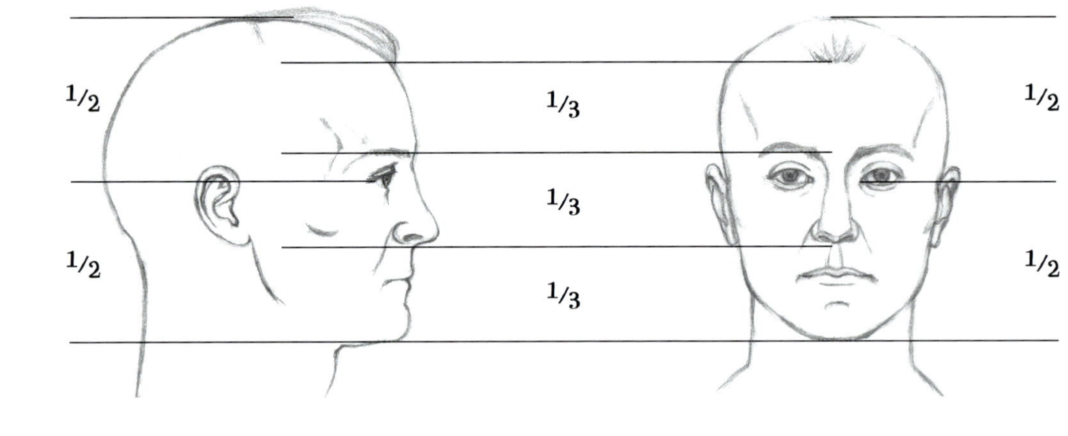

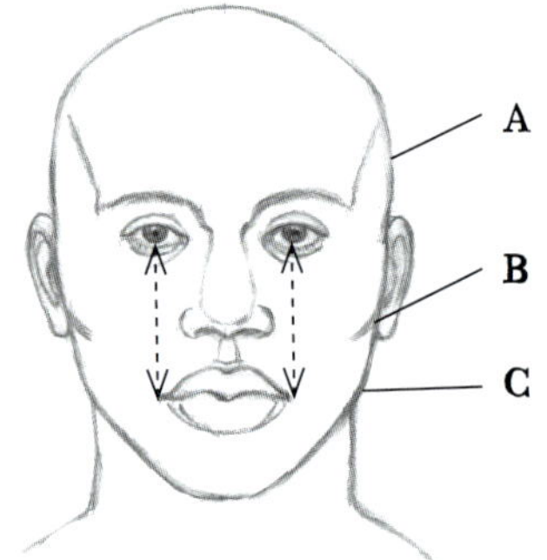

The mouth is usually the same width as the distance between the pupils. This particular model's tear ducts are higher than the midpoint.

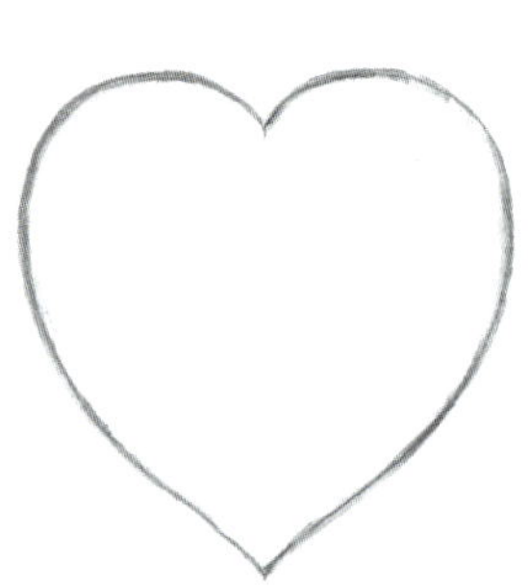

Heads are somewhat heart shaped. The temple (A) is wider than the cheekbone (B), which is wider than the jawline (C).

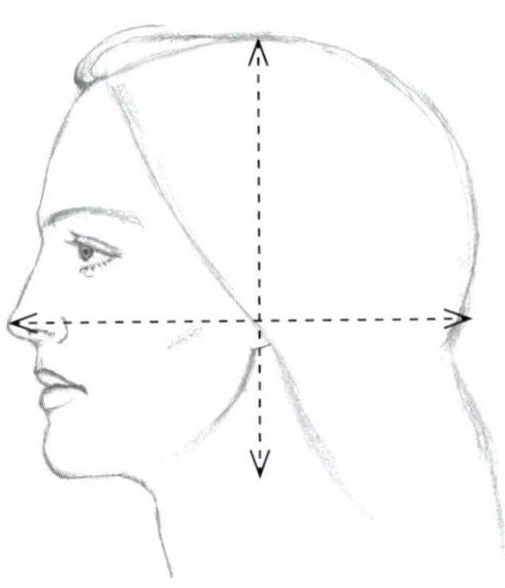

Generally, the distance between the tip of the nose and back of the head is longer than the distance from the top of the head to the bottom of the head.

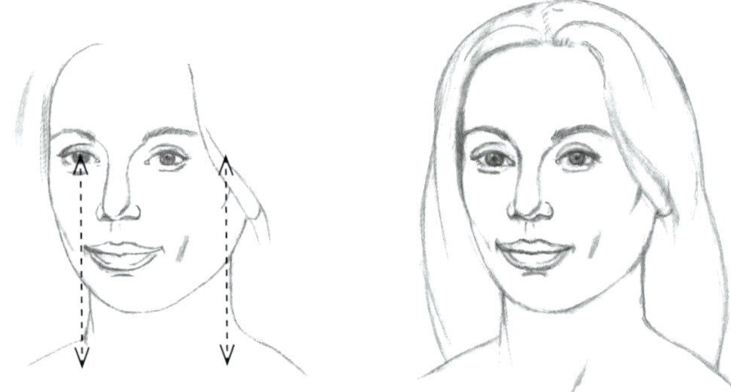

To determine the width of the neck, use the features directly above each side of the neck to serve as a guides for placement. To easily see this, hold up your pencil vertically in front of you, lining it up with the side of the model's neck.

PROPORTION SUBTLETIES

- The neck pitches forward slightly.
- The neck doesn't narrow as it goes up to the jaw.
- You can usually fit another eye between the eyes.
- If you've diligently measured and the model's face is asymmetrical or involves different proportions than I've given here, that's okay. These are guidelines—not strict rules.

SHIFTS IN GUIDELINES

When drawing the tilted head, it's essential to first measure to find the midpoint to see where it has shifted (A). Next draw lines to indicate the new positions of the features (B). Apply a bit of shading because horizontal lines alone aren't enough for you to judge by.

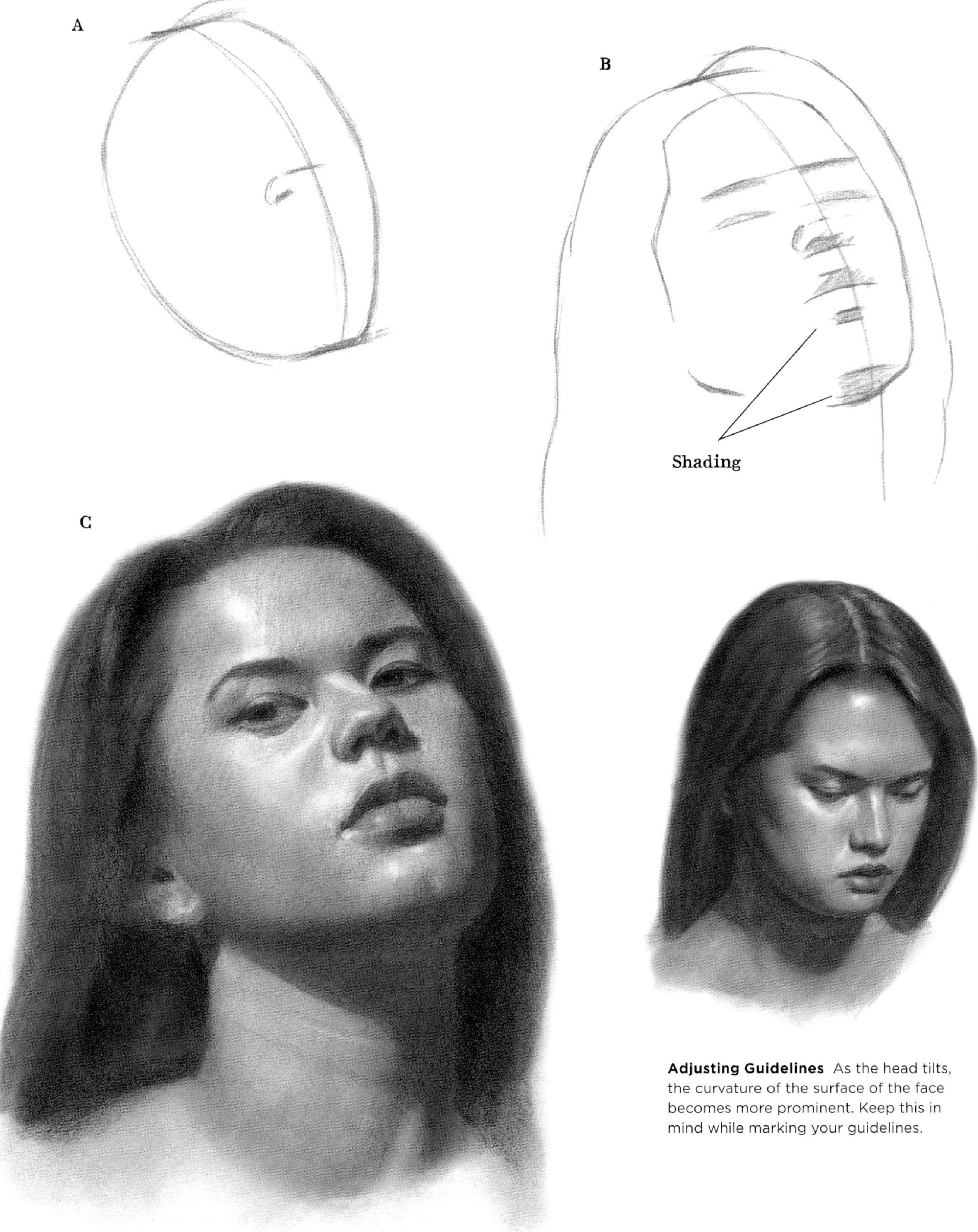

Adjusting Guidelines As the head tilts, the curvature of the surface of the face becomes more prominent. Keep this in mind while marking your guidelines.

Planes of the Head

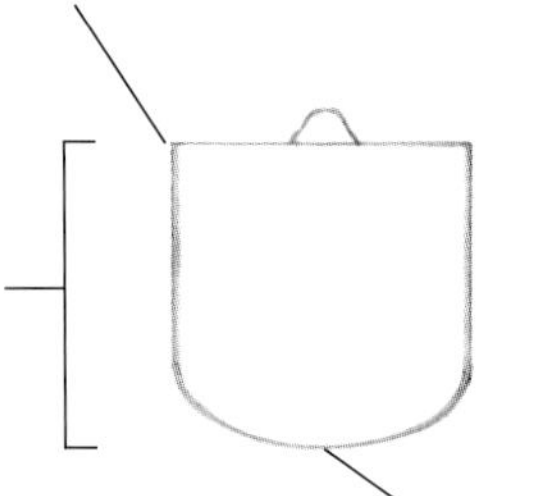

Brow and forehead
too square

Head too short

Back of head
too flat

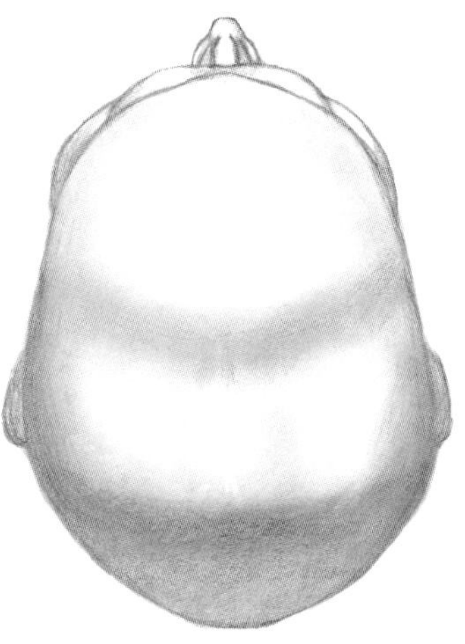

Artists unfamiliar with the top view of the head make errors at the brow, with the shape of the forehead, and in the head's overall length and width.

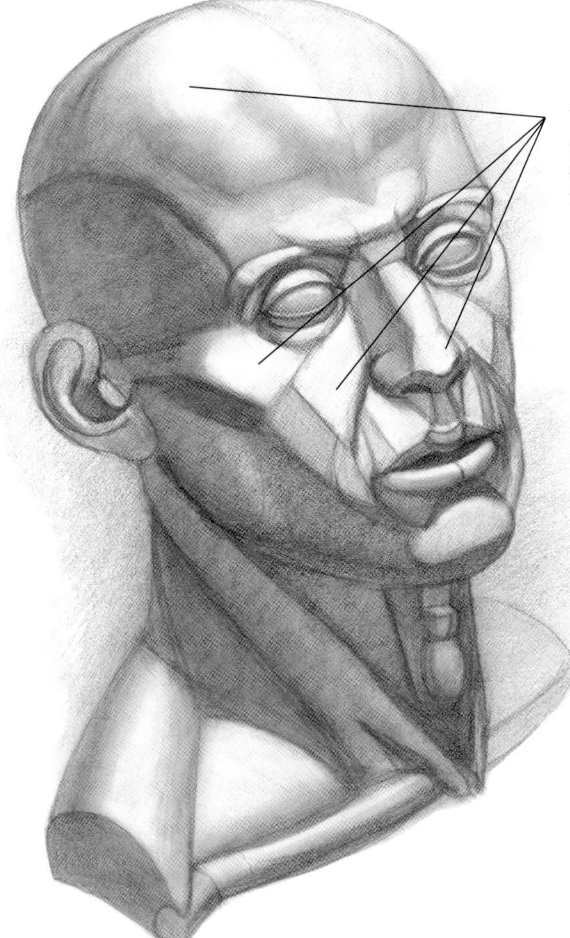

The light is brightest on the planes that are perpendicular to the light source.

The neck doesn't narrow at the top, and it isn't concave at the sides (A). The body's forms bulge out (B). They can be flat but not concave (except in tiny transitions that are barely visible).

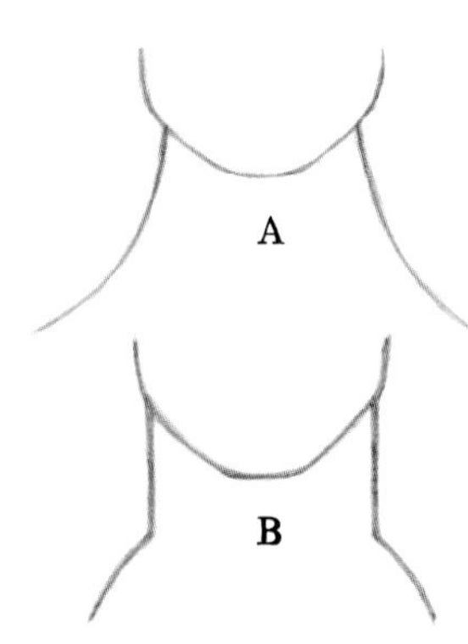

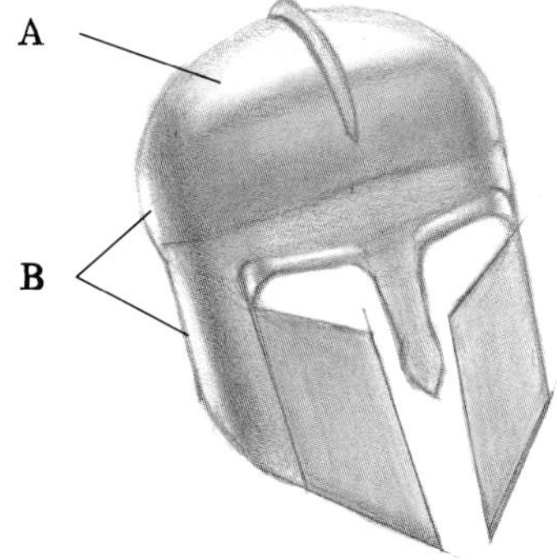

The face wedges toward the nose like this helmet. Notice the exaggerated highlights (A) and reflected light (B) on the metal.

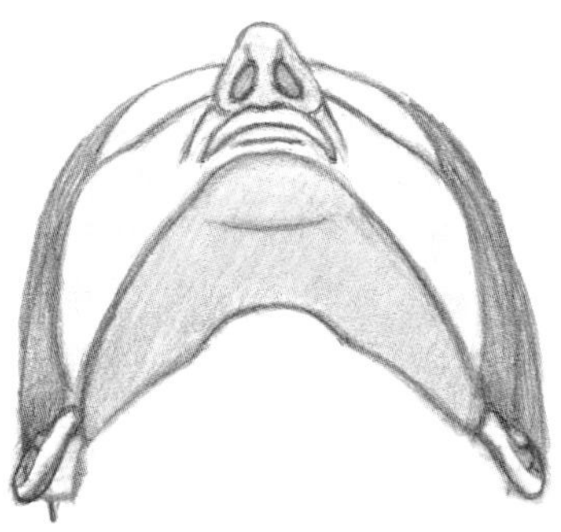

This first example shows how the face wedges toward the center.

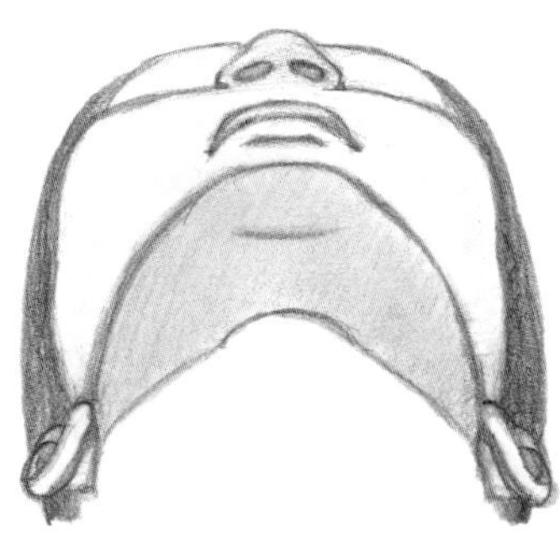

This second example shows a wider face with sharper angles at the sides of the head.

Ears

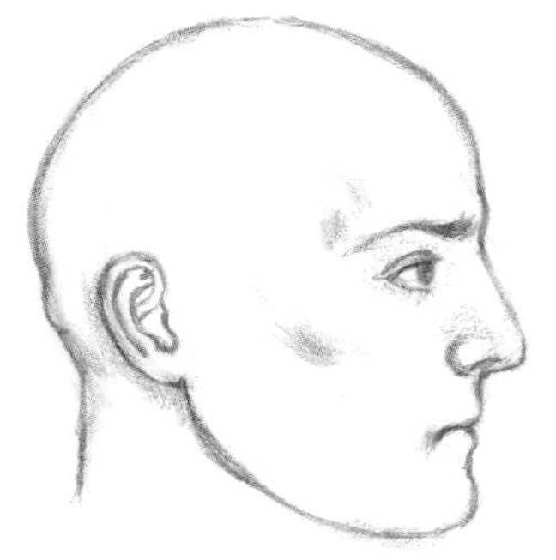

Ear too far back

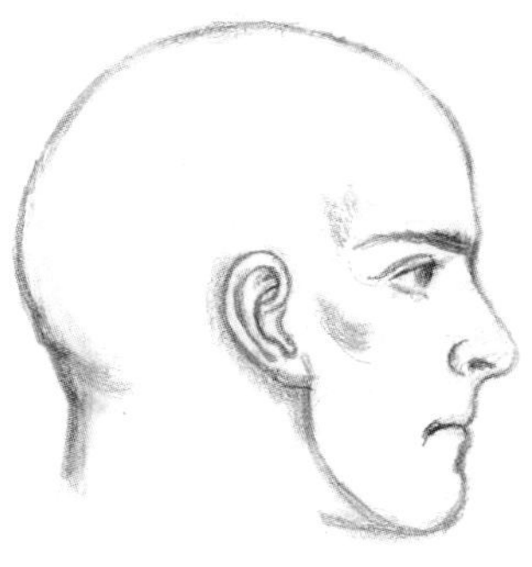

Ear too far forward

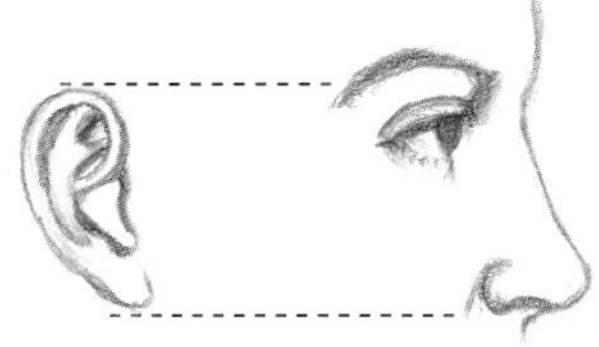

The ear is situated between the brow and the base of the nose. It tends to be more in line with the lower part of the eyebrow, not the arch.

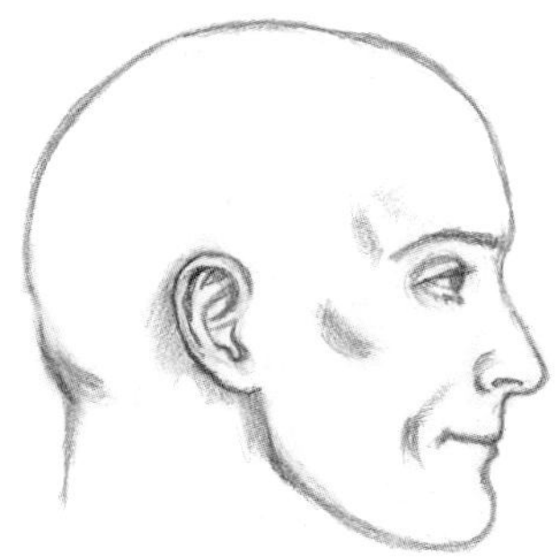

Ear is just right

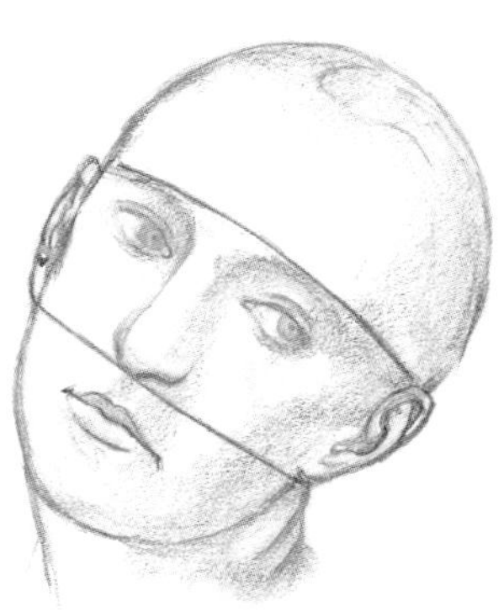

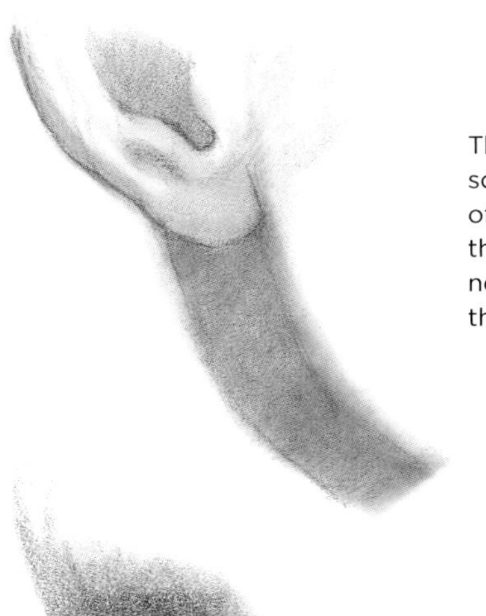

There's a soft transition of the jaw from the lobe to the neck. The back of the jawline isn't sharp.

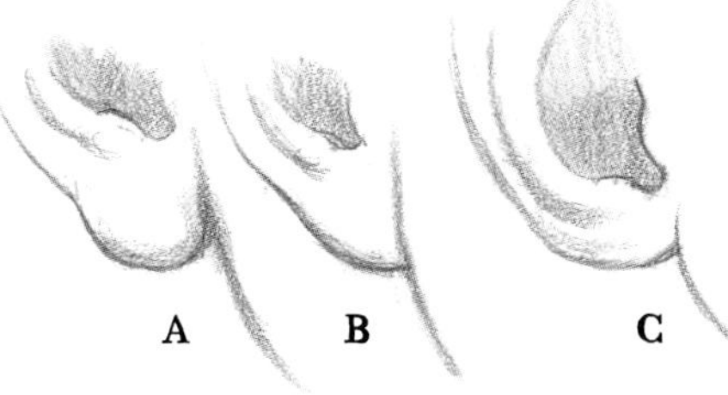

Earlobes can hang (A), be attached (B), and even be underdeveloped (C).

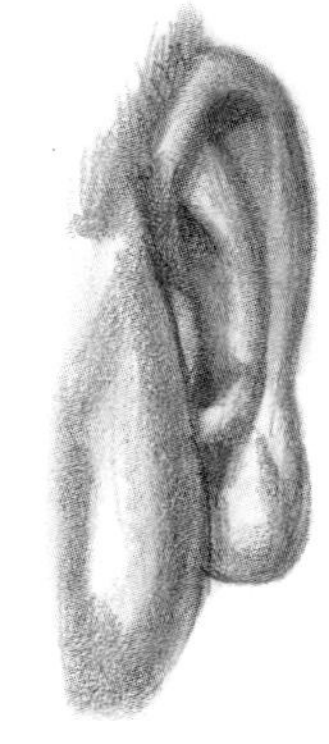

Some people have lobes that are pushed out from their faces.

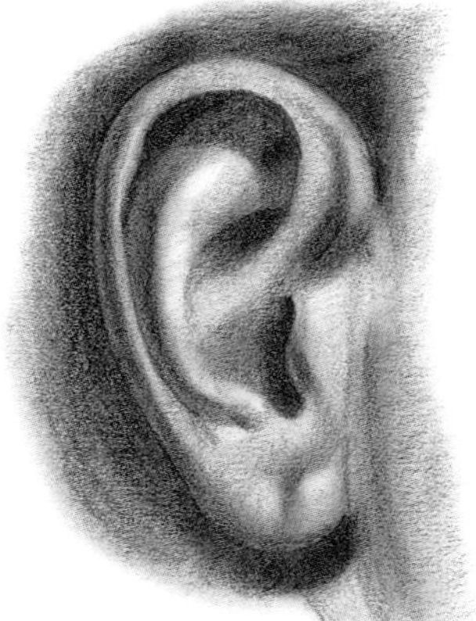

A baby's ears are rounder and more concave than an adult's.

Ears have a confounded habit of having extra forms. Notice the doubled helix and two lumps on this lobe.

Eyes

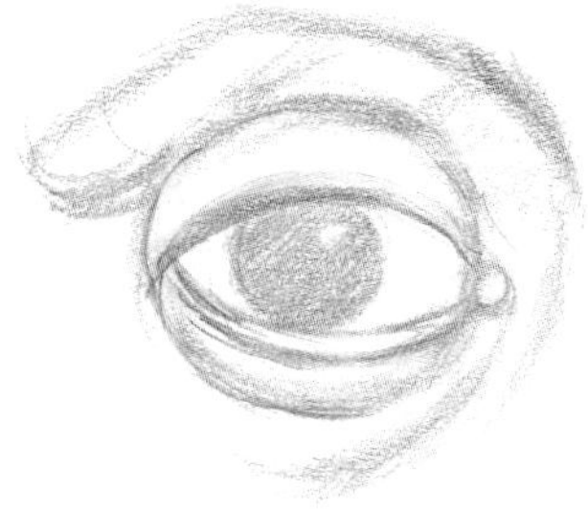

Step 1 Lay in the size, location, and folds of the eye.

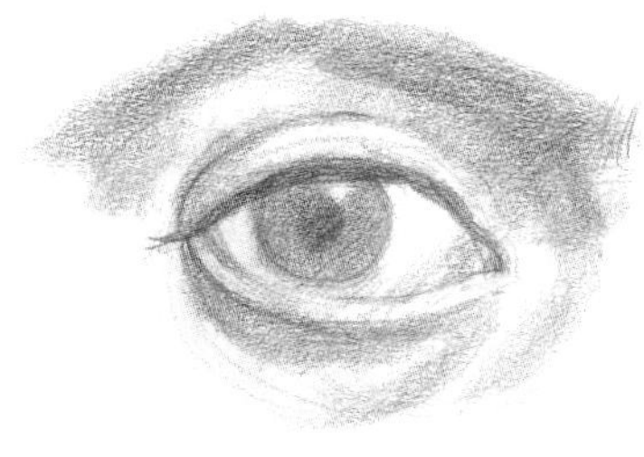

Step 2 Build the volume by adding tone for the form and cast shadows.

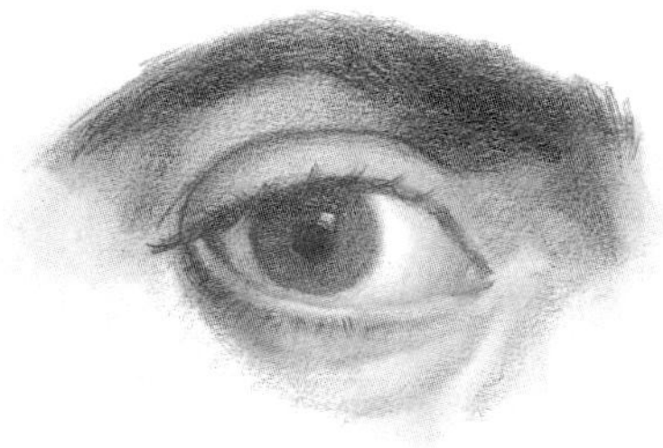

Step 3 Stump, pull out highlights, and give clarity to edges.

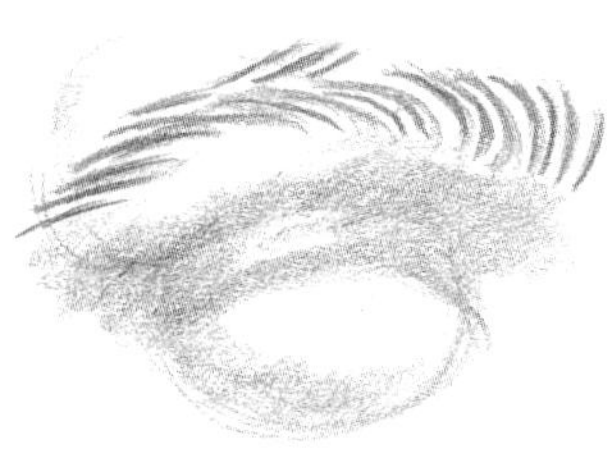

The eyebrows start vertically and end horizontally.

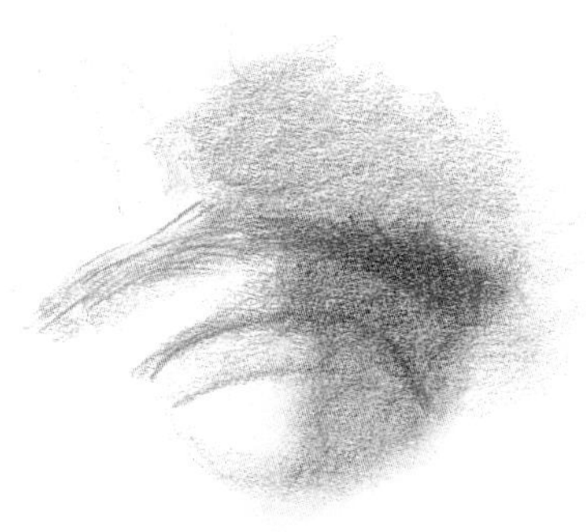

The eyebrow is rarely the same tone all the way across because it's located on both the front and side of the face.

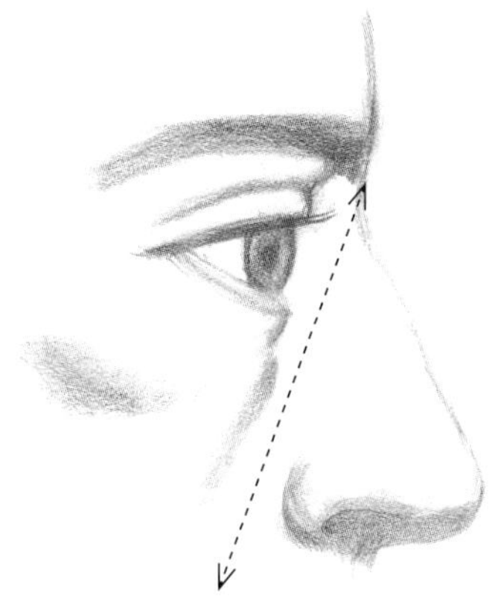

There's a clear diagonal from the brow to the cheek.

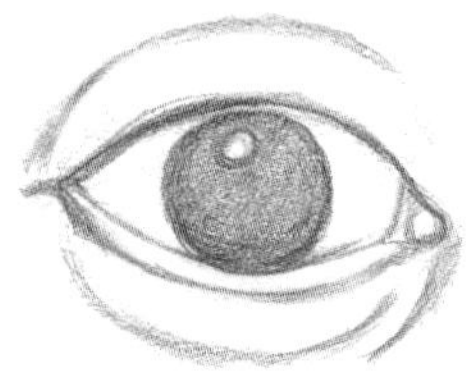

Showing the top of the iris looks unnatural.

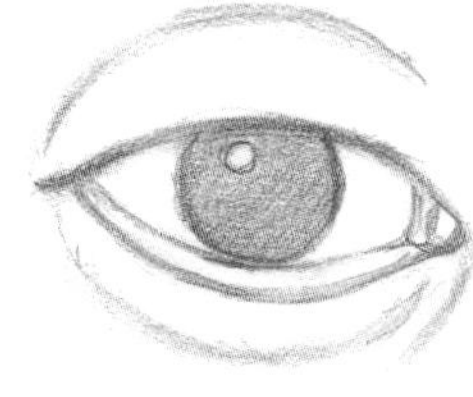

The lid should always partially cover the top of the iris.

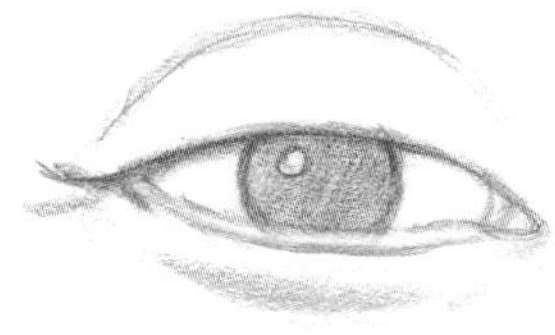

When a person smiles, even more of the iris is covered (especially at the bottom).

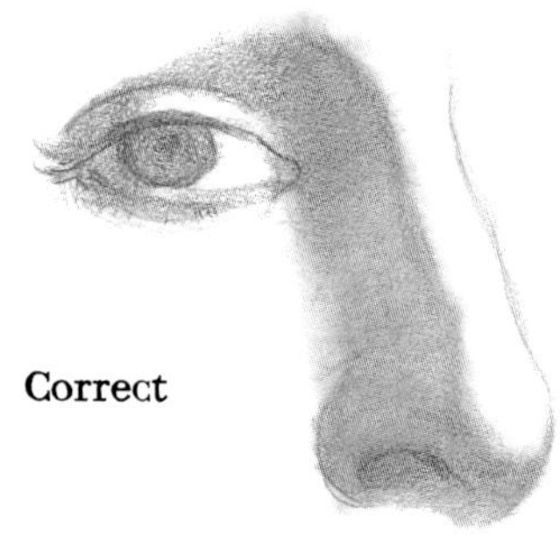

To correctly place the eye in relation to the nose, there must be a side plane between the nose and the eye.

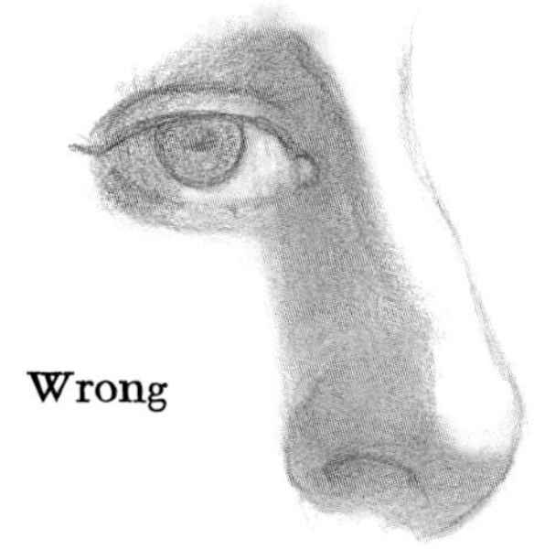

Students often make the mistake of letting the eye creep up the side of the nose.

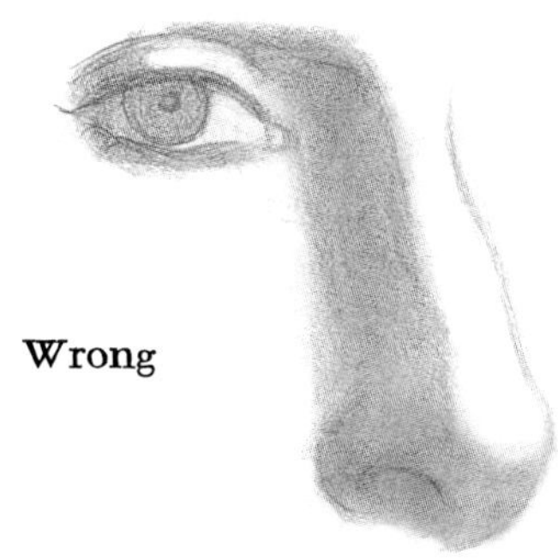

Students also often place the eye at the top of the nose. The eye is to the side of the nose.

Noses

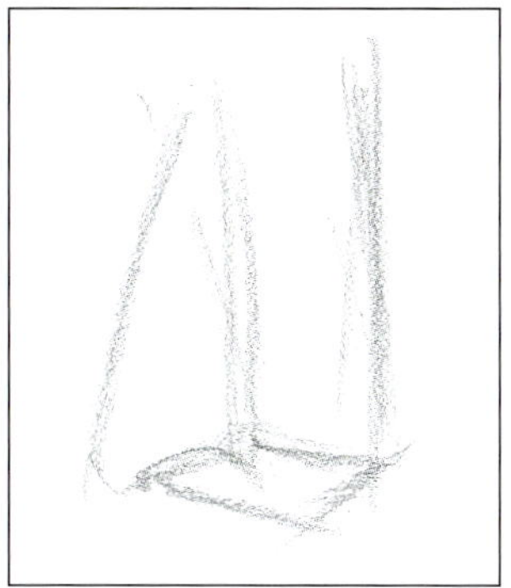

Step 1 Check the nose's vertical angles and size compared with other features.

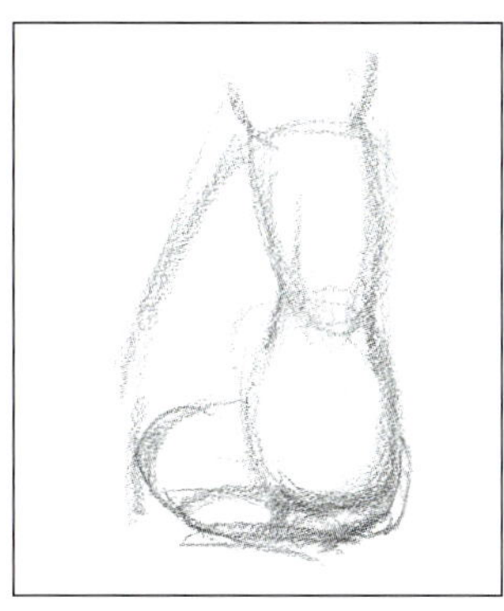

Step 2 Identify the planes and forms of the nose.

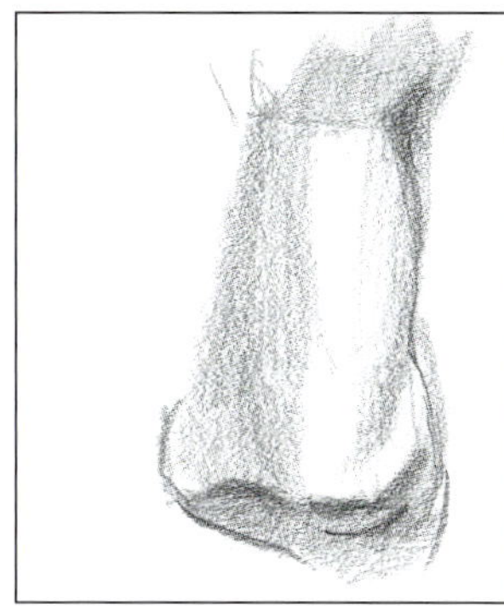

Step 3 Add tone to the nose to represent the core and cast shadows.

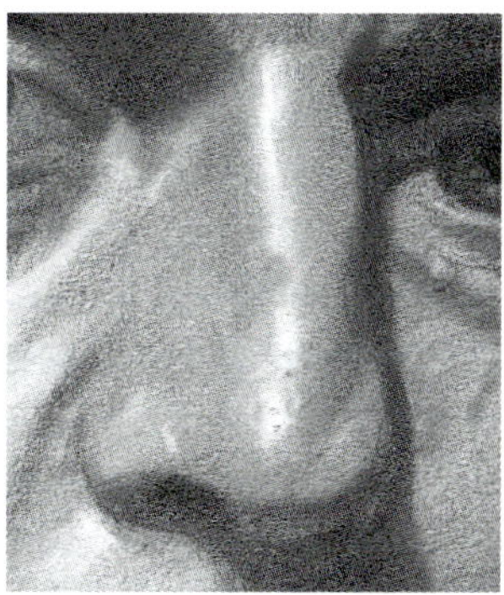

Step 4 Stump, and then pull out highlights for a realistic effect.

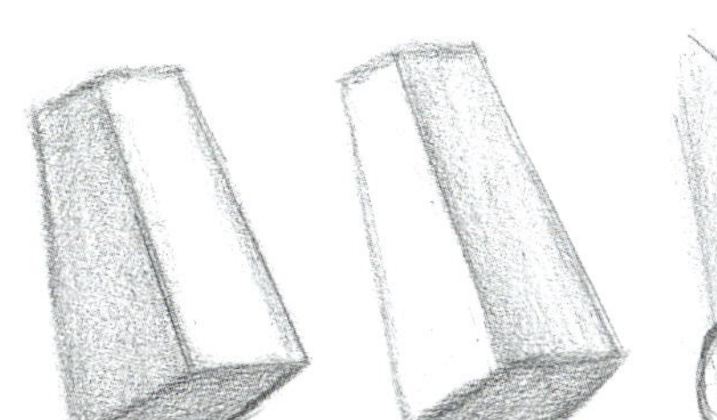

Make simple forms before adding character.

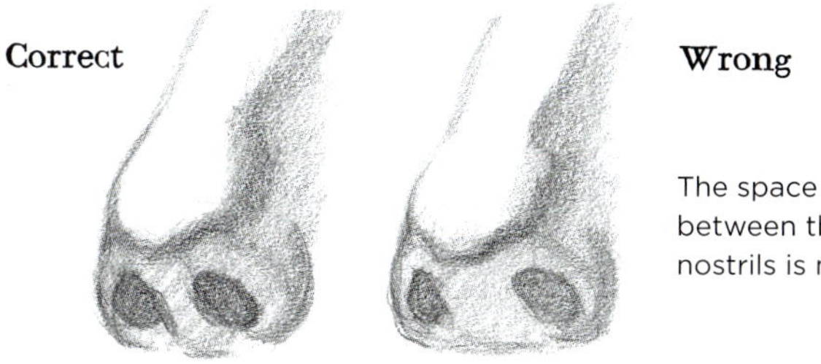

Correct   Wrong

The space between the nostrils is narrow.

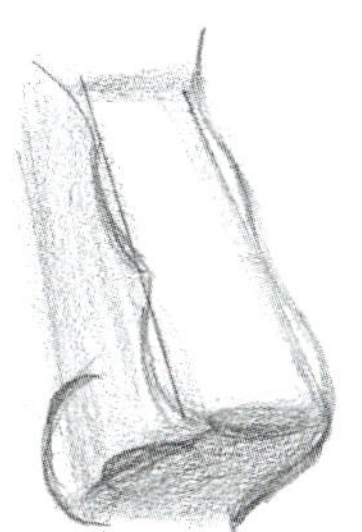

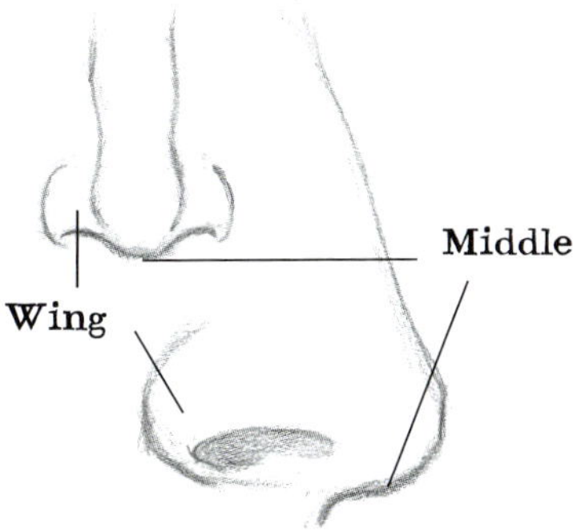

The middle of the nose is usually lower than the wings.

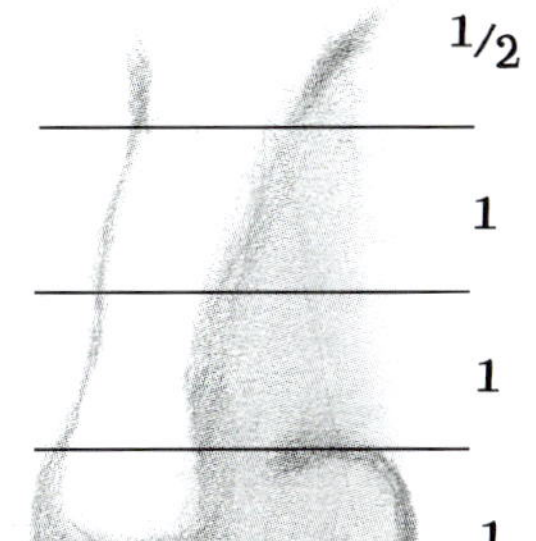

The height of the nose is about 3 1/2 wings high.

Correct   Wrong   Wrong

Carefully place the nose at the correct level before developing it. The seven-eighths view (shown above and below) is especially tricky.

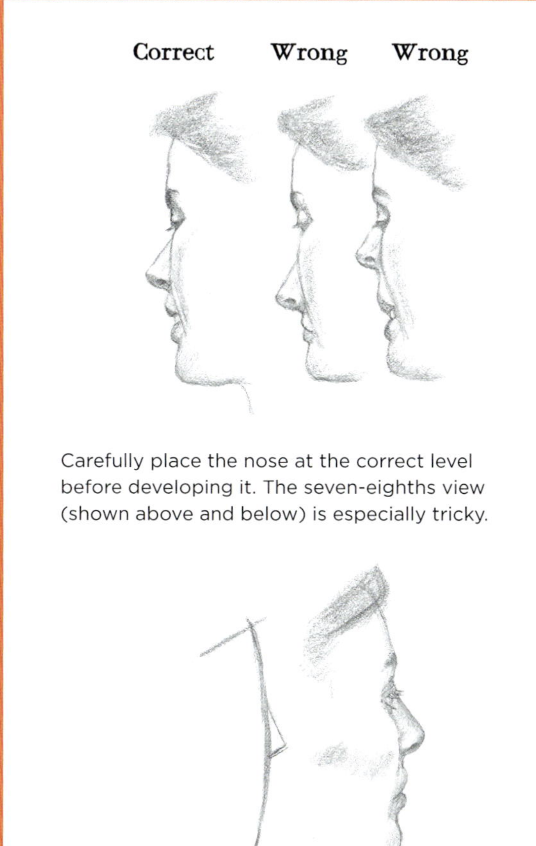

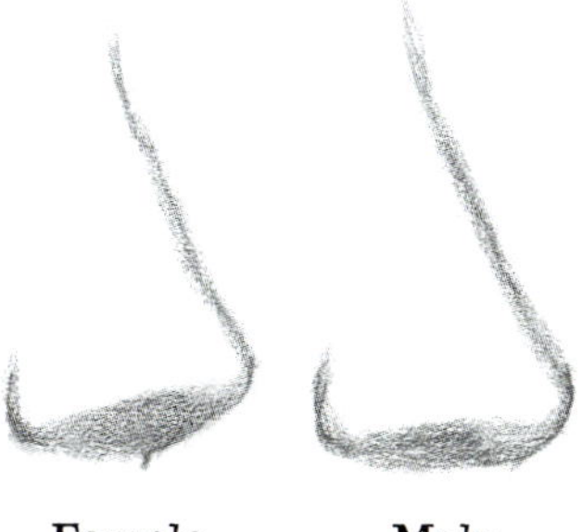

Female noses tend to be smaller and tilted upward a bit when compared with a male's.

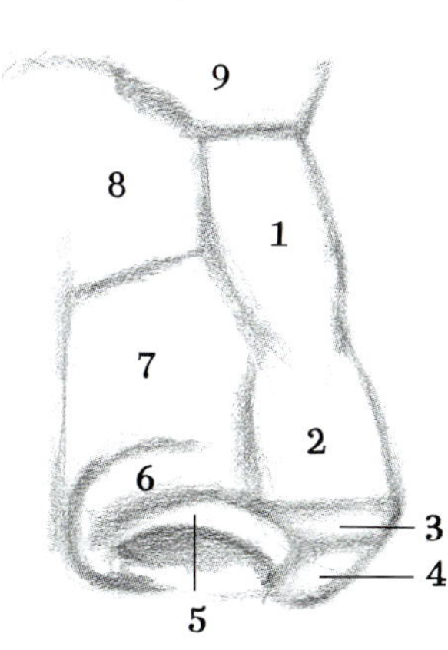

These are the nine typical planes to look for on noses.

The Face & Mouth

Unfortunately, many portrait artists neglect to render the mouth. Look at how many different shades can be seen here. The line between the lips is also a shadow rather than a random stroke. The upper lip points upward, and the lower lip points downward. This means they can never have the same gray tones.

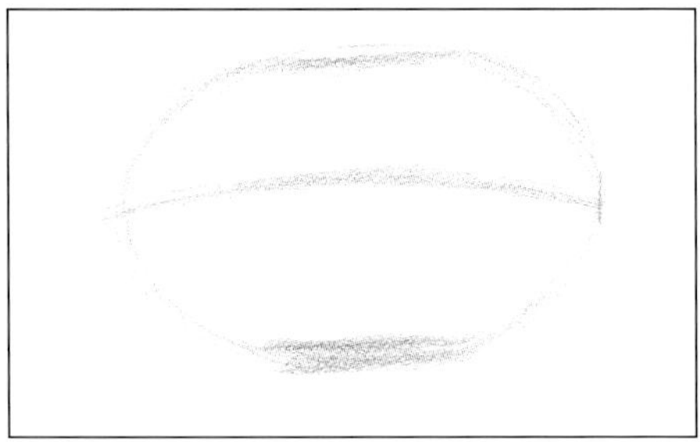

Step 1 Lay in the size, location, and angle of the mouth.

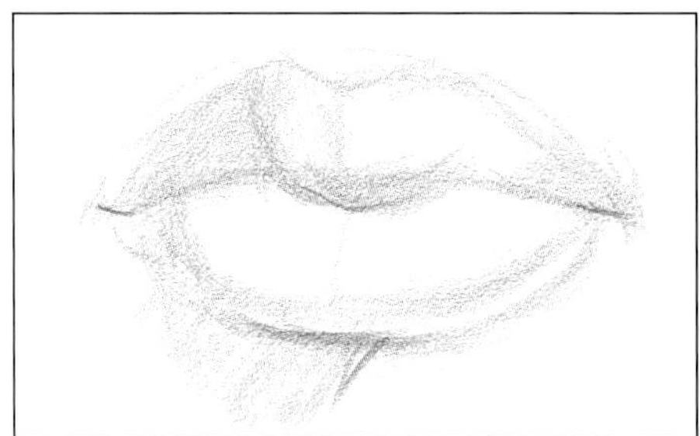

Step 2 Build the volume, and add tone for the core and cast shadows.

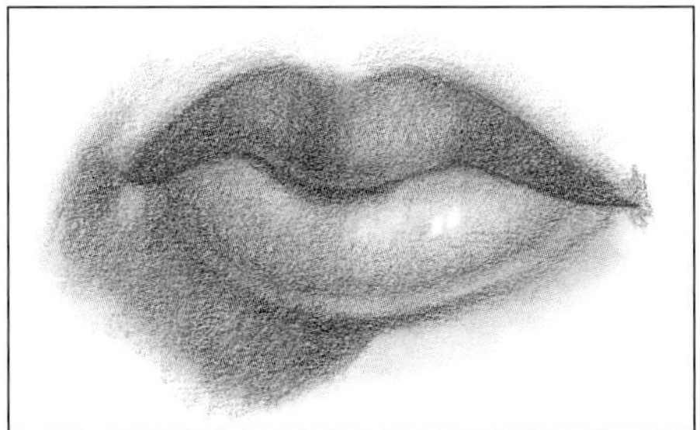

Step 3 Stump, and then pull out highlights for a polished look.

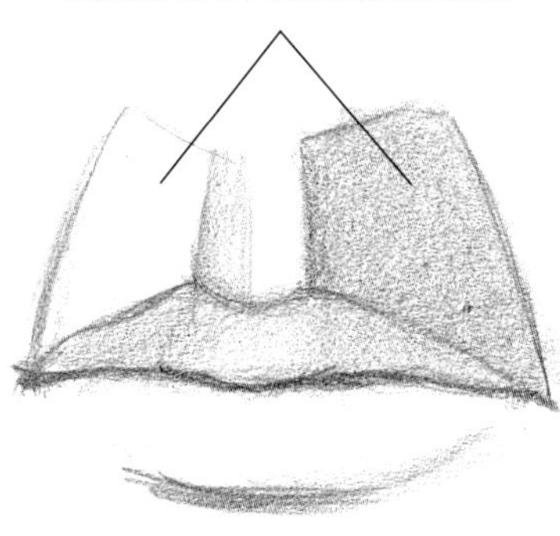

It's rare for both sides of the muzzle to be the same shade.

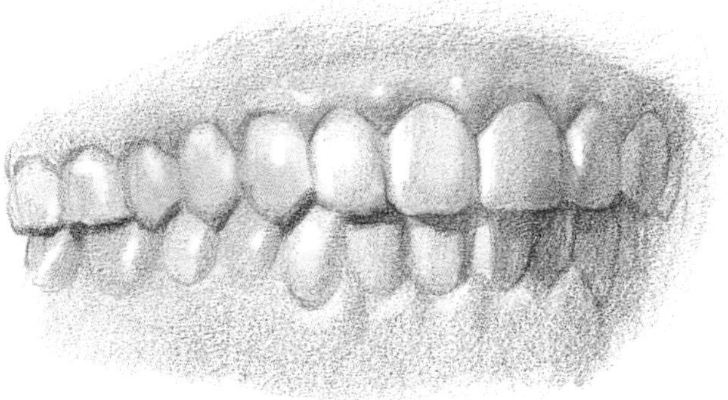

Err on the side of too light when adding lines between teeth.

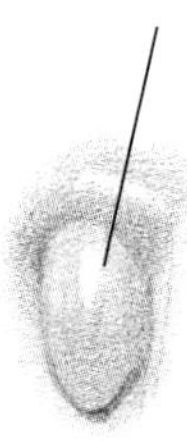

Every tooth has a highlight.

FACIAL EXPRESSIONS

These images show how closely the mouth conveys facial expressions. Take a close look at the shape of the mouth. When we are angry, our mouths form a rectangle. Surprise is expressed in a round shape of the mouth, whereas fear shapes the mouth into a trapezoid. If you would like to draw such extreme facial expressions, you can imitate and draw them using a mirror.

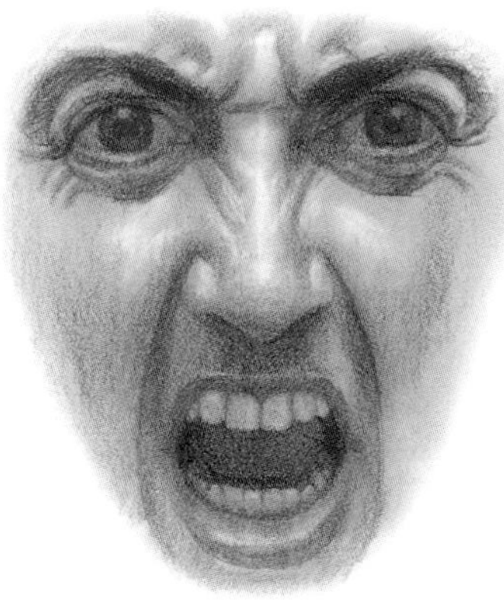
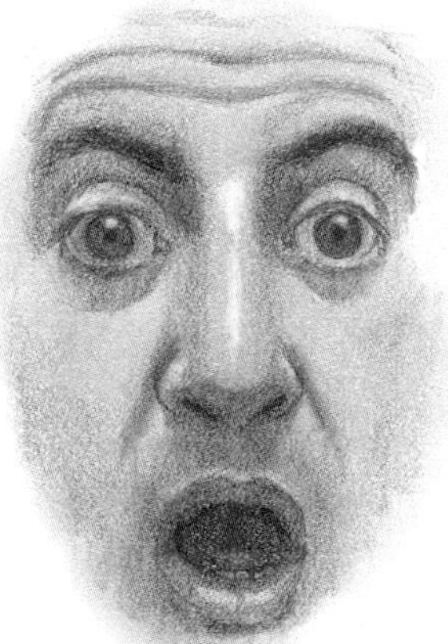
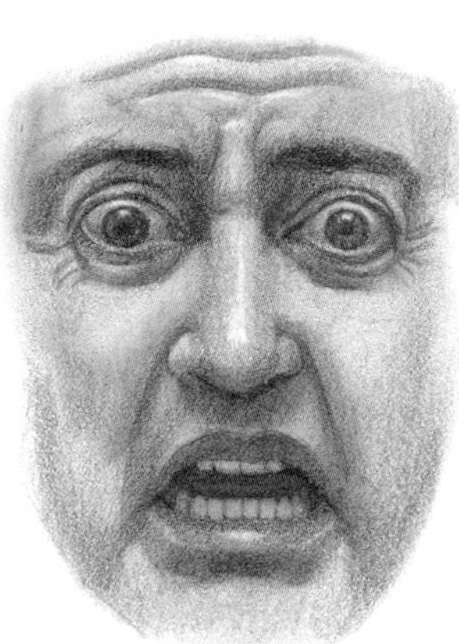

The Mouth and Expression The mouth assumes predictable shapes for the emotions. Note the square for anger, the small circle for surprise, and the trapezoid for fear. The handsome gent in the examples above was drawn with the aid of a mirror—a great tool for checking the veracity of an expression.

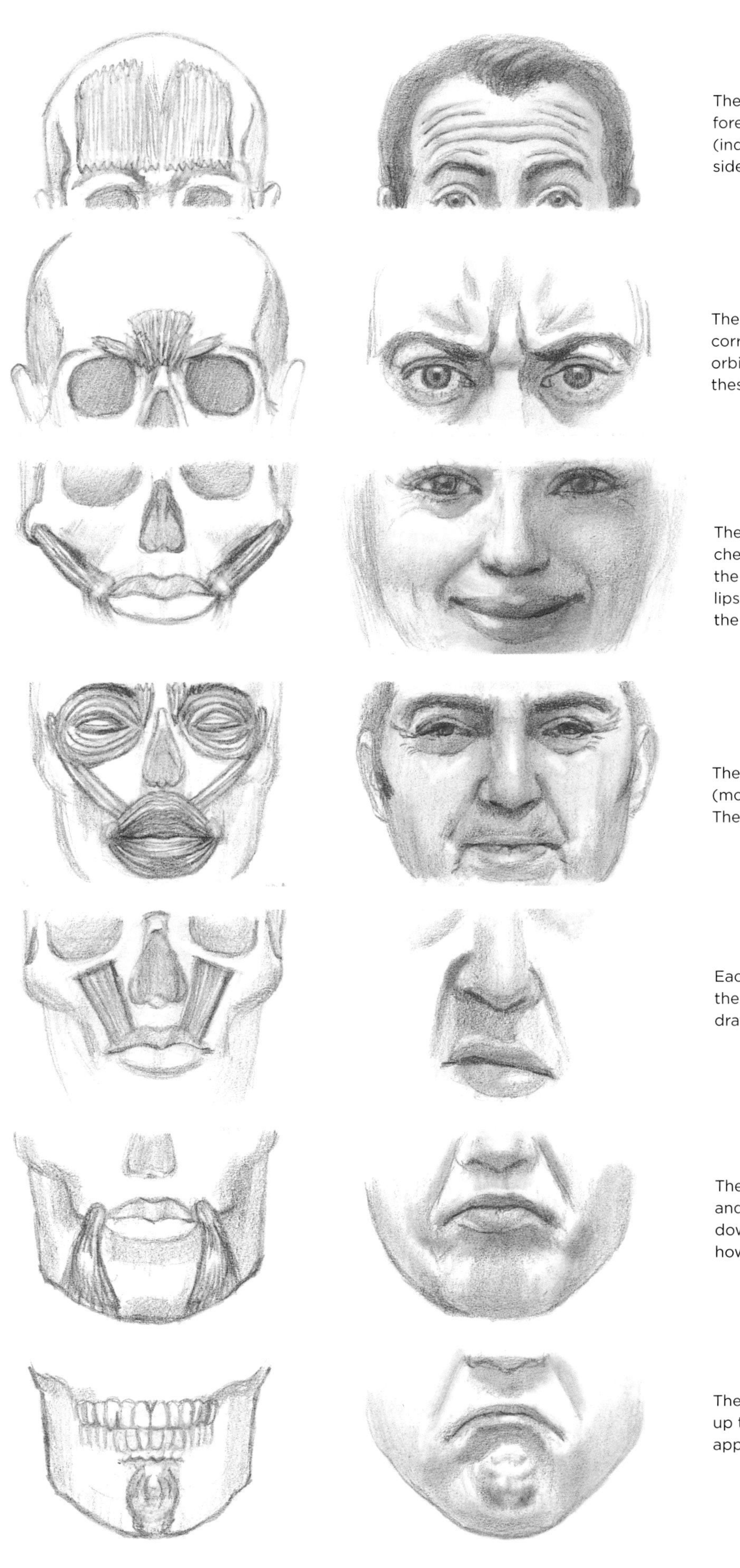

The frontalis contracts to create wrinkles on the forehead. It can contract in the middle alone (indicating sadness) or in the middle and on the sides (indicating surprise).

The procerus is in the middle of the browridge; the corrugator is on each side, like little wings. The orbiculares oculi (see below) work together with these muscles to create a frown.

The zygomaticus major is anchored on each cheekbone and inserts into a node at each side of the lips. When they pull, they widen and raise the lips, forcing a cheek bulge under each eye. These are the main muscles for smiling.

The orbicularis oculi (eye) and the orbicularis oris (mouth) squeeze and narrow the eyes and mouth. They also close the eyes and mouth, respectively.

Each levator is anchored to the skull and yanks up the side of the lip so you can sneer at other artists' drawings.

The triangularis muscles are anchored on the jaw and tug at the nodes on the sides of the lips, pulling down the corners of the mouth when you realize how little money artists make.

The mentalis is anchored below the teeth and pulls up the flesh of the chin. This creates a pout or the appearance of someone thinking (mental—get it?).

Expressions

For this section on facial expressions, the artist drew the models from life and coaxed them into specific expressions. However, fleeting expressions are best captured with a camera. A photo can be copied on its own or—ideally—used in combination with sessions with the live model.

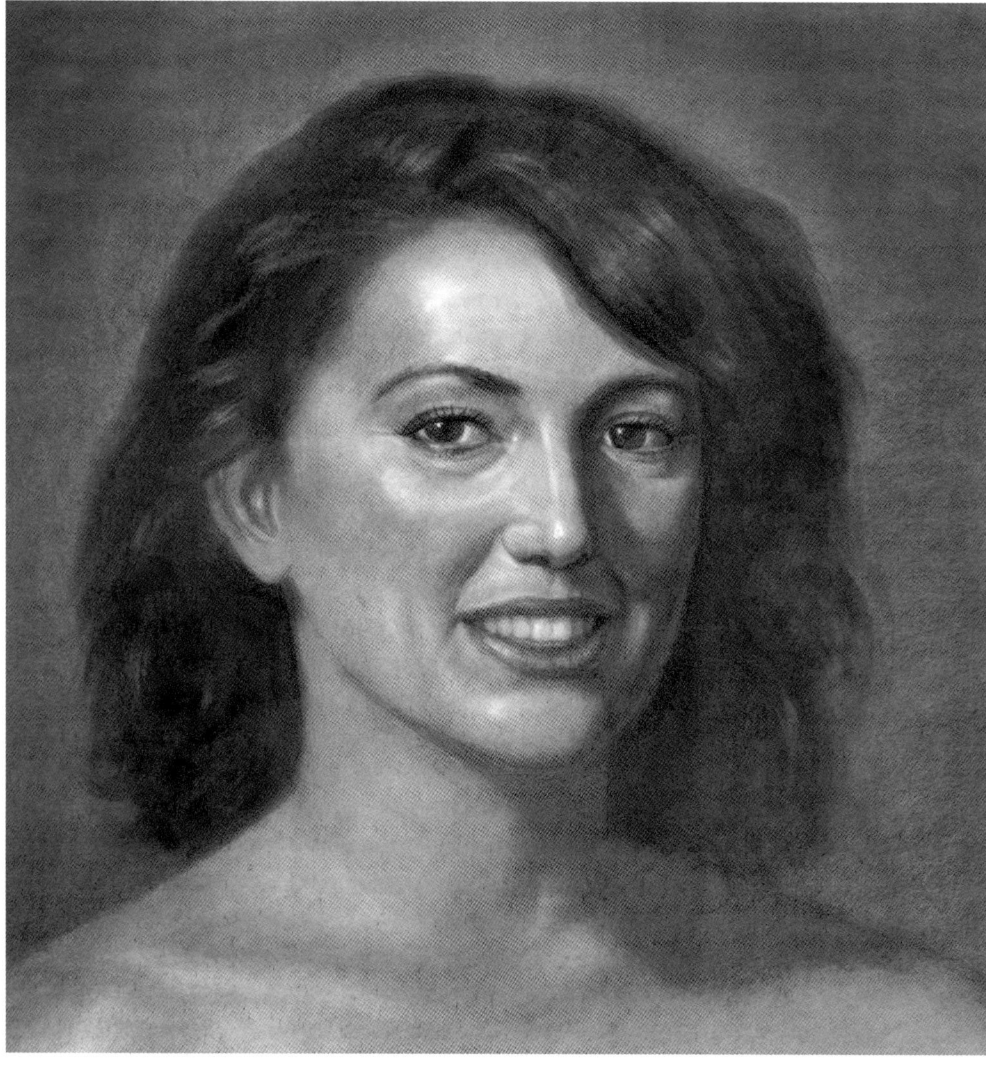

Broad Smile Regardless of how you work, an artist is expected to know a few rules of how to achieve his or her purpose and not arrive at "accidental" moods. Below is a list of important changes that you must check when drawing a broad smile. As you work, remember that the lines at the corners of the mouth shift and sometimes disappear. Check out the Mona Lisa!

Indicators of a Broad Smile

A. The areas above and below the mouth become shallower as the lips widen.

B. Lips stretch and fold in at the sides, which leaves more light in the middle.

C. The cheeks bulge up and should have a highlight indicating this.

D. The upper eyelids lower slightly, but the lower eyelids rise, covering the bottoms of the irises. This is essential to depict.

E. Laugh lines form around the eyes and mouth. It's tempting to minimize these to flatter the model, but don't. Without the appropriate wrinkles and folds, your drawing will not look correct.

F. Be very selective about when to show lower teeth. They're barely visible unless the expression is very intense.

G. The nostril wings widen and rise.

H. The eyebrows remain relaxed.

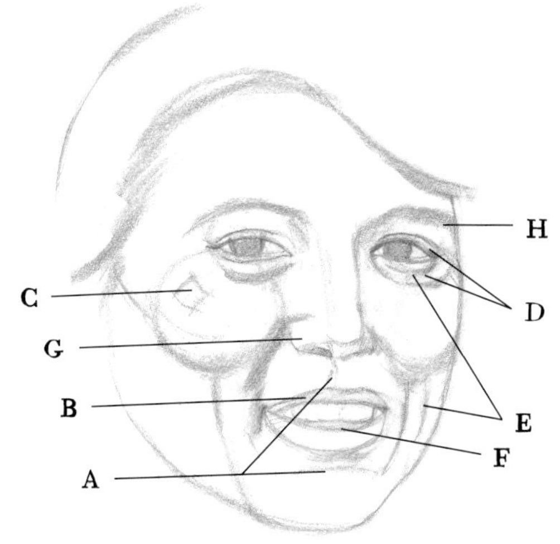

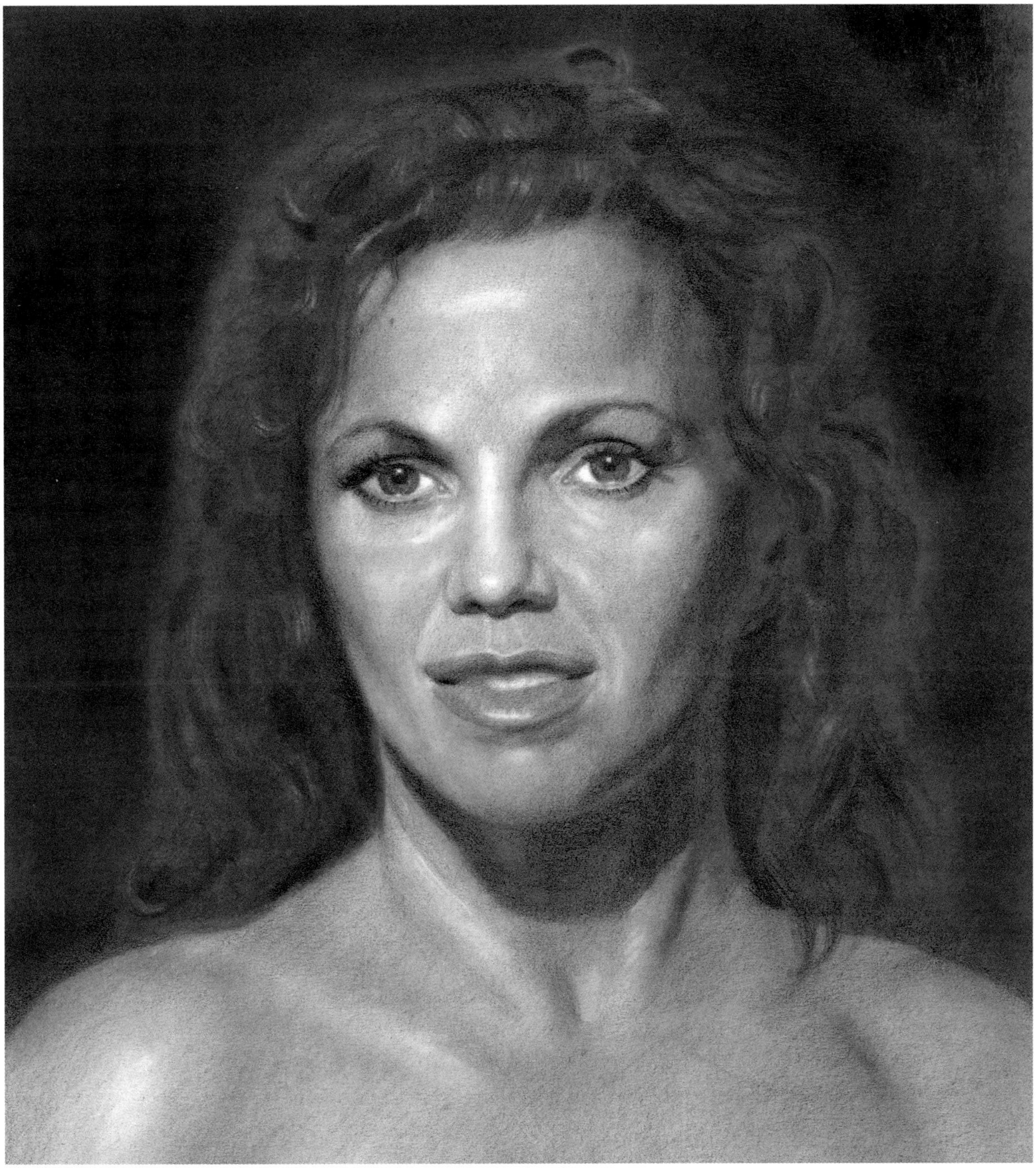

Gentle Smile Depicted here is a hint of a smile that one might have in mid conversation. (Items A through H from page 156 are repeated here.) If your model can't hold a smile for long, try the following strategy. Ask the model to smile for 30 seconds, and quickly check an item from your list. Then let the model relax for 5 minutes, and ask again. Notice how the lines between the teeth are drawn as lightly as possible. Also, the teeth are shaded as they turn away from the light. If you forget this, they will appear to jut forward and out at the sides of the mouth.

Indicators of a Gentle Smile This diagram shows important areas involved in a gentle smile. A slight covering of the bottom of the iris will help create the smile (A). Careful—if you raise the nasolabial fold too much at the nostril, the model will have a sneer (B). The positions of highlights C and D depend on the intensity of the smile. Notice that the highlight on the forehead (E) is brighter than the one on her chin (F).

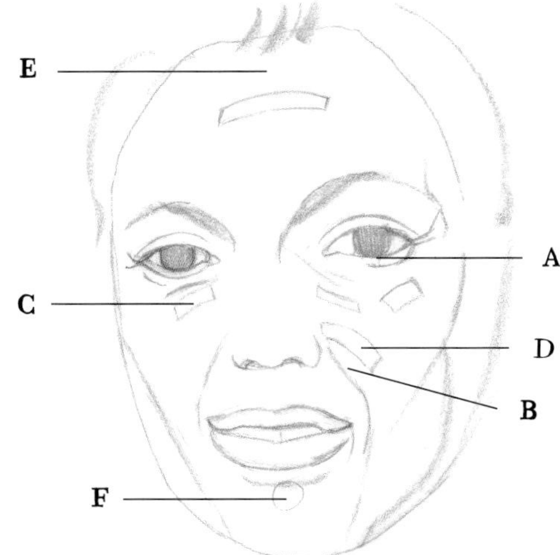

Hair

Don't think of hair as a series of lines or squiggles; instead, treat it as a mass with texture. Following the steps and tips below will help you draw it realistically.

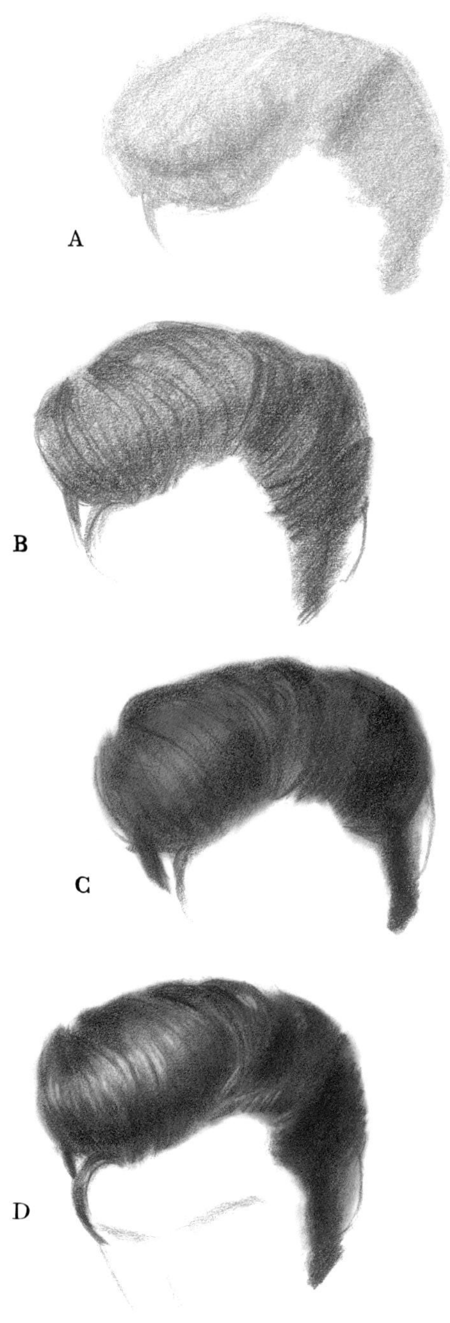

A

B

C

D

Drawing Hair Lay in a pattern of light and dark with core shadows (A). Add striations and details of the forms (B). Stump and rub; then reinforce the striations (C). Form a kneaded eraser into a point and pull out highlights. Erase parallel striations of light to mimic hair (D). The highlights in black hair aren't white.

Loose Curls   Tight Curls

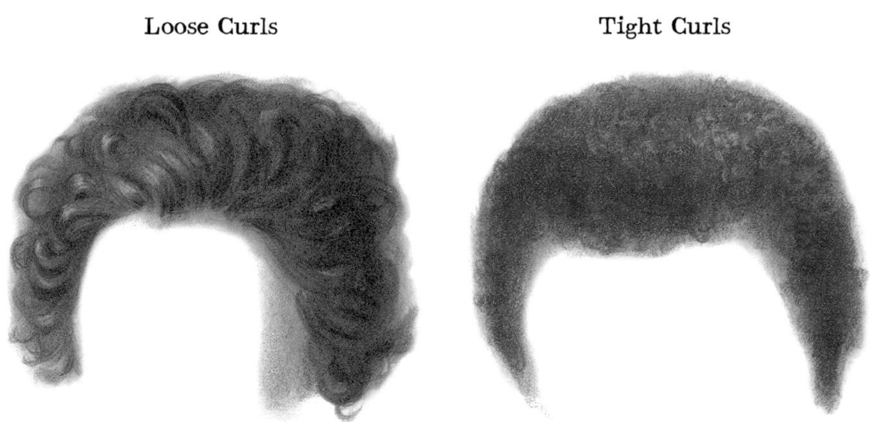

Curly Hair When encountering curly hair, don't panic. You don't have to draw every curl. Just lay down a tone and draw a few curls. Highlight some of them, and deepen some of them. Have fun with it.

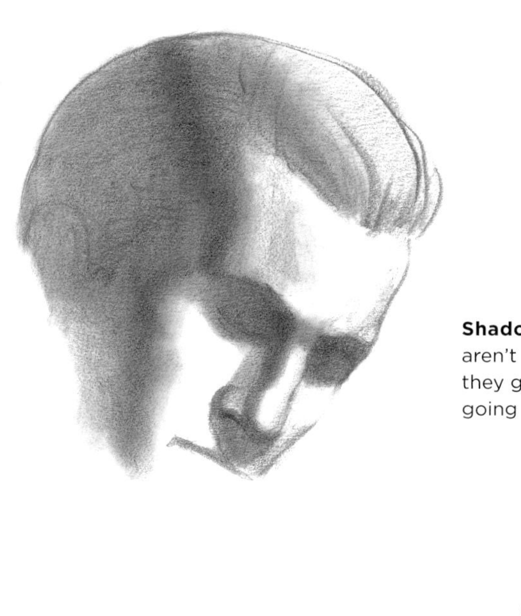

Shadows in Hair Core shadows aren't smart enough to stop when they get to the hairline. They keep going through the hair.

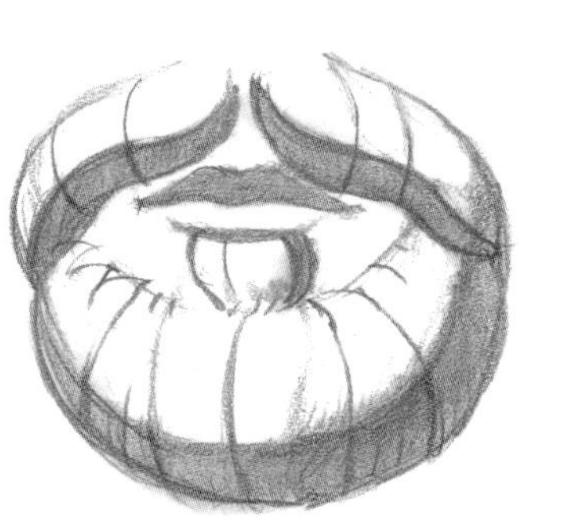

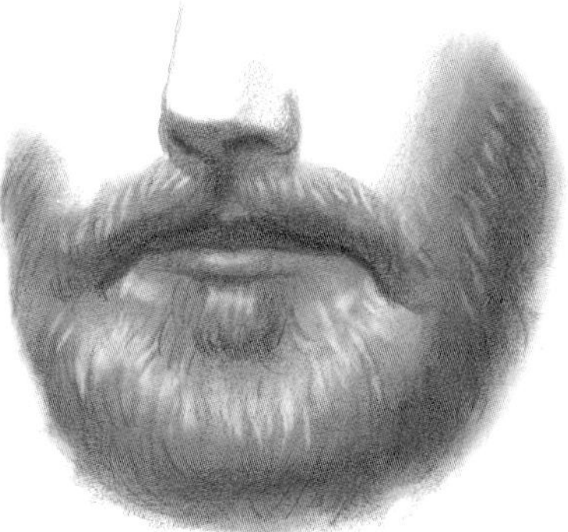

Creating Beards Beards aren't cotton candy—you must bear in mind a structure as you render the volumes.

The danger for the student artist is rubbing too soon or shading chaotically. Therefore, shade methodically, first addressing the whole head with halftone. Emphasize the edges of the core shadows and cast shadows. Then, when the structure is nailed down, you may rub and darken. Remember to shade either along the core or across it—multiple directions will result in a mess.

▶ **No Hair** When working with a model with no head hair, achieving a likeness relies on capturing the distinct curves and bumps that make up the shape of the head.

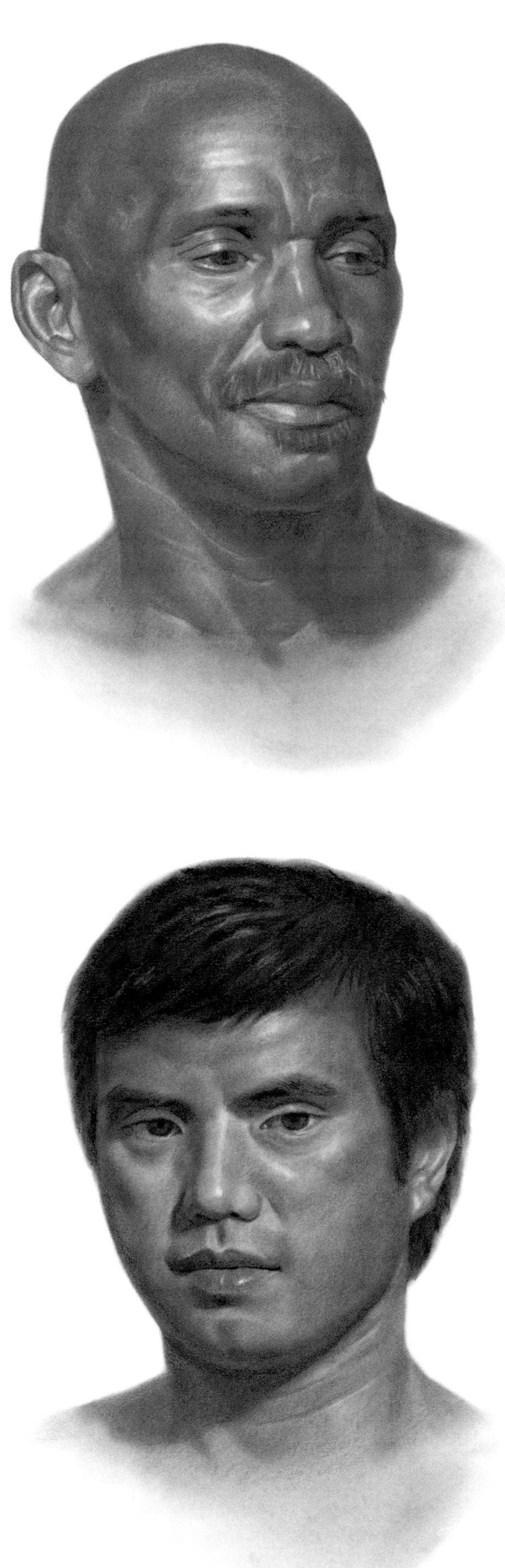

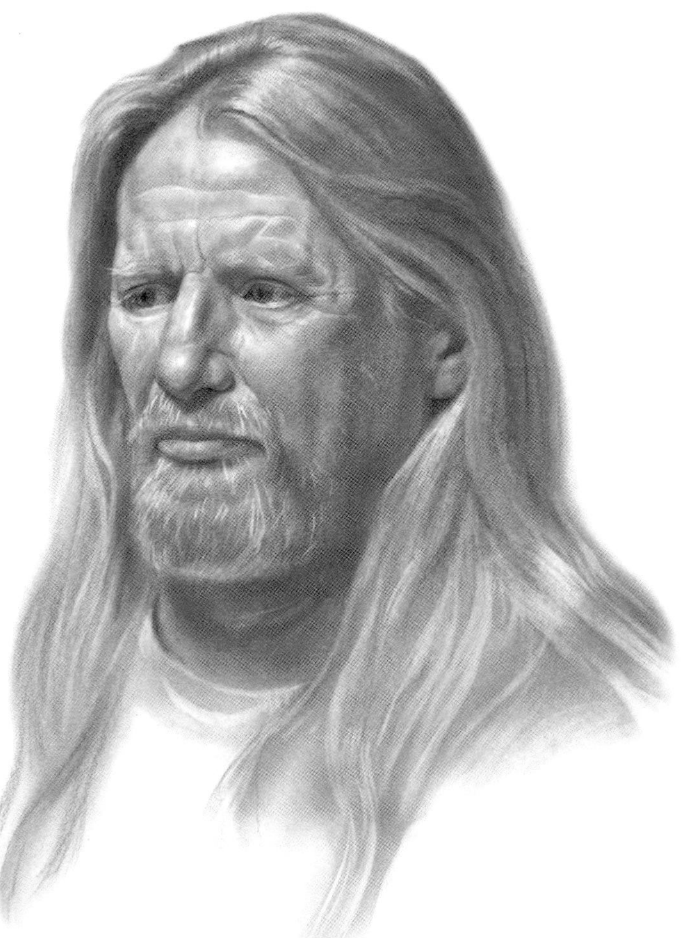

▲ **Drawing Realistic Hair** Hair should be composed of tones and striations—not bundles of spindly lines.

▶ **Rendering Dark Hair** The tricky part about drawing Adrian was replicating his inky black hair. For a small head, you can get away with grinding in a Staedtler® 8B for a quick black. But for a life-size head, lay the drawing flat, pour on the graphite powder, and rub it in with a powder puff and make-up applicator. Even then you still may have to grind in the pencil here and there for the darkest darks. Fortunately, the Staedtler® 8B stays matte while providing dark tones.

Project: Man

This project shows the step-by-step method for drawing. Each project is broken down into seven stages of drawing: the lay-in, plumb lines, volume, edges and outlines, tonal pattern, finishing, and polishing. The first project provides the most detail on these seven stages, so it's best to start here. However, it's a good idea to read all the projects because each one includes slightly different information. Actually copying the stages (drawing each step over the previous) would be commendable. (Note that all projects call for the 9B pencil, only switching to 5B or 2B for small details.)

STAGE 1: THE LAY-IN

Because the lay-in and the next step, plumb lines, seem so basic (and ugly), artists tend to rush through them. But these steps ensure the success of the drawing. You can always adjust your shading, but if sloppy work now leads to bad proportions, then the drawing will require major surgery later. The first measurements must be exact to achieve a likeness.

Step 1 Draw an oval; then add a vertical arc (A) that follows the curvature of the model's face. Place horizontal marks at the top, bottom, and midpoint (B) of the oval. Next determine the midpoint of the model's face by extending your arm—elbow locked—and placing the tip of the pencil where you imagine the center to be. Place your thumbnail in line with the model's chin (see diagram below).

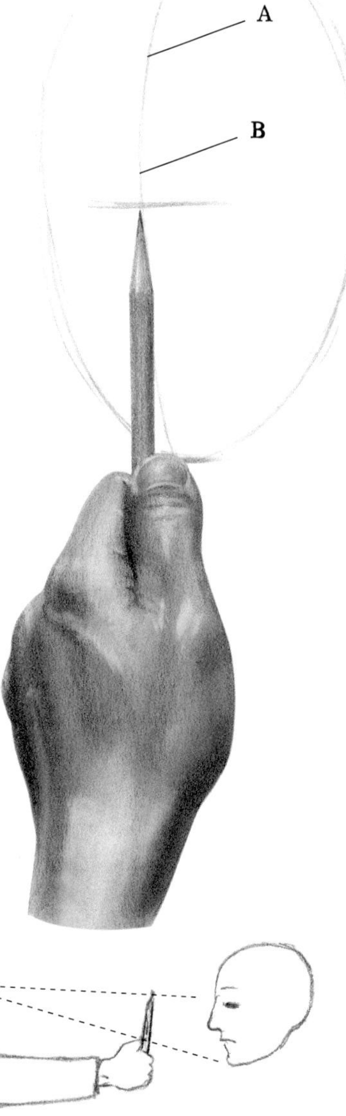

NOTE: All hands in this chapter used to show measurement are drawings.

Step 2 Raise your arm so that your thumbnail is where the tip of the pencil was. If the tip is now at the top of the model's head, you've found the center. If not, simply keep adjusting the pencil and your thumb, repeating steps 1 and 2 until your nail and the tip consistently fall halfway up the model's face (the midpoint).

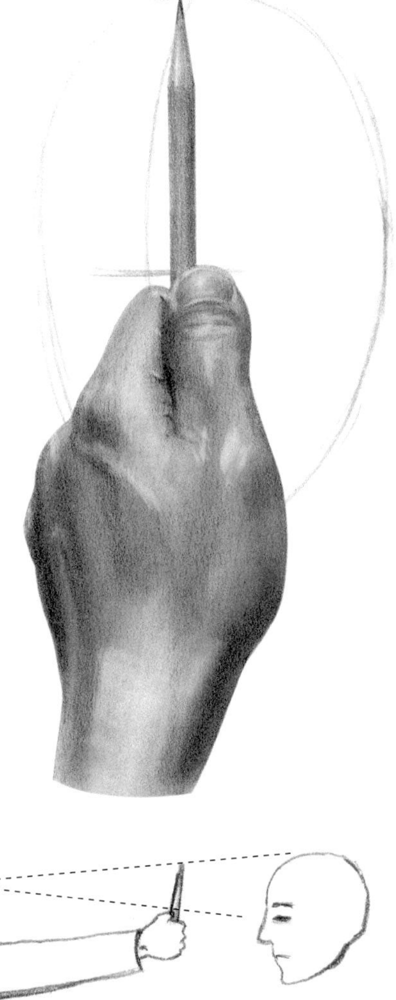

NOTE: If this is a private session and you're working at life-size, you should actually measure the distance from the inner corner of the model's eyebrow to the bottom of his chin with a ruler, and place this measurement on your paper. It's not the center, but it's very accurate.

Step 3 Note the form that you found at the midpoint of the face (for example, the tear ducts). Then use this to guesstimate the distances of other features from top to bottom, including hairline to browridge, eyes to bottom of nose, lips to chin, top to browridge, nose to chin, and so on. Don't measure these with the pencil because the forms are so small that it's easy to make a mistake. If you put the drawing next to the model, it may be obvious what the distances should be.

Make sure these horizontals are placed along the vertical arc so you can establish the center of the face. Draw lightly—these guidelines are for you, not for art history. Also, remember basic proportions of the head: Hair line to brow is roughly one-third of the head's length, brow to bottom of nose is roughly one-third, and bottom of nose to bottom of chin is roughly one-third.

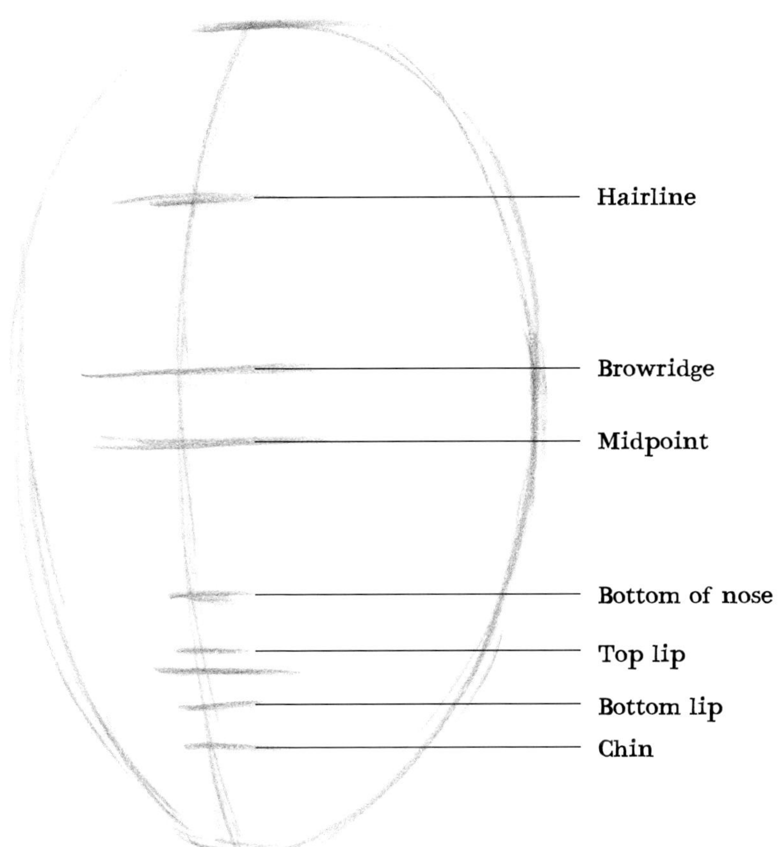

STAGE 2: THE PLUMB LINES

Now that we have the proportions roughly laid out from top to bottom, we can work on the widths. Always work out the vertical measurements first because it's easy to narrow a form but big trouble to lengthen one (in this case, everything has to move).

Step 1 In this step, you'll use your eyes to guesstimate a rough shape that would fit between the marks you measured in stage 1. This will not be a precise outline. We just want a shape that has the basic width and size of the model's features. To do this, first mark a width for each feature that corresponds to the marks you made for the lay-in (A). Then compare general sizes: How much space does the nose occupy on the face? Which takes up more space—the lips or one eye? Compare back and forth between the features. Then begin to suggest the basic shape of each feature (B).

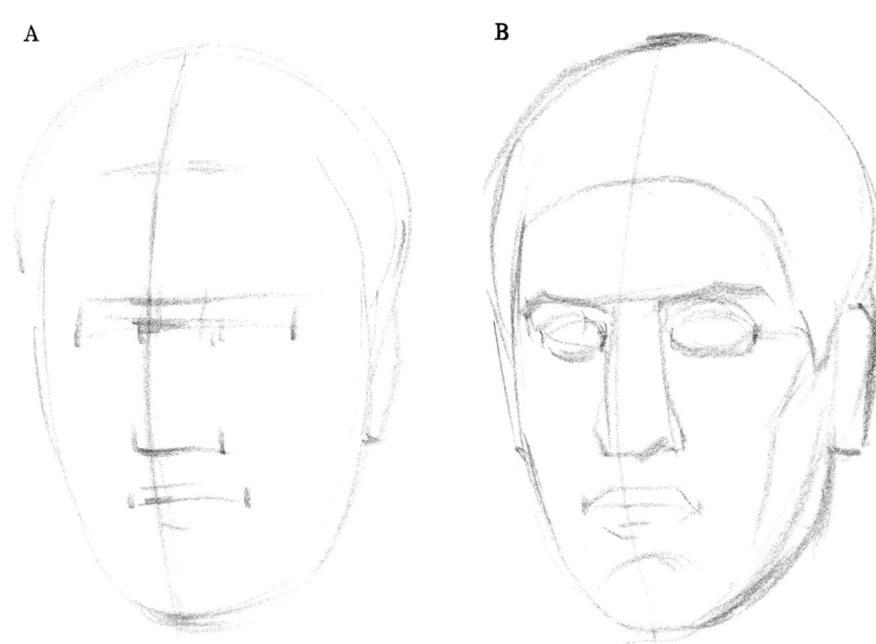

Step 2 You now must use plumb lines to make sure the forms are aligned properly above and below one another. Wouldn't it be helpful to know if the tear ducts are directly above the nostrils? Does the side of the neck line up directly below the corner of the mouth? Put your pencil in front of the model's face vertically and check (A). Then place the pencil horizontally to gauge the alignments, including earlobe to nose, mouth to corner of jaw, and so on (B). Adjust the drawing accordingly.

Don't forget that there is a slight skewing effect from perspective. Here it's exaggerated to make a point.

Step 3 Pay attention to negative space (the space between the forms). If you ignore it, you won't achieve a likeness and may never figure out why. The space between the forms is as important as the forms themselves. Continue checking these distances as you draw.

Always compare the two key measurements above. Hold your pencil out and have your thumbnail touch the bridge of the nose while the tip touches the ear (A). Now turn the pencil and see how this length compares with the same point on the nose to the chin (B).

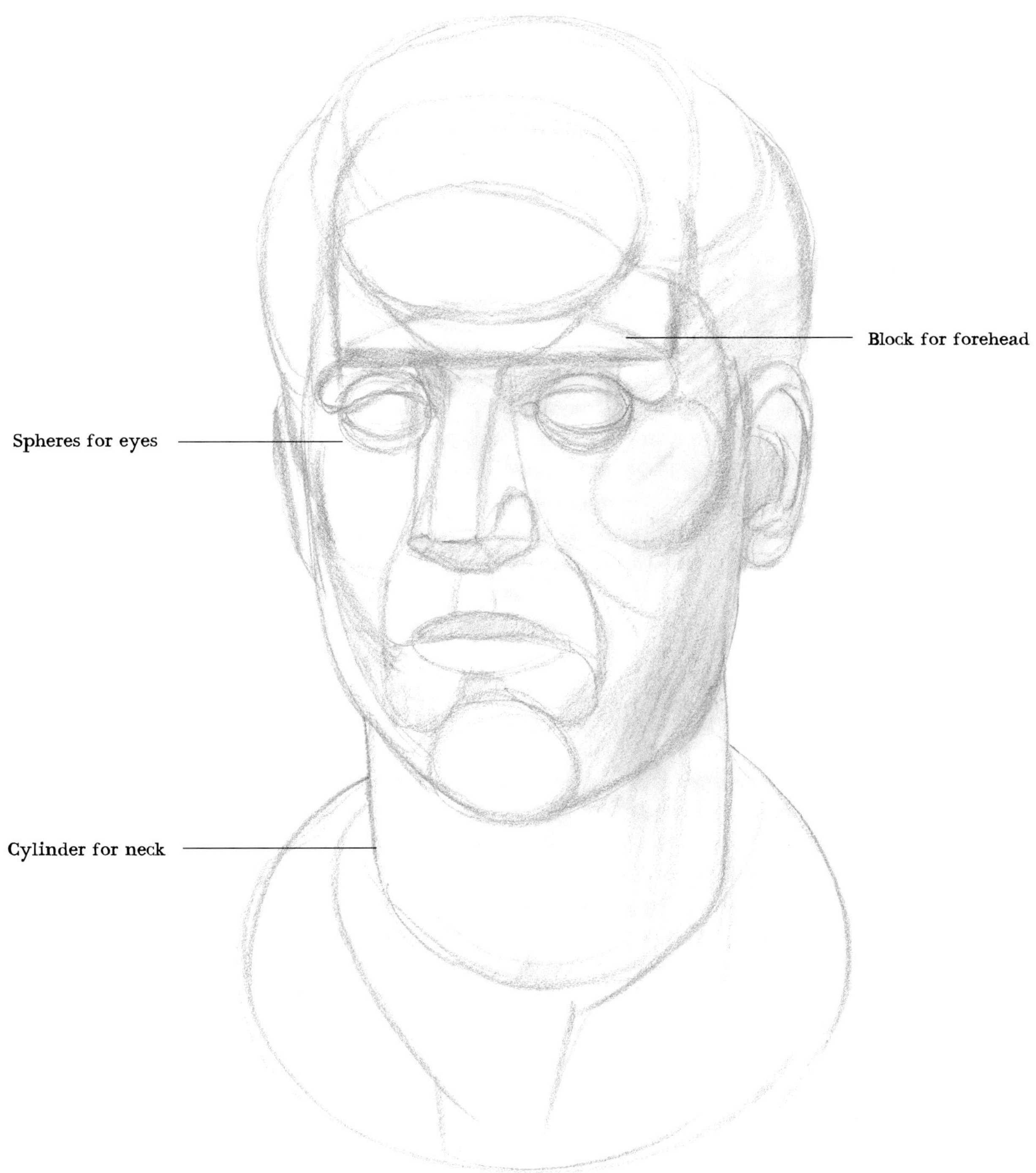

STAGE 3: VOLUMES

With an accurate lay-in on the paper, there's no chance of making a huge mistake, so you can relax and develop the structure on top of the plan. Faintly draw a simple volume that might protrude beneath the surface of each form. Beginners sometimes resist this practice, but it can provide your drawings with more structure and a greater sense of three-dimensionality. If the model were hollow, the volumes could fit inside the skin; but they are obscured by the surface of the skin. Therefore, you will shade over the volumes, erase them, and leave them, depending on what makes the drawing look more real. But having them there initially gives you a guide—a framework upon which to add details and lighting. You can't be distracted by the surface because the volumes remind you of the mass underneath. The realist always draws the big mass, integrating smaller masses into it. The way to do this is to draw a large shape—an egg or a cube for the head—and then spheres and blocks on top of it. The shapes of these forms are your choice, as they're suggested to you by the model's appearance.

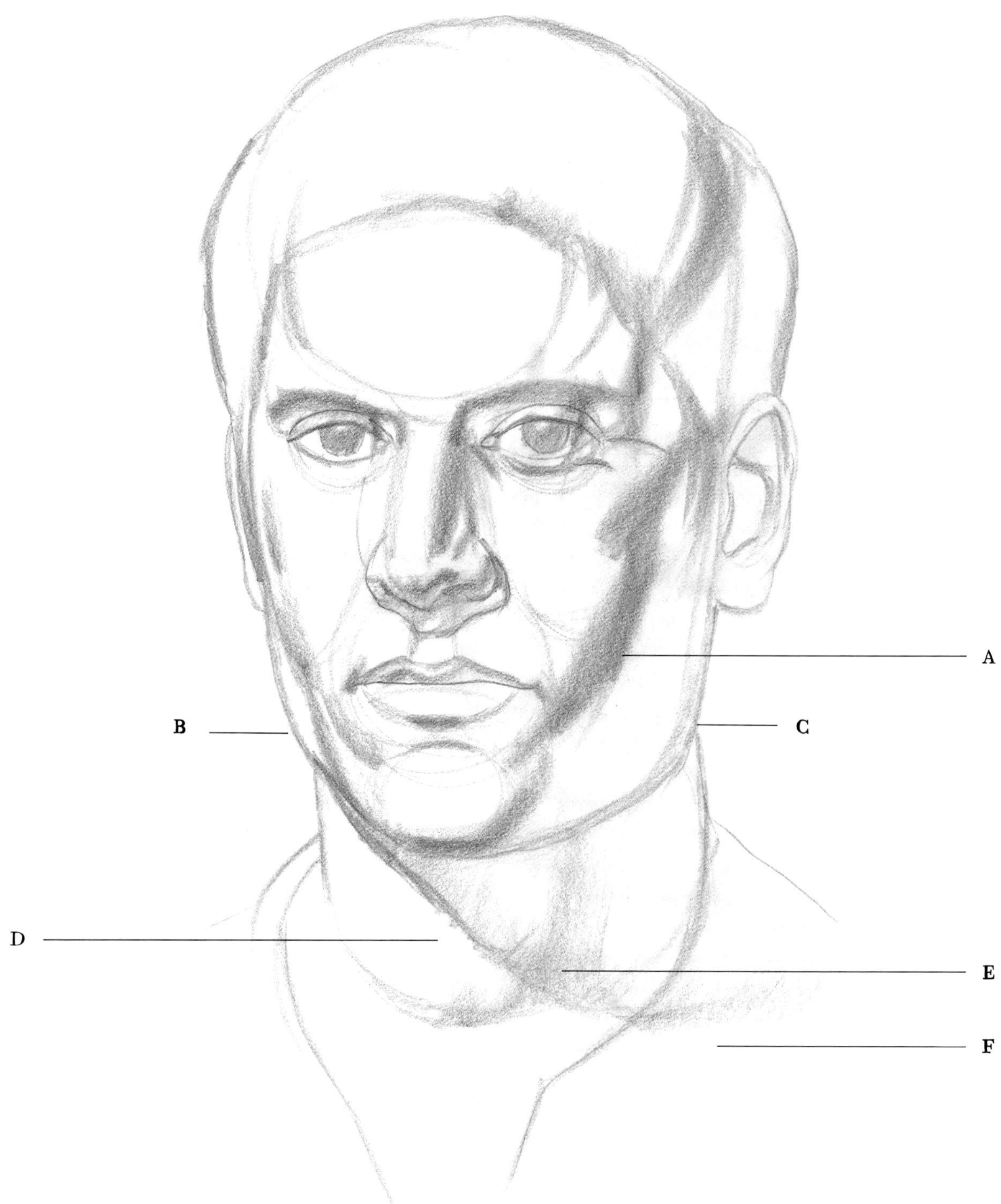

STAGE 4: EDGES & OUTLINES

Using the volumes as guides, draw the outlines and the core shadows. The core shadows are on the edges of the shadows (A). Amateurs leave out core shadows because they don't notice them, but core shadows give the forms corners and, hence, a three-dimensional quality. Core shadows are darker parts of the shadows, and they're always soft. Don't draw them as sharp lines. Please don't. Just don't, OK? When they happen to be darker than the outline, the form really protrudes.

When drawing the outline, try to draw one side of the form (B) and then the other (C). You can do this with the jaw, cheekbones, nostrils, and so on. Sometimes, as on this nose, you must outline one side, then turn your pencil to the side and shade the core shadow. Keep the

outline faint—it is not a thick, black stroke. In some places, it fades away entirely, and by the end of the drawing you should have shaded up to it so that it no longer appears as a line. Don't grind it in now, but you must have a clear point where the form stops, so an outline must be there.

You must also draw the edges of the cast shadow (D). The edges aren't razor sharp, but they must be very clear—especially compared with the softness of the core. The shadow edge on the form is core (E); the edge thrown by the form is cast. The shadow's edge will soften and lighten as it travels away from the form casting it (F). Note your model's softest and sharpest shadow edges.

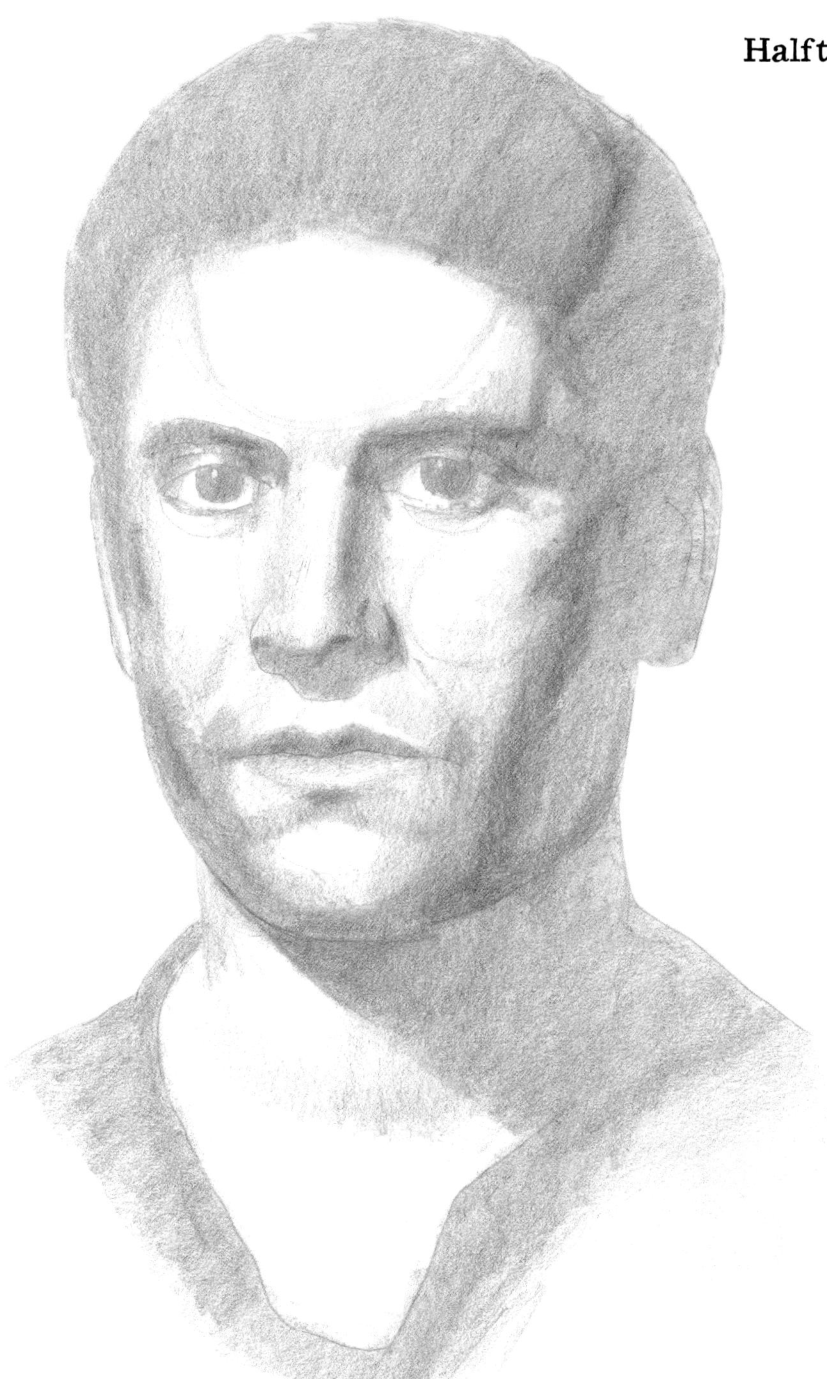

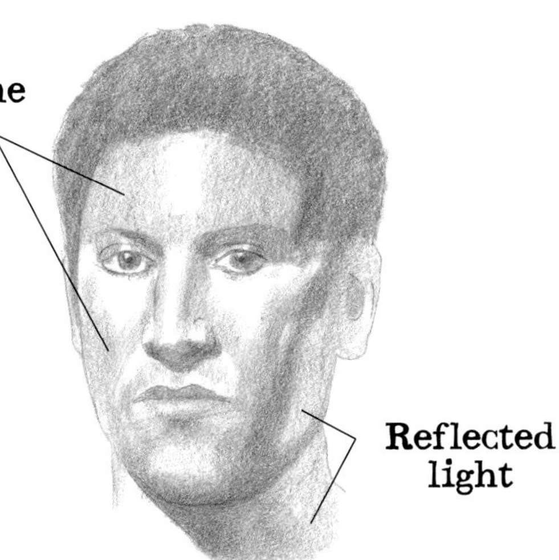

Adding Halftone It's okay to put some halftone in now as your pencil glides across the cores, but adding the darkest parts of the shadows is most important. Shade right over the reflected light. It will come back when you darken around it.

STAGE 5: TONAL PATTERN

This should be the simplest stage. It's actually better if you think very little during this stage. Just squint your eyes, and the model's face will become blurry and simplify into a pattern of dark and light. If you squint hard enough, the halftones in the light area and the reflected lights in the dark area will no longer distract you. The brain wants to exaggerate every tone, but if you draw only what the eye sees, your drawing will be more accurate. To judge tone correctly, you must squint often. This fresher eye will tell you when an area has fooled you into inaccuracy; correct tone is the mark of a master realist.

If the model has a lot of shadow on his face, you can experiment with drawing this tonal pattern at earlier stages (though never before the lay-in and plumb line stages). A little toning can be valuable to judge proportions and decide where to outline.

Try to shade in one direction for the whole head (along or across the cores). Fill in gaps, and shade evenly. This pattern initially will be of medium darkness. Shade over several forms with the same strokes (e.g., face through hair through ear).

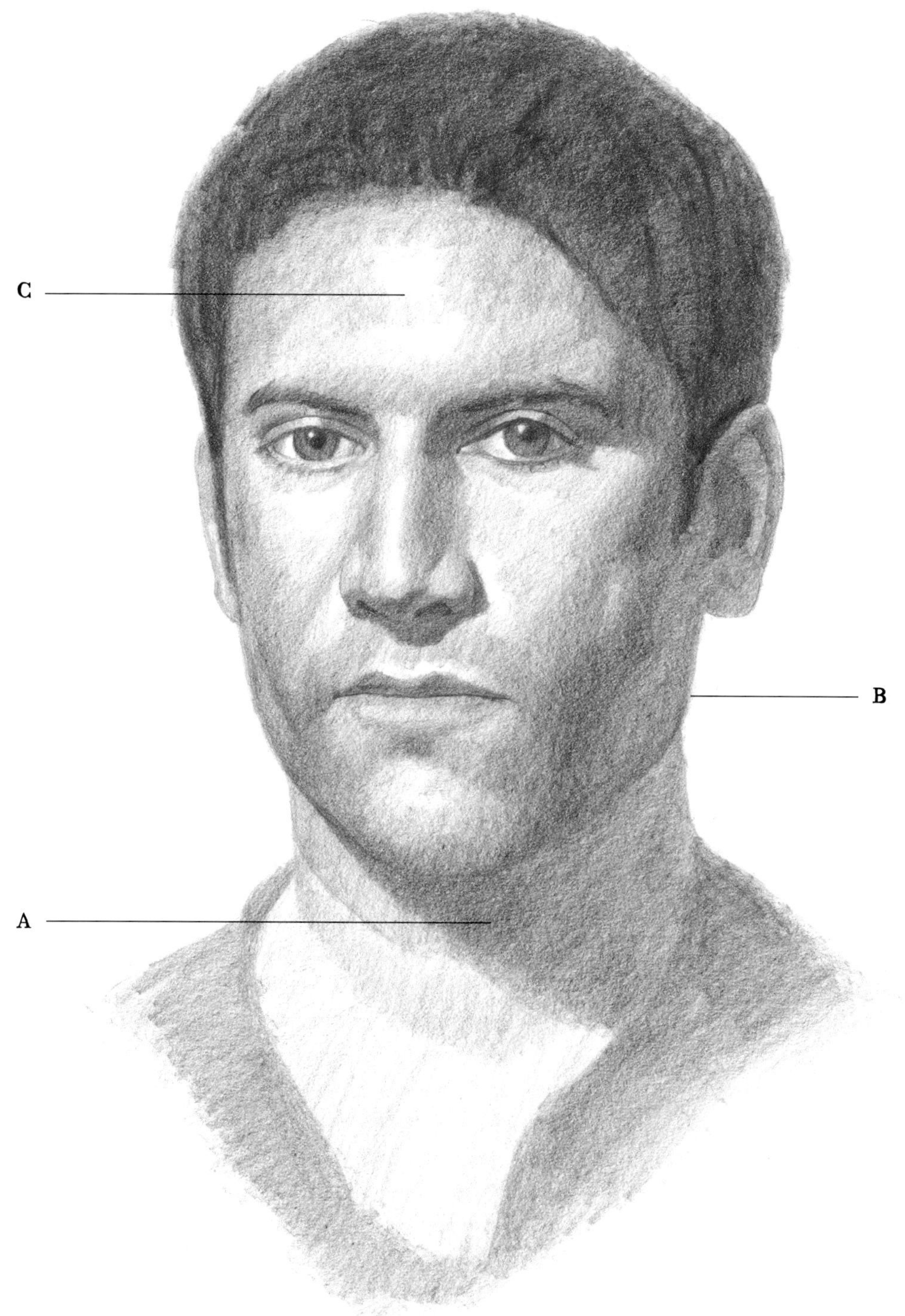

STAGE 6: FINISHING

It can be helpful to draw with a kneaded eraser in your opposite hand so you can continually clean up mistakes as you go along. Moreover, you've now had five stages to achieve accuracy of outlines and proportions. Between the erasing and constant checking, the drawing should be extremely accurate.

Now you need to concern yourself only with adding correct tone (value). This consists of adding darks and halftones. The darks must be gradually blended into the halftones by repeatedly caressing the side of the 9B into the "bed" of tone (A). Darks must be shaded up to any lines either on the outline or on the edges of the cast shadows (B).

Lines must be hunted down and eliminated like vermin. They are the enemy of realism and must suffer accordingly. Eliminate them by shading up to them. Caress halftones from the outlines or the core shadows all the way up to the highlights (C). Feckless students shade over the highlights, hoping to erase them, but this will result in flatness. By stopping at the highlight, a clear plane change emerges. Later you can, and should, rub over and erase them out, but first you must establish a clear division between the highlight plane and the halftone plane to avoid the charge of vagueness.

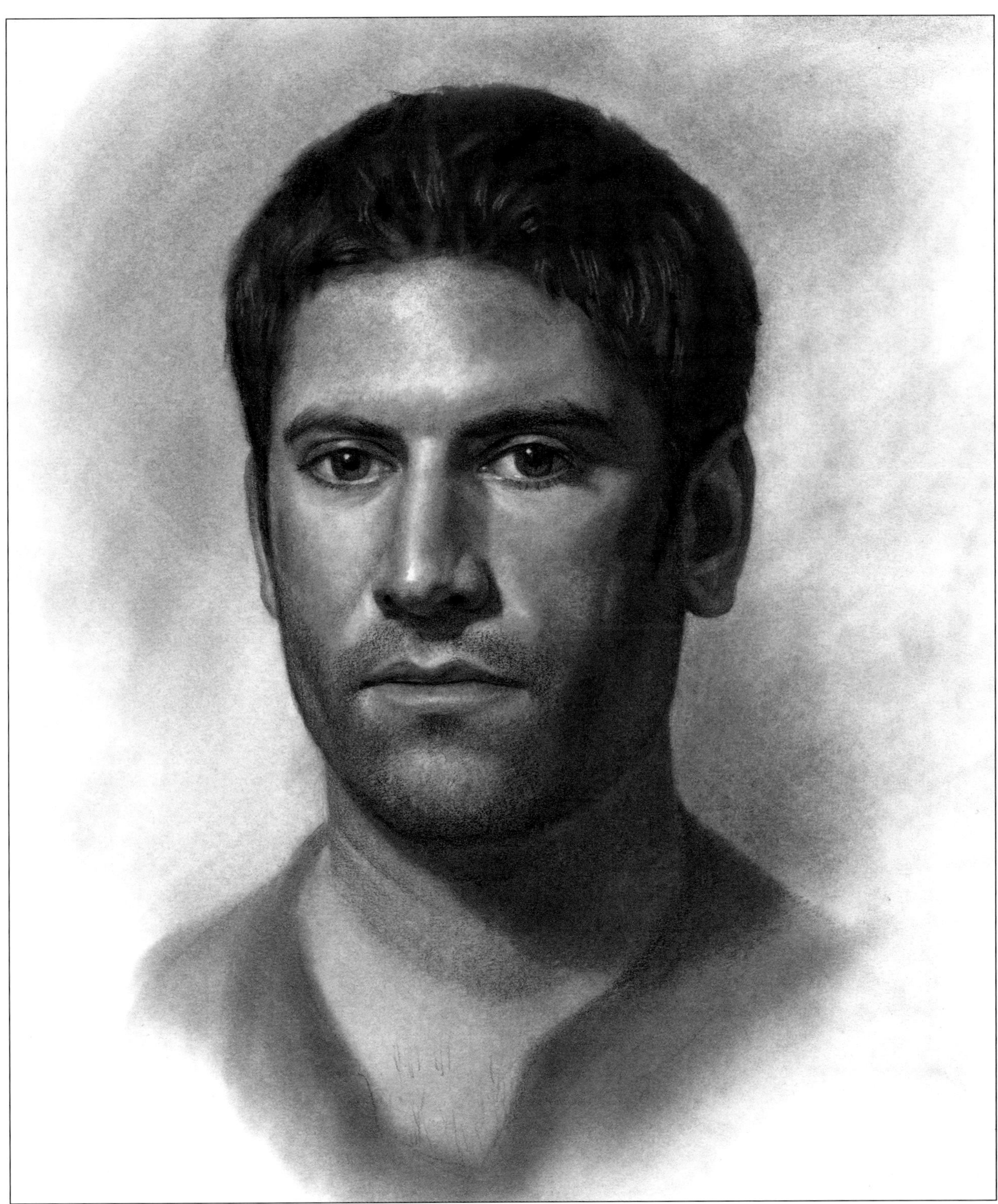

STAGE 7: POLISHING

This stage will be time consuming and can be messy. As you stump, rub, and highlight, note that the head gradually darkens as it turns away from the highlight. Any deviation in tone will look like a bruise. Your blends must transition smoothly. Don't leave patches of light or dark. Begin by using your stumps to rub the core shadows. Remember to stump with the core—hatching across it just creates patches. Use the "cone" of the stump, not the tip—the tip also creates patches. Use the tip in small areas. At this point, it's OK to grind in the Staedtler® 8B for extreme darks. Put an object that's truly black up to the model so you can see how dark to go. Rub most of the drawing with the powder puff. You can also go in with the make-up applicator in place of the stump— experiment to see which tool works best for different areas. This smearing may change the tones, forcing you to reevaluate them. At stages like this, you may have to flatten your kneaded eraser and press it onto areas to lighten, but not erase, them. Pull out highlights with your mechanical and battery erasers. Finally, drag a 9B over the chin and leave it rough to create stubble. The project is now complete!

Project: Woman

STAGE 1: THE LAY-IN

First draw an oval with a 9B pencil. The straight-on view calls for a somewhat symmetrical shape, but don't worry about making the shape of the head accurate at this point; the oval simply is a tool to establish the size of the head. Mark the midpoint of the oval. Now you must find the midpoint on your model so you can place reference marks for nearby features, such as the eyes and browridge. To do this, hold your pencil vertically with the pencil tip up. Extend your arm with your elbow locked, and place the pencil tip where you estimate the midpoint to be.

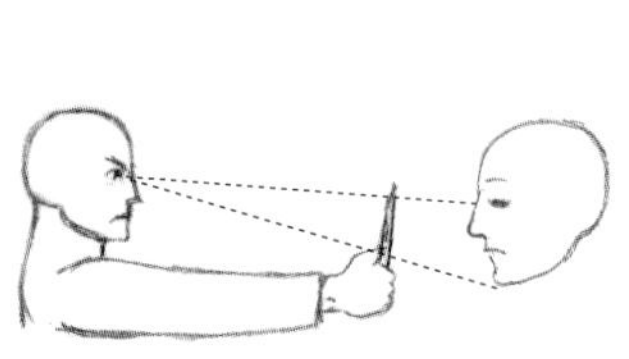

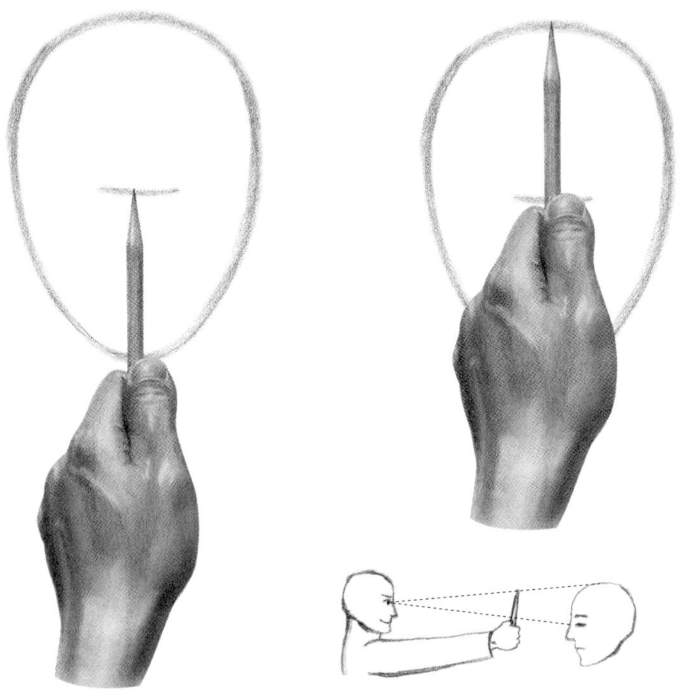

STAGE 2: PLUMB LINES

During this stage, you'll nail down the placement of the facial features by checking your verticals, horizontals, and negative space. Begin by marking an estimated width for each horizontal line along the vertical line; then roughly block in the features. Compare the sizes of the features with one another, and continue to check the horizontal and vertical plumb lines, adjusting your drawing as necessary. As you draw, remember that the negative space between the forms is as important as the forms themselves, so compare the spaces in your drawing with your model often. As you check the verticals and horizontals, assess the negative space (as shown by the arrows at right), which will help you find any shapes that might differ from those of your model.

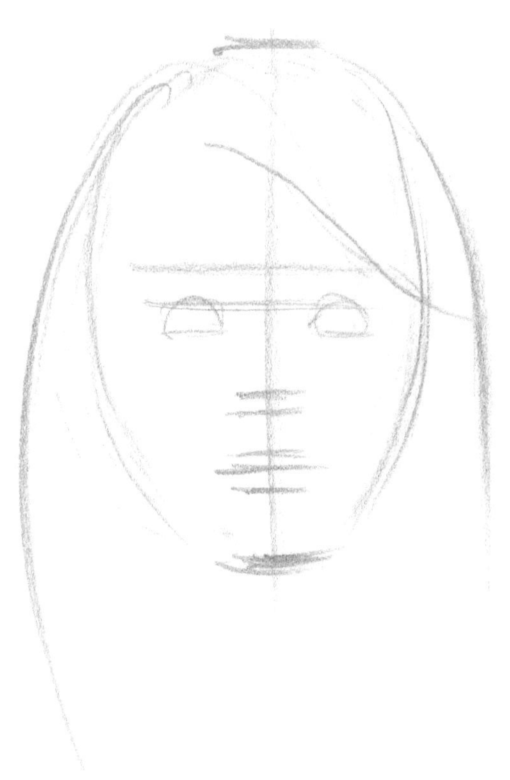

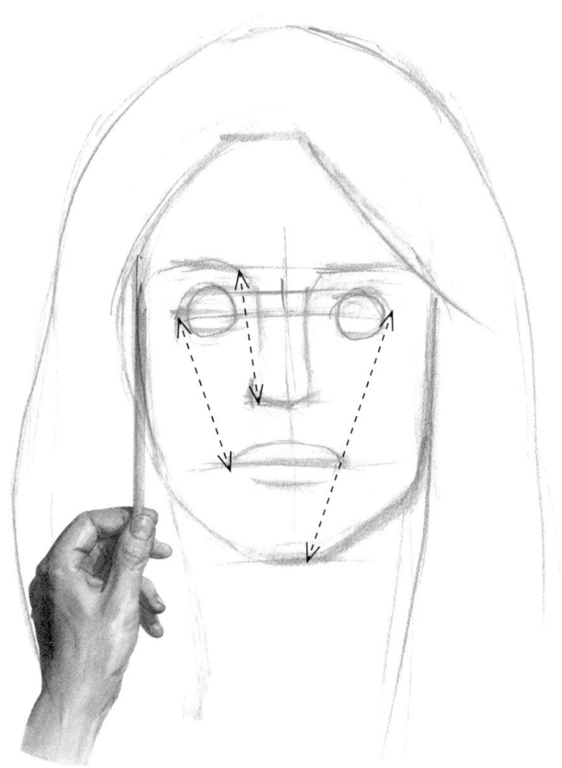

Add a line to establish the vertical center of the oval; then estimate and check other vertical distances, marking the bottom, top, and center of the lips; the tip and base of the nose; the browridge; and the hairline.

STAGE 3: VOLUMES

With all the measuring complete, you're now free to draw more intuitively. Try imagining simple forms that would fit inside the face under the surface that you see. The forms will help guide you—although the forms may look robotic, the human quality will emerge as you refine their shapes and tones. Using an underhand grip (hold the pencil with your hand over it, with the pencil between the thumb and index finger) for loose, light strokes, start with the largest forms and draw the smaller ones into them. Represent the forms with basic volumes—spheres for eyes, eggs for cheekbones, and so on. Imagine that you are overlapping transparent forms, building up from larger to smaller forms. This stage should take only a few minutes. Also, every model is different and suggests a different set of volumes.

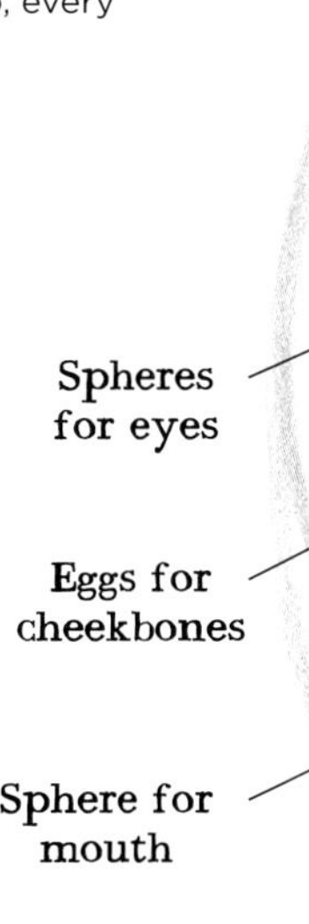

STAGE 4: TONAL PATTERN

This stage can come after stage 5 (see page 170), depending on what works best for you. If you think you're at the point at which you can create an accurate outline, skip ahead to stage 5, and then return to this stage. However, first establishing a shadow pattern can help you find where to place the outline. To begin this stage, look at your model, and squint your eyes to see the face as a pattern of light and dark. The extreme highlights and darkest accents will blend into the main pattern. Now begin blocking in this pattern of tones on your paper, turning your pencil to the side and shading diagonally for quick coverage.

Keep your strokes close together, and shade all the dark areas in the same direction to keep the drawing from appearing chaotic. (However, in more developed stages, one may shade in different directions when adding core shadows and dark accents.)

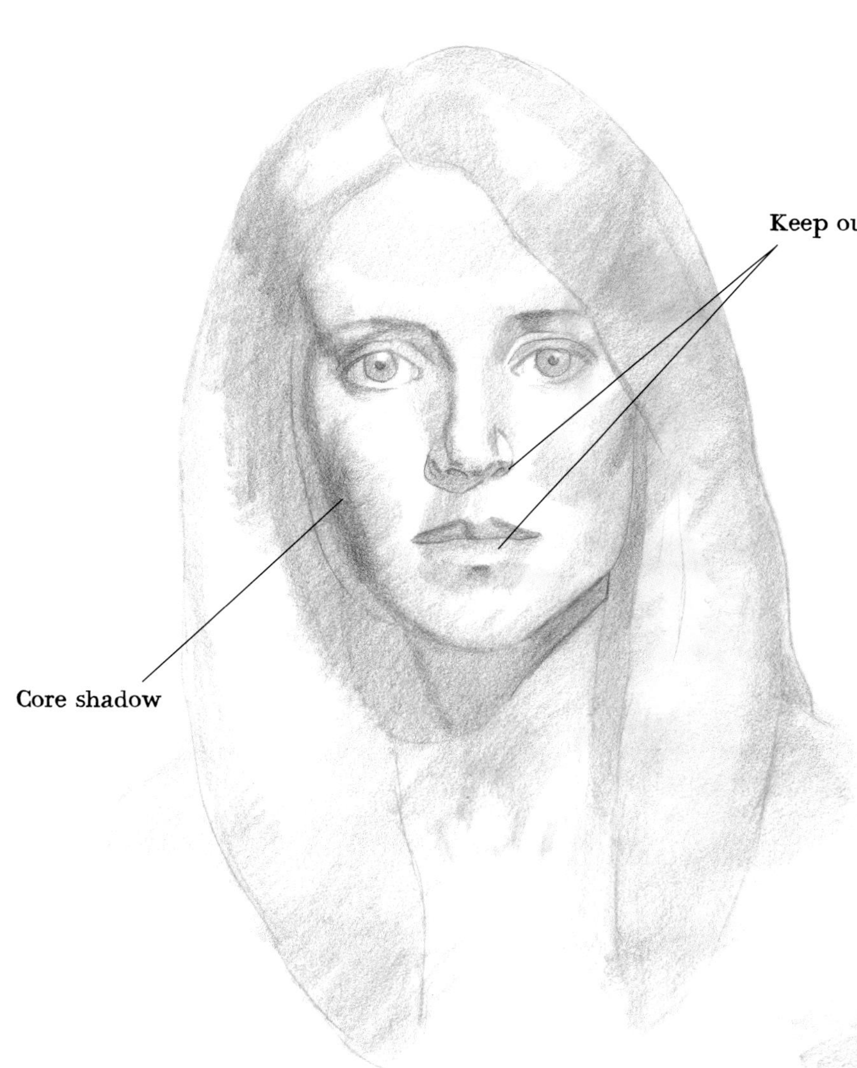

STAGE 5: EDGES & OUTLINES

Every form on this model's face has a side plane, front plane, and sometimes a clear bottom plane. The softened corner where the planes meet is the core shadow. Turn your pencil to the side, and shade a thick bar of tone—not a line—from her hair to her temple, around her cheekbone, and all the way to her chin. The core shadows overlap and soften where the forms soften. Don't ignore core shadows on the sides of the eyes or tip of the nose. As you add the core shadows, also add the subtle outlines. The outlines work like a parenthesis for each form. Try to outline one side of the form, then the other; then add the core and go back to the sides again—all in one operation. Now sharpen the edges of the cast shadows, keeping them sharpest where they are closest to the forms casting them.

STAGE 6: FINISHING

Work within the new outlines to continue developing your shading. Caress your pencil over the core shadows to pull halftone across them, diminishing the tone as it reaches the highlight. Notice how the halftones softly and gradually emerge from the core. They aren't isolated islands of tone; they mass against the core. As you shade, squint your eyes often to compare the relationships of tone on the model with those of your drawing. To make sure you're shading thoroughly, try holding a piece of white paper up to the model's face. With the exception of a few small white highlights, the entire face should have tone. Now switch to a harder pencil, such as a 5B or 2B, and develop and darken details on the face.

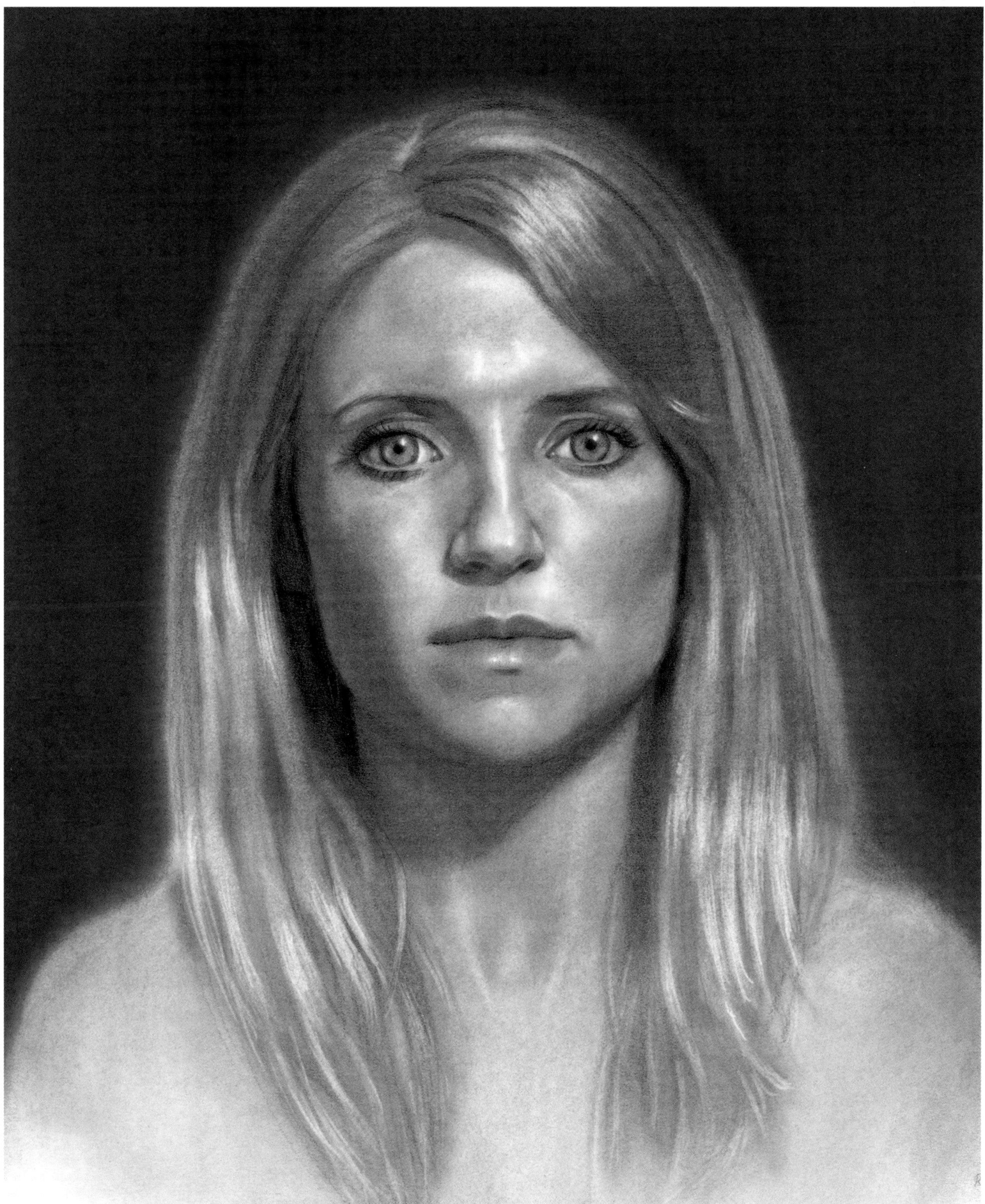

Elizabeth T. Gilbert, one day, life-size

STAGE 7: POLISHING

This is the longest stage; within it, the previous stages usually have to be repeated to some degree. Begin stumping the core shadows, and rub a make-up applicator over the dark details to soften and blend them. Burnish the entire drawing by caressing it with a powder puff, and then pull out the highlights with your kneaded eraser. If the highlights are too sharp, soften the edges with a clean stump. If the highlights won't easily erase, a battery-operated eraser should do the trick. After burnishing, your drawing may lose a bit of value. In this case, simply go back in and re-introduce the darkest darks of the face. Black is a good choice for this model's background because it creates a wonderful contrast with her blond hair. (To determine the best value for the background, it often helps to place a white, gray, or black sheet of paper behind the model, which allows you to see the different balances of tones.) To create a dark background quickly, dump out a pile of graphite powder, and use your powder puff to rub it across the paper, repeating if necessary. (Remember that faces are never perfectly symmetrical; for example, your model's nose may veer slightly to one side.)

Master Class: Drawing Portraits in Graphite | 171

Project: Young Girl

STAGE 1: THE LAY-IN

The tricky part about drawing young children is getting them to sit still. This photo of a young girl was drawn from life with the aid of a television. The drawing was created at life size in two sessions of two-and-a-half hours. Sometimes a child can be transfixed by video games, as motionless as Mount Rushmore. Using photos to draw children is often necessary, but try to adjust the halftones from life.

Step 1 The face is slightly tilted, so draw an oval with an arced midline. Check the angle of the tilt against the 90-degree vertical of your pencil.

Step 2 Measure the midpoint from top to bottom. With children, the proportions change every year, so rely on measurement rather than memorized rules.

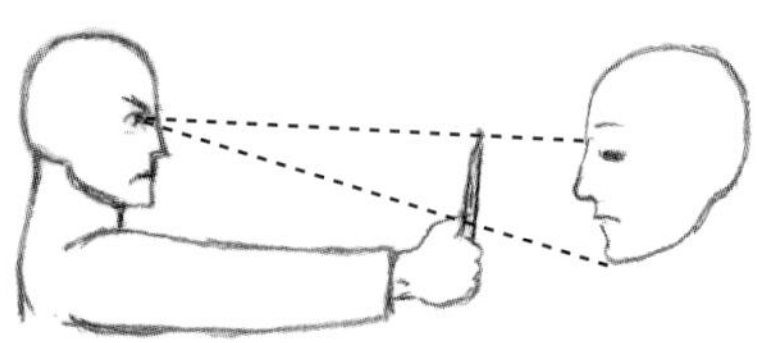

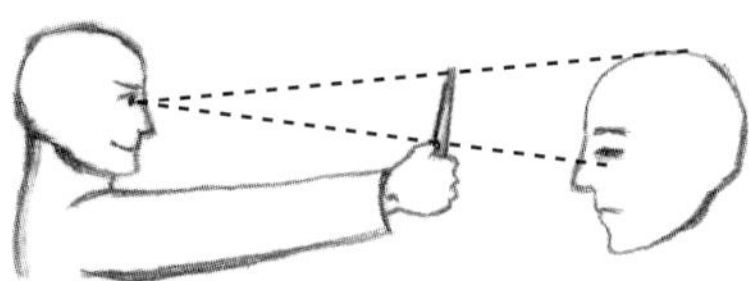

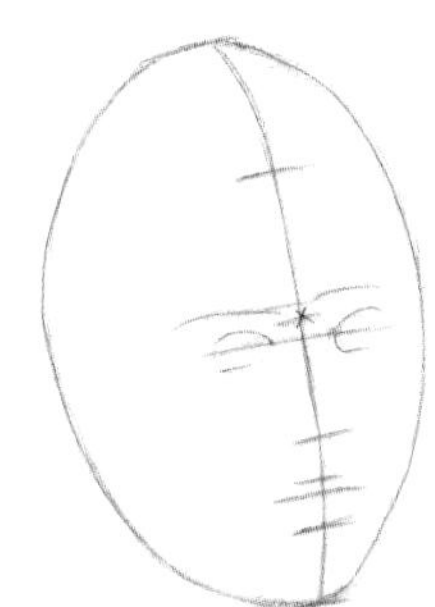

Step 3 Guesstimate the distance of each form from top to bottom. Although it's natural to make slight adjustments up and down later, one should not be careless in placing these points. Remember this: It's easy to adjust the widths of the forms, but lengthening and shortening forms requires a lot of erasing of adjacent forms.

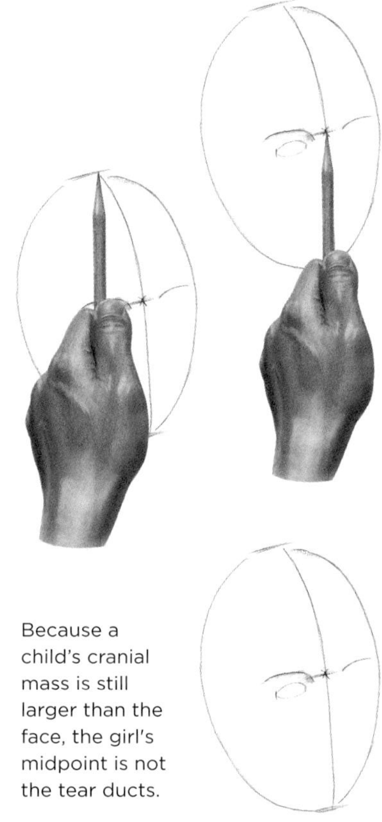

Because a child's cranial mass is still larger than the face, the girl's midpoint is not the tear ducts.

STAGE 2: PLUMB LINES

Now indicate the width of the head and check the horizontals. It's easiest to judge a tilted angle by placing a true horizontal below it (A). Next check the verticals and adjust as necessary (B); then check the spaces between the features (C).

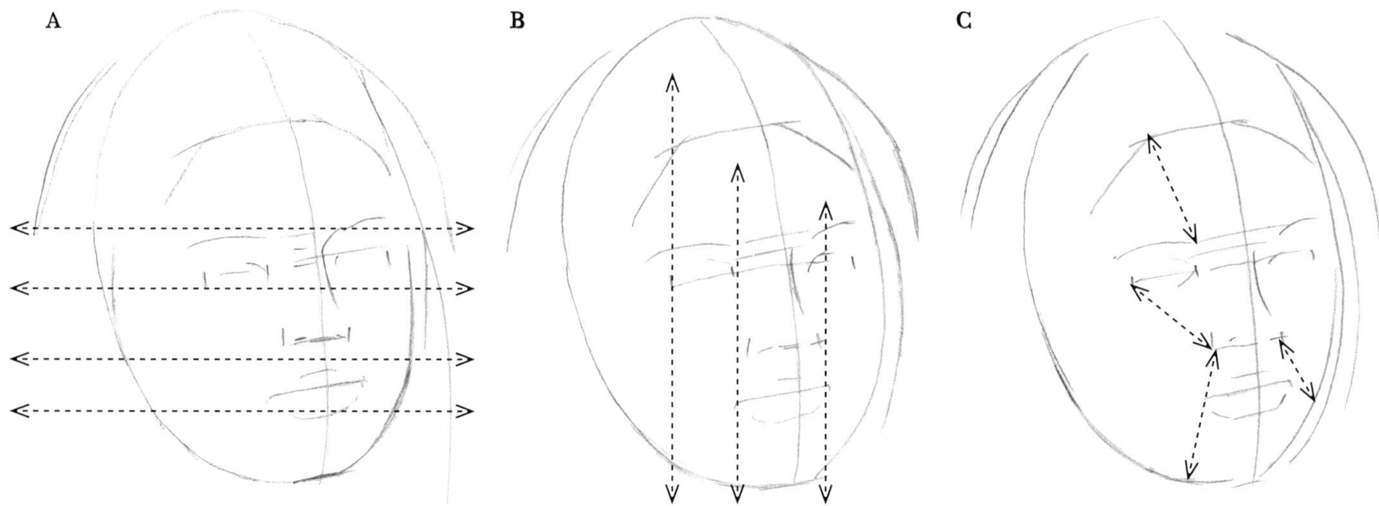

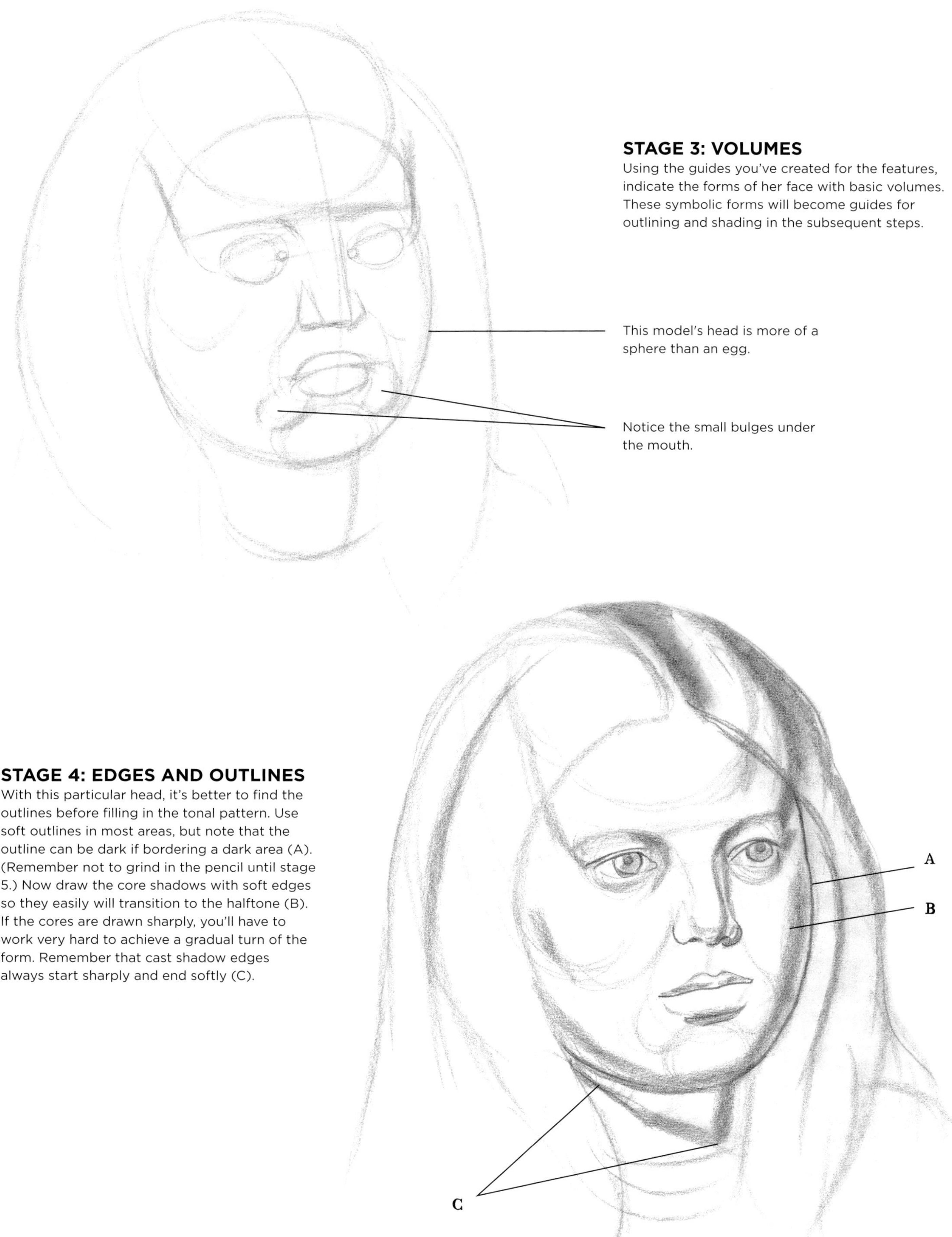

STAGE 3: VOLUMES

Using the guides you've created for the features, indicate the forms of her face with basic volumes. These symbolic forms will become guides for outlining and shading in the subsequent steps.

STAGE 4: EDGES AND OUTLINES

With this particular head, it's better to find the outlines before filling in the tonal pattern. Use soft outlines in most areas, but note that the outline can be dark if bordering a dark area (A). (Remember not to grind in the pencil until stage 5.) Now draw the core shadows with soft edges so they easily will transition to the halftone (B). If the cores are drawn sharply, you'll have to work very hard to achieve a gradual turn of the form. Remember that cast shadow edges always start sharply and end softly (C).

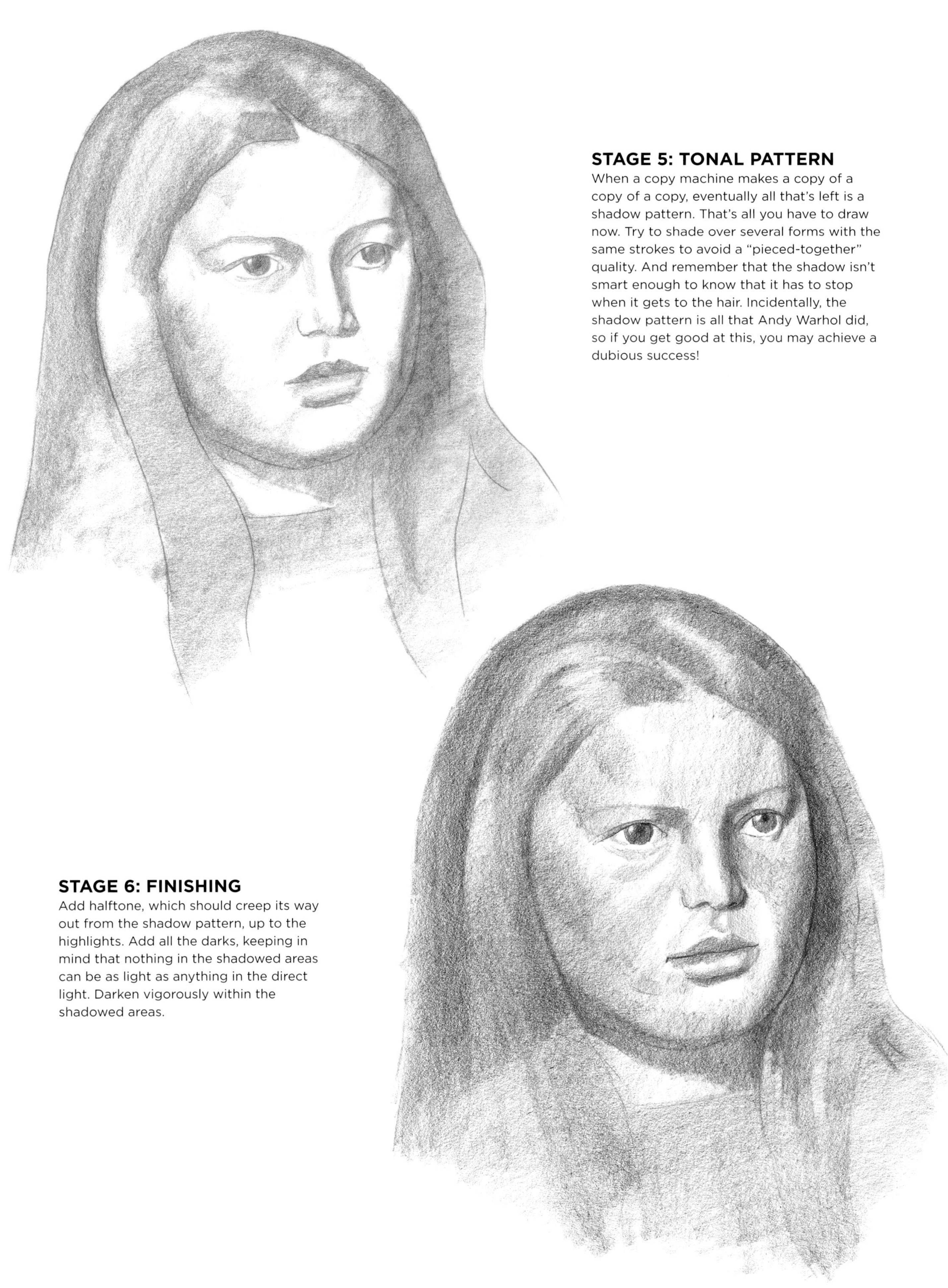

STAGE 5: TONAL PATTERN

When a copy machine makes a copy of a copy of a copy, eventually all that's left is a shadow pattern. That's all you have to draw now. Try to shade over several forms with the same strokes to avoid a "pieced-together" quality. And remember that the shadow isn't smart enough to know that it has to stop when it gets to the hair. Incidentally, the shadow pattern is all that Andy Warhol did, so if you get good at this, you may achieve a dubious success!

STAGE 6: FINISHING

Add halftone, which should creep its way out from the shadow pattern, up to the highlights. Add all the darks, keeping in mind that nothing in the shadowed areas can be as light as anything in the direct light. Darken vigorously within the shadowed areas.

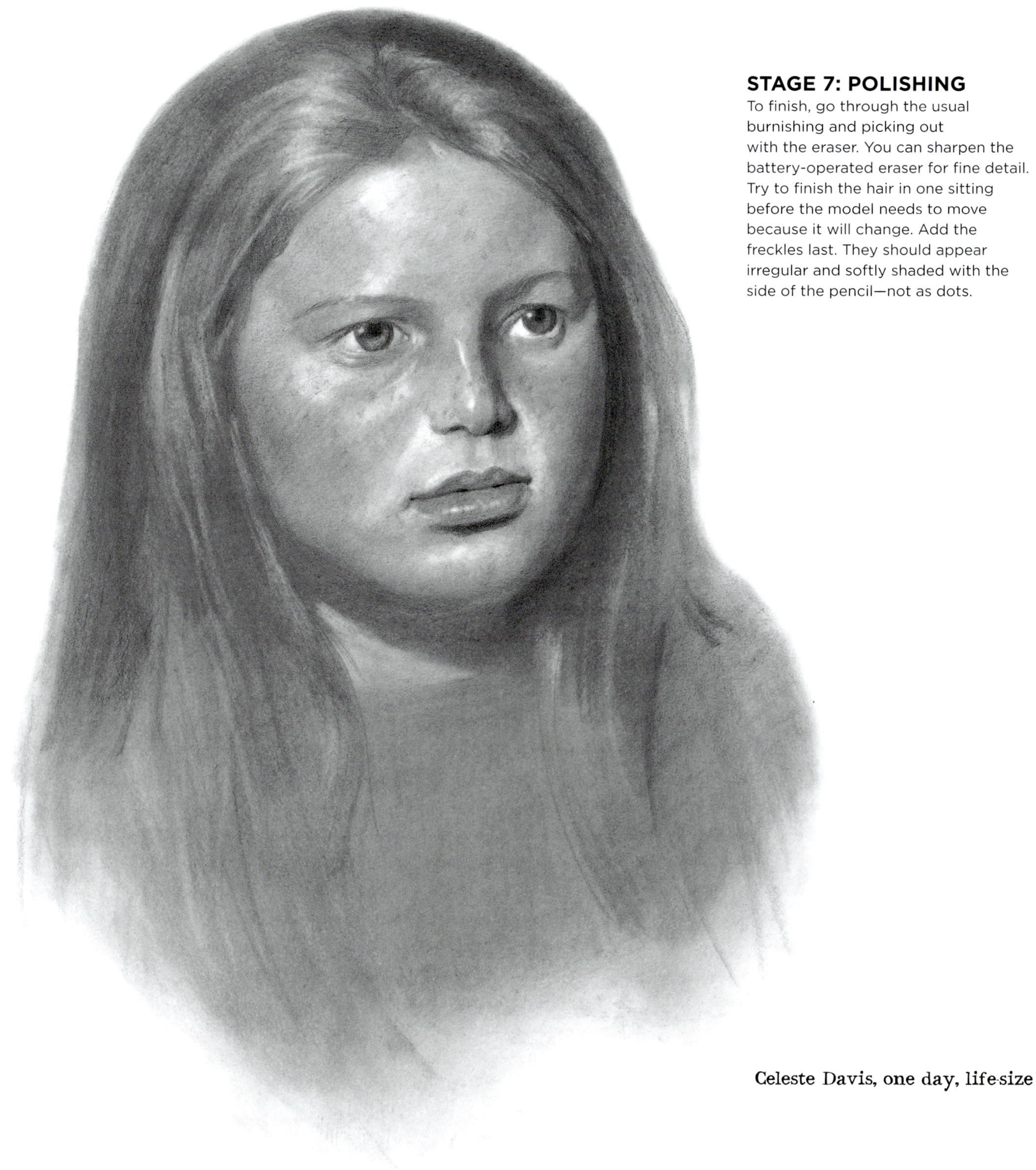

Celeste Davis, one day, life-size

STAGE 7: POLISHING

To finish, go through the usual burnishing and picking out with the eraser. You can sharpen the battery-operated eraser for fine detail. Try to finish the hair in one sitting before the model needs to move because it will change. Add the freckles last. They should appear irregular and softly shaded with the side of the pencil—not as dots.

ALTERING THE EXPRESSION

The girl's expression in this drawing is not particularly a happy one—it's one of concern or concentration. To make her look happier, you could gently arc the lips upward, raise the lower eyelids, and relax the inner corners of the eyebrows. A slight bulge in the cheeks might be called for at the nasolabial fold (the lines that run from the nostrils to the corners of the mouth) and above the cheekbone.

Project: Young Boy

Very often in a portraitist's career, he or she is forced to use photos exclusively. Sometimes it makes everyone's life easier, and sometimes there's simply no choice. Even if given an old, weathered, blurry to work with, your knowledge of the subject can allow you to improve your portrait beyond the photo. Endeavor to trace photos instead of copying them freehand. The client has sent you a reference, and you might as well give them back the exact outlines they've given you. Any creative alterations can come after the photo has been traced.

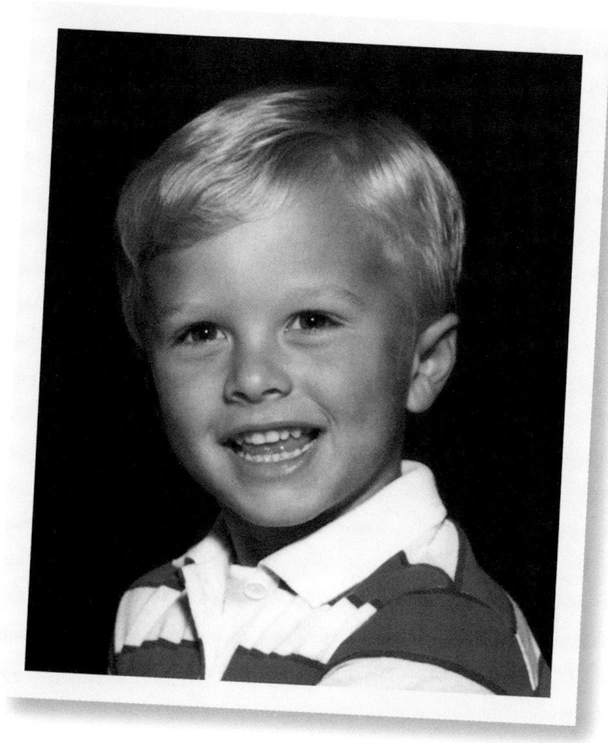

▶ **Selecting a Reference** Choose a good photo that the client has already approved. Ideally the lighting will flatter the model's features, and the expression will capture the model's true likeness.

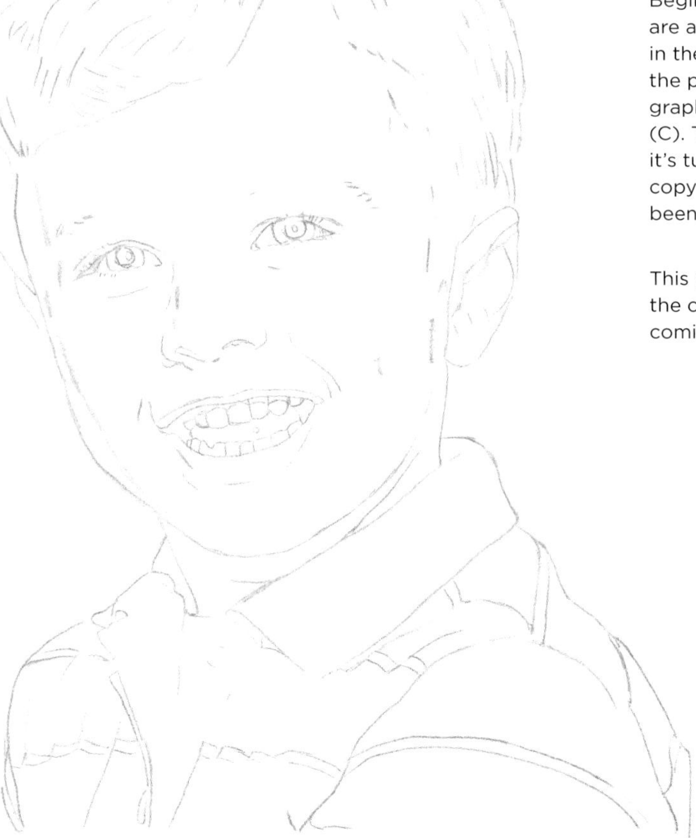

STAGE 1: TRANSFERRING OUTLINES

Begin by making black-and-white photocopies of the reference that are a bit lighter than the actual photo, which helps avoid losing detail in the dark areas. The copy can, of course, be bigger or smaller than the photo. Using artist's tape (A), secure the photocopy to a piece of graphite transfer paper (B); then place this over your drawing paper (C). Tape only at the top so you can lift the transfer paper to see how it's turning out as you draw. Then trace the important outlines over the copy using a colored pencil, which makes it easy to see where you've been (D). The lines then transfer to the drawing paper (E).

This process is more practical than using a projector. You also can tape the copy to a window, put your paper over it, and trace. The sun coming through the window creates a free lightbox.

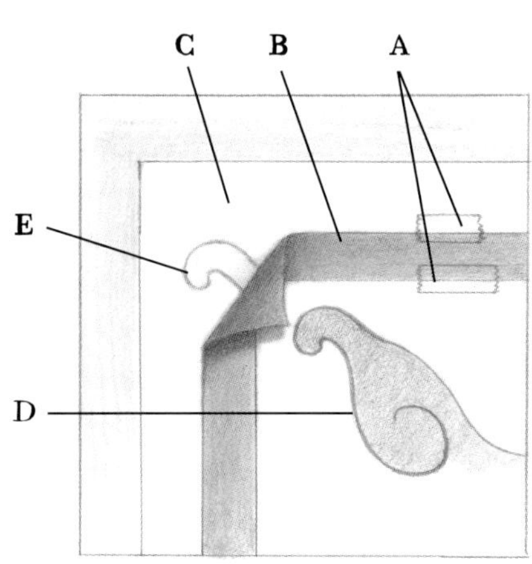

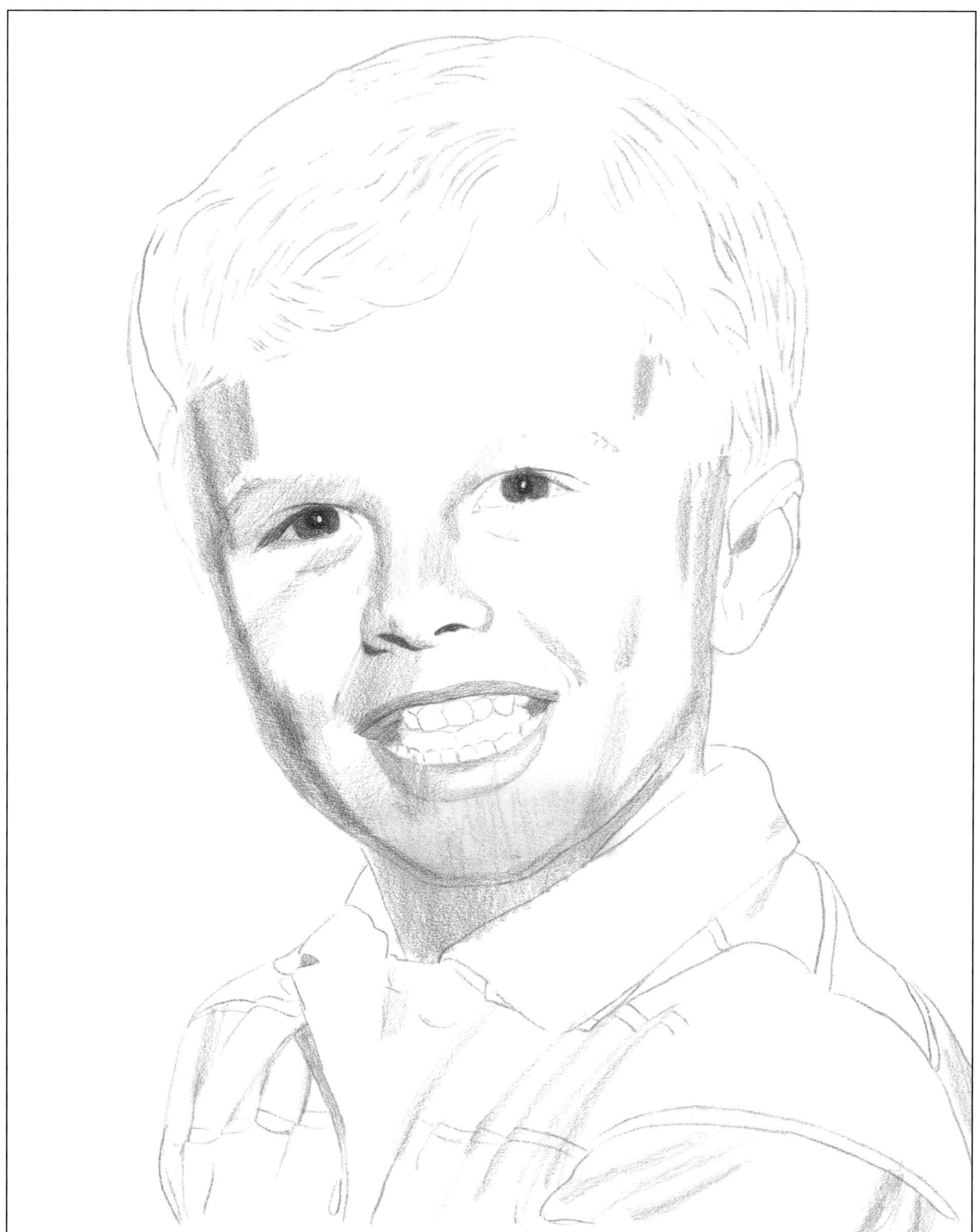

STAGE 2: ADDING DARKS

With a traced photo, no guidelines are necessary. Therefore, you won't need measurements, plumb lines, or volumes. You can go right to the shading. In fact, there's no reason to hold back on the darks because you shouldn't have to erase them. Typical commissions are around 8" by 10" in size, which is smaller than life. At this size, it's necessary to use a harder range of pencils, such as 2B, H, and 2H. These pencils produce fine, precise lines that are perfect for drawing teeth and eyelashes at this size.

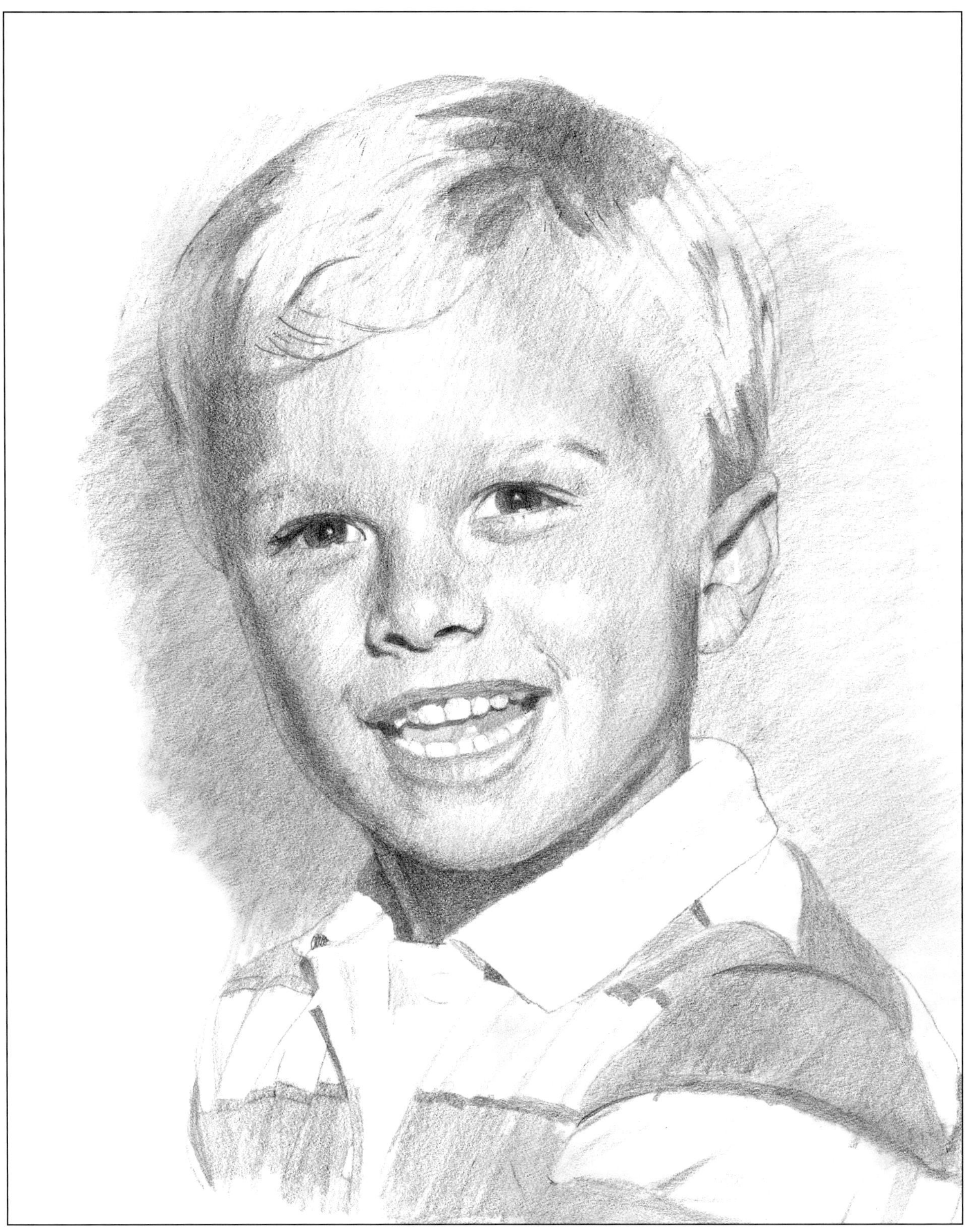

STAGE 3: BUILDING TONE

Now develop the forms using tone and detail. To prepare for the final look of polished realism, you need to have the shaded areas in their final locations. The surface must have enough graphite for you to begin stumping and blending in the next stage.

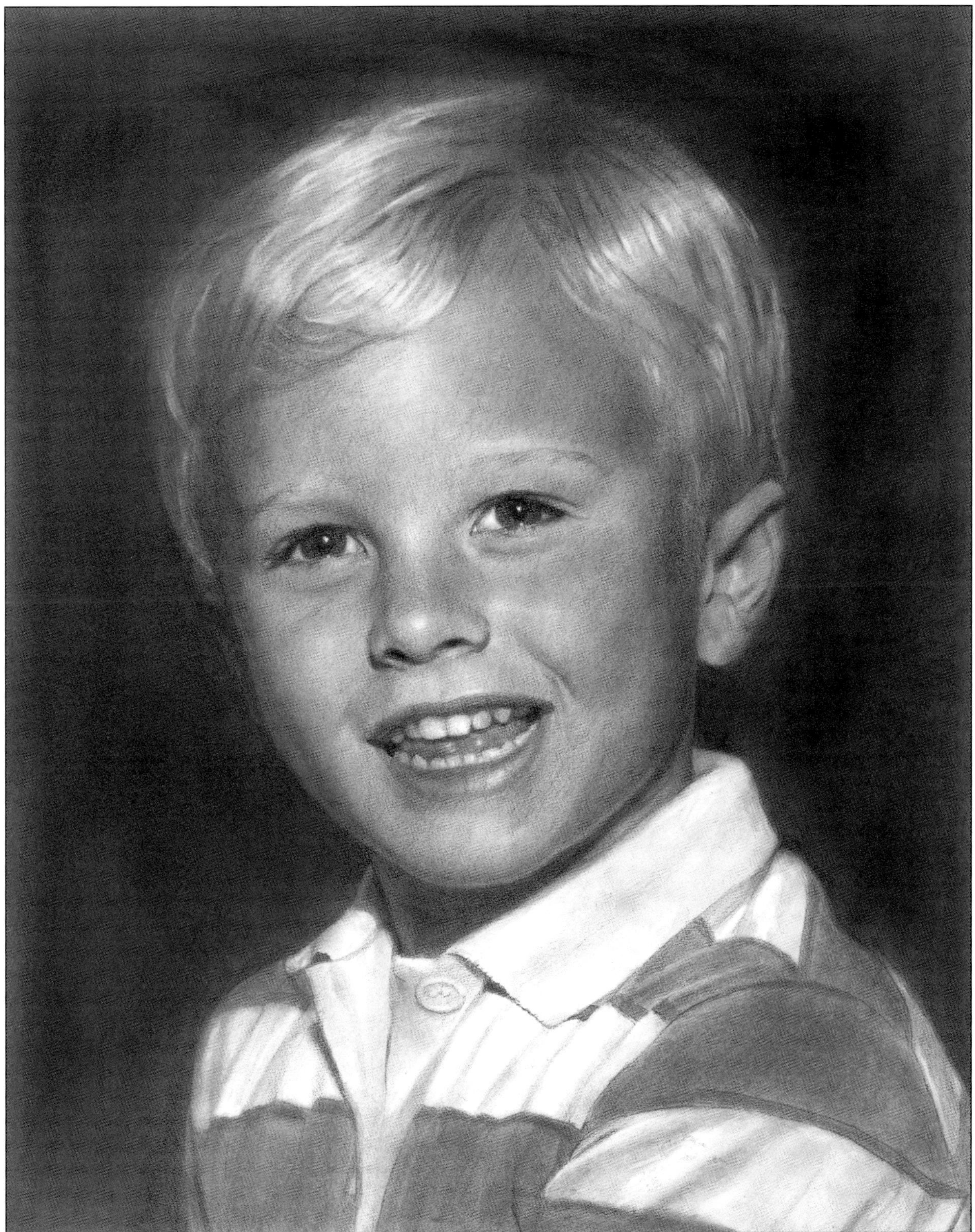

STAGE 4: FINISHING AND POLISHING

Polishing your drawings is an important final stage. To go from the previous step to this one, reach for the powder puff, the stump, and the make-up applicator. Don't just rub the whole drawing; start by stumping the shadows, darkening them and dragging the graphite across the forms. Then rub the powder puff everywhere, and pull out the lights and highlights with a kneaded eraser. Be careful to soften the edges of the highlights so they don't look like lightning bolts. Repeat all of these steps until you're happy. Blacken the background with graphite powder and the puff. You could go darker by grinding in an 8B pencil, but this may not be necessary. Note that the reference photos shows darker stripes in the shirt; the artist lightened these stripes so they wouldn't compete with the face.

Drawing a Profile

Drawing a portrait in profile is less common than drawing one from a front or three-quarter view, and it requires a slightly different approach. Follow the stages below for a profile.

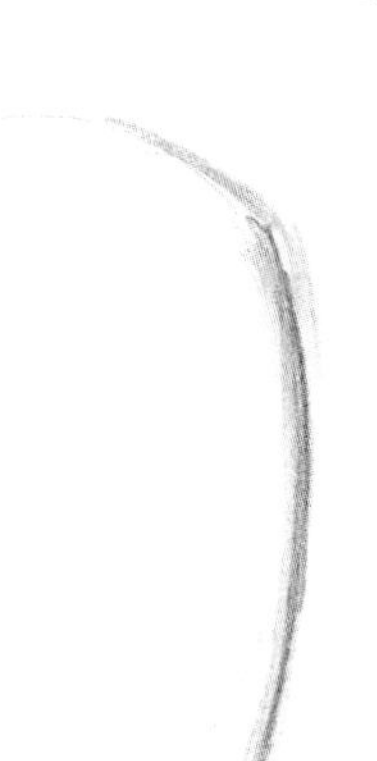

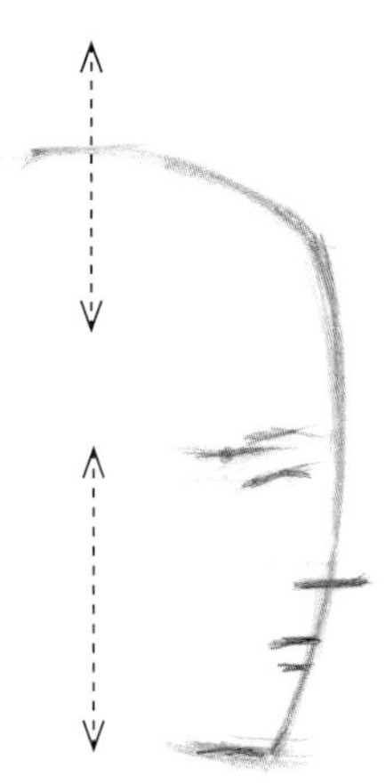

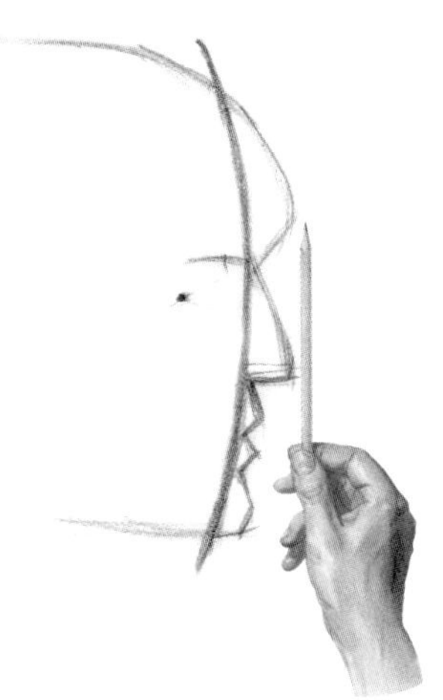

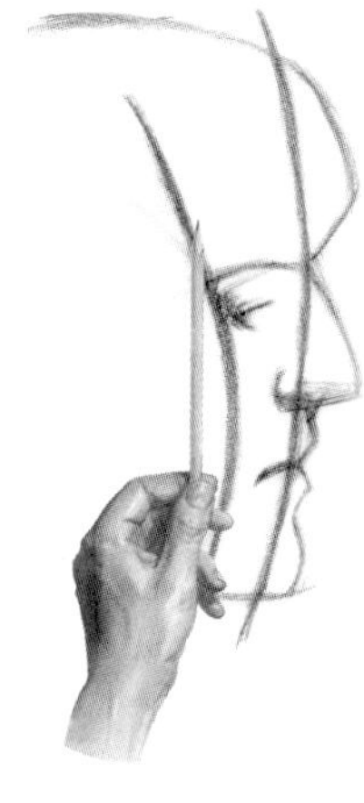

Stage 1 Try to discern a basic arc from the forehead to the chin, and put it down on paper. This is a guess that you will build on.

Stage 2 Extend your arm, and measure to find the halfway point between the top and bottom. Mark it. Then guesstimate where the brow, bottom of the nose, lips, and so on fall on your arc. Now mark them.

Stage 3 Hold a pencil vertically to the model's silhouette, and determine which form goes out farthest (e.g., brow or chin, upper lip or lower lip, etc.). Add them to the arc.

Stage 4 Hold the pencil vertically on the inner silhouette to compare the corner of the eye, the nostril, the mouth's corner, the neck, and so on. Place them correctly in relation to one another.

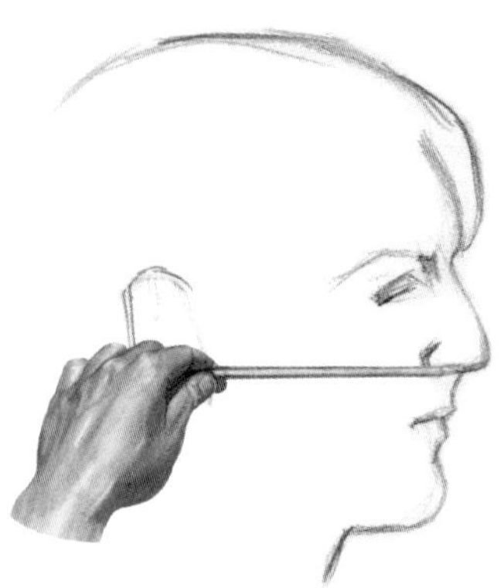

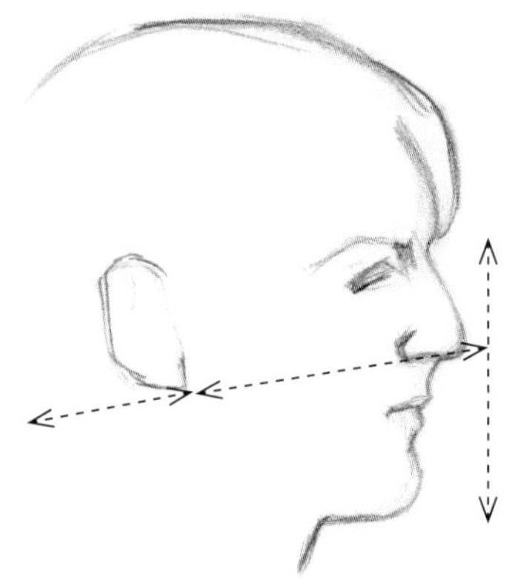

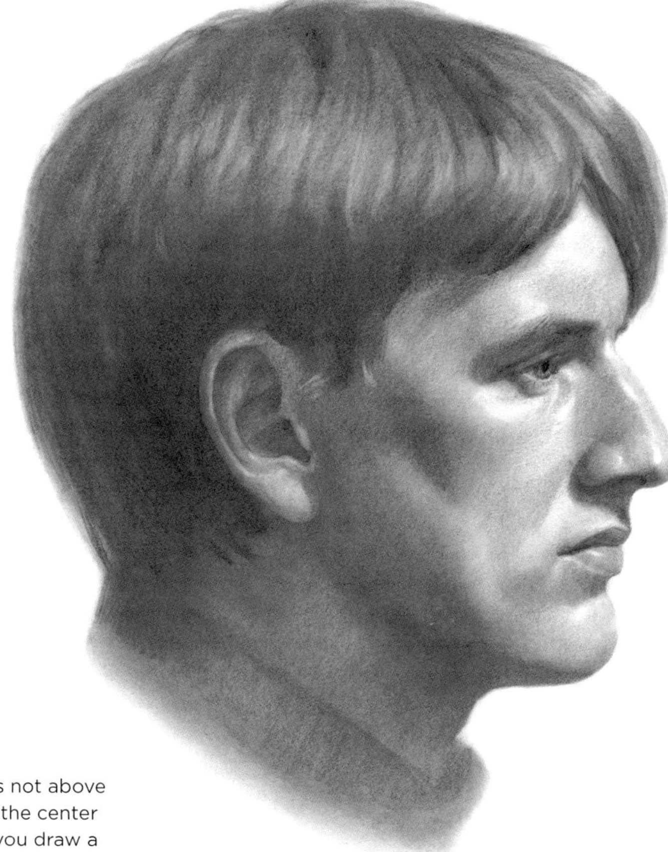

Stage 5 To place the ear, hold the pencil horizontally to check it against the base of the nose and the eyebrow. This will show you how high the ear should be.

Stage 6 Continuing to place the ear, extend your arm, and measure the distance from the chin to the brow. Compare this with the distance from the nose tip to the earlobe. This will enable you to decide how far back to draw the ear. (Also measure from the lobe to the back of the head.)

Notice that the high point of the head is not above the forehead. The top is near or behind the center of the head. Remember this fact when you draw a tilted head.

Working with Limited Time

When drawing a head from life in a limited amount of time, you must make adjustments to the seven-stage process. Keep the following three points in mind as you draw: (1) You must draw at a smaller size: the final drawing on this page (bottom right) is shown at actual size and took an hour; (2) you should use 18-lb marker paper and rely less on the 9B and more on the 5B and 2B pencils (these are harder and better suited for small details); and (3) you must combine stages.

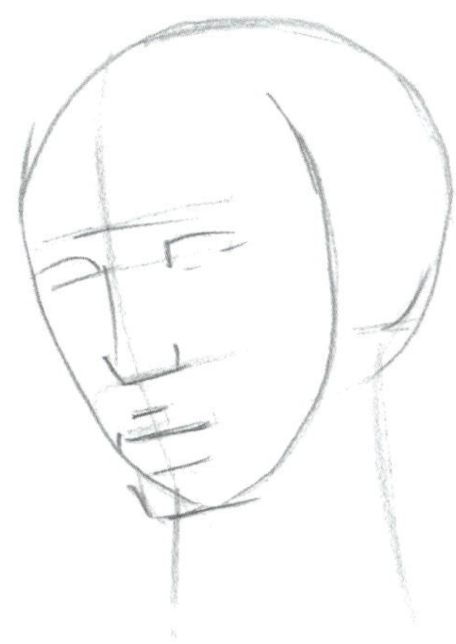

Stage 1 Create the lay-in, but leave out plumb lines and only check if you sense inaccuracy. Leave out the volume stage because you can imagine it as you draw around the edges and outlines.

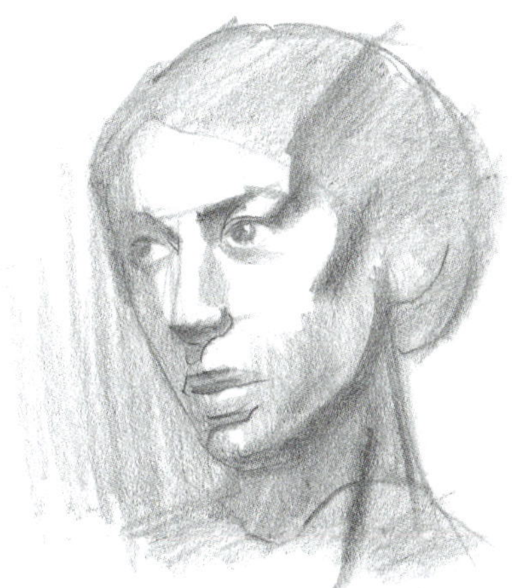

Stage 2 Combine edges and outlines with the tonal pattern. Draw the outline, and then draw the opposite core shadow. Throw on the tone as you go back and forth. The main tone will help you decide where to put the next line. If the face has a lot of shadow, rely more on the tonal pattern. If not, rely more on outlines and edges.

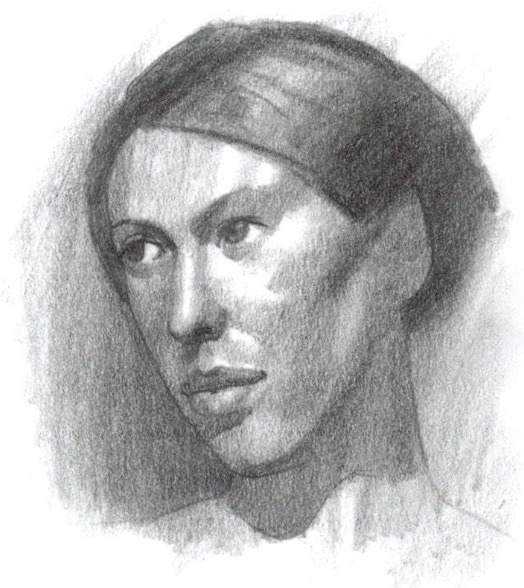

Stage 3 Move on to finishing. "True up" the drawing from the previous stage by nailing down the darks and erasing to make adjustments as you go.

IDENTIFYING FORMS

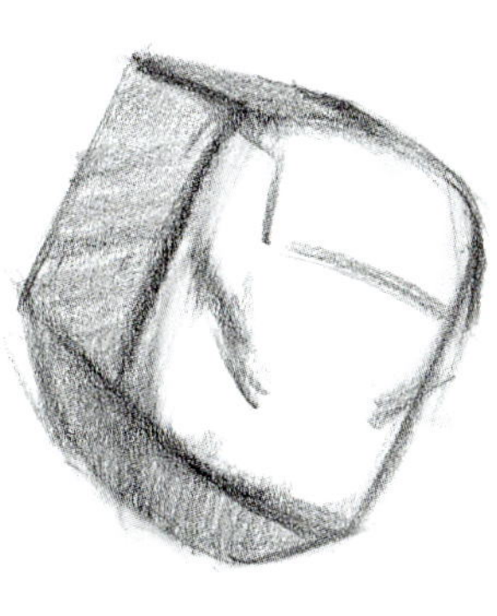

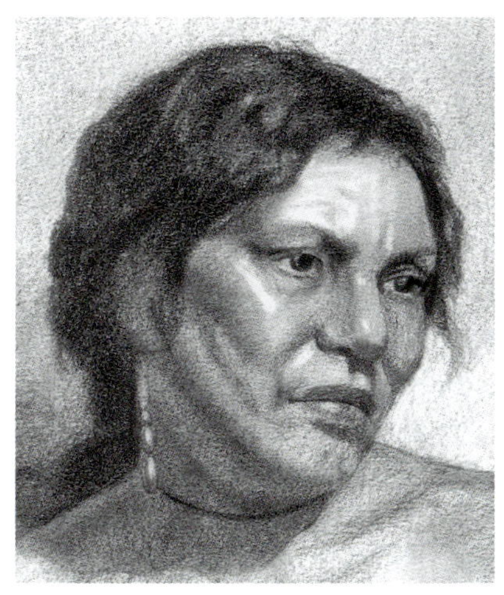

When working within a limited scope of time, begin by identifying the simplest form that best represents your model's head shape. This portrait started with a cube. Notice how the model's slightly furrowed brow creates a sense of melancholy.

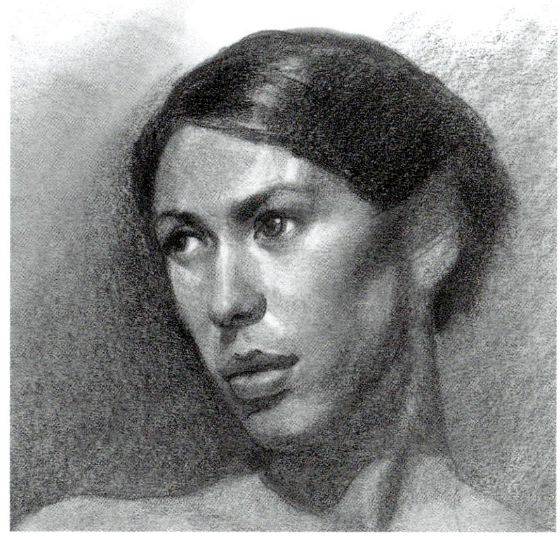

Stage 4 Darken, stump, and pull out highlights to polish the drawing.

Drawing Babies

The only difficult thing about drawing babies is their radically different proportions. It's a good idea to memorize the diagram below and even lightly draw these guidelines before you draw a baby—after all, you don't have much time for mistakes. When drawing a baby from life, consider allowing ten minutes of drawing for every hour of waiting. But the wait is charming. The drawing at right was created from a photo. Although drawing from life is generally considered ideal, it makes perfect sense to use a camera for a baby due to their frequent movement. Photos are often poorly lit, so remember to shade sensitively or the forms may look flat. Even without heavy shadow patterns, people still look three-dimensional—just use the lights and darks that are there, even if they're subtle.

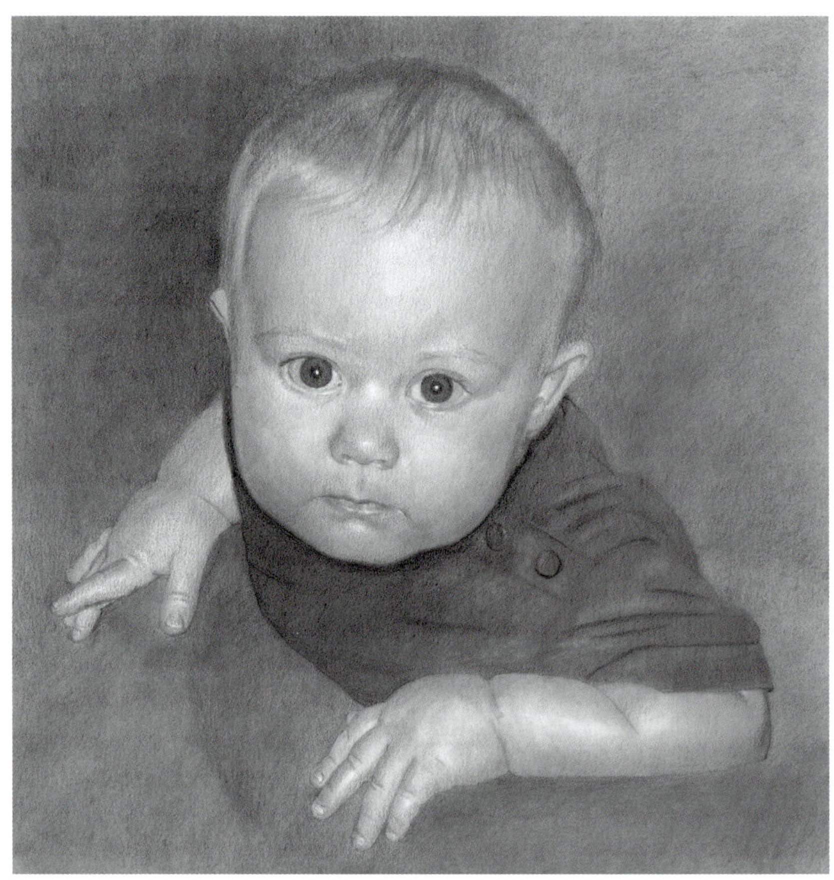

BABY PROPORTIONS

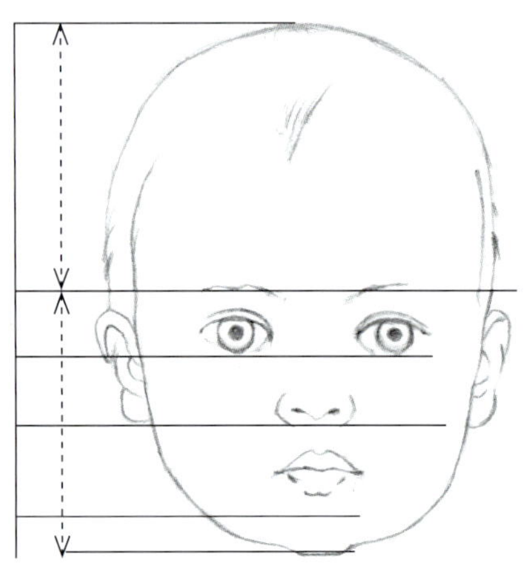

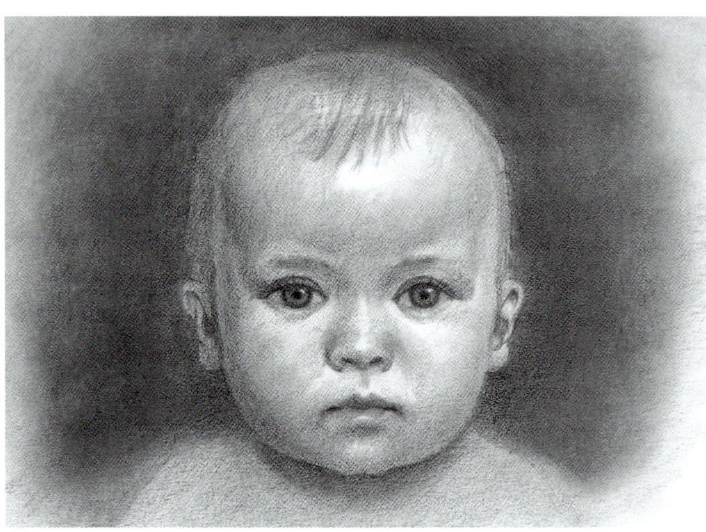

The proportions of a baby are much different than those of an adult. The eyebrows are halfway up the head, the bottoms of the eyes are about three-eighths of the way up the head, the bottom of the nose is about one-fourth of the way up the head, and the bottom of the mouth is about one-eighth of the way up the head.

Drawing Older People

S eniors are excellent subjects for exploring texture and character. Notice how the side lighting on the model below brings out his rugged look.

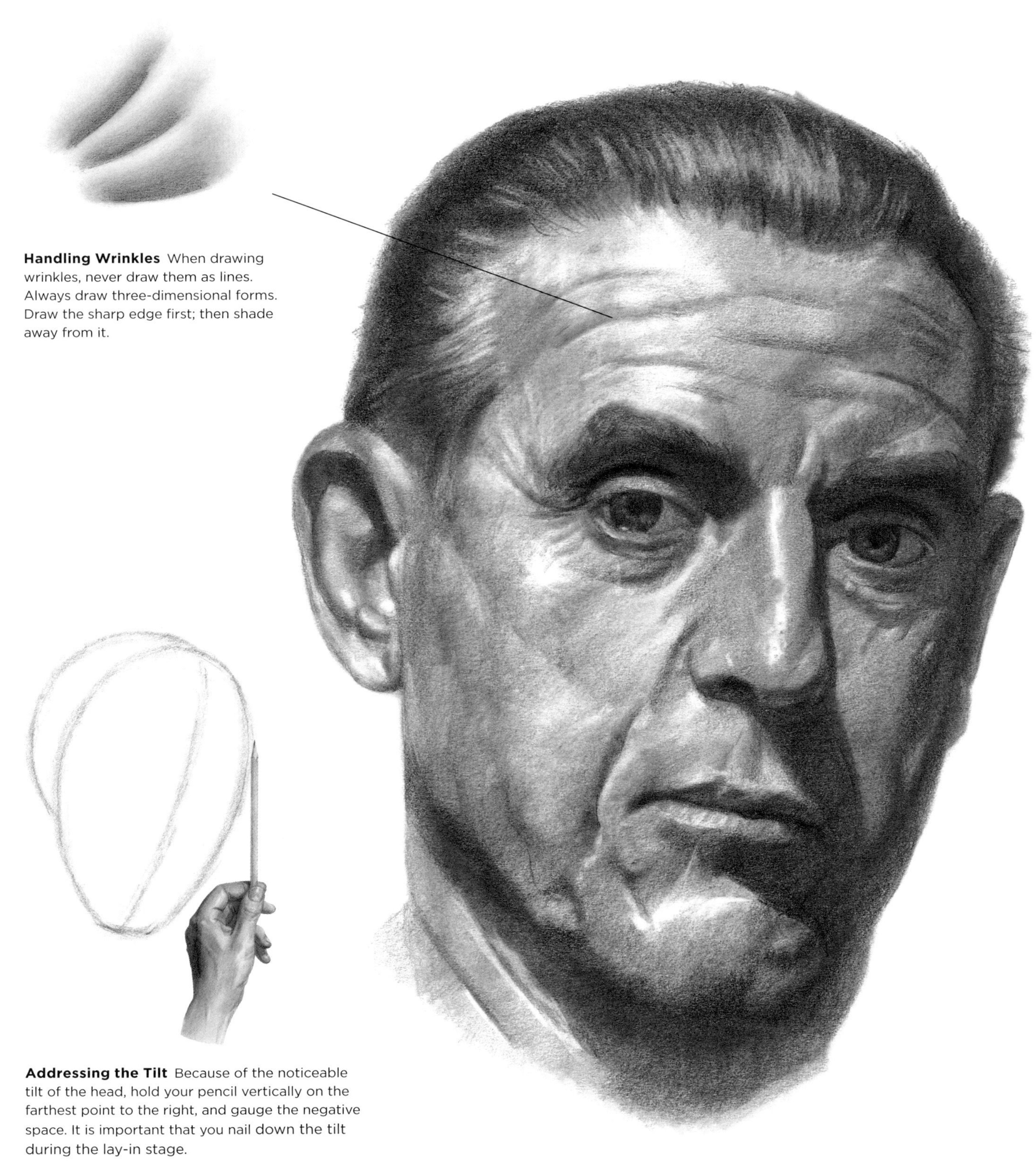

Handling Wrinkles When drawing wrinkles, never draw them as lines. Always draw three-dimensional forms. Draw the sharp edge first; then shade away from it.

Addressing the Tilt Because of the noticeable tilt of the head, hold your pencil vertically on the farthest point to the right, and gauge the negative space. It is important that you nail down the tilt during the lay-in stage.

Mastering Proportion

Once the head is correct, it's easy to determine the proportions for the rest of the body. First hold out your arm, and measure how many heads it takes to reach the waist. This gives you the appropriate length. (Remember that it's easier to adjust a form's width than its length.) To estimate the body's width, it's also vital to measure the breadth of the shoulders. Once you have the shoulders, you can run verticals down to see where the rest of the body aligns. Of course, you also should check verticals down from the sides of the head, the nose, and so on.

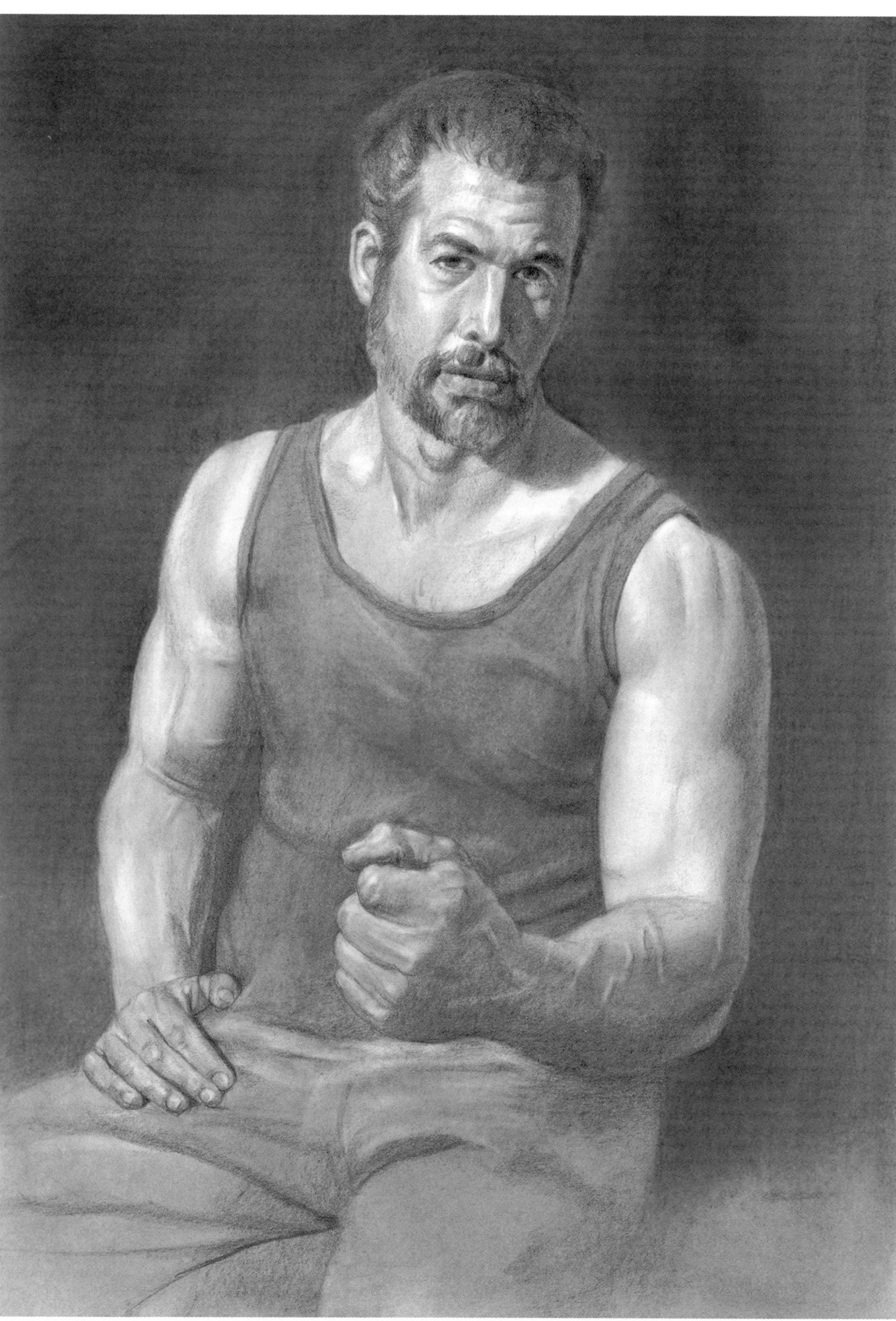

Avoiding Distortion This artist sat only 4 feet from this model, which created extreme foreshortening (the way objects closer to the viewer appear larger than those farther away) of the fist. This seemed acceptable because it added drama—and drama helps art. But if you want to avoid the apparent distortion of foreshortening, do the following:

1. Sit about 10 feet from your model, or far enough away that the proportions regularize.
2. Mark all the proportions (See page 185.)
3. Creep forward when you need to see the details.
4. As you move forward, adjust the height of your chair so your line of sight remains constant. You must see the forms from the same angles.

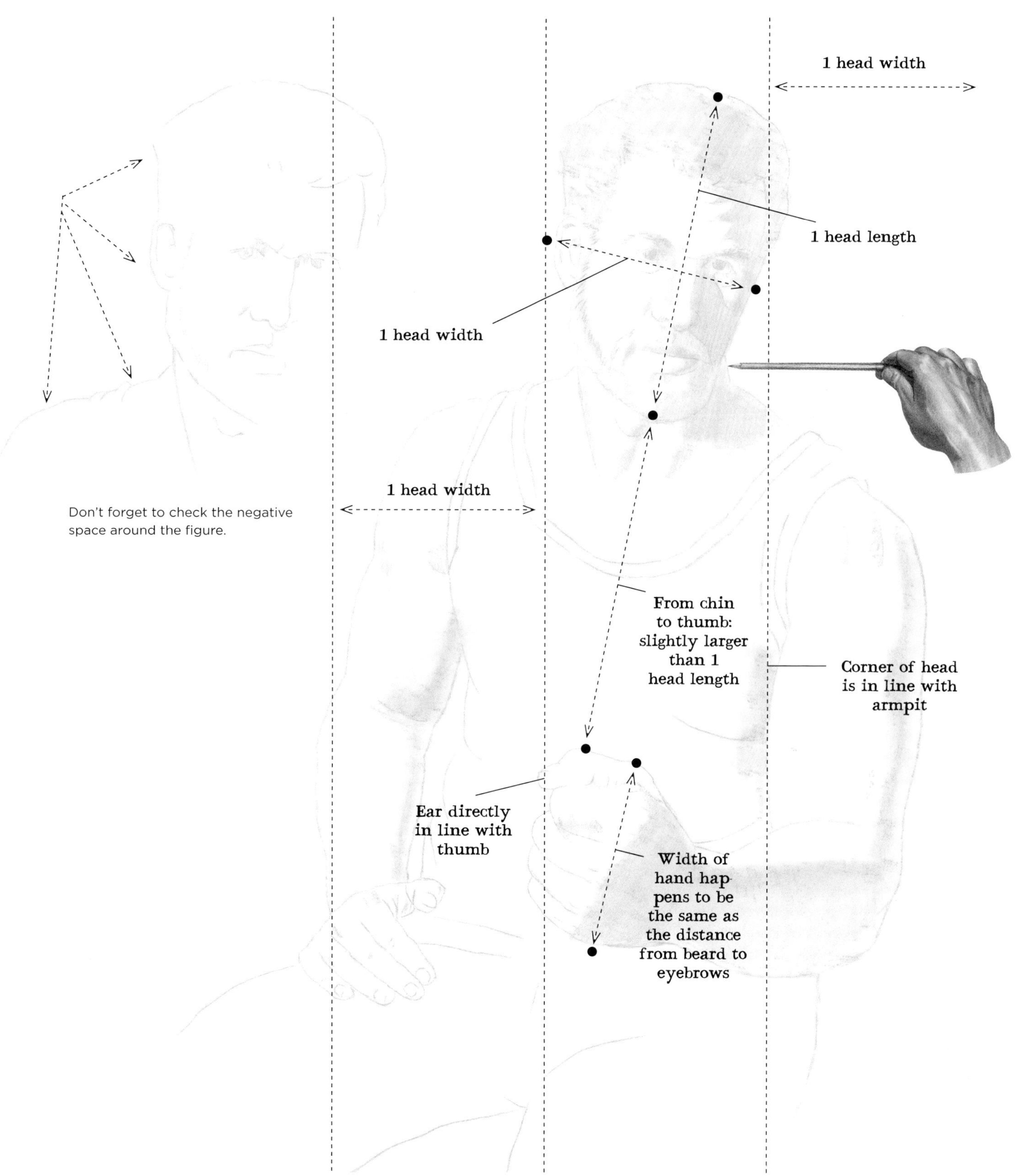

Mapping Out Proportions Follow the steps below to achieve accurate proportions in your figure drawings. Measuring carefully is especially important in a drawing with foreshortening—the size of this model's left fist is larger in proportion to the head than you may expect. Reflect these counter-intuitive measurements in your drawings to ensure accuracy.

1. To determine the width of the shoulders, compare them with the width of the head. Also look at the shape of the negative space.
2. Check verticals down from the shoulders and head to determine the rest of the body's locations.
3. Measure head lengths down for proportions. Fore example, compare a single hand (or foot) to the size of the head.
4. Ask yourself questions along the way. For example, which is longer—the distance from the shoulder to the neck or the distance from the neck to the top of the head?

Improving Your Work

This section is designed to show you how to correct yourself during the portrait drawing process. In general, there are four basic categories of mistakes that prevent a drawing from appearing realistic: negative space inaccuracies, overmodeling, outline issues, and tonal problems. This section will show four versions of our model Karolina (drawn accurately to the right), demonstrating each mistake. Refer to the accurate drawing as you examine the mistakes of each version.

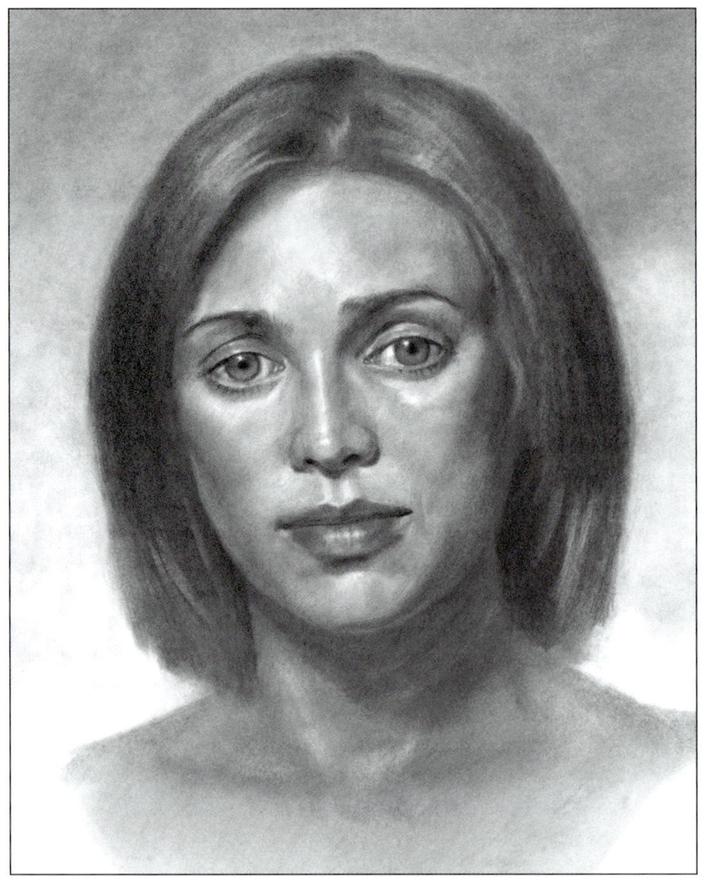

Karolina Rosinska, one day, life-size

THE FOUR PERILS OF KAROLINA

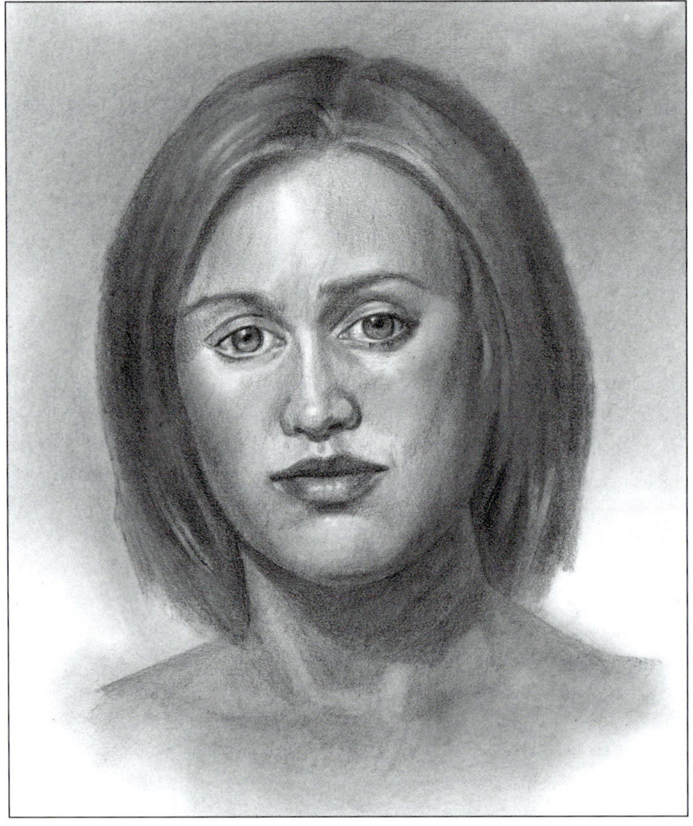

Negative Space Inaccuracies This artist draws details well but either doesn't know how to—or want to—spend time on the lay-in or plumb line stages; this is evident in that the mouth and eyes are too close to the nose. (Remember: The space between the forms is just as important as the forms themselves.) Of course, the artist should master stages 1 and 2 of the first two projects. But an artist like this also should try drawing the nose and comparing its size with the space around it, or he or she should check verticals up and down from the sides of the nostrils. He or she also should ask questions: Which is bigger—the lips or the space above the lips? Does this woman have a big jaw or a delicate one?

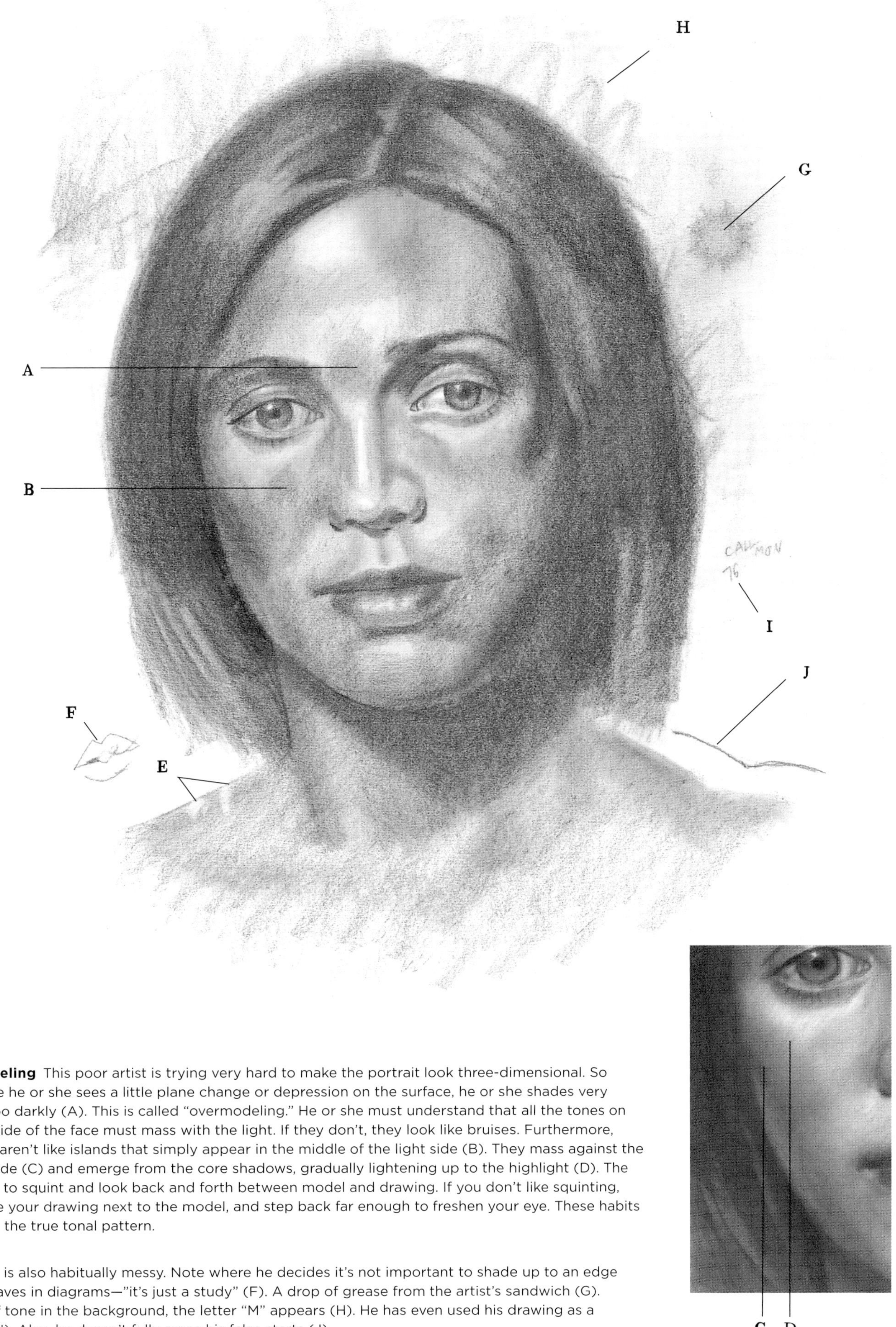

Overmodeling This poor artist is trying very hard to make the portrait look three-dimensional. So every time he or she sees a little plane change or depression on the surface, he or she shades very darkly—too darkly (A). This is called "overmodeling." He or she must understand that all the tones on the light side of the face must mass with the light. If they don't, they look like bruises. Furthermore, halftones aren't like islands that simply appear in the middle of the light side (B). They mass against the shadow side (C) and emerge from the core shadows, gradually lightening up to the highlight (D). The remedy is to squint and look back and forth between model and drawing. If you don't like squinting, then place your drawing next to the model, and step back far enough to freshen your eye. These habits will reveal the true tonal pattern.

This artist is also habitually messy. Note where he decides it's not important to shade up to an edge (E). He leaves in diagrams—"it's just a study" (F). A drop of grease from the artist's sandwich (G). Instead of tone in the background, the letter "M" appears (H). He has even used his drawing as a notepad (I). Also, he doesn't fully erase his false starts (J).

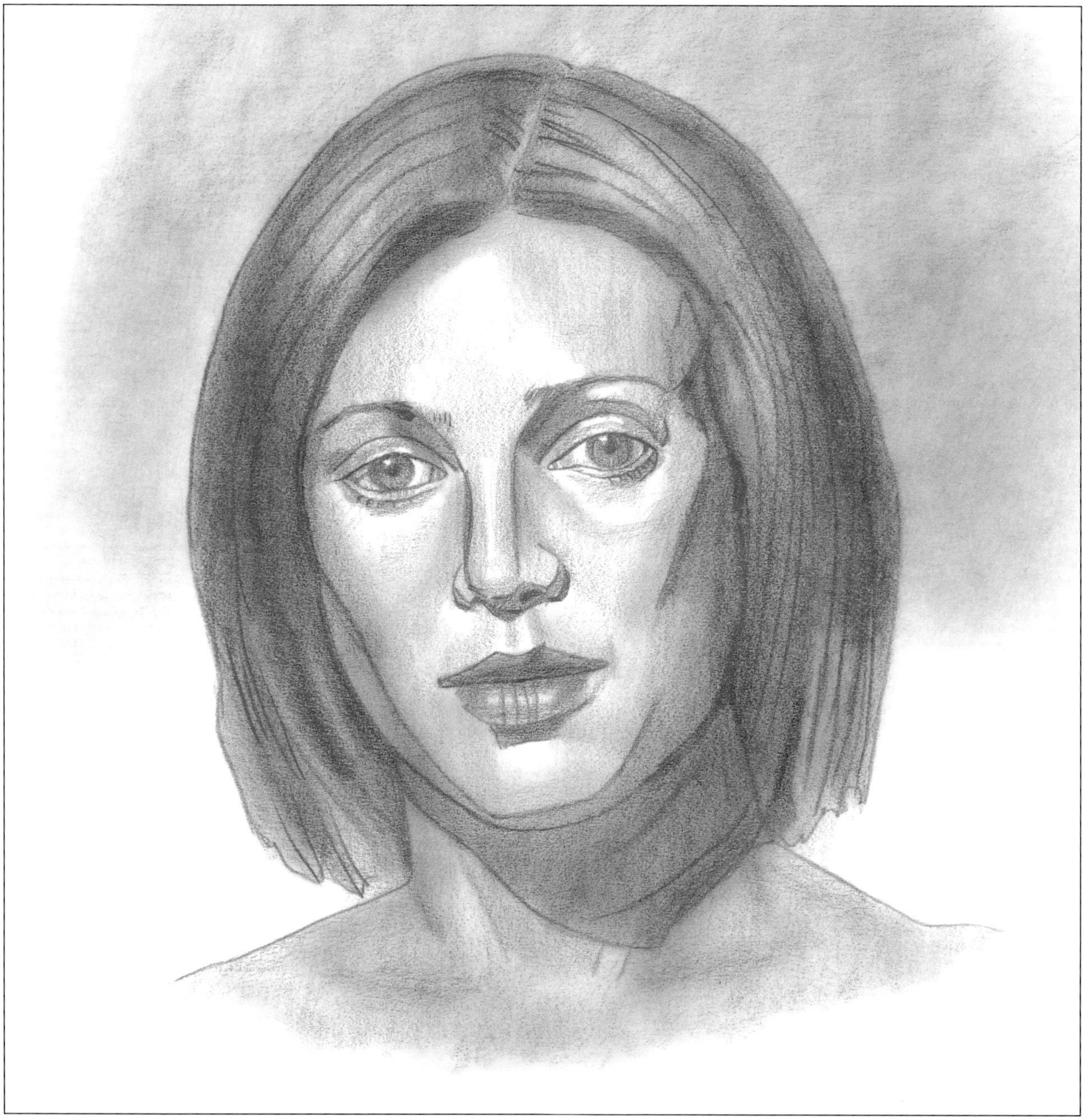

Outline Issues A percentage of every population will become "outliners." If you are trying to overcome this behavior, the first steps are to admit to yourself that you are an outliner, that people don't have outlines, and that lines are for plane changes on robots, not people.

The solution is to draw the sharpest edge (A); then draw the softest edge (B). All other edges must be between the two. As for the silhouette, it's true that the forms have to come to a stop somewhere, so go ahead and draw a line—but shade up to it so it becomes lost (C), or draw it clearly but lightly, even fading it out (D). After all that, if you still can't control your outlining habit, don't punish yourself with guilt. Nobody's perfect.

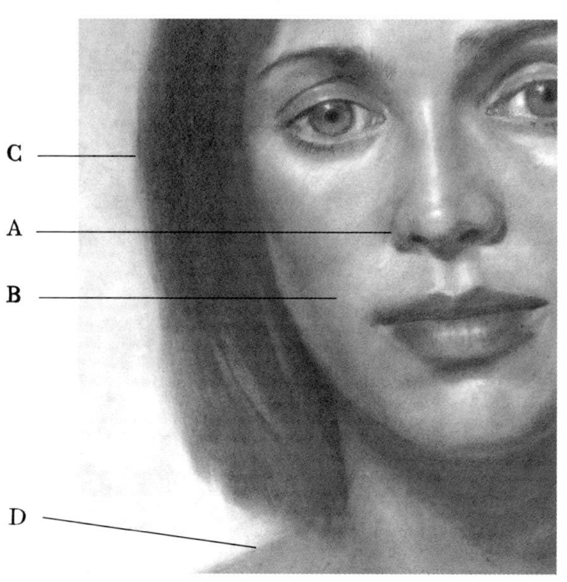

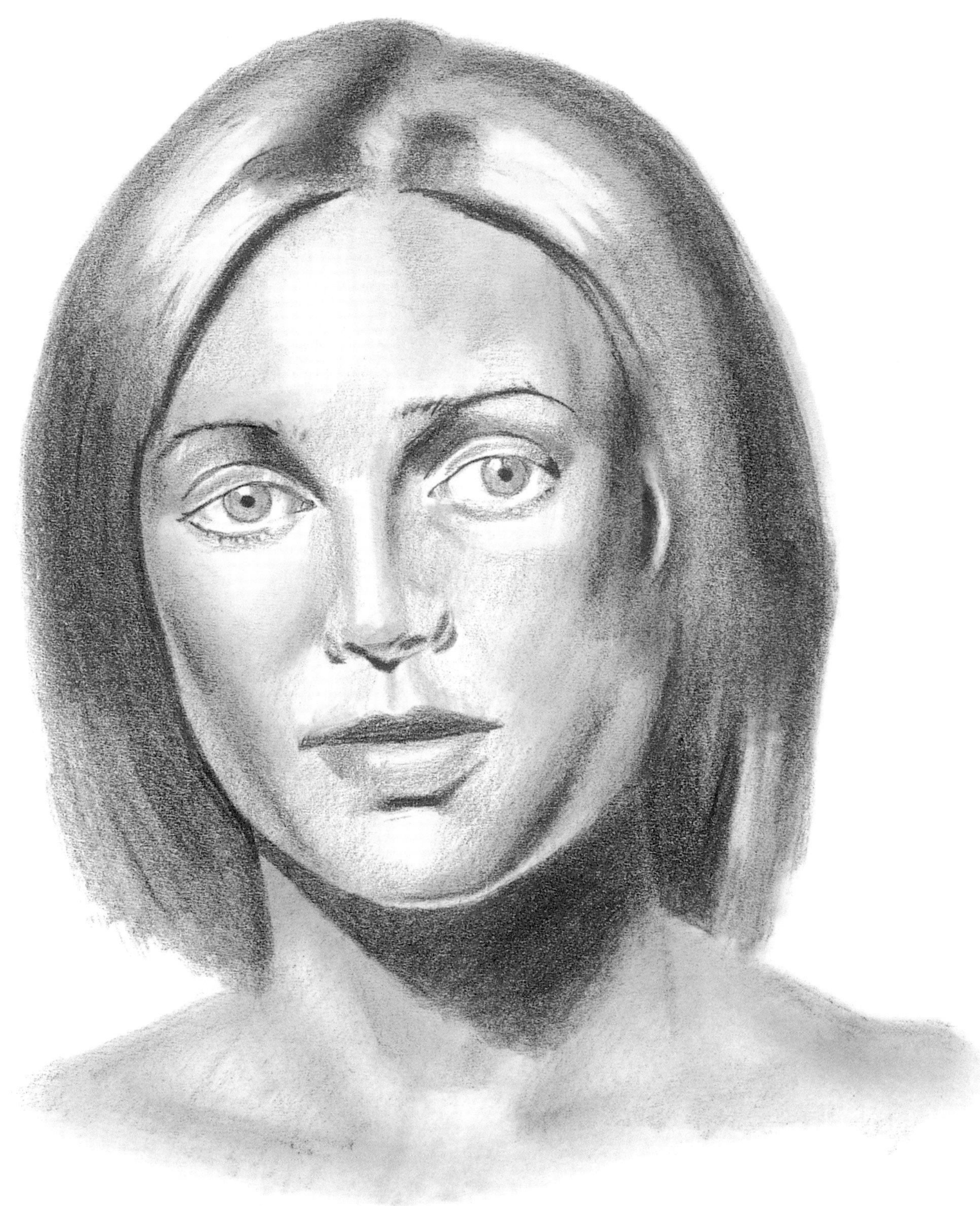

Tonal Problems When this artist sees anything light, he or she makes it too light (for example, look at the highlights in the hair and the reflected light under the jaw). And when he or she comes to the "white of the eyes," guess what happens. The solution is for some well-meaning soul to put a piece of white paper next to Karolina's hair—the highlights in brown hair are light brown, not white. Reflected light isn't light in tone—it's still part of the shadow. Remember: Nothing in the shadowed areas can be as light as anything in the direct light. If you find that the reflected light under the chin is competing with the halftone on the front of the cheeks, you should worry. Squint—the reflected light will mass with the shadow. And please shade the "white" of the eye; the "white" of the eye is only an expression. Unfortunately, this student also makes his or her cast shadows black. It can be very helpful to find a black object to place next to the cast shadows, showing their true value.

Index

Quarto.com • WalterFoster.com

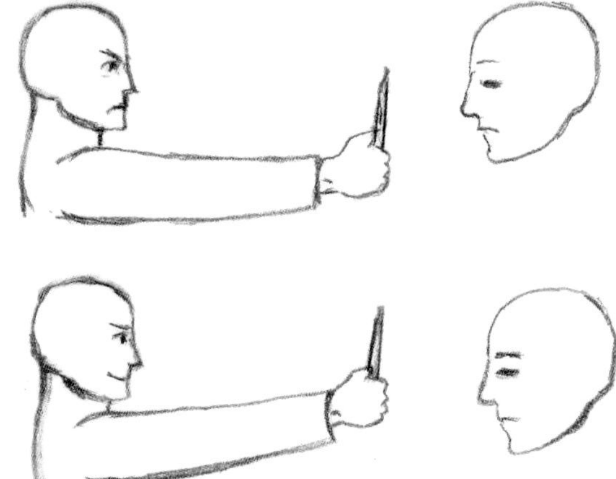